MW01029924

THE ISLAND

THE **ISLAND**

WAR AND BELONGING IN AUDEN'S ENGLAND

NICHOLAS JENKINS

THE BELKNAP PRESS *of* HARVARD UNIVERSITY PRESS

Cambridge, Massachusetts   2024

First printing

Published in the United Kingdom (as *The Island: W. H. Auden and the Last of Englishness*) by Faber & Faber Ltd, London

Library of Congress Cataloging-in-Publication Data

Names: Jenkins, Nicholas (Nicholas Richard), author.
Title: The island : war and belonging in Auden's England / Nicholas Jenkins.
Description: Cambridge, Massachusetts : The Belknap Press of Harvard University
   Press, 2024. | Includes bibliographical references and index.
Identifiers: LCCN 2023041006 | ISBN 9780674025226 (cloth)
Subjects: LCSH: Auden, W. H. (Wystan Hugh), 1907–1973—Criticism and
   interpretation. | Auden, W. H. (Wystan Hugh), 1907–1973—Friends and
   associates. | World War, 1914–1918—Influence. | Nationalism and literature—
   England—History—20th century. | England—In literature.
Classification: LCC PR6001.U4 Z75345 2024 | DDC 821/.912—dc23/eng/20231024
LC record available at https://lccn.loc.gov/2023041006

FOR ENID BROWNE AND JOY HOLMES

Every Englishman is an island.

—NOVALIS, *DAS ALLGEMEINE BROUILLON*
(1798–1799)

CONTENTS

CHRONOLOGY

FEB 1907	born in York, the third son of George and Constance Auden
CA SUMMER 1908	Auden family moves to Solihull, near Birmingham
APRIL 1912	first memory of a public event: the sinking of the *Titanic*
SEPT 1914	Dr. Auden joins the Royal Army Medical Corps
SUMMER–AUTUMN 1915	Dr. Auden serves at Suvla Bay during the Gallipoli campaign
OCT 1915	with brother John starts boarding at St. Edmund's School in Surrey
JAN 1916	Dr. Auden is invalided out of frontline medical duties
AUG–SEPT 1917	Dr. Auden on leave; dispute with Mrs. Auden about a mistress in Egypt
SEPT 1917–FEB 1919	Dr. Auden serving as a military medical administrator in Britain and France
CA WINTER 1917	shamed for his appetite in front of the school: "I see, Auden, you want the Huns to win"
CA FEB 1919	Dr. Auden is demobilized and returns home
SUMMER 1919	Auden family moves to Harborne, a Birmingham suburb; Dr. Auden suffers an attack of encephalitis lethargica
CA AUG 1919	visits the North Pennines for the first time
CA MARCH/APRIL 1920	sex with the school chaplain at St. Edmund's
OCT 1920	starts at Gresham's School in Norfolk
JULY 1921	plays Ursula in the Gresham's production of *Much Ado About Nothing*
MARCH 1922	as Auden walks with Robert Medley in a ploughed field, Medley inspires him to start writing poetry

JULY 1922	plays Katharina, the "shrew," in the Gresham's production of *The Taming of the Shrew*
AUG 1922	walking tour in the Lake District with his brother John and Dr. Auden
CA 1924/1925	the Audens buy Wesco in the village of Threlkeld in the Lake District
JULY 1925	plays Caliban in the Gresham's production of *The Tempest*
CA JULY 1925	writes "The Dying House"
AUG 1925	first journey abroad: with Dr. Auden to Salzburg and Kitzbühel
OCT 1925	goes up to Christ Church, Oxford, intending to read natural science
MARCH– APRIL 1926	writes "'Lead's the Best'"
MAY 1926	drives a car for the Trades Union Congress in London during the General Strike; reads *The Waste Land* and adopts a modernist poetic style
SEPT 1926	switches to reading for an undergraduate degree in English literature
DEC 1926– JAN 1927	visits Austria again
JUNE 1927	submits a book of poems to T. S. Eliot: rejected in September with mild encouragement
JUNE / JULY 1927	drops his Eliotic modernist style and writes "I chose this lean country"
JULY–AUG 1927	spends a tortured holiday with his father in Yugoslavia; perhaps writes his first poem abroad
AUG 1927	writes "Who stands, the crux left of the watershed"
OCT 1927	meeting with Eliot in London
DEC 1927	starts drafting *Paid on Both Sides*
JAN 1928	writes "Control of the Passes was, he saw, the key"
JUNE 1928	examinations in English literature at Oxford result in a Third Class degree

CA JULY 1928	finishes first version of *Paid on Both Sides*
AUG 1928	undertakes a form of psychoanalysis in Belgium
CA SEPT 1928	is engaged to a Birmingham nurse, Sheilah Richardson
SEPT / OCT 1928	Auden's first book, *Poems,* is privately published by Stephen Spender
OCT 1928	moves to Berlin, stays first in a suburb and later in the year in a slum
CA NOV 1928	meets John Layard in Berlin
DEC 1928	sends a second version of *Paid on Both Sides* to Eliot
MARCH 1929	Christopher Isherwood visits Berlin; Auden meets Gerhart Meyer
APRIL 1929	John Layard attempts suicide in Berlin; Auden begins long, four-part poetic sequence
APRIL–MAY 1929	John Auden visits Berlin
MAY 1929	meets Otto Küsel
MAY–JULY 1929	living in Rothehütte in the Harz Mountains
JULY 1929	returns to England; breaks off engagement with Sheilah Richardson
OCT 1929	completes his long, four-part poetic sequence; starts tutoring in Kensington, London; writes "Sir, no man's enemy, forgiving all"
FEB 1930	stops tutoring, leaves London
MARCH 1930	undergoes surgery in Birmingham for an anal fistula
MARCH / APRIL 1930	writes "Consider this and in our time"
APRIL 1930	writes "Get there if you can and see the land you once were proud to own"; starts teaching at Larchfield Academy, Helensburgh, Scotland
AUG–NOV 1930	writes a now-lost play, "The Fronny"
OCT 1930	*Poems* published by Faber and Faber
JAN–NOV 1931	writes most of *The Orators*
OCT 1931	has "a most important vision about groups"

FEB 1932	writes "A Happy New Year"
LATE MARCH–APRIL 1932	holiday on Dartmoor with Gerald Heard
APRIL 1932	visits Dartington Hall in Devon
MAY 1932	*The Orators* published by Faber and Faber; writes "Prologue" ["O love, the interest itself in thoughtless heaven"]
CA JUNE 1932	finishes teaching at Larchfield Academy
JULY–AUG 1932	starts writing an alliterative "epic" ("In the year of my youth when yoyos came in")
AUG 1932	writes "A Communist to Others"
CA SEPT 1932	starts teaching at the Downs School at Colwall in Herefordshire
MARCH / APRIL 1933	abandons his "epic," unfinished
APRIL 1933	writes "The month was April"
MAY 1933	writes "Hearing of harvests rotting in the valleys"
CA JUNE 1933	falls in love with Michael Yates
JUNE 1933	has another vision; writes "Out on the lawn I lie in bed"
JUNE / EARLY JULY 1933	writes letter to Spender about politics, poetry, and "national emblems"
JULY 1933	Michael Yates leaves the Downs School and starts at Bryanston in the autumn
LATE SUMMER / AUTUMN 1933	writes "Here on the cropped grass of the narrow ridge I stand"; starts affair with Peter Roger?
JAN 1934	first broadcast on the BBC
AUG–SEPT 1934	trip by car to the Carpathians with Michael Yates and Peter Roger
LATE 1934	sends sequence of sixteen love poems, mostly inspired by Yates, to Isherwood
MAY 1935	Auden and Isherwood's play *The Dog Beneath the Skin* published by Faber and Faber

JUNE 1935	marries Erika Mann in rural Ledbury, Herefordshire
JUNE–JULY 1935	writes "Madrigal"; starts composition of "Night Mail"; begins collaboration with Benjamin Britten; leaves the Downs School
AUG 1935	holiday on the Isle of Man with Michael Yates and his family; composes "August for the people and their favourite islands"
SEPT 1935	officially joins the GPO Film Unit in London; living in a London flat with Basil Wright
OCT 1935	first showing of *Coal Face*; visits the Manns, his in-laws, in Switzerland
NOV 1935	writes "Look, stranger, at this island now"
DEC 1935	appears briefly on camera as Father Christmas in scene for the film *Calendar of the Year*
CA DEC 1935 / JAN 1936	moves in with William and Nancy Coldstream in Belsize Park, London
JAN 1936	first performance of *The Dog Beneath the Skin*
FEB 1936	first showing of *Night Mail*
CA FEB / MARCH 1936	writes "Dear, though the night is gone"; starts affair with David Impey?
CA MARCH 1936	writes "Fish in the unruffled lakes"
MARCH– APRIL 1936	working in Sintra, Portugal, with Isherwood on *The Ascent of F6*
MARCH 1936	resigns from the GPO Film Unit by airmail letter
CA APRIL 1936	writes "Stop all the clocks, cut off the telephone" for *The Ascent of F6*; writes "Casino"; meets the German exiles Ernst Toller and Christiane Grautoff; writes "Epilogue"; returns to England
CA APRIL / MAY 1936	completes his new book of poems
MAY 1936	participates in the marriage celebrations for Therese Giehse and John Simpson in Birmingham
JUNE–SEPT 1936	in Iceland, gathering material for a travel book, *Letters from Iceland*, with Louis MacNeice; joined for part of the time by Michael Yates

JULY 1936   suggests to Eliot his new book of poems be called "It's a Way" or "The Island"

OCT 1936   Auden's new collection published by Faber and Faber under the title *Look, Stranger!* (in the United States, the book appears in 1937 as *On This Island*)

NOV 1937   receives the King's Gold Medal for Poetry from George VI

DEC 1937   at Wesco in the Lake District, spends his last Christmas in England for 35 years

THE ISLAND

PROLOGUE

CALIBAN'S ISLAND

The price of nationality is war.

—W. L. GEORGE (1915)

IMAGINE ONE AFTERNOON in an eighteen-year-old poet's life—the afternoon of 4 July 1925. The scene is rural Norfolk, the marshy eastern haunch of England, at a spot barely three miles from a beach where the land shelves down into the North Sea. It is Speech Day at Gresham's School. In overcast weather, a prosperous, straw-hatted audience is outside watching the school's annual production of a work by Shakespeare. This year, the play is *The Tempest*.

On the grassy stage, a gawky Caliban lurches forward from the trees. "This island's *mine*," growls this spindly figure with a plummy voice, played by W. H. Auden.[1] His face is hidden behind a false beard, and his body is covered by a crudely patched cloak over a fur jerkin, like the kind soldiers wore in the trenches during what is referred to as simply "the War." This *Tempest* is being acted in the still reverberating aftermath of a gigantic military storm. Such were the numbers of men who fought in the conflict that there are combat veterans among the spectators in Norfolk this afternoon, as well as families observing today who lost a relative in the violence. Like someone coming out of the line, Caliban stumbles into the clearing, claiming an audience for his griefs.[2] He is part ghoul, part stevedore, part victim, part shaman.

Wystan Hugh Auden is already a poet. But, dressed up as the endlessly allegorized Shakespearean renegade Caliban, this is one of his last days as a schoolboy. Without anyone, not even Auden, exactly knowing it, as Caliban puts into spellbinding language his feelings of

1

FIG. 1   *W. H. Auden, aged eighteen, plays Caliban in the Gresham's School production of* The Tempest *in July 1925. Auden sought the Shakespearean role of the disinherited inhabitant of an island as a way of making a covert protest against the disciplinary regime he suffered under at Gresham's.*

anxiety and injustice and his love for the island world where he lives, Auden is acting out part of his own literary life to come. Imagine how, if we were there that day and we were sensitive enough to see them, many of the important things about this poet might already be discernible, brought out by the role, the clothes, and the script—the fiction says something true, the old drama is a window onto this poet's future.

Gresham's, the setting for the play, is a small, relatively progressive but firmly upper-middle-class, fee-paying school, situated a discreet half mile or so from the small Norfolk town of Holt. A social enclave in the midst of salt marshes and woods, Gresham's is mainly a clutch of large, modern brick buildings. The school functions as a sort of island, like the one where *The Tempest* takes place. It is a cut-off world where a domineering, recently deceased headmaster has ordained special rituals, arcane traditions and rivalries, and where he tolerated (or promoted) idiosyncratic forms of common sense and logic.

While the national news that day in the summer of 1925 is dominated by industrial conflict—especially deadlock in the coal industry between pit owners and miners—here the classic drama unfolds decorously and undisturbed (unless, that is, you see dark, disruptive Caliban as the living projection of the workers from that far-off realm of misery and discontent). In Shakespeare, the natural world is a place for revelations, and *The Tempest* is staged where all such performances at Gresham's occur, in a theatrical space like a small amphitheater, excavated from the side of a hill in the school wood.[3] In an uncanny way, as the young Auden wears this stage costume among the trees, something hidden in him appears.

In previous summers, Auden has played a female part in the school Shakespeare plays—Ursula, a "waiting gentlewoman," in 1921's *Much Ado About Nothing* and Katharina, the "shrew," in 1922's *The Taming of the Shrew.* In the run-up to 1925's production of *The Tempest,* there has been predictable competition for the best parts. In Auden's final year at Gresham's, rather than aiming for the starring role of Prospero, he has been set on acting Caliban.[4] He has his own purposes in playing that "monster," based on an instinctive grasp of and identification with Caliban's condition as a disinherited outcast constantly kept in painful thrall by the all-seeing eye of Prospero, the priggish master-magician who takes over Caliban's island. The play is about power and the abuses of power, and Auden has told Robert Medley, one of his closest friends and the boy who inspired him to begin writing poetry in 1922, that he has chosen the role of Caliban—a "thing of darkness" like the miners about whom Auden has composed poems—in order to "express his dislike of 'the Masters.'"[5] Referring to the school's emotionally coercive system of inducing pupils to self-report for their own violations of the moral code and to divulge one another's lapses, Medley, later a painter, will write: "With extraordinary psychological insight, Wystan perceived that, implicated in Caliban, was a protest against the honour system, under which he had suffered so much; the occasion for making a witty, personal and deeply felt 'send-up' of the system was not to be missed."[6] Auden has probably noticed that, early on in the play, Prospero refers to himself as a "schoolmaster," and now Auden is here in the wood, acting the rebel whom the master cheats out of his home.[7]

Apparently celebrating the victory of a socially and morally superior mage over the brutish embodiment of sedition, *The Tempest* is a safe choice for this privileged English place on a summer afternoon. Numerous pairs of eyes gaze at Auden playing the island's "savage and deformed slave." The audience's murmurs and smiles that greeted his first appearance are fading now. Hunched, he moves as he speaks. "Which *thou* takest from me," he snarls as he commands more of the stage, pointing at Prospero. The magician and his daughter, Miranda (played by the future biologist David Lack, author of the evolutionary classic *Darwin's Finches*), draw back.[8]

"I loved thee | And show'd thee all the qualities o' the isle, | The fresh springs, brine-pits, barren places and fertile," the mooncalf tells the old man plangently, waving his hand toward the Norfolk countryside. But quickly, bitterly he realizes that he has been a fool: "I am all the subjects that you have, | Which first was mine own king: and here you sty me | In this hard rock, whiles you do keep from me | The rest o' the island."[9] It is an imaginative fantasy, but Auden is making it seem real.

Confined to "this hard rock," Caliban / Auden mentions his "island" three times during his first substantial speech. It is the nub of his grievance, the symbolic token of all his life's losses and the object of his desire, the possession he wants to regain. "Thou most lying slave, | Whom stripes may move, not kindness!" the boy playing Prospero roars back. Perhaps at this point, hearing of "stripes," the schoolmasters in the audience exchange glances and archly raise an eyebrow. For is not anarchic Auden the only Gresham's pupil from this period whom the school's own Prospero, the headmaster J. R. Eccles, has caned humiliatingly?[10]

In the play's final lines, like a Speech Day orator wishing a favorite pupil every success in life, Prospero liberates Ariel, his devoted, primly asexual servant, to a life of his own: "to the elements | Be free, and fare thou well!"[11] But as a counterpoint to these insipid, concluding notes of conformist success, there remains a deep problem: Caliban. Every school, every island, every nation has its Calibans, those it categorizes as failures, dissidents, disruptors, and outcasts. Before his death in 1919, exhausted by his labors and depressed by the loss of one hundred Old Greshamians during the 1914–1918 war, G. W. S. Howson, the austere and dynamic renovator of Gresham's reputation during the first two decades of the twentieth century, loathed the "professed rebel" and allowed "not a grain of hero-worship for the opponent of authority" in the little world of Gresham's. Howson thought that his duty was, like a potent magus, by force of will to "mould the characters of his boys" into decent, public-spirited, and loyal citizens who, both at school and later in life, would feel that they "had a moral 'stake in the country.'"[12]

In effect, Howson and his sedulous successor, Eccles, wanted Gresham's to be a place entirely populated by Ariels.[13] (Howson's grave, by the school chapel's south wall, is adorned with a quotation, carved in stone and ominous in this context, from Hebrews 11:4: "He being dead yet speaketh.") For a disturbingly large number of pupils, Howson's and Eccles's unreal goal would have devastating psychological effects, as we will see. Along with a distinguished roster of Ariel-like scientists, artists, and industrialists such as the inventor of the hovercraft Christopher Cockerell, the computer scientist Christopher Strachey, the property developer Charles Kearley, the modernist architect and designer "Kit" Nicholson, the actor Sebastian Shaw, and the ambiguously establishmentarian composer Benjamin Britten, Gresham's would produce an impressive number of real-life Calibans in the first half of the twentieth century. These include the diplomat and spy Donald Maclean, as well as a number of senior members of the Communist Party of Great Britain, some of them probably Soviet moles.[14] And it turns out that the boy who is taking part in *The Tempest* and who will become Gresham's most famous pupil is a Caliban too. (In 1934, Auden will call the school in his time "a Fascist state"; unfazed, today Gresham's puts on plays in a structure named the Auden Theatre.[15])

Imagining this Shakespearean moment in 1925, we can begin to forget the things we might vaguely think we already know about Auden—the supposed poet of a Red-decade socialism quickly abandoned, the supposed poet of rumpled, garrulous urbanity, the supposed versifier of bourgeois hyper-cleverness, the ostensibly cerebral bard.

After his death, Hannah Arendt, who was close to him, acutely referred to Auden as possessing "the necessary secretiveness of the great poet."[16] It is probably the single most telling phrase in all the millions of words of Auden criticism and biography. Just as his protest against Gresham's was hidden inside a familiar dramatic role, Auden's poetry, shielded by that "necessary secretiveness," came from a place far below his surface idiosyncrasies and far beyond his looming intelligence. His comments about his identity as a writer often emphasize deep feeling over intellect: he once defined a poet as "before anything else, a person who is passionately in love with language," and he referred to himself as "in love . . . with the muse of poetry."[17] Auden's passion for words (not ideas) was at the core of his identity as a writer.

Two of the key lines in the younger Auden's oeuvre (they come in his poem "The Composer") describe his vocation as being an inspired version of a lucky dip: "Rummaging into his living, the poet fetches | The images out that *hurt* and *connect*."[18] In this sonnet, poetry, composed by a madcap, Auden-like figure who digs around distractedly in the overlooked or discarded debris of daily existence and memory, looks for "images," not themes, and the artistic goal is an emotional epiphany produced through intuitions, remembrances, and luck. Correspondingly, in thinking about Auden's poetry, we find rich seams of meaning in his dreams, fears, fantasies, and visions, even (at one moment near the end of this book) in his drunkenness. Theodor Adorno rightly insisted that a "collective undercurrent provides the foundation for all individual lyric poetry."[19] Auden's writing, in the period covered by *The Island*, is neither anecdote nor lofty philosophical or moral rumination. Rather, it is an urgent reaching down to that pre-rational, communal undercurrent, a groping into the hidden sources of group meaning for access to experiences painful and shared, for "images . . . that hurt and connect."

But if the foundation is collective, the process of composition is individual. Poets have to stand alone in a culture's rain, waiting. Every so often some are fortunate enough to have lightning strike them. Auden was someone whom the downward blaze of inspiration hit again and again.[20] So, put to one side the clichés of Auden biography, and of intellectual and literary history, of recycled "truths," of self-aggrandizing gossip, thrice-told tales, and giggly portraits—almost all of which tend to emphasize the purported sadness or eccentricity of a gay man's life.

Instead, as a way of recovering the eeriness, beauty, and deep power of the young Auden's work, imagine with me an Auden in the 1920s and 1930s very unlike the cliché portrait. Imagine a raw, intense, wounded, politically ambiguous, prophetic figure. And, as a way of beginning that effort, hold in mind this dramatic spectacle of *The Tempest* being performed in East Anglia in 1925. Auden starts as he means to go on: as a Caliban, the role he chooses for himself. Throughout this book, we will see that there is something uncannily revealing in the times when Auden dresses up as a stage character. These are Wildean moments when a mask discloses something true. Now, in 1925, Caliban incarnates Auden's disruptiveness, dispossession, lyrical knowledge, pained memory, and uncertain hope. He is the Dionysian force in this artist so often and so misleadingly understood as an Apollo.

Seeking to show love both to the arias of poetry and to the recitative of life, *The Island* examines Auden's work from 1922, when he began writing, until around the time when his epochal second full collection of poems was published. That ardent, ambivalent volume (called *Look, Stranger!* [1936] in the United Kingdom and *On This Island* [1937] in the United States) is simultaneously the high point and the end in Auden of a positively valued commitment to England and Englishness and of a desire for national representativeness.

This is not a familiar story about the young Auden's poetry. In the first half of the 1930s, many readers saw, or thought they saw, political messages in Auden's work. But in the postwar period and over many ensuing decades, the social and political dimensions of his early poetry were largely debunked, erased, or ignored. Psychology and ideas took their places. Typically, critics have interpreted Auden's writing from the later 1920s or the early 1930s as an investigation of divisions within the mind or as a probing of ethical matters.[21] This book brings politics back, but not as a discussion of party slogans, philosophies, or programs. The politics in question here concern personal life and personal identity, often in relation to Auden's fascination with Englishness and the meaning of England.

By 1937, when this book concludes, Auden had developed a highly ambivalent relationship to ideas about nationalism and his own relationship with his home nation. His poetry had lost most of its belief in the virtue of belonging, and Auden had already embarked on a period of almost continuous travel. Over the next few years, he went to, among other places, Iceland, Spain, China, Japan, Belgium, Germany, and the United States. He put down roots in New York in 1939, although he spent a few months in Germany again in 1945, this time in uniform, as a member of a US military intelligence-gathering mission. Reporting on the transatlantic trip and punning on "major," which indicated both his literary prestige and his temporary rank, he commented to a friend: "My dear, I'm the | first major poet to have flown | the Atlantic."[22] (Perhaps, in the background, he was also thinking here about his "flight" from England in the later 1930s.)

Between 1937 and 1945, as a noncombatant Auden was in or very near the front lines of three separate war zones: those of the Spanish Civil War, the Sino-Japanese War, and the European theater of operations in the Second World War.[23] In Munich in 1945, he met hospitalized survivors shortly after their release from the Dachau concentration camp. When Adorno wrote in 1949 that it was barbaric to write poetry after Auschwitz, Auden was in a position to know the full force of the statement. He did continue to write, of course, but it was poetry of a different, increasingly chastened and melancholic kind: "we shan't," he said in a work from the 1960s, "not since Stalin and Hitler, | trust ourselves ever again."[24]

In 1946, he became a US citizen amid consternation and derision in Britain over his absence. That same year, once the poet of "the island," he was now maintaining that humanity had reached a "a further stage of development in which it may well be as necessary at least for intellectuals to leave their country, as it is for children to leave their homes."[25]

In the beginning, though, Auden's attitude toward England and Englishness was very different. In his work up until 1936, as if he were following in the tracks of one of those ghostly miners who haunt his earliest poems, Auden explores the obscure depths of some of the most profound and ambiguous elements of recent existence. In particular, he returns frequently to a thing imposed: the mind's pull toward national belonging. He asks questions about what it meant, or means, to be English. Auden's early writing can fundamentally be described as one poet's emotional expression of this specific, localized facet of modern humanness: the condition of having a national identity. This subject, subtle but ubiquitous in his work, he dramatizes with moving literary brilliance as experiences of selfhood that "hurt and connect."

In seeking to excavate these meanings in Auden's poetry, *The Island* tries to make his poems unfamiliar and new—not only for readers who are just encountering them but for those who are already well acquainted. My aim is to make his poems vividly remote, evocatively historical, to allow the atmosphere of the past, and of that lost world, England in the 1920s and 1930s, in all its subtle strangeness to breathe out of these pages and, ultimately, out of Auden's writing itself. Auden's poetry is completely alive, but he is not a contemporary writer. With a few exceptions, most of the people who knew Auden at all well are dead. He is a poet whose worldview and responses belong to a different era than the present—his birthdate of 21 February 1907 is closer chronologically to those of Tennyson and Darwin than it is to any child's born today. So, I turn back to Auden's beginnings to reimagine him and his work within as clearly articulated a social setting as possible. Auden's genius as a writer is neither reducible to nor separable from his historical context. The culture he lived in was passing through extraordinary convulsions: his poems register that turmoil. We exist amid the aftershocks.

The ambition to dramatize Auden in his own external and internal worlds has corollaries. Often Auden is treated as a sage or philosopher who teaches lessons (which by chance are written as poems) to the present. But Auden is not speaking didactically to contemporary readers about eternal verities of human experience. Rather, he is a voice brilliantly transmitting the contours of life in a specific time and place to whomever wants to listen to this signal from a world that is both distant and somehow still close.

Auden grew up in the aftermath of the First World War, and he matured through a series of further national crises. More than most, he is a "something has just happened" poet—overtly or tacitly, almost all his poems are a response to an occurrence, sometimes small, sometimes large. It is "the case with most poems," he once wrote, that the germ is "a real historical event."[26] His poems emanate from a particular location and often clearly emerge in reaction to a particular predicament. Again and again, his poetry rises to an occasion—although at times it works hard to disguise that circumstantiality. And in his work, Auden is as much intuitive as analytic, more vulnerable, perhaps even traumatized, than dispassionate, not so much eminent or idiosyncratic as movingly representative of common concerns. And, like so many great poets, he is someone who turned to this great verbal art not to articulate an opinion that he already held but to discover what he thought.

And what did he think? Auden the man defined himself, probably sincerely, as a "selfish pink old Liberal."[27] But for a while in the 1930s, Auden the poet was a consistently quietist, nostalgic figure, one whose aesthetic politics crossed into a genteel but intense version of nationalism. The painter and art critic Andrew Forge, whom Auden taught at a prep school in the 1930s, once commented that Auden "was naturally anarchic but had inside him a demon which was deeply conservative."[28]

The difference between a historical individual and the persona that speaks in their works is a commonplace of literary criticism, but not less useful for that. In what follows, I distinguish between Auden the person and the speaker in his poems because I sense a split between his own opinions and the sometimes conservative "demon" that appears in his poetry. Which is the "real" Auden? Perhaps we should say that the record in art is truer than the evidence in life. In *The Prisoner* (1923), as Marcel Proust's narrator plays over Vinteuil's sonata at the piano, he wonders: "Was there in art a more profound reality, in which our true personality finds an expression that is not afforded it by the activities of life?"[29] Perhaps the real Auden is the one in the poems.

The "speaker" in Auden's poems is a "true personality" different from the one known in the flesh by Auden's family and friends. There often seems to be a gap between the opinions and values of Auden, the living individual, and those that emerge in his poetry. Because the poems are ultimately what matter most, in cases of obvious conflict I focus on what the poems say. For Auden, the split seems less aggravated when he is writing in dramatic forms or in prose, especially in his published prose where he sounds much more like the person his friends knew. But Auden's plays and prose are weaker during this period than his poetry; poetry is his enabling genre. There are many great poems by Auden in the 1920s and 1930s, but are there any great (as opposed to very good) essays? I do not believe so: in his prose, the early Auden rarely seems to go as deep as he so often does in his poetry. Nevertheless, from time to time the voice of truth does speak oracularly but clearly in this young poet's letters and essays. Whenever it has, for me, sounded that authentic note, I have drawn on those statements.

It is also clear that Auden's personal relationships—with his family, his romantic partners, his friends and schoolmates—are essential clues that help us discern meanings in his early work. The people around the man light up the poet's mind. So this book emphasizes the role of some of these relationships and the parts they played in Auden's evolution as a writer. Unlike many other accounts, *The Island* treats Auden's father—and especially his father's medical career and his military service—as being at least as important as his mother's religious beliefs in the formation of Auden's poetic identity.[30] In addition, the book offers details about, and attributes large significance to, Auden's relationship with Michael Yates, a boy he had fallen in love with while Yates was his pupil, as well as to his flings with other young men he met in and through his jobs at schools in the early 1930s. These affairs—like the role Dr. Auden played in his son's imaginative life—illuminate deeply important aspects of Auden's identity as a writer.

What is genuinely new can often begin by seeming wrong or monstrous. In 1925, the year when Auden was performing as Caliban, Freud wrote that "the content of a repressed image or idea can make its way into consciousness, on condition that it is *negated*. Negation is a way of taking cognizance of what is repressed; indeed it is already a lifting of the repression, though not, of course, an acceptance of what is repressed."[31] Auden's role as Caliban, the unacceptable pariah upstart, and his own stark, abrasive, often hermetic poems of the next five years or so, from 1925 to 1930, look like they are acts of negation—negations of a polite social order and of advanced literary fashions. But as negations, they herald the emergence from darkness of a new kind of modern English poet making his way into the light, of a new dispensation in modern literary history, and of a profound shift, or retrenchment, in national cultural values.

Auden's austere, modern but antimodernist poetry, set in bleak but symbolically freighted northern landscapes, was the vital early phase in a journey toward his role as the representative voice of a new Englishness, the voice of an insular, inward-looking, cloistered, closeted, and confined world. It was (and it is), in its own way, a traumatized world—guilty, sad, and beautiful. And his early, idiosyncratic poetic landscapes, filled with mine shafts and tunnels, were intended as a means of connecting to the culture as a whole. So this is the study not just of a particular artist but also of one version of a collective sensibility. It is an English sensibility that has survived, mutated but still recognizable, into the twenty-first century: the national imaginary often still seems obsessed, as Auden was, by the idea of "the island."

How can someone who saw himself as Caliban, an outsider, cast himself, or be cast, as the true embodiment of a culture, even if that culture is just the little world of a school? The idea that a society's best representatives are not its leaders but its pariahs was by 1925 one that had become thinkable, at least in a literary context. For example, in poems written during 1918, Wilfred Owen, soon to become one of Auden's poetic heroes, suggested that the soldier-victims of the war, although literally killed or shoved aside by the nation they served, were in fact England's truest subjects. In "Smile, Smile, Smile," one of the last poems Owen wrote before he died in action in the First World War, he imagines the "sunk-eyed wounded," convalescing and reading in the *Daily Mail* reports of politicians' chauvinistic platitudes. "The greatest glory will be theirs who fought, | Who kept this nation in integrity," the bully-patriots say in the newspaper. Owen insists, though, that the soldiers, in losing their own bodily wholeness to uphold the country's spiritual (rather than merely territorial) "integrity," have separated the self-sacrificing, displaced English wheat from the patriotic home-front chaff. With distinctly queer overtones (as if to say that dissident sexuality, martyrdom, and national representativeness were all somehow linked together), Owen presents England as no longer a place or a state but a select, battered group of "secret men," many permanently exiled in foreign graves:

> Nation?—The half-limbed readers did not chafe
> But smiled at one another curiously
> Like secret men who know their secret safe.
> (This is the thing they know and never speak,
> That England one by one had fled to France,
> Not many elsewhere now, save under France.)[32]

The idea that an aristocracy of outsiders represents "this nation" echoes through many other war texts published during Auden's opening years as a poet. For example, the final scene in Henry Williamson's novel *The Patriot's Progress* (1930), published in the same year as Auden's first full collection, is a confrontation in London on 11 November, Armistice

Day, between the disenchanted amputee ex-soldier John Bullock and a bleary-eyed "old toff." The toff tells Bullock sententiously: "We'll see that England doesn't forget you fellows!" He receives a humbling reply: "'We are England,' said John Bullock, with a slow smile."[33] In this line of thought, already visible during Auden's early years as a writer, the outsider *is* the central figure, and the true nation *is* its outcasts, its dead, its poets.

In July 1925, the same month that the eighteen-year-old Auden acted in *The Tempest,* he wrote "Friendship," a poem about a "weary," solitary speaker, walking through a country storm, to whom the rain means "no more than tree or stone." The fact that "Friendship" is derivative of Wordsworth poems such as "Resolution and Independence" (1802) in no way muffles its convincing sense of isolation or its strange, suggestive mood. Suddenly, Auden's speaker meets "An old man picking flints, wet and alone, | Who gave a meaning to the rain at last." (The stranger, who seems like a wild man of the woods, is probably a "runner"—one of the tramps who earned money each summer in rural England by picking flints off the hillsides and selling them to farmers, who used the stones to repair country roads.[34])

The words of this soaked vagabond "picking flints," reminiscent of Caliban carrying logs, leave an impression on the nature-sensitive protagonist like the sound of a "thrush's song," which is superficially "Heard and forgotten" but whose reverberations are destined, in the deeper layers of the mind, "not perhaps to end."[35] The old man who "gives a meaning"—whose flints strike the spark of inspiration in the speaker—is both an archaic outcast and an authentic inhabitant of the island. He clears the fields of useless debris, bringing back order and restoring an unsullied greenness to the landscape.

The itinerant flint picker also suggests the commonplace figure of the First World War veteran, tens of thousands of whom were never fully reintegrated into the society they had left behind when they went to fight. In the postwar period, the threatening ex-serviceman, now returned from overseas and like a kind of living Caliban or like the young Auden's "old man . . . wet and alone," was often not seen as a hero but as someone who represented "everything that is presumed to lie 'outside' the boundaries of domestic existence." He was "the initiate of death . . .

stripped of every social superfluity, stripped to his essence."[36] Auden's poems about such wanderers and, a little later, about mysterious, larger-than-life but vanished miners raise the same question of inheritance that emerges in the performance of *The Tempest*. Who will revive the island? The answer is: its outsiders. Auden begins as a dissident or outcast in the heart of the country. By 1937, and the end of this book— after he has embraced and been temporarily embraced by English literary culture—as an act of artistic survival, he will make himself dissident again, casting himself out of England.

It is a central truth about Auden's poetry that its deepest sources lie not in other books but in the world. The crucial historical forces driving his early work were twofold and interrelated: the catastrophe of the First World War (often evocatively known at the time as "the War" or "the Great War") and, in reaction to the conflict, from the mid-1920s onward, an influential section of English society's gradual, dazed, selective rediscovery and reenchantment of the rural English landscape. It is impossible to understand the early Auden without connecting his work both to the mass trauma of war and to the subsequent mass psychological compensation for the conflict's horror. This compensation, even among those who had not fought, took the form of a deep and almost manic concern with pastoral Englishness.

But the war first. Auden was seven when it started and eleven when it ended. His late-in-life comments about this European Armageddon often seem oddly flat, as for instance when he claimed that he was "too young for the First World War to be real."[37] That notion defies innumerable accounts of the period in British cultural history, both contemporary and those more recent. "The War is such a tremendous landmark that locally it imposes itself upon our computations of time like the birth of Christ. We say 'pre-war' and 'post-war,' rather as we say B.C. or A.D.," wrote Wyndham Lewis, one of Auden's favorite authors, in the 1930s.[38] What Lewis implied was that at the center of this four-year moment of transition, this "landmark" in modern history, was not a birth but a horrific, sacrificial mass death paralleling in depth of meaning Christ's murder. How could it not matter to anyone alive then? Closer to the present, the literary historian Samuel Hynes called the war "the peculiar shaping force" for people of Auden's generation in

Britain: "Every memoir about the time makes clear that the First World War dominated the lives of those who were children then as much as it did the lives of their elders. Perhaps more so, for the young had no real experience of the Edwardian world before the war; for them, awareness of the world and awareness of the war came at the same time."[39]

A journalist only slightly younger than Auden remembered: "I was five years old when the first war began and nine when it ended. Some of the most deeply impressive emotional experiences of my boyhood were concerned with the effects of the war." He added: "On a winter evening in my 13th year the memorial in . . . honour [of the fallen old boys] was dedicated in the Chapel; for six years, Sunday after Sunday, I sat and faced four panels which bore the names of four successive heads of the school, all of whom had been killed in battle before they were 21."[40] At Auden's school, Gresham's, the chapel's war memorial (completed in 1921) included an oak screen into which were carved, entirely in capitals, the names of one hundred old boys, "OUR COMRADES WHO FELL IN THE GREAT WAR."

Auden's claim that the war meant little to him would not matter if this were simply a case of his having a different experience than most people did. In fact, though, as is so often the case, Auden is representative as well as unique. The accounts of his contemporaries corroborate the deeper, more painful story that his older self either avoided or forgot but that his early poetry insists on telling.

Auden's father, a doctor and public servant, volunteered for the Royal Army Medical Corps (RAMC) in September 1914. He spent most of his time in uniform far from home, caring for the wounded and dying, and experiencing unspeakable horrors as he did. Serving in various theaters of operation until 1919, Dr. Auden narrowly escaped death at least twice, fell sick, and began a love affair in Cairo that rocked the Audens' marriage in Britain.[41]

Auden did admit that his father's departure for the war, if not the war itself, was formative: "I did not . . . lose my father physically by death, but to some degree I lost him psychologically. I was seven . . . when he enlisted in the R.A.M.C., and I didn't see him again until I was twelve and a half."[42] Loneliness suffuses a vignette from the long poem "Letter to Lord Byron," written in 1936, of the three Auden brothers on a wartime holiday with their mother hymning an absent God. Auden recalls "those summer Sunday evenings, when | Along the seafronts fled a curious noise, | 'Eternal Father,' sung by three young boys."[43] And, rightly or wrongly, Auden told an interviewer that he related his homo-sexuality to his father's absence: "My father was away during the 1914–18 War and I'm sure that's why I am the way I am."[44] Sex and war are never truly distinct subjects in Auden's imagination.

Even if we accept that the young Auden was insulated from at least some of the home front's emotionally bullying, grief-stricken atmo-sphere, and even if he truly did not worry for his father's, his brothers', or his own safety (Auden's eldest brother, Bernard, was in training camp, like a calf at the abattoir, when the war suddenly ended in 1918), his nonchalance is suggestive. In its blandness, it evokes a wartime child's version of Walter Benjamin's description of the storyteller who survives the conflict "not richer, but poorer in communicable experi-ence."[45] Children like Auden, though noncombatants, went through the war as well, and their experiences too were sometimes unspeak-able, even to themselves. Yet, inevitably, those experiences found voice in other ways. Auden's poetry evokes war anxieties constantly but not often in literal terms.

This expressive indirectness raises a broader question about Auden's autobiographical statements. How open was Auden habitually about significant, and even traumatic, events? Probably not very. For a prom-inent figure whose emotional life was considered unacceptable by many, some of that reticence was (in the words of his 1939 elegy for Freud) "a protective coloration | for one who'd lived among enemies so long."[46] This almost pathologically prolific and capable author left in his oeuvre many gaps and silences about his identity and his experiences, treating them, as a character in one of his poems does, like wounds "to keep hidden from the world."[47] Arendt identified Auden's "necessary secretiveness"—there were even secrets in his writing that he kept hidden from himself.

The most obvious instance of Auden's selective reticence about sub-jects that are everywhere present but only occasionally touched on explicitly concerns the profound subject of his queerness. "He could be very cagey about such matters," the novelist Christopher Isherwood once remarked, speaking of Auden as a person but also providing a useful clue to the enigmatic, ambiguous qualities in his close friend's poetry.[48] Given the moral norms of the time, perhaps there was often no other way for Auden to give literary expression to his sexuality except by circling it, signaling its presence not by a direct view but by the visible perturbations it creates around the subject.

But other crucial moments provide further instances of this oblique mode, closely akin to Auden's habitual "necessary secretiveness." Because sex and conflict were intertwined at some level for Auden, so, besides his indirection about homosexuality, many of his elisions center on the witnessing of war, actual or impending. For example, Auden said and wrote very little about his disillusioning journey to Spain in 1937, when he seems to have intended to serve as an ambulance driver on the Republican side in the civil war. He never commented on his visit with Isherwood to Nagasaki in 1938 during a round-the-world journey home from observing the Sino-Japanese War. And he wrote nothing about his brief stay in Nazi Berlin in early 1939, though he told a correspondent he "often [thought] of" his visit there and "how awful it was."[49] Yet, in spite of thinking about it often, in the huge number of words that Auden published, there is not a single mention of Berlin in 1939.

Although Auden had a contract with another writer for them to produce together a book on their time with the United States Strategic Bombing Survey in Germany in 1945, he never began work on the text. Conspicuously, he said nothing in print about his experiences there, although he saw extraordinary, historic scenes such as firebombed cities; researched and wrote reports on topics such as prostitution in the Third Reich, the 20 July 1944 assassination attempt on Hitler, and Christianity and Nazism; and, as mentioned, spoke to Dachau survivors—all experiences that must have widened the horizons of his heart and imagination and that often brought him to tears.[50] The point is not that these events did not enter Auden's poetry. It is that, like sexual love, they did not enter it explicitly. Auden's poetry says everything, but slantwise.

Given that many of the traumatic lacunae in Auden's accounts of his life concern war, it is obvious too that often these gaps also relate directly or indirectly to Germany. Because of the power of poems such as "September 1, 1939," in criticism about Auden's work the standard historical reference point is the Second World War. But an even deeper connection is with the First World War. In Auden's poems, the First World War appears like a light, always on, that is discernible as a glow even through the fabric of a closed curtain. At a thematic level, Auden was obsessed with weak leaders, with spiritual renewal, with the dead soldier poets of the war, including the poets Wilfred Owen and Edward Thomas, with Germany and German-speaking culture, and even with Thomas Hardy, who "looked like my father," the father who (to use the terminology of the time) went "missing" for his young son. These subjects, to which he returns again and again, testify to Auden's camouflaged fascination with the First World War and its aftermath.[51]

All Auden's protestations to the contrary, then, it is not simply the subjects he wrote about that make clear how real and, in a painful sense, how *inspiring* the war was for him. The war is most profoundly a landscape, a history, and an atmosphere in the poems that made Auden famous at the end of the 1920s and start of the 1930s, precisely in the era of the sudden boom in films, novels, memoirs, and histories produced by those who had lived on the conflict's battlefronts. As in a dream, the story of the war's violence is there in the bleak, empty northern spaces described in Auden's early poems, in the roll calls of the names of obscure hills and villages, in the deserted moors filled, like the recent battlefields, with tunnels, holes, and shattered machinery, ghosted with missing heroes, and the scene of lethal exploits now growing mysterious. It is there in the terrifying and alluring, grass-blown entrances to an underground world in the Pennines where Auden first approached the line between "Self and Not-self, Death and Dread." Here, in his imagination at least, as a young man he heard chilling German words being whispered back to him in the northern English countryside—almost as if he were suddenly thinking of himself as a dazed British soldier kneeling by an enemy trench.[52]

Whatever Auden's own "official" account of the conflict's lack of relevance to him, his art suggests a haunted writer for whom the significance of what happened in 1914–1918 is never distant. In a very real sense, the young Auden is a war poet—a First World War poet. In his imagination, there is no true escape from the Great War, just as perhaps, up to the present day, in prescriptive rituals like the wearing of the November poppy, there never has been an escape for British culture.

The unavoidable memory of war is related to another important thread in the story of Auden and his poetry: his absorption with German and Austrian culture. German-speaking culture had a broader impact on him than it has had on any English writer since nineteenth-century figures such as Samuel Taylor Coleridge and George Eliot. Auden once described himself as "in love with the German language."[53] He made sixteen trips abroad between August 1925 and May 1936. At least ten of those trips, and probably more, involved time in Germany or Austria. During the same period, he never visited France. (Tellingly, intense dislike of the French was a commonplace, boorish attitude among British war veterans in the 1920s.)

Germanic culture had been part of Auden's childhood. His early home life included an Edwardian aesthetic diet involving plenty of music by German composers—he told a friend he was "brought up on Bach and heard him all the time when [he was] young."[54] He also recalled playing the Grand March from the German-British G. F. Handel's *Athalia* on the piano with his mother.[55] Sometime around the start of the First World War, she taught him to sing the "Liebestod" duet from Wagner's *Tristan und Isolde*. They sang the parts together while they were squeezed up next to each other at the piano playing the music as an accompaniment, fingers stretched out and almost interlacing.[56] By the time Auden was eighteen, he was a competent enough pianist to enjoy playing Beethoven duets.

Beyond music, Auden remembered an incident (to which I will return in Chapter 1) in Surrey during the war when a schoolmaster vindictively accused him of preferring Germany to Britain. Ruminating later on his interest in the country, including his interest in its sexual freedoms, Auden commented that "I may . . . have had an unconscious bias in favour of Germany because, when I was a little boy in prepschool during the First World War, if I took an extra slice of bread and margarine, some master was sure to say: 'I see, Auden, you want the Huns to win'—thus establishing in my mind an association between Germany and forbidden pleasures."[57]

Auden's first trip abroad came in the summer of August 1925, a month or so after he had played Caliban. He and his father attended the Salzburg Festival of music and drama that year. Auden *père et fils* also spent some time in Kitzbühel, about forty miles southwest of Salzburg, where they stayed as paying guests in the house of Hedwig Petzold, widow of the poet Alfons Petzold, who had died from the flu in 1923. The ostensible purpose of the Kitzbühel visit was to start Auden learning German. He went back to visit Petzold at least once and possibly twice in the next couple of years, and they had a brief fling. (Auden explained to his Oxford friend Stephen Spender, "we fucked in the woods."[58]) Around the time of that initial visit, a phrase in German appeared in his poems for the first time, and after another visit to Petzold in the winter of 1926–1927, a few more words of German appeared. Within three years, he was speaking the language fairly easily and writing some competent poems and jingles in German.[59]

The story of "the forbidden pleasures" with which Auden associated Germany is usually construed simply in terms of the emancipated sexual atmosphere he found when he lived in Berlin in 1928–1929, supplemented by the artistic innovations of interwar German culture.[60] But the appetite for German life that many in Auden's generation, like Auden himself, displayed was historically conditioned, and the desire among young English people for experiences in Germany had a symbolic dimension. Isherwood wrote that it "was natural for us, the members of the immediate post-war generation, to be the first to react from the blind chauvinism of the war years."[61] One of Auden's favorite poets, Hardy, bemoaned war between "kin folk kin tongued," and Owen, another favorite, had a vision of a dead German soldier "Lifting distressful hands, as if to bless" the British enemy he calls "my friend."[62] Auden's fascination with German-speaking culture and life was not just a search for personal freedom but also an emblematic quest for reconciliation between warring peoples, often transacted through friendships and sexual love.

The aftermath of the war also emerges in the young Auden's poetry through the common presence of the English countryside and the ideological values associated with the rural world. War and national belonging feed on each other. Although there is a historical truism connecting political dissidence and revolutionary thought, Auden's poetic concerns had more to do with the attempt to restore lost worlds than they did with promoting social upheaval. Eden meant more to him than Utopia. And this too was representative of wider currents of feeling. "To be 'young' is to be in impulsive 'revolt': so a youth-movement must be a 'radical' movement, it is felt," Wyndham Lewis wrote in 1927. "*But the most characteristic, and the most admirable, 'youth-movements' in Europe to-day are not at all 'radical,' but quite the reverse. . . . Europe has had the* lessons of War and Revolution burnt into it."[63] Auden and his contemporaries had all been "burnt" in imagination by war; their characteristic writing is pragmatic, restorative, and, in Auden's case, even conservative and nationalistic. Auden began as a rural writer, and the way that he cultivated his poetry in the English countryside is an example of a widely shared reaction to the recent historical trauma of war.

This book is a story, then, about a variant of middle-class English nationalism, hegemonic but somehow invisible to the mainstream in ways that other indigenous nationalisms in the British Isles during this period were not. English nationalism often metonymically conflated England with Britain. But this is not a general tale about an overarching nationalism spread across all parts of the multinational political entity of the United Kingdom in the interwar period. This concerns a specifically English form of nationalism, with its own distinctive landscapes of marshes, moors, and walled gardens, its own seigneurial sense of its iconographic centrality, its own cozy, sheltered habits of mind, its own pride in deep but selective historical continuities, and its own faith in the symbolic value of rural existence.

Some of Auden's early poetry offers biting satire, verging on excoriation, of English cultural exhaustion. At first glance, this mode might seem to come from a leftist perspective. But, after an initial period in which Auden's poems survey a ruined world, again and again in the earlier 1930s they swing toward a lyrical exaltation of a new vision of England as a blessed, if morally compromised, haven that is momentarily exempt from the terrifying pressures of history. England, geographically a part of an archipelago, is figuratively an island. And within this mythic island, Auden's imagination often seeks out further nest-like, provincial, or rural enclaves, places protected, for example, by the "creepered wall" of an "English house" that shuts out threatening "multitudes" and offers "gardens where we feel secure" and, "gentle, do not care to know, | Where Poland draws her Eastern bow."[64]

Why are there so many urgent, and often celebratory, references to the "nation," to "England" and the "English," in the early work of a writer who was purportedly a progressive, left-leaning poet and therefore one for whom the "nation" might have been a deeply suspicious concept? And what is at stake in these appeals to "England" and the "English" made by the first major poet born in Britain in the twentieth century? Up to the year 1936, the young Auden wrote often about small

English communities (frequently schools)—privileged places that generated poems of intense feeling set among a tightly knit, often same-sex, group of friends in spaces sheltered from the pressures of change, intrusion, and struggle. In such worlds, an amalgamation of the real and the imagined, Auden and others of like mind hoped that a new, more modest and humane national character, decontaminated of the Empire's moral and aesthetic legacies, might emerge. For example, in a 1932 lyric set in a provincial academy, Auden pleads with his tutelary deities, the "Lords of Limit":

> Permit our town here to continue small,
> What city's vast emotional cartel
> Could our few acres satisfy
> Or rival in intensity
> The field of five or six, the English cell?[65]

The community Auden is writing about was actually in Scotland, but his visionary Anglocentrism slides over that detail. The dominant monosyllables of the stanza's last line set off, and add an emotional richness to, the disyllabic, breathy word "English." The language of English nationhood recurs strikingly in a constellation of important poems from this period in Auden's career: as, for instance, when he writes about "our English land" (from "Get there if you can and see the land you once were proud to own") or "English earth" (from *The Orators,* an "English study") or "the English heart" (in "In the year of my youth when yoyos came in"), or, in the example just cited, "the English cell" (from part 2 of "A Happy New Year").[66] Nationalism fueled the First World War that Auden lived through, and the First World War produced the ruralized but modern variant of English nationalism that Auden's early poetry is feverishly caught up in and inspired by.

In Auden's poetry, the "*English* Auden" of this book was not a socialist or left-leaning writer. The young poet imagined that his work might play an important role in the creation of a specifically modern, specifically English, culture in the early 1930s—until he began to realize, around 1936, that this ambition was an empty one.

He wrote in a time when there was a receptive audience for a poet with aspirations for a national voice. The lyrical belonging realized in

Auden's early work derives in part from poetry's historical role in defining nationality, one of the primary constituents of personal identity in the modern world. From "the start," Benedict Anderson wrote in his classic work *Imagined Communities,* "the nation was conceived in language, not in blood."[67] From the mid-1920s onward, Anglo-American poetic modernism, now alienated from its transcultural origins, became steadily more nationalistic, more deeply obsessed with roots, community, tradition, and belonging. In 1943, T. S. Eliot summarized this trajectory when he insisted that "No art is more stubbornly national than poetry."[68] The cultural prestige of poetry in the 1930s stemmed from the assumptions that a poem ought to be as much a collective as a personal utterance and that the best poets would speak representatively on behalf of a large social grouping, typically a nation. Poetic language indeed was part of what constituted the national community. In *The English Vision,* published in 1933, just when Auden was becoming prominent within advanced circles in English culture, the influential critic Herbert Read asserted: "Without a consciousness of national language, there can be no consciousness of a nation."[69]

Auden's poetic voice, using the "national language," coalesced during a period when the "anglicization of Continental styles and values was being openly contested by a militant cultural nationalism."[70] In this context, some readers even saw Auden as, deep down, a dangerously right-wing writer. It was not just committed socialists who held this view and questioned Auden's eccentricity, his bourgeois values, and his artistic individualism. The impeccably liberal Isaiah Berlin wrote to a friend in 1935: "it is as though Auden, fundamentally a patriotic poet, writes most eloquently when vaguely fascist, & conscientiously has to transfer this to the enemy because people he respects are all left-wing."[71] When Auden himself looked back on his book *The Orators,* largely written in 1931, he commented that his name on the title page looked like a pseudonym for "someone talented but near the border of sanity, who might well, in a year or two, become a Nazi."[72]

What kind of writer would Auden seem like now if he had stopped writing in 1936? He would sound like a voice from a modernizing but still pastorally fixated England, like an oddly conservative figure. In the early 1930s, Auden (with an ingrained masochistic tendency to be his own harshest critic) went so far as to acknowledge his "tendency to National Socialism" in an English context, and he longed in one poem for the deity of "love" to show itself in England, "our little reef . . . | This fortress perched on the edge of the Atlantic scarp."[73] In a country traumatized by war, class strife, economic malaise, and cultural pessimism, the young Auden started by searching for the country's wounds, and he hoped that his poetry could play a regenerative, healing role within English culture.

This is a story, then, about one poet's engagement with what it meant to be English in the period between two world wars. But, at the same time, it is a story about an entire cultural formation of Englishness coming to an end, a culture that Auden, among others, tried for a while to shore up among its landscapes, ghosts, and ruins. No reimagining of Auden's work could take place without a parallel reimagining of the cultural world in which it was embedded. And a new account of Auden also entails a different account of literary history.

Just as I attempt to describe Auden without the disadvantage of hindsight, so I also pay close attention to the ways his contemporaries, with no knowledge of how it would end, understood the period they were living through. One of the best methods to compass the meaning of Auden's poetry is to listen to other literary voices from the era. Many volumes on the movement now known in shorthand form as modernism have framed twentieth-century literature, inaugurated (in Wyndham Lewis's account) in 1914, as reaching its zenith in the year 1922 with the publication of T. S. Eliot's *The Waste Land* and James Joyce's *Ulysses*. Literary modernism, culminating in 1922, has been associated with the cosmopolitan, the international, and the polyglot, with formally fractured verse and a broad range of experimental literary practices. Yet many of Auden's contemporaries saw the crucial year in recent literary history as being not 1922 but rather 1926, the year of the General Strike in Britain. (The General Strike, lasting nine days in May, was a widespread, coordinated, and unsuccessful action by numerous trade unions to force the government into concessions to over one million locked-out miners.) And for these contemporaries, 1926 marked not a rise or peak of anything. It was instead a moment of termination, of closure and narrowing.

On or around 1926, metropolitan modernism died in Britain and a new, or new-old, formalist poetry, often rurally based and centered on a rueful, intimate individual speaker, emerged. At the same time, a broad and connected shift in national sensibility was taking place. The literary historian Alison Light puts it like this: in the two decades after the First World War there was "a move away from formerly heroic and officially masculine public rhetorics of national destiny and from a dynamic and missionary view of the Victorian and Edwardian middle-classes in 'Great Britain' to an Englishness at once less imperial and more inward-looking, more domestic and more private—and, in terms of prewar standards, more 'feminine.'"[74] Auden became a poet of that new nonimperial, domestic, and conservative, "feminized" inwardness. His introspective poems set in schools among children he watches and worries over are one manifestation of this change in sensibility. Nonetheless, a subtle feeling of violence close at hand, like something inescapable, casts shadows across his domestic or institutional poetry. Auden's private worlds, like the country itself, are always full of historical and literary ghosts.

For many Europeans, the First World War was an event unimaginable in scope, duration, and intensity, and unreckonable in financial and human costs. In 1930, the journalist H. M. Tomlinson called it "the greatest disturbance of mankind since the glaciers pushed our hunting forefathers down to the South."[75] After a stunned lull when the war ended, the mid-1920s saw a sea change in class and industrial politics. The period from 1925 to 1926 was the most radical phase of what one commentator has called "the most intense industrial and class confrontations" in Britain of the interwar years in Britain, focused on the struggle over the future of the coal industry.[76] (The mining that deeply fascinated the young Auden was also a national preoccupation.) In literary terms, these same years marked the waning of modernism's deformations, fracturings, and aleatory expansions.

The two most influential members of the "Men of 1914" living in London in the mid-1920s were Wyndham Lewis and T. S. Eliot.[77] For both, the modernist world ended in 1926. Lewis wrote: "I find a good way of dating after the War is to take the General Strike, 1926, as the next milestone. I call 'post-war' between the War and the General Strike. Then began a period of a new complexion."[78] In the second half of 1925, Eliot, who would within a very few years become Auden's publisher and his aesthetic doppelgänger, put together a collected edition of his own work: *Poems: 1909–1925*, which appeared in late November of that year.[79] In doubt about the value of his latest poem, "The Hollow Men," Eliot nevertheless gathered that poem's fragments together in five parts (a formal parallel to the five parts of *The Waste Land*). He wrote to Ezra Pound in October that although the poem seemed "bad," he felt that he "want[ed] something of about this length (I–V) to end the volume as post-Waste."[80]

The evocative term "post-Waste" (meaning "post–*Waste Land*" but with conspicuous echoes of "post-haste" and "post-war") indicates that Eliot wanted to close his 1925 volume with a diminuendo, with a self-consciously minor statement: not with *The Waste Land*'s thunderous mantra and formal ending of "Shantih   shantih   shantih" but with something fainter, more enigmatic.[81] Besides appearing in Eliot's letter to Pound about the poem, the verb "to end" occurs three times, like a broken record repeating the same sound in the final four lines of "The Hollow Men":

> *This is the way the world ends*
> *This is the way the world ends*
> *This is the way the world ends*
> *Not with a bang but a whimper.*

Eliot closed *Poems: 1909–1925,* which is essentially one poet's version of modernism's life and death, with a verbless, inert, negatived last line: "*Not with a bang but a whimper.*"[82] The postwar and "post-Waste" worlds, and Eliot's own book, thus "end" with a tremulous cry, the semiconscious moan of a dying victim or, conceivably, the plaintive squeal of a newborn creature. Or both at once. At the close of 1925, Eliot's concluding note was that of a self-elegy for a cultural world dwindling into stasis and silence. It is as if, like Prospero, he were saying, "Now my charms are all o'erthrown, | And what strength I have's mine own, | Which is most faint."[83]

Much later, at the very end of 1938, Eliot, a constant reference point for Auden, wrote an account of the termination of literary modernism in the last issue of his periodical *The Criterion* (the place where *The Waste Land* had first appeared). From the journal's beginning in 1922, Eliot argued in "Last Words," he had envisaged it as internationalist in character. But this was a short-lived aspiration: "Only from about the year 1926 did the features of the post-war world begin clearly to emerge—and not only in the sphere of politics. From about that date one began slowly to realize that the intellectual and artistic output of the previous seven years had been rather the last efforts of an old world, than the struggles of a new."[84] Gradually after 1926, Eliot added, "communications became more difficult," and the "'European mind,' which one had mistakenly thought might be renewed and fortified, disappeared from view." In this context, a new parochialism set in, and "alien minds took alien ways." Eliot aligned this new condition with the emergence "here in England" of a "definitely post-war generation." And he added: "our efforts turned to what was possible in a situation of enforced insularity; to the introduction of younger British writers."[85]

Eliot marked "about the year 1926" as the date for his own political and cultural watershed, of the turn from internationalism to "enforced insularity." His entry into the Anglican communion took place in the Cotswolds at the end of June 1927; his naturalization as a British subject came in November of the same year.[86] Late in 1927 he composed "Journey of the Magi," commonly seen as the first poem of a new phase in his work. And, at the end of 1928, after living in England for some eighteen years, he suddenly declared his viewpoint as "classicist in literature, royalist in politics, and anglo-catholic in religion."[87]

Eliot's sense of a new paradigm's emergence, a paradigm of demarcation, definition, and closure, anchored in a national identity, is evident in his imagery of islands, landings, and settlings. "Last Words" describes the way in which international modernism was succeeded by an insular poetic conservatism in which the "definitely post-war generation," including both Eliot himself and Auden, was enmeshed. Coincidentally, June 1927, the month that Eliot formally became an Anglican, is the same month that Auden first sent his poems to Eliot.[88]

To insist that 1926 is the most important year in English literary culture between the wars is not merely to draw attention to an episode in a certain strand of English poetry, and it is not just to voice a perception about the way in which one member of an older, self-consciously avant-garde generation, such as Eliot, or an ambitious young poet, such as Auden, experienced recent history. In England, many of the period's writers of different backgrounds saw the date 1926 as the watershed. Vera Brittain, for example, younger and far to the left of Lewis and Eliot, ends her autobiography *Testament of Youth* in 1925. For her, too, "the whole War and post-war period" are a single chronological and emotional unit, concluding around the midpoint of the 1920s.[89]

Something came to an end in 1925–1926, and something else, in the "period of a new complexion," sprang into being. Modernism did not effect a once-and-for-all revolution in poetic consciousness, even among those who are most identified with modernism's highest points. At the time, the movement seemed just another phase in an endless cycle of stylistic and imaginative paradigms. The next was an insular reworking of modernism—Auden, who in 1932 called himself a "Little Englander" (that is, someone patriotic but anti-imperial), was its first and most prominent youthful exponent.[90] In the work of later writers, the afterlife of this "insular" mode still widely endures.

The dwindling of international modernism in the mid-1920s, coupled with the presence of lingering traumas caused by the First World War, explain why "the island" reemerged as such a powerful symbol for English identity in the same period. The war historian Eric J. Leed wrote that there were "constant citations and complaints" from soldiers that the "war imposed upon its inhabitants a restricted and fragmented consciousness that made it ever more difficult to distinguish what was true, what was false, and what was rightly to be feared."[91] One defense against this experience of incomprehensibility and illimitable violence was the ideal of a circumscribed, protected space, a container with knowable boundaries and character. And the natural images, sanctified by tradition, of contained, delimited, isolated spaces were an island, and on the island, a garden.

These motifs have had a long presence in iconography related to English identity. The late eighteenth and early nineteenth centuries had seen a substantial consolidation of the imagery of England as "the island" within the national imagination. Romanticism gave "England" (rather than the United Kingdom) a unique mythic landscape in which land and water confronted each other. The "island story," which is Tennyson's phrase in his elegy for the Duke of Wellington, was visible everywhere—in poetry, in song, in history books.[92] In the first half of the twentieth century, even the contemporary codes of espionage, like the languages of politics and popular history, were shot through with connections people made between Britain, or its elision into England,

and a mythic island status. Even its enemies agreed on that. In the interwar period, the Soviet Secret Service in Britain wanted a code name to use for the country in the ciphers it was sending back to Moscow. The name the Russian spies chose for Britain was "the Island."[93]

In reaction to the First World War and its vast psychological toll, to class conflict and to economic uncertainty, one of the most marked tendencies in the writing of the 1920s and 1930s was a renewed fascination with England's rural cultures, its history, its geography. A certain section of England was fixated by the countryside. The postwar period saw the pastoral world of country landscapes and towns become popular as never before. In this period, a whole phalanx of writers set out to enact the re-enchantment, and by extension the moral and even economic rebirth, of rural England. Auden's writing belongs among the work of these writers at a time when an idealized country world was often associated with a "true" England. (The comforting double meaning of "country" as both "nation" and "rural scenery" is obvious.) From the mid-1920s onward, there was a surge of interest in English pastoral settings. Vita Sackville-West's long, ruralist poem *The Land* (1926), conspicuously subtracting the metropolitan "waste" and despair from the title of Eliot's most famous poem, is one early manifestation of the rage for the countryside. This new level of interest in rustic life is also expressed in the founding of antiquarian organizations such as the Place-Names Society in 1923.[94] Another prominent organization, which coalesced in 1926, was the Campaign for the Preservation of Rural England.[95]

Country specialists, preservationists, agriculturists, scholars of rural architecture, and antiquarian experts abounded, ready to meet demand with a large supply of Anglophilic reading material. Catering in part to literary enthusiasts, in part to the large influx of weekend visitors to the provinces, books of varying kinds, but all with a concentration on the English countryside, began to proliferate.[96] H. V. Morton's travelogue *In Search of England,* published in the summer of 1927, had gone through twenty-one impressions by 1934.[97] Guidebooks reached new levels of popularity in the postwar world when cars became more common and railway companies, through posters, pamphlets, and guided rambles, began "selling" rural landscapes that were accessible by train. English publishers produced reams of heavily illustrated books about the countryside.

The "Old English Life" series, for example, launched by Batsford in 1925, was relaunched and repackaged as the "English Life" series in 1932. The content was largely unchanged, but the revised title suggests that the publisher felt the qualifier "old" was now superfluous. "English Life" signaled the fantasy that the best and truest parts of contemporary society were simply the ones that preserved the English past.

The interwar period saw the decisive emergence of the "Heritage Britain" iconography of the English countryside—a world of gently swelling southern fields, neatly sectioned by hedgerows and meandering lanes gleaming in afternoon sunlight. This became the nostalgic emblem of true Englishness.[98] It was in the same period that Auden established his reputation as an iconic English writer. In 1932, the critic F. R. Leavis spoke of Auden's work as "remarkable. His imagination tends to the creation of myth. The hints he drops lead one to dream of a representative modern English poem—such as it seems extravagant to hope for."[99] Auden's poetic imagination, then, had a profoundly social dimension. In exquisite language, his poems worked through communal longings and ambivalences about Englishness and about what it meant to belong on the island.

Within a few years, though, Auden was gone. "Musée des Beaux Arts," composed in 1938, is one of the century's most complicatedly simple poems. Its second half focuses on Icarus, the mythological figure, a "boy" who becomes immortal after he dies falling into the sea as he is trying to escape from the island of Crete, his "white legs disappearing into the green | Water."[100] Auden's own escape from an island was similarly ambiguous in its aesthetic consequences. The emotional pull of the world he had left behind gave his immediately post-English poems, as he was "disappearing," an extraordinary flush, glow, and equivocation. These poems of expatriation are filled with a sublime historical melancholy. In 1932, he had longed for "us" to have, in mythic simplicity, "an eternal tie" with England. A mere nine years later, in 1941, he was insisting, in a poem written in New York that is a pastiche of a poem by Cavafy (a Greek-speaking Egyptian) as translated by Marguerite Yourcenar (Belgian / French in exile in the United States), that his readers should "honour the fate you are, | Travelling and tormented, | Dialectic and bizarre."[101]

After the Second World War, the persona of the cosmopolitan Auden crystallized as he divided his life between autumns, winters, and early springs in New York and long summers (typically from the start of April to mid-September) in Europe, first in Italy and then Austria, where he died during the night of 28–29 September 1973. By the end, he was a man who looked and sounded (and perhaps wrote) like he was past eighty but who was only sixty-seven. Images of Auden from later years bring to mind Yeats's words in "Among School Children," where he wonders what "youthful mother" contemplating her child would "think her son, did she but see that shape | With sixty or more winters on its head, | A compensation for the pang of his birth"?[102] When Auden fell asleep for the last time, he was five years younger than his mother had been at the time of her relatively early death.

Very few poets have uninterruptedly organic and predictable career arcs, a reflection of the fact that success in writing is desperately hard to achieve and is often subject to factors not within an artist's control. From the late 1940s onward, Auden's voluminous writings, both in poetry and in prose, are full of remarkable achievements: ravishing, bittersweet, airy songs; piercing moments of lyric introspection; and acutely sensitive registrations of contemporary alienation. But his poetry was no longer designed to terrify or enthrall an audience. It "Rummag[ed] into his living" still, but it did not seem to have mythic, collective roots. Instead, it grew glitteringly formalist as he became the great modern poet of aloneness—or, to put it another, perhaps truer way, the great modern poet of of loneliness—the prototypical emotional ache of Euro-American twentieth-century life. Auden's later career withdraws very deliberately from drama, historical resonance, or even a simple story line (qualities it is important to note that he said he did not desire). That is especially true when the tenor of his post-1945 poetry is compared to the intensity of his first two decades as a poet. In a poem from the 1960s, admitting that he usually went upstairs alone and needed alcohol to help himself fall asleep, he wrote about the bedroom in his Austrian home, reflecting: "Ordinary human unhappiness | is life in its natural color."[103]

In *The Island*, I have tried to write as if the young Auden's future were largely unknown. But in that effort, the older Auden, displaying an author's not-uncommon urge to control the meaning of their work, stands in our way. After many extraordinary changes of scene and style, the Auden of the 1960s and early 1970s lost some authorial battles because of the sheer complexity, strength, and diversity of his poetic canon. For instance, he was unable to persuade readers to approve of his revisions to iconic works such as *Spain* and "September 1, 1939." In the 1960s he even wanted to drop from collected and selected editions of his writing his most famous love poem, "Lay your sleeping head, my love," until he was successfully urged not to.[104]

However, having lost those battles, the older Auden mostly won the interpretive war. He was successful at stage-managing his reputation and rewriting (usually not for the better) not only his work but also, to a certain extent, his personal and poetic history. I am intent on returning to Auden's beginnings as a writer, on seeing his early work and world, if possible, in a dawn light. He once remarked that a poet's ideas about their poems and "the nature of poetry" when considered as "objective statements . . . are never accurate, never complete and always one-sided."[105] I have taken that comment to heart.

Suppose that the only Auden we knew about was the young, ardent, slightly puritanical, shaman-like poet, posh-voiced and visionary, from the moment in 1922 when he began writing poetry until around 1936–1937? Suppose that we focused on the young writer who during his last year at school "went for long solitary walks . . . and was extremely happy," the country boy who was spotted "very early one day several miles from school, standing alone on the shore at Weybourne, looking at the sea," the renegade who saw himself as a righteous, abjected Caliban?[106] This is the Auden I try to describe.

This book's broader arguments about Englishness sit deep within the specificities of Auden's own work and career. And they are informed by a long history of Auden scholarship that has cleared the way for an account that zeroes in on Auden's early poetry in relation to a specific set of poetic and historical preoccupations.[107] At the same time, I have tried wherever feasible to go back behind the published accounts of Auden's poetry and career to the raw materials, making extensive use of primary sources—notebooks, typescripts, letters, newspaper reports, and interviews.

While I discuss the significance of events and people in Auden's personal world, this is not a biography. (There is a chronology of some of the main events in Auden's life between 1907 and 1937 at the beginning of the book.) It is concerned first and foremost with Auden's dazzling poems. Auden is sometimes reticent, as we have seen, and sometimes amazingly frank, as we will see. But he did not use the lyric "I" to tell the world his secrets. His poems often have a self-dramatizing power; but he is not a confessional writer, and one could not glean an accurate history of his life simply from a reading of his poems.[108] And, just as this is not a "Life," so it is also not an exegesis of every poem or piece of prose that Auden wrote during the period between 1922 and 1937. The immense bulk of his work, poetic, dramatic, and essayistic, would make such an analysis impossible. Instead, because I want to the best of my ability to understand something about the depths of Auden's artistry, I choose for discussion the poems that open most fully onto the issues—war, trauma, identity, nationality, belonging, love—that are central to Auden's early writing, and I try to explore these representative works as intensively as possible.

My focus on Auden's explorations of the condition of nationality does not reduce his poems to a set of ideological polemics but is rather an attempt to expose more clearly the collective history distilled into their aesthetic structures. The Auden portrayed here looks more like a kind of lyric novelist than he does a poetic essayist or philosopher. He is a writer more focused on the feel and workings of the social world and on relations between people in that world—especially as those relations touch on the deep, profoundly personal, even existential, issues of identity embodied in the modern experience of being a "national"— than one impersonally, abstractly focused on theories, dogmas, or ideas. I operate on the principle that Auden's dreams and his love life, both of which I discuss in some detail, are as relevant to understanding his early poetry as are the works of Thomas Aquinas or the German physician Georg Groddeck, whom for a time Auden showily lauded to friends and acquaintances. The critical reference point I return to most often in understanding the motivations within Auden's poetry is the melancholic, stoical Freud. However invalidated by contemporary medical science, Freud remains for me one of the subtlest introspectionists and best recorders of the mind's reactions to modern life.

To bring some daylight to Auden's emotional and sexual history and to describe Auden as for a while a type of conservative, inward-turning, nationalistic poet might suggest moral judgments on his poetry and life. The many violent and extreme manifestations of ethnic nationalism that erupted in the 1930s in the lead-up to the Second World War are obvious. But it would be beside the point to claim that the idea of the nation, the experience of being national, and the existence of nationalism are, in themselves, wrong or unjust. The phenomenon of being born into an identity that pulls one toward national belonging—and many people's troubled but continuing existence within this cultural paradigm—is too varied and too pervasive a feature of recent life to be judged by moral criteria first or alone. It is, in the words of one leading scholar, "the central thread binding, and dividing, the peoples of the modern world."[109]

The nation-state and the collective solidarity that nationalism promoted in the 1920s and 1930s are historical facts; they were the dominant patterns through which many individuals in the period organized and reflected on their experiences. For this reason, I try to contextualize Auden's early poetry, rather than aspiring to sit in judgment on a historical figure. One of the sobering lessons of writing *The Island* has been the need for me to reconcile myself to the reality that so much of English culture in Auden's time (and perhaps even today) was a fundamentally conservative field of force and to acknowledge Auden's place in that field. Yet, as the sociologist Georg Simmel wrote, it "is our task not to complain or to condone but only to understand."[110]

For a couple of hours on 4 July 1925, looking more like one of the local Norfolk tramps than a public schoolboy, Auden swaggers, plots, cowers, and moans onstage as he speaks the most stunning Shakespearean poetry. He will get a few cursory reviews for his performance, but they probably will not matter much to this introspective and privately rebellious teenager who has already decided that he is, more than anything else, a poet.[111] (The senses of alienation and marginality in the young man playing Caliban as a protest against school life come through in knowing that, at around the same time as he is taking part in the play, he is writing poems about a dead soldier, about meeting a mysterious stranger in the rain, and about weeping over the sight of a sinister, crumbling house in the woods.[112])

While the play lasts, Auden lumbers about in a clearing—the rebel, the cerebral oddball, the sexual freak, the despised native islander, and, unbeknownst to anyone, the island's future. Prospero reproaches Caliban yet again, and Caliban seethes: "You taught me language; and my profit on 't | Is I know how to curse."[113] Within a mere ten years, using with extraordinary dexterity the artistic language that he had begun learning at Gresham's, this Caliban will be transformed into a figure who casts spells as often as he utters curses. He will imagine himself, and be imagined, as the visionary poet of a reenchanted England, the island. Emerging from a darkened childhood in an apocalyptic war, he will try to find words to summon for a moment a brighter, better society into being and, just a few years after that, as if the drama were finally over, he will recognize the limits of the beautiful fantasy that a poet can remake the world.

PART ONE   MARSH

THE HISTORICAL CHILD
MUSIC, WAR, AND SEX, 1907–1922

In the confusion of wartime in which we are caught up, relying as we must on one-sided information, standing too close to the great changes that have already taken place or are beginning to, and without a glimmering of the future that is being shaped, we ourselves are at a loss as to the significance of the impressions which press in upon us and as to the value of the judgements which we form.

—SIGMUND FREUD (1915)

ARTISTIC LIVES BEGIN before poets actually start composing their works. "Most of what I know about the writing of poetry, or, at least, the kind I am interested in writing, I discovered long before I took an interest in poetry itself," Auden said toward the end of his life, suggesting sources for his writing that existed behind, or beyond, simple linguistic prowess.[1] What was it he discovered during that poetic foretime before March 1922, when he wrote his first poem?

Prose accounts of Auden's early years (including his own accounts) are remarkable not for what they reveal but for what they veil: society, history, culture, ideology, class, and family secrets. W. B. Yeats claimed that he remembered "little of childhood but its pain."[2] Auden's memories of early life mainly seem to recall with exaggerated emphasis his security and happiness. Different notes emerge only occasionally— notes of danger, loss, isolation, confusion, and anxiety. He once called his childhood a time of "intense emotion."[3] But a crucial determinant in his early life is one that he later dismissed almost completely. As a fledgling writer, Auden was a boy in a country saturated by the experience of war and then by war's aftermath. It was in this haunted atmosphere that he learned most of "what I know about the writing of poetry."

Auden's father, Dr. George Auden, who was fascinated by children and childhood, described in one of his essays the "ceaseless stream of suggestions of social import from his immediate environment which stamp upon the still plastic material of [a child's] mental make-up an impression which stands out even clearer and in stronger relief with his increasing years."[4] As if W. H. Auden were recollecting again and again the "stream of suggestions" he had once experienced, his poems are always eager to return to the sensations and traumas of childhood. "I think we shall find that all intelligent people, even the great doctor himself [Auden was not referring directly to his father but to Freud, though one could be forgiven for believing that in a fashion he was thinking about Dr. Auden as well], are the product of psychological conflict in childhood, and generally share some neurotic traits," he wrote in 1936.[5]

The poetic obsession with childhood wells up in these lines from 1934:

> Certain it became while we were still incomplete
> There were certain prizes for which we would never compete;
> A choice was killed by every childish illness,
> The boiling tears among the hothouse plants,
> The rigid promise fractured in the garden,
> And the long aunts.
>
> And every day there bolted from the field
> Desires to which we could not yield;
> Fewer and clearer grew the plans,
> Schemes for a life and sketches for a hatred,
> And early among my interesting scrawls
> Appeared your portrait.[6]

Semi-surreal conjunctions link "choice" with "illness," "boiling" with "tears" and "hothouse," "promise" with "fracture," and "sketches" with "hatred." These unexpected couplings disrupt the momentum of the poem's rational argument. Alongside the odd stanzaic amalgam of rhyming and nonrhyming lines and the nervous fluctuation between five long lines and a truncated sixth line (as if the poem were suddenly having to check its own headlong excitement or panic), the rampant strangeness of Auden's language testifies to the magical power that the idea of childhood held over his mind. The subject seems to cause a quickening of the literary pulse. Childhood was father to this man's poetry—and the childhood he describes in poetry (unlike in his prose) is usually a fraught one.[7]

Auden was born at home in the northern city of York on 21 February 1907 (a Pisces, one of the water signs, as he later made a point of saying), the last of three brothers.[8] Linking his own presence to the precondition of someone else's absence, he told a friend's daughter in 1944 after she had suffered a miscarriage: "My mother had a miscarriage before me, for which I cannot be sorry, because if she hadn't, perhaps I shouldn't exist." Edward Mendelson calls this "a blithe tone that concealed the private depths of his theme," and that blithe tone is a familiar one in many of Auden's comments about his childhood.[9]

In York, Auden's doctor father was in private practice from 1905 to 1908; the family resided in a substantial house in the city center not far from the cathedral. However, in spite of Dr. Auden's early financial success, Auden's brother John remarked that the children "had the impression in later years that our mother slightly disapproved of [Dr. Auden's] proficiency in gynaecology."[10] It was perhaps partly to remove the cause of this disapproval that Dr. Auden applied for a position in public service as Birmingham's first school medical officer in 1908. According to his third son, who was using information he must have picked up much later as if it were still a family sore point, Dr. Auden's York practice "had been lucrative, and abandoning it to enter the Public Health Service meant a considerable financial loss."[11] After Dr. Auden was appointed to his new post, the family moved to the outskirts of Birmingham when Wystan Auden was only one year old. Auden spent the next few years in Solihull, then not much more than "a large village" to the southeast of Britain's second city. There his everyday world had a pre-twentieth-century, class-bound character, complete with "earth privies, oil lamps, gas jets, horses, domestic pianos, maids, governesses, and silence . . . [and] open space."[12]

During the entire span of his life, Auden lived in "horrible London" for only two periods of just a few months when short-term jobs required him to.[13] In this he was unlike other literary and artistic friends of his own age, such as Christopher Isherwood, William Coldstream, and Stephen Spender, or older acquaintances such as T. S. Eliot, all of whom spent prolonged periods in the capital. Instead, Auden identified himself as a "raw provincial," writing about life in rural landscapes and sympathizing with the provinces' traditional suspicions of the metropolis.[14] "I am grateful for having a country background," he said.[15] And he began his poetic life as a writer of plain descriptive lyrics set in nature: "All features of the wood are known to me | For I have latched the gate which borders it | And scrambled through its fences many times" is how one typically direct, bare, simple country poem from his earliest period as a writer begins.[16]

This was not a scene he copied from someone's book. Young Auden was an upper-middle-class, small-town boy who emerged as a rural poet at boarding school in the English countryside. Direct experiences of the natural world gave him his subject matter, though because, in the early years of the twentieth century, "the fastness of rural England" was considered the source of English poetry, just as it was considered to be, in Ralph Vaughan Williams's words, "the wellspring of English music," Auden as a youthful country poet could not help but write poems with a distinctly "English" flavor.[17]

Dr. George Auden and Constance Bicknell had married in June 1899 at All Saints' Church in Notting Hill, London, a bastion of Anglo-Catholicism. The year of their wedding, like the temporal hinge between two eras, was very near the end of Queen Victoria's long reign, as well as the one in which Freud published *The Interpretation of Dreams*, a symbolic intellectual inauguration of the twentieth century.[18] The prewar domestic world on the edge of Birmingham where the Audens raised their sons (Bernard, born in 1900; John, 1903; Wystan, 1907) was, for them, exceedingly comfortable.[19] There were cooks, nannies, toys, and plenty of food, all secured by a small private income as well as by Dr. Auden's somewhat meager municipal salary. It was in some ways a conventional home, typifying the tastes and values common among the higher echelons of the professional classes in Edwardian Britain.

That society had foundations that were exploitative, nationalistic, and materialistic. The country welled with patriotic encomia about the historic civilizing mission of the British Empire and it indulged in vast, vulgar displays trumpeting the splendors of supreme power, such as the coronation of George V in London in 1911 and the huge Delhi Durbar held in India later that year to celebrate the king's and Queen Mary's coronations as emperor and empress of India and rulers of "the British Dominions beyond the seas."[20] It was a gaudy, theatrical culture. It was also an increasingly militaristic one. Britain was a "military-industrial-scientific complex, which believed in being in the phrase of the time, 'second to none.'" The historian David Edgerton writes that the country was a "pioneer of modern, technologically focused warfare," which "saw itself as a global, liberal power, as world political-economic policeman, an arbiter of the fate of nations."[21] All these brazen notions were part of the atmosphere in Auden's childhood world in the provinces.

An empire has few morally uncompromised spaces. In the 1900s, the light of imperial splendor gleamed dimly from millions of everyday objects in the mother country and in hundreds of contexts apparently far removed from Britain's rapaciously gathered possessions abroad. The glint of empire flickered on patriotically emblazoned biscuit tins and cigarette packets, in the nonnative shrubbery of English front gardens (filled with new species of rhododendron from India), in the words of popular songs, and in quasi-military boys' clubs.[22] There is nothing to suggest that either the Audens or their sons ever showed any special enthusiasm for the imperial ideal. If anything, the opposite is the case. But they lived in the midst of a world that valued power, wealth, and display.

Mrs. Auden, whom Auden once told Isherwood he was aware "was a bit dotty" and whom he "used to wish [was] . . . more like other mamas," was immured within the otherworldliness of her strongly Anglo-Catholic religious beliefs.[23] Dr. Auden made a cult of the North and of ancient Scandinavian culture, tastes strongly associated with the anti-imperial, anti-industrial politics of the Victorian socialist William Morris, "half of whose *Collected Works* are translations of sagas, poems based on Old Norse literature, romances derived from Icelandic sources or travel literature about Iceland."[24]

But the Audens' lives were at least partly founded on the social and economic privileges accruing to the English upper-middle classes from the spoils of the country's overseas possessions. Family links implicated them in networks of financial and industrial power. One of Auden's grand-uncles on his mother's side was once a tutor to the Prince of Wales, another was a governor of the Bank of England, another was lieutenant-governor of Ceylon. On his father's side, one of Auden's uncles, Harold, was a successful industrial chemist at the conglomerate United Alkali, another, Thomas, was a well-to-do solicitor and district judge. In the mid-eighteenth-century, Auden's great-great-grandfather had profited from the rents he received for mines on the Staffordshire land he owned and had purchased a coat of arms for the Auden line.[25] Auden's family was not noble, grand, or completely stolid. Nonetheless, Auden was, the historian Carolyn Steedman notes, the "product of the Edwardian three-servant household," with many of the inherited attitudes and expectations such a background entailed.[26]

In other ways, the Audens' house in Solihull was subtly isolated and unconventional, as Auden himself said:

> The study was full of books on medicine, archaeology, the classics. There was a rain-gauge on the lawn and a family dog. There were family prayers before breakfast, bicycle-rides to collect fossils or rub church-brasses, reading aloud in the evenings. We kept pretty much to ourselves. Mother was often ill.
>
> In one way we were eccentric: we were Anglo-Catholics. On Sundays there were services with music, candles and incense, and at Christmas a crèche was rigged up in the dining-room, lit by an electric-torch battery, round which we sang hymns.[27]

Besides the unusual, Anglo-Catholic religious fervor in the Auden household, this was a mildly "eccentric" home in another sense too. An acquaintance who visited the Audens wrote that "the arts (especially music) and the sciences were valued far above material luxuries. . . . Books were plentiful; the piano was in daily use."[28] The family made music "inseparable from religion and equally important."[29]

Birmingham, where Dr. Auden was responsible for the health of every child in school in the city, was a huge, and economically important, metropolis, the political power base of the pro-imperial Chamberlain family of politicians, a manufacturing redoubt with slums that, as Auden later said, made it "disgraced before the cats and dogs."[30]

Middle-class Birmingham had an exceptionally active musical life in which the level of artistic sophistication was treated as a reason for civic pride. There were numerous symphony orchestras and chamber music groups in the city. From the mid-Victorian period onward, it was a standard port of call for the major choirs, orchestras, and celebrity performers on their British tours. By the last quarter of the nineteenth century the

Hallé, London Symphony, and Queen's Hall orchestras had become regular visitors for concerts held mainly at the Birmingham Town Hall. And between the 1850s and the 1930s, almost every famous English singer or player performed in the city, often at the triennial Birmingham Music Festival.

Choral singing, with its appeal to collective emotions and its experience of individuality subordinated to a powerful communal effort, was very popular in Victorian and Edwardian Britain, especially at the provincial music festivals, such as those in Birmingham and Leeds. As a result, at the time when Auden was growing up, Birmingham taste favored the wordy surge of the oratorio as the privileged musical form. By the 1880s, the tradition of performing works by Handel and Bach had given way to a vogue for huge, neo-Wagnerian, religious set pieces, welling with moral righteousness. English composers, such as Stanford and Parry, wrote many pious oratorios for chanting choir and booming orchestra. Most were performed at one time or another in Birmingham.

This Victorian fashion climaxed in *The Dream of Gerontius* (1900) by Edward Elgar (a frequent visitor to the city from his home in the Herefordshire town of Malvern), a work commissioned by the Birmingham Music Festival.[31] Auden was so attuned to childhood memories of the "beautiful roar of the chorus under the dome," that in 1941–1942, when he wrote the words for his own oratorio, "For the Time Being," to commemorate his deceased mother, he did so in part because this form was so deeply associated with her and the musical culture she had inducted him into.[32]

Although the oratorio form, more earnest and thus less morally suspect to Protestant taste, took precedence over the opera in Victorian and Edwardian Britain, operatic overtures were regularly included in concerts. It was natural that Auden, growing up in such a world, could already play the piano in a rudimentary but proficient way by the time he left for prep school in 1915. There he took more lessons, as he would also do at his public school.[33] Poems are often said to have a "music," but how many modern English-language poets, aside from Auden and Frank O'Hara, even partially mastered an instrument?

Religion was the inseparable complement to music. Dr. Auden had a dogged attachment to Christian practices. He served at least for a while as a sidesman (an assistant churchwarden) at St. Alphege's, the family church in Solihull, and from time to time he took on various other lay roles.[34] Mrs. Auden, more extrovertly emotional in temperament, was more enthusiastically doctrinal in her opinions than her husband. Both Auden parents were "devout Christians," regular churchgoers motivated in their daily lives by upper-middle-class Christian ideals of industry, service, and (what often goes with them) a self-esteeming sense of noblesse oblige.[35] The couple belonged to the same generation of workaholic Britons as the novelist John Galsworthy, the architects Edwin Lutyens and Detmar Blow, the poet John Masefield, the musicians Ralph Vaughan Williams and Gustav Holst, the horticulturalist Gertrude Jekyll, the literary patron Edward Marsh, the soprano Clara Butt, and the psychiatrist C. S. Myers (later the popularizer of the term "shell-shock"), who was a professional associate of Dr. Auden.

These highly educated and economically secure people attained public prominence in the late Edwardian period and, after the nightmarish hiatus of the Great War, in the 1920s. The men were products, the historian Martin J. Wiener wrote, of the "ethos of later-Victorian Oxbridge, a fusion of aristocratic and professional values, [which] stood self-consciously in opposition to the spirit of Victorian business and industry," and exalted "a dual ideal of cultivation and service against philistine profit-seeking."[36] Almost all were uniconoclastic, serious and public-spirited, self-denying, choosy in their moral attitudes, and politically moderate. The influential members of this generation formed an overwhelmingly patriotic group, whose class-based values placed an almost spiritual significance on the ethical aesthetics of John Ruskin and Morris. (These virtues notwithstanding, Auden mentioned a few of the flaws his parents shared with many of their contemporaries. They included "a mild and for the most part quite unthinking anti-Semitism" and the "typical snobberies" of the professional middle class: "contemptuous attitudes towards businessmen . . . and toward Dissenters."[37])

The services that the Auden family attended in Solihull, at one of the Birmingham diocese's very "highest" Anglo-Catholic churches, were artistic as well as religious experiences, dramatized with "music, candles, and incense."[38] When Auden was five, he served for a year in the family church as a boat boy (one who helps the thurifers with the wafting incense holders during services).

Predictably for someone who had such an intense Anglo-Catholic faith, his mother was Francophile. She loved Mediterranean cultures, and her first trip abroad, made when she was eighteen, was to a popular resort in Italy with her favorite uncle, a "bachelor" mathematician, Rev. Charles Bicknell.[39] Three years later, she graduated from Royal Holloway College in London with a diploma and a gold medal in French. Mrs. Auden retained her fluency in that language, and in the 1920s and 1930s, she held popular "soirées" at her home for students studying French at the University of Birmingham.[40] Perhaps partly by reaction, little of her affection for French culture passed to her youngest son.

Mrs. Auden, some of whose family believed she had married beneath herself in wedding a doctor, had more than a touch of the poet in her genes. Her mother, Selina Acton Bicknell, claimed to be descended from John of Gaunt, the warrior renowned, thanks to Shakespeare, as the most grandiloquent of all English patriots.[41] Mrs. Auden's granddaughter remembered her as a spiritual person "always bathed in sunlight," as "tall, rather austere, seeming to me dressed in mauves and grays," and as "an expert seamstress, making sewing and embroidery work that was absolutely beautiful."[42] Some of her apparent otherworldliness may have stemmed from the fact that she seems to have suffered quite early on from heart disease, which shadowed her for the rest of her life. With his painter's eye, Auden's friend Robert Medley noted that Mrs. Auden "had a refined and remote dignity, a withdrawn circumspection. Her face had many fine lines, so fine that at first glance they would not be noticed."[43]

But she was also vehement and unrelenting in her seriousness. Auden later wrote down a conversation he remembered between his brother and an aunt. The aunt said: "I expect Mummy often plays with you like this." John replied, becoming "quite rigid": "Mummy doesn't play; she punishes."[44] Auden later told friends that Mrs. Auden could become so furious during arguments he had with her when he was a teenager (some of them no doubt to do with his sexual habits) that he was certain "my mother would kill me."[45] A neighbor from the 1920s remembered her as "an unattractive, domineering kind of woman, who ruled all her three boys with a rod of iron."[46]

The social conservatism of her class and times meant that Constance Auden was unable to have the kind of professional, or religious, life for which she was fit. (As a young woman, she had wanted to become a missionary in Africa but eventually only finished training as a nurse before she married.) She occupied herself with the management and embellishment of her home and with her family's spiritual life, copying out "anthologies of prayers in her beautiful handwriting, with capitals in Gothic red."[47] Passionate about music (she played the piano expertly), she also loved to read aloud about the lives of the saints and owned an ivory, devotional crucifix that she took with her when she attended, as she frequently did, church retreats in Anglican convents.[48] In an essay about John Betjeman in the 1940s, Auden asked of his fellow poet: "How . . . could he have entered so intimately into my childhood? How else could he be so at home with the provincial gaslit towns, the seaside lodgings, the bicycles, the harmonium, above all, the atmosphere of ritualistic controversy?"[49]

Constance Auden's fascination with religious martyrs cannot have been divorced from her own experiences in an intensely patriarchal society that enforced a daily reality of self-sacrifice for women of all classes. In similar fashion, her fondness for *recherché* religious rites, sacred objects, special dates in the Christian calendar, and highly theatrical communal ceremonies was not detached from a specific and modern set of social dilemmas. For all the surface eccentricity and tinges of snobbery in her beliefs, they articulated some poignantly typical modern anxieties. During the late nineteenth century, the Anglican Church as a whole had begun a concerted move toward the kinds of "higher ritual" that appealed to Mrs. Auden: the senior clergy took to wearing more ornate and highly colored vestments, their religious regalia and badges became more elaborate, sacred interiors were more richly decorated, and candlelight and scents were added to the sensory atmosphere in many churches.[50] This ornamental extravagance was a reaction against the prevailing cults of sobriety, mercantilism, and pragmatism in Victorian culture.

Even though they often collaborated in making what they bemoaned, intellectually inclined Victorians and Edwardians worried that the world was becoming increasingly technocratic and utilitarian and that there was a withering of intuitive communal feeling, of unselfconscious religious practice, and of a social memory "affective and magical."[51] Like a candle flame flickering but not yet extinguished, around which someone protectively cups a hand, the numinous remnants of a collectively shared world could only survive the brusque, materialistic atmosphere of Edwardian and then Georgian England in the deliberate renovations of ancient rites—or, on a different but parallel level, in the lavish ceremonial displays cultivated by the British monarchy in the same period. Invented traditions, the vigilant sacralization of a few specially chosen secular moments and fetishes, were, for Mrs. Auden as for numerous other citizens, a means of relieving nostalgia for a more secure, holistic (and hierarchical) past.[52]

All of these ritualistic reconstitutions, including self-consciously dramatic religious ceremonies as well as iterations of "glorious" school traditions and "splendid" royal occasions, had a synthetic, stagy air. But that was inevitable. When there is "no spontaneous memory," the historian Pierre Nora wrote, "we must deliberately create archives, maintain anniversaries, organise celebrations, pronounce eulogies, and notarise bills because such activities no longer occur naturally."[53] In early twentieth-century England, especially for marginalized people of faith like Mrs. Auden, more often than not these varied activities in which they joined together conjured up the ancient religious community of the church of true believers. However, such moments of belonging also constituted acts of worship, covert or explicit, of that modern, secular, but still mystical entity—the nation. Through these ceremonies of connection, "a deep, horizontal comradeship" was incarnated that *was* the nation.[54] Auden grew up in a home in which aesthetic worship was a fundamental part of life; he grew up in a country in which a sense of national belonging was virtually a religious value. It is likely that at times religious experience and national feeling—for instance, when Elgar's "Land of Hope and Glory" was being sung—may not have seemed so different from each other.

Instead of artistically copying out prayers as his wife did, the phlegmatic Dr. Auden carved wooden screens and made oak tables.[55] His cultural interests pointed not south, like Mrs. Auden's, but north toward German and Scandinavian cultures.[56] Aside from publishing a few minor medical articles in the 1890s, almost all of Dr. Auden's publications until 1910 were on northern, antiquarian themes. There were strong connections between the cult of the North and the Arts and Crafts movement in the decorative arts that flourished in Britain during the second half of the nineteenth century.

Several generations of the Arts and Crafts movement were highly patriotic, with a particular reverence for the English countryside and for craft traditions predating the industrial revolution and the empire. For furniture, the movement's designers favored the use of "native" woods such as walnut, yew, elm, and especially oak, which Dr. Auden worked with frequently.[57] At a political and social level, the Arts and Crafts movement strongly opposed mass production, wage slavery, factories, and industrialization, with the attendant ills that these created among a vast, unhealthy proletariat in modern cities. Such ideas were key tenets of Auden's father, who every day of his professional life dealt with children living in the Birmingham slums.

For Ruskin, it "would be well if all of us were good handicraftsmen in some kind."[58] The sorts of ethically serious crafts that Auden's parents practiced (embroidered fabrics and calligraphic renderings of sacred scripture for her; useful tables and chests, often embellished with sententious phrases, for him), as well as their contempt for entrepreneurial commerce, were a result of exposure to Ruskin's and Morris's ideals. Their veneration of manual skills and the physical characteristics of textiles, paper, ink, and wood evoked Arts and Crafts ideals that are evident too in their son's later veneration of poetic technique and his sensitivity to the material qualities of language.

Dr. Auden's career evolved rapidly in Birmingham. His hope for a greater degree of marital harmony may have been one reason why he decided to move from private practice into public service. The change may also have been motivated by his embrace of Edwardian philanthropic traditions in which paternalism, scientific rationalism, and altruism were fused. Giving up his work in York, he became the first school medical officer of the City of Birmingham and the honorary psychiatrist to the Birmingham Children's Hospital at a moment when it became mandatory for every education authority in the country to appoint such an official.[59] Dr. Auden decided to concern himself with public service and administration as the state was taking a larger role in welfare and hygiene responsibilities, which had previously been left to parents or private charitable organizations.

After annual inspections of every elementary school and every schoolchild in the nation were made compulsory in 1908, Birmingham's school medical officer was responsible for the health (and medical care) of the many children—often ill-treated and malnourished—who inhabited the city's tenements. With an interlude for wartime service, Dr. Auden held his position in Britain's second-largest city until his retirement in 1937. Although it was not an especially well-paid post, it was nonetheless a very important role: in any given year, during the mid-1920s, he was accountable for the health at school of approximately 150,000 children.[60]

For more than forty years, this polymathic doctor and civil servant was also a prolific contributor to various professional congresses and journals on subjects varying from juvenile delinquency, "feeble-mindedness," mental retardation, and emotional maladjustment to sanitary conditions, prisons, medical education, Viking surgery, the head louse, and psychology.[61] Dr. Auden was also deeply interested in extrascientific, un-"modern" approaches to understanding the world. His son, making his father sound like a proto-poet, would write: "'Healing,' | Papa would tell me, | 'is not a science, but the intuitive art | of wooing Nature.'"[62] This remarkable, vigorous, but strangely self-suppressing man was, among much else, at times the honorable district secretary for the York chapter of the Viking Club as well as secretary of the local Classical Association. From 1905 until 1910, most of his published writing was archaeological and antiquarian and chiefly on the subject of Scandinavian antiquities discovered in Britain. Even at the start of the First World War, he was still serving on a committee of the British Association for the Advancement of Science dedicated to investigating the "Age of Stone Circles."[63]

In its obituary for Dr. Auden, who died in 1957, the Lancet remarked: "His wisdom as a physician was matched by his learning as a scholar and antiquarian, and in letters to our columns he would quote from Sanskrit writings as easily as from the Saga of St. Olav."[64] The range of his professional interests may even have been underplayed in the obituaries, perhaps for reasons of tact. In his early years in York and then Birmingham, Dr. Auden became interested in the then-fashionable medical specters of degeneracy, feeble-mindedness, and criminality. Earnest Edwardians who worried about the condition of the empire and nation foresaw the end of the middle classes, who, "with all their good and bad qualities,

would soon follow the bison and dodo to extinction, while the population became increasingly recruited from a 'tabid and wilted stock.'"[65]

For a while, and in a limited way, Dr. Auden also endorsed Edwardian
eugenic theories. Compounded from a mixture of positivistic and materialistic science and from fears about the intractability of poverty, crime
rates, and the threatening fertility of the working classes, eugenics was a
divisive response to social and political dilemmas that seemed to threaten
the middle classes as well as the efficiency and order of the country as a
whole.[66] Before he arrived in Birmingham, the city, under the aegis of the
educational theorist Ellen Pinsent, had become especially concerned with
new ideas about treatment of the "feebleminded" and mentally "defec-
tive" children and adults. In the early 1900s, Pinsent was a member of the
Birmingham School Board and (from 1903) the chair of the Birmingham
Special Schools Subcommittee, as well as the first woman elected as a
Birmingham city councilor.

Pinsent may have played a decisive part in Dr. Auden's appointment in Birmingham. It seems certain that, with Pinsent in the senior
role, the pair worked closely during his early years there, since they
shared interests and belonged to some of the same municipal organizations. His first two publications on the issue of "feeblemindedness" came
in 1910, less than two years after he began his job in Birmingham.[67]
Dr. Auden also took an interest in the work of Francis Galton, the primary intellectual benchmark in the field of eugenics; and in 1910, he
may have been one of the founders of the Birmingham branch of the
Eugenics Education Society, of which Pinsent was also a member.[68]

In the postwar period, Dr. Auden distanced himself from eugenicist
ideology, even criticizing the "fallacy of the eugenist standpoint" in a 1926
article for a professional journal.[69] Still, throughout his later career he remained interested, perhaps slightly obsessively, in "feeble-mindedness."
He was continuously involved as both an author and administrator with
issues surrounding mental functioning in childhood. Like his father,
Auden, the polymathic son, worked with children as a young man, although as a teacher rather than a researcher; and as a poet, his fascination
with disease and renewal echoed Dr. Auden's interests. Reflecting on his
time as a schoolteacher, Auden wrote: "The children who interested me
were either the backward, i.e. those who had not yet discovered their real
nature, the bright with similar interests to my own, or those who, like
myself at their age, were school-hating anarchists."[70] The "backward"

children who caught his imagination were a later generation of the children who had preoccupied his father.

At the end of Auden's career, as if seeking to explain something about the cast of his mind, he commented that the first public event he remembered was the sinking of the *Titanic* in April 1912, when he was five. If this is accurate, Auden's symbolically important first recollection of his place in the wider world was fixed by the announcement of a catastrophe. The shipwreck was a brutal blow to national pride that, in the words of Thomas Hardy, whose poetry would be among Auden's deepest influences, "jar[red] two hemispheres."[71]

Decades later, Auden mostly continued to look back on his prewar home as a place filled with love, music, books, financial security, good food, and faith. But, whatever Auden thought he remembered, imperial Britain in the 1900s was not a society of complacent stability, peace, and security. For many years, the ethical underpinnings of laissez-faire Victorian liberalism had been in slow decline as a newly belligerent and expansionist order took shape. The historian Adam Tooze describes the world system in the early twentieth century as a radically new and unstable arrangement of "uninhibited military, economic, political and cultural competition."[72]

Even as Britain initially dominated this new system, it shook under the strains like a building riding an earthquake. It had been engaged in a costly naval arms race with Germany since 1898, with ever vaster and more heavily outfitted ships being built year by year. The campaign for women's voting rights, Home Rule for Ireland, and industrial strife all caused further tension in the prewar period. In 1911, there were violent bouts of industrial action, riots, and looting in the mining areas of South Wales. A huge strike by dockers, seamen, and firemen took place in the summer of the same year. Soldiers fired on and killed striking workers in Liverpool and Llanelli. The army was ordered to be ready at all times to come out to assist the police in breaking up strikes.

In 1912, the year the *Titanic* sank, 41 million days of work, representing an enormous amount of production, were lost to industrial action.[73] By the summer of 1914, the Ulster crisis had reached the boiling point: there was an almost mutinous mood among senior British army officers faced with the possibility that they might have to enforce a

Home Rule policy in Ireland.[74] The king told the Unionist and nationalist leaders from Ireland who convened at his initiative in London in
July 1914 that "today the cry of civil war is on the lips of the most responsible and sober of my people."[75]

By then, though, two pistol shots fired in June in far-off Sarajevo had
already started the process that would change British life forever. Later, in
the wake of one of the bloodiest conflicts in human history, a few pre-
1914 strikes and some laborers' deaths here and there were hard to recall.
Many people in Europe, both professional soldiers and civilians, greeted
the conflict with ecstatic excitement, not least because it seemed to annul
the factional struggles of normal political life. A contagion of patriotic
euphoria swept through Britain, which was sustained even after brutal
early setbacks such as the British Expeditionary Force's costly retreat
from Mons during late August and early September 1914.[76] Soon, John
Garth writes, wounded soldiers "were filling the military hospital that
had just been set up in the University of Birmingham, and Belgian refugees were arriving in England with stories of German atrocities."[77]

In September 1914, not long after the conflict began, Dr. Auden
volunteered for the Royal Army Medical Corps. About 10 percent of the
country's medical professionals freely joined up in the first few months
of the war, as Dr. Auden did. This was a far higher rate of enlistment than
that of most other professions.[78] Auden recalled that "one of the last
times" he saw his father before Dr. Auden disappeared into the services
was when his parents surprised him by appearing "in drag. . . . She had
on his clothes and a false moustache and he was wearing hers. They were
going to a masquerade, I think, and I suppose they thought it would
amuse me." Instead, Auden (seven years old at the time) was terrified and
burst into tears, confused by seeing his strong-willed mother dressed as a
man and his mild-mannered and kindly father as a woman.[79]

Dr. Auden soon put on another set of unfamiliar clothes: a tailor-
made army officer's uniform purchased, like the rest of an officer's
equipment, by the soldier himself.[80] It was almost as if a seasonal
change in the human foliage was taking place. The architectural historian J. M. Richards, who would be an exact contemporary of Auden at
their public school in the 1920s, remembered that in 1914 there were
"no signs of war in our suburb except the proliferation of khaki."[81]

After the oldest Auden brother, Bernard, went back to Shrewsbury
School in the autumn of 1914 and their father departed for military

service, John and Wystan Auden spent a year or so alone in Solihull with Mrs. Auden. It must have been during this lonely period, with all of them mourning in their separate ways the disappearance of Dr. Auden, that Auden remembered his mother "taught me the words and music of the love-potion scene in *Tristan,* and we used to sing it together."[82] Mother and son sat side by side and played the piano, as remembered in the early poem "The Happy Tree," where Auden puns on the meanings of "quavers": "Once at Ryde | We played duets, she turned the page, | More quavers on the other side."[83] The "quavers" are musical notes but also bodily tremors or pangs of grief. So strong an impression did this physical-musical closeness with his mother make on Auden that he later noticed recapitulations of the scene when he played piano duets with Hedwig Petzold and Elizabeth Mayer, two older, German-speaking women, to both of whom he had strong emotional attachments.[84]

The gender confusion that had disturbed Auden when he saw his parents in drag continued in modified form during these private performances as his mother took the tenor part of Tristan while her seven-year-old took the soprano's role of the illicit lover, Isolde, in a doomed but ecstatic love affair. The counterpoint to an absent father was an eerie intimacy between mother and son, something Auden often wrote about later in notes to himself—for example: "Mothers treat their sons as lovers," or "The possible family situations which may produce an artist or intellectual are of course innumerable, but those in which one of the parents, usually the mother, seeks a conscious spiritual, in a sense, adult relationship with the child, are probably the commonest."[85] These were the thoughts of a poet who had spent his childhood living in what was in effect a one-parent family in a country at war. When Auden slowly reapproached religion at the end of the 1930s, at the onset of another global conflict, he would do so by way of a sudden passion for the works of Wagner.

Dr. Auden's career as an army doctor began when he was commissioned at the acting rank of lieutenant in the Field Ambulance unit attached to the Second South Midland Mounted Brigade, a yeomanry brigade commanded by the Earl of Longford.[86] In close proximity to the front line, Dr. Auden would at first have had the terrible task of overseeing a section of stretcher bearers and working in a tent where he gave initial treatment to the wounded.[87] For the next four and a half years, until Dr. Auden was decommissioned in February 1919 at the age of forty-six, his family hardly saw him at all, in uniform or out. In spite of the sometimes momentous nature of his life in this period, like many veterans he seems to have been unable to communicate directly about his experiences: his granddaughter Jane Hanly commented that "My grandfather never would talk of the war."[88] But, like many other men and women in the services, Dr. Auden broadcast his sense of wartime stress and trauma to the people close to him. Perhaps reticence or even withdrawal were two of the ways in which that happened. His family rarely met him, and apparently there are no surviving letters home.

The Field Ambulance unit was in camp, mainly at Fakenham, Norfolk, until April 1915, when it departed for Egypt. The medics were stationed at Ismailia until August 1915, when the brigade left for Suvla Bay, where a series of landings were being made in an attempt to end the bloody deadlock of the Gallipoli campaign. On 18 August 1915, Dr. Auden's ambulance unit landed with the brigade from small boats on "A" beach, the "pitch dark night being periodically illuminated by gun flashes and shells bursting on the hills."[89] Three days later, they marched across a salt lake bed under constant fire before joining an attack, made by three divisions, into what a few nights later developed into the Battle of Scimitar Hill. This was the largest and most costly one-day battle in the entire Gallipoli campaign and ended in a brutal defeat for the British. Over one-third of their troops became casualties that night and day, while the defending Ottoman forces also suffered heavy losses. Undergrowth that the Turkish shells had set on fire burned wounded men alive. Lord Longford, leading a suicidal charge with remnants of his brigade, was killed in the engagement.

Dr. Auden was probably in the advance dressing station at what the British Army referred to as Chocolate Hill (part of Yilghin Burnu). Throughout the night of the battle, the ambulance unit, very close to the front line, dealt with a "constant stream of wounded" as they were "being brought in by the bearers under a heavy fire."[90] It was probably during this action that Dr. Auden himself carried a badly wounded sergeant to safety on his back.[91] The historians of the Field Ambulance unit laconically call it "a memorable night" from which "certain incidents . . . remain indelibly fixed on the mind."[92] One man, who claimed he had sprained his ankle, was examined by the doctors and pronounced fit for duty. He was preparing to return to the front line when he was shot through the heart at the dressing station.

In the morning, the medical facilities themselves were shelled, leading to a retreat, then further Turkish shelling and another retreat to a previous position at Lala Baba. There, in the words of the official history, "they remained for a fortnight, busy with the treatment and evacuation of casualties."[93] Dr. Auden worked, caring for the living and dying, but also, as if preserving a little piece of sane, civilian existence, he pursued his scholarly interests, recording Greek inscriptions on two ancient graves he found in the vicinity.[94]

W. H. Auden later said, seemingly implausibly, that the "thought never entered [his] head" that his father "might be in danger." But Dr. Auden barely escaped during the Gallipoli debacle, when over the course of eleven or so months about 44,000 Allied and 87,000 Ottoman troops perished. Once the two sides dug in in the area in September 1915, the Field Ambulance had its main dressing station near the beach at Suvla Bay and had to deal with very large numbers of men suffering from dysentery, jaundice, and other diseases. According to John Auden, Dr. Auden one day crawled out to rescue a tortoise that had got stuck between the Turkish and Allied trenches. While he was there, a Turkish sniper almost hit him.[95] Armies of bloated flies fed on the corpses of dead soldiers and animals; a third of the Second South Midland Mounted Brigade's remaining force was evacuated as sick or wounded.

After Dr. Auden survived such an intense period of service, and perhaps also in light of the wastage in the Field Ambulance unit, in October 1915 the army promoted him at Suvla Bay to the rank of captain.[96] As the Turkish summer turned to autumn and then winter, there were storms, floods, blizzards—soldiers drowned on land, some froze to death, and thousands suffered from frostbite. Dr. Auden, by now forty-three years old, was affected. Army medics later reported that he had "had fever, and muscular rheumatism on and off for some months."[97] The Field Ambulance finally left the peninsula on 13 December 1915: "only three officers and sixty men remained with the unit to embark in H.M.T. *Anchises*." Dr. Auden was probably one of those officers. They withdrew to Moudros, Greece, where Dr. Auden got soaked during freezing weather, afterward suffering more muscle aches and stiffness. At last, they reached Egypt. In January 1916, he was admitted to the hospital there with a fever and was subsequently invalided out of battlefront duty and sent to teach at the Imperial School of Instruction in Cairo.[98]

Trauma is isolating and contagious. Given Auden's "blitheness" about his father's experiences at Gallipoli and Dr. Auden's own silence on his wartime life, it is impossible to know what the impact of these events might have been on Dr. Auden or what he might have transmitted to his son. The closest we can come at one remove to the unconscious mind of the young wartime and postwar Auden lies in the poetry of another great anatomist of modern Englishness, Ted Hughes, whose father, William, also served in the war. In August 1915, William Hughes was with the Lancashire Fusiliers around Krithia, only about ten miles south of Dr. Auden's position. In Ted Hughes's 1967 collection *Wodwo,* he describes his father and himself at home together in the 1930s with brilliant, pessimistic vividness:

> His outer perforations
> Were valiantly healed, but he and the hearth-fire, its
>   blood-flicker
> On biscuit-bowl and piano and table-leg,
> Moved into strong and stronger possession
> Of minute after minute, as the clock's tiny cog
> Laboured and on the thread of his listening
> Dragged him bodily from under
> The mortised four-year strata of dead Englishmen
> He belonged with. He felt his limbs clearing
> With every slight, gingerish movement. While I, small and four,
> Lay on the carpet as his luckless double,
> His memory's buried, immovable anchor,
> Among jawbones and blown-off boots, tree-stumps, shellcases
>   and craters,
> Under rain that goes on drumming its rods and thickening
> Its kingdom, which the sun had abandoned, and where nobody
> Can ever again move from shelter.[99]

In the later 1920s and the 1930s, Auden, like Hughes later, wrote as a "luckless double" of his father, anchored in the trauma of combat experience. Although never as close to the surface as it is in Hughes's writing, the memory of war suffuses the young Auden's poetry.

In the autumn of 1915, while Dr. Auden cared for medical cases in a tent at Suvla Bay, the eight-year-old Wystan and his brother John were sent away to prep school in the Home Counties' countryside. Once they had left for St. Edmund's in Hindhead, Surrey, Mrs. Auden gave up the lease on the house in Solihull. She put the books, china, and furniture into storage and "for the duration" went to live with relatives during term times. "When our school holidays came round," Auden remembered, "she took furnished rooms for my brothers and me, each time in some new and exciting part of the country."[100] From 1915 until 1919, when the family moved into a house in the Harborne suburb of Birmingham, Auden had plenty of fatherless excitement with his mother and brothers in some of the more austerely beautiful rural corners of England and Wales. But he had no home.[101]

Isherwood remembered Auden at St. Edmund's as a "sturdy, podgy little boy" nicknamed "Dodo Minor," a sobriquet he acquired there by family entail because "of the solemn and somewhat birdlike appearance of his bespectacled elder brother." The young Auden's "normal expression was the misleadingly ferocious frown common to people with very short sight." This odd newcomer to the tribal atmosphere of the school looked out at the world from a "narrow scowling pudding-white face" surmounted by hair "like bleached straw" and waved around hands that were "nail-bitten and stained."[102] Here was the very raw human material that institutions such as St. Edmund's were designed to shape into an English gentleman. Auden spent "six years of schooling" in Surrey, where his classroom energies were "devoted largely to Latin and Greek."[103]

Ever since the major reforms of the British public schools in the mid-nineteenth century, the underlying purpose of the upper echelons in the country's educational system had been not simply to improve moral and intellectual standards for their own sakes but to prepare fresh, more competent generations of managers and administrators for the British Empire. The sacred imperial mission required huge cadres of unattached, self-disciplined young gentlemen brought up to obey and be obeyed. The literary historian Peter Parker writes that they were to value above all the "subordination of self to the community, personal striving for the common weal, the upholding of traditions and loyalty to the community."[104] Preparatory and public schools, like human factories, were planned to turn out such men on an industrial scale and with as little variation as possible.

A supercilious conformity, manifested in youth as "house feeling" and "honor" and in adult life as "decency," "character," and "team spirit," became one of the cardinal gentlemanly virtues inculcated in schools. It was intended in coming years to fortify these scions with a feeling of moral superiority in their adult roles as bureaucrats, officers, overseers, and fixers.[105] An expected feeling of mystical reverence for the institution of house and school prepared the way for a religion of country and duty in later life. A few years after Auden had passed through St. Edmund's, the *Times*' obituary for the school's long-serving headmaster Cyril Morgan-Brown (known as "Ciddy" to the boys) saluted him with unselfconscious candor for rendering "50 years of good and faithful service to the State."[106]

During the late nineteenth century, and most particularly after the Second Boer War of 1899–1902, the elite schools of England developed an increasingly close and symbiotic relationship with the British Army. In the early 1900s, the War Office took overall charge of the Officer Training Corps (OTC) program for the nation's schools and universities, thus preparing to its own specifications a wave of young men whom it could confidently commission as junior officers once a long-expected European war had been triggered.[107]

Britain, like most of the rest of Europe, was becoming in myriad ways a more pervasively bellicose and tightly organized society. Naturally, this involved the increasingly thorough militarization of childhoods, especially for boys. Alongside the OTC, quasi-military organizations such as the Boy Scouts—and for the working class, the Church Lads' Brigade and the Boys' Brigade—had large memberships. At the same time, magazines like *Boys' Own Paper* and *The Captain* propagated the romance of war, imagined in distinctly officer-worshipping terms, into almost every section of British society.[108] Most of the public schools in England cultivated the ethic of aggressive, self-sacrificing heroism, justified by appeal to muscular Christian values such as patriotism and duty. This process was made subtler and more intense by the messages circulating not just on the playing fields or in the dormitory but also in the classroom and the dining hall. Nationalistic indoctrination was a *Gesamtkunstwerk*.

In 1915, when John and Wystan Auden arrived at St. Edmund's prep school, they found it situated in the semirural, "conifer-and-ravine" depths, or rather heights, of Surrey and housed in an "aggressive gabled building in the early Edwardian style, about the size of a private hotel."[109] St. Edmund himself was a soldier: a youthful East Anglian king who had resisted a Danish invasion of his kingdom and had, in St. Sebastian–like fashion, been shot to death with so many arrows that his corpse resembled a thistle. In keeping with this noble example, the school's main dining room was decorated with "frescoes of British heroes (Raleigh, Chaucer, the Black Prince), saints (Augustine, Michael, George and, of course, Edmund) and allegorical figures (Faith, Hope and Charity)."[110] There was also a large copy of G. F. Watts's 1888 picture of the virginal Grail seeker and holy warrior Sir Galahad, the original of which hangs in Eton Chapel.

Around the school, the town of Hindhead stretched, a desert of "big comfortable houses in grounds of rhododendrons and firs, the traditional image of Surrey."[111] On the school lands, among stands of pine trees and numerous, lonely acres of ragged gorse bushes, there were playing fields and a rifle range—the latter an obvious sign of the increased emphasis that most Edwardian public and prep schools, with encouragement from the War Office, placed on military training for boys.[112]

Near the end of Auden's life, he mentioned that during the school holidays, the only "war work" for him and his brothers had been the typical tasks of "collecting sphagnum moss [for surgical dressings] . . . and knitting mufflers [for soldiers and sailors] in the evening" while Mrs. Auden read aloud to them.[113] His memories of prep school emphasized the mundane dangers of St. Edmund's more than the horror of the war:

> My political education began at the age of seven when I was sent to a boarding school. Every English boy of the middle class spends five years as a member of a primitive tribe ruled by benevolent or malignant demons. . . . For the first time I came into contact with adults outside the family circle and found them to be hairy monsters with terrifying voices and eccentric habits, completely irrational in their bouts of rage and good-humour, and, it seemed, with absolute power

of life and death. Those who deep in the country at a safe distance from parents spend their lives teaching little boys, behave in a way which would get them locked up in ordinary society. When I read in a history book of King John gnawing the rush-mat in his rage, it didn't surprise me in the least: that was just how the masters behaved.[114]

And in "Letter to Lord Byron" (1936), he wrote about his days at St. Edmund's in this way:

> The Great War had begun: but masters' scrutiny
>   And fists of big boys were the war to us;
> It was as harmless as the Indian Mutiny,
>   A beating from the Head was dangerous.
>   But once when half the form put down *Bellus,*
> We were accused of that most deadly sin,
> Wanting the Kaiser and the Huns to win.[115]

The grammar is a little blurred. Although Auden clearly means that the "Great War" was harmless, "it" here should logically relate to the war of "masters' scrutiny | And fists of big boys," implying that the "Great War" was not in fact harmless. And he gives the game away with his comparison between the First World War and the harmless "Indian Mutiny": two of his distant relatives had been killed during the "Mutiny."[116]

For Auden at St. Edmund's, it was "dangerous" to make a mistake in Latin—by putting the word for "beautiful" (*bellus*) in place of the word for "war" (*bellum*), evoking in Ciddy's outraged mind the destroyers of Rome, Attila and his Huns, who did not speak Latin properly. It was "dangerous" not only because of the headmaster's crazily choleric moods, often ignited by lapses in Latin grammar and vocabulary, but because schoolchildren learned a set of beliefs about war, patriotism, and duty, even when they were apparently engaged in studying ancient languages or in memorizing dates and episodes from distant English history.[117]

To get the Latin wrong not only meant risking a beating. It was also letting the side down. It was as bad as wanting the "Huns to win," leaving a child saddled with the feeling that he had compromised the safety of the entire "primitive tribe ruled by . . . malignant demons." In this war, the "demons," not only at St. Edmund's but in the country as a whole, *were* overwhelmingly "malignant." The language in Auden's descriptions of life at the school—"monsters," "terrifying voices," "completely irrational," "bouts of rage," "absolute power of life and death," "locked up," "gnawing," "rage"—evokes a mood of hysteria lurking beneath the poised prose surface.

The madness was not simply a result of personal pathologies among the schoolmasters whom Auden encountered. The global conflict of 1914–1918 set off convulsions that reached into every corner of life for civilians as well as soldiers, children as well as adults. A new feeling spread, slowly and inexorably penetrating every nook and cranny of existence, including the world of schools. In *Kangaroo* (1923), D. H. Lawrence wrote about the atmosphere that his central figure, Richard Lovat Somers, had known in Britain during the war years, the years when Auden was at St. Edmund's:

> During the later years of the war, [he experienced] a true and deadly fear of the criminal *living* spirit which arose in all the stay-at-home bullies who governed the country during those years. From 1916 to 1919 a wave of criminal lust rose and possessed England, there was a reign of Terror, under a set of indecent bullies like [Horatio] Bottomley of *John Bull* and other bottom-dog members of the House of Commons. Then Somers had known what it was to live in a perpetual state of semi-fear: the fear of the criminal public and the criminal government. The torture was steadily applied, during those years after Asquith fell, to break the independent soul in any man who would not hunt with the criminal mob.[118]

Lawrence's chapter in *Kangaroo* on wartime England is called "The Nightmare." Many troops returning to Britain on leave were appalled by the levels of abrasive ignorance and the spiteful bellicosity they found in the public on the home front. Robert Graves, for example, wrote about the amazement he felt when he came back from the trenches to find "war-madness" in England that "ran about everywhere looking for a pseudo-military outlet."[119] This was the psychotic world in which Auden was growing up.

Between 1914 and 1918, it was almost impossible for anyone in Britain not to know at least one person involved in the war. But even if this *were* possible, the presence of war, in places where there was no fighting, was unavoidable. On the streets, in public buildings, and in homes, visual reminders of the government-sanctioned carnage were ubiquitous. The war was in newspapers, in jokes, on boxes of tea, in children's games, on municipal walls. Alongside Field Marshal Kitchener's crooked finger pointing directly out from recruiting posters at the furtive observer—"Britons [Lord Kitchener] Wants You! Join Your Country's Army!"—legions of other hectoring notices became familiar sights on station platforms and street corners as troop levels dwindled in late 1914 and throughout 1915, before the government introduced conscription in 1916.

As the able-bodied marched away, so the crippled, the blinded, and the mad limped back, and the slowly dying were carried home. (Bodies of men who died in France, Belgium, or elsewhere were not repatriated.) War casualties increased to such an extent that the kinds of people one might expect to encounter in English towns also changed. Geoffrey Gorer, the English social anthropologist, who was a boy during the First World War and later became a good friend of Auden, wrote that in wartime Britain, the war widow was "a tragic, almost frightening figure in the full panoply of widow's weeds and unrelievedly black, a crepe veil shrouding her (when not lifted) so that she was visibly withdrawn from the world."[120]

Along with the bereaved in black, the walking, twitching, hobbling, or wheeled wounded were impossible to miss. More than 41,000 British soldiers underwent an amputation during the war. Maimed or disfigured ex-servicemen were visible in every city and town.[121] Even when their bodies were whole, the men who returned from the conflict into the young Auden's world almost all bore some kind of mental wound. The war correspondent Philip Gibbs wrote that "all was not right with the spirit of the men who came back. Something was wrong.... They were subject to queer moods, queer tempers, fits of profound depression alternating with a restless desire for pleasure. Many of them were easily moved to passion when they lost control of themselves. Many were bitter in their speech, violent in opinion, frightening."[122]

The last poem of C. H. Sorley, killed at Loos in October 1915, recognized that the awareness of mass death was so deep and sickening that it had invaded the unconscious lives of people on the home front.

He imagined civilians, lying in their beds, having nightmares in which "millions of the mouthless dead | Across your dreams in pale battalions go."[123] If there is one truth about Auden's childhood that needs to be fully absorbed and not deflected, it is that he grew up in a culture in which war and death were everyday preoccupations and in which their traces were everywhere in actual, and psychic, landscapes.

After Isherwood's mother visited St. Edmund's school in June 1917 (around the time when her son met Auden there), she described the atmosphere as being "very military now."[124] The intense, introverted world of school was filled with reminders of the war; the conflict's material culture was absorbed seamlessly into the hothouse atmosphere of boys' rivalries, friendships, and intrigues. Isherwood's story "Gems of Belgian Architecture," set in a St. Edmund's–like school during the war, describes a craze among the pupils for collecting cigarette cards from their contacts among the "thousands of Canadians down at the Camp" not far from the school. The most prized set is the sequence "Gems of Belgian Architecture," patriotically and profitably immortalizing on cheap cardboard the treasures of the Flemish architectural patrimony—buildings such as the Cloth Hall at Ypres—damaged or destroyed by the Germans at the start of the war.[125]

Poor food and mindless drilling were further staples of the St. Edmund's war experience. When Auden recalls, in "Letter to Lord Byron," how Ciddy accused the boys of the "most deadly sin" of "Wanting . . . the Huns to win" because they failed to use the Latin noun for "war," he seems to allude, privately, to a different incident from his school days (one that is glanced at in this book's Prologue). Memoirs of the war years make clear that any hints of home-front sympathy in Britain for Germany, or of kinship with the German people, were rapidly stigmatized.[126] Toward the end of his life, Auden recollected that he had once leaned forward in the St. Edmund's dining hall to take "an extra slice of bread and margarine." Helping oneself to another piece of bread was permitted by school rules. But a master—an invalid? a geriatric? a wounded veteran?—muttered audibly, "I see, Auden, you want the Huns to win."[127] The remark's sadistic bitterness suggests how deeply cynical and anguished moods infiltrated the texture of school life.

But who can know what that master had himself been through? In schools such as St. Edmund's, the roster of the male staff changed with ominous frequency, as Auden describes in "Letter to Lord Byron":

The best were fighting, as the King expected,
  The remnant either elderly grey creatures,
  Or characters with most peculiar features.
Many were raggable, a few were waxy,
One had to leave abruptly in a taxi.[128]

There was, for instance, Reginald Oscar Gartside Bagnall, affectionately recalled by Auden as having a "moral character" that was "all at sea," distributing "beer and biscuits" to his awed favorites, confiding to them his skill as a "first-class shot" and reading aloud "in a Henry Irving voice" from his play *The Waves* ("a barefaced crib . . . from *The Bells,*" Irving's great, melodramatic, Victorian star vehicle, composed for him by Leopold Lewis).[129] When Gartside Bagnall, who was either a captain or a second lieutenant depending on whom you asked (if you asked Gartside Bagnall, he was a captain), met Mrs. Bradshaw-Isherwood, a war widow, she described him as "a very keen soldier somehow now unfit for service."[130]

As the raggable and waxy like "Reggy" and his ilk came and went, Auden and his St. Edmund's schoolmates "drilled with wooden rifles and had 'field days' when we took cover behind bushes and twirled noise-makers to represent machine-gun fire."[131] There is a description in the school magazine of Auden taking part in a compulsory OTC exercise, staged at a scenic local spot, The Devil's Punchbowl, near Hindhead in June 1917. "Corpl. Auden (junior)" was stationed behind a wooden machine gun. During "the [enemy's] charge, the Corporal [i.e., Auden] gave them a good deal of lead, but was unable to stop them."[132] His role in this official game must then have been to lie dead.

Isherwood's diary records that, besides practicing for combat, the boys at St. Edmund's also received frequent lectures on the progress and aims of the war.[133] They must have been regaled with maps very like those that the poet C. Day Lewis saw at his school: "maps of France and Flanders, the Western front a snaking line of flags, Allied and German, which from time to time were moved, a centimetre westwards, a few millimetres to the east—tiny shifts which marked, we were told, great victories or strategic withdrawals" but not that "another fifty thousand or five hundred thousand men were dead or maimed or driven insane."[134]

In *Lions and Shadows*, Isherwood wrote that he had been "emotionally messed about [by the masters and mistresses] at my preparatory school, where the war years had given licence to every sort of dishonest cant about loyalty, selfishness, patriotism, playing the game and dishonouring the dead."[135] As a result, he believed that, "like most of my generation," he became "obsessed by a complex of terrors and longings connected with the idea 'War.'"[136] The home-front atmosphere that Isherwood breathed at St. Edmund's was one he shared with his friend Auden at the same place during the very dark depths of the war.[137]

If the struggle haunted school life for Auden, it also lurked in the countryside he visited. The Auden family, minus Dr. Auden, spent most of their wartime holidays together in the northern and western parts of Britain. Yet, the war sprang up in front of them wherever they went, especially when they ventured south from Birmingham. At Easter 1917, for example, they traveled to the Isle of Wight (this was the trip during which Auden remembered playing piano duets full of "quavers" with his mother). The youngest Auden recorded that they talked to some "nice New Zealand nurses" who told the family they had recently been on a "hospital ship coming from Havre with 600 wounded on board." The ship had rammed a cliff at four o'clock in the morning, and in remorse, the chief officer had shot himself. Auden noted the minor but ghoulish incident in the family's holiday diary.[138] In the days after they met the nurses, while they pottered around collecting fossils, visiting churches, or making brass rubbings, the Audens could probably hear the rumble of the giant guns firing across the Channel in France— the sounds made by the Allied and German artillery indistinguishable from each other.[139]

Even if the practical effects and deprivations of the war itself (worse food, strange masters, more boring forms of physical exercise, agonizingly dull lectures by twitching, beribboned cripples) had a limited impact on Auden, as he implausibly claimed, then the psychological impact of growing up during what, as seen earlier, H. M. Tomlinson called the "greatest disturbance of mankind" in tens of thousands of years, and with a parent away at the war, was far greater.[140] Auden was a subtle child (a school friend at St. Edmund's described him as "a good deal more sensitive, and even thin-skinned, than he cared to appear") in a country seething with bewilderment, fear, anger, and a huge, dark, half-repressed feeling of mass grief.[141] In an article written at the end of the 1920s, Dr. Auden acknowledged the psychological damage that the "anxious days of the War" had caused in young children's minds when he noted that the "difficult maladjusted child" had been identified as a phenomenon of "modern social life" in which war played a major role.[142] A few years later, in 1934, his own son, as if recalling his father's remarks about the impact of war on boys, decided that he too had been a "difficult child."[143]

Any boy at school during this time was constantly adjured against "dishonoring the dead"—by which "dishonest cant" the headmaster and his educational subalterns meant in part besmirching the memory of the large numbers of fallen old boys from the school that these children were now attending. And he would have felt an eerie shadow spread over his sense of what the future might bring. Many young children around Auden had parents, uncles, or elder brothers who had already died in the conflict. Lieutenant-Colonel Frank Bradshaw-Isherwood was killed at Ypres in May 1915; his body was never found.[144] Reared in institutions to which traditions of self-sacrifice and service (often with a military inflection) were so profoundly important, young men in their school years would have felt that they were already being, in Siegfried Sassoon's phrase, sped "up the line to death."[145]

Until the very end, it seemed to many people as if the war was likely to go on forever. Lord Northcliffe, the minister of information, said as late as September 1918, about two months before the Armistice, that "None of us will live to see the end of the war."[146] Auden's older brother Bernard was already in training camp when the war suddenly stopped, and their cousin Geoffrey Auden, a cadet in the Royal Air Force (RAF), died of pneumonia in Hampstead Military Hospital at the age of eighteen during the war's last month.[147] At the Dragon School in Oxford, John Betjeman and his classmates listened in morning assembly as "the Skipper would announce | The latest names of those who'd lost their lives. . . . Sometimes his gruff old voice was full of tears | When a particular favourite had been killed."[148] At St. Edmund's, "lists of 'old boys' who had fallen were read out in chapel each week" to the assembled school.[149] There were thirty-seven young soldiers, former denizens of the school's OTC, who "played up" and died during the war.

The etymological root of "infantry" is in the Latin *infans, infantis,* or "child." As the war went on, and as the army relied more and more heavily on conscription of those who were just finishing school, the typical recruit became younger. And France and Flanders, where so many were sent, was by far the deadliest theater of operations.[150] There, the chances of death for young men in service were much greater than for older men: the mortality rate was highest throughout the war among twenty-year-olds. The greatest rate of loss was among junior officers, who were expected to keep calm, to model courage for the soldiers under their command, and to lead from the front. Because of the rigid class structure in the British Army, the subalterns, at least in the early stages of the war, were overwhelmingly upper-middle-class young men who had either been attending university or had been about to do so.[151] For a change, the class system worked against those who were the most privileged. Only a small fraction of the overall population of men in Britain attended university at all in this period, and Oxford and Cambridge undergraduates had disproportionately high casualty rates compared with those who were at other universities.[152]

During the war, there were around fourteen new pupils at St. Edmund's each year. Had the conflict continued, as many people thought it well might, until 1925 (the year when Auden and his classmates would have been conscripted) and had the killing rate remained constant, then approximately three out of the fourteen could have been expected to die in uniform.[153] This casualty rate is roughly in line with those for public schools where "one old boy out of every five who served" was killed.[154] If all had served, a family with a father and three brothers, such as the Audens, would have faced very significant odds of losing at least one of its members.

In Britain and Ireland alone, hundreds of thousands had died before their time; millions of lives had been ruined; millions more would be lost in the postwar epidemics that swept around the world. "In every year between the wars," the historian Jay Winter wrote, "men died of wounds or disease contracted on active service. Mourning began, for many, after years of caring for ex-servicemen."[155] This is the bleak reality underwriting David Cannadine's assertion that, as the scale of the loss sank in during the interwar years, "Britain was more obsessed with death than at any other period in recent history." In this period, Can- nadine declared, "the all-pervasive pall of death" hung "sorrowful, stag- nant and static" over the country.[156] Auden became celebrated as a writer in a country still "obsessed with death," and his poems faithfully reflect that truth.

After Dr. Auden was temporarily invalided out of a frontline medical unit as a result of his experiences at Gallipoli, he spent most of 1916– 1917 in Egypt at the Imperial School of Instruction on the outskirts of Cairo. Perhaps, as someone who had now seen mass death close at hand, he was ready to live a bit differently. In Cairo, he began a serious, long-lasting affair with an English nurse (a profession she shared with his wife). Her name was (probably) Ann Haverson, and she and Dr. Auden met in Cairo or Alexandria.[157] When he came home on leave for the first time in nearly three years in the summer of 1917, his wife had somehow learned about the romance. There was, in John B. Auden's words, "a mammoth row" that all three brothers heard while the family was on a holiday at Clitheroe, a town with an old lead mine on the southern edge of the Yorkshire dales.[158]

The war put the Audens' union under pressure, as it did many tens of thousands of other marriages in Britain.[159] The divorce rate in 1919 was three times the level it had been in 1913. Perhaps something cracked irreparably in the Auden marriage, even if it remained tenu- ously intact. Their granddaughter thought that what Dr. Auden "missed most in his marriage was a sense of fun and gaiety."[160] Mrs. Auden's feelings about the matter were not recorded.

Dr. Auden's solution to this 1917 marital crisis was to apply for a home transfer on compassionate grounds. The family had quickly moved from Clitheroe on to Rhayader in Radnorshire, Wales, perhaps hoping to recapture the harmony of their prewar world since they had visited the town in the innocent days of 1913. (Rhayader, only about eighty miles west of the Audens' home in the Birmingham suburbs, is the site of a massive set of dams and reservoirs designed to bring clean water to Birmingham's population—the industrial engineering may have been an attraction for the youngest Auden boy.) From there, Dr. Auden wrote to the War Office: "I have been away from home since August 1914. . . . During this time my wife's health has undergone pro-

FIG. 2 *W. H. Auden (left), John Auden (center), and Bernard Auden (right) with their father, Dr. George Auden, at Rhayader, Wales, in early September 1917. The photographer is probably the boys' mother, Constance Auden. W. H. Auden is ten years old. Although wearing uniform on leave was not required, Dr. Auden is dressed as a captain in the RAMC and has on his cord riding breeches. This picture was taken not long after the "massive row" between Dr. Auden and Mrs. Auden (overheard by their sons) about Dr. Auden's nurse mistress in Egypt.*

gressive deterioration. She underwent an extensive operation in November last and since then her heart has given cause for anxiety and she can now bear very little exertion. During the past 3 years she has had no settled home and the burden of the upbringing of our 3 sons has fallen entirely upon her shoulders. It is now imperative to make some permanent home for her and to relieve her from further mental and physical strain."[161]

How much of the information in Dr. Auden's request was true and how much was equivocation is unknowable. His transfer was approved, and he was posted to Norwich by the end of the same month. In the event, it took some time for Mrs. Auden to reestablish a home for herself and her family, and the Audens were mostly separated until Dr. Auden was demobilized in early 1919. But they reached some kind of understanding about this episode, and their marriage seems to have been relatively stable and happy in the following years until Mrs. Auden's death in 1941. Yet in old age, or perhaps earlier, Dr. Auden carved a wooden screen on which was incised in Greek an adage from Marcus Aurelius praising self-sufficient solitariness in the face of death: "Live as on a mountain."[162] What message might that have sent to his wife if she was still alive when he made the screen? Dr. Auden's involvement with Ann Haverson continued sporadically for the rest of his life and included some later meetings in Repton, the village in Derbyshire to which he retired in 1949. As a last wish, he asked for his lover's letters to him to be burned with his body.[163]

Besides introducing a deep source of parental discord into the family, Dr. Auden's war was, as we have seen, physically very risky. Though an army medic carried no weapon, Dr. Auden was not insulated from lethal dangers. Doctors had to be near the fighting to have any hope of saving the wounded. High explosives blew people apart and maimed bodies indiscriminately; and, besides, army physicians were a favored target for snipers. Dr. Auden told his middle son, John, that he was again lucky to escape death in France after he was sent there in late 1917.[164]

When Dr. Auden returned home in 1919, he contracted encephalitis lethargica—commonly known as "sleeping sickness"—during an epidemic of the illness, which was virulent from around 1918 to 1926, killing roughly a million people. His case was a mild one and, although he continued to be troubled by a foot frozen during the Suvla Bay retreat, he must have largely recovered from the effects of sleeping sickness because, during the 1920s, he was both a busy public-health official in Birmingham and a prolific writer on a range of issues related to children, psychology, and disease. In fact, he became one of the country's experts on encephalitis lethargica in children.[165]

About one subject relating to the First World War, Auden was consistently frank. Near the end of his life, he explained in an interview: "At seven, which is just the age a child really needs a father, my father went away to the war. He didn't come back till I was twelve, so in a certain sense I lost him. . . . in a way he was always a stranger."[166] When Auden claimed that he "lost" his father during the war, he was playing with the term most often used to indicate "losing" a parent to death. Elsewhere he wrote that "we never really came to know each other."[167]

Curiously, both Dr. Auden and Mrs. Auden had had little or no experience of their own fathers. *His* father had died at the age of forty-five when George Auden was only four years old; *her* father had died at the age of forty-seven, when she was barely eleven months of age: their "fathers both went suddenly to Heaven | While they were still quite small and left them here | To work on earth with little cash to spare."[168] Wystan, their son, believed that, at least as an inner presence, his father died for him, or to him, during the First World War. Physically he returned; psychologically he was gone.

This was an emotional earthquake, which altered the landscape of Auden's entire life and shaped his career as a poet. But its significance was not confined to a merely private level. The "loss" of a father in the war was exactly the fate suffered, whether actually or imaginatively, by millions of others in Britain and across Europe and in the populations of the European empires. As such, each private "loss" was also symbolic of social loss, of the crisis of authority, and of the rage against the "old men," which lay at the heart of many political and poetical dilemmas of the 1920s and 1930s. The trauma of a lost authority figure within his psyche gave Auden's poetic mind a deeply representative cast; it is a part of what made his poetry resonate in postwar England.

The war also shaped Auden's view of his sexual identity. Aside from being a learned authority on sulfuric acid, Auden's "favourite uncle," Harold Auden, was a "life-long homosexual" who collected pictures of naked choirboys and had got into trouble over sex while he was studying for his doctorate in chemistry at Tübingen.[169] But Auden primarily connected his own emerging sexual identity as a young man with his father's absence. Not long before he went away to prep school in 1915, the youngest Auden was circumcised at an unusually late age. He told a friend thirty years afterward that the operation had a significant impact on him and had been "really something."[170] Perhaps the fact that he underwent the disfiguring procedure around the age of seven or eight, when his father was gone, is part of what made it such a harsh experience.

Moreover, it was a psychological commonplace of the period that homosexual men, when they were children, had been smothered with affection as "mummy's boys" and that their homosexuality resulted from a weak or absent father and an excessive identification with the mother. Auden believed that the war had helped make the kind of sexual being he was.[171] Nietzsche, the exponent of revelatory diagnoses in a pre-Freudian era, claimed that the "degree and kind of a man's sexuality reach up into the ultimate pinnacle of his spirit."[172] It is just as true that the nature of the contemporary world reaches down into the "degree and kind" of a person's sexuality. Sex lives are historically conditioned.

The configuration of W. H. Auden's erotic imagination was deeply imprinted by his social moment—evident, for example, in his transgressive but common fascination with men from a lower class or a different nation than his own and in metaphors from military life that creep into the descriptions of his emotional world. For example, in an unpublished poem he wrote in 1930, he described one would-be lover (lightheartedly but not altogether lightheartedly) as being thrillingly like a "Commander, | Head of the storm-troops."[173] In a haiku chain he composed toward the end of his life, when it had become just slightly easier to raise such topics in a public context, Auden described an incompatible couple whose sexual "day-dreams" were the same, like their "natures," which are imprinted by military fantasies: "Both wish to play *Officer*, | Neither *Other Ranks*."[174]

And in a poetic recollection of his wartime years, Auden made his father's absence disrupt the normal division of sex instruction between parents and hence nurture the forms of his own homosexuality. In a confessional tanka from the late cycle "Marginalia," Auden wrote, referring to himself in the third person (perhaps taking a cue from Isherwood's favorite mode of self-portraiture):

> Father at the wars,
> Mother, tongue-tied with shyness,
> struggling to tell him
> the Facts of Life he dared not
> tell her he knew already.[175]

The imaginative connection between "Father at the wars" and the "Facts of Life" (the two phrases are linked with a capitalized "Fa") was created in Auden's mind by the conflict that raged as he was growing up.

Isherwood recalled Auden at St. Edmund's during the war as precociously "clever, untidy, lazy and, with the masters, inclined to be insolent," and he remembered that Auden had a "playbox full of thick scientific books on geology and metals and machines, borrowed from his father's library." The cleverness of "Dodo Minor," his untidiness, his unusual armory of "forbidden knowledge and stock of mispronounced scientific words, portentously uttered," gave him the status of "a kind of witch-doctor" among his "semi-savage credulous schoolfellows."[176] Dodo Minor was interested in sex, medicine, and (like many clever schoolboys at this period) religious controversies. A schoolmate recalled that "On one occasion, when two forms that were accustomed to share a single room for prep were sundered for disciplinary reasons, [Auden] dubbed the event 'The Great Schism' and treated us to a short discourse on the late fourteenth century."[177] But, above all, he was obsessed with thoughts about life underground; his "ambition was to become a mining engineer."[178]

Isherwood left St. Edmund's at the very end of 1918, just after the Armistice, so his comments about Auden and his interests probably refer to the years 1917–1918, the last two years of the war, when Auden was ten or eleven years old and when Dr. Auden was still almost completely absent from his son's life even during the school holidays. On a number of occasions, Auden himself reported that from around the age of "seven until twelve," he "spent a great many of my waking hours in the construction and elaboration of a private sacred world, the basic elements of which were a landscape, northern and limestone, and an industry, lead mining."[179] In another essay he described himself during this period as the "sole autocratic inhabitant of a dream country of lead-mines, narrow-gauge tramways, and overshot water-wheels."[180] This dream country is at the core of Auden's imagination as it existed before he started writing poetry.

It is important to note three basic, interconnected points about this crucial facet of Auden's artistic psyche and the "discoveries" he referred to making before he "took an interest in poetry itself." First, the dates imply that Auden's initial interest in mines was coterminous with the war and with the time when his father had left home for military service: from roughly 1914 to 1919, he thought of himself in a literal sense as a future "mining engineer" (as an upper-middle-class boy, Auden expected to become a mining engineer, not a miner). That is, his interest in mines evolved while he was living in a country caught up in a desperately costly and unfamiliar kind of conflict, a war in which the earth was a source of both life and death. One of an infantryman's primary tasks was to stay hidden most of the time by digging himself down into the safety of below ground, while one of the most terrifying ways of dying at the front was to be buried alive in the huge, heavy showers of earth that rained down after a shell blast.

Second, and relatedly, Auden's imagination became saturated in images of a landscape dotted with abandoned mine workings and industrial machinery before he became a poet. At first, Auden read about mines as much as he visited them—for a while they were just a "[day]dream country." As an adult he told a friend: "My landscapes aren't really the same as Wordsworth's. Mine . . . came from books first."[181] And Auden insisted that he spent much of his time as a child thinking about mines "in a kind of daydreaming that was of immense importance to my childhood."[182] In one sense, an escape into reading about mines is like going into a private bunker and sheltering from the world.

One childhood book that was especially important to him was George MacDonald's fairy tale *The Princess and the Goblin* (1872), "set, for the most part, in the huge caverns, great deep pits and subterranean passages that transect the interior of a mountain whose possession is contested by miners and evil-minded troglodyte goblins."[183] The hero, a young poet-miner named Curdie, can use his rhymes to magical effect to liberate a princess whom the goblins have captured. He is a literary prefiguration of Auden's own poetic and symbolic interest in mines. Auden also owned such mine- and tunnel-centered children's fictions as Jules Verne's *Journey to the Centre of the Earth* (1867) and *The Child of the Cavern* (1877), as well as H. Rider Haggard's *King Solomon's Mines* (1885). As his mind grew more analytic and his fascination with mines increased, his parents provided him with technical books on mining: at Christmas 1918, for example, his mother gave him E. H. Davies's *Machinery for Metalliferous Mines* (1902).[184]

The idiosyncratic Auden family was interested in geology and industrial machinery, but Auden's interest in lead mines was obsessive

even for them. Auden remembered being taken to the Solihull gas-
works when he was a small child because it was believed at the time
that gas fumes were a cure for coughs and inflammations of the lungs.
The sick child was mesmerized by the machines there, "gazed at in awe
| by a bronchial boy."[185] He visited the North Yorkshire moors with his
family as early as 1913, when he was six.[186] And the family diary (compiled mainly by Mrs. Auden and John B. Auden) for a visit to Rhayader
in mid-Wales in the summer of 1913 reports that they learned about
rocks, climbing, and geology from going on walks with their father. On
"rainy days," there were visits to "local factories and other places with
machinery."[187] These included a tannery, a ginger beer bottling facility,
a woolen mill, and a waterworks. But there were no visits to mines.[188]

At Easter 1914, the family took a holiday at the summer resort of
Fairbourne on Barmouth Bay, near Snowdonia, a region filled with
spectacular mountains and working slate quarries, and a town boasting
an unusual small-gauge railway.[189] But although they were repeatedly
in quite close proximity to mines on their Welsh holidays during the
first half of the war, the Audens' collective holiday diaries talk of quarries but make no mention of ever visiting a mine.

Thus, although he seems to have read about mines for a while, Auden
probably first visited a mine only in the spring of 1916, when he was nine
years old and his father had been away from home for about a year and a
half. Then, Auden, his brothers, and their mother spent a holiday at
Bradwell in Derbyshire, from which base they visited the famous mine at
the Blue John Cavern in Castleton. Blue-John is the local name for the
abundant blue fluorspar mineral found in Derbyshire (the name comes
from the French for blue-yellow, *bleu-jaune*). Auden later referred to the
Cavern as one of the names on his "numinous map" of sacred spots.[190] In
all likelihood, during the same holiday the Audens visited the Speedwell
Cavern, also in Castleton, the site of an ancient lead mine. These first visits
in the depths of the war were likely to have been prompted by Auden's
bookworm obsession with mines.

This fascination appears to have been a largely private concern, fed
at first more by books and his imagination than by the relatively few
visits he made to mines themselves. It was also, in a nonjudgmental
sense, a "neurotic" concern, which germinated as he came to terms
with his father's absence. The fantasy allowed him a place to retreat to
from the pain of the outer world as if to what he once called a "private

[island] of schizophrenic bliss."[191] There was an old lead mine at Clitheroe in Lancashire, where in 1917 Auden's mother and father had a bitter
argument about Dr. Auden's mistress in Egypt.[192] Perhaps the mine was
the reason they had chosen to visit the town. Auden recalled that in
1919, when he was twelve, he saw the North Pennine moors—and the
many abandoned lead mines on what is technically called the "North
Pennine Orefield"—for the first time.[193] This must have been the moment
when, according to his own statements about his obsession, he was beginning to lose interest in mining as such and when his father had returned permanently from the war.

Third, and finally, Auden's technical mining fixation, as he spoke of
it, sprang up when his father was away at the war, and it seemed to disappear—or at least to become more moderate—after his father's return.
But mines and their heroic, invisible inhabitants, the miners, were already imbued for Auden with imaginative connections to an absent
father and to violence. Even thinking about them was in effect part of
his psyche's war work within a landscape where the subjects of mines,
lost heroes, conflict, and sexual longing intermingled.

Isherwood's description in *Lions and Shadows* of Auden as he remembered him at St. Edmund's is one of the most remarkably detailed descriptions ever given of a major poet who had not yet written
a line of poetry.[194] Sometimes the delicate ideas suggested by Isherwood's penetrating gaze point to the presence of truths that might
otherwise be overlooked. For example, Isherwood insightfully associates Auden's "lost" father with the subjects of "geology and metals and
machines." He recognizes that the "scientific" volumes on these subjects in W. H. Auden's playbox came from his father's library, not necessarily because they actually originated there (although many of
them may well have) but more importantly because he wants to suggest how deeply Auden's imagination connects his father with mineral
science and engineering. For his young son, Dr. Auden symbolically
owned the subjects of "geology and metals and machines"; in the son's
imagination, these subjects *held* Dr. Auden, and the impact of war,
symbolically within them.

Mining was an anomaly among industries in England in the early
part of the twentieth century. It was a highly technical, intensively capitalized process, but it primarily took place in desolate, rural areas,
among "tenements on sombre hills" and "gaunt in valleys," not in the

country's main cities or its overbuilt industrial centers.[195] Its workers had a reputation for enduring extreme dangers, which associated them both with the physical prowess and resourcefulness characteristic of heroes of an earlier age and with wide, unspoiled spaces. Thus, after Auden began to write poetry in 1922, where there are abandoned mines, there is also—realistically but eerily—silence, grass, and open land.

Auden's father returned home to his family in February 1919. On the following 11 November, in his last year at St. Edmund's, Auden had to attend the Armistice Day memorial service. There, two minutes' silence was observed for the old boys who had died, or, in the chivalric euphemism, had "fallen," during the war. It was probably in connection with this somber ritual in 1919 that Auden's pious mother gave St. Edmund's a wooden crucifix for the chapel.[196] An intelligent boy might, in this context, have viewed the cross as a disturbing emblem of the Son dying in agony, with the consent of the Mother, to save the world and the Father's name. That day the flag "on its newly-erected flag pole was flown at half-mast," and "in the evening a bonfire was lit on the playground and, joining hands," everyone "sang 'Auld Lang Syne.'"[197]

Some time after the somber bonfire ceremony, one of Auden's final notable experiences at St. Edmund's occurred. He had probably already experienced some forms of erotic contact with his contemporaries at the school. He told an American friend in the 1940s that after a boy was sent away to boarding school in Britain, "an older boy or a man might take charge of a young child. And when a master whipped or punished a child, there was the older boy, or a dormitory proctor, waiting to take him in bed to comfort him. Really, it was quite natural to become queer, like them."[198] But, when he was thirteen years old, he had his first full homosexual encounter with an adult: the school chaplain at St. Edmund's. The Rev. G. G. Newman was a man in his mid-thirties at the time, ordained and with an Oxford degree. Not insignificantly, he was (like Dr. Auden) a returned veteran, only recently back from France, where he had served as an army chaplain at the end of the war. (He also spent a period in the same role in the navy.) For reasons unknown, but guessable, Newman did not remain at the school long, leaving in 1921.[199] Auden was going through a confusing period of "ecclesiastical Schwärmerei" (originally Luther's word for a fanatical, overemotional, and confused faith) at the

time, centered on his enthusiasm for Rev. Newman, whom, as a schoolmate explained, "we boys believed, quite erroneously, to be some sort of
nephew of the cardinal."[200] Newman may not have discouraged the idea.
Auden later put the sex between a child and a man down to a "quite
straightforward and unredeemed eroticism" on his own part.[201]

Although Auden associated mines with his father's favorite point on the
compass, the North, he began as a poet not in the North or West of
England among industrial machines or workings of any sort but deep
in the more "maternal" eastern stretches of the English countryside. He
began, that is, in a landscape that English writing, music, and painting
had codified over the course of centuries of internal and external conflict, of trading, industrializing, empire-building and empire-losing history, as the source of the nation's moral and spiritual values. This was
the country's mythic center, the shaper of its aesthetic traditions, and a
microcosm of organic, "English" social integration, set against the universe of unrest in the nation's cities. Auden found that these kinds of
rural landscapes could absorb his imaginative world of mines and miners
because mining was not an antithesis to nature but a complement to it—
as if miners were like heroic, subterranean farmers harvesting the
earth's riches beneath the surface instead of above it.

In the autumn of 1920, Auden went on from St. Edmund's to
Gresham's School in Holt in Norfolk, the "most easterly public school
in England."[202] Like many other such schools, Gresham's is situated
deep in the countryside. It sits on the edge of the small town of Holt, in
a beautiful, mellow, largely flat part of north Norfolk, only about twenty
miles northwest of Salthouse, where Auden's mother was born in 1869,
and nearby Wroxham, where his grandfather once had the parish.[203]
Auden lived here for much of the year from September 1920 (when he
was thirteen) until the summer of 1925 (when he was eighteen), and it
was here that he eventually began writing poetry.

All around Gresham's there are still salt marshes, mudflats, and salt-
water lagoons, which form an important sanctuary for numerous birds.
Many of them appear in Auden's first poems. Describing the area, the
1937 edition of Baedeker's guide to Great Britain mentions bird sanctu-
aries, nature reserves, and the "pretty coastal village" of Weybourne.
(Gresham's itself is briefly noted as a "minor public school."[204]) Auden

loved bicycles in his youth, and all of these places were within walking or bicycling distance for a Gresham's schoolboy. As Baedeker's description of Weybourne indicates, Gresham's is only a few miles from what the volume's foldout map of Britain's coastline calls "the German Ocean." A friend of Auden's from this time remembered that Auden enjoyed "walking over fen or through wood; and he was always didactic, as he is still today; the walk would be accompanied by a discourse on whatever subject might crop up."[205]

Gresham's had begun to develop a reputation for educational excellence only at the start of the twentieth century. When Auden arrived there in 1920, it was still a fairly small, and not very grand, single-sex public school of around 250 boys. Gresham's infrastructure, curriculum and, more questionably, its morals had been improved by G. W. S. Howson, who was headmaster from 1900 to 1919. J. R. Eccles, Howson's successor and the headmaster during Auden's time at the school, continued the reforms. As a result, Gresham's was an odd mixture of the beautiful and the sinister, the earnest and the quirky, the predictable and the unforeseen.

There were the obligatory exhortation-filled visits by bishops and colonels. The "school's regime was very spartan (only cold water to wash in, even when ice on the jug first had to be broken; a compulsory cold shower every morning and another cold shower after the weekly hot bath), it was bracing to an uncomfortable degree."[206] There was "fagging," and, as at more traditional English public schools at the time, there was also a ceaseless mantra about forming the inner steadfastness of "character" while, as a matter of course, and perhaps even more so at Gresham's than elsewhere, the boys were never trusted to conduct themselves properly.[207] An extreme prudishness about decency and manliness coexisted with the annual chance for boys to play all the girls' parts in the school play. Auden saw Gresham's basic raison d'être as being very like that of the more traditional public schools, such as Repton, where Isherwood was being educated, or Marlborough, where John Auden and the poet Louis MacNeice were sent. As Auden put it in 1934, such places were dedicated to the "mass production of gentlemen."[208]

By the standards of the period, though, Gresham's was, on the surface at least, a relatively benign place. Although founded centuries earlier in 1555, it was cautiously modern and liberal in ethos for an English public school. It appealed to the values of the country's new professional and business elites, who, with social consciences or philanthropic impulses, "wanted some alternative to the old regime." It also attracted a number of eminent Liberal parents such as C. P. Scott, editor of the *Manchester Guardian,* and Walter Layton of the *Economist,* both of whom sent their sons there.[209] As a token of "modern" attitudes, there was almost no corporal punishment at the school. In fact, Auden was probably the only pupil beaten at this time: after much consternation and debate, he was caned by the headmaster J. R. Eccles in front of the school prefects for having been seen with a "prostitute" during a school expedition to the South West of England.[210]

For a public school, Gresham's was also pro-intellect to an unusual degree—Auden credited it with having "a magnificent library"—and it had a policy of discouraging the normal hero-worship of school athletes.[211] Both Howson and Eccles had, like Auden's father, trained in the natural sciences. The school emphasized science and history rather than, as at St. Edmund's, Greek and Latin; Auden said that he spent his "last two years at school in the exclusive study of chemistry, zoology, and botany."[212] Music, presided over by the eminent organist and hymn writer Walter Greatorex, was an important part of school culture.[213] Auden continued to play the piano and take part in concerts, for example performing "The Holy Boy," a work for solo piano by John Ireland, in a school recital in the spring of 1924.[214] He also enjoyed the teaching of the senior classics and English master, "Tock" Tyler, and of the modern languages master, Frank McEachran, only seven years older than Auden and by the end of the 1920s, like him, a contributor to T. S. Eliot's *Criterion.*[215]

School plays, sometimes reviewed in the *Times,* the country's quasi-official newspaper of record, were a prominent feature of Gresham's life, though all productions had to be, according to Howson's *diktat,* "ethically 'helpful.'"[216] In July 1922, Auden participated in the production of *The Taming of the Shrew,* just a few months after he wrote his first poem. In what was probably the first review of any kind that he received, the *Times* opined that "W. H. Auden suggested very well the spitfire nature of the Shrew, a part difficult for a boy."[217] Auden hated the master in charge of the annual Shakespeare play, E. A. Robertson, who taught modern languages and was also Auden's housemaster in "Farfield" (the new name for a house that had previously been known as "Bengal Lodge"). But playing a part in Shakespeare meant enough to Auden that he continued appearing in the school's productions in spite of Robertson's supervision.[218]

In "The Liberal Fascist," the essay that Auden wrote about Gresham's in 1934, he emphasized many of the school's advantages. But his most famous comments concern the "Honour System," the military-sounding disciplinary and ethical code by which Eccles, "a fussy, precise, bustling bachelor with the manner of an over-energetic scout leader," laid such great store.[219] Gresham's was a "modern" school, not only in its openness to science but also in the way its disciplinary practice centered on creating a society of total surveillance, substituting an internalized ethos of self-observation and self-policing for a regime of spectacularly public, physical punishments in the manner of Rugby or Eton.

Not long after arriving at the school, each boy was interviewed separately by the headmaster and his housemaster. At these meetings, Auden explained, the new pupil "was asked—I need hardly say how difficult it would have been to refuse—to promise on his honour three things." These were "Not to swear. . . . Not to smoke. . . . Not to say or do anything indecent."[220] Any boy breaking these promises was supposed to report himself. If he saw someone else breaking a promise, he was supposed to give the offender a chance to turn himself in and, if that did not happen, to report the boy in question to the school authorities.

Auden's friend Robert Medley found that the system was "a really very vicious affair."[221] In 1934, Auden asserted that the Honour System formed a "potent engine" for turning pupils "into neurotic innocents, for perpetuating those very faults of character which it was intended to cure."[222] It "meant that the whole of our moral life was based on fear, fear of the community." Small wonder, then, that it produced such a large number of (mostly) morally impressive dissidents.[223]

In Auden's discussion of the "honour code," Auden added that at school, as a result of the code, he had "lived in a Fascist state."[224] However outrageous this claim about the Honour System at Gresham's might have appeared when it was published in 1934, it seems in retrospect extraordinarily acute. The school during this period placed a very high premium on conformity: Howson had been enraged by any criticism of his methods from the masters he employed at Holt—"it was disloyalty to the community, striking therefore at the foundation of his work."[225]

Gresham's had a uniform not only for boys but also for masters: "ridiculous black clothes . . . which made them look like unsuccessful insur-
ance agents." Auden wrote, calling it a "shameful thing," that he had
heard "a master was sacked for taking part in left-wing politics outside
the school."[226] No regime, whether of a family, a school or a country,
which demanded such a degree of loyalty could have hoped to extirpate
dedicated rebels from its midst. Perhaps it ended up creating the kind of
dissidents whom it appeared to abhor, in much the same way that Prospero seems to bring Caliban's rebelliousness into existence.

The school's Honour System, with its obvious sexual puritanism,
was connected with a mercantile, and not just a moral, fear of "smut."
For a school that was also, necessarily, a business, a scandal would have
been financially threatening. Gresham's apparently did not have much
of the brothel- or prison-like atmosphere characteristic of some of the
"great" English public schools where Auden might have been sent, nor
did it have the mellower, "sexy" flavors of the schools where he was to
teach in the 1930s.[227] At Gresham's, Auden wrote, "One almost never
saw anyone smoke, heard anyone swear, or came across any smut."[228]
It seems likely instead that there was plenty of intense romance and
little sex. While there, Auden's romantic feelings centered on his love
for Robert Medley and later, less intensely, for the future poet and novelist John Pudney, neither of whom he slept with at the time.[229] Medley
understood that the young Auden was already very sure of his sexual
identity but that "he did suffer from a bad conscience about it."[230]

Howson had felt that the "end of every activity . . . was, in an adult
and not always very wide sense of the word, a *moral* one."[231] As a result,
boys were supervised in everything down "to the most intimate details
of their private lives."[232] Because of anxieties about masturbation, "all
Gresham's boys had their trouser-pockets sewn up."[233] But Howson's
obsessive need to maintain moral purity was more than merely financially pragmatic. It was, at its base, pathological. The novelist John
Lanchester, head boy at Gresham's in 1980, comments that Howson's
loathing of moral impurity "shaded into an obsession with germs and
with ideas about contamination." As a result, "Gresham's never played
other schools at sports, because [Howson] was so worried about germs,
and only ever had house matches. Also, [Howson] was very preoccupied with cutting off contact between the school and Holt, again for
reasons to do with germs."[234]

Around 1903, the school's Tudor buildings in the center of Holt had been "handed over to the preparatory school, and new buildings were erected outside the town." Howson opened the main school on a more secluded site beyond the town limits, coincidentally allowing space for such things as an outdoor theatre in the woodlands.[235] For a doctor's son, as Auden was, such paranoia about germs, especially in the depths of the Norfolk countryside, must have seemed phobic rather than modern.

Gresham's, then, was a microcosm of a society set in an area of great natural beauty but requiring total conformity to the group, organized according to a set of deeply irrational and manipulative "rules," and, in its programmatic insularity, based on an overwhelming fear of contamination by the outside world. What better metaphor than this strange place could there be for a society that, as a whole, gloried in its anticonstitutional system of government, encouraged loyalty at all costs, and for more than a century had officially attempted, in its diplomatic policy, to exist, island-like, in "splendid isolation" from foreign entanglements?

Given Gresham's relatively small size, from the 1910s through to the 1930s it was the seedbed for a remarkable number of engineering, medical, and artistic geniuses as well as an impressively large ring of lifelong political activists.[236] In this sense, the impact of Gresham's on British culture in the first half of the twentieth century was at least as deep as that of any other public school. Sadly, the school also produced an extensive cohort of the psychologically wounded among its former pupils. The emotional toll of adapting to the rigid Honour System, of the "license to spy on one's peers," as Medley put it, or of course of the feeling of being spied on by them, was very high.[237] Alongside all the distinguished old boys whom the school turned out, it minted psychic wrecks by the dozen.

One observer was impressed by the outwardly placid character of the Greshamians under the Honour regime: "to a quite remarkable extent boys adopted and carried out, when they were by themselves, the standards set before them by authority."[238] Yet inwardly the mental strain experienced by many ex-pupils for years afterward was intense. Auden explained the effect of the system on the boys once they had left the school: "all those with whom I have spoken, whether old boys or others who have come into contact with old boys, have borne out my conclusion that the effect is a serious one in many cases."[239] According to one later headmaster of the school, subsequent nervous breakdowns or serious psychological disturbances of one kind or another afflicted nearly one-third of all old boys who had been subject to Gresham's Honour System in the 1920s and 1930s.[240]

Auden described himself at Gresham's as "mentally precocious, physically backward, short-sighted, a rabbit at all games, very untidy and grubby, a nail-biter, a physical coward, dishonest, sentimental, with no community sense whatever, in fact, a typical little highbrow and difficult child."[241] Medley, more succinctly, said Auden was "isolated."[242] Partly he was isolated by his powerful intellect; he seems to have owned an edition of Freud's Collected Papers by the time he finished at Gresham's, though perhaps for show as much as for reading.[243] In the 1910s and 1920s, upper-middle-class English culture, especially in the public schools, often associated the emancipatory promise of psychoanalysis—with its aura of antimoralism, hedonism, and bisexuality—with the "Uranian poetry of love between men." There was, in other words, "a nexus between Uranism, classicism and the new science of the mind."[244]

Surprisingly, although Auden claimed to be a "rabbit at all games," at Gresham's, he continued to take part in at least a few enactments of war, the shadows of which hung heavy and stagnant on the national mind. While participation in OTC had been compulsory at St. Edmund's, it was voluntary at Gresham's. Yet Medley mentions that during one of Auden's last years at Gresham's, he volunteered to attend the annual OTC Camp, where boys from a number of public schools would be trained for a week by "professional army officers."[245]

At the same time, Auden recognized that Gresham's was not all genteel "Fascism" and panoptical sexual paranoia. The school's tribe-like atmosphere and the moral surveillance system that alienated him so much also deepened his interest in nature and in the rural landscape. In a gesture that he would dramatize again and again in his poetry, Auden turned "away from the human to the non-human." He was an intense, homesick, introverted youth, unhappily in love, who sought out "not his mother, but mountains or autumn woods" and, "friendless," would "observe the least shy of the wild animals."[246] Auden loved the countryside as much as he loved books. It was that sensitive, uncertain, and nature-loving boy, as much as the dogmatic autodidact, who wrote Auden's early poems.

Toward the end of Auden's time at Gresham's, life improved a bit for him, largely because he was able to roam more freely through the school's "beautiful situation" in the Norfolk countryside, sometimes ignoring school limits on the extent of the walks.[247] Pudney, a schoolmate and potential lover, remembered that on his tramps through the Norfolk woods and marshes with Auden, "we followed paths carefully chosen because they were out of bounds."[248] Auden himself said that he "went for long solitary walks, played the organ . . . and was extremely happy" during his last year at the school.[249] A naturalist at Gresham's out looking for specimens spotted Auden "very early one day several miles from school, standing alone on the shore at Weybourne, looking at the sea."[250] And Auden himself recalled the formidable beauty of the surroundings: "Watching a snow storm come up from the sea over the marshes at Salthouse [his mother's birthplace], and walking in a June dawn . . . by Hempstead Mill are only the two most vivid of a hundred such experiences."[251] This rural world is where Auden emerged as a poet, and natural phenomena were to play an important part in his writing throughout his artistic life.

In the period between 1920 and 1923, every week the British state was shipping 4,000 headstones to France and Belgium as the vast Commonwealth war cemeteries were painstakingly assembled.[252] It was a time when memorials of all kinds were also emerging on the English scene. Most obviously, there was a huge surge of public statuary in the early 1920s. Some of it was on a grand scale. George Frampton's memorial to the nurse Edith Cavell near St. Martin-in-the-Fields in the British capital was one of the first such works. Unveiled in March 1920, it was followed by a string of high-profile London monuments by artists and architects such as C. S. Jagger, Eric Gill, and Edwin Lutyens.

But most of the war monuments were humbler in scale than these, and they were established not at significant points in major cities but were dispersed at crossroads and in churchyards in thousands of small towns and villages throughout the country. During the war, and with even greater frequency in the years immediately after it, memorial crosses and unofficial, temporary wayside shrines proliferated on streets, lanes, walls, and greens—as the country grappled with the aftermath of bereavement and violence on an unprecedented scale.[253] The art historian Richard Cork wrote that "Now that memorials to the Great War are so often taken for granted and even overlooked, it has become easy to underestimate the significance they possessed when unveiled. Even modest communities insisted on erecting them as a tribute to the men from their locality who had died."[254]

In November 1919, Auden had participated in the memorial service for old boy casualties at St. Edmund's. In late March 1921, after Auden had been at Gresham's less than a year, the school installed a large, very bright stained-glass window representing the "City of Peace" at the east end of the chapel.[255] On a scroll unfurling near the foot of the window, the long admonition reads in part: "LET THOSE WHO COME AFTER SEE TO IT THAT THEIR NAMES BE NOT FORGOTTEN. 1914–1919." Shortly after, the chapel's oak screen, with the names of one hundred fallen Old Greshamians carved into it, was completed. Auden would have attended the dedication ceremony and, in the time until mid-1925, must have seen these messages about the war over and over during Sunday services.

The painter Stanley Spencer, who served in the RAMC as an orderly in Macedonia, later created a number of masterpieces based on his experiences there. His little-known but extraordinary picture *Unveiling Cookham War Memorial,* finished in Hampshire during the summer of 1922, is unique within his cycle of paintings about the war, in that it portrays the war's impact on the home front.[256] The scene is the official dedication of the Cookham War Memorial in September 1919, on the High Street of a picturesque little Thames-side village in the northeast corner of Berkshire. Spencer shows the moment just after the Union Jack has been pulled off the large white granite cross, revealing the gleaming memorial to the eyes of the gathered ranks of local people.

Unveiling Cookham War Memorial confronts us, as it does with the teeming crowd of villagers in the picture, with the pathos of silences and absences, with knowledge of the many deaths of village men, with the pain and blessing of memory. In Spencer's Cookham, as almost everywhere else where memorials were erected, the "absence of hatred, or triumph, or worship of the military *per se* is evident."[257] The national flag, still settling after it has fallen, lies crumpled and ignored in the

FIG. 3 *Stanley Spencer,* Unveiling Cookham War Memorial *(1921–1922),* *oil on canvas, 61 by 58 inches. This painting is anomalous within Spencer's work in that it commemorates a specific historical occasion: the unveiling of the war memorial in the village of Cookham, Berkshire, on 19 September 1919. The name of Spencer's brother, Lt. Sydney Spencer, MC, killed in France in September 1918, is listed on the Cookham cross's plinth. In the postwar period, ceremonies like this took place all over England on village greens, in city streets, and in churches and school chapels. At the schools Auden attended, he was present for two such events.*

bottom right-hand corner of the picture, symbolizing a transcendence of the patriotic rhetoric that had played its part in sending villagers to their deaths during the recent conflict.

Some of the onlookers, those not closest to the monument, are bored, sleepy, or indifferent. But with psychological acuity, Spencer has made the crowd denser and more anonymous as it gets closer to the memorial cross itself. Those with some deep personal stake in the war seem to be jostling to get as near to the cross as possible. In an age when almost everyone wore hats, nearly every male head is bared in awed, awkward reverence; numerous hands clutch caps and programs. Young women around the cross's plinth are laying pots and vases of flowers as dedications to the memory of the dead. Many heads are bowed; some people bury their faces in their hands in grief. Some stare awkwardly at the stone.

Most poignant of all are the men and boys immediately adjacent to the white-clad girls. Almost all the faces in the front and center of the painting are of young men or teenagers. Some look at the ground. Others gaze in shock at the monument. One gnaws anxiously on the edge of his program. The sight of these young men is especially moving because, although they may have lost older brothers or fathers or male relatives, they have themselves miraculously been spared, by good luck and the Armistice, from death in the war and the fate of having other young eyes read their names on the tablets of memory. (Spencer's eldest brother, Sydney, who served with the Norfolk Regiment, was killed at Épehy in late September 1918. His name is on the Cookham memorial.) The cross, symbol of both death and resurrection, looms over them, a tangible reminder of the cataclysmic event that has darkened their young lives.

When Spencer finished this painting in 1922, a fifteen-year-old Auden had been making his own creative efforts for just a few months across the country in Norfolk. All the while, hundreds of unveiling ceremonies like the one at Cookham were taking place in villages and towns across Britain and the rest of Europe. As each monument was disclosed, young men must have looked on in mute disbelief, in sadness, in guilt, in terror. The young Auden could have been any of the youths who stand close to the monument in Spencer's painting, staring at the white cross, the island of the plinth, and the names of the recently fallen. The war lingered powerfully not just in the minds of those who had fought but also in the minds of those who had remained behind.

In their own ciphered ways, Auden's first poems were a memorial to the war and its impact on his life. Even when the young poet was ostensibly writing modest traditional lyrics about the English countryside, his youthful poetry finds memories, traces, residues, and ghosts of the war wherever it looks. The fear and impact of conflict linger in the shadows and corners of his first poems, even—perhaps especially—when these poems are set in the depths of one of the most beautiful and tranquil parts of the English countryside.

PART TWO   MOOR

2   MINING THE COUNTRYSIDE
HAUNTED PASTORALISM, 1922–1925

The farther forward one goes the more scattered and meagre every-thing is. The nearer to danger the fewer and the more hidden the men—the more dramatic the situation the more it becomes an empty landscape.

—JOHN SINGER SARGENT (1918)

UNEXPECTEDLY, SUDDENLY, THE GREAT WAR ended when an armistice came into effect on the morning of 11 November 1918. In a poem called "'And There Was a Great Calm,'" Thomas Hardy imagines soldiers "in the now familiar flats of France" pausing, looking up, and murmuring, "'Strange, this! How? All firing stopped?'" Quiet had returned to the natural world: "no flying fires inflamed the gray, | No hurtlings shook the dewdrop from the thorn, | No moan perplexed the mute bird on the spray." Hardy presents the moment as a maelstrom interrupted; his negated phrases ("No moan perplexed," for example, rather than "Peace reassured") suggest that noise and violent shocks have become the normal state, one that has only been temporarily put into abeyance. Renewed pastoral peace is still haunted by its opposite. "From Heaven distilled a clemency," Hardy concludes eerily, "There was peace on earth, and silence in the sky; | Some could, some could not, shake off misery."[1] Inside many minds, not least the minds of those who were children during the conflict, the war went on, there was silence in the sky, and the misery was not shaken off.

The artist and art historian Andrew Forge, mentioned earlier, whom Auden taught at prep school in the 1930s, remarked on the pervasiveness of wartime language in young people's psyches in postwar culture. Forge said it was hard to realize "how general the imagery of World War One was all through the 20s and 30s. . . . Getting a ticking off from your parents was always called 'being strafed.' Lots of German words like that. . . . [There was] this vocabulary, these terms, these words, these patterns of thought that were absolutely burned into people's minds."[2] And Ted Hughes, whose father had been in hell at Gallipoli like Auden's father, wrote in the 1960s that the Great War was the "number one national ghost": "It's still everywhere, molesting everybody. . . . Somewhere in the nervous system of each survivor the underworld of perpetual Somme rages on unabated. . . . We are still living in the thick of it, as well as being far out of it."[3]

The "national ghost" also haunts the young Auden's innocent-looking first poems about the countryside, written in the early 1920s. At first, this "ghost" does not seem to be there at all. But then, like the allusions to sexuality that are everywhere and nowhere and with which Auden connects his feelings about the war and his father's absence, the conflict appears almost ubiquitously. Deep down, war is one of this young poet's main subjects.

Auden's creative psyche was shaped by the distinctive nature of his parents' home, by the experience of living through a war, and by his childhood's symbolic, war-related obsession with mines and machines. But his active life as a poet began at the age of fifteen on a Sunday in late March 1922 as he walked in a stretch of rural Norfolk. Auden was with his platonic crush Robert Medley. They had recently met on a field trip that the Gresham's sociological society made to a boot factory in Norwich. Auden had been determined to sit next to Medley and introduce himself on the bus ride to the city.[4] A few days later, according to Auden, the flash of inspiration over his vocation happened in a small field near the bird-rich salt marshes surrounding the school where he and Medley, more or less clandestine rebels within the system, were pupils. Medley recalled that, walking together, they had been arguing about the Church. The religiously inclined Auden was "flushed, frowning and offended."[5] A silence fell. The first time Auden describes the moment in print, he treats it almost like a Damascene conversion. In "Letter to Lord Byron," he writes that

> indecision broke off with a clean-cut end
> One afternoon in March at half-past three

> When walking in a ploughed field with a friend;
>> Kicking a little stone, he turned to me
>> And said, "Tell me, do you write poetry?"
> I never had, and said so, but I knew
> That very moment what I wished to do.[6]

It was the location in the rural landscape, as well as the person, Medley, that called Auden into being as a writer. From the moment of its appearance, Auden bound his literary identity up with the "ploughed field" of the English countryside, its scenery, its creatures, and its organic rhythms, and with things found there, like the "little stone." And, since there are ancient tropes connecting writing and farming, he matched the nature of the place where the revelation occurred with the activity that began there. The association of a ploughed field with verse on a page descends from Greek literature through Virgil, whom Auden had probably read Latin extracts from during prep school. The furrows in the field where Auden and Medley were walking looked like a page written on with lines of natural poetry.

Auden's personal familiarity with the English countryside and its inhabitants meant that, as a young writer, he overwhelmingly found his subjects and his inspiration in the landscape. People are somewhat rare in these early poems. He wrote either about his own immediate rustic environment in Norfolk or, only slightly later, about the central and northern parts of the Pennines, a vast, almost empty area near to the Lake District, the sacred ground of English Romanticism.

In "California," apparently the first Auden poem to survive, and perhaps his first at all, he describes being in the Norfolk countryside at night and looking up a gentle hill "Past the farm and past the mill."[7] His first published poem in anything other than a school magazine is "Woods in Rain," also probably about a Norfolk scene. In the latter, Auden writes about "raindrops kissing the green ground" in a wood.[8] His *Juvenilia* is crammed with poems about landscapes, country sights, and rural life. In this, Auden's first poems were traditional and representative of common literary themes of the time. The non- or anti-metropolitan and anti-industrial vision of a true England located in the southern or south-eastern English countryside had emerged in the 1880s. By 1914, this ruralist ideal had spread widely across English culture and into the work of the poets published in the *Georgian Poetry* anthologies.[9] Like these writers, Auden's early poetry set in the East Anglian world dealt, perhaps only half consciously, not just in symbols or conventional literary ideas but in mythic commonplaces about the nation.

However, Auden's knowledge of this rural landscape was anything but borrowed or abstract. There is a rich history of bird symbolism in poetry reaching back at least as far as the Greek poet Pindar's soaring eagles. But one can gauge how fully Auden was empirically committed to and "versed in country things" (as a poem about birdsong by one of his early favorites, Robert Frost, puts it) through the extraordinary number of bird species that inhabit his earliest lyrics. In number and variety, these birds go far beyond a few larks and nightingales mandated by poetic tradition.[10] In addition to a plethora of vaguely identified backdrop "birds" that, watching or flying, singing or silent, swarm through his earliest poems, his first lyrics include references to the following species: blackbird, buzzard, chicken, chiffchaff, coot, cuckoo, dabchick, finch, greenfinch, goldfinch, hawk, jay, kestrel, lark, linnet, martin, misselthrush, nightingale, owl, pheasant, plover, raven, robin, rook, seagull, sparrow, sparrowhawk, starling, stonechat, swallow, swift, thrush, wagtail, woodpecker, wren, and wryneck.[11] The youthful Auden mentions each of these birds at least once, and in a number of cases several times, in the poems he composed from March 1922 through to Easter 1926. During these formative, bird-rich years, his persona as a rural, English poet slowly crystallized.

Auden was the most bird-sensitive English poet since John Milton. Birds, connected in poetry with "flights" of the imagination and with augury, prophecy, and visions, are so fundamental to his imagination that, at many crucial stages in his career, they constitute the literary equivalent in his poetry of an indicator species in nature. Their health and presence, or their vulnerability and absence, are signs of change in Auden's literary ecosystem and in the social world he wrote about. Birds chronologically precede, and play just as prominent an imaginative role as, other early and more frequently discussed symbols in his poems, such as drystone walls or defunct industrial machinery.[12] In fact, birds soon start to interact in organic ways with these other common features in Auden's poetry. For example, elusive, and often unseen, creatures of the air sometimes channel the mysterious ghost voices of Auden's favorite vanished lead miners, the unseen denizens of the earth. In a poem from as late as 1930, the sound of a "bird stone-haunting, an unquiet bird" is imagined as the spectral call of one of Auden's provocative, frightening heroes trapped forever underground.[13]

When Auden went up to Oxford in 1925, he characterized himself even then as:

> A raw provincial, my good taste was tardy,
>   And Edward Thomas I as yet preferred;
> I was still listening to Thomas Hardy
>   Putting divinity about a bird.[14]

The reference to Hardy's "The Darkling Thrush" (1899) prompts a comparison with Auden's own bird-crowded, early poems. In 1930, in the Villon-like "Last Will and Testament" that he inserted near the end of the now-lost play "The Fronny," Auden remembers another telling incident, probably drawing on a conversation with an acquaintance whom he met while he was at school:

> Item, my naval range-finder and case
> To Captain Edward Gervase Luce
> With whom on seawall at King's Lynn
> I talked of bird-migration in the rain.[15]

Auden could talk about "bird-migration" because he had observed the phenomenon at first hand and had read about it to understand it better. Moreover, he was also deeply interested in two of the major determinants for all life in the countryside, including birds: weather and climate. Both are "much more important for a poet," he once told a journalist, "than most people like to believe is true."[16]

Birds and birdsong were characteristic properties in many of the poems Auden must have seen in Edward Marsh's anthologies of Georgian poetry, which he pored over at Gresham's between 1922 and 1925. They were also common in other standard literary fare of the time, which Auden absorbed as a teenage boy: for example, it abounds in *Come Hither!*, the 1923 anthology edited by Walter de la Mare, as well as in the volumes of Wordsworth, Keats, Hardy, and the country poet W. H. Davies that he read at school.[17] But birds primarily come into his poems from his life in the English countryside, where he cultivated knowledge about the details of natural phenomena. He once had to instruct the more bookish and urbane Christopher Isherwood, who complained that the description of birdsong in Auden's 1925 Norfolk poem "The Mill (Hempstead)" was inaccurate. Glossing the lines in question, the "weir's music, more ancient than the bird, | . . . hushes not for rain or wintry days," Auden patiently explained that a "bird does stop singing for rain and a weir doesn't."[18]

Given his sustained interest in the rural world and its inhabitants, it is not surprising that Auden entered university partly as a result of the naturalist expertise that he had developed as a bird-watcher and schoolboy scientist. Interviewed by Julian Huxley, a zoology lecturer (and Aldous Huxley's younger brother), for admission to Christ Church, Oxford, as an undergraduate, Auden correctly identified a bone that Huxley showed him as the "pelvis of a bird."[19] He began at the university with an exhibition, a small scholarship, in natural science, the same subject his father had studied in the 1890s at Cambridge.

In the 1920s, Auden repeatedly characterizes himself as a country dweller and, what is almost synonymous, an "*unsocial* English boy."[20] His poetic and personal world in his teenage years was one that, as he put it looking back in 1940, "had nothing to do with London, the stage, or French literature."[21] His early poems belong in the rural world not because they do not know anything else but because they respond to it so deeply. The young Auden was a bookish *and* rural writer, with, even later on, "a feeling for landscape" that a friend described as "profound."[22]

"California" is a brief, neo-Georgian poem of three coupleted quatrains, ostensibly about a quiet country scene.[23] It must have been written very shortly after he and Medley had walked in the "ploughed field" together, contending over religion. Here are the first two stanzas:

> The twinkling lamps stream up the hill
> Past the farm and past the mill
> Right at the top of the road one sees
> A round moon like a Stilton cheese.
>
> A man could walk along that track
> Fetch the moon and bring it back
> Or gather stars up in his hand
> Like strawberries on English land.[24]

The poem is about ambition (literally a reaching for the stars), about fear and about a desire for connection with a mythically rich landscape. The title is probably a reference to a tiny village, improbably called California, on the Norfolk coast not far from Gresham's and only about ten miles south of Hempstead, another hamlet on the same stretch of shoreline that Auden explored while he was a schoolboy.[25]

Auden sets "California" at night, which makes it a characteristic beginning to his work. That is because throughout his career he was to write so many great poems set in darkness, in dark rooms, or on the borders of sleep. (Auden is a bird poet and also, and again like Milton, a night poet.[26]) Already, in "California," he demonstrates psychological astuteness: in the suggestive state that darkness creates, the poem's consciousness is freer to speculate, foretell, and remember. The speaker in "California" looks inland up a slope and into the sky above it. The glimmering moon, appearing to be "Right at the top of the road," seems mysteriously close. Auden's comparison of the moon to a Stilton carefully reworks the old idea that the moon is made of cheese; here, the shadowy craters of the moon's surface evoke for him the irregular blue veins of a dimpled, round Stilton.

The slight but definite sense of verbal mastery in the opening stanza prompts, in the second, the thought that "A man," that is, a *real man* or a *real poet,* "could walk along that track | Fetch the moon and bring it back | Or gather stars up in his hand." The fifteen-year-old Auden, not yet "a man," seals his pat but revealing thought by imagining, through metaphor, what the stars in the sky so invitingly resemble. They seem "Like strawberries on English land." The poem turns here on the verbal similarity of "star" and "straw"; briefly the stars appear as if they could be plucked out of the heavens' dark fields like succulent, ground-growing fruit. In the third and final stanza, though, the possibility of such triumph generates an anxiety-ridden self-cancellation, as if, like a good Greshamian who is out of bounds, the speaker were preventing himself from giving in to temptation:

> "But how should I, a poor man dare
> To meet so close the full moon's stare?"
> For this I stopped and stood quite still
> Then turned with quick steps down that hill.[27]

Stanza 1 presents simultaneously a poetic and a naturalistic perception of the world. The "twinkling lamps" introduce the impending appearance of stars via the association with the lullaby "Twinkle, twinkle, little star," suggesting a human power to give shape and order to the night. At the end of the first stanza, the "seer" sublimates the realistic mastery, evidenced by the phrase "twinkling lamps," into the higher power of conceptual mastery when he links the moon and a Stilton cheese just as he joins sky (moon) and earth (cheese). In stanza 2 he contemplates moving up the hill to gather stars. But, in the last stanza, as if having been drawn by the metaphor and "stream[ed]" up the hill himself, he abandons the flight of fancy and rushes back down. Now an observed being, "a poor man," he humblingly cannot return the "full moon's stare." If in the first stanza Auden plays off the folklore of the moon being made out of cheese, the third uses the popular myth of the full moon's appearance as a time of unusual levels of lunacy among humans.

The most suggestive tension in the poem is one that the teenaged Auden is innately skillful enough to avoid acknowledging explicitly. "California" hints that in order to move toward the ennobling world of poetry, associated with height, the sky, planets, and stars, one must leave the shared, social world. The moon hangs in the distance, "Past the farm and past the mill | Right at the top of the road." To "walk along that track" past those human habitations would take the speaker out of communal space into the loneliness and glory of the heavens. (In the context of English verse, a canonical example of this common poetic move into nature, with a hesitation at the end, is Keats's first published poem, the "O Solitude!" sonnet.) Walking "along the track" in "California" would mean a risky abandonment of the human world and a reach for something delicious but prohibited. That is a course that the young, emotionally vulnerable Auden, having internalized his parents' self-denying ethic, may have felt was morally suspect or perhaps just frightening.

His parents' strictures on indulgence come across in an anecdote told by one of the Audens' granddaughters. Mrs. Auden once took Bernard Auden's daughter, Jane, outside: "I was taken into the garden and shown red, juicy apples. I was told they were lovely, but were not for me!"[28] And the austere Dr. Auden constantly stressed the need for individuals to merge themselves into the social group and to place its needs above their own. In his 1929 essay "The Difficult Child," he cautions dourly that "the cohesion of the social group depends upon the degree in which each individual member of the group is prepared to subordinate his own interests and desires to the dictates and inhibitions of the group as a whole."[29] It is a sentiment that every school authority figure at Gresham's would have echoed.

At this point in "California," though, poetic logic overcomes maternal strictness or paternal dutifulness. In that isolated, desirable world into which the speaker of the poem wants to go, "Fetch[ing] the moon" or "gather[ing] stars up" would be like finding a kind of spiritual and pointedly traditional sustenance (Stilton cheese and strawberries) for the inhabitants of farm and mill whom the speaker has just left behind. Paradoxically, by rejecting a world, one might in fact be sustaining it with sacred nourishment while also "feeding" oneself with a sense of visionary or metaphysical power. Already, in this first poem of his to survive, Auden experiments with the trope of a "turning away" from a vital subject, but only in order to connect with it better.[30] Here the turn away promises to provide for the world that it appears to ignore. Variants of this poetic tactic will occur again and again in Auden's later career, not least in relation to traumatic subject matter such as sexuality and war, where the painful content, apparently ignored, is hidden inside a poem ostensibly about an innocuous topic, precisely so that it can appear more mesmerizingly powerful, like a light gleaming underwater.

At a literal level, "California" finally draws back and confines itself within the world of the community, a change that is associated with a failure to lay hold of the moon and stars. However, Auden never disowns the rightness of the ambition to walk alone and create a regenerative poem that could "feed" the people of the "English land." It is the weakness of his lyric protagonist, not the justice of the ideal, that is in question.

In this tiny poem, the phrase "English land" expresses a desire for unity between the human and natural worlds. The countryside is England, almost as if the soil itself were English. In the young Auden's subsequent juvenile work, he almost always uses "English" or "England" in a vague but positive sense. In "March Winds" from March 1924, he writes that "This English Spring is lovelier than we."[31] In "The Gypsy Girl" of Autumn 1925, he declares: "Blessed be England for so fair a face."[32] "England" and "English," as these simple lines show, are to the young Auden poetic words in themselves. To deploy a Freudian idea metaphorically, if we look in this first surviving poem for the scene that shows the secret pages of Auden's poetic mind, it suggests his ambitions are associated with the issue of a regenerative closeness to the English community and "English land."[33] And to dwell intensively on Auden's early poems is to uncover a blueprint of his artistic psyche, a psyche that had already been forming by the time he began to write.

While at Gresham's, Auden was mainly interested in the works of Edward Thomas, Walter de la Mare, Robert Frost, A. E. Housman, and, above all, in Thomas Hardy's lyrics and poetic dramas. For many young English poets in the first decades of the twentieth century, the most consequential established writers were Housman and Hardy.[34] Auden started reading Hardy's poems in the summer of 1923, twelve months or so after he composed "California." In a later essay, "A Literary Transference," he mentions that for about a year after he discovered Hardy's work, "I was never without one volume or another of the beautifully produced Wessex edition in my hands: I smuggled them into class, carried them about on Sunday walks, and took them up to the dormitory to read in the early morning."[35]

Auden saw Hardy's poems, like those of Frost and Thomas, as a genuine poetry of the countryside, revealing the relative shallowness of the weekend tripper's knowledge of the natural world that the Georgian poets displayed. In Auden's earliest poems, he often presents himself in terms similar to those he found in Hardy's and Thomas's works, as a custodian of rural values. There is "so much I can share with you," one love poem announces,

> Which once was only dear to me alone:
> The new day's lambent secrecy,—the yew
> Casting her shadow on the greening stone,
> The solemness of pines, the finch's voice
> Like a creaking gate.[36]

The "finch's voice | Like a creaking gate" sounds like a tentative, self-critical young writer projecting a brief self-portrait onto a bird.

Many of Auden's first efforts at poetry do not address a human "you" but speak to, or ponder, the natural world and its inhabitants. In this respect, his early writing seems particularly close to many Hardy poems about small animals, birds, and insects, such as "An August Midnight" or "The Fallow Deer at the Lonely House" or "Afterwards"—a poem specially important to Auden throughout his life. In its refrain, Hardy, speaking as if posthumously, prides himself on having been a person attuned visually to the subtle manifestations of creaturely life in the countryside. There, Hardy claims he was a watcher "who used to notice such things" as how during "nocturnal blackness, mothy and warm, | . . . the hedgehog travels furtively over the lawn."[37]

Auden's early poems often resemble fragments of the huge verse-drama that he treasured during his adolescence, Hardy's Napoleonic war epic, *The Dynasts,* published in three parts between 1904 and 1908.[38] At the time when Auden was growing up and discovering Hardy, *The Dynasts* was a work of great prestige among both educated general readers and younger writers.[39] Today, the famous parts of *The Dynasts*—and the parts that Auden critics have often associated with his writing—are Hardy's stage directions to his epic. These survey the petty strivings of humanity on earth from a vast, detached aerial perspective. "What I valued most in Hardy," Auden wrote, "was his hawk's vision, his way of looking at life from a very great height."[40] (Hawks have exceptional vision: their sight is about eight times as powerful as that of human eyes.)

But, in addition to the memorable panoramas of Hardy's huge drama, it is also filled with almost microscopic observations of the natural world. For example, Hardy writes in *The Dynasts* about the evening before the Battle of Waterloo in June 1815. In *terza rima,* he describes the terror of the small animals and the destruction of their homes caused by the human preparations for war:

> Yes, the coneys are scared by the thud of hoofs,
> And their white scuts flash at their vanishing heels,
> And swallows abandon the hamlet-roofs.
>
> The mole's tunnelled chambers are crushed by wheels,
> The lark's eggs scattered, their owners fled;
> And the hedgehog's household the sapper unseals.[41]

In his image of the panicking rabbits with "their white scuts flash[ing] at their vanishing heels," Hardy shows once more his fascination with minute signs and movements of natural life. This preoccupation with life on a small scale reappears in many of the young Auden's poems, such as "To a Field-mouse," written perhaps in 1923. Here, the poet recounts how he spotted "a pair of round brown eyes | Gleaming between the stalks so homely wise."[42] The mouse "fled" from him through the grass just as the parental larks have fled in horror in *The Dynasts*. In other poems, the young Auden writes about small creatures such as a nightingale, a wren, a dragonfly, an owl, a cat, a robin, and buzzards.[43] Another of Auden's favorite's, Edward Thomas, also gazes at this natural landscape of small things, though in a less bloody mode than Hardy's. For example, with a melancholy feeling for micro-beauty, Thomas describes the "shell of a little snail bleached | In the grass; chip of flint, and mite | Of chalk; and the small birds' dung | In splashes of purest white."[44]

T. S. Eliot anatomized the anti-rhetorical, anti-moralizing Georgian ethos in a 1917 essay in the *Egoist*, "Reflections on Contemporary Poetry." In Eliot's words, it "is not unworthy of notice how often the word little occurs; and how this word is used, not merely as a necessary piece of information, but with a caress, a conscious delight."[45] Auden might even have remembered that observation when he describes the moment he decided to become a poet, coloring it with a memory of Medley "kicking a little stone."[46] Although Auden does not often use the word "little," his early poems are densely preoccupied by small things, down to the movements of the tiniest of creatures. Consider the field mouse's brown eyes or the poem "Ploughing," which opens by describing the speaker and a friend "Watching what an ant would find to do when | Stones blocked its path."[47]

What matter most in the scenery of young Auden's poems are sky, water, weather, birds, and other animals. He experienced the natural world not as an encounter with a sublime inhuman immensity or with the otherness of large, powerful creatures but instead as something delicate and consoling, refracted as subtle or faint sounds—the "distant splash" of a stone dropping into an old shaft or rain dripping off leaves—or as sudden brief glimpses of a bird.[48] "Woods in Rain" describes, with a note of mild sensual ecstasy, birds listening to the innumerable minute plops of rainfall, their small ears registering a gentle whispering noise:

> silent, drunk with sound
> Of raindrops kissing the green ground,
> They sit with head tucked under wing
> Too full of joy to dare to sing.[49]

In such poems, though, nature is never just itself; it always has a mythic, social dimension. Writing in this pastoral mode when he was a schoolboy, Auden introduced neo-Georgian themes about belonging and the natural world that would become structuring tensions in his later work.[50] Eliot diagnosed some of these tensions in "Reflections on Contemporary Poetry," describing the Georgians as parochial. He wrote with dismissive suavity that "contemporary English verse has borrowed little from foreign sources; it is almost politically English."[51] And he connected the Georgians' love of the "little" with their "positively patriotic" insistence on the English countryside.

Bound by their narrow ideological horizons, these poets associated "little" too naturally with "England," the modernist Eliot implied. And from there, he moved to play on the adjective "insular" derived from that most England-associated noun, "island." The poet Harold Monro, Eliot wrote toward the conclusion of his review, was unlike the Georgians because he is "less a Little-Englander" than they and therefore "deserves a public not purely insular." (As we saw in the Prologue, Eliot would metamorphose as a writer in the later 1920s, abandoning his hostility to the "insular." He recognized that from 1926 or so, against his expectations, a new literary paradigm had emerged.[52] His poetry began to move within the new paradigm: his last major poem, written between 1941 and 1942 and the final work in the highly patriotic *Four Quartets,* is set deep in the Cambridgeshire countryside and is titled "*Little* Gidding."[53])

Eliot's 1917 essay rightly implied that there is always a politics— usually a conservative and "positively patriotic" politics—implicit in pastoralism and in the poetry of the countryside and small things. But Auden's early poetry almost entirely lacks the stolid traditionalism and rural-nook coziness of the more complacent Georgian writers. It hews much more closely to the examples set by skeptical or astringently melancholy poets such as Hardy or Thomas. However, it *is* nonetheless "positively patriotic." But, in writing in this mode, Auden was not simply copying Hardy or Thomas. Rather, they were all poets caught up in a set of ideas about where the truly deep symbols and sources of their country's identity existed. In ways that were typical of so much writing in England about the countryside since the 1880s, for Auden, like for Hardy and Thomas as well as a host of much less gifted writers, Englishness inheres in nature and the rural world, not in the city.[54] Auden was inexorably led, by imitation of his poetic models, to broach issues about what constituted "true" Englishness and where it was to be found. Thomas's answer in "Home" is that nation and nature are one: "'Twas home; one nationality | We had, I and the birds that sang, | One memory."[55] Auden's faithful itemization of English fauna and flora suggests that similar feelings underlie his poems as well.[56]

To be sure, something more unsettling than a simple celebration of country values characterizes both Thomas's work and Auden's early poetry. But, like Hardy's vision of nature being desecrated by preparations for war and Thomas's poems about threatened peace in the rural world, the darker quotient in Auden's writing is partially hidden because it is so traumatic as to demand repression.

None of the nations in the United Kingdom experienced widespread revulsion against the war in the years immediately after it ended. One dominant feeling was that the victory was a glorious, if extraordinarily costly, achievement. Virtually the entire country seems to have been on a quest to leave behind the trauma of the recent past by glossing over its pain or by stressing the "positive."

As just one instance of this phenomenon, Dr. Auden hardly ever spoke about his experiences after returning home in 1919, and the same need for silence afterward held for many civilians, especially children, who lived through the war on the home front, where the air hung heavy with grief, anxiety, incomprehension, envy, and suppressed anger.[57] Many accounts of the period describe the ways in which memories of the war on the home front seemed to vanish among young people in the early 1920s. For a while, Samuel Hynes wrote, it was as if "1914–18 had dropped out of time."[58] In his well-known 1918 lecture "The Repression of War Experience" (also the title of a poem by his patient Siegfried Sassoon), W. H. R. Rivers declared that "It is natural to thrust aside painful memories just as it is natural to avoid dangerous or horrible scenes in actuality, and this natural tendency to banish the distressing or the horrible is especially pronounced in those whose powers of resistance have been lowered by the long-continued strains of trench-life, the shock of shell-explosion, or other catastrophes of warfare."[59]

Formerly a captain in the RAMC like Dr. Auden, Rivers was an important British anthropologist and psychologist, a heroic figure to many people. He had died suddenly, of an intestinal obstruction, at the age of fifty-eight in 1922. Rivers was an author of great interest both to Auden and to his father, from whom the young Auden probably first learned of Rivers's work. Dr. Auden looked to Rivers, whom he had known slightly, as a groundbreaking physician and psychiatrist. Auden did too, although he probably soon also learned through literary contacts or gossip about Rivers's treatment of Sassoon, the traumatized war-hero poet, at Craiglockhart Hospital in 1917.[60]

At first glance, Auden might seem to have been writing in 1922 and the immediately following years as if the disaster of the war had never happened. Relatedly, the rural poems he composed at the time might seem like exercises in technique, emulations of older poets' work, or descriptions of his favorite spots in nature, but with little strong or deep subject matter of their own. This is how Isherwood, to whom Auden sent many of the poems, described them: "neither startlingly good nor startlingly bad; they were something much odder—efficient, imitative and extremely competent."[61] That comment would become influential with critics, but Isherwood was wrong about Auden's empty skills as a young poet, and his misperception suggests that Auden, to whom he was extremely close, may also not have discussed, or understood, exactly what he was writing about. Just as the apparent national evasion of the subject of the war in the early 1920s created a false calm, or a queasy, evasive quiet, so Auden's poems are superficially silent on subjects they continually dwell on. But the repressed subject was bound to return, like the surviving soldiers coming home, if only because its traces could never be completely cleared from sight.

The postwar world was filled with veterans, many of whom carried the unmistakable scars of their experiences and haunted the streets like wraiths. It was impossible to avoid them. Some had obvious war injuries that would once have been fatal. But medical knowledge had developed to the point where horribly mutilated individuals could be saved from death, only to lead a tortured post-combat existence. Injured veterans were preserved from oblivion to walk or limp, glare or cower through modern cities and villages. "Mass-mutilation," the historian Joanna Bourke writes, "was there for all to see."[62] About 1.2 million men—or roughly one-quarter of the armed services in Britain—were eligible for some kind of disability pension after the war.[63]

Moreover, the number of psychological casualties produced by the Great War was much larger than that from any previous conflict. Rivers wrote: "the medical administration of our own and other armies was wholly unprepared for the vast extent and varied forms in which modern warfare is able to upset the higher functions of the nervous system."[64] One-third of all discharges from the army during the war were on psychiatric grounds.[65] Paradoxically, Eric J. Leed noted, in the wake of the Armistice and for a decade or more afterward, "'war' neurosis was a condition more prevalent in 'peace' than in war."[66] British medicine struggled to understand the sudden flood of "neurasthenic" and "hysterical" soldiers, like the officer who hallucinated "jewelled spiders of enormous size" all over a Gallipoli beach. Many veterans—along with the traumatized women who had cared for them as nurses in army clearing stations and hospitals—returned from combat in France and Belgium and other places physically uninjured but psychically wrecked. The culture that Auden grew up in was reluctantly learning that not all mental events have an immediate material cause.[67] In 1920, there were 65,000 ex-servicemen receiving disability pensions for neurasthenia; 9,000 were still receiving hospital treatment.[68] From 1919 to 1929, nearly double that number, 114,600 ex-servicemen, applied for psychiatric pensions.[69]

Cases of mental or physical injury were ubiquitous in the world that Auden and his friends inhabited. For example, there is the hatless young man with "a powerful, curiously wooden stride which suggested some unseen injury" (as likely to be psychological as physical) whom Isherwood describes meeting by chance on the Isle of Wight in 1927.[70] Or consider Ted Hughes's father at home in the Calder Valley outside Halifax in the 1930s:

> Your day-silence was the coma
> Out of which your night-dreams rose shouting.
> I could hear you from my bedroom—
> The whole hopelessness still going on,
> No man's land still crying and burning
> Inside our house, and you climbing again
> Out of the trench, and wading back into the glare.[71]

Almost everyone had a memory of a healthy male relation or neighbor who had marched down to the station or recruiting office at some time during the war; and, after the war, everyone knew a veteran. Both Auden's and Isherwood's fathers, like hundreds of thousands of other fathers, had served in the war. (As already mentioned, Isherwood's never came back.) And ex-servicemen appeared repeatedly in every setting in the young Auden's life as teachers, lovers, or friends. At St. Edmund's, there was the mysterious ex-military eccentric Reginald Gartside Bagnall, whom Auden described as the "oddest" of the masters to arrive at the school during the war."[72] There, too, was Rev. Geoffrey Newman, the first man Auden had sex with, who had until very recently been a chaplain in the armed forces in France. At Gresham's, Auden was taught mathematics by a veteran, A. Bruce Douglas, whom he seems to have liked.[73] And in 1922 or 1923, at around the time Auden was taking up poetry, he formed a chaste friendship with a journalist, Michael Davidson, who was working in Norwich on the *Eastern Daily Press*. Davidson had been wounded at Passchendaele in 1917.[74] At Oxford, when Auden studied there from 1925 until 1928, as everywhere else, veterans abounded. His entrance interviewer, Julian Huxley, had served in the Intelligence Corps from 1917 to 1919; an economics tutor, Roy Harrod, whom Auden briefly studied with informally, had been in the Royal Garrison Artillery in 1918; and he knew or attended lectures by other Oxford don-veterans, including J. R. R. Tolkien (Lancashire Fusiliers), C. S. Lewis (Somerset Light Infantry), and his English tutor, Nevill Coghill (Royal Field Artillery).

Traditionally, Death is a reaper, an icon drawn from the rural world. There are many reasons why fear haunts the countryside where Auden sets his first poems. One should never forget that the unspoken anxiety pervading Auden's early writing in part reflects the psychological attrition through microaggressions that were inherent in everyday life for a young man like Auden growing up in a society hostile to the most fundamental parts of his emotional and sexual makeup. Some of that aggression was internalized. As noted earlier, Auden's closest friend at Gresham's, Robert Medley, believed that Auden was both sure about his sexual orientation and suffered from "a bad conscience about it."[75]

But other crucial factors were in play as well. In the aftermath of war, many soldiers with artistic gifts turned back to life in the English countryside while finding it impossible to escape fully from memories of combat. The musicologist Michael Kennedy noted: "Vaughan Williams's immediate post-war period yielded some of his quietest, most meditative music," adding that "Ivor Gurney returned to the lyrical poets and the Gloucestershire scene which had been his first inspiration. Arthur Bliss, who had been a Guards officer, wrote a rhapsody, a pianoforte quintet and a 'witchery' none of which reflects his experiences at Cambrai and on the Somme."[76] And Paul Fussell argued that, for wartime poets, an often ironized "recourse to the pastoral is an English mode of fully gauging the calamities of the Great War and of imaginatively protecting oneself against them. Pastoral reference . . . is a way of invoking a code to hint by antithesis at the indescribable; at the same time, it is a comfort in itself."[77] The war in France and Belgium had mainly been fought in the countryside, and the English rural worlds that soldiers retreated into afterward often proved to be filled with the traces of a subtle war "witchery" pursuing them there.

A note of war-related anxiety in Auden's poetry emerges in his first literary landscape, rural East Anglia, a region that zeppelins had passed over on their way to London, leaving their ghost trails lingering in the air. "November at Weybourne" (1924), ostensibly a simple, two-stanza poem about an autumn day at a small coastal town not far from Gresham's, exemplifies the process by which undertones of war (the poet and veteran Edmund Blunden's phrase) begin to reverberate in Auden's lyrical world. The poem opens on a vague note of struggle and grief:

> The starlings gather on the eaves
>> And shiver stiff with cold
> The elms still bear bewildered leaves
>> That dare not lose their hold
> Yon willow stoops as one who grieves
>> For a Spring that is old.

In a cold, bare, and sinister environment, the speaker, alone, sees the almost-deathly "starlings . . . shiver stiff with cold." Ghostly sounds seem to this sensitized listener like those of corpses talking. In the second stanza, he hears the "surge of wind through writhing trees | The huddled clouds of lead, | The waste of cold dark-featured seas | And the men that are dead."[78] The presence of "the men that are dead" uncannily diffuses into the rural, postwar world through words and phrases like "stiff with cold," "writhing," "huddled," and "lead," as well as "bewildered" and "grieves" in the first stanza.[79] The "men that are dead" cannot, in postwar England, mean all the earlier generations of humanity. It means here the soldiers slaughtered in the recent war, much as it does in the exhortations at Auden's and Isherwood's prep school not to "dishonour the dead" or in lines by Sassoon such as "dumb with pain I stumbled among the dead."[80]

To fantasize about hearing the spirits of dead men, as Auden does here, would not have seemed so odd in the 1920s. Gathering as a force during the war itself but continuing to build into peacetime, there was a wave of public interest in spiritualism, séances, books about communication with the dead, psychic photography, telepathy, ghosts, and the like, promoted by eminent figures like the physicist Oliver Lodge and the author Arthur Conan Doyle.[81] Auden's favorite uncle, Harold Auden, was both a scientifically trained chemist and a devoted séance-goer. "November at Weybourne," filled with the sounds of "the men that are dead," is a poem of anguished, death-obsessed irrationality perfectly in key with the country's mood at this period.

Other early poems set in an East Anglian landscape also refract a sense of wartime violence. For instance, in "The Sower," from 1922 or 1923, the "sun had stained the roofs with blood," and the speaker relates how he was "Wearied and sick at heart."[82] His rhetoric here closely follows Wilfred Owen's in "Mental Cases," a poem written during the First World War, which describes shell-shocked soldiers, slumped in a hospital ward, "whose minds the Dead have ravished" and to whom "Sunlight seems a blood-smear."[83] In one poem, "sun . . . stained . . . blood"; in the other, "Sun . . . blood-smear." Although both poems luridly associate sunlight with bloodstains, this is not a case of "influence" because Auden did not discover Owen's work until 1926. Rather, these are two poets independently exploring how perceptions of the external world away from the battlefield can nonetheless be imbued with, or ravished by, the traumas of war.[84]

Auden encountered this commingling of the worlds of rural life and war most powerfully in the work of Edward Thomas. In Thomas's great poem beginning "As the team's head-brass," an enigmatically footloose narrator, resting on an elm that was "felled" by a blizzard, talks to a ploughman, activating, as in "California," the equation of ploughing and writing. The ploughman has not been able to remove the elm from the field because the friend who would have helped him with this task has been killed in France. If that friend had been alive the speaker remarks, "I should not have sat here. Everything | Would have been different. For it would have been | Another world," and the ploughman answers "Ay, and a better."[85] The poem ends with the speaker leaving, probably contemplating enlisting, even though he is old enough that he does not need to fight. But he is now guiltily aware that his useless presence in the English countryside requires the sacrifice of someone else in France. And he knows that the landscape is suffering because the competent laborers are not at home to work it while reflective, middle-class strangers and the "stumbling team" are still, superfluously, on the land.

Thomas's poem goes beyond this simple point, subtly delivered though it is, to engage with the nightmarish foreboding and horror that haunt the country scene. The war spreads everywhere in the poem, suffusing natural objects, humans, and weather and atmosphere. As the conversation ends, the speaker watches from the fallen elm as the "clods crumble and topple over | After the ploughshare." He contemplates what would once have been an innocent rustic sight in England, a simple description of ploughing, but that, because of the Armageddon elsewhere, is now a phantasmagoric image of his own future death (his harrowing, as it were) amid the "flash[es]" of "brass" on the fields of France. Like the "clods" he sees in front of him here (a "clod" can mean a lump of soil or a bumpkin), he will "crumble and topple over" there, ploughed under by the iron blade of war.[86]

Auden's poems likewise see the subject of war as a contagion that moves opportunistically into whatever hosts it can find. He often practiced a Thomas-like mingling of field and wood with a place of death. An example is "September," written in 1923 or 1924, which describes an ambush during a hunt. The poem takes up a familiar wartime persona: the soldier so shocked and calloused by exposure to death that he can no longer feel any sorrow or guilt.[87] In this poem, set in a "barley field," the speaker watches "with undimmed eye" as "guns scream out." Soon a dozen hares, scared out of hiding, lie "either killed or maimed."[88] The way Auden specifies "barley" here, establishing plausibility while at the same time suggesting a link between "barley field" and "battlefield," is characteristic of his instinctive ingenuity as a writer.

"The Owl," apparently a simple account of a bird catching a mouse at night, replays in the nonhuman world another common war story: a sniping death in the trenches occurring when a flare temporarily lights up the scene. (Sassoon's "A Working Party" is a vivid example of this subgenre.) Here is Auden:

> Two bright eyes peer
> Through dew-drenched grass.
>
> In trembling fear
> There waits a mouse;
> No hiding near,
> And far his house.

The mouse waits, "Forlorn, alone," but protected by darkness,

> Till through a tear
> In cloud-thick skies
> Moon shows him clear
> To watching eyes.[89]

Already expert at using indirection to increase poetic tension, in "The Owl" Auden dramatizes the moment of death by switching suddenly from the sense of sight to the sense of hearing: "No sound to hear | Save one small cry" from somewhere in the dew-drenched grass.[90] The shriek of the tiny animal in the darkness discloses the physical collision of claw and fur. Death is almost instantaneous, as fast as a sniper shot.

Other early poems also obliquely stage themes of abandonment and violent death. The young Auden can make a poem that looks at first merely like a simple translation of a classical inscription uncannily evoke contemporary death. "On a Greek Tomb Relief" (perhaps like the tomb inscriptions in Greek that Dr. Auden had copied out on the battlefield at Gallipoli) describes a young man whom Death has sent for.[91] The slightly feminized victim, seemingly someone who died thousands of years ago, behaves with the same careless elegance that young English officers were said to have shown facing death in France: "You paused one moment more to dress your hair | And went."[92] Most freighted of all is "J. S. Bach," a poem about a dead musician (and a father of musicians) who is a "beacon fire to lost humanity." Auden, who listened to and played Bach's music all the time in his childhood home, imagines hearing in Bach's notes both the voice of a mother grieving for her children and a dying son accusing his father of having abandoned him.[93] None of these poems can be fully understood simply in terms of their ostensibly bland subjects.

In this context, one might wonder again about the young Auden's fascination with smallness—in poems about a mouse's "pair of round brown eyes | Gleaming between the stalks so homely wise" or about a toadstool, a dragonfly, a cat, an ant, or a "small Buddha."[94] A focus on the minute can be a traumatic marker, the sign of an extremely distressed psyche. The classic instance in a literary context comes from Fyodor Dostoyevsky's *The Idiot,* where Prince Myshkin gives an account of the terrified focus on insignificant details of a man about to be guillotined: "The brain, tremendously alive and active, must, I suppose, be working hard, hard, hard, like an engine going at full speed. I imagine all sorts of thoughts—all unfinished and absurd, too, perhaps, quite irrelevant thoughts—must constantly be throbbing through his brain: 'That man is looking at me—he has a wart on his forehead—one of the buttons on the executioner's coat is rusty.'"[95]

The passage glanced at earlier from *The Dynasts,* the poetic drama about a vast multinational war in Europe, shows Hardy indicating his own mind's anxiety by describing the unnoticed deaths of small animals in the lead-up to the enormous human massacre of Waterloo. Perhaps Auden had been sensitized to Hardy's poetics by knowing that his own father had almost died in a Hardyesque incident at Gallipoli when he was trying to rescue a single tortoise lost in the vortex of that gigantic battle and was almost shot?[96] Veterans of the Great War remembered that during times of intense stress, they tended to level their attention on the smallest things: "The most profound impressions came to me later, with some distance. On the spot, I attended to small matters and this detail often prevented me from judging the whole."[97]

Auden's poetry of the rural world, of the (literally) overlooked, the small, the abandoned, is at one level a means of dramatizing indirectly a sense of pervasive anxiety and fear. Every way his speakers turn, the landscape seems bathed in a mood of barely repressed grief and terror. The poetic eye that intently watches an ant trying to find its way around a stone uncannily re-creates the dazed eye of someone shocked by the world's brutality and sadness.[98] In coded form, the lyrics that Auden began to write in the period between about 1923 and 1926 are a kind of "war work": a working through of the war's unearthly psychological impact even when human conflict is never mentioned.

Though he belonged to a younger, noncombatant generation, Auden's work therefore belongs alongside the kind of haunted pastoralism hinting at "the indescribable" that many English veterans produced in the 1920s. As if it were perfumed by a faint smell of cordite or emanated from the unnatural, absolute silence that follows a huge explosion, Auden's pathologized nature poetry set in provincial England is obsessed with the violence and heroism of war, with its wounding effects on the psyches even of those who did not directly experience it, with the shame of not having taken part in it, and with sadness and guilt over the bodies and minds destroyed.[99]

Auden's projections of war onto a rural landscape are underwritten both by an identification with widespread social trauma and by his personal anguish about his absent, military father, the father he had lost to the war. His poetic world in these early poems is a violent and entropic one, and it is associated with legendary deeds and men now dead. In these imaginative landscapes, the dead are different from the living not only because they are heroic but also because they are unreachable. In a poem about "Arthur's Quoit, Dyffryn," the site of a Bronze Age burial chamber in Gwynedd, Auden's speaker inspects the "Cold grey stones" named after the mythological British king and wonders, "What mighty warrior lies beneath thy shade? | What deeds of valour wrought his battle blade?"[100] This poem, written in 1923 or 1924, reflects in a cryptic way on Auden's experience of the wartime years. But there is also a direct connection between this lyric about a vanished English hero and Auden's "loss" of his father in the war. Dyffryn, the site of Arthur's Quoit, is where Auden, his brothers, and his mother spent their holidays in August 1915 and August 1916. By the end of the second visit, Dr. Auden, a "mighty warrior" as a doctor serving Britain's cause, had been away for nearly two years.

Where there is sadness, there is also reproach. In "Punchard," written in July 1925, the month that he played Caliban and then left Gresham's, Auden describes a remote farmstead where the old owner has died and the body is awaiting burial. The poem's landscape reverberates with the familiar violence: "a gun | Tells that some jay will suck no eggs again | In pheasant woods across the valley." As if implying a connection between them, this gunshot leads directly to Punchard's corpse laid out:

> now and then a gun
> Tells that some jay will suck no eggs again
> In pheasant woods across the valley; hot
> It is out upon the fell here but not
> Within the farm where old Joe Punchard lies
> On the cool kitchen flags until to-morrow.[101]

The sequence of thoughts in the poem is "gunshot—death—hot outside—cool inside—corpse." Punchard was a decent man, sounding much like Dr. Auden does in his youngest son's numerous descriptions: "Toil he knew, and love, but mostly toil—wise | And kind."[102] ("Kind" is a richly ambivalent adjective that Auden often associates with fathers and never in a purely honorific sense, as though he were hinting that there is weakness or destructiveness in being kind.[103]) But, because so much needs to be done on the farm, Punchard's "son has not an hour for sorrow | The farm is his now, he must reap the corn." The speaker passes by, "Shading [his] eyes with one rose-glowing hand" to shield himself from the sun's rays and muttering that there is no way to "find the word | Fit to speak of beauty and the dead."[104]

In a poem about a son beginning to stand in the place of his dead father, performing the tasks that the dead man is no longer there to do, Auden's "rose-glowing hand," protecting the eyes from the sun, is an evocative image; it implies that the poem contains themes, centered on the father, that are too powerful to look at directly. But they can be sensed indirectly through the defensive screen of the poet's hand, which turns the blinding white light to a warm, aesthetically pleasing "rose-glowing" one. "Punchard" suggests a strong sense of ambivalence in a younger generation; the speaker feels both guilt and anger, with no "fit" word to say about the death of the old farmer.

As in "The Death of the Hired Man" by Frost, another of Auden's favorite poets at this time, there is guilt hinted at because the speaker may feel responsible, if only at an unconscious, irrational level, for the death that has occurred. In addition, perhaps Auden's readers wonder if the son had something to do with the father's death. In "Punchard," the son (who now owns the farm and "has not an hour for sorrow") and his counterpart, the poem's speaker, are both unable to mourn Punchard's passing with eloquence. But there are also feelings of anger and abandonment in both because Punchard's death has left his son alone to cope with the task of keeping the farm going. As a result, the farm's viability is at stake, just as, in all Auden's war-infused poems, the existential struggle against death threatens the survival not just of particular individuals but of a whole culture and way of life.

Around 1923, when the gamekeepers' guns began to "scream out" in Auden's rural poems and when he started to write lyrics such as "Arthur's Quoit, Dyffryn," Auden was intensively reading Hardy, the poet whom he called his "poetical father."[105] By keeping the volumes of this father with him constantly, Auden was symbolically attempting to heal the breach between himself and the parent he had lost. By echoing or mimicking Hardy in his writing, he was reidentifying at a stylistic level with the father who in psychic terms had become distant, had become a "stranger"—to use a word that always seems to carry a special weight for Auden.

Hardy was alive at the time when Auden was reading and imitating him at school; he died only in January 1928, during Auden's last year at Oxford.[106] The old man was fascinated by uncanny facial resemblances. For example, his poem "Heredity" from *Moments of Vision* (1917) describes the ghostly "family face" or "years-heired feature that can | In curve and voice and eye | Despise the human span | Of durance."[107] Prompted by a frontispiece portrait or a reproduction of a photograph in a book or magazine, Auden identified so strongly with Hardy's writing partly because he felt its author resembled his own absent parent: "he looked like my father: that broad unpampered moustache, bald forehead and deeply lined sympathetic face belonged to that other world of feeling and sensation (for I, like my mother, was a thinking-intuitive)."[108] The parenthesis here, connecting Auden to his mother in a relation they share to his father, even seems to hint at a feeling of attraction.

Children often find themselves haunted by turns of phrase or physical gestures that they instinctively make and in which their parents' mannerisms and vocal tics seem to survive. Auden's mimicry in his early poems of Hardy's rhythms, phrases, and situations is partly an attempt to re-create a sense of familial poetic relation with this literary father figure. It is at the same time a symbolic effort to augment an otherwise missing or diminished sense of relation to his own father. Similar motivations also seem to have animated Auden's dedication to writing Edward Thomas–like poems. Thomas had been killed at Arras in 1917 and was buried in a military cemetery at Agny in France. He was another lost soldier with whom Auden could imaginatively identify his father. Thomas had even demonstrated interests like those of Auden's father, publishing a book of translations of Norse myth in 1912.[109]

Auden started reading Thomas around 1924. In June of that year, in a moment that encapsulates the variety of his intellectual interests as a teenager, he chose Thomas's *Collected Poems,* published in 1920, as his reward for winning the Eccles Science Prize at Gresham's.[110] And in the summer of 1925, he wrote a poetic tribute, "To E.T.," in which he stressed the way Thomas, like Hardy before him, had taught the young poet how to look at the countryside. "To E.T." is addressed to Thomas's body in the grave, where "beneath the rumbling wheel | No scratch of mole nor lisping worm you feel." But the speaker tells Thomas that by reading his poems, "someone learns what elm and badger said | To you who loved them."

In "To E.T.," Auden even goes so far as to suggest that he is something like a poetic reincarnation of Thomas: "when the blackbird tries his cadences anew | There kindles still in eyes you never knew | The light that would have shone in you."[111] The word "kindles" suggests kindredness as well as the kindled metaphoric light that shines "in eyes you never knew." By focusing on eyes, one of the most familiar indicators of shared genes in different generations, Auden's lines hint at an almost blood relationship between a surviving son (Auden) and a dead poet-father (Thomas), implying a family relation between them as poets of the same kind. The "I" whom Thomas "never knew" now sees the world as though through Thomas's own eyes. Writing to, and in the styles of, these soldier "fathers"—one ancient (almost pre-dead but still living in the countryside), Hardy, the author of the war epic *The Dynasts;* one younger but dead, Thomas, the author of poems that hardly ever confront war directly but that are imbued in almost every line with the atmosphere of a country at war—Auden was joining them at a fantasy level. But he was also attempting to stand in their places, much as Joe Punchard's unnamed son was forced to do with his dead father.

Often, though, Auden as a young poet is barely able to inhabit the literary worlds of his favorite writers. In that first surviving poem,

"California," the speaker's courage fails, and he never gains the visionary power he seeks: "For this I stopped and stood quite still | Then turned with quick steps down that hill."[112] This scenario of failure plays out a number of times in Auden's earliest poetry as he seeks height, literally and metaphorically, only to find himself driven back, often by something menacing but intangible. This is true, for instance, of "'The Road's Your Place,'" in which the speaker is walking along a road, tired by "the crunch of stones" under his feet. The sight of a stream persuades him that "A tarn [a lake] lay somewhere at the end of it."[113] Typically, Auden's poetic desire leads him off the beaten path: "I left the road and struck up by the burn | Along a track which heaved and plunged and leapt." ("Burn" is a northern English and Scottish word for a stream or small river, though of course it also poetically evokes the other meaning: a wound from heat.) This poem and "California," as if they were paired, share not just similar scenarios but crucial words including "stream" and "track."

In "'The Road's Your Place,'" the burn bends to the left: "I hurried on, eager and out of breath | And soon had turned the corner." Then, three mountain crags appear to rise up, "overshadow[ing]" him. A spectral voice, projected onto the crags, asks, "What are you doing here, the road's your place." "Between [the crags'] bodies," the speaker sees in the distance the tarn he had hoped to find. But, as in "California," he feels repulsed:

> What could I do but shift my feet awhile
> Mutter and turn back to the road again
> Watched out of sight by three tall angry hills.

Auden alludes here to an episode from book 1 of *The Prelude* in which Wordsworth, rowing a boat at night, feels he is being chased by a huge, threatening cliff.[114] Yet Auden emphatically separates himself here from Wordsworth's integrative model of the relation between humanity and nature. The incident stands alone in Auden without any Wordsworthian moral commentary or connection to a broader sense of life and without any positive relief from the fear. The poem ends simply, starkly, with the speaker harried back down to the road and his proper place by the "three tall angry hills."

Unlike "California" or "'The Road's Your Place,'" where Auden's speaker cannot reach the summit that will give him satisfaction or a clear perspective, "Below me Ticknall lay but in the light" opens on a height. But this poem, which Auden wrote in May 1925, shares the same mood of fear. Ticknall is a village in Derbyshire, near where Auden's paternal grandmother lived, and the poem begins with Auden's speaker on top of a hill looking down on the village, which is "Below me." Dismayingly, the lofty vantagepoint brings no visual or conceptual clarity. The speaker stands above the village, "but in the light | Which yet remained the roofs looked strange and blurred." His footsteps "rang aloud but nothing stirred." Instead, he hears the cry of the "fern owl." ("Fern owl" is another name for the nightjar, a bird with a strange rising and falling cry and a ghostly, almost sinister reputation because of its ability to fly absolutely silently.) It "Seemed an old man calling at the edge of night."[115]

Unable to see the "fern owl," the speaker is free to imagine its cry, at first, as being like that of a sentry on the hill, reassuring the anxious "hearts" in the village below. But then, "some change of mood as home I came" makes the speaker compare the bird's call to the cry of a ghost in the ears of the ancient inhabitants of Britain who,

> Hearing that cry, woke sleeping logs to flame
> Shivered and huddled closer to the fire
> Feeling the dead peer downward through the trees.

By the poem's end, unable to clarify anything from his hilltop vantage-point, the speaker has retreated and has become prey to the dreads and superstitions of those "shagged men, who had | An older name for home than Derbyshire | Or Britain." Where the village lay "Below me" at the start of the poem, ghosts now "Peer downward" at him through the gathering dark.[116]

The summer 1925 poem "The Dying House," a dark and complex lyric filled with the flavors of an Edward Thomas poem, is perhaps the best example of the way in which fatalistic themes, and preoccupations with personal vulnerability, align with intuitions about the fate of postwar England in Auden's early poetry.

> The house was dying when I saw it; gaunt
> And hollow its eyes looked, which once had shone

So bravely from the wood on winter mornings
Across the fields; now even moss and leaves
Were getting ready for the burial

I knew but little of the house save what
They told me at the inn; a woman lived
There last who bore a boy and dropped him
Three days later—That stair was always dark—
She would not live in houses after that.

The house still seemed an old and kindly one
Which shut no door on martin or on ghost
I only stopped to watch a silver squirrel
Chasing a red across the broken tiles
My odds were on the English one, I lost

Nought could be done to help it so I left
Like Hagar wishing not to see the end
There are worse ways of death than this to choose from
Beneath the sky and rain, alone, with birds
And no grief but a stranger's casual tears.[117]

"The Dying House" strongly recalls such Thomas poems as "Gone, Gone Again," with its "old house, | Outmoded, dignified, | Dark and untenanted."[118] Auden's chastening narrative—a traveler comes upon a ruined house among the trees, where he learns about the death of a child there and the tragic story of the woman who was the child's mother and the home's last inhabitant—also reaches back to Wordsworth's "ruined cottage" in *The Excursion*. There, a "roofless Hut" stands in the "gloom | Spread by a brotherhood of lofty elms." As Wordsworth explains, the "Last human tenant of these ruined walls" was the mother of "a little babe" who died in the house.[119]

"The Dying House" is written in a relatively unusual, consistently lineated five-line pentameter stanza, which Hardy, Thomas, and Frost used so often as to imprint the stanza form with something of their quietly but firmly individualist literary personalities. Hardy's "The Sunshade" in *Moments of Vision* (1917) and "'And There Was a Great Calm'" in *Late Lyrics and Earlier* (1922) use this five-line stanza, as do Thomas's "The Bridge," "It Rains," and two of his very last poems, "The Sheiling" and "Out in the Dark."[120] Frost uses the stanza form often in his first book, *A Boy's Will* (1913), in such poems as "Ghost House," "My November Guest," "In a Vale," and "Pan with Us."[121]

Hardy, Thomas, and Frost deploy a more or less gently rhyming form of the stanza, sometimes (in Thomas's case) using truncated or irregular line lengths, whereas Auden's stanzas are unrhymed and consistently lineated.[122] But "The Dying House," with its solidly blocked cinquains, is the first poem Auden wrote in a form that, with small modulations, would become a vehicle for some of his most important canonical poems, such as part 2 of the 1932 diptych "A Happy New Year."[123] When he first experimented with the five-line pentameter stanza in "The Dying House," the form was already associated with poets who wrote about the countryside and its fraying communities, as he knew. In Auden's later poems in cinquains (because poetic form is never without its own social content), he will continue to use this stanza to evoke similar themes and to suggest thoughts about cultural decay and possible renewal.

In "The Dying House," the outsider happens upon a rotting, lightless edifice in the depths of a wood. Its windows, like living eyes, "once had shone | So bravely from the wood on winter mornings | Across the fields."[124] The chiastic opening lines contrast the state of dying and being sightless with the state of living and being able to observe: "The house was dying when I *saw* it; gaunt | And hollow its eyes *looked*." While the speaker "sees" the dying house, the building itself "looks," but intransitively and with the sense in the latter verb of "seems" rather than "observes" or "looks at." It is as if the idea of sight is dying from the word "look" just as life is ebbing from the ruined building. In the middle of 1925, Auden was particularly fascinated by imagining human eyes about to pass over into the glazed unresponsive state of a corpse's eyeballs or, conversely, of inanimate, "dead" objects that seem uncannily to see. In a poem about the nature writer Richard Jefferies, Auden thinks about the dying man watching the sky "with eyes as bright | As kestrel."[125] And in "To E.T.," as mentioned, Auden reassures Thomas that "There kindles still in eyes you never knew | The light that would have shone in you."[126] The latter notion feels very different from the "gaunt | And hollow" eyes the visitor sees in "The Dying House."

In "The Dying House," these themes of seeing and not seeing are mirrored formally in the poem's commitment to enjambment. Enjambment suggests the idea that the poetic line cannot always see where it is going (no poet writing in English enjambs more than the blind Milton). Auden emulates Edward Thomas's extensive use of run-on lines to create the impression of a tentative, careful groping for meaning, like the movements of a hand in a darkened room searching along a wall for the light switch. Here, in Auden's poem, enjambment helps to create a sense of inconclusive, inexorable process—linked to decay and death— where the lines continuously fail to stabilize themselves at the natural boundary of the line end.

A contrast between direct knowledge, gained with the eyes, and hearsay or appearance continues to modulate throughout the rest of the poem. In stanza 1, the speaker's visual observations of the house prevail. In stanza 2, information, rumor, and conjecture rather than personal observation predominate: the poet-speaker learns, at a nearby inn, of the house's tragic history.[127] By the third stanza, the terrible story told in stanza 2 has not quite eradicated the pleasantly melancholic look of the house in the speaker's eyes, but it has shaken his confidence in his perceptions of the place: "The house *still seemed* an old and kindly one | Which shut no door on martin or on ghost." Nothing, whether the creatures of the natural world (embodied by the "martin," with its bright, French-derived name) or of the supernatural world (the weighty Saxon-derived "ghost"), appears barred from shelter. But a new atmosphere, at once macabre and symbolic, enters the poem. The tone of confident perception announced in the opening line ("The house was dying when I saw it") has dwindled to the point where the speaker's judgments have become uncertain: "The house still seemed an old and kindly one."

The subsequent lines insist that the house is a symbol of a vanished England that, having been abandoned, is now being taken back by nature and overrun by creatures without a "native" origin:

> I only stopped to watch a silver squirrel
> Chasing a red across the broken tiles
> My odds were on the English one, I lost

The speaker's patriotic but mistaken faith is in the "English" squirrel, the red animal, which is being chased by the "silver" or gray one. As the English house slowly crumbles into a shell, the native red squirrel on a natural ground of conflict is being overcome and displaced by the foreign import.[128]

The defeat of the native creature is implicitly linked to the demise of the three-day-old "boy" that caused his mother to leave the house and let it fall into decay. The death of the English heir, the ruined English house, and the symbolic death of the English animal—a lost child, a falling building, and a lost wager—are all imaginatively one. The poem ends on a laconic, stoical, and deeply enigmatic note. As at the ends of many Frost poems ("Two Tramps in Mudtime," for example), here we seem to be among people who observe a world they do not genuinely belong to; and, as readers, we have little notion of who the protagonists, and especially the narrator, of the poem really are. As Auden's speaker leaves the red squirrel losing the race across the "broken tiles" and the house preparing for its own "burial" in the encroaching world of nature, he shrugs:

> There are worse ways of death than this to choose from
> Beneath the sky and rain, alone, with birds
> And no grief but a stranger's casual tears.

Knowing how often Auden referred implicitly or indirectly to war in the poems he was writing in these years, one wonders which "worse ways of death" he could be imagining here. The last stanza, where the speaker turns away from the ruin, is the only one in which the word "house" does not appear in the opening line—a choice that emphasizes the emotional gulf finally separating speaker and building. Moreover, in this final stanza, the speaker for the first time refers to himself not as "I" but as "a stranger" (one of Auden's talismanic words appears again), a characterization that deepens the poem's portrait of a ruined and emptying world in which old communities and homes alike are falling apart or being displaced.

The tight-lipped quality of the closing lines may also serve as a foil to a new and surprising level of meaning that is introduced immediately before the end. As the speaker turns away from the house, he brings in a note of parable by likening himself to "Hagar," who wished "not to see the end." Hagar is the second mother mentioned in this short poem who is involved, either actually or potentially, in the death of her child. First, there is the unnamed "woman" of the dying house who fatally "dropped" her son on the dark staircase—a suggestive use of the verb "drop," as it can mean "to let fall" and "to give birth to." Second, there is Hagar, despairing in the desert, after she has been expelled by Abraham. Fearing the worst, Hagar moves away from her child, Ishmael, the prototypical exile, so as not to see him dying.[129]

"The Dying House" is an early instance of Auden's anxiously misogynistic fascination in his poetry with the idea of cruel or devouring mothers, associating the derelict home with two boys ill cared for by the women who gave them life. But, since the speaker compares himself to Hagar, his turn away from the house implies that the house stands in the same relation to him as Hagar's temporarily deserted offspring stands in relation to her. At a symbolic level, the speaker repeats the mothers' neglect of their offspring in his own, parallel abandonment of the house. But, at the moment when Hagar moves away from her son, God hears the boy's cries and descends to save them both. The paradoxical implication is that, as the speaker turns away from the moldering house and the English squirrel being displaced by a foreign interloper, a regeneration of the house's "English" life is about to begin—just as it is only after Hagar has turned away from her child that God rescues them. Northrop Frye wrote that "The lyric is the genre in which the poet . . . turns his back on his audience."[130] Here, as in "California" and as in many poems Auden will write in the coming years—and perhaps also, by the mid-1930s, in his relationship to English culture as a whole—the deep lyric impulse to turn away from something is mysteriously to participate in redeeming it.

Complex undercurrents of Oedipal desire and resentment, directed toward the Mother, flow through these associations with Hagar and the mother in "The Dying House." But the poem's rage at the Father is even deeper and colder, all the more so because it is largely silent. Although no father is so much as mentioned and the adult male absence is never explained, in the context of 1925, the year Auden wrote the poem, it is natural to interpret the missing father as someone lost in the recent war and to connect his disappearance with the reasons for the ruin of the house and the boy's death.

Neither this poem nor any other of these early poems is merely a piece of autobiographical self-expression on Auden's part. Auden's models at the time made it likely that he would address subjects in terms of the health or sickness of life, human or animal, in the English countryside. But his themes are communal and historical, not private, ones. Even while attending to the psychological subject matter in "The Dying House," it is impossible to ignore its social dimension, which expresses an anxiety about the decrepit condition, or disappearance, of English rural life. The people are gone; the house's windows are smashed; the English squirrel, chased across the rotting roof, is finally overcome. The poem is an elegy for abandoned sons, forsaken houses (this one looks like a human skull with its "gaunt" and "hollow . . . eyes"), and native nature overwhelmed by foreign trespassers. And, as such, it is a sentimentally conservative lament for a declining country.

In book 1 of *The Excursion,* Wordsworth provides an account of social and human decline that combines both natural and human blights. Living during the period of Britain's conflict with Napoleonic France, the people of the country cottage he describes suffer first under the weight of two poor harvests. But this is followed by "A worse affliction in the plague of war."[131] In "The Dying House," the family disaster is obvious, but the background of the war is more faintly sketched. Yet the fears about endangered boys and the declining national home are, at an imaginative level, one and the same. The poem subtly touches on feelings about the death of a large part of an entire generation of young men, consigned by the motherland to their fates during the recent Great War, just as the mother of "The Dying House" "dropped" her son when he was most in need of her. And the issue of the war inevitably brings up questions of national loyalty. War has often been the event that precipitates the emergence, or fabrication, of such loyalties. For Auden's generation, conditions of national emergency, conflict, and the fever of puritanical patriotism that they induced brought feelings about England and Englishness to a crisis point.

Much of the description in "The Dying House" evokes familiar tropes of war literature. For example, the decaying house with "gaunt | And hollow" eyes and its tragic male ghost hint at the familiar scenery of ruined homes, shattered barns, and collapsed spires on the battlefields of rural France and Belgium. For younger writers, such as Auden, rural verities and the implicit innocence and safety of the pastoral scene were one more value that had been desecrated during the war. The old country world, with its network of secure (or rigid) social relations and a harmonious interplay between humanity and nature, is dead, gone with, in Edmund Blunden's words, the "last rat and last kestrel banished."[132] The pastoral English world is no longer the peaceful antithesis to the battlefield but its double.

In the preface to a collected edition of his poems in 1930, Blunden noticed that he had been "labelled . . . among the poets of the time as a useful rustic, or perhaps not so useful." But because of the historical situation in which he had found himself, he claimed that "War became part of the author's experience at a date so early (that is, in comparison with ordinary times) as to mould and colour the poetry almost throughout this book."[133] The best-known instance of this molding and coloring of a rustic subject in Blunden's work is "The Midnight Skaters." Here, under the darting skaters on the ice in the English countryside, "With but a crystal parapet | Between, [death] has his engines set."[134] Death is like an enemy, planting mines beneath his enemy victims. The poem almost literalizes the title of Blunden's 1928 autobiography: *Undertones of War.*

Although Auden was too young to go to war himself, he lived it vicariously in his poems, where imagined war experiences "mould and colour" the representation of the rural world. Blunden first collected "The Midnight Skaters" in *Masks of Time.* The book was published in June 1925, the same month that Auden wrote "The Dying House."[135] In Auden's poem, the chase of the "red" and "silver" squirrels across the "broken tiles" might easily be read as a displaced account of two soldiers from different nations, identified by different uniforms (one "red," one "silver") fighting each other through the warren of a splintered building on a battlefield. In "The Dying House," the "silver" squirrel hounds the "red" as a gray-clad German soldier in the trenches might have rushed a khaki-clothed Tommy. In a similar way, Blunden, war-traumatized, gazes in "Water Moment" from *To Nature,* published in 1923, as an eel ambushes a fish with "*red* gold wings": "The *silver* death writhes with the chosen one."[136] In the postwar world, natural ferocity at its most realistic becomes a metaphor for human conflict.

In these ways, even as an eighteen-year-old, Auden was a poet of "national" themes. That such themes appear in a covert or displaced form is a testimony not only to their importance but also to their aura of menace. As Rivers said, describing a young officer who had come into his care at Craiglockhart: "painful thoughts were pushed into hidden recesses of his mind only to accumulate such force as to make them well up and produce attacks of depression so severe as to put his life in danger."[137] The young Auden was perhaps not literally in danger (though surely one can see that somewhere inside he must have suffered throughout his life from unusually high levels of anxiety), but he was beginning to write a poetry in which "painful thoughts were pushed into hidden recesses of his mind" only to "well up" again in new contexts with memorable force.

That process was never more evident than in the way that Auden's old obsession with mining between 1914 and 1920 suddenly blossomed in the mid-1920s into poems that talked of northern mines to speak of war. The Auden family had almost always taken holidays in regional parts of Britain—Wales, Derbyshire, the Isle of Wight.[138] In the 1920s, they started to return repeatedly to the Lake District and the North Pennines. Auden visited the North Pennine moors, the site of numerous abandoned lead mines, for the first time in 1919 when he was twelve.[139] He may have toured the nearby Lake District in the summer of 1921, and in August 1922 he, his father, and his middle brother, John, went on another holiday to the region, staying at Derwentfolds farm near Threlkeld, also in the Lake District.[140]

During this 1922 trip, Auden visited Rookhope in Weardale in the North Pennines. This holiday, in the same year that he began to write poetry, was a crucial one for his imagination.[141] He reverted several times in his poems to the experience at Rookhope of dropping a stone down a disused mine shaft and listening (as his first poem on the subject puts it) to a "distant splash, a whispering, a laugh" and of feeling the "icy hands of fear" weigh "heavily on the bone."[142] The following year, in August 1923, he stayed with Medley and his family at Appletreewick in the Yorkshire dales, where there is a nearby lead mine. (The town's name is pronounced "AH-trick.") Because Auden did not start writing about the Pennines until 1924, Appletreewick is the scene of his first surviving northern poem, written in the winter of 1923–1924, when he reminisced about his summer visit.[143] He went back to the North Pennine region repeatedly, when his interest in mines and deserted workings appears to have shifted from a literalist obsession to a poetic, figurative one.

As Auden began to visit the North of England more often in the early 1920s, the poetry he had made from the natural world around Holt in Norfolk and in various holiday spots began to be complemented by poems about the North Pennines. The latter area seems connected for Auden with the eruption of powerful, almost Dionysian feelings that had never emerged in such stark form in other contexts. Auden recalled to his friend James Stern that during the 1922 trip to the North

Pennines, "I was on a walking-tour with my father, and we were sharing a bed: I suddenly had a violent longing to be fucked by him," adding dryly, "(Not being a novelist, I have to confess that he didnt)."[144] It seems to be the case that, on the same holiday in 1922, Auden and his brother John had sex together at Derwentfolds farm.[145] In later life, Auden believed (or claimed to believe) that "male sexuality as such is playful, frivolous and impersonal"—and perhaps this incident should be put down simply to those hedonistic impulses.[146] But the turmoil during this tour also offers a glimpse of the psychic intensity obtaining within the superficially decorous Auden family.

By 1924, as Auden gained in technical dexterity as a poet, he started writing with much greater force about experiences of primal fear and anxiety in a northern landscape. The first poem set in the Pennines is "The Old Lead-mine," composed in February 1924, in which Auden's speaker feels the "icy hands of fear" weigh on him.[147] Many of the scenarios of violence in Auden's poetry leave the southern world into which they somewhat awkwardly fitted and, intensifying, migrate north into a rural but industrial world like the "sunless courts of death" that Auden described in a poem about Christ's descent into hell.[148] For instance, "Elegy," which, like "'The Road's Your Place,'" uses the distinctively northern English word "tarn" (meaning a small lake), seems to be about an older man who has suddenly died:

> Little [we] guessed that in the splendid morning
> One we loved would lie as cold, as strangely still
> As the black tarn deep-hollowed in the hill.[149]

A violent death in these early poems often functions as a poem's terminal, conclusive moment, its "point," as it had in "The Owl."[150] In fact, the words "death" or "die" or "dead" occur with marked frequency in the last two lines of many of Auden's early poems about northern landscapes, as if he were intent on finding ever new ways to approach the same traumatic subject.[151]

The North, already made numinous by his father's obsession with northern myths and archaeology and from Dr. Auden's reading Wordsworth's poetry aloud to his son, became inseparably connected in Auden's imagination with the world of the northern mines he visited. In addition to the experience of dropping a stone down into a disused mine shaft, which Auden recounted in "The Old Lead-mine," a terrifying presence seems to lurk at the bottom of every darkened shaft or over every windswept ridge. In "Stone Walls," written in 1923 or 1924, Auden's speaker wonders what would happen if he were to follow the walls as they stretch up over the fells:

> What if I come to
> Where burns no star,
> Dark hidden places
> Where memories are,
> And cold dead faces
> Despairs do mar?[152]

It is precisely into the world of "cold dead faces" that Auden's poetic lines—snaking across the page like the slender stone walls snaking through the Pennine grass—lead him. It is a world of bleak weather, emptied landscapes, abandoned mine workings, stories of death, and subtle signs of danger and distress. "The Dying House" centers on a ruined building associated with dead people, and Auden's northern landscape is replete with rotting or half-collapsed edifices, with tunnels and stilled or decaying machines appearing in such poems as "The Old Colliery" or "Allendale."[153] A sonnet written in April 1924, "Rookhope (Weardale, Summer 1922)," begins: "The men are dead that used to walk these dales"—dead and, so the speaker says, largely forgotten. Yet, the sonnet's sestet reveals that the poet, as if he were a veteran haunted by memories of war even during years of peace, still remembers, or imagines, the men as if he had established some mystical link with the dead. While the poem does not explicitly make the connection, the place that the poem describes is like a Great War battlefield, which looked empty but was in fact filled with human presences:

> Yet—I have stood by their deserted shafts
> While the rain lashed my face and clutched my knees,
> And seemed to hear therein their careless laughs,
> To glimpse the spirit which engendered these.[154]

In many other poems, too, the dead watch, speak, or listen in the darkness. In "'Lead's the Best'," for example, the speaker hears water drip "like voices from the dead" in the mine's "dark holes opening onto hollow hills."[155] In later life, Auden was able to recognize that in the landscape of mines he wrote about, there was an "unconscious relation between [his] sacred world and death."[156]

Auden and his father and brother had stayed at Derwentfolds farm near Threlkeld in 1922; in 1924 or 1925, the family acquired half of Wesco, a farmhouse in the same village. (They bought the second half of the property a few years later, probably sometime before 1928.) Auden went back there often well into the 1930s.[157] The large cottage, built around 1600, is only about twelve or fifteen miles north of Wordsworth country around Grasmere, and to the east, it has what Auden's father described as views of "transcendent beauty" toward Ullswater.[158] The North Pennines, separated from the Lake District proper by the Eden Valley, begin about twenty miles east, northeast of the Audens' Threlkeld home. Much of Auden's exploration of the area as a young man must have relied on short journeys on foot or by car, bicycle, or motorcycle.[159]

A starker version of the nearby Lake District, this North Pennine landscape that Auden explored was primarily a region of abandoned or decaying lead mines, jagged scarps, vast, lonely fells, and looming skies. These moors and hills were at the time largely deserted. Signs of present human activity were rare, but crumbling reminders of the mining past were abundant: they formed a material incarnation of the world in which Auden had already immersed himself through mining literature.

As "California" and other early poems show, Auden's first lyrics had not fully engaged with—and often swerved away from—the subjects toward which he was instinctively edging. It was not until a few years after he began writing that Auden was able to combine successfully his feeling for natural scenery and the countryside with the psychological subjects that mattered to him. In looking back into the darkness of the past, he found himself writing about mines. And to write about mines was to tap into a mythical reservoir of images that allowed him to address, in even more concentrated and energetic forms than before, war and its aftermath, both its personal costs, like the absence of his own father, and its national costs, like the huge army of the country's dead.

Mining slang bolstered an association between Dr. Auden and mines. In Stanley Smith's *Lead and Zinc Ores of Northumberland and Alston Moor* (1923), one of Auden's treasured manuals on lead mining in the North Pennines, the author notes that "encountering the 'old man'" is "a term commonly employed to denote any workings of which no records exist."[160] Auden may also have known from conversations with Pennine inhabitants or from his other reading that, to miners, the "old man" was a term for an enigmatic, lost figure who dwelt underground making forays deep into the earth. In writing in his early poems about mines, war, death, and the "old man," Auden—whether consciously or not—had stumbled onto archetypal, *Hamlet*-like terrain, where a son's search for connection with his father takes place in a kingdom that is "contracted in one brow of woe."[161]

Auden himself later said that he had "no practical mechanical gift whatsoever" and that he understood his youthful interest in mines and bleak, deserted, postindustrial landscapes as "a symbolic one."[162] These imaginative cipherings of war and death, in which feelings about dead heroes, absent fathers, and life-and-death struggles between men who are, as a father and son are too, at once friends and enemies, are displaced in Auden's imagination onto an apparently empty but profoundly worked landscape.

Auden recognized that his poems had a "deep" and not just "surface" meaning, as is evident in a little lyric of 1925:

> Like other men, when I go past
>   A mine shaft or a well,
> I always have to stop and cast
>   A stone to break the spell
>
> Of wondering how deep they go;
>   And if the clatter end
> Too soon, turn grieved away as though
>   Mistaken in a friend.[163]

The mine shaft that is not "deep" enough to yield its symbolic secret, and ends its "clatter" after only a short span of time, causes grief in the poet. But what do these shafts and wells symbolize? No one, including on most occasions Auden, ever seems to say. Once, though, Auden *did* try his "hand at a little self-analysis." When that happened, he was thinking more associatively than symbolically, connecting his juvenile "passion for lead-mines" with the world of death: "I note, firstly that the word *lead* rhymes with *dead* and that lead is or was used for lining coffins: secondly, that mining is the one human activity that is by nature mortal."[164] By "mortal," Auden apparently intended to say only that mining is an activity of limited duration because a mine will, sooner or later, "become exhausted, and be abandoned." But at the same time, "mortal" also reinforces the connection he has already established between "lead" and coffins and hence the "dead," between mines and death. "Mortal" means "limited," "subject to death," and also "lethal."[165]

Knowledge about the dangers of working in mines was hardly a profound revelation, even for people whose social status removed them from direct contact with working miners. Mining for all kinds of metallic ores and minerals was a huge industry in the Britain of Auden's childhood. At the end of the Edwardian era, about one British laboring man in thirteen worked in a mine or quarry; there were over a million miners in the country—almost like a vast industrial army—and there were many casualties annually.[166] Given the connotations of the words "lead" and "mortal," mines must have seemed to Auden's young, upper-middle-class imagination like fascinating but terrifyingly remote places, enigmatically eroticized, where a band (or brigade) of mysteriously heroic, sinister, and anonymous working-class brothers engaged together in a physically exhausting, potentially fatal activity in the dark.[167]

These feelings spotlight one further "mortal" meaning of the noun "lead," which is clearly relevant to Auden, although he did not mention it himself. Lead was used not only for the lining of coffins but as the basic material for boys' toy soldiers and (along with a small amount of tin) for bullets. Indeed, during Auden's childhood, "lead" was a common slang term for "bullets." (We saw in Chapter 1 that when "Corpl. Auden (junior)" participated in an OTC "field day" in Surrey in June 1917, he "gave them a good deal of lead."[168]) And of course, numerous war poems and stories use the word "lead" almost as frequently as they use the word "bullet."[169]

In coming to terms with hidden or buried traumas, Auden's lead-mine poems draw on a common, quite realistic connection made in this period between modern warfare and mining. Once the German army dug in on the Western Front in mid-September 1914 by constructing trenches near the Aisne, the whole character of warfare was transformed.[170] "Trench warfare in general was a war of engineers, but the theatre of war that was dominated exclusively by engineers was the war of mining and counter-mining under no-man's-land," wrote Eric J. Leed about the First World War.[171] Leed added: "This war was a matter of holes and ditches, a place where the sewer worker, the miner, and the ditch-digger were at home."[172] All the infantry carried entrenching tools, but more specialized mining warfare was a relatively well-known

part of the war effort: *Mining Activity on the Western Front*, a short propaganda film made by the same unit that shot the famous *The Battle of
the Somme* (1916) and including scenes from underground, was shown
in British cinemas during 1916, the same year when Auden visited his
first mine.[173] On both sides, thousands of men (many of them miners
and engineers in civilian life) participated in these lethal activities, constructing hundreds of miles of tunnels deep beneath the trenches in
France and Belgium.

The trenches themselves were only a step away from being mines.
There a filthy, dangerous life was eked out in dank excavations and
gloomy tunnels; they were what one literary combatant, Henri Barbusse, called a "troglodyte world."[174] The descriptions in Barbusse's war
novel *Le Feu*, published in 1916, were drawn directly from Émile Zola's
brutally realistic 1885 account in *Germinal* of a disaster in a northern
French mine.[175] Fighters on both sides frequently spoke of the journey
to the front as being like going underground to live, fight, and often die.
H. M. Tomlinson, the journalist, wrote: "An army had become, for the
first time in history, a continuous ditch of hidden men."[176] For another
soldier, the battlefield was a "country deserted. No sign of humanity—a
dead land. And yet thousands of men were there, like rabbits concealed."[177]
On the battlefields, "thousands [were] huddling nigh," Blunden wrote.
"The scarped holes hid not stoats but men."[178]

From the other side of the line, Ernst Jünger's writing similarly
presents the war as creating a hellish, Hades-like, underground existence. It was a "subterranean war" fought in a world in which "we killed
each other out of sight."[179] These descriptions evoke a zone exactly like
the one in Auden's early poems filled with bleak landscapes, ruins,
abandoned mines, and slaughtered heroes.[180] This is the atmosphere
that Isherwood called up too when, in *Lions and Shadows,* he wrote
about the "abandoned tin-mines" around St. Michael's Mount in
Cornwall: the "bare hillside was pitted with them; they looked like
shell-craters, surrounded with barbed wire."[181] By the time Auden was
writing in the 1920s, mines and modern battlefields had become imaginatively interchangeable.

Using this imagery, Auden's accounts of miners become a semiconscious way of writing about soldiers and war. Mines were, and are, often
extremely dangerous places: pits were already easy to associate with
death and the underworld. But the relationship between mining and

modern war added an extra, and urgent, new dimension to this age-old linkage. The word "mine" joins together the excavation of minerals and military weaponry. A mine is a place, but it is also an object. As the sociologist Lewis Mumford once said, sounding Audenesque, "taking mining regions as a whole, they are the very image of backwardness, isolation, raw animosities and lethal struggles."[182]

It is as if, when Auden walked alone in the Pennines, he were like one of the millions of bereaved who visited the sacred grounds of First World War battlefields throughout the 1920s in search of the locations where their loved ones had died. As Auden played on the symbolic interrelationship between trenches and mines, the latter became for him places of eerily modern death, places where the voices of vanished men linger. In "The Old Colliery," for example, an "iron wheel hangs | Above the shaft | Rusty and broken | Where once men laughed."[183] In "The Miner's Wife," a "young man white and pale" informs a woman of bad news, like one of those young messengers who at front doors handed over the fatal telegram from the War Office.[184]

"The Tarn," a poem that describes two boys bathing naked, mixes the themes of eroticism and war. According to Paul Fussell, "Watching men (usually 'one's own' men) bathing naked becomes a set-piece scene in almost every memory of the war."[185] In "The Tarn," Auden camouflages and relocates the naked bathing topos. His speaker describes having seen two naked boys "splendid of limb" bathing in the "bottomless" tarn, in the presence of a stonechat that twitters like a "ghost asking to be let out of Heaven." They have since vanished, and "Now | The place seems haunted by their laughing voices."[186] What could have been a straightforward poem about an erotic encounter has become, instead, a fantasy of desire and death in a "haunted" landscape of spirits.

Since Auden did not discover Wilfred Owen's work until later in 1926, he would not have known Owen's poem "Miners" when he began writing these poems about desolated landscapes. But Owen's poem, prompted by news of an explosion at a Halmer End, Staffordshire, mine on 12 January 1918 that killed 140 men and boys, draws on the same equations between mining and war. In "Miners," Owen's placid speaker listens to the "whispering" of burning coal in his hearth. Expecting to hear sounds that evoke the prehistorical ages when the coal was formed from carbonized vegetation, he hears instead the coals "murmuring of their mine, | And moans down there | Of boys that slept wry sleep." These sounds lead him to move mentally from mines to trenches. It is no journey at all: "I thought of all that worked dark pits | Of war, and died | Digging the rock where Death reputes | Peace lies indeed." This linkage established, the speaker (implied to be a soldier on leave) begins to talk of himself and the miners as a single group, identified by a collective "we." By the end of the Owen poem, soldiers and miners have become a kind of macabre mineral deposit in the earth: coming centuries "will not dream of us poor lads, | Lost in the ground."[187] After writing "Miners," Owen told his mother in a letter that he had composed "a poem on the Colliery Disaster: but I get mixed up with the War at the end. It is short, but oh! sour!"[188]

Owen is not the only English war poet who evoked the atmosphere of the mine in descriptions of the trenches. Sassoon, in "The Rear-Guard," writes about how a soldier, like a miner, "Groping along the tunnel, step by step, | . . . winked his prying torch with patching glare | From side to side, and sniffed the unwholesome air." In the same poem, he describes "a shafted stair | To the dazed, muttering creatures underground."[189] Elsewhere Sassoon evokes the darkness and danger of the largely underground world in which he and his comrades lived. On a number of occasions, he refers to them as being in a "pit," as he does in the poem "Remorse": "Lost in the swamp and welter of the pit, | He flounders off the duck-boards."[190]

Everything is now old or dead in the young Auden's northern world: a traction engine, for instance, lies, suggesting to a reader a corpse or the husk of a wrecked tank in no-man's-land, "unsheltered, undesired" and is only "Companioned by a boot heel, and an old cart-wheel, | In thistles attired."[191] A building with a chimney has "rotten" rafters and "mighty bulwarks shattered." It stands "Mute and lonely" like "a stark figure in the land."[192] "Allendale," a town in the North Pennines, is similarly a ruin:

> The smelting-mill stack is crumbling, no smoke is alive there,
> Down in the valley the furnace no lead ore of worth burns;
> Now tombs of decaying industries, not to survive here
>   Many more earth-turns.[193]

One of the most noticeable features in these lines are the words and phrases wrought with odd, Hardyesque locutions, such as "earth-turns," and repeated negations: "no smoke is alive . . . no lead ore . . . burns . . . tombs of decaying industries, not to survive." From here, it is only a short step to the danger-freighted, past-obsessed, feud-riven, entropic world of Auden's first canonical poems, the world, for instance, of the northern charade *Paid on Both Sides,* which he wrote mainly in 1928.[194] This is a world always shadowed by ambushes, disasters, and the "watch-fires of a stronger army," a world where there is "no news but the new death."[195] On Auden's northern battlefields, there is an extreme economic, emotional, and linguistic harshness: "Life stripped to girders, monochrome."[196] And the whole landscape is animated by mysterious "Sounds of conclusive war."[197]

For Auden, the departure of his father correlated with the perceived loss during the war of something deep within English culture, a loss that his poetry would explore at length.[198] In some lines from "Letter to Lord Byron," Auden expresses this loss in terms of the death of a mythic icon of English national pride, John Bull: "his acres of self-confidence for sale; | . . . [he] passed away at Ypres and Passchendaele."[199] Auden's enigmatic minescapes are places where ruin has set in after authoritative, competent men have been destroyed. The beautiful but disfigured and ghostly landscape of the Pennines becomes not only a contemporary war zone but also a representation of England's declining industrial might. Feeling the weight of the nation's fraught history, Auden's poetry forges deep imaginative links between his father's wartime absence and mines, between warfare and mines, between mines and the entropic condition of England.[200]

These links expressed a personal anguish; but they were also a social vision—a fundamentally patriarchal one—of a country in which the absence of "strong," capable men has generated disorder, confusion, and danger. Personal feelings concerned with Auden's "lost father" are present in these poems, but their full meaning includes a public, social component. For all the originality of some of his scenery, Auden was still writing from deep within a conservative literary tradition in which the rural landscape was associated far more closely than English cities with English national identity. The dangerous, ramshackle mine workings, abandoned or going to ruin, and the vast, deserted moors in his poems are dramatizations of the landscape of his own psyche. But they are also symbolic accounts of a nation in crisis because of social losses and failures. Auden's youthful poems suggest a finite and uncertain future for a huge empire and industrial culture that has hollowed itself out—both in terms of raw materials and of ideology.

Yet although Auden's poems about mines and deserted, battlefield-like moors and about the rural world offer symbolic representations of England and Englishness, they do not focus on the visible presence of the state. They are not about monarchs, statues, magnificent buildings, sacred national institutions, or hallowed tombs or, indeed, traditionally beautiful landscapes. Rather, they reach into a sphere far beyond the tangible manifestations of the modern, imperial, and quasi-democratic nation, probing instead the extra-political world for spectral, uncanny symbols of England's spiritual condition.

By 1936, in "Letter to Lord Byron," Auden was openly criticizing the boosterish optimism that claimed technology would solve all of humanity's problems. To people in the North of England, he insisted, this was a lie. There, the truth was laid bare. There, what Ted Hughes would later call the "national ghost" is visible. When Auden made his assertion, he described the North in words that sum up a whole era of his own writing, mixing class struggle and industrial conflict with the wounds of modern war:

> There on the old historic battlefield,
>   The cold ferocity of human wills,
> The scars of struggle are as yet unhealed.[201]

In the early autumn of 1925, soon after Auden arrived at Oxford as an undergraduate, birds began to die in his poems. In "Frost," which was written in late 1925 or early 1926 when Auden was just eighteen years old, he reproaches "us" for being complacent "in our delight" over pretty winter scenes.

> The wind that blew the clouds away so silently
> Has gone, leaving nothing but bright stars and the frost
> These and a half moon wandering about the sky
> Bewildered like a market-woman tired and lost.
>
> Tomorrow there'll be the beacon glittering beyond
> The elms, and icicles to snap off from the roof
> For us too, skating then perhaps on Winster Pond
> If boys snowballing are not beautiful enough.

We do not notice every thing in our delight
The frozen buzzard caught upon the mill-hatch bars
Forget, what the farm dogs do not, this starry night
All who must walk the lanes of darkness blind to stars[202]

"Frost" is set on a clear winter night in a house in countryside otherwise full of "nothing but bright stars and the frost." Secure, warm, well fed, Auden's boyish speaker imagines in chastely exciting detail the activities that the following day will bring. The beautiful sight of "boys snowballing" is winsome and erotic at the same time. The word "delight" in the last stanza reminds the reader that, although Auden is already intellectually robust as well as poetically very skilled, in 1925 he is still a young, enthusiastic person. "Frost" begins as an amazingly innocent, almost sappy poem—the intense and cloistered family life of the Audens had placed this writer's imagination in an enclave that protected him against cynicism.

But the poem darkens as it ends, turning in a new direction in the final stanza. Inside our snug, cheery homes, Auden writes, "we do not notice every thing." He gives one vivid example of this indifference: the bedraggled corpse of a buzzard "caught upon the mill-hatch bars."[203] Another example is far harder to visualize precisely: we forget "what the farm dogs do not, this starry night | All who must walk the lanes of darkness blind to stars." Here, there is a palpable beauty in the vagueness of these lines. Auden might have had in mind one of the aimless legion of disabled or shell-shocked unemployed war veterans, many of them missing a limb, or disfigured, hobbling around the country in the 1920s as tramps.

The shadowy vagrant out there in "Frost," who nightly "walk[s] the lanes of darkness," might be "blind" to the beauty of the winter stars because of cold, hunger, and alienation. For the "soul grown strange in France," to use another of Blunden's phrases, postwar England was hardly a happy place.[204] Blunden writes in one poem about an ex-serviceman back in England: "still you wander muttering on | Over the shades of shadows gone."[205] Or, as the historian Graham Wootton put it, the "land for heroes turned out to be a land in which heroes were selling bootlaces and matches, going with their families into the workhouse and tramping the heedless countryside in vain search of work."[206]

"Frost" hinges on a simple contrast between the either literally or figuratively blind tramp in the darkness and healthy people like "us," who "do not notice." The idea is that "we," in contrast to the tramp, although we can see, are usually morally blind: we are unable, because of spiritual rather than physical shortcomings, to look into the darkness that lies beyond our well-illuminated little province of self-concern. We cannot glimpse, or care about, the suffering animals and unknown people hidden in the folds of the night. And unknown people *are* there in "the lanes of darkness." The poem seems clumsy at first (as Hardy's often do too) as well as innocent, but Auden's language is in fact extremely subtle. Although he presents the farm dogs as "not" doing something, he really offers a double negative: "We . . . Forget, what the farm dogs do not." They *are* doing something that Auden's poem only implies: they register ominous noises they have heard and, in accord with the dictates of their neural wiring and their training, are tensed for further clues about a hidden presence in the darkness. The poem's speaker must have become aware of this as he hears the dogs' barks or growls at strange sounds of movement in the night air. He is listening to the dogs listening.

The anonymous figure of a night traveler in the "lanes of darkness," much like the speaker in "California," gestures toward what will become another of the crucial scenarios in Auden's poetry: a person looking into, or walking through, the night. Again and again, Auden's later poems characterize the poet as someone who stares into or moves into a darkened world. It is Auden's version of the classical *neukeia*, the hero's orphic journey through the shadows of the underworld as a test of endurance and courage, and it stands as one of his most potent and deeply felt emblems of poetic making.[207]

It is not surprising that the blind tramp stumbling through the darkness at the end of "Frost" acts as a figure for the poet. A reader thinking about a blind, wandering character remembers Homer, the archetypal sightless, homeless bard about whom next to nothing is known. Of course, "Frost" does not literally suggest that the tramp in the darkness is Homer or even a poet. But the faceless, alluring, sinister figure out there somewhere, in a darkness as complete as the darkness in a mine, is a composite presence, standing not only for the poet's displaced self (independent and yet ostracized) but also for a paternal figure such as Odysseus apparently far from home and lost (like Auden's father) to a war. That shadowy presence is the stimulus to the poem's visionary climax.

It is hard to fathom how simple joyfulness coexists with the burden of psychic scars—but "Frost" shows that it does. The real poetic countryside, according to the poem, is not found in the bright, picturesquely sunlit, daytime jollity of skating and snowballing but rather in the realm of the night, of loss, death, fear, and other themes that can best, or can only, be broached in symbolic form. "Frost" fully discloses what Auden's conventional but nonetheless inspired beginnings as a writer had been struggling to achieve: using lyric symbols, this young poet has taught himself to sense the presence of the country's ghosts.

3   THE RHINO AND THE CHILD
ABJECT MODERNISM, 1925–1927

As in dreams so also in poetry.

—ROBERT GRAVES (1925)

IN RETROSPECT. T. S. ELIOT UNDERSTOOD THAT "only from about the year 1926 did the features of the post-war world begin clearly to emerge—and not only in the sphere of politics."[1] As the cultural field in England reshaped itself as a result of underlying economic and political forces, the period between late 1925 and 1927 saw a shift of literary paradigms, a reorientation within a situation of, to use Eliot's phrase again, "enforced insularity." In the world of poetry composed in England in the mid-1920s, Eliot and Auden are the literary equivalents of the birds that are Auden's indicator species in the landscape. But literary history is not beautiful, and they did not move in perfect synchronization. In fact, for a time, they even seemed to be moving in opposite directions.

Around the time when Auden went up to Oxford in 1925, Eliot was rapidly becoming a figure of intense interest and rumor in artistic circles. But for a while after the bomb of *The Waste Land* detonated in 1922, Auden, though he read some contemporary poets intensively, seemed to know little or nothing about the work of the man who would soon become not only his publisher but one of his main aesthetic reference points. It was only in the pivotal year of 1926 that Auden read *The Waste Land* and understood the challenge it put to his own work. For a time, as he grappled with the changes Eliot had wrought in his imagination, Auden set aside his rural and industrial scenery with its evocative atmosphere of violence and mystery. Instead, as an Oxford undergraduate Auden self-consciously struggled to make himself "modern," a term that evoked for him not only the poetry of Eliot but also that of W. B. Yeats and the fashionable aristocratic trio of Edith, Osbert, and Sacheverell Sitwell, poets, authors, and provocateurs, who produced six volumes of their *Wheels* anthology between 1916 and 1921. (The 1919 edition, dedicated to the war poet Wilfred Owen, who had been killed months earlier, printed seven of Owen's poems and was the first major public showing of his work.)

Changes in Auden's writing did not happen linearly or all at once. After arriving in Oxford, he continued trying to write poems about the countryside and ruined industrial sites. In 1926, for example, he composed "'Lead's the Best'," his most ambitious poem to date. He then almost immediately encountered, and was temporarily overwhelmed by, Eliot's internationalist, modernist style—ironically, just at the moment when Eliot himself was abandoning that mode. Auden eventually shakily recovered his "English" poetic equilibrium in 1927, when he wrote the poem "I chose this lean country." But paradoxically his own slow emergence at Oxford as one of the leading voices of Eliot's "definitely post-war generation" was marked by a deep sense of failure and crisis. For much of his life, Auden valued dreams and even, on occasion, "visions" as a source of insight and creative inspiration.[2] As is so often the case with this extraordinarily intelligent writer, in 1927, revelation and reorientation of his poetic path came to him through a dream.

Auden's artistic history in the middle part of the decade maps onto one of the century's most consequential transitions in English literary history: the rapid flood and then ebbing of poetic modernism, followed by the incoming tide of more traditional, constrained, and nationally specific styles. Although Auden projected to some contemporaries an aura of powerful independence, the new stage in his poetry emerged out of personal confusion, even out of misery and vulnerability. English cultural norms for men of all classes in the 1920s were narrow and repressive, and it is against this background that Auden's reactions can best be understood. These years saw Auden struggling with his parents, losing direction as a poet, and failing to cope with the highly stratified world of Oxford society. Are there records of any other major English-language poet from any era whom friends at the time so often saw weeping? It happened with Auden in Oxford. The first phase in his career, up until 1930 or so, was about suffering, individual and social. And the period from 1925 to 1927 was its chaotic, disorienting core.

Isherwood once explained that when Auden began writing, he had "forebodings of catastrophe in England" and that he "chose an uncompromising, obscure way of voicing his intuitions and prophecies."[3] The Romantic notion of the poet representing a culture's zeitgeist may seem obsolete. But which writer does not harbor, somewhere inside, a fantasy of being able to speak on behalf of a group of some kind, of finding a genuine way to say "we"? And which reader of poetry does not search for a poet capable of using lyric language to articulate community? Understanding the true dimensions of Auden's poetry of forebodings, intuitions, and prophecies means situating them within a broader, more-than-personal story about fear, confusion, loss, and violence. That is to say, Auden's story, for all its idiosyncrasy, also offers itself as a parable about twentieth-century English history.

For a few months after Auden started as an undergraduate at Oxford in the autumn of 1925, he studied natural science (his father's degree subject at Cambridge), reading academic work about plants, animals, and physical processes, some of which he knew about at first hand from his rural childhood.[4] During this time, he lived as a poet largely off the emotional and scenic funds he had accumulated in the worlds of Norfolk, the Lake District, and the North Pennines, composing poems about the countryside and its inhabitants. For instance, in the deliberately threadbare lyric "The Carter's Funeral," which Auden wrote in the grandiose surroundings of the Junior Common Room at Christ Church during his first term at university, he described the endpoint of a rustic life: "Sixty odd years of poaching and drink | And rain-sodden waggons with scarcely a friend." When the carter is buried:

> Little enough stays musing upon
> The passing of One of the Masters of things;
> Only a bird looks peak-faced thereon
> Looks and sings.[5]

"The Carter's Funeral" is not only an elegy for a rather unreal-sounding rustic and not merely a lament for a rural world from which Auden was now temporarily separated in his new, socially exclusive academic setting. It is also a threnody for the subject matter out of which he had until now felt that he could make poetry. The poem says that in the imposing purlieus of Christ Church, almost no one "muses" on the lives or deaths of uncouth peasants in the countryside, except for the solitary "peak-faced" bird who is the poet's surrogate and who with only a smidgen of confidence and steadfastness "Looks and sings."

"The Carter's Funeral" suggests Auden's doubts about his ability in metropolitan Oxford to remain connected to his subject matter and scenery in the countryside. The preposition "on," appearing twice in these lines (in the rhyme of "upon" and "thereon," with near echoes as well in "One" and "Only"), describes merely a spatial relation and not a temporal continuity. The bird cannot keep "on" singing forever about these things; it only "thereon | Looks." By following "thereon" with "Looks," Auden signals, across the line break, the noun "onlooker," implying the bird's—and by extension his own—essential indifference to the scene. They are both just onlookers. The bird, notably unidentified by species, is not an involved participant like the "Sexton" who "has stamped down the loam" and "blows on his fingers" or the "Parson" who "turns to his home."[6] Rather, it functions as a Hardyesque solitary observer and elegist.

The implication is that Auden too is looking at this world from the outside, without any profound involvement in the life and death chronicled in his poem. He was by now sufficiently self-aware and well-enough "versed in country things" to believe, and to compel his readers to believe, that this "peak-faced" bird is just singing, not weeping over the death of a man. And, deep down, in Oxford, so was the undergraduate Auden.

Auden continued to write "raw provincial" poems in his first year at Christ Church; they linger on in this period, like the last examples of a dying species wandering aimlessly through a changed ecosystem.[7] In one of Oxford's wealthiest colleges, surrounded by dully gleaming aristocrats and winsome, upper-class aesthetes, as well as spectacular sportsmen and other variants of the "hearty," Auden went on nostalgically imagining himself back in rural landscapes. In "Rain," he describes "This careless striding through the clinging grass" during a storm, the future prospect of "sunshine on the weir's dull dreamless roar," and the temporary peace of the body after an orgasm:

> for this brief hour or so
> I am content, unthinking and aglow.

Made one with horses and with workmen, all
Who seek for shelter by a dripping wall
Or labour in the fields with mist and cloud
And slant rain hiding them as in a shroud.[8]

But the unity with this better world will last only "for this brief hour or so." The country scene is starting to be obscured "as in a shroud," not only because it suddenly seems, historically speaking, a dead or moribund world but also because, at Oxford, Auden as a poet is losing contact with it, like someone standing at a ship's rail and watching the shoreline recede. His early work at college includes other rural poems, reminiscent of Blunden, Hardy, and Thomas, about country railway stations, ploughing teams, and cuckoos singing in the trees.[9] But "The Carter's Funeral" and "Rain" obliquely acknowledge that Auden's provincial poetry is coming to a crisis point.

During his first year at Oxford, Auden's most searching nonmetropolitan poem was "'Lead's the Best'," composed in the spring of 1926.[10] When he was writing it, he was contemplating changing his field of study from natural science to politics, philosophy, and economics (PPE), perhaps because of the country's political crisis that led up to the General Strike in May of that year. (Winston Churchill, the Chancellor of the Exchequer, wanted to have machine guns, tanks, and armored cars on the streets during the General Strike as if it were simply a new battlefront.) Indeed, as Auden composed "'Lead's the Best'," he was having informal tutorials in this new academic subject with the Christ Church economist Roy Harrod.[11]

Eventually, at the end of his first year, Auden decided to switch not to PPE but to English literature. However, in "'Lead's the Best'," he made an ambitious attempt to represent poetically the workings of a national economy and to grasp imaginatively what cannot be understood in purely rational terms: a massive economic system that operates, as Marx said of history, "behind men's backs" and outside full comprehension or control.[12]

Here is the opening of the poem, where the poem's speaker talks to old miners in a northern inn. When interlocutors have spoken in Auden's poems before this (if they did), they have been folkloric figures or middle-class characters. In the 1920s, very few young people attended university at all, and only a fraction of a percentage of those who did studied at a college as socially rarefied as Christ Church. Another sign of the poem's broadened scope is visible in the fact that this is the first time voices unmistakably marked as working-class enter Auden's poetry in a (relatively) unmediated way:

> The fells sweep upward to drag down the sun
> Those great rocks shadowing a weary land
> And quiet stone hamlets huddled at their feet;
> No footstep loiters in the darkening road
> But light streams out from inn doors left ajar,
> And with it voices quavering and slow.
> "I worked at Threlkeld granite quarry once,
> Then coal at Wigan for a year, then back
> To lead, for lead's the best"—
>   —"No, sir, not now,
> They only keep a heading open still
> At Cashwell"—
>   —"Yes, the ladder broke and took him
> Just like a pudding he was when they found him"—
> "Rich? Why, at Greenearth Side the west vein showed
> Ten feet of ore from cheek to cheek, so clean
> There weren't no dressing it"—[13]

The poem is a remarkable work for a nineteen-year-old. Filled with echoes of Hardy and Thomas (the use of direct speech to record a conversation with the poem's speaker is redolent of both writers, as it is of Sassoon) and crammed with real but obscure place-names, it is Auden's longest work to date: sixty-nine lines of wide-ranging blank verse. It has, partly for this reason, a summative quality. But the poem also marks the point at which, like a firework dying spectacularly at its peak, Auden's rural themes, already seen attenuating in poems such as "The Carter's Funeral," temporarily vanish.

At the time when Auden wrote the poem in 1926, Britain's General Strike, centering on disputes about wages and conditions for miners, lay no more than two months ahead. But long-running struggles in the declining coal industry meant that, before the strike, mining and mine workers were already controversial in Oxford, as everywhere else in the country. On 29 January 1926, the miners' leader A. J. Cook spoke, with a special police guard, at a noisy meeting in the city center. Barracked and threatened by a crowd of students, he stood his ground, insisting that "There is not a University undergraduate who could endure [the miners'] conditions for a week."[14] No one, especially in the densely populated world of an Oxford college, escaped knowledge of the intensifying class conflict.

One undergraduate in Oxford at the same time as Auden wrote later that as "a General Strike became increasingly likely, many [in the university] became perturbed at the possibility of violent strife."[15] Auden had several close Oxford friends who were politically committed on the left: for example, his Christ Church friend David Ayerst, who gave Auden the insightful nickname of "The Child." Ayerst was active as the chair of the University Labour Club. Both Richard Crossman, at New College reading Classics, and Tom Driberg, at Christ Church reading the same subject, were similarly involved with politics (as well as sex, parties, and, in Crossman's case, intensive academic study).[16] Auden met both of them in the spring of 1926, and it is difficult to imagine that he did not talk about politics with either one or with other Oxford friends.

Auden must have been at least half aware that, in his private world of emptied pits and defunct machinery, there was a rich seam of symbolism about the nation's traumatic industrial past and present. Even if he wrote "'Lead's the Best'" alone, like a wan hermit in his room in Christ Church's Meadow Building with the curtains drawn, Auden let in a strong political valence to this story about exhausted mines and the "afterglow of an old country's greatness" (409).

As the poem begins, the unidentified speaker (whose motivations we never know with certainty) notices the sun begin to set over a barren moor somewhere in the North Pennines. He turns back from the stark, open countryside where he has been wandering to one of the "quiet stone hamlets huddled" at the foot of the fells. There, in taverns, he talks about the mining activities that once took place all over the area. The earth's mineral riches have been almost used up so that there is little work left. The men he meets converse with him about mining "in voices quavering and slow." No one young gravitates toward a mine now except this presumably youthful, tourist-like inquirer with his unexplained air of loneliness. One man, responding to a question from the middle-class outsider about whether there is much lead mining still going on, says, "No, sir, not now, | They only keep a heading open still at Cashwell" (407).[17]

The speaker-listener leaves the inn: "steps closed the door | And stopped their mouths." The phrase almost suggests that what he has learned from these interlocutors is too much to bear and he needs to "stop their mouths." He retreats, as so many Frost- and Thomas-derived wandering protagonists in Auden's early poems do, to reflect alone, outside the social collective symbolized by the inn. Borrowing a phrase from *The Tempest,* the speaker ponders how the "last of generations | Who 'did their business in the veins of th' earth'" were integrated into a larger social whole, and he reflects on what the decline of mining means for an English identity (408).[18]

References to the sinking "sun" and the "great rocks shadowing" in-augurate a cycle of darkness and light, obscurity and illumination, that runs throughout the poem: we see it in the contrast of the "darkening road" and the "light" that "streams out from the inn doors" or the juxtaposition of "torchlight and the glare of blazing homes" and afterward the "torrent, darkness, and the rain" (407–408). Moreover, the dragging down of the sun in the first line not only establishes a chain of images of obscurity and illumination, actual, and figurative. It also broaches another of the poem's themes: sunset, understood literally as the time of day when the poem takes place and poetically as the end of both a historical era and, more covertly, a phase in Auden's work.

Remembering an anecdote about a miner who was accidentally squashed "Just like a pudding," the speaker in the gathering darkness thinks about the wealth generated by lead mining. That wealth has placed "a roof on noble Gothic minsters | For the glory of God" and bought "Some damask scarf or silken stomacher | To make a woman's body beautiful" (408). The attempt to work out what lead is *for* and not just where it comes *from* is an ambitious advance from Auden's previous poems. Here he integrates lead mining within a network of disparate social practices, which include the exchange and consumption of commodities, linking miners, managers, ecclesiastics, armies, thieves, and international rivals in an economic web of dependency and exploitation.[19] Auden's first poem with working-class voices is also his first attempt not just to find evocative symbols of the nation but to "see" it as a multifaceted totality.

When Auden refers to the "great rocks shadowing a weary land | And quiet stone hamlets huddled at their feet" at the beginning of the poem, these descriptions of the landscape also suggest the way in which localized subjects (such as "quiet stone hamlets") are set within a much larger context of "great rocks shadowing." Similarly, the place of the mines and "barren farms | Up wind-swept northern dales" is contextualized by the "shadowing" immensities of metropolitan wealth and style as well as by the crusade-like "adventure" of knights who (in a detail that suggests death on a battlefield) "died where there was none to bury them" (408). Mining, with its world of subterranean connections, its pathways and circuits not visible on the surface, becomes a metaphoric system for trying to imagine the labyrinthine immensity of the vast, differentiated capitalist economy Britain had become by 1926. The hamlet overshadowed by great rocks is a figure for the way in which the ostensible subject matter of "'Lead's the Best'," and Auden's best poetry more broadly, is shadowed by something larger.

It is striking that Auden should try to expand his grasp of the country, or of the empire (remember the details about the "Knights . . . in far desert lands"), by thinking in terms of economic relations between mines and minsters, wealth and wars. From this point of view, the allusion Auden makes in "'Lead's the Best'" to *The Tempest* (a crucial play for him throughout his life) is vital. The speaker thinks about how the people he has met are "the last of generations | Who 'did their business in the veins of th' earth'" (408). That quoted phrase is Prospero's as he berates his fairy servant Ariel for being reluctant to carry out tasks assigned.[20] The speaker's Shakespearean quotation evinces sympathy for the miners who work underground. But it also suggests that the poem aspires to know the whole of the economic system in which mining is involved in the same way that Prospero seems to know about whatever is going on anywhere on "the isle." It might even hint that a poet-magician's ambition could be not just to see everything but also—at the level of fantasy at least—to control it.

For now, though, that possibility of control lies beyond reach. In "'Lead's the Best'," Auden's ideas about the nation return repeatedly to perceptions of violence and injustice. The market in which lead becomes a commodity is not a just one, guided by a benign, hidden hand. Rather, it is exploitative, regulated neither by reason nor by need. This understanding of the market as an anarchic, irrational space was becoming a fashionable view among economists themselves, as Auden probably learned from Harrod, who was a protégé of John Maynard Keynes. In the 1920s, when Auden was taking tutorials with him, Harrod was doing neo-Keynesian work on aggregate demand and fluctuations in economic growth.[21]

Near its end, "'Lead's the Best'" reverts to a less conceptual and more naturalistic key:

> Here speak the last of them, soon heard no more
> Than sound of clarinets in country churches;
> Turf covers up the huge stone heaps, green ferns
> The dark holes opening into hollow hills
> Where water drips like voices from the dead.
> A pile of stone beside the stream is all
> Left of the "Shop" where miners slept at nights;
> (Within, tired crowded sleepers, far from home;
> Without, the torrent, darkness, and the rain);
> Nor will they start again in early dawns
> With bags like pillows slung across their shoulders
> And watched by children enviously, who wish
> Themselves grown-up to climb like that, for whom
> Soon after it was all the other way;
> Each wished himself a child again to have
> More hours to sleep in. (408)[22]

From the evidence of a "pile of stone beside the stream," the speaker manages to reconstruct the "Shop" where the "miners slept at nights." He imagines how, as they set out again for the mine in the early mornings, they were "watched by children enviously, who wish | Themselves grown-up to climb like that." But, since generations grimly succeed one another in the mine, each of those envious children soon "wished himself a child again to have | More hours to sleep in."

The idea of the sleeping child marks another moment of transition, this time to the poem's final section, beautifully handled by Auden, as the lines pass from the notion of a boy asleep to a figure from a child's fairy story, a "two-headed giant slain by Jack" who lies on his back, like a vast, supernatural version of a sleeping child, "for years in the combe-bottom." ("The combe" strongly evokes Edward Thomas's 1914 poem with that title.) Auden then shifts to an image of children playing in the bleached and crumbling skeleton of the double-headed giant:

> only children visited the spot to play
> At hide-and-seek in the dark, cavernous skulls
> Or gather berries from the thorns which hid
> The arched ribs crumbling in the grass. (409)

Auden's fantasy makes a point about the national imaginary. The dead giant is a mythic emblem of a vital national strength that has been laid low. It is because the seams of lead have petered out and because the "memory fades" of the heroic miners that the symbolic wealth (represented by the giant), as well as the material power of the nation, begin to dwindle, like "arched ribs crumbling in the grass." A world without these mine workers is also a world without vivid, lively symbols of Englishness. The two-headed giant's bones are moribund in "the combe-bottom," and, correspondingly, the archetypal English peasant Hodge, celebrated by Jefferies and Thomas and so many others, is also now corrupted. He becomes a tawdry figure with disagreeably perverse ("continental") tastes:

> Hodge himself becomes a sottish bawd
> Who takes his city vices secondhand
> And grins, if he hears Paris mentioned.[23]

What remains in this aftermath, once the personifications of a true England have vanished or gone to seed, is only "wind-sough over barren pastures | The bleak philosophy of Northern ridges" (409).

"'Lead's the Best'" takes place as the sun goes down: having appeared and disappeared in line 1 of the poem, the sun reappears and disappears too in the poem's final lines, as the speaker announces that all the intervening ideas and scenes have been nothing but "Harsh afterglow of an old country's greatness | Themes for a poet's pretty sunset thoughts" (409). Those themes that provide "pretty sunset thoughts" in "'Lead's the Best'" are joined to the "Harsh afterglow of an old country's greatness" ("afterglow" suggests the diffused light characteristic of the minutes after sunset). As Auden sits in Christ Church and recollects his experiences in the Pennines, his "sunset" theme describes how organically connected with the fate and identity of England as a whole are his landscapes of heroic miners—workers who now, like vanishing creatures, in a "final valley went to ground."[24]

Auden later claimed that political and existential uncertainties never intruded on his insular world at Oxford in the 1920s, any more than the war had on his life at St. Edmund's: "Ah! Those twenties before I was twenty, | When the news never gave one the glooms."[25] He told an interviewer later, "The city as such didn't affect us in any way. We were totally self-centered."[26] But this was at best only superficially true; his feeling for injustice was already alive. For example, in around 1926 or 1927, he joined a group of students who were picketing an Oxford restaurant that had refused to serve an Indian customer.[27] Even if, as Auden said, he never opened a newspaper at Christ Church (a statement that he seems unlikely to have meant literally), the contemporaneous political reverberations from the coal-mining industry in Britain at the time he was writing "'Lead's the Best'" were powerful enough to have breached the walls of an Oxford college.[28]

Compounding the effects of industrial conflict, the Great War continued to live in the minds of Auden's generation in the mid-1920s. Isherwood's account in *Lions and Shadows* makes this clear. There, he describes how the "young writers of the middle 'twenties were all suffering, more or less subconsciously, from a feeling of shame that we hadn't been old enough to take part in the European war."[29] Memories about the war years were made more complex for Isherwood and others by the manner in which the war became a kind of emotional black hole into which many other subjects, not necessarily related to it on a logical level, were inexorably dragged. With its mythic status, the war became for young writers like Auden and Isherwood a way of camouflaging, or alluding indirectly to, other subjects: class, for example, or political allegiance or, in the ritual ambushes carried out by undergraduate hearties on the precious aesthetes of Oxford, issues of belonging and conformity. To Auden and his friends, even sex was connected—in "Letter to Lord Byron," he would indicate that the impact of the war did register in his personal experience at Oxford. In that poem, he uses rhyme to link postwar styles of "Amor" (Love) in his "debauched, eccentric generation" to having grown up with "fathers at the War":

> We were the tail, a sort of poor relation
> To that debauched, eccentric generation
> That grew up with their fathers at the War,
> And made new glosses on the noun Amor.[30]

For many writers in the postwar period, social conflict in Britain was conceptualized as a war between classes. At the center of these struggles were the miners, around whom Auden focused his private poetic obsessions. The General Strike began in the late spring of 1926, when personnel across many sectors of the economy took industrial action to support colliery workers who had been locked out by mine owners. Isherwood felt that, during the period of the strike, "'war' was in the air: one heard it in the boisterous defiant laughter of the amateur bus drivers, one glimpsed it in the alert sexual glances of the women."[31] During the strike, Henry Yorke (who later wrote novels as "Henry Green"), then an Oxford undergraduate, met Siegfried Sassoon, decorated veteran of the Western Front, who reacted as if he was reliving postcombat exhaustion: "Siegfried spoke of the civil war wh. (he said) wd. begin, and then, sitting down on a tub in which a tree grew, laid his head against the tree, shut his eyes, and agonised in silence."[32]

Auden's Oxford friend Tom Driberg was arrested while working for the Communist Party during the General Strike, while another friend, probably Ayerst, arranged for Auden to drive a car in London for the Trades Union Congress (TUC).[33] (More undergraduates signed on as "special constables" for the government than in support of the unions.) Auden later recalled an incident when he was accused of betraying his own side (or class). He does not directly connect it with the moment at St. Edmund's, also occurring at a dining table, when he had been accused of wanting "the Huns to win," but his story from 1926 seems strongly evocative of the earlier episode: "One day, I had driven R. H. Tawney to his house in Mecklenburgh Square. It happened that a first cousin of mine, married to a stockbroker, lived a few doors away, so I paid a call. The three of us were just sitting down to lunch when her husband asked me if I had come up to London to be a Special Constable. 'No,' I said. 'I am driving a car for the T.U.C.' Whereupon, to my utter astonishment, he ordered me to leave his house. It had never occurred to me that anybody took the General Strike seriously."[34] The way Auden described the incident to Isherwood, around the time that it occurred, is more dramatic and less whimsical: "During the strike I worked for the TUC and have quarrelled bitterly with certain sections of the family in consequence, which is all to the good."[35]

The rhetoric around the General Strike often fed on, or reverted back to, the mood and language of the Great War. A decade earlier, in March 1916, Hubert Parry's choral arrangement of "Jerusalem," made from William Blake's opening lyric in *Milton: A Poem,* at the poet laureate Robert Bridges's suggestion, was premiered for a choir of 300 voices at a bellicose "Fight for Right" meeting at the Queen's Hall. (The scholar of mysticism Evelyn Underhill was one of the speakers at the same meeting, offering the audience that night "much practical exhortation."[36]) On 12 May 1926, Prime Minister Stanley Baldwin made a broadcast to the nation about the end of the General Strike and the vanquishing of the miners. After he finished speaking, the BBC played the wartime anthem "Jerusalem," as if to equate the miners' defeat with the vanquishing of a sinister national enemy and to evoke feelings of national pride and unity.

Isherwood felt that his own shame about having missed the war was mentally "suppressed by the strictest possible censorship" ("censorship" is itself a term with obvious wartime connotations) but that it persisted nonetheless.[37] In "Lions and Shadows," the unpublished novel that he began working on in 1923 and finished in 1925 (not the memoir published in 1938 with the same title), "the War is hardly mentioned."[38] Nonetheless it pervades the work, completed in the same year that he reencountered Auden, with whom he had lost touch after St. Edmund's. In Isherwood's novel, the war is "disguised" as the daunting prospect of the battle for survival that the young hero knows he will have to undergo when he enters "Rugtonstead," an English public school. Under the compulsion of his self-censorship, the war, Isherwood explained, "which could never under any circumstances be allowed to enter in its own shape, needed a symbol—a symbol round which I could build up my daydreams."[39] School was the symbol.

As Isherwood had done in "Lions and Shadows," Auden might claim to remain aloof or sheltered from feelings about the war (and everything else) in his poems. Nonetheless, the conflict, albeit disguised, still infiltrated work that at a manifest level seemed to have nothing to do with it. This happens, for example, with "'Lead's the Best'" in a historical vignette about a violent raid, after which "torn men lay, that clutched their wounds, | And bonnie forms face downward in the grass" (408). It happens also in "The Carter's Funeral," where the strange compound adjective "peak-faced" is attributed to a "bird."[40] The ghost of a military memory, in this poem about a hasty burial, is secreted in this small detail: the "peak-faced" creature is imagined like someone wearing a peaked military hat low on their forehead. And when the "Parson unvests," he takes off his religious regalia with a military-sounding phrase: "Duty done."

"Rugtonstead," Isherwood later came to understand, was an example of his own simultaneous displacement of, and obsession with, the war that had taken his father. He believed that Auden's "own personal variety of 'War'-fixation" had to do with his "feelings about the heroic Norse literature" of the sagas, which Dr. Auden had read to him as a child.[41] In 1926, when Isherwood told Auden that the saga world, with its "warriors, with their feuds, their practical jokes, their dark threats conveyed in puns and riddles and deliberate understatements," reminded him of the "boys at our preparatory school," Auden was "pleased with the idea."[42] Just as Isherwood displaced the war onto an "English public school," so he associated the Icelandic sagas and their chronicles of deadly intergenerational feuds with St. Edmund's in Surrey, the educational institution where he and Auden had spent most of the war years.

The loss of an "old country's greatness" is related to Auden's inability as an Oxford undergraduate to continue writing poems about the English countryside and lead mining. "'Lead's the Best'" was the last major poem Auden composed before he discovered T. S. Eliot's poetry. Strikingly, given the length of "'Lead's the Best'" and the prevalence of small animals in Auden's early work, the poem is also (with the exception of the "cattle" stolen by the Scots in the raid vignette that the speaker mentions in passing) a completely creatureless work, without even the white mice or canaries taken into mines because of their sensitivity to gas and hence known as "the tunnellers' friends."[43]

Around the time of writing the poem, Auden begged his Oxford friend A. S. T. Fisher to come and stay with him in Harborne during the Easter 1926 vacation and act as a peacekeeper, because "Family relations have been tres difficile."[44] During his visit at the start of April,

Fisher witnessed several explosions (between mother and son) and fits of tears (on Auden's part). When he wrote a bread-and-butter letter to Mrs. Auden afterward, in which he tried to make a case for her youngest son's ways, she responded darkly: "I do not know how much you know of his past life, but there has been much to cause his father and me real anxiety."[45]

Easter was always an important festival of transformation for Auden, even when, as at Oxford, he was not a practicing Christian, and it was at about this time that Hardy and Edward Thomas were displaced as his poetic models by a new literary reference point. As he put it, in the spring of 1926 T. S. Eliot won the "battle of Oxford" in his imagination.[46] The military metaphor is striking but not surprising. In the 1920s, a language of war-imbued violence and enigma pervaded much of Eliot's own writing as well as the reactions to his poems. For example, Eliot liked to envisage literary relations as a kind of desperate physical or psychic struggle. He called his early relation to the poet Jules Laforgue "a sort of possession by a stronger personality."[47] And he asserted in "The Metaphysical Poets" (1921) that the "poet must become more and more comprehensive, more allusive, more indirect, in order to force, to dislocate if necessary, language into his meaning."[48] Eliot's implication was that there was a salutary violence at the heart of authentic poetic language.

Many contemporary testimonies to the impact of reading *The Waste Land* in the 1920s are likewise filled with metaphors of force, aggression, and ferocity. Critics, such as Edmund Wilson, were immediately attuned to the poem's importance, which they saw as landing like a blow. For example, in a letter of 22 September 1922 to John Peale Bishop, Wilson called *The Waste Land* "the great knockout up to date."[49] And Ezra Pound told Eliot shortly after the poem was completed that he was "wracked by the seven jealousies."[50] The percussive, aggressive nature of frontline experience in the recently ended war echoed in the way that early readers, especially its sympathetic readers, experienced *The Waste Land* as a type of assault on their senses and aesthetics.

Auden too "fell" under the poem's overwhelming influence. He was apparently first introduced to Eliot's work by his friend Tom Driberg. Driberg knew the Sitwells, arranged for readings by them in Oxford, and wrote Sitwellian poetry himself—as Auden was soon doing too in the spring of 1926.[51] It was probably Driberg who led to a temporary expansion in Auden's literary range of reference, first sharing the Sit-wells' poetry with him and then Eliot's early work. And it says some-thing about how isolated Auden had been from smart poetry circles among his Oxford contemporaries that he came to the poem long after *The Waste Land* had become notorious among advanced undergradu-ates with literary tastes. Auden and Driberg read it together in early 1926 in the version printed three and a half years earlier in the first number of the *Criterion* in October 1922. Driberg remembered that they "read it, at first, with incredulous hilarity (the Mrs. Porter bit, for instance); read it, again and again, with growing awe."[52] Personally and poetically, the effect on Auden was marked. If his testimony in "Letter to Lord Byron" (1936) is to be believed, soon Auden "faced life" in a self-consciously modern, Eliotic, and Continental "double-breasted suit," strolling around Oxford's quadrangles with a copy of the medieval Italian St. Thomas Aquinas's works carefully positioned for maximum visibility under his arm. He claimed to be "mute" at the "verdict" of this periodical edited by an expatriate American with an overarching es-teem for Mediterranean cultures, and he parroted Eliot's "dogmatic words . . . 'Good poetry is classic and austere.'"[53]

However, Auden's poetic imitations of Eliot were neither classic nor austere. This is the opening (complete with fashionable, Eliotic epi-graph from Jacobean drama) of "Thomas Prologizes," written in April or early May of 1926:

> "Nay, an thou'lt mouth, I'll rant as well as thou."
> —*Hamlet*

> They are all gone upstairs into the world
> Of candlelight. The Prodigal is left
> Beneath to work his own salvation out,
> Helped by the sordes of the past which taught him
> Well how best to set his codpiece in order.
> Have I forgot young Desmond whom I met
> Behind the fives-courts every Sunday night?
> Or Isobel who with her leaping breasts
> Pursued me through a summer?[54]

A companion piece, "Thomas Epilogizes," written a month or two later, shows that Auden had also been reading Eliot's Sweeney poems:

The poodle has returned to her old vomit,
We to our model homes like crouched Ophelias,
Where Job squats awkwardly upon his ashpit,
Scraping himself with blunted occam razors,
He sharpened once to shave the Absolute.
A cold wind clutches at his scraggy knees.[55]

Other 1926 poems in this broken modernist mode include "Consequences" and "Cinders."[56]

On the basis of Eliot's poetry and his voluminous prose writings from the later 1920s through to his death in 1965, literary history has often construed him as a deeply conservative figure.[57] But to young readers such as Auden and Driberg in the mid-1920s, the poet in Eliot probably appeared otherwise. The literary historian Michael North points out that "A. L. Morton and other young communists like Edgell Rickword" were "thrilled by the 'strange and unexpected transitions'" in *The Waste Land* and viewed the poem as a "liberating experience." For these young readers, North writes, citing Morton, "Eliot was 'a standard around which certain forces of revolt gathered.'"[58]

There may have been other "revolutionary" undercurrents that appealed to Driberg and Auden too. Rumors and presumed mysteries about Eliot in the 1920s included suggestions about his sexuality.[59] (In January 1922, in a squib called "Sage Homme," Eliot's friend Pound described Eliot's poetry as "By the Uranian Muse begot." By the late nineteenth century, in a poetic context, "Uranian" had come to mean pederastic.[60]) The rumors circulated so intensively in London literary circles in part because Eliot's deep personal secretiveness opened a space for speculation, informed or uninformed.[61] He was not just fascinating to contemporaries like Virginia Woolf. He was also a figure of great mystery and interest for younger writers too. Gossip and speculations about him abounded; there were stories about drinking, madness, drugs, strange costumes, sex, and a tortured domestic life.[62] The satiric disdain for heterosexual union and for women evident in much of Eliot's work (the young man carbuncular and the typist in *The Waste Land*, for example), combined with stories about his marriage, probably contributed to a grapevine rumor that Eliot was homosexual. This may have added to the impact he had on Auden's and Driberg's imaginations.[63] Auden's poems in the Eliotic mode are replete with ambiguous references to sexuality.

For a while, Auden sublimated the social concerns implied in "'Lead's the Best'" into an attempt at a revolutionary, emancipated, modernist style that he tried to borrow from Eliot. At the same time, his self-image as a poet briefly became an Eliot-derived one of the dispassionate, expert scientist or physician of words. In his memoir *Lions and Shadows*, Isherwood recalled a declaration that "Weston" (Auden) made while visiting in July 1926, that "to be 'clinically minded' was . . . the first duty of a poet. Love wasn't exciting or romantic or even disgusting; it was funny. The poet must handle it and similar themes with a wry, bitter smile and a pair of rubber surgical gloves. Poetry must be classic, clinical and austere." Over the next few days of this visit from "Weston" (during which, Isherwood's biographer believes, Isherwood and Auden became lovers), Isherwood writes that he "got very tired of the word 'austere.'"[64]

Eliot never uses the word "austere" in his poetry and only infrequently deploys it in his prose. But perhaps Auden found it in the 1919 essay on Ben Jonson that Eliot reprinted in *The Sacred Wood* (1920): "The words themselves are mostly simple words, the syntax is natural, the language austere rather than adorned."[65] In "Tradition and the Individual Talent," another 1919 essay reprinted in the same volume, Eliot spun a variation on the idea of austerity, likening poetry to a chemical experiment: "It is in this depersonalization that art may be said to approach the condition of science. I therefore invite you to consider, as a suggestive analogy, the action which takes place when a bit of finely filiated platinum is introduced into a chamber containing oxygen and sulphur dioxide."[66]

In *World within World*, Stephen Spender spoke of Auden (sounding very Eliotic) telling him at Oxford that the poet was "a kind of chemist who mixed his poems out of words, whilst remaining detached from his own feelings." Auden had, Spender said, a "clinical view of living."[67] Auden's choice of "rubber surgical gloves" as part of the poet's professional uniform and the idea of a "clinical" attitude show how he adapted Eliot's poet-as-chemist metaphor from "Tradition and the Individual Talent" to a poet-as-doctor ideal, evidently in emulation of, or rivalry with, Dr. Auden's professional work. But just as Eliot's own dicta about "impersonality" now seem to conceal as much as they illuminate, so Auden's clinical stance prompts further investigation of the relation between his ideal of the "clinical" in poetry and his doctor father, who dealt with horrific bodily traumas during the war with "a pair of rubber surgical gloves."

Auden's poems from around the spring of 1926 until the summer of 1927 mark a temporary abatement of his poetic fascination with the English countryside. Birds virtually disappear from his poetry, as does his sense of connection to the "English land," both the countryside and the nation more broadly. Many of the writers whose work had attracted the young Auden—Walter de la Mare, for example, and Edward Thomas— filled their poems with a deep and subtly nationalistic mood. It makes sense, then, that almost all of Auden's references in his *Juvenilia* to "Britain," and more frequently to "England" and "English," occur before May 1926, that is, before Auden began imitating the cosmopolitan, modernist poetry of Eliot.[68] After Eliot exploded into Auden's imagination, the young poet loaded his poems, according to Katherine Bucknell, "with arcane allusions, used the most difficult and awkward-sounding words he could think of, added epigraphs and footnotes, and splintered his verse into syntactically discrete shards."[69]

As early as May 1926, an exasperated Isherwood, to whom Auden was sending almost all his poems for critique, was accusing Auden of "Eliotian Intellectual Bombast."[70] Throughout the next year or so, Auden continued to model his poetry and his own conduct on Eliot: the ideas of discipline and austerity that he absorbed from Eliot were one of the factors behind his claim (probably theoretical) that he was practicing a self-imposed celibacy. "As to sex," he wrote to his brother John, "I am becoming convinced that for myself, asceticism is the only thing."[71]

However, as Auden temporarily abandoned an "English" style for a version of Eliot's macaronic, metropolitan, internationalist, fractured manner and the "dogmatic" opinions he found in the *Criterion,* several writers produced personal sketches of the poet that hint, for all Auden's intellectual extroversion, at an underlying sense of shyness and depression. The poet John Betjeman, a friend, was impressed that Auden "was not in the least interested in the grand friends I had made in the House": "He would not come to the fashionable luncheons with peers and baronets and a sprinkling of dons which I liked to attend and sometimes myself gave. . . . He belonged to no clique. When he asked me to tea in his rooms high up in the north-west corner of Peck (Peckwater Quad) I felt I was district-visiting, so snobbish was I, so other-worldly he."[72] Auden himself felt far from tough and self-confident or, perhaps, "other-worldly." Betjeman was a member of, and by one estimate the "chief clown in," one of the most glamorous literary circles in Oxford at the period, the group of aesthetes gathered around the future dean of Wadham College, Maurice Bowra.[73] Auden was not included.

Ultimately, Auden's self-consciously modernist phase was short-lived. As if Eliot had proved a false poetic father, even by the end of 1926, Auden was beginning to swerve symbolically away from his experiments in modernist poetry and from what he understood to be the Eliotic worldview, which had so far, at least in public, been so profoundly centered on esteem for French literature and the classical languages of Greek and Latin. When Isherwood came to stay with Auden in Oxford at the end of 1926, he discovered that his friend had a new favorite adjective. Explaining his temporary fascination with the races at the local dog track, Auden called them "marvellously *English.*" Isherwood added, "'*English,*' I soon discovered, was his latest term of approbation. 'All this continentalism won't *do,*' he declared. 'It simply doesn't suit us. And we do it so frightfully *badly.*'"[74]

"Continentalism" means, for Auden, roughly "French." And during the Christmas vacation of 1926–1927, the leitmotif of Auden's involvement with German-speaking culture reemerged when he went on a three-week return visit to Austria with a resolutely straight Christ Church friend, William McElwee, who was reading history. They stayed in Kitzbühel with Hedwig Petzold, who had put up Auden and his father during the summer of 1925. There might be a memory of McElwee in Austria in Auden's 1927 poem "Quique Amavit," where he recalls, "You in a kitchen, drinking, wet with snow."[75] Auden had fallen in love with McElwee, but they seem not to have been lovers. Indeed, Auden's letters to friends, as well as his letter to his brother John, suggest that, at around the time of the Austria trip, he may have committed himself to some sort of half-effective regime of celibacy for one or perhaps two years as a way of managing his unrequited love for this stolid public schoolboy, making disappointment seem like a choice. After he and McElwee returned from Austria, Auden told a friend that it had been "a very good three weeks . . . and no complications thank God!"[76]

Just as Auden did not lose his relationship with the countryside and lead mining all at once, so his commitment to an already-out-of-date international modernist style only gradually faded in 1927. Auden communicated with friends several times about his feelings of torpor in the first half of the year. In mid-April 1927, he told McElwee about a "week of abject depression which culminated in my getting flu." In another letter to the same correspondent, written only a bit later, he complained: "I am suffering badly from the 'waking alone' sensation, a slightly sick medical feeling like the smell of iodoform."[77] "Out of sight assuredly, not out of mind" from the early summer of 1927, a verse letter to McElwee, along with the virtually contemporaneous poem "The Megalopsych," were, Bucknell writes, "the last of the pedantic miscellanies Auden wrote in his pseudo-high modernist phase."[78] The end of "The Megalopsych" suggests a semiconscious recognition that parodying or imitating Eliot had not allowed Auden to say something in his "own voice": "I wake with a dry mouth," the poem says, "Something, important once, on the tip of my tongue."[79]

Auden was about to lay aside all his self-consciously evolved metaphors about rubber gloves and his allusions to Aquinas. Eliot would continue to have an enormous effect on his poetry throughout the rest of the 1920s and the 1930s. But it was a wholly different Eliot from the cosmopolitanized modernist poet of *The Waste Land* whom Auden was primarily aware of at this stage. The Eliot who would influence Auden was a poet only just coming into being in 1927, when he, and Anglo-American modernism as a whole, began to reject polyculturalism and formal fracturings in favor of commitment to the tribe, to "order," to rootedness, to aesthetic pattern, and to insularity.

Discussing Eliot's "turn" in the mid-1920s, the literary historian Roger Kojecky commented that "After 1926, the year of Britain's General Strike and of the papal condemnation of the Action Française, . . . Eliot devoted more attention to social and political issues."[80] When Eliot wrote about a new, post-1926 condition of "enforced insularity," as he described it in "Last Words," he was aligning this broad cultural shift with many developments in his own life, marking the emergence of a "new Eliot," an insular, English one. These developments included his delivery of the Clark lectures in Cambridge at the start of 1926 (the first of several endowed, university lecture series that Eliot would use through the coming years as a credentialled launching pad for the composition of his prose books); the confidence-proclaiming addition of "edited by T. S. Eliot" to the cover of the *Criterion*, starting with the May 1927 issue; his entry into the Anglican communion, which took place at Finstock Church in the Cotswolds at the end of June 1927; his naturalization as a British subject in November 1927; and the composition in the last half of 1927 of "Journey of the Magi," the first poem he wrote after thawing out the writer's block that had formed once he finished "The Hollow Men" in 1925.[81]

In "Journey of the Magi," the speaker admits to nostalgia for the exoticism of a lost world of sensory, cosmopolitan pleasures and the company of an "alien people": "The summer palaces on slopes, the terraces, | And the silken girls bringing sherbet." But he is now "no longer at ease here, in the old dispensation, | With an alien people clutching their gods."[82] The use of the morally loaded adjective "alien," with its connotations of foreigner, outsider, and heathen, bears a heavy ideological weight. Eliot's shift of poetic coordinates comes with political messages that, through the use of a persona to speak the poem, he can voice but also remain carefully distanced from. Nonetheless, the austerity and conservatism of his own worldview are clear.

All these changes in Eliot's work and life were cryptically telescoped into the announcement of his new English coordinates as a "classicist in literature, royalist in politics, and anglo-catholic in religion," which he made in the preface to *For Lancelot Andrewes* a year or so later, in the autumn of 1928.[83] For those close to Eliot, and for Eliot himself, these events, taken together, indicated a divide in his life, the passage over a Rubicon. In March 1928, after his first confession, Eliot himself told a priest friend, W. F. Stead, who had baptized him the year before, of his feeling of having "crossed a very wide and deep river . . . I feel very certain that I shall not cross back."[84]

Eliot's sense of a new period of demarcation, clearer cultural definition, and stylistic retrenchment—evident in his imagery of islands and enclosures, of landings and settlings—was deeply in tune with contemporary political language as well as with forward-looking literary developments in England. Many of Eliot's most important poems written between 1927 and 1930 seem to be centered on past or concluding journeys, on the falseness of movement, on the necessity of, spiritually and literally, sitting still, of remaining self-contained. "Journey of the Magi" is an obvious example. Another poem in the "Ariel" series (again, a reference to the enisled Prospero's supernatural servant in *The Tempest*) is "Marina," which Faber and Faber would publish in September 1930, less than a month before they issued Auden's first book, *Poems*. "Marina" begins with the end of a voyage, with a boat making landfall on an island: "What seas what shores what grey rocks and what islands," asks the opening line.[85] It is as if Eliot were now starting to provide in poetry glimpses of some of the ideas that he would codify in the prose of "Last Words," nearly a decade later, about "alien minds [taking] alien ways" and "a situation of enforced insularity" beginning.[86] These poems enact Eliot's own move into inwardness and wholeness in the face of the fragmenting, disharmonious condition that he saw taking over European culture.

Auden could have had little to no idea of what was happening in the ultra-secretive Eliot's personal or creative lives. But, in June 1927, coincidentally within days of Eliot committing himself to the Anglican Communion, Auden submitted a collection of poetry to the poet at Faber and Gwyer. He had been encouraged to do so by the youngest of the Sitwell siblings, the writer Sacheverell Sitwell.[87] It is not known which poems were in this collection, but the irony, strangeness, confusion even, of this act is that the proposed book probably featured a preponderance of poems, such as "The Megalopsych," which showed an almost abject dependence on an Eliotic style that Eliot himself had now abandoned. And although Auden continued to tinker with a few of these poems for a year or so, he himself was about to jettison the Eliotic mode of the collection that he had just submitted to Eliot.

In fact, even in the period when his poetry was in literary exile from the English countryside and from a post-Georgian poetic, and when it was locked into a creative winter from which most of the birds that normally inhabit his poems had temporarily migrated, Auden had not lost his basic grounding as an amateur naturalist or his deeply felt identity as a provincial artist. After an April 1927 visit to William McElwee's home near Wellington in Somerset, he asked McElwee in a letter: "Do let me know if you have time about the nests we found. Was the one in the single tree a crow's?"[88] He even put an imagistic memory of the climb into a new poem: "The first hand bent into the swaying nest."[89] There is something tellingly idiosyncratic about a sophisticated twenty-year-old poet during a holiday with a would-be lover scrambling around to look at birds' nests. It seems unlikely that other comparably ambitious and talented young writers from Auden's circle, such as Isherwood, would ever have been found up a tree.

The earliest poem to appear (much revised) in the collection of Auden's poetry that Faber published in 1930 was an unrhymed Hopkinsian sonnet of unrequited love, probably for McElwee, which Auden wrote in June 1927 and originally included in the compendium poem "The Megalopsych." It begins, "Bones wrenched, weak whimper, lids wrinkled, first dazzle known," one of the most turgid opening lines in modern poetry in English.[90] The poem contains germs of imagery that point towards the mood of doom and alienation that Auden would perfect in coming years: "gun-barrel burnishing | In summer grass," for example. But the dominant impression is one of words being dragged recalcitrantly, laboriously out of darkness into the blinding sunlight of the page. It is as if Auden were using Gerard Manley Hopkins's style to dramatize what he sensed was a pathology in his own current way of making poetry.

While he observed birds' nests and continued to chip away at "The Megalopsych," Auden also wrote the first poem that marked, as Bucknell says, his "move away from the cerebral, multi-layered, artificial Eliotic productions of his middle Oxford years."[91] At the end of the farraginous "The Megalopsych," Auden mentions "Something, important once, on the tip of my tongue." This something turned out to be the poem "I chose this lean country," composed when Auden paid a one-week return visit to Appletreewick in Yorkshire with Cecil Day Lewis at the end of June 1927. This is where he had stayed four years earlier at the family house of his friend Robert Medley. While with Day Lewis, Auden turned back toward an English identity and English themes. (Unbeknownst to him, and probably within the same week, Eliot took the important step along his own path toward the new mode of English "insularity" with his entry into the Anglican Church.)

Auden and Day Lewis had gone to Appletreewick to write a preface to the 1927 edition of the yearly *Oxford Poetry* anthology.[92] The time of their visit was a good one for inaugurating momentous change. Starting at around 6:23 in the morning of 29 June 1927, a twenty-three-second, heavily publicized total eclipse of the sun was visible in the North of England. A few days before, Auden had written to McElwee with mock exasperation from the New Inn in Appletreewick. He made it seem as if Dr. Auden, at long distance, were treating his son like the subject in a clinical experiment: "My father insists on my getting up for the eclipse to record my psychological experiences."[93] Even though the weather was poor that morning, Auden probably did see the eclipse—or, as he put it the poem beginning "I chose this lean country," written in York-shire, the "sponge[ing] away | [of] The idiotic sun." In any case, the partial disappearance of his old Eliotic style and the appearance of a new surge of poetic energy were associated with a temporary disap-pearance and then reappearance of the sun itself. It was an auspicious correlation. The poem starts:

> I chose this lean country
> For seven day content,
> To satisfy the want
> Of eye and ear, to see
> The slow fastidious line
> That disciplines the fell,
> A curlew's creaking call
> From angles unforeseen,
> The drumming of a snipe,
> Surprise where driven sleet
> Had scalded to the bone
> And streams were acrid yet
> To an unaccustomed lip.[94]

The eclipse heralds a return to a simpler, terser, more sinewy style in Auden's poetry and, with it, a re-embrace of his favorite landscapes. It also marked a return to a variant of English Romanticism. Casting himself and Day Lewis as latter-day equivalents of Wordsworth and Coleridge, Auden declared portentously in a letter to Isherwood that the preface to *Oxford Poetry* "should be as important as the preface to lyrical ballads."[95] But his excitement was more a spillover from having written "I chose this lean country" than the result of composing the dutiful prose in the preface.

In spite of the poem's references to particular people ("Margaret the brazen leech, | And that severe Christopher") and its report of a dream, it is far from a simple, diary-like account of the experiences Auden had during the holiday with Day Lewis (392). For example, some of the poetry had been written earlier in the year: parts of the third stanza are recycled from an earlier poem, "Hodge Looks toward London."[96] "I chose this lean country" is a triumph of a new literary style, not the inauguration of a poetry of empirical, autobiographical truthfulness.

Auden's experiments with discontinuities and modernist fragmentation of form that he had made during his brief Eliotic phase were not pointless dead ends. Even in the rural setting of "I chose this lean country," there is an anxious energy, learned from Eliot, that also reads as the literary correlate of what Dr. Auden described as "the increased turmoil of daily life with its feverish and restless activity; the clamour and noise of urban life."[97] Each slender, driving verse of the four-stanza poem is confined to a specific moment—and with modernist formal jaggedness, each stanza is a moment sharply juxtaposed with the others in the poem. Stanza 1, in a generalized past tense, focuses on the speaker's solitary rediscovery of the natural world of birds, streams, and fells that his senses have long "want[ed]" to encounter again. Stanza 2 switches tone, describing "yesterday" and the conversation at a "deserted mine" with "a poet," while stanza 3 shoots forward chronologically to "Last night" and shifts to the interior world in which a dreamer has a feverish conversation with a therapist-like "Professional listener" (391–392).

The poem reaches the present tense in the last of the four stanzas. But it cannot rest content with, or even long tolerate, the present. As readers arrive at "Now," the poem anxiously folds back on the scene of its naturalistic and lonely beginning with the poet solitary at a "waterlogged quarry." His rueful meditations on how in the future "death shall | . . . lead this people to | A mildewed dormitory" are broken up, in another vivid moment of discontinuity, by the "sudden scurry" of a blackbird that "Lets broken treetwigs fall | To shake the torpid pool" (392–393). The poet frees himself from the living death of "torpid" poetic introspection, the twigs' writing-on-water fades, and he returns to a shared social world:

> breaking from the copse,
> I climb the hill, my corpse
> Already wept, and pass
> Alive into the house. (393)

The idea that because he is late, his "corpse" will already have been "wept" for, as if he was assumed to have drowned or fallen into a hole, sounds strangely frantic. Reinforcing the intermittent use of Wilfred Owen–like pararhymes such as copse/corpse, "I chose this lean country" draws heavily on diction redolent of infantry experience and of trenches: "angles unforeseen," "Surprise," "acrid," "scrambled," "crumbling," "deserted," "ecstasy of pain," "sallow," "death," "breaking from the copse," "my corpse," "wept," "Alive." (The "snipe" seems an especially relevant bird to find in the first stanza because "sniper" is derived from the name given to someone who hunts from cover for snipe.) The final lines suggest that the speaker is like a soldier missing in action. In terms of the dynamic of Auden's career, he is one lost and presumed dead on the battlefield of Eliotic international modernism before in this poem at last he returns "Alive" to his native poetic house (393).

Besides Owen, Auden had recently added another ex-soldier poet to his pantheon of literary models: Robert Graves (who served in the Royal Welch Fusiliers). In *Poetic Unreason* (1925), Graves suggested that the "best poetry appeals in turn to all the senses."[98] And in Auden's highly Gravesian poem, the "*lean* country" suggests muscularity in those who enter it, connoting both the bareness of the landscape and the posture of hikers who must tilt their bodies forward as they climb the landscape's hills. A new vivacity is conveyed in the first stanza by the strong rhythms that draw in references to the five senses: the sight of the "slow fastidious line," the sound of a "curlew's creaking call," the feeling of "driven sleet" that has "scalded to the bone," and the taste (and smell) of streams "acrid yet | To an unaccustomed lip." The sense of energy accrued from activating the complete range of the human sensorium is transmitted into the second stanza by a flurry of strenuous verbs in the opening lines: "stepping," "climb," "twist," "see" (391–392).

The rugged country that had been so important once to Auden was about to become important again, and he "scrambled in a hurry" to reach it (392). And when Auden returned to writing about familiar northern scenes, he hinted that these remote landscapes were representative of the nation itself. The poem is set in a particular piece of "country" within a nation. But "country" can also *mean* "nation," and Auden again offers his northern world as a synecdoche of the national whole. As if to indicate a renewed literary health associated with this return to the North, birds play an almost heraldic role in "I chose this lean country." For example, the sounds made by two named and voluble birds dominate the first stanza: a "curlew's creaking call" and the "drumming of a snipe" (392). The synergy evident between birds and Auden's renewed focus on English landscapes develops further in the second stanza, where the speaker and "a poet" watch silently a "singular vision," the beautiful, stark sight and sound of a "defiant bird," probably a ring ouzel, which "Fell down and scolding stood | Upon a sun-white boulder" (392). The naming and description of birds dramatize Auden's reawakening sense of connection to this world.

"I chose this lean country," written in late June or early July 1927, draws on the imagery of the third section of Yeats's "The Tower," which Auden had recently seen in the latest number of the *Criterion*. Like his reading of Graves, his new interest in Yeats came from Day Lewis, with whom Auden spent the week in Yorkshire. "Have you seen Yeats' poem in the June *Criterion*[?]," he asked Isherwood. "It is very good."[99] Auden's restless, heavily enjambed trimeters are distinctly Yeatsian, as is the decision to cast himself in a symbolic role; here, Auden is a youthful version of "everyman" concerned with premonitions about "this people" (393). His image of the blackbird dropping twigs into the water also draws on Yeats and specifically on his description of the jackdaws making a nest in one of the vertical slit openings in his Norman tower at his home, Thoor Ballylee in Galway. In Yeats, "The daws chatter and scream, | And drop twigs layer upon layer."[100] In Auden's poem, though, the blackbird's dropped twigs breaking up the smooth surface of the pool at the "water-logged quarry" disrupt the speaker's narcissistic reveries and shake him back into action, returning him to society (and poetry) as he enters "Alive into the house" (393).

Auden's poem also draws on the landscape and the language of Graves's "Rocky Acres," a bird-dominated poem that begins, "This is a wild land, country of my choice, | With harsh craggy mountain, moor ample and bare."[101] Both of Auden's source poems share a common thematic background: war. And both poems experiment with depicting how the atmosphere of modern conflict has come to suffuse domestic spaces (in the case of Yeats) and natural ones (in the case of Graves). In Yeats's poem, the war is the Irish Civil War. But the "Violence upon the roads" (of "Nineteen Hundred and Nineteen") that infects "The Tower," with its language of "battlements," severed ears, blindness, darkness, and "Rough men-at-arms . . . shod in iron" comes very close to the representations of First World War violence in the poems of younger English poets whom Yeats affected to despise.[102]

Meanwhile, Graves's wartime experiences clearly underlie "Rocky Acres," a poem about a place far off from "fat burghers," and outside time and civilization. Life is a "hardy adventure, full of fear and shock," voices are never heard, weather has an "armour," and a terrifying, machine-like buzzard scans "his wide parish" from the sky, "catches the trembling of small hidden things, | . . . tears them in pieces, dropping them from the sky."[103] Both "The Tower" and "Rocky Acres" also insist pridefully on self-assertion through decisive action and choices in the face of their brutal worlds. Yeats writes: "It is time that I wrote my will; | I choose upstanding men | That climb the streams."[104] For Graves, "This is a wild land, country of my choice."[105] In fact, the verb "choose" in Yeats and the noun "choice" in Graves are crucial load-bearing elements in these almost Nietzschean poems, both very similar in worldview, associating power with the vantage point of height, decisiveness, assertion, and somewhat stereotypical versions of masculinity.

With these two conflict-filled works towering over Auden's poem, one critic has asserted that "I chose this lean country" shows that a "new strength," deriving from Yeats and Graves, is entering Auden's writing.[106] But the poem's most important trajectory is its passage from the opening moment of "masculine" vigor to the threat of debility, passivity, and a possible death-like state. That degenerative movement emerges very clearly in the second stanza, where the initial verbs of propulsive self-rising yield to a vision of physical ruin:

> So stepping yesterday
> To climb a crooked valley,
> I scrambled in a hurry
> To twist the bend and see
> Sheds crumbling stone by stone,
> The awkward waterwheel
> Of a deserted mine;

The speaker, all momentum gone after his scramble up the valley, soon turns to "sitting by the fall" and speaking "with a poet there" (392).

In biographical terms, the poet spoken with clearly seems like a version of the gossipy Day Lewis. The alteration in physical register from climbing and scrambling alone to sitting and talking with another person is emphatic, and it is telling that the first subject of conversation is "Margaret the brazen leech." In other words, as soon as the speaker sits down and starts to talk, the first subject that comes up is a threatening woman who is "brazen," being both socially unconventional and, metaphorically, metallic like a robot. She is also a "leech," a bloodsucker, or, more prosaically, a psychoanalyst.[107] To talk critically about absent friends as "the poet" and the speaker do (after discussing Margaret, the pair turn to "that severe Christopher" Isherwood), only adds to the sense of weakness that, after an initial show of vigor, is now emerging.

Then, deepening the mood of passivity that has replaced the active striving of the first part of the poem, "both dropped silent" and began watching a "defiant bird" that stood "scolding" them (392). We are meant to understand that the bird is, symbolically at least, "scolding" the two speakers for their feckless gossiping. The bird also draws attention to the emotional frailty that characterizes the speaker and differentiates him from the self-reliant and assertive protagonists in Yeats's and Graves's poems.

As the poem moves forward, the languid protagonist is pulled even further downward. Here is the third stanza:

> Last night, sucked giddy down
> The funnel of my dream,
> I saw myself within
> A buried engine-room.
> Dynamos, boilers, lay
> In tickling silence, I
> Gripping an oily rail,
> Talked feverishly to one
> Professional listener
> Who puckered mouth and brow
> In ecstasy of pain
> I know, I know, I know
> And reached his hand for mine. (392)

The abjection becomes even more pronounced, when, after having "dropped silent" in stanza 2, the speaker now finds himself "sucked giddy down | The funnel of [his] dream." "Sitting by *the fall*" (emphasis added) prepares the way for "Dropped," which prepares the way for "sucked . . . down." In the speaker's dream, another stage in his evolving passivity is described, as he is pulled into the dream's "buried engine-room," where power is dormant: "Dynamos, boilers, lay | In tickling silence." The person with whom the dreamer talks—a "Professional listener" who "puckered mouth and brow | In ecstasy of pain"—is, like a mirror image, an ineffectual male who is unable to help the dreamer and instead seems intent on seducing him (392).[108]

The poem's final stanza flirts with the only further stage of passivity possible: death. The speaker sits alone "in a brown study | At the water-logged quarry" ("water-logged" presumably because the "Dynamos, boilers" have long been out of action) thinking pensive, poetic thoughts about how "everyman" shall "Sit, querulous and sallow | Under the abject willow" (393).[109] The weeping willow is a drooping tree fit to cover a moping everyman who sags with melancholic torpor. As seen earlier, it is only the life force embodied in the "blackbird's sudden scurry" that draws the speaker out of his melancholic reveries about death even after his friends or hosts have come to believe that he is irretrievably lost.

"I chose this lean country" is like a robust Yeats poem housing quivering Eliotic emotions. Auden's ending, with the blackbird's help, pulls his surrogate speaker-dreamer back from the brink of despair or death. But it also shows clearly that Auden's pose of decisive poetic vigor, borrowed from Yeats and Graves, is shaky and provisional. Even after he abandoned Eliot's cosmopolitan tones and fractured forms, Auden retained in his poems much of the nervous fragility and dejection that Eliot had dramatized in *The Waste Land*. For Auden, the representative psyche for a male poet in the 1920s is nervous, loss obsessed, and vulnerable.

During his self-consciously "modernist" performance of intellectualism and self-confidence at Oxford between 1926 and 1927, Auden publicly lauded the importance of St. Thomas Aquinas and parroted in "dogmatic words" Eliot's ideas from the *Criterion* "Commentaries." Yet although he gave a conspicuous display of the advanced nature of his new opinions, Auden, in fact, was a reclusive, reticent figure at university who failed to break into the smart sets of advanced 1920s aesthetes and poets. He spent much of his time alone.

In contrast to legendary undergraduates such as Mark Ogilvie-Grant of Trinity, who once entered the fashionable George restaurant in Oxford "in a bathing dress with seaweed in his hair and carrying a looking-glass," Auden took walks "past the gas-works and the municipal rubbish dump" like a neurasthenic, sexually wounded, Eliotic antihero. He worked in isolation. in the style of a Proustian invalid, "in a darkened room with the curtains drawn, and a lamp on a table at his elbow." He was often paralyzed by anxiety about his academic progress and his poetry, troubled by bouts of "abject depression," and prone to fits of tears.[110] And for all his sexual knowledge and his fondness for running his friends' love lives, at Oxford, Auden himself was forlornly and probably chastely in love with a series of cheery, rather puzzled heterosexual men such as William McElwee and, later, Gabriel Carritt.[111]

John Betjeman was aware of Auden's apparent indifference as an undergraduate to literary vogues. He recalled Auden coming into his rooms at Magdalen one day, "looking at my bookshelves and seeing there all the books that were fashionable at the time, but among them were several volumes of Edmund Blunden's poems. 'These are what you really like' he said, and he was quite right."[112] Auden also loved Blunden's work, deeply outmoded though it was in Oxford by this point. Betjeman noticed too that Auden's attitude to his parents was different from that of most undergraduates: "At this time it was fashionable, in my set, for undergraduates to regard their parents as brutal philistines. Auden, on the other hand, much reverenced his father. . . . He often spoke with affection of his parents and brother."[113] In referring to Auden's attitudes toward his parents, Betjeman was venturing onto more complex and ambiguous terrain than he had when he noted that Auden shared his affection for Blunden's poems. Predictably, Auden's relations with his mother and father, and his awareness of "the immense bat-shadow of home," were far more difficult and ambivalent topics for him than his remarks to Betjeman and others indicated.[114]

The subject of Auden's family now comes into the foreground, because Auden wrote "I chose this lean country" not long before he went on a strange, disturbing holiday with his father in Yugoslavia (or "the Kingdom of Serbs, Croats and Slovenes," as it was officially known until 1929). This was a new country, which had been diplomatically engineered into existence in the postwar peace treaties only a few years earlier and which included within its borders the city of Sarajevo. During this holiday in the Balkans, Auden was unusually troubled by a dream and a disturbing coincidence, just as he seems to have been afflicted by a panicked dissatisfaction with Dr. Auden's unassuming mildness and taciturnity. In poetic and psychological terms, the holiday in Yugoslavia was a painful, tortured moment in Auden's life. It is also one of the most illuminating.

How Auden understood the equivocal feelings about authority and endangered self-realization expressed in his 1927 poems like "I chose this lean country" can only be grasped in the context of another underemphasized, or ignored, aspect of his intellectual bearings. Isherwood noted that by 1926, the period of Auden's brief capitulation to and escape from a fragmented, cerebral modernist style, his "magpie brain was a hoard of curious and suggestive phrases from Jung, Rivers, Kretschmer and Freud."[115] One might expect a young poet to search for new authority figures who can emotionally and ideologically replace the standard familial ones. But it is striking that three out of the four physicians mentioned by Isherwood were German-speaking and that they were all writers whom Auden discovered through his father's enthusiasm for their works. In the same year that Isherwood noted Auden's verbal addiction to Jung, Rivers, Kretschmer, and Freud, Dr. Auden mentioned *each* of these physicians in a single article—an overlapping of reference points that is too complete to be accidental.[116] And what that overlapping implies is that Auden was probably reading his father's writing and perhaps discussing it with him too. The ideas that animated Dr. Auden also became important to his son.

Although Dr. Auden occasionally alluded to Jung, Kretschmer, or Freud elsewhere in his work, the most important writer by far for Birmingham's school medical officer was W. H. R. Rivers, the recently deceased English physiologist, social anthropologist, and psychologist whose name and ideas, as we saw in Chapter 2, come up again and again in Dr. Auden's writing. Dr. Auden had known Rivers personally before the war when they had served together on committees of the British Association for the Advancement of Science. Rivers died suddenly of a strangulated hernia in 1922. Not long afterward, Dr. Auden began to take a deep, almost obsessive, interest in Rivers's work, citing him repeatedly in his medical essays during the 1920s, his most prolific decade. It is no exaggeration to say that professionally and personally, Rivers gave Dr. Auden an articulated worldview.

Rivers's work was equally central for Dr. Auden's son. Although Auden apparently owned a set of Freud's *Collected Papers* in his final year or so at Gresham's, these books may well have had a decorative status similar to the one enjoyed by his volume of St. Thomas Aquinas at Oxford.[117] In rudimentary form, Freud's ideas were already becoming popular and even cultish among self-consciously modern readers in postwar England. But they were primarily known and applied through the highly modulated use that psychiatrists such as Rivers had made of them in their writings about shell shock. To the younger Auden, for whom, as Isherwood discovered, "'*English . . .*' was his latest term of approbation," the English doctor Rivers preceded the Austrian Freud in importance and in date of influence.[118]

With a single joking exception, there are no references to Freud in Auden's letters before the 1930s, nor any notes on Freud's work before the detailed set that he took on "Mourning and Melancholia" and *Beyond the Pleasure Principle* in Berlin in 1929.[119] The first time he mentioned Freud by name in a poem was in "Get there if you can and see the land you once were proud to own," composed in April 1930.[120] And no commentator has been able to cite any specific allusion to Freud's work in Auden's poetry before the period of *The Orators*, which was primarily written in 1931. By contrast, the writing of Rivers was central and inspirational to both Dr. Auden and his son throughout the later 1920s. As a poet, W. H. Auden was far more interested than his father in what Rivers had to say about dreams and symbols, and his interest was surely piqued as well by Rivers's connections to Sassoon (whom Rivers had treated at Craiglockhart Hospital in Scotland in 1917) and indirectly to Sassoon's friend Wilfred Owen. But Riversian ideas about regression to primitive states associated with perversion, antisocial habits, and mental degeneration, which so captivated Dr. Auden, were also important to his youngest son. When Auden thought about psychology and psychoanalysis during his first years as a poet, he did so mainly in terms of Rivers's physiologically inflected English adaptation of Continental psychoanalytic theory.

Rivers's work reverberated through British medical and psychiatric circles all through the 1920s as physicians absorbed his paradigms into their own particular specialties—as Dr. Auden did, for example, in his work with Birmingham's maladjusted, "difficult," and postencephalitic children. Auden's father was professionally interested in new developments in psychology, buying "books by pioneer psychologists as soon as they were published."[121] He read and contributed to some of the same medical journals for which Rivers had written (*Psyche* and the *Lancet*, above all). Dr. Auden's earliest reference to Rivers comes in the essay "The Biological Factors in Mental Defect," which he probably wrote in the summer of 1922 shortly after Rivers's death. It was published in a June 1923 issue of *Psyche,* where C. S. Myers's lengthy tribute to Rivers had appeared in October 1922.[122]

From "The Biological Factors in Mental Defect" onward, Dr. Auden started to mention Rivers regularly in his essays and articles. Most of these references involved Rivers's theory of the differences between the "protopathic and epicritic forms of sensibility to stimuli from the outer world." The protopathic and the epicritic "represent two distinct stages in the evolution of the nervous system" and implied, as Dr. Auden put it, lengthily quoting Rivers, that "the instincts associated with the needs of the individual and with the early preservation of the race are mainly of the protopathic kind, whereas the epicritic group of instincts first appeared with the development of gregarious life."[123] That is, Dr. Auden asserted that the contrast between these "forms of sensibility" within each individual reproduces the history of human culture. The child, like early humans, is "primarily, and essentially, an individualist" and protopathic. It gradually learns, as our human ancestors did, to develop an epicritic "altruistic attitude," to "subordinate or suppress his individual wishes and desires in conformity with the demands of his group," to become what Dr. Auden, citing Aristotle, called a "social animal."[124] However, physical illness can allow psychological regression to an early stage of development to occur, producing "moral changes," "aberrations of conduct," and the "persistence of certain perverse habits."[125]

Fusing physiology and psychology, the Riversian idea of a basic "protopathic" seam of lower, more violent, individualistic, and "primitive" reactions that underlies civilized, "epicritical," altruistic, and higher responses had a powerful appeal to doctors and psychiatrists such as Dr. Auden in the 1920s. In his 1923 essay, Dr. Auden remarked that Rivers "had formulated a biological theory of the genesis of morbid mental states, based upon our knowledge of the evolution of the nervous system, which appears to give us an entirely new view-point" for understanding mental deficiencies. From the start of 1925 onward—as his son was gaining experience as a poet—Dr. Auden returned again and again, and with special intensity, to Rivers's basic schema: the distinction between two layers in the nervous system, the more "primitive" protopathic layer, which always lies beneath later psychic developments, and the more "advanced," and higher, epicritic layer. The Riversian protopathic/epicritic distinction, where under healthy conditions the "higher" faculties control and subdue the "lower," was the conceptual bedrock on which Dr. Auden built much of his writing on psychology.

It was also to be of primary significance, though in a less positive sense, for W. H. Auden's poetry. Indeed, the context in which Dr. Auden almost always took up Rivers's distinctions between the epicritic and the protopathic, the intelligence and the emotions, higher and lower levels in the mind, the socially well-adjusted and the deviant or maladjusted, was one that must have had a special, painfully intimate resonance for his youngest son. For the context in which Dr. Auden used the distinction time and again was in the study of unhealthy or problematic children.[126] And his son's poems often explore the protopathic base layers of the mind, associated with individualism and deviancy, where the lower faculties supposedly reside.

Dr. Auden may have felt rather pleased with himself when he and his youngest son set off on their journey to Yugoslavia on 21 July 1927, a few weeks after Auden had finished "I chose this lean country" and just after Dr. Auden himself had published a strange piece of new work. The University of Birmingham had conferred a doctorate of philosophy on Dr. Auden in 1926 in recognition of his published essays on character formation and infantile feeble-mindedness. He was now an accredited scholar and writer as well as a qualified medical professional. And in July 1927, he saw into print one of his oddest and most suggestive articles, "An Unusual Form of Suicide" in the *Journal of Mental Science*.[127]

In the 1920s, this mild but energetic man wrote mostly about children and their physical and psychological problems; many of these professional writings emerged from his experiences as Birmingham's school medical officer. In the case of "An Unusual Form of Suicide," though, Dr. Auden did not write about a child under his care but about a nameless working-class twenty-four-year-old male (to whom, in the custom of medical literature at the time, he referred, using the final letters of the alphabet, only as "X.Y.Z., aet. 24"). Dr. Auden gave no indication of how he came to know about this unfortunate man's death, which had taken place earlier in the year, calling it merely a narrative with "considerable psychological interest" that was "worthy of permanent record" (428).[128]

Yet the case's "unusual" contents are of "considerable psychological interest" not only in relation to the dead person but also in relation to the author of the essay and to his son. If W. H. Auden often seems to reflect on his father in his writings, here is a moment, in a story about a father and son, when Dr. Auden seems to reflect parabolically and perhaps unconsciously on his relationship with his youngest child. Just as Auden tried to bring his father's epicritical medical world into his own world of poetry, so here Dr. Auden seems to have tried to write something in a medical context that has a poetic, emotional, protopathic, and even transgressive quality. Auden must have been reading his father's work, because traces of Dr. Auden's article appear ciphered into the poetry Auden wrote while on holiday with his parent in Yugoslavia, and his state of mind, already a vulnerable one, seems to have been deeply affected by the essay as well.

In "An Unusual Form of Suicide," parental anxiety, like the kind Mrs. Auden wrote about to her son's friend A. S. T. Fisher, is on full display, as is some parental guilt. This story, from outside his field of professional competence, was one that had clearly piqued Dr. Auden's imagination and thus presumably evoked a preexisting interest or concern of his own. Professional earnestness and personal asceticism make it unlikely that he invented the story; however, it is fair to say that this case history is used as a form of self-expression. Dr. Auden's article mainly focuses on describing at fastidious but prurient length how a "normal"-seeming male who ran a small "fish business" with his father in an unnamed city or town met his end.

Dr. Auden related how, on the morning of 4 February 1927, X.Y.Z.'s father, who suffered from epilepsy, left the house where they lived together, apparently alone, "to go on his daily fish sale round." The "fish business" that the pair in the article "carry on" together also suggests the phrases a "fishy business" and a "carrying on" of foolish or improper activities. The detail about the father suffering from epilepsy is also significant. For Dr. Auden, as he had explained elsewhere, the "automatism of epilepsy" was a Riversian instance of the "removal of epicritic control" allowing the mind to regress, or descend, to lower levels of functioning, equivalent to "an earlier period of infancy or childhood (which itself reflects a corresponding stage in man's phylogenetic development)."[129] Although the son does not suffer from epilepsy, the regressive nature of his own problems makes it clear that there is a hereditary weakness that the epileptic father has passed on to his child.

After the father had gone out, Dr. Auden explained, X.Y.Z. spoke briefly to a police constable—appearing to the constable "quite right and jovial" as they talked. The officer had called about the trivial possibility that X.Y.Z. had been seen (and heard) "driving a motor cycle without an efficient silencer." "No summons was being issued," and after a further short chat the officer left (429). Dr. Auden reported that in the late morning, X.Y.Z. also had a hurried conversation "from the cellar" with a cleaning woman in the house. This, again, happened without incident. On the evening of the same day, the unnamed father returned to their house and found his son's body stretched out cold on the floor of the front bedroom, which "was not in general occupation." Pressing on the dead man's neck was a woman's "high-heeled suede outdoor shoe." A cobbler's last had been fixed inside the shoe, and a piece of wood was wedged in it as well; all this was held in place with some newspapers and "a woman's stocking." The wood protruded from the top of the shoe, and its upper end was positioned under one of the raised bottom legs of a "heavy double bedstead, in such a way that the whole weight of the bed was transmitted to the shoe, and so to the throat" (429). X.Y.Z. had died of asphyxiation as the high-heeled shoe crushed his windpipe.

Dr. Auden told his readers that the coroner had recorded a verdict of "suicide during temporary insanity," but in the *Journal of Mental Science* he ventured to disagree, suggesting that the bizarrely careful and well-balanced nature of the shoe-wood-bedstead mechanism that had killed the young man pointed to "a masochistic impulse" or "symbolism of subjection" that, being so minutely and successfully calibrated, implied "previous experiment or use to induce some pleasurable gratification" (428–429). In other words, Dr. Auden saw the shoe and bedstead arrangement, which left the young man's hands free for other purposes even as the bed's weight pressed down heavily on his neck, as having been set up not to kill X.Y.Z. but for the purpose of giving him the kind of dangerous sexual gratification usually known as autoerotic asphyxiation (AEA or "breath play"). In this practice, the reduction of the amount of oxygen reaching the brain while sexual stimulation occurs heightens the pleasure because, as asphyxiation nears, the body is producing more than the normal quantity of endorphins. Dr. Auden, in his stolid, professional style, was saying that this was a case of a masturbatory sex game gone wrong. For that reason, he suggested "misadventure" as the reason for death and not "self-destruction" (429).

This kind of case study is so far outside the norm of Dr. Auden's work that it provokes many questions and induces many observations, not least about his overt, if demurely expressed, fascination with the event. In particular, as described by Dr. Auden, this death seems like a way of narrating something disturbing about his relationship with his youngest child: a father abandons his son for a while and, when he returns, finds his son dead, apparently the victim of an accident attendant on his sexual deviancy. The father's tendency to regress to a lower, protopathic psychological level is manifested as epilepsy, the son's as a sexual perversion: Dr. Auden saw "sexual offences, crimes of violence, arson and stealing" as instances in which there "has been a failure of function in the hierarchy of mental control."[130] The scenario of the father who, to attend to "business," leaves his son vulnerably alone replays Auden's own sense of having "lost" his father during the war. The father, like everyone else, is apparently unaware of the extremely disturbed state of his son's mind; readers of Auden's work might feel that, in a sense, the fishmonger father and son "never really came to know each other."[131] And, as Dr. Auden himself pointed out, the symbolism of choosing to be crushed under a woman's "high-heeled suede" shoe points to a sexual proclivity bound up with a fear about women's supposed destructive power over men, about the (literally, in this case) "downtrodden" man, an etiology that strongly echoes the psychoanalytic

narratives prevalent at the time about the reasons for a boy's development of homosexuality.

Bucknell has argued that for all Dr. Auden's evident learning, stamina,
and kindness, his son saw him as dismayingly mild-mannered and
conflict-averse: he "understood his father to be the source of what he regarded as inherited weakness in himself" and resented that, "as a husband," Dr. Auden was "often henpecked."[132] The symbolism of a dead
young man suffocated by a woman's shoe must have resonated with W. H.
Auden, given his own anguish about the way he believed his mother dominated his father and caused her son fits of weeping. It might have resonated as well with Dr. Auden, who perhaps harbored similar prejudicial
feelings about his wife. Nothing can be said definitively, but Dr. Auden
was never willing to give up completely his ties with Ann Haverson, the
nurse he had fallen in love with in Cairo during the war; there were strains
between the Audens over the ownership of the Wesco house; and Dr.
Auden's woodworking hobby allowed him the chance to carve stark but
challenging mottoes like "Live as on a mountain" into the household items
he fashioned.[133] "An Unusual Form of Suicide" points to self-pitying guilt
over the author's delinquency in leaving his family alone while he attended
to the business of war (and, in Egypt, the business of love) and fear for a
son victimized or spoiled by his wife's overwhelming psychological pressure. Perhaps there is even a hint of jealousy over the portrait of a father
out at work while the son at home indulges in alluring sexual play.

"An Unusual Form of Suicide," for what it said in ciphered form about a
dead son and a delinquent father, was exactly the wrong piece for W. H.
Auden to have read immediately before he set off on a journey to Yugoslavia with his stolid parent, a trip that apparently lasted from 21 July to
19 August 1927. It was their second trip abroad together, two years
after they had traveled to Salzburg and Kitzbühel.

The next poem Auden wrote after "I chose this lean country" was
probably the short lyric beginning "On the frontier at dawn getting
down," and it shows that the third part of Yeats's "The Tower" lingered
in his mind. Auden composed this as a travel poem, a sonnet, which he
wrote in Zagreb in July 1927. As far as I can tell, it is the first poem
Auden ever wrote outside England.

On the frontier at dawn getting down,
Hot eyes were soothed with swallows: ploughs began
Upon the stunted ridge behind the town,
And bridles flashed. In the dog days she ran
Indoors to read her letter. He in love,
Too curious for the East stiffens to a tower;
The jaw-bone juts from the ice; wisdom of
The cooled brain in an irreverent hour.

At the half-close the muted violin
Put cloth and glasses by; the hour deferred
Peculiar idols nodded. Miles away
A horse neighed in the half-light, and a bird
Cried loudly over and over again
Upon the natural ending of a day.[134]

Beginning with the swallows at dawn and ending with another bird's cry in the twilight, the sonnet covers a whole day in fourteen lines, as if each line stood roughly for an hour of wakefulness. It can be read straightforwardly as a "life goes on" poem, a stoical description of how each day brings a succession of sights and challenges that, however painful, do not last but appear and disappear like the sun rising and setting. But there is a less straightforward reading, as well, one that concentrates on the refusal of Auden's words to resign their individuality and serve only the higher order of the poem's ostensible narrative. Modernist discontinuities and zigzags, often consisting of a network of images at odds with the "message" of the poem, are hidden beneath the apparently traditional, discursive verbal surface.

By now Robert Graves had given Auden an analytical language in which to understand and justify this kind of psychoanalytically motivated reading of poetry. In his critical book *Poetic Unreason*, Graves had written in Riversian fashion that "poetry is a record of the conflicts between various pairs of Jekyll and Hyde" in a poet's mind. This conflict was recorded as a tension between the "manifest content," which Graves linked to the intellectual, propositional level of the poem, and the "latent content," which he connected with the poem's emotions and with images. Graves argued that the conflict between latent and manifest could appear in "an outburst in symbolism" against the "victor" of intellect.[135]

Here, the opening lines of Auden's poem can mean—and do mean—that the sight of the swallows, the traditional harbingers of summer, swooping and dipping in the air is soothing to the tired, sweaty traveler, disembarking from the train "at dawn" to go through passport control on the frontier between two countries (a formality that had become far more commonplace in the period after the First World War).[136] The swallows are soothing, perhaps because their characteristic irregular darting movements are a relief after the monotonous progression of telegraph poles running by the side of the tracks or (to use a word shared with poetry) "lines" and glimpsed hour after hour through the train window. But they might also be soothing because these migratory birds with their streaming tails are beyond the reach of officials and bureaucratic protocols of the kind that harass the poem's speaker by making him climb down "at dawn."

Just as the poem takes place on a spatial "frontier" between two countries, and at a temporal boundary between night and day, Auden tries to balance his poetic language on a threshold between denotation and connotation. Coexisting with this manifest content, in Graves's terms, in which the language proceeds from left to right, then drops a line and returns to the left, from which it sets off again rightwards, there is a kind of latent underground tunnel network linking words together through association. Or, as Auden once put it, in poetry—unlike in prose or scientific formulas—there is "an aura of suggestion round every word through which, like the atom radiating lines of force through the whole of space and time, it becomes ultimately a sign for the sum of all possible meanings."[137] Here, for example, the word "hot," in the phrase "Hot eyes were soothed with swallows," suggests the human need to drink liquids when the body is too warm, and this leads, further down the line, to the secondary association of "swallow," meaning a gulp of something taken at one go.

In this poem, written immediately after his father published "An Unusual Form of Suicide" about an asphyxiated young man, Auden's poem emphasizes the throat and mouth. As he probably expected his reader to know, the dullness of the swallow's main body color is countered by its throat, which in some species is a bright, eye-catching, wound-like red. From here, images and ideas connected with the mouth and throat proliferate: the "bridles," the "jaw-bone jut[ting] from the ice," the "muted violin" (an instrument held between jaw and collarbone), the horse that "neighed," and, in the poem's final lines, the "bird" that "Cried loudly over and over again."

Why is this poem so sensitized to images and ideas related to the throat and mouth, the physical locus of speech in the human body? The poem's reiterations of these motifs suggest a camouflaged memory of the asphyxiated son of whom Auden had just read in his father's article and with whom, "forced by the feeling of identification," the poem links itself, not least in the lines about "He in love, | Too curious for the East stiffens to a tower."[138] The poem's ending (as in "I chose this lean country") recalls the end of the third part of "The Tower," where death and old age begin to seem to Yeats, when weighed against the significance of soul-making, no more important than

> the clouds of the sky
> When the horizon fades;
> Or a bird's sleepy cry
> Among the deepening shades.[139]

Auden's Zagreb poem also ends with what is, for him, the familiar note of birdsong. Besides Yeats's poem, we also hear in the background the end of John Keats's "To Autumn" (1819), where at evening the "redbreast whistles from a garden-croft; | And gathering swallows twitter in the skies."[140] But, in Auden, there is not an ending note of peace or harmony. While Yeats's bird gives a "sleepy cry," Auden's traveler-speaker recalls a call filled with a sense of desperation and lostness: "a bird | Cried loudly over and over again | Upon the natural ending of a day."[141]

The throat and mouth were highly erogenous zones for Auden. They were also imbued with symbolic significance for him as a poet, as *The Poet's Tongue*, the title of an anthology he compiled with John Garrett in the mid-1930s, implied. In his introduction to that book, Auden emphasized the orality of poetry, praising the "stimulus" of the "audible spoken word, to which in all its power of suggestion and incantation we must surrender."[142] "On the frontier at dawn getting down" is a somewhat empty poem if one focuses on the "Dr. Jekyll" of its manifest content. But the "Mr. Hyde" of its subversive latent content, centered on fears about threatened poetic and personal selfhood, emerges when one focuses on the meanings of its birds, their creaturely cries, and ideas and emotions associated with the throat, jaw, and mouth. The abjection of the bird that cries "loudly over and over again" is the

displaced cry of a poet fearful over his own future, still partially in
thrall, as he is aware, to older poets such as Eliot and Yeats and to his
own vigorous but somehow distant and bemused parent, who, recapit-
ulating the original trauma of loss during the war, day after day disappeared just like X.Y.Z.'s father, who "left the shop early to go on his
daily fish sale round."[143]

Auden felt deeply disturbed while he and his father were in Yugoslavia together. "I once went to Yugoslavia with father and wished I was
dead," he wrote in a later travelogue.[144] While he was away, he sent at
least one despairing and mildly fevered letter to Isherwood from Cro-
atia.[145] He also seems to have been physically ill. In a note in a journal
written a couple of years later, he said, almost certainly with reference to
this trip, "Young men, Travel abroad but go alone. To travel with one's
family is a contradiction in terms. It gave me indolent ulcer."[146] Almost
nothing is known about this illness or how Auden eventually overcame
it, but the mention of it is an index of his distress in the summer of 1927.
At the same time, after producing the initially vigorous rhythms and
ideas of "I chose this lean country," Auden's poetry weakened while he
was on the holiday and shortly afterward, as he produced a number of
unmemorable poems.

"On the frontier at dawn getting down" mirrors the imagery of the
asphyxiated young man in Dr. Auden's latest article. And Bucknell
points out that Auden composed two other poems, either during or
immediately after the Yugoslavia trip, that in different ways take up the
"theme of paternally inherited illness."[147] These poems are "Truly our
fathers had the gout" and "We, knowing the family history." The latter is
written as an impersonation of a doctor's dry, fatalistic manner, exactly
the kind of authorial voice that Dr. Auden had used in writing up "An
Unusual Form of Suicide." (The poem also mentions an indolent
ulcer.[148]) Both of these works do not draw much attention outside the
context of their author's fraught psychological state, and both figure
the disasters that they describe as irremediable, as if Auden felt himself
too enmeshed in the "family history" to be able to see it poetically. "The
eagle strangles in the snare," says the first of these poems. "The tide is
out | And the ash-pit bare."[149] The word "ash-pit" recalls the sonic con-
tours of the first part of the verb *asphyx*iate. (Auden's original first line
for this poem was, "Hanged men swing in the air."[150]) Auden may still
be thinking of "An Unusual Form of Suicide," since this poem is about

people "born on the wrong side of the line," just as X.Y.Z., as a member of the working class, had belonged on the wrong side of the tracks.

While in Yugoslavia with Dr. Auden on their troubled holiday, Auden also had a disturbing meeting and a nightmare so powerful that he was still able to remember it more than a decade later when he described it to his friend the anthropologist and psychoanalyst John Layard—who was an old pupil and patient of Rivers.[151] Unsurprisingly, Dr. Auden figures unheroically in both the meeting and the dream.[152]

The meeting probably occurred first and triggered Auden's dream. Maurice Bowra, small in build but with a large head and a loud voice, which some people described as akin to a bittern's boom, served with the Royal Field Artillery during the war and was a scholar of ancient Greek literature. Nicknamed "the Rhino," Bowra was a formidable and disturbing figure on the Oxford social scene among aesthetes in the 1920s when Auden was an undergraduate. John Betjeman was a member of Bowra's circle of protégés, as were Isaiah Berlin, David Cecil, L. P. Hartley, Nancy Mitford, John Sparrow (a lifelong Auden enemy), and the Etonians Cyril Connolly, Kenneth Clark, Anthony Powell, and Robert Byron. Day Lewis was one of the more somber members of Bowra's brilliant but pretentious flock.[153] Powell wrote that Bowra and his acolytes were ready to insist on "the paramount claims of eating, drinking, sex (women at that early stage somewhat derided, homosexuality and auto-eroticism approved), but to accept, as absolutely normal, open snobbishness, success worship, personal vendettas, unprovoked malice, disloyalty to friends, reading other people's letters (if not lying about, to be sought in unopened drawers)—the whole bag of tricks."[154]

Auden felt excluded from this golden group of second-rate first-raters: "To the youth I then was, uncertain of himself, gauche, shy, and, therefore, brash, [Bowra] embodied all those qualities, social poise, elegance, wit, worldliness, which I most longed to possess and despaired of ever possessing. . . . To belong to 'Maurice's' circle was to be 'in,'" Auden wrote, a little masochistically, late in life. "I was not 'in,' but dearly wished I could be."[155]

Not to be "in" was to be "out" and to be vulnerable. Bowra could be a formidably cruel opponent: "I create rebuffs before I am rebuffed," he told Isaiah Berlin.[156] Auden later admitted: "When I was twenty, I was more scared of 'Maurice Bowra' than I have been of any other human being before or since."[157] In these comments (taken from "A Don in the World," his late review of Bowra's *Memoirs*), Auden mentions in passing, and forty years on, the dream he had in 1927: "He [Bowra] appeared as an accusing figure in a nightmare and when, while I was traveling with my father in Yugoslavia, we unexpectedly ran into him, I was so petrified that I could not remember his name."[158]

"A Don in the World" makes it seem that the meeting with Bowra in Yugoslavia in 1927 was *preceded* by the "nightmare." Yet when he reported his dream to Layard much earlier, in 1938, Auden recalled that it had occurred one night while he was *in* Yugoslavia. This detail makes it almost certain that Auden and his father unexpectedly met Bowra while they were in the country and that after being "so petrified that I could not remember [Bowra's] name," Auden had a nightmare about him in which "he appeared as an accusing figure."[159]

Auden related the dream to Layard thus, perhaps giving some clues about where the unexpected meeting with The Rhino had taken place:

> I was sitting in a café talking to someone. In the same café was a man called Morris Bowra (an Oxford don whom I used to be frightened [of] because of his social success and who represented what I should then have liked to be). I made some disparaging remark about him. He came over to me and said "When you came up (to Oxford) you were very promising, but now, of course, you know you're no good."
>
> Then I was on the road that runs round the Devil's Punchbowl (close to where my prep school used to be). There was a taxi there with Morris Bowra sitting in it. I thought (? or said) "If I apologize, all will be all right." Then my Mother appeared and screamed out to Bowra "You promised to give him 6ᵈ."[160]

This dream involves the two people who had inspired greatest fear and anxiety in the young Auden. There is his religious, highly strung, highly intelligent mother, with whom his relations were "intimate and intense in childhood" and "turbulent and painful" later.[161] By the time that Auden was at Oxford, his relationship with his mother had become especially difficult, probably largely because of her awareness, and disapproval, of his homosexuality. A. S. T. Fisher, the friend who stayed with the Audens at Easter 1926, "noticed that Auden was deeply upset by the frequent quarrels with his mother; after a particularly stormy breakfast one day, Auden went upstairs and burst into tears."[162] The dream's second protagonist is Bowra, of whom Auden, at the age of twenty, "was more scared . . . than I have been of any other human being before or since."

One topographical detail from the dream as related by Auden needs clarification: the location of the Devil's Punchbowl. This is a large hollow situated on a hillside not far to the west of Hindhead in Surrey, where Auden was at prep school from 1915 to 1920. It was also the place where "Corporal Auden" had taken part in the St. Edmund's OTC field day in 1917, ten years earlier than the time of the dream, and had been overrun by the opposing forces, obliging him to role-play his own violent death.[163] The "road that runs round the Devil's Punchbowl," the place where in the dream Auden meets Bowra sitting in a taxi, is cut along the side of Gibbet Hill, overlooking the Punchbowl. Charles Dickens mentions the folklore connected to this sinister spot in a passage in *Nicholas Nickleby*, during his account of the walk that Nicholas and Smike, refugees from Dotheboys Hall, make from London to Portsmouth: "They walked upon the rim of the Devil's Punch Bowl; and Smike listened with greedy interest as Nicholas read the inscription upon the stone which, reared upon that wild spot, tells of a murder committed there by night. The grass on which they stood, had once been dyed with gore; and the blood of the murdered man had run down, drop by drop, into the hollow which gives the place its name. 'The Devil's Bowl,' thought Nicholas, as he looked into the void, 'never held fitter liquor than that!'"[164] The stone marks the place where a sailor was killed; his attackers were later caught and hanged on the summit of Gibbet Hill.

Auden's dream has two parts. This dyad immediately signals the basic duality of early emotional life: the infant's relation to its father and mother. A totemic "father," very different from Auden's actual father and represented by the powerful and socially established figure of Bowra, of whom Auden is frightened and "who represented what I should then have liked to be," dominates the dream's first episode. Indeed, he almost literally dominates the dreamer's consciousness since in the café the dreamer is talking to an unidentified "someone" who is a nobody (probably this is Auden's own less-than-colorful father). The dreamer is making remarks about Bowra, of whose presence he is already aware, even though Bowra is not sitting with them. The threat of the Bowra figure generates a feeble, preemptive attack. Bowra comes over in the café and delivers a crushing rebuke, commenting on the abjected Auden's failures, academic and poetic, at Oxford: "When you came up . . . you were very promising, but now, of course, you know you're no good." From "now" to "know" to "no good," the sound of the word "no" is repeated three times in rapid succession.

Like Prospero's dismissive chiding of Caliban at the end of *The Tempest*—"disproportion'd in his manners | As in his shape"—Bowra's remark, indicating that there is no possibility of acceptance from the world he represents, ends the first part of the dream.[165] But there is a wrinkle to this train of thought in the dream: even as Auden is rejected by Bowra, he is himself rejecting his father. Bowra—savage, witty, glamorous, worldly, homosexual, and morally empty, ensconced in his famous white rooms in an Oxford college—was the antithesis of Auden's real father, the stolid, practical, down-to-earth Dr. Auden, part-time lecturer at a provincial university, carver of oak screens, author of notes on Viking antiquities, and chief physician to the children in a city filled with slums. In Auden's description, there are hints of terror, envy, and perhaps even desire: Bowra was something his own father was not.

If the first part of the dream belongs to Bowra, Auden's mother looms over the second part and over Bowra, too. Even before she appears, Mrs. Auden is symbolically present through the idea of a scenic place, a deep natural hollow, which is the site, drenched in blood, where a man was brutally murdered. This makes it clear that the "Devil's Punchbowl," a place whose very name is symbolic of these associations, is identified by Auden's unconscious with the mother and, more particularly, with her sexuality and fertility.

The second part of the dream is rich with maternal symbolism but also with clear references to violence in the atmosphere created by the dreamer's knowledge of the legends about the Devil's Punchbowl, by the continuing menace in the presence of the dismissive Bowra, by Auden's memories of a wartime spent in that location, and by his mother's vehement "scream." In this part of the dream, Bowra, the all-powerful father substitute in the first part, is silent and seated. In a sense, the dreamer is by this stage even more threatened and feeble, not only because he has now regressed to a place associated with his childhood but also because he is eager to try to conciliate the terrifying paternal figure of Bowra by apologizing for his transgression.

Then, chastizing Bowra like the ring ouzel that scolds the two poets in "I chose this lean country," his mother screams at the Oxford don, "You promised to give him 6ᵈ." The dream concludes as if her words have successfully broken the spell. Money often has a symbolic relation to sex in dreams (and in poetry), and Auden's dream (like his poetry) seems to suggest this connection. Auden once explained to an American friend that the word "sixpence" has "an underground relation to sex and penis."[166] Auden's mother's speech in the dream—"You promised to give him 6ᵈ"—thus means something like, "You promised to give him a penis" or, figuratively speaking, "You promised to give him adult strength."

The petrifying "Bowra," the epitome of an Oxford culture of cutting remarks, appears on Gibbet Hill, where "the blood of the murdered man had run down, drop by drop, into the hollow which gives the place its name." He has apparently symbolically castrated Auden the dreamer or has at least denied him the strength symbolized by a phallus. The dreamer feels that all he can do is propitiate the father figure rather than fight back: "If I apologise, all will be all right." Is Bowra in part a screen here for another father figure from Auden's time at Oxford: T. S. Eliot, whose poetry Auden had weakly tried to imitate? The Mother's reproach, spoken on behalf of the dreamer, is that the Bowra figure, or more broadly Oxford, or the modernist Eliot, has failed to give her son a penis—that is, to give him strength, independence.

At Gresham's, a new boy had to make three promises about his behavior: not to swear, not to smoke, and not to say or do anything indecent.[167] Looking back later in a poem, Auden mock-bequeathed the school "three broken promises" from him.[168] In this Yugoslavia dream, Bowra declares that Auden's "promise" at Oxford has come to nothing, and Mrs. Auden screams that Oxford has not kept its "promise" to her son. The dream is a catastrophe of disturbing reproaches over broken promises. In the feud, Auden's mother seems to prevail loudly.

After some time in Yugoslavia with his father, Auden's unhappiness (wishing "I was dead") seems to have been tipped toward desperation. He almost free-associated when he wrote to Isherwood, "Sugar in rectangles again, cognac, and the Blue Danube waltzes under undistinguished trees. Bezahlen bitte. Jesus wept. . . . Am writing in the heat of the day, while Memory drones on like a Satirist reciting in the Dog Days. The recrudescence of Atmosphere is too much for me."[169]

The Bowra dream occurred during a crucial, crisis-bound phase in Auden's development as a writer, after he had been at Oxford for two years. He was struggling as a poet, and with his final examinations in English (a subject that he began studying late and that he did not apply himself to systematically) looming at the end of his third year, he had realized "very well what sort of degree I was going to get and what a bitter disappointment this was going to be to my parents." He had also intuited that "The poems I was writing were still merely derivative, that I had not yet found my own voice, and I felt certain that in Oxford I should never find it, that as long as I remained there, I should remain a child."[170] (Recall that "The Child" was Ayerst's astute nickname for Auden.) The dream seems to say that as long as Bowra and all he stands for reign over him, Auden, without his "sixpence," will remain a child personally and poetically. His anxieties at Oxford centered on his confused identity as a writer and on his sense of social marginality. It is striking to note that almost all the "action" in his dream is concerned with words: remarks, charges, accusations. That makes it reasonable to conjecture that the dream at a deep level is not merely about Auden's relation to his parents or to Oxford but also about his still-fraught relation to language, to poetry, and to his stylistic models.

By the dream's end, a poetic "scream" has become the way to manifest personal and poetic decisiveness. In dream logic, to make loud sounds is a sign of vigor; it is to "find a voice," as Auden put it in his later reminiscence about his time at Oxford. X.Y.Z., accused of having an inefficient "silencer" on his motorcycle and abandoned by his father, soon accidentally crushed his own throat while trying to obtain an abject form of sexual gratification. In one of the poems Auden wrote while he was in Yugoslavia, he parodied his own sense of a futile laconicism in his writing by criticizing a poetic "story" that, like his father's case history, "never was more reticent | Always afraid to say more than it meant."[171] By contrast, it is in the countryside that Auden can hear the primally poetic birds of his imagination singing: the "curlew's creaking call," the "drumming of a snipe," and the "defiant bird" that "stood | Upon a sun-white boulder" in "I chose this lean country" or the bird that "Cried loudly over and over again | Upon the natural ending of a day" in "On the frontier at dawn getting down."[172] Here, too, was part of what Auden found energizing in Yeats's poetry—its vibrant cacophony of noise and speech, all of which signified poetic life and independence. In the third part of "The Tower" alone, for example, there are the human verbs to "declare," "sing," "mock," and "cry"; there is the "bird's sleepy cry" at day's end; there are the jackdaws who "chatter and scream."[173] In the dream, Mrs. Auden silences his son's detractor when she screams.

Auden's greatness as a writer is inseparable from his vulnerability, and his exploration of postwar national identity exposes a side of his persona that was fragile, chaotic, and representative. Talking in an "icy voice" to an Oxford friend, Auden would say, not much later, as if he was pronouncing an unchallengeable truth: "Art is born of humiliation."[174] (Of course, that idea held for himself as much as it did for anyone else.) In the summer of 1927, he seemed in a slough of despond as a poet. But the abjection caused by his failed experiments with international modernism, by his feeble mimicking of Eliot's now-anachronistic early style, and by his inability to break into Oxford's elite literary circles now forced him in directions that would transform his poetry. Sunk low in Yugoslavia, he was soon to mount high in the Pennines. This "child," who was a student (of a sort) of English literature, was about to write a new kind of English poem, one that he would later title "The Watershed."

THE ENGLISH KEYNOTE
VIOLENT WORDS, 1927–1928

In a war in which all combatants were victims of material, in which an industrial technology was the "true" aggressor, identification with the enemy and his dominant motive—survival—was logical, even necessary. . . . [But] however admirable and humane was the "identification with the enemy," it was also the source of a profound, deeply felt conflict, in which the combatant was forced to repudiate self-conceptions sponsored by his society and often shared by himself. Unquestionably the breakdown of the "offensive personality" in the realities of defensive war was one of the major causes of war neurosis. Indeed, for extreme cases of departure from official norms there was even a pathological category: "neurotic sympathy with the enemy."

—ERIC J. LEED (1979)

W. H. AUDEN TURNED TWENTY in February 1927, and just a few months later he began writing the first poems of his that survived into his mature canon of work. In progressing, he was also turning back—to his mining landscapes in the North of England, to earlier poetic models such as Hardy, and to the traumatic inspiration of a country still obsessed in shadowy, indirect forms with the aftermath of the First World War. If anything, Auden's poetry from 1927 onward becomes even more intensely focused on the psychic consequences of war. And, after a period of absence, the conflict bursts back into Auden's poetry as—in some of the same ways and at exactly the same time—after a lull in literary production, a spate of disillusioned war memoirs and novels (some of them, like Robert Graves's *Good-Bye to All That* and Erich Maria Remarque's *Im Westen nichts Neues* [*All Quiet on the Western Front*], destined to become classics) appeared toward the end of the 1920s. Auden was a haunted poet, led by visions, memories, and dreams as much as by books, just as England was a haunted nation.

On the morning of Sunday, 24 July 1927—shortly after Dr. Auden and his son began their troubled holiday in Yugoslavia—at Ypres in Belgium, a crowded ceremony took place on the town's eastern edge. Albert I, the king of the Belgians, the British ambassador to Belgium, and Field-Marshall Lord Plumer unveiled the gigantic Menin Gate Memorial to the Missing. It marked the place through which huge numbers of men, many of them doomed, had filed on their journeys toward the battlefields and the German lines. Plumer had been the commanding officer of British and Commonwealth troops at the Second Battle of Ypres in 1915, during which Christopher Isherwood's father was one of tens of thousands killed.[1]

Once the speeches were over that day, there was a "terrible minute of silence." Then, as the crowd sang "God Save the King," a contingent of British soldiers with drums marched out of the gate. The *Times* correspondent covering the ceremony wrote: "They always make one shudder, those drums. But here, at such a place and in such surroundings, the splendour and the terror of them were beyond words."[2]

The Australian artist Will Longstaff, who had served at Gallipoli and in France, witnessed this ceremony. That night he too walked through the great gate and along the road stretching into the countryside beyond. When he did, he experienced a vision of "steel-helmeted spirits rising from the moonlit cornfields around him."[3] Returning to London, Longstaff painted a large, blue-hued canvas, some five feet by ten feet, evoking the silvery glow of the moon in the darkness that night and showing an army of anonymous, skeletal ghosts milling outside the Menin Gate in fields of blood-red poppies. They wear helmets, carry packs, and bear bayoneted rifles. These are not the risen but the unburied. In the distance, a building is burning. The following year, Longstaff added another image to what became a cycle. This one, called *Immortal Shrine (Eternal Silence),* shows similar ghost-soldiers marching in darkness and rain past the Cenotaph in London's Whitehall. The vast Tannenberg Memorial to the German dead on the Eastern Front was dedicated in the same year, 1927, as the Menin Gate Memorial. (It stands near what is now Olsztynek in Poland.) Years after the Armistice, the First World War and its victims still weighed like a nightmare on the brains of the living in the victorious as well as in the defeated nations.

At the same time, and because war memories and a sense of nationality are inextricably linked, in the United Kingdom, "Englishness" was becoming a matter of widespread discussion. What was Englishness? Was it static or evolving? The word "Englishness," meaning, simply, the quality of being English, denotes a modern concept. It does not appear in the works of any of the classic poets, playwrights, and novelists who are so often taken as the constituents of an English literary canon: it is nowhere in Chaucer, Spenser, Marlowe, Shakespeare, Milton, Behn, Pope, Burney, Austen, Wordsworth, George Eliot, or Dickens. In fact, the term is not in any English poem written before the twentieth century or in any novel I have been able to find published before 1900 or in any piece of drama from the medieval Mystery Plays through to Oscar Wilde's comedies. The first recorded citation of "Englishness" in the *Oxford English Dictionary* (*OED*) is from 1804 during the Napoleonic Wars; but it lists only three recorded uses of the word from the entire nineteenth century. Over the same period up to 1919, the word appeared a mere five times in the country's foremost establishment newspaper, the *Times*.

Between just 1920 and 1929, though, the word surfaced in the same newspaper twelve times in phrases such as "the peculiar Englishness of the English landscape" and "a certain arrogant Englishness that most of us conceal under our subscription to the now cosmopolitan world."[4] The nature of Englishness is a modern problem, a modern ideal. The word, which has a subtly defensive flavor, gained currency because in the country's postwar culture, writers and commentators began to discuss the question of what "Englishness" was, and they searched for existing definitions or, failing that, engineered their own. The last quotation from the *Times*, cited earlier, comes from a May 1927 review of works by William Blake. Later the same year, in August 1927 (only about a month and a half after T. S. Eliot was baptized and became a member of the Anglican Church), on the centenary of Blake's death, the *Times* praised him again as "more truly English" than any of his literary and artistic contemporaries, lauding Blake's "peculiar Englishness" and calling "Jerusalem" (in the Parry setting) "Almost a second National Anthem— nay, if it be not disloyal to say so, it has come to stand for something the National Anthem fails to express: the private loyalty to some Little England—the white and secret Albion of Blake's imagination—upon which public loyalty to the larger England of the National Anthem ultimately depends."[5] (The phrase "Little England" goes back at least as far as *Henry VIII*, the play that Shakespeare had a hand in writing with John Fletcher in around 1601. But in the context of the late nineteenth century and the early twentieth century, it specifically refers to the ideal of a constituency of nationalists and patriots, mainly identifying as liberals and often called "Little Englanders," who believed in England's moral and social superiority to other nations but who were opposed to the vast military expenses and moral corruption attendant on possession of a far-flung overseas empire.[6])

The *Times* article added, sounding almost Eliotic as it pronounced on Blake, "Certainly the mystical England of his imagination—not here and perhaps never to be realized—has become the ideal of our intenser patriotism with its hundred local attachments."[7] Like Eliot's conversion, the paper's encomium, with its emphasis on Blake's "native genius" and his "Englishness," on "private loyalty" and "local attachments," illustrates the pervasiveness of a new, more apprehensive, insular and nationalistic mood that was circulating in English culture during the second half of the 1920s while Auden was at university.

Another sign of the same developing phenomenon was the waning prestige of France. You could calibrate this shift in taste among the culture-consuming professionals and upper-middle classes in England at the time by tracing the chiastic decline in sympathy for France and rise in sympathy for Germany. "The violent, even hysterical, hatred of Germany during the war, and the moral zeal for her punishment in 1918–19," the historian Correlli Barnett wrote, "had given way to pity for poor Germany in her plight of defeat and ruin, oppressed as she also was by the hard-hearted French."[8] In the 1920s "Anti-French feeling among most ex-soldiers amounted almost to an obsession," Graves maintained. "Edmund [Blunden], shaking with nerves, used to say at this time: 'No more wars for me at any price. Except against the French. If there's ever a war with them, I'll go like a shot.'"[9]

In the second issue of *The Enemy*, published in 1927, Wyndham Lewis launched strikes against the French capital. He crowed that "in Paris you can be certain that, if nowhere else, *The Enemy* will justify its name."[10] Developing the "critical attack on the grand scale" that he had already started "against the 'radical' institutions in the ascendant in the world of art and letters," Lewis broadsided the "activities of many people, politicians much more than artists, not french, who make Paris their headquarters" and "propose to dictate to the world of Western art and letters, from that address, policies that are as alien to most of us as they are to France." He blasted the tourist ambience in Paris: "Jazz-parties of *Campus Owls* arrive and are absorbed; spunging and super-annuated pathics, who have lost their last pair of professional pyjamas in their last moonlight flit, touring fairies, cultured, obliging and vigilant; 'five-dimensional' ex-bar-tenders, many many 'poets,' arrive as particles or in parties: this Paris is a great holiday camp." As a result, "No independent individual is likely to succeed there."[11]

Some of the same controversies, albeit in a more decorous register, were taking place in Oxford, where Auden was spending the academic terms writing poetry, suffering in love, and, on occasion, studying.

In August 1927, the same month that the *Times* exalted "the private loyalty to some Little England," Auden returned from his disturbing Yugoslavian holiday with his father. Soon after he got back, he wrote his first great poem. It begins: "Who stands, the crux left of the watershed" (for brevity's sake, referred to hereafter as "Who stands"), and it is a blank verse lyric aggressively asserting a vision of Auden's own "private loyalty" to a particular English landscape, his own secret, dystopian Albion. He wrote it not in the spot it describes but at his parents' home in Harborne, Birmingham, which perhaps accounts for some of its intensity. The poem reads almost like something from a vision or a state of trance.

In this poem, Auden returns to the same sort of landscape that he had described in "'Lead's the Best'" in the spring of 1926 and in "I chose this lean country" in the early summer of 1927. The new poem Auden wrote recapitulates the experience of being in fell and lead-mine country, doing so to gain a better cognitive control over it, to master it imaginatively to a degree that the other works could not. However, it is the way that the poem's speaker is shown falling short in that effort that makes "Who stands" such a success. The poem gains memorability from its expression of the failure of the effort at mastery, of the failure to hold a divided society within a single visionary frame. Here is the poem:

> Who stands, the crux left of the watershed,
> On the wet road between the chafing grass
> Below him sees dismantled washing-floors,

Snatches of tramline running to the wood,
An industry already comatose,
Yet sparsely living. A ramshackle engine
At Cashwell raises water; for ten years
It lay in flooded workings until this,
Its latter office, grudgingly performed,
And further here and there, though many dead
Lie under the poor soil, some acts are chosen
Taken from recent winters; two there were
Cleaned out a damaged shaft by hand, clutching
The winch the gale would tear them from; one died
During a storm, the fells impassable,
Not at his village, but in wooden shape
Through long abandoned levels nosed his way
And in his final valley went to ground.

Go home, now, stranger, proud of your young stock,
Stranger, turn back again, frustrate and vexed:
This land, cut off, will not communicate,
Be no accessory content to one
Aimless for faces rather there than here.
Beams from your car may cross a bedroom wall,
They wake no sleeper; you may hear the wind
Arriving driven from the ignorant sea
To hurt itself on pane, on bark of elm
Where sap unbaffled rises, being spring;
But seldom this. Near you, taller than grass,
Ears poise before decision, scenting danger.[12]

The poem's first verb, "stands," surges with energy and independence, in contrast to the passivity embodied in "sitting in a café" with a no-body, as Auden had dreamed of doing not many days before he wrote "Who stands." Indeed, the poem's active primal verbs are its first two: the interrelated "stands" and "sees."

These two verbs in the first sentence of Auden's first canonical poem offer mutual strengthening because the actions of standing and seeing are so intimately linked to each other that they have sometimes been taken as jointly constituting the essence of being human. In two long footnotes to *Civilization and Its Discontents,* both added in 1931,

Freud conjectures that one of the momentous developments in prehistory came when humanity's ancestors raised themselves up from the ground, enabling them to see further (and to react to dangers and opportunities earlier) because their vision was unimpeded by grasses, scrub, and undergrowth. The "fateful process of civilization," Freud writes, set in with "man's adoption of an erect position," making "visual stimuli" become "paramount."[13] The loftily situated speaker in "Who stands," flooded with visual stimuli from the landscape, seems at first to hold a position of absolute cognitive mastery over the world that he (taking the speaker as a stand-in for the poet) surveys. But the poem ends on a conflicted note with a powerful sense of alienation from the people and animals—and they from him—in this terrain spread out before him. In Gravesian style, "Who stands" dramatizes the poet trying to recognize rather than avoid conflict so as to stand a chance of becoming the "physician of his mental disorders."[14]

In forswearing any false note of synthesis or harmony and insisting instead on a sense of division as fundamental to poetic utterance, Auden writes here a poem of genuine social scope. The fissures and rifts within "Who stands" are at once maps of the geological fissures and rifts in the poem's northern landscape, the rifts in the poet's own psyche, and the divisions within English culture. As such, written in a period when concerns with the nature of Englishness were becoming widespread, it is a poem not just, or not so much, about epistemological or psychological issues (as some commentators argue) but about the riven condition of postwar England and about the difficulties of national belonging.[15]

Through the strong association of blank verse with the works of Milton and Wordsworth, Auden's choice of poetic form here links his poem to a tradition of stylistic and moral sublimity. Correspondingly, he could not have set the poem's opening at a much higher or more dramatic spot. The "stranger" is probably standing on Cross Fell in the North Pennines, and the sense of primary power connected with standing and seeing is reinforced by situating his poem in this special place.[16]

The Pennines, running roughly north-south and sometimes known as the "backbone of England," stretch for about 160 miles from the Scottish border to the Peak District in Derbyshire.[17] Cross Fell is around twenty-two miles as the hawk flies east-northeast of Wesco, the home on the edge of the Lake District that the Auden family had bought in the mid-1920s.[18] The vantage point for this poem is the loftiest spot on the Pennine range and the most elevated place in England outside the Lake District. These desolate, boggy hills, often played over by a shrieking wind, form the watershed in northern England—as Auden mentions in the poem's first line. Cross Fell, where the speaker probably "stands," is the highest position on the island's main geological dividing line between west and east. As such, it is a location of great symbolic and physical significance in the context of English topography. The rivers Eden, Ribble, and Mersey rise here in the Pennines and flow west to the Irish Sea. The Tyne, Tees, Swale, Aire, Don, and Trent also rise in the vicinity and flow east to the North Sea. On clear days from Cross Fell, you can see both coasts.

Symbolically, the mountain top is the lonely place of truth, speculation, absoluteness. Following classical and biblical exempla, peaks have long been associated with poetry and revelation, as they are, for instance, in Wordsworth's visionary poetry set in the Alps in *The Prelude*. The ascent to a great height is a familiar scenario for a human confrontation with divinity, as happened in Moses's encounters with God on Mount Horeb (Sinai) and Mount Pisgah. These biblical episodes were the symbolic context for Dante's revelations at the top of Mount Purgatory and Petrarch's celestial visions on Mont Ventoux. To Milton, one periphrasis for God's majesty is "the power of the most high."[19] And in his description of Michael's conversation with Adam on the topmost hill in Paradise, Milton writes that from that vantage point, Adam's "eye might there command wherever stood | City of old or modern fame."[20] In noting that Adam specifically "command[s]" such immense spatial and temporal perspectives, Milton emphasizes that to see from on high is not only to perceive an object or a space at a distance but also to feel mastery or ownership of it. Height is power. In Auden's poem, the prospect offers the poet an apparently "commanding" overview of England's landscape—and, by extension, its economic and spiritual conditions.

The appeal of a lofty position from which to scrutinize, understand, and deliver judgment had first appeared in Auden's work around 1923 and 1924, in poems such as "Arthur's Quoit, Dyffryn" (see Chapter 2).[21] That poem, and others like it, date from the period just after Auden discovered Hardy's poetry, and he later associates this high, steeply angled perspective with his enthusiasm for Hardy's work, and especially for the war poem *The Dynasts*.[22]

However, literary precedents for this strategy of surveying from a great height are inseparable from more mundane contemporary practices. For example, a vogue for hiking and walking trips—as well as tours by car, bus or bicycle—to "discover" the English countryside reached mass proportions in the 1920s. Beginning "before 1914 but reaching its peak in the interwar period, a great movement 'to the outdoors' completed the process [of rediscovery] by making the countryside an accessible and popular site of leisure," Alun Howkins wrote.[23] The view from above, on a hill or from a tower, was a standard recommendation for postwar tourists and hikers who wanted to "know" an area they were visiting. The fascination conjured up by Hardy's aerial viewpoints in *The Dynasts* thus matches the sensitization of the public imagination in the 1910s and 1920s to the advantages of looking down at landscape from new angles and standpoints.

Many poems lose something when they get too far away from at least some relation to simple, widely shared experiences. Reflective poems, like Auden's here, can base their success on allowing uniqueness and normality, vision and everydayness, to intermingle. Matthew Arnold's "Dover Beach" is another august, generalizing poem about human fate, and at the same time it is recognizably an almost sociological portrait of a middle-class person's pleasant sentimentality as they watch the world from a hotel balcony on holiday. "Who stands" does something similar. In it, Auden manages to dramatize himself as both prophetic and representative, a poet and an energetic but commonplace tourist. It is part of his genius that, even at his most discursive and abstract, a recognizable, mundane world still grounds Auden's writing.

"Who stands" is divided into two unequal paragraphs of blank verse, the first of eighteen lines, the second of twelve; and in this way, on a larger scale, it comes close to matching the ratio between octave and sestet in a sonnet, suggesting that poetic form's inbuilt sense of complicated self-division.[24] Auden's subtly delineated hiker scenario organizes these two elements. The formal asymmetry of the two parts reflects two different vantage points on the landscape and two contrasting modes of address. The first part, which by its clarity of detail implies a daytime setting (no one can see "dismantled washing-floors" and snatches of derelict tramline in the distance, once darkness has fallen on this remote, unilluminated world), is spoken in the cool, knowing voice of someone who has a mastery of visual specifics and local lore. Perhaps this part of the poem mimics the verbally assured manner of a guidebook, describing what a viewer would see who looked down and out across the mine-dotted and sheepfold-speckled landscape from this high place in the Pennines.

The poem's short, but altogether more urgent-feeling, second part, with its mention of "Beams from your car" (an homage to the father-poet Hardy's 1924 lyric "Nobody Comes" and its passing car with "lamps full-glare, | That flash upon a tree"), is set at night; and, correspondingly, its mood is emotionally darker.[25] Moreover, it is articulated in a different, counterpointing voice. Now, eerily, the country itself seems to speak, rejecting the stranger's attempt to know the land or its people. That the region suddenly acquires a voice gives the second part of the poem a strikingly dreamlike quality. But the entire nighttime journey through the landscape of the second part of the poem is a phantom one, since it is conjured up by the landscape's voice. The poem's first voice *knew* and *saw* the landscape and its human society from a great height. But the anonymous observer through whose eyes the poem looks in part 1 has now become the observed and confronted stranger in part 2.

The poem's second voice, answering back, tells the stranger to "Go home . . . turn back again" because the land "cut off, will not communicate." The stranger (this term, a key one for Auden, is used twice in two lines) will never be able to interest the people who live there, those "Aimless for faces rather there than here." Although the poem does not rhyme, the line endings are revealing. In particular, the final words in each of the poem's last seven lines form a beautiful, right-hanging chain of nouns: *wall, wind, sea, elm, spring, grass,* and *danger.* Nouns denote, so to speak, things in themselves, and this stark right border of thing-words emphasizes the uncontaminated self-sufficiency of this world with which the stranger cannot communicate.

The reference to "cut off" land occurs just after the point when the split or fissure between the two parts occurs. The sudden break shows, again, that not everything from Auden's study of early Eliot's fracturing mode was lost when Auden reverted to a more insular, antimodernist, and "English" style. The split within Auden's poem mirrors the subtly different temporalities of the two parts. The first is written in a generalized, unspecific present tense and is focused largely on incidents from the past, with reflections on "an industry already comatose," and on "acts . . . Taken from recent winters." The second, full of injunctions and assertions, is written in a simple present: "Go home, now, stranger. . . . Ears poise before decision."

But a poem that broke completely into two would be two poems, not one. So, at the same time that Auden produced this emphatic gap between the two voices and two parts in the center of "Who stands," he also found ways to suggest that the two verse paragraphs were not completely dissociated, to create a faint web of connections between the different sections. Auden's studies of Eliot and of Graves had allowed him to reach the point where he could write a poem that was fractured in structure but not entirely sundered. Many of the linkages between the poem's two parts, such as the miner who "in wooden shape . . . *nosed* his way" in part 1 and the hare "*scenting* danger" in part 2, may not have a logical connection in terms of paraphrasable content, but they signal that Auden's poem is looking for modes of formal coherence that will survive rational judgments about similarity and dissimilarity, linkage and separateness.

There is a quiet but profound sensitivity on Auden's part here to the constructed and contingent nature of perceived differences. Cultures draw lines, define categories, and make boundaries; yet it is obvious that there are connections across boundaries that show the limited validity of common sense, demarcation, and even some forms of logic. It was this formal awareness of connections and ruptures that enabled Auden to write about a country in crisis, "already comatose, | Yet sparsely living." Auden's method of finding subtle relationships between apparently unlinked objects or phenomena was perfect for representing an entity in conflict with itself—and in this poem, that entity is not only the speaker but also, and above all, postwar England. "Who stands" ends with an image of instinctive wariness. An animal of which the stranger is unaware, a hare with a sensory apparatus far more powerful than a human's, is about to be triggered into flight by the stranger's presence. Even the region's animals will flee from the stranger: "Near you, taller than grass, | Ears poise before decision, scenting danger." But the "grass" in which the hare is hiding at the end, without being explicitly connected, is the same "chafing grass" in which the stranger is standing at the very opening of the poem. "Who stands" works like a straight line that is also somehow a circle.

Auden dramatizes his stranger moving visually and emotionally across and down a landscape, back into history, and into a confrontation with an uncanny and frightened spirit of the land. But the protagonist does not physically move an inch from the spot where he starts. The whole journey of the poem is an inner one. Moreover, it is an entirely conjectural and conditional inner journey with a spectral, unreal quality: Auden imagines an observer who surveys the landscape, and then the observer's own imagination takes a journey through it. True to the Gravesian ethos of poetry as intrapsychic "conflict," the final lines abruptly, almost violently, terminate the poem in very much the way a dream might suddenly stop on a note of panic, without any attempt at harmonization, reconciliation, or even stasis. For example, there was the recent plug-pulling moment of Mrs. Auden's scream at Bowra at the end of Auden's 1927 Yugoslavia dream. And here the hare is about to race away from the stranger, bringing the dream / poem to a sudden stop.

Freud was an unwilling genius of figurative language, distrusting the distorting pull of metaphors, similes, and what he once curtly called the "pictorial mode of expression." And yet, as if the mind's structure could only be talked about in analogical terms, he felt obliged to have recourse to such figures as a way of throwing "light from different directions on a highly complicated topic which has never yet been represented."[26] Of these similes or metaphors, perhaps none recurs with more frequency in his work than that of the mind as an entity with a surface and hidden depths. Sometimes this idea takes the form of metaphors of the mind as an archaeological site, sometimes as a labyrinth or as a tomb. Freud talked of the analyst taking "the path" that "leads into the depths" and, in the same essay, of work that becomes "more obscure and difficult . . . the deeper we penetrate into the stratified psychical structure."[27] He described how an analyst might even believe that "we have penetrated through all the psychological strata and have reached bedrock."[28]

Freud's concept of the analyst as an explorer journeying into the mind's dark inner depths resonates powerfully with the language of mining so prevalent in Auden's poem. Chapter 3 described how Rivers, too, thought insistently of the mind in terms of higher and lower strata, theorizing, for example, that there was in the human psyche "an arrangement of mental *levels* exactly comparable with that now generally recognized to exist in the nervous system, an arrangement by which more recently developed or acquired systems control the more ancient."[29] These terms match usefully with the language in Auden's poem. For instance, Rivers's idea of "mental levels" that can be "ancient" jumps like a spark in the reader's mind to Auden's vignette of a miner's body being brought back through "long abandoned levels" inside a Pennine excavation. (A "level" is an old mining term for a roughly horizontal undergound passage or gallery in a mine.) Rivers and other British physicians, including Dr. Auden, were trained—as Freud had been—within a nineteenth-century medical culture that conceived of the mind, like society, in pseudo-evolutionary terms as consisting of "higher" and "lower" functions; W. H. Auden maps that common schema onto the *mined/mind* landscape of "Who stands."

The psychological journey downward that the poem undertakes is an attempted Riversian descent through the "mental levels," represented here as both geological and human-made strata. In his writings, Rivers makes clear that journeys through physical landscape can be correlated with the progress downward in the mind to what he termed "tendencies belonging to an older social order."[30] The senses of land as a representation of mind and of the plot of the poem as an attempt at an internal descent into the lower levels of consciousness are strongly suggested by the use of the medical term "comatose" to describe the nonfunctional state of the industry in the region.[31] The poem's observer/stranger uses rare language like "crux" and "frustrate," which marks him as a symbolic representative of sophisticated, more recently evolved "epicritical" control, a rationally based faculty associated (in the Riversian paradigm) with higher-level functions in the mind. That higher level is connected, naturally, with a superior vantage point and (as the guidebooks advised) with climbing upward to gain the power to understand space and topography accurately. In the opening verse paragraph of Auden's poem, knowledge comes from observation, which organizes the confident coordination of objects in space and the temporal coordination of events in time.[32] But the epistemological command has a social dimension as well.

The masterful, and intensely self-conscious, marshaling of observations and information about the landscape not only produces the effect of an accurate report, a sense of objective knowledge. The cogency also helps to suggest the effect of listening to an authoritative speaker, an expert. The tone is subtly technocratic, scientific, and managerial; the impression given is of a modern allegory in which the higher mental faculties, used for conceptual and analytic labor, are controlling the lower. But there is something slightly one-sided or excessive about this expertise; and the voice projected sounds lonely. The attempted encounter is with the "cut off" and uncommunicative land of the lower, protopathic levels of the mind. This is enacted as the passing down the social scale from the middle-class, intellectually active observer on the mountain to the lower-class, physically active miners to the world of the unwakeable sleeper, sinking into the unconsciousness that returns us to infantile levels of experience and finally to the nonhuman world of the hare. But that journey downward is a failure: the speaker cannot make contact with the inhabitants of the world he is looking down on.

The anonymous figure on high could see and judge, could imaginatively own the landscape from Cross Fell. But if the first paragraph was the "intellectual moment" of the poem, dramatized by the height from which everything was seen, the second paragraph is the "emotional moment." And they fail to mesh fully or organically. The anonymous stranger-speaker in the first part "commands" and knows the landscape and its history. In the second part, the stranger has in imagination moved down and into the world of people. But he is without identity, anonymous, almost a ghost. When he comes down into the world of the villagers, the speaker is defined for the first time—ironically, though, as a stranger, because one only becomes a stranger in relation to other people who are locals. In this way, "Who stands" is a poem that seems to dramatize a feeling of superiority and privilege, but it does so only to show that this privilege produces isolation, and then it dramatizes that privilege crumbling and failing. Seen like this, Auden's poem reads, parabolically, as a great exploration of class divisions, unrequited longing, emotional alienation, and a culture broken apart.

The attempt to enter the inhabited parts of the landscape, and to reconcile the lofty and the grounded, the epicritic and the protopathic, the visual and the auditory, the upper and the lower, collapses. But Auden's frustration contains within it the germ of possible future success and regeneration. The poem fails to "prehend" experience "emotionally and intellectually at once"—as he and Day Lewis insisted that poetry should in their preface to *Oxford Poetry 1927*. But it shows, as they also demanded, the poet's mind bearing "the brunt of the conflict" to bring the psyche's higher and lower levels (and, by implication, different levels in the social world) into contact with one another.[33] In this sense, the conflict—the baffled effort by the conscious, middle-class mind as it enters the communal, working-class world of the unconscious—represented but not resolved in the poem, is valuable because, as Graves said, it is "half-way to a solution, which may be expected to occur both in our practical life and in some poem or dream of the future."[34] In that "half-way" point is a glimmer of the ardent and beautiful poems about moments of togetherness and unity that Auden will compose in the southern part of England in the first half of the 1930s.

When Auden wrote "Who stands" he was a mere twenty years old, a student of English literature with a pallid academic record, who within a year was to leave university with an ignominious Third Class degree. But regardless of Auden's poor efforts as a scholar, this poem is an interesting early example (and there will soon be many others) of the feedback loop by which university modes of analyzing literature influence the making of one of the primary objects of disciplinary study, poems. There is something faintly but deliberately academic in tone or material about so much that is genuinely creative (in, for example, the work of Pound or Eliot or Marianne Moore) from the 1920s onward. Similarly, as a result of Auden's college reading "Who stands" is situated within the frame of the neoclassical genre of the picturesque "prospect poem," often said to have been inaugurated by the Royalist poet Sir John Denham's "Cooper's Hill" (1642), set on a prominence just outside Egham on the south bank of the Thames in Surrey.

"Who stands" records with merciless, militant flatness a scene of "dismantled washing-floors, | Snatches of tramline running to the wood.... | A ramshackle engine," and so on. Denham's smooth, bland poetic "flow," awash with vowels and running, like the Thames, "deep, yet clear, though gentle, yet not dull," is wholly absent from the ragged, discontinuous rhythms of the modern poet.[35] Instead of a poetry modeled on the gentle, inexorable movement of an amenably smooth river, the consonantally clashing "ramshackle engine" of Auden's poem laboriously "raises water" at Cashwell. But it is impossible to understand Auden's poem without recognizing that what gives it life at the same time is what it is rejecting.

Instead of focusing, as Denham's poem does, on the privileged heart of the country, on its capital and court, Auden's poem is located on a periphery, an entropic and largely deserted area where a dangerous industry associated with deaths has all but collapsed. Auden's speaker in "Who stands" is not someone securely embedded in the culture that he surveys. Denham spoke as an aristocrat, as a landowner, as a courtier, someone who had a stake in the world surveyed by his poem. By contrast, the sociological positioning of Auden's speaker is complex. The high vantage point suggests both a sophistication and a cognitive power that might be taken as signs of social prestige in the observer. But Auden's well-educated protagonist is also cast as a stranger here, someone not at home in a town and not at home in this landscape either, someone who is longing for psychic and social integration but who is, as the speaker fears, of no interest to those "Aimless for faces rather there than here." Unlike Denham, the speaker neither owns the particular stretch of land in question nor sees the property he surveys as a reflection of his own economic interests; he is someone who has no obvious reason to defend or idealize the landscape that he describes.

By bringing into consciousness and highlighting the parallel divisions within the psyche and within the nation, "Who stands," a poem built around a whole system of formal and thematic asymmetries, shows how Auden begins to imagine (idealistically and by negation) a role for poetry in the creation of a new harmony—that of a psyche reintegrated with itself and a country regenerated to social wholeness. For now, though, the sense of violent conflict is not very far below the surface of "Who stands" and other poems like it that Auden wrote during this period. It juxtaposes two antagonistic entities: the observer who desires to enter the world he has surveyed and the voice of the land that warns him, as a stranger, to turn back from the "cut off" place that will not communicate with him.

The poem is resolved in the image of a hare's ears poking out of the grass and its (hidden) nose "scenting danger," a moment redolent of many war narratives about the dangers faced by jumpy frontline troops from either side catching glimpses of the enemy in No-Man's-Land. As in a dream, Auden's poem distributes its subjectivity into many places— the poem's center is in the dominant stranger on Cross Fell, and yet it also lives in the phantom embrace of two headlight beams crossing a bedroom wall like a pair of outstretched arms in a lover's frustrated imagination. It is in the engine "grudgingly" working at Cashwell and in the nervous twitching nose of the hare anxious not to be exposed and harmed in the way that Auden had dreamed of himself being exposed in the Bowra nightmare. This poem, written only a short while after that nightmare, is so powerful not because it is unified but because it is so beautifully and honestly fractured.

On 9 September 1927, around three months after Auden had sent a collection of poems to Eliot at Faber and Gwyer, the poet of *The Waste Land* wrote back gently rejecting Auden's submission but hinting that Auden could send him future work.[36] They met in London in mid-October, probably around the time when Auden returned to university for his final year of study and exams. Eliot perhaps gave Auden a copy of his Ariel poem "Journey of the Magi," which had been issued that August as a pamphlet with a distinctive yellow cover. Eliot was preparing to become a British subject that November. Although neither yet knew it, Auden had now written a poem, "Who stands," that Eliot would publish within a few years and that he would ensure remained in print for the rest of his life and beyond.

Back in Oxford that autumn, Auden met two other people who would play significant roles in his creative and emotional life: Gabriel Carritt and Stephen Spender, both of whom came up to the university for the Michaelmas term of 1927. Carritt, at Christ Church like William McElwee, had likewise been at Sedbergh, an austere, ancient school in a desolate part of the West Riding around which Auden's imagination wove some ripe sexual fantasies. (He eventually visited the school with Carritt and a fellow old Sedberghian in December 1927.[37]) Carritt was another straight, athletic type, albeit a person already with very strong left-wing political convictions: he would work in various roles for the Communist Party for most of his life. The emotional connection between Carritt and Auden started when Auden fell in love at a rain-soaked rugby game between old Sedberghians at Oxford in November 1927.[38] Auden had known Stephen Spender's older brother, Michael, at Gresham's, and it may have been through Michael Spender that he and Stephen met in Oxford at around the same time that he met Carritt. Spender's place in Auden's life is extensive, and it includes his role as, in 1928, the first person to publish something resembling a chapbook by Auden.[39]

In the poems that Auden wrote after "Who stands" and in the six months or so up to January 1928, one of the most prominent features of the work he produced is the sudden appearance of motifs directly, rather than symbolically, related to war. At most a month after completing "Who stands," Auden wrote "Suppose they met, the inevitable procedure," a poem about frustrated love. He describes "two pathics" whose passivity and indifference he contrasts with the "epic life," which includes an epic death with "the bayonets closing in."[40] Another poem, "The crowing of the cock," mainly about the inability to find emotional satisfaction, ends with a new note in the line "Sounds of conclusive war"—a quietly momentous point in Auden's oeuvre since, although he had been writing lyrics haunted by war memories for five years now, this marks the first time he actually used the word "war" in a poem.[41] In "Because sap fell away," from November 1927, Auden writes about "cold night's attack" and "Love" as the one "Fought at the frozen dam."[42] Poems from further into the winter of 1927–1928 contain more evidence of this new lexicon of war in Auden's work. For example, one small poem is built enigmatically around a military execution and its lethal aftermath:

> The colonel to be shot at dawn
> Plays a harmonium on the lawn.
> Though stimulated by the tune
> The subalterns will die in June.[43]

And in "The weeks of blizzard over" from January 1928, Auden describes his familiar North Pennine landscape and an incident when, "trespassing alone | About the village," his speaker reads on a memorial "The written names of three" who had "died beyond the border | Sent to a recent war."[44]

All these poems show some flashes of war imagery, moments that might be related to war or glimpses of military language. But, in another poem from January 1928, "Control of the Passes was, he saw, the key" (from now on, "Control of the Passes"), Auden introduces a further key word into his militarized lexicon: "spy." "Control of the Passes," an unrhymed sonnet, has a special importance because it is his first poem with an explicit and completely worked-out war scenario:

> Control of the Passes was, he saw, the key
> To this new district, but who would get it?
> He, the trained spy, had walked into the trap
> For a bogus guide, seduced with the old tricks.
>
> At Greenhearth was a fine site for a dam
> And easy power, had they pushed the rail
> Some stations nearer. They ignored his wires.
> The bridges were unbuilt and trouble coming.
>
> The street music seemed gracious now to one
> For weeks up in the desert. Woken by water
> Running away in the dark, he often had
> Reproached the night for a companion
> Dreamed of already. They would shoot, of course,
> Parting easily who were never joined.[45]

The plot set out in the opening two quatrains is of a "trained spy" who feels he has understood the tactical imperatives in the country that he is assigned to monitor: "Control of the Passes was, he saw, the key | To this new district." But he is uncertain about how the struggle for domination will develop. More urgently, he has blown his cover—"walked into the trap | For a bogus guide." And just as he realizes that he has been exposed to the enemy, he also begins to feel that he has been abandoned by his own side: "they ignored his wires." For all his abstract knowledge and understanding of the terrain, acquired while he has been for "weeks up in the desert," he has no control over his circumstances. The spy's secretly assembled knowledge is no key to practical power.

After the poem's volta, the sestet counterpoints and matches the octave's professional disaster with a set of private frustrations, implying a link between private and public failures: "he often had | Reproached the night for a companion | Dreamed of already." For the "trained spy," speaking in the flat, generic idiom of restrained emotion, the end is inevitable: "They would shoot, of course, | Parting easily who were never joined."

In another respect besides its fully worked-out scenario of war, "Control of the Passes" was a prophetic poem—its verbal dryness and gauntness, its "lean[ness]," signaled the taste for angular directness and hardness soon to come into Auden's early canonical poems. In the opening quatrain, for example, the language is halting, plain, argumentative, certainly not "beautiful" or mellifluous. John Betjeman called Auden "the new type of Oxford undergraduate": the "tough youth in corduroys" who was "already aware of slum conditions in Birmingham and mining towns and docks. . . . He combined with this an intense interest in geology and natural history and topography of the British Isles."[46] But this new, hard-edged quality to Auden's poetry in his final year at Oxford is not solely the result of personal characteristics but also of the moment that Wyndham Lewis pinpointed as the birth within English culture in 1926 of the "period of a new complexion," a complexion that was starker, more abrasive, and more combative.[47]

It is in this period from 1926 to 1927 that words such as "war," "bayonets," "attacks," "shooting," and "spies" appear in Auden's poems, to be joined within a few years by other terms such as "soldier," "bomb," and "fighter."[48] As Auden begins to write more explicitly about the aftereffects of "a recent war," he also begins to insert proper names into his poems, perhaps as a note of intended realism. In "The houses rolled into the sun," for example, from the autumn of 1927 or from early 1928, he refers to the enigmatic but suggestive names of "Fagge and Clotters."[49] And in the poem just mentioned, "The weeks of blizzard over," the three dead heroes whose "voices in the rock | Are now perpetual" are given the posh names "Foot, Cockshutte, Tesser-Coop."[50] At least two of these odd names are derived from boys Auden had known at prep school at St. Edmund's during the period of the First World War, further imbuing these poems from 1927–1928 with links between school and the war that had consumed so many British ex-schoolboys.[51]

"Who stands" was indeed a "watershed" poem in Auden's career. Alongside the increasingly military cast of Auden's language, it inaugurated a feeling of crisis without solution or ending in which realistic-sounding characters are obscurely involved. The appearance of a new martial type of poetry in "Control of the Passes" marks another poetic milestone. Its ending—"They would shoot, of course, | Parting easily who were never joined"—sets the tone for many of Auden's despairing, doom-laden poems about social and psychological disorders in the next few years. Part of that tone comes from the fact that the ending is a trans-lation from the famously enigmatic Old English poem *Wulf and Ead-wacer*—a lament spoken by a woman for her illicit lover, "Wulf is on iege, ic on oþerre" (Wulf is on one island, I on another), as she foresees disaster, "þæt mon eaþe toslited þætte næfre gesomnad wæs" (you can easily part what was never joined).[52] The cryptic way in which the ancient poem deals with unsanctioned love must have appealed to Auden, as surely also did the Anglo-Saxon lyric's sense of tragedy and frustration.

By the first part of 1927, not long after praising what was "*English*" to Isherwood, Auden was starting to consolidate the insular tenor of his new poetic style by evoking in his own lines the stark, primal, melan-cholic quality of the Old English poetry that he was studying academi-cally at Oxford.[53] He had mentioned the monster Grendel (from *Beowulf*) in a casual manner in "Thomas Epilogizes," a poem written in the early summer of 1926. But it is only in his poetry of a year or more later that serious stylistic imitations of Old English start to occur in his work. For example, the poem "Suppose they met, the inevitable procedure," written in September 1927, ends with the phrase "Sorrow they had after that." Auden explained in a letter to Isherwood that the line was "not as far as I can remember a direct quotation from OE verse" but "only a typical remark" of the kind found everywhere in Anglo-Saxon poetry.[54] How-ever, shortly afterward, in the autumn of 1927, a steady stream of allu-sions to, and imitations of, Old English poetry rises to the surface in his verse. The fact that Auden joined the library of the English School in October 1927, allowing him to borrow books, seems related to the flow of poems he subsequently wrote including Anglo-Saxon themes or phrases.[55] Poems from 1927 and 1928 cite or allude to *The Dream of the Rood, The Wanderer, The Seafarer, The Battle of Maldon*, and, as just seen, *Wulf and Eadwacer*.[56]

By the mid-Victorian period, it had become a racial commonplace in Britain to stress the shared Saxon and Teutonic heritage of the nations of northern Europe. The German scholar Max Müller, who came to Oxford in 1861 and was made professor of comparative phi-lology there in 1868, declared that the "grammar, the blood and soul of the [English] language" was Saxon, "a branch of the great Teutonic stem of the Aryan family of speech."[57] Thomas Carlyle insisted that the true

English were "blond and blue-eyed nordic, threatened and infiltrated by decadent Celts and Latins."[58] And the critic W. P. Ker, a president of the antiquarian Viking Club, to which Auden's father and his uncle Harold both belonged in the early 1900s, asserted that the English were "a Teutonic people who had inherited along with their language a form of poetry and a number of stories which have nothing to do with Roman civilisation."[59]

Correspondingly, many specialists viewed Old English, pre-Norman poetry as a defining element of English literature, the bedrock on which the canon had been built, its protagonists being the heroic benchmarks against which later adventurers could be measured. The patriotic literary historian Stopford Brooke claimed that the Anglo-Saxon "Widsith is our Ulysses."[60] Around the turn of the twentieth century, the notion that an essential Englishness could be located in Old English poetry was a familiar one. Ezra Pound wrote that in bitter poems such as *The Seafarer* and *The Wanderer*, he could find the "English national chemical" and the "English keynote."[61] When Auden introduced Old English echoes into his poetry, as he did in "Control of the Passes," with its reference to *Wulf and Eadwacer*, he was therefore embedding his writing in a very specific and nationalistic (not to say highly prejudicial) tradition, one that was made vital for him by the figures he encountered at Oxford in the second half of the 1920s.

When Auden came up to the university, Oxford had long been a special bastion of Anglo-Saxon and Old English scholarship. It had conducted its first examinations in English language and literature in 1896, and philology and the study of the ancient Teutonic languages, such as Anglo-Saxon, were central parts of the curriculum. By the time of Auden's arrival in Oxford nearly thirty years later, an influential group of younger scholars of Old English and medieval English literature was gathering there. These included Nevill Coghill, who was elected to a fellowship at Exeter in 1924 and who would be Auden's main tutor in English from 1926 to 1928 (though not for Anglo-Saxon, for which Auden went to the austerely philological C. L. Wrenn); J. R. R. Tolkien, who arrived from Leeds University at Pembroke in 1925; and C. S. Lewis, who became a fellow of Magdalen in the same year. Fired in their writings by what Tolkien called "love of the land of England," these scholars found something primally English about what Lewis later described as "our own ancient system, the alliterative line," suggesting its aptness for contemporary poets now that the "general reaction . . . has set in against the long reign of foreign, syllabic metres in English."[62]

Most of the main members of this prolific academic circle had been marked by the experience of war. Tolkien (1892–1973), Lewis (1898–1963), and Coghill (1899–1980) were all former army officers.[63] Coghill's service was the briefest and apparently the least traumatic: he served as a second lieutenant in the trench mortar division of the Royal Artillery in Salonika and Bulgaria during the last few months of the war and escaped without being wounded or taken seriously ill. But for Tolkien and Lewis, things were different. Tolkien was already sketching out elements of what would become his vast mythological world of epics and tales, dramatized in works such as *The Hobbit* (1937) and *The Lord of the Rings* cycle (1954–1955)—which are packed with poetry as well as narrative prose—when, after graduating from Oxford in 1915, he was commissioned into the Lancashire Fusiliers (the same regiment that Ted Hughes's father served in, though William Hughes [1894–1981] came from a different class and was in the ranks). Tolkien recalled writing some of the "Lost Tales" and elements of what would become the posthumously published *Silmarillion* mythological cycle "in grimy canteens, at lectures in cold fogs, in huts full of blasphemy and smut, or by candle light in bell-tents, even some down in dugouts under shell fire."[64] He served at the Somme and was invalided off the battlefield on 28 October 1916 with a severe case of trench fever, a sickness that bedeviled him for the rest of the war. Later he wrote to a correspondent that the corpse-strewn landscape of the Dead Marshes and the "approach to Morannon" in *The Lord of the Rings* owed "something to Northern France after the Battle of the Somme."[65]

Like Tolkien (and Dr. Auden), Lewis had become passionate about northern and Germanic culture as a boy in the late-Victorian atmosphere of enthusiasm for things Nordic. By October 1917 he had joined the Somerset Light Infantry, and in November of the same year he left for France with the rank of second lieutenant. Lewis was badly wounded on 15 April 1918 at Mount Bernanchon, near Riez, when a misaimed British shell exploded near him.

Old English poetry, like many of the other ancient literatures of northern Europe, is a poetry of lonely travel, of exile and loss, and, above all, of brutal fights between armed men in battles, feuds, hunts,

ambushes, and duels that, to compound the horror, are often fratri-
cidal. As George Dasent grimly rendered it in his mid-Victorian trans-
lation of Snorri Sturluson's *Prose Edda*, "Brothers shall fight together, |
And be one the other's bane; | Sister's children | Their sib shall spoil."[66]
But, as much as subject matter, it was the quasi-abstract, estranging
sound of this poetry, and particularly the ringing, clanging sound of its
alliterative meter, that inspired twentieth-century writers. For Pound,
the prosody was gloriously "riotous and noisy."[67] In a subtly programmatic introduction to "our native metre," Lewis explained in 1935 that
in responding to alliterative poetry, the "reader must learn to attend
entirely to *sounds,* and to ignore spelling. . . . The thing to aim at is
richness and fullness of sound."[68]

Auden's father had read the Icelandic sagas to his youngest son as a
child, but it seems likely that (as Auden later reported) he was first captivated by Old English poetry when he heard Tolkien reciting *Beowulf*
in his "*Beowulf* and *The Fight at Finnesburg*" lectures, delivered at Oxford in the Michaelmas term of 1927. (As we saw just now, it was in
October 1927, shortly after this lecture series started, that Auden suddenly joined the English Faculty library, although he had already been
reading for a degree in English for about a year.) Auden was mesmerized not by the sentiments or themes in the poetry, which he could as
yet read only in translation, but by the sonority of the language. He listened stunned to the Somme veteran Tolkien's performance of a long
passage from *Beowulf:* "I remember one [lecture] I attended, delivered
by Professor Tolkien. I do not remember a single word he said but at a
certain point he recited, and magnificently, a long passage of *Beowulf.* I
was spellbound. This poetry, I knew, was going to be my dish. I became
willing, therefore, to work at Anglo-Saxon because, unless I did, I
should never be able to read this poetry."[69] It was, Auden later wrote,
"my first introduction to the 'barbaric' poetry of the North."[70]

By the time that "introduction" happened, the loose grouping of Oxford scholars working on northern literatures had crystallized into something slightly more formal: an unglamorous, unworldly circle centered
on a shared fascination with northern languages and legends. In the
spring of 1926, the clubbish Tolkien had founded the "*Kolbítar*" (Icelandic for "the Coal-biters") circle. Its first members were R. M. Dawkins
and Coghill. The idea behind Tolkien's group was to proselytize for the
return of Old Norse to the degree syllabus by showing colleagues "how

enjoyable the reading of Icelandic can be."[71] Merton's John Bryson soon joined, and Lewis became a member in January 1927.[72] The Coal-biters started by working their way through the Icelandic sagas in the original language and moved on to the prose *Eddas*.[73] As an undergraduate, Auden is very unlikely to have been included in the group, but he gravitated toward its interests and was in close contact with several of its members, including his tutor Coghill and Dawkins (both queer), as well as being an enthusiast for others, such as Tolkien. Auden, according to Betjeman, "really admired the boring Anglo-Saxon poets like Beowulf whom we had read in the English school; and . . . was a close friend of John Bryson and Nevill Coghill, real dons who read Anglo-Saxon, Gutnish, Finnish and probably Swedish and Faroese as easily as I read the gossip column of the *Cherwell*."[74]

The *Kolbítar*, with a cluster of war veterans who shared a love for the North and for Germanic literatures as its nucleus, formed a countergrouping within Oxford's literary culture to the more fashionable, glamorous circle of *Sonnenkinder* (sun-children) and lovers of the Mediterranean world gathered around Bowra at Wadham.[75] In different ways, both circles were manifestations of the Great War's lingering emotional aftermath. Writing about the 1920s' cult of sunlight and Mediterraneanism, Paul Fussell argued that the "fantasies of flight and freedom which animate the imagination of the 20s and 30s and generate its pervasive images of travel can be said to begin in the trenches." His tradition of "flight and freedom" is almost exclusively south oriented, and its canon is made up of such works as Norman Douglas's novel *South Wind* of 1917, set on the island of Nepenthe (loosely modeled on Capri), where, as Fussell remarks, "the 'broiling' sun shines daily, the cause of 'paganism and nudity and laughter,' and the benign climate is specifically contrasted with that of the northern countries, 'lands adapted only for wolves and bears.'"[76]

By contrast, Tolkien admired the "'Germanic' ideal" that had appealed to him as a young man "in reaction against the 'Classics'" and that in 1941 he described as "that noble northern spirit, a supreme contribution to Europe. . . . Nowhere, incidentally, was it ever nobler than in England."[77] In the 1920s, an affiliation with the ancient literature of the Mediterranean or, conversely, with that of the North also implied a contemporary literary positioning. Eliot (until his insular turn) and other influential modernists were oriented toward the classical and Romance literatures of Europe. But the Germanophilic, counter-Bowra group of dons at Oxford such as Tolkien, Lewis, and Coghill were all antimodernists. Insofar as they rejected the Mediterraneanized aesthetes as well as their tastes and manner, undergraduates such as Auden, as well as the circle of pro-northern "Coal-biters," were also rejecting one possible artistic reaction to the emotional heritage of the Great War. Their style, too, was a performance—dourer, more elegiac, nationalistic, and melancholic than that of the aesthetes gathered around Bowra but likewise conditioned by memories or visions of the battlefields.

The notion of a parallel between contemporary warfare and epics of conflict among ancient northern clans was a common one among the younger generation. Robert Graves, who, along with Edmund Blunden, studied English at Oxford earlier in the 1920s than Auden, wrote that "Beowulf lying wrapped in a blanket among his platoon of drunken thanes in the Gothland billet; Judith going for a *promenade* to Holofernes's staff-tent; and *Brunanburgh* with its bayonet-and-cosh fighting—all this was closer to most of us at the time than the drawing-room and the deer-park atmosphere of the eighteenth century. Edmund [Blunden] and I found ourselves translating everything into trench-warfare terms. The war was not yet over for us."[78] Equally, Coghill's, Lewis's, and Tolkien's fascination with the austere, blood-soaked worlds of Old English and Old Norse literatures was a displaced return to the "dark world" of the front in an attempt to master it or understand it. Far from being merely dispassionate academic specialists, they gazed intently at their personal wartime experiences through the lens of their studies of Old and medieval English and through their own creative efforts.[79]

For example, one of Tolkien's poems in alliterative meter was "The Homecoming of Beorthnoth Beorhthelm's Son," a modern supplement to the Old English poem *The Battle of Maldon* but one that can also be read as a clear, if oblique, evocation of traversing a battlefield in modern France. Tolkien's poem is set in the disastrous aftermath of the Maldon battle, which took place in 991 and permitted the invading Danes to gain a foothold on "English" soil because of a heroic but imprudent (in fact suicidal) decision by the leader of the Anglo-Saxons, Byrhtnoth, who, "for his ofermōde" (because of his overconfidence), as the poem says, allowed the Vikings to cross a narrow causeway to the mainland before engaging the Anglo-Saxons in battle. In the ensuing carnage, Byrhtnoth and many of his closest retinue were slaughtered in an episode that one

might feel foreshadows, along with so many other military disasters involving the British Army, the mad, chivalric death of Lord Longford and
his senior officers at the Battle of Scimitar Hill in 1915.[80]

For most of Tolkien's poem, a cultivated young man, Torhthelm, son
of a minstrel, and Tídwald, an old farmer, move around the battlefield in
the darkness after the fighting has ended, stepping over numerous dead
in search of their slain lord Beorthnoth. As they do, Torhthelm groans,
"What a murder it is, | this bloody fighting!" and Tídwald sighs:

> Aye, that's battle for you,
> and no worse today than wars you sing of,
> when Fróda fell, and Finn was slain.
> The world wept then, as it weeps today:
> you can hear the tears through the harp's twanging.
> Come, bend your back! We must bear away
> the cold leavings. Catch hold of the legs![81]

They heave their lord's mutilated body onto a cart, ready to dignify it as
far as possible for burial. The poem is cast in an updated version of a
familiar Old English mode—stoical, elegiac, tender, pragmatic. It is
like, for instance, one of Wilfred Owen's poems, "Futility," which describes a dead soldier's body being tidied up:

> Move him into the sun—
> Gently its touch awoke him once,
> At home, . . .
> Always it woke him, even in France,
> Until this morning and this snow.[82]

C. S. Lewis had no trouble in recognizing the parabolic quality of Tolkien's writing about ancient or mythic worlds. When he reviewed *The
Lord of the Rings* in 1955, he was categoric: "This war has the very
quality of the war my generation knew. It is all here: the endless, unin-
telligible movement, the sinister quiet of the front when 'everything is
now ready,' the flying civilians, the lively, vivid friendships, the background of something like despair and the merry foreground."[83]

Passages like this one notwithstanding, biographers have remarked
that Lewis himself went out of his way to deprecate his own war experience and to claim it had no deep impact on him. But he admitted to a
friend that, like so many others, "memories of the last war haunted my

dreams for years."[84] And in his autobiography, he referred to "the frights, the cold, the smell of H.E. [high explosive], the horribly smashed men still moving like half-crushed beetles, the sitting or standing corpses, the landscape of sheer earth without a blade of grass."[85] His creative writing too bears the imprint of war experiences. The book-length poem in nine cantos, *Dymer*, which Lewis started in 1916, rewrote between 1922 and 1925, and eventually published in 1926 under the pseudonym "Clive Hamilton," is, according to Coghill, "a long, romantic story, told like Masefield's *Dauber*, in rhyme-royal" (a standard meter for narrative in the later Middle Ages and one used extensively by Chaucer in, for example, *Troilus and Criseyde* as well as in some of *The Canterbury Tales*).[86]

But Coghill leaves a lot unsaid. In truth, Lewis's *Dymer* is a disturbed work centered on a man who begets a dragon that he must then destroy. In this macabre and feverish tale, there is an abundance of First World War–like violence—"men with splintered faces, |—No eyes, no nose, all red—were running races | With worms along the floor"—in landscapes where humans "Torn raw with briers and caked from many a swamp" come "among the wild flowers dripping blood | And churning the green mosses into mud."[87]

These indirect, analogical (but often horrific) approaches to the experience of war were possible for Tolkien and Lewis and others like them at least in part because many nineteenth- and early twentieth-century readers heard the sounds of percussive violence sublimated into the emphatic rhythms and "clashing stresses" of Old English poetry. Pound linked the "clatter" in Old English poetry (especially anomalous to ears trained to listen for accentual-syllabic patterns) with intense, sometimes violent, physical effort, with "the raw, muscular vigour that he associated with 'The North.'"[88] The poetry's dinning sonorities often match the action or place being described. For example, in a specimen of poetry in alliterative meter that Lewis composed to illustrate its prosodic rules, he wrote about "trouble in trenches, with trees splintered | And birds banished. . . . [Mars's] metal's iron | . . . was hammered through hands into holy cross, | Cruel carpentry."[89]

For Auden too, like the Oxford scholars who taught him, violence and the North went together. For him too, the alliterating consonants of the Old English line readily offered themselves as a vehicle for the description of conflict. Auden's most intensive use of Old English idioms and style comes in the "charade" (as Auden called it) *Paid on Both*

Sides, whose title is drawn from *Beowulf.*[90] Written in a language that oscillates into and out of Old English, *Paid on Both Sides* is also his most ambitious early picture of the nation and his most pessimistic account to date of poetry's inability to do anything but record and mourn.

Paid on Both Sides, Auden's longest work so far, is an intense and extensive literary exploration of the scars of war in the English psyche. It is the bridge, too, that leads from his generalized fascination with Anglo-Saxon, Nordic, and Scandinavian cultures to his immersion in modern German culture in Berlin in 1928–1929. The action centers on the story of how violent blood feuds are inescapably inherited, like a society-wide disease, from generation to generation, leading to ceaseless murder, revenge, betrayal, and isolation. The feud in question is between two families or clans, the Nowers and the Shaws, speaking the same language and inhabiting the bleak landscape of the North Pennines. Violent death is a thematic constant from start to finish; the play begins with prose (as it will end with poetry) inflected frequently by the omission of definite articles, conjunctions, and explanatory clauses. In the opening scene, a character breaks the news of an ambush: "A breakdown at the Mill needed attention, kept me all morning. I guessed no harm. But lately, riding at leisure, Dick met me, panted disaster."[91] The "disaster" is the murder by members of the Shaw family of George Nower, the head of the other clan involved in a feud whose origins are ancient, obscure, and, by this time, irrelevant. Nower's death triggers the premature birth of his son John, who grows up to avenge his father by having Red Shaw, the head of the Shaw clan, killed one Christmas Eve as he "lay with woman | Upstairs together tired after love" (11).

Superficially, John is determined to "destroy the whole lot of you," as he tells a Shaw spy just before ordering the spy's execution (12). On a more profound level, though, John is searching for a way to end the feud between the two families. After a dream sequence in which John comes to identify with the spy he has just had killed, he arranges to be married to Anne Shaw, the daughter of Red Shaw. Anne begs John to leave with her: "John, I have a car waiting. There is time to join Dick now before the boat sails. We sleep in beds where men have died howling" (21).

John rejects her idea, apparently because his aim is not so much personal survival as a lasting social peace. At the wedding celebration for John and Anne at the Shaw clan's redoubt, Red Shaw's widow encourages her son Seth to kill John: "Have you forgotten your brother's death, . . . taken out and shot like a dog?" (23) After first demurring, Seth agrees in order to prove the courage that his mother has implicitly called into question. John Nower is shot to death, but some of the Nower party escape and the play ends with news that they are returning with fresh companions to avenge their leader. Anne is left alone on the stage surrounded by "the dead," as at the end of a revenge tragedy:

> Now we have seen the story to its end.
> The hands that were to help will not be lifted,
> And bad followed by worse leaves to us tears,
> An empty bed, hope from less noble men.
> I had seen joy
> Received and given, upon both sides, for years.
> Now not. (24)

The feud is revived and, because he refused the chance to escape, the story of John Nower's life, precipitated by the death of his father, has been one solely of murdering and being murdered and ensuring fresh murders after his own death.

Paid on Both Sides is a work in which, as in a crime film, we see only violent episodes and not the day-to-day, banal business and domestic activities of the two houses. In this world, there is "no remedy | . . . but the new death; | A Nower dragged out in the night, a Shaw | Ambushed behind the wall" (11). With violence at its center, it presents itself not as, or not merely as, a quasi-realistic description of life in the harsh northern regions of England but, as what Auden called it, a "parable."[92]

Stylistically, Paid on Both Sides uses Old English to lay bare the desperate stress and hostility lying underneath the placid surfaces of middle-class life. In writing about the tragic nature of a clash between two "families" and the inevitable loss of life "on both sides," Auden may have remembered Hardy's poem "The Pity of It," which had appeared in his 1917 volume Moments of Vision. That poem is set in "loamy Wessex lanes" as the speaker walks in wartime near rural "field and farmstead." There he hears the linguistic evidence of cultural closeness between Germans and the inhabitants of South-West England, between the speech, that is, of two peoples who are now at war with each other. Hardy discerns "many an ancient word | Of local lineage like 'Thu bist,' 'Er war' | ... and by-talk similar." Reflecting on the now firmly established links between the German language and this English dialect, he curses the people who have "flung this flame | Between kin folk kin tongued even as we are."[93]

Hardy's poem had a great impact on Owen, whose work Auden took up at around the same time as he began to imitate an Old English style. (The literary historian Valentine Cunningham calls the war poet Owen "one of the most potent of memories haunting the young writers of the '30s."[94]) In the original version of Owen's famous preface to his unpublished book of poems, written in the spring of 1918, he declared that his subject was war and "the pity of it," borrowing words from the title of Hardy's poem. (Owen later changed the phrase in his preface draft to "the pity of War."[95])

Auden's "charade" owes something to the Hardy poem that so impressed Owen. Like Hardy's poem about "kin folk kin tongued," *Paid on Both Sides* takes up the theme of a war or feud between two essentially similar groups: "Sharers of the same house | Attendants on the same machine" (17). Just as Hardy saw almost no difference between the people he heard "in loamy Wessex lanes" and the Germans who were officially their enemies, so Auden observes a trivial demarcation between his "hostile parties" solely in terms of "different coloured armbands." Indeed, this detail hints at the German dimension of this charade set in the North of England: at the time, it was common for competing political factions in Germany to display allegiances with the use of differently colored armbands.[96]

The description by Nower, George, and Sturton of their attack on Red Shaw is a good example of the frequent use in *Paid on Both Sides* of a pastiche Old English poetic style:

> Day was gone Night covered sky
> Black over earth When we came there
> To Brandon Walls Where Red Shaw lay
> Hateful and sleeping Unfriendly visit.
> I wished to revenge Quit fully
> Who my father at Colefangs valley
> Lying in ambush Cruelly shot
> With life for life. (11)

Auden stylistically mirrors the theme of a fight between two parts of the same culture, since the verse form used in Anglo-Saxon poetry and re-used here in loosened form is one common to the Germanic cultures of the fifth century CE onward. (It was brought to Britain by tribes migrating from northern Europe.[97]) Auden preserves some of the ruggedness of the ancient form, described by the poet Seamus Heaney as having a "kind of foursquareness about the utterance, a feeling of living inside a constantly indicative mood, in the presence of an understanding that assumes you share an awareness of the perilous nature of life."[98] Alliteration usually joins by devices like repeating sounds and capitalization the halves of a line visually separated into two parts. The fact that the old alliterative line is divided into two, or, as one of the luminaries of Auden's Oxford, C. S. Lewis, describes it, into "two half-lines, which are independent metrical organisms, connected only by the alliteration," also furnishes a formal analogue to the idea of two warring parties, held together by forces beyond their control, in poetry for which the alliterative price must be paid on both sides (of the line).[99]

In one of the speeches from *Paid on Both Sides,* a work started in Oxford, the redoubt of Anglo-Saxon studies, Auden uses the thudding qualities of alliteration to suggest mimetically the explosive impacts of flying lead in a gunfight:

> Shot answered shot Bullets screamed
> Guns shook Hot in the hand
> Fighters lay Groaning on ground
> Gave up life Edward fell
> Shot through the chest (12)

The passage is freighted with objects that seem to speak like people and with people who seem to vocalize like animals: here "Shot *answered* shot Bullets *screamed* | . . . Fighters lay *Groaning* on ground." The sounds, and the jarring sonorities, often match the action or place being described. And these philological excavations from Old English verse style dovetailed with, or mirrored, the traumatized psychology with which Auden was most familiar.

As noted earlier, Dr. Auden frequently used W. H. R. Rivers's distinction between the higher and underlying lower human faculties to explain disease. And the images he deployed to explain the process could have strongly spatial or material connotations. Thus, Dr. Auden

FIG. 4 *A portrait of Auden taken by his brother John, around 1928. Auden, during a brief pipe-smoking phase, is wearing the "very broad-brimmed black felt hat" that Christopher Isherwood (writing in* Lions and Shadows*) wrote he "disliked from the start": "It represented, I felt, something self-conscious and sham, something that Oxford had superimposed upon [Auden's] personality. . . . He wore it with a certain guilty defiance: he wasn't quite comfortable in it; he wanted me to accept it, with all its implications—and I wouldn't."*

remarked in delinquent children a "reduction of this epicritic control, which may be compared with the geological process of denudation whereby the younger sedimentary rocks are removed by the action of the various physical agents, leaving bare the ancient primitive rocks upon which they had been deposited."[100] In his son's stark, Saxonizing poetry, the reduction or "denudation" of English down to the "ancient primitive rocks" of its elemental nouns and verbs is the parallel phenomenon. For Dr. Auden, reduction of "epicritic control" yields disease, unrestrained selfishness, or social barbarism. For W. H. Auden, the linguistic version of the same process lays bare, just as the First World War had also done, the violent appetites and enmities, the thrilling but antisocial savagery underlying the smooth veneer of English manhood, as well as the illicit kinship between enemies.

Here "no remedy | Is to be thought of, no news but the new death," a character named Trudy, one of the boss John Nower's men, announces ruefully in *Paid on Both Sides* (11). Even though Trudy is old and expects to die soon, he predicts, in the clipped, laconic idiom Auden uses in the play, that "more than once [I] shall hear | The cry for help, the shooting round the house" (11). These words sound like a translation from Anglo-Saxon, but (after all, shooting does not happen much in early literature) they simultaneously evoke another genre and moment altogether: popular culture's dramas of spectacular contemporary violence, which everyday citizens looked to for entertainment. In the period when Auden was about to embark on *Paid on Both Sides,* the popularity (there is no other word for it) of horrifying news stories, plays, and within a short time, films about American gangsters was growing rapidly in Britain.

The first English citation of the word "gangster" in the *OED* is from July 1928, just the time when Auden is finishing the first version of the charade. However, the word had begun to infiltrate even the staid columns of the *Times* before that date. This happened, for example, in connection with reviews of American films, as in a 1923 article describing Milton Sills's character in *Skin Deep* as "a repulsively ugly New York criminal 'gangster,'" as well as in stories about crime in the United States.[101] During the bloody feuds and "gang wars" that were especially intense in New York and Chicago following the introduction in 1920 of

Prohibition and that peaked in the later 1920s and early 1930s, the word became even more common in English publications. In 1928, the year when Auden was composing much of *Paid on Both Sides,* the *Times* reported, "Election Day in Chicago. Police versus 'Gangsters.'"[102] It also headlined, "Another Gangster Shot in New York. Silver Coffin to Be Used."[103] Among the American and British publics, mob violence was becoming enjoyable to read about and to watch. The first film usually recognized as a gangster classic is *Underworld,* directed by Josef von Sternberg in 1927. As if medium were aligning with message, Sternberg called *Underworld* an "experiment in photographic violence and montage." (Sergei Eisenstein insisted that the latter technique, through shock cutting's violent collisions between images, incorporated a basic aura of violence in its very form.[104])

Gangster films may seem a long way from *Paid on Both Sides,* but the composition of Auden's northern English charade and the growing vogue for this film genre were contemporaneous. Auden himself saw a connection, as he once noted in relation to the Icelandic sagas, filled with blood feuds between families, on which *Paid on Both Sides* was partially based: "I love the sagas but what a rotten society they describe, a society with only the gangster-virtues."[105] And *Paid on Both Sides* shows two close thematic similarities to gangster films. The first is the importance of kin loyalty in both the charade and a typical gangster movie such as *Little Caesar* (1931). Loyalty to the family or tribe and a willingness to defend or avenge it at any cost are more important than any other duties. John Nower, the central figure in Auden's work, is obligated by this ethos to strike back for the death of his father by killing his father's killer. He does so only to be killed by the son of his victim. Though the gangster, like the central figure in Auden's play, John Nower, is a hero, he is also trapped and doomed by the tribal protocols he must obey.

The second similarity lies in the story's inexorability. Death lies predictably at the end of *Paid on Both Sides,* exactly like a contemporaneous gangster movie, which (in the words of the midcentury film critic Robert Warshow) "progresses by inalterable paths to the point where the gangster lies dead."[106] Indeed the tension between group loyalty and individualism, central to *Paid on Both Sides,* mirrors the fatal predicament of the gangster. To be a hero in either fictional world, you must die. At the end of *Paid on Both Sides,* the result of John Nower's attempt to break with the feud, underpinned by the logic of family loyalty, has been a failure. Filled with bullets, John lies dead in the arms of his grieving wife, who laments:

> Now we have seen the story to its end.
> The hands that were to help will not be lifted,
> And bad followed by worse leaves to us tears,
> An empty bed, hope from less noble men. (24)

One other cultural strand is woven into this set of connections. The growth of enthusiasm for popular genres such as gangster movies at the end of the 1920s happened virtually simultaneously with the often-noted, sudden emergence of a burst of overwhelmingly violent, disillusioned war literature, not just in Britain but in Germany too. By the end of the decade you might, in a copy of a British newspaper, read sensational reports on the news pages about gunfights in Chicago or murders in suburbia or massive pilgrimages by forlorn relatives to the battlefields of the Great War, then turn to the book reviews for a piece about the latest murder mysteries or the most recent war memoir, check showtimes for a gangster film, and then glance in the sports pages at the description of an especially noteworthy prizefight (which was another exploding genre of broadcast entertainment showcasing combat). Auden's work, in his lyrics as in his charade, is both highly idiosyncratic and completely contemporary—to miss the connections he makes with popular tastes and forms is to understand only half the story and to underestimate his efforts to connect his own obsessions with broader psychic preoccupations, including the widespread fascination with violence.

Britain's overt preoccupation with the war, suddenly obvious rather than mostly repressed or subliminal, at the end of the 1920s follows the same trajectory that the war took in Auden's poetry, where it emerged in works such as "Control of the Passes" and in *Paid on Both Sides* from symbolic expression into almost direct representation. The national appetite for war narratives manifests itself at the end of the 1920s most obviously by the large number of skeptical, antiwar books by soldiers, mostly by young, well-educated former junior officers. These works turned the publishing focus away from issues of tactics or weaponry and political or military history toward the predicament of the individual combatant.[107] Graves's *Good-Bye to All That* and Blunden's *Undertones of War* were not the first disillusioned books about the war to appear. But by 1928, the year when Auden wrote most of *Paid on Both Sides,* the number of such books, both novels and memoirs, was rapidly increasing and by now included significant prose volumes by well-established English (officer) poets. The first part of Siegfried Sassoon's very lightly fictionalized autobiography, *Memoirs of a Fox-Hunting Man,* appeared in this year, as did *Undertones of War. Good-Bye to All That* was published the following year, 1929.

These are not isolated examples. Radclyffe Hall's taboo-breaking *The Well of Loneliness,* published in the summer of 1928, includes a long section on Stephen Gordon's service in an ambulance unit during the First World War.[108] Almost simultaneously, Wyndham Lewis published his strange science-fiction satire about the walking dead of the postwar world, *The Childermass.*[109] And, although David Jones's epic poem *In Parenthesis* was not published by Faber and Faber until 1937, Jones began working on the book in 1928, the year of *Paid on Both Sides* and the high-water mark of books about the Great War.[110] Notably, this British obsession with the war was being mirrored by contemporaneous developments in Germany. There were some 200 books about the war issued in Germany in 1926. In 1930 the number had doubled to 400.[111]

In Britain, fascination with the war was never a purely chauvinistic phenomenon. (The period also saw a large number of German and French memoirs of the war translated into English.) But Samuel Hynes cautions that wartime frenzy was not suddenly and wholly replaced by antiwar sentiment in England. Throughout the 1920s, there continued to be in the country "two cultures, separate and mistrustful of each other, a conservative culture that clung to and asserted traditional values, and a counter-culture, rooted in rejection of the war and its principles."[112] Speaking at an Armistice Day ceremony in Folkestone in 1929, one clergyman bewailed the fact that "I did not think that I should ever live to read books written by my own countrymen which are like the dirty work done by enemy propagandists."[113]

However, a historian notes that there "were signs in the late 1920s and early 1930s of a political as well as a cultural reappraisal of Britain's role, and the war books boom must be seen as part of something larger."[114] This became especially clear with the enormous (and surprising) success of R. C. Sheriff's play *Journey's End,* first staged in London in December 1928. The play, about a group of Tommies stuck in a trench dugout as the

German army advances toward them, ran for some 600 performances at the Savoy Theatre in the West End. The following year, 1929, saw the publication of other landmark novels, such as Ernest Hemingway's *A Farewell to Arms* and Richard Aldington's *Death of a Hero*. It was also in the spring of 1929 that the English translation of Erich Maria Remarque's best-selling and extremely controversial *Im Westen nichts Neues* appeared, lightly bowdlerized, as *All Quiet on the Western Front*.

Although neither began the fashion for works about the war, Sheriff's play and Remarque's novel intensified it. The peak period of the war boom began in 1927, in which eight war novels were published, and continued with ten in 1928, twenty-five in 1929, and thirty-six in 1930.[115] London publishers—including Faber and Faber, the firm that would shortly publish Auden's first book—hurried to capitalize on this widespread taste for reading about the war.[116] There were new textbooks, new books of military analysis, psychological studies, books applying the lessons from the war of yesterday to the war of tomorrow, books about commemorative monuments, books about the ways in which the great public schools created memorials for their fallen old boys, collections of letters, guidebooks to the battlefields, and books of reminiscence about pilgrimages to soldiers' graves.

This banked-up surge of interest shows that England had never recovered from the impact of the conflict and that the prose- and drama-centered literary outpouring was a symptom of a broader national, and international, mood, much of it reflecting awareness of the continuing suffering of ex-servicemen throughout the following decade. Even as late as 1928, 6,000 new artificial limbs were issued by the government to war-wounded soldiers.[117] At the end of the decade, 65,000 ex-soldiers were still in British asylums being treated for shell shock.[118] Records of war veterans' psychoses increased in absolute terms throughout 1920s. Will Longstaff's painted wraiths were fictionalized but essentially truthful versions of the damaged people who walked Britain's, France's, and Germany's streets (as well as the streets of the European empires' colonial possessions whose subjects had fought in large numbers) and of the ghosts that haunted traumatized minds.[119]

One historian has noted that in 1929, the same year that the greatest number of war novels and memoirs was published and that Auden completed the final version of *Paid on Both Sides,* more ex-soldiers than ever before fell victim to psychological traumas caused by combat: "More pensions for psychotic illnesses were granted by the British government in 1929 than had been granted in the four years immediately after the war."[120] In other words, not only were more veterans developing disabling psychiatric conditions as the years passed, but the number of veterans officially recognized as suffering from previously undiagnosed psychological aftereffects of the conflict was also increasing with the distance from the war. By the early 1930s, 36 percent of all wounded men entitled to war pensions were receiving them for psychiatric illnesses.[121]

Legislation, too, was affected by the widespread preoccupation with the war's impact. In 1929, the year when the British government paid out a record number of pensions for veterans' mental illnesses, Parliament first debated abolishing the death penalty for cowardice and desertion. The measure was passed in 1930 and joined a number of other offenses struck from military law's list of capital crimes throughout the mid- to late 1920s.[122] If Auden's poetry is forever circling around the subject of war, this is because his imagination had tapped into a whole culture's nightmares and regrets.

At the end of the 1920s, the main literary outlets for this cultural anxiety were novels and memoirs; new publications of poetry had relatively little prominence in the war-books boom. This relative lack of new poetry about the conflict in the late 1920s opened a space for Auden's work. His post-1926 poetry of bleak northern battlefield-like moors, abandoned mine works, dead heroes, and endless feuding surfaced within British culture at a time when the country remained obsessed by the human cost of the First World War and by the long, lingering shadows the conflict cast. As Auden's poetry gained a readership, a synergy emerged between the appearance in his poems of a set of imaginative recreations of war and a readership in search of such representations.

In *The Waste Land,* Eliot had allowed memories of the war to infiltrate his poetic cityscape with, as Paul Fussell wrote, its "archduke, its rats and canals and dead men, its focus on fear, its dusty trees, its conversation about demobilization, its spiritualist practitioners reminding us of those who preyed on relatives anxious to contact their dead boys, and not least its settings of blasted landscape and ruins."[123] Part of the reason why Eliot could respond so immediately to *Paid on Both Sides,* calling it "quite a brilliant piece of work" in a letter to a friend at the time it was published in the *Criterion,* was that Auden's method of dealing with the shadows cast by the war onto the civilian and natural worlds of the postwar period had such a close analogue and precedent in his own writing.[124] The audience that Auden's poetry found in Britain at the end of the 1920s was generated in part simply from the way in which he shifted the huge image bank of modern war's desolation onto a recognizably English landscape, giving a dramatic sense of a nation in crisis. In a country still psychologically working through the costs of conflict, Auden's first substantial collection, *Poems* (1930), which included *Paid on Both Sides,* was, in effect, a kind of war poetry, a phantom war poetry written by a member of the generation obsessed by the struggle, having read or heard about it or watched films about it, without having fought in it.

Faber and Faber published *Poems* in October 1930. Just a few weeks earlier, it had brought out Sassoon's *Memoirs of an Infantry Officer,* the second volume in a trilogy. Sassoon's narrator, George Sherston, writes about watching from behind the front lines as exhausted troops return toward dawn from an engagement with the enemy: "Soon they dispersed and settled down on the hillside, and were asleep in the daylight which made everything seem ordinary. None the less I had seen something that night which overawed me. It was all in the day's work—an exhausted Division returning from the Somme Offensive—but for me it was as though I had watched an army of ghosts. It was as though I had seen the War as it might be envisioned by the mind of some epic poet a hundred years hence."[125] *Paid on Both Sides,* Auden's dramatic poem, is the "epically" rendered version of the war that Sassoon had imagined could only be written "a hundred years hence" but that Auden showed could be represented now in just lightly ciphered form.

Many of the critical readings of *Paid on Both Sides* have construed the charade as a kind of modernist psychomachia, that is, primarily as a dramatization of the divisions within a single mind.[126] The dream interlude exploring John Nower's inner conflict, which Auden added to the middle of the drama in Berlin in the autumn of 1928 (perhaps after seeing examples of contemporary German Expressionist theater there),

offers support for this viewpoint.[127] But the charade is as much a portrait of a divided society as of a divided mind or of a divided mind
within a divided society or of a divided mind caused by a divided society. The struggles within John Nower's character are primarily social
in origin. He is trapped by the feud, the education in violence, the bond
with the dead, the care for his subalterns, and the obligation to uphold
family honor.

From the dramatis personae on, an alignment with the conflict of
the First World War is obvious. The names of some of the Nowers'
lieutenants—Walter, Kurt, Culley, Zeppel—sound (to an English ear)
German, and yet these people speak in the same mixture of contemporary
English and Anglo-Saxon pastiche as their enemies, the Shaws.[128] Moreover, as if to emphasize its own culturally divided condition, *Paid on
Both Sides* has both an "English" and a "German" component: the un-
adorned Old English verse and the parodies of middle-class life and language, on the one hand; and on the other, the Expressionistic central
section—added after Auden reached Berlin in late 1928—more evocative of Continental dramatic styles than anything surrounding it.

The charade's themes of "no news but the new death," of slaughter,
spying, sniping, ambush, revenge attacks, and endless, futile struggles
endemic to a doomed warrior culture that kills off the young on both
sides, are the themes of the war (11). Indeed, the very word "war" occurs frequently, as in John's complaint, "Our fathers. . . . taught us war,"
or the Doctor's menacing reference to the "criminals of the war"
(13, 16). In addition, the text is full of diction taken from the lexicon of
modern conflict: "ammunition," "base for operations," "flares," "bullets,"
"treaty," "bomb," "armies," "enemies," "revolver," "barbed wire," "prisoner
of war," "field glasses," and "burning town" (7–21).

The charade also draws heavily on the rhetoric of contemporary war
in which foreign or exotic place-names acquired a numinous, tragic
quality during the war years, if only from schoolroom "maps upon the
whitewashed wall" (19). The starkly foregrounded place-names in *Paid
on Both Sides,* mundane in themselves but tolling like the names of places
where battles occurred, have a magical sense of heroic achievement and
sacrifice: Colefangs, Rookhope, Brandon Walls, Eickhamp, Nattrass, the
Barbon Road, Lintzgarth, Garrigill (7–20). Auden alludes as well to the
familiar use, in war memoirs, of references to rural-sounding landmarks
on a battlefield, such as "the Mill" or "the Farm."[129] Moreover, if "the Mill"

mentioned in the charade's opening scene is Rookhope Smelt Mill, next to the Nower home, Lintzgarth, at Rookhope, near Weardale, as seems to be the case, then the work's connection with lead mines and miners is a further link to Auden's private mythology of the industrial landscapes of the North as doubles of the war's battlefields.[130]

The poet and Auden scholar John Fuller has mentioned another point of contact with the war: the dream sequence at the center of *Paid on Both Sides* is taken directly from Rivers's *Conflict and Dream* (1923).[131] Rivers remarks early in the book that it was only when the recent war brought him "into touch with dreams as prominent symptoms of nervous disorder and as the means of learning the real nature of the mental states underlying the psychoneuroses of war" that he began to study Freud's theory of dreams.[132] His modest (desexualizing) revisions of Freud's theory are marked by the wartime moment in which he thought them through. Rivers, who, as noted, had treated Sassoon in 1917, gives an analysis of what he calls the "Suicide Dream," related to him by another of his patients, a doctor who was a captain in the RAMC—someone with the same rank in the same corps as Dr. Auden. In *Conflict and Dream,* this captain's anxieties are directly rooted in traumatic war experiences "centering round the death of a French prisoner who had been mortally wounded during his escape from the German lines," the shock of which had made the captain "extremely reluctant to return to the practice of his profession" after being demobilized.[133]

The central metaphor in Rivers's description of dreams is one of "conflict" within the mind. Rivers's comments on the "Suicide Dream" dismiss the loosely Freudian idea of a dream as "wish-fulfillment" and instead describe the traumatized doctor's dream as "an attempted solution of a conflict of a very complicated kind which is going on in the mind of the dreamer."[134] He remarks that the patient's dream was a dramatization of a struggle between the "manifest opinions that the war must be fought to a finish and deeper feelings that a struggle involving such horrors" should not continue.[135] When Auden took over from Rivers the contents of the "Suicide Dream" for *Paid on Both Sides,* he simply substituted the notion of a blood feud for the idea of a war.

In *Paid on Both Sides,* some people do try to escape from the effects of the violence. At the very start, John's father—whose name is George, like Auden's own "lost" father—is killed riding to "speak with Layard," a guide who might have helped end the feud (7).[136] Once George Now-er's counterpart, Red Shaw, has been murdered in revenge, there are no fathers left in the work, only men who struggle to stand, unsuccessfully, in their fathers' places. In rapid succession, we also learn that Dick, from the Nowers' group, wants to emigrate to the Colonies and that Trudy is "sick of this feud." Toward the end, after their wedding, Anne wishes John and herself to "join Dick before the boat sails" (11, 21). The plans come to nothing, not because of a lack of will on the part of the would-be exiles but because the feud has such a brutal grip on the society that it frustrates individual efforts to escape or change it. *Paid on Both Sides* becomes tragic because Nower's resolution to try to end the feud by marrying Anne Shaw (the daughter of the man who killed his father and the sister of the spy he has had executed earlier in the drama) is foiled by two decisions. The first is his own: to continue living in a place where, as Anne says, they must "sleep in beds where men have died howling" (21). The second decision belongs to Anne Shaw's mother, who urges Seth to kill Nower in revenge for Nower's murder of Seth's brother.

Comparing Nower's dream sequence in *Paid on Both Sides* with the "Suicide Dream" of the captain in Rivers's book, we see a very similar pattern at work. The disease is social rather than personal. Neither the captain nor Nower is a maladjusted individual in a sane society: both are suffering from the madness of their social situations. Writing about the American psychiatrist Trigant Burrow's *The Social Basis of Con-sciousness* in Berlin in April 1929 (the same month in which he sent corrections of *Paid on Both Sides* to Eliot), Auden noted with approval Burrow's claim that "Freud's error is the limitation of the neurosis to the individual. The neurosis involves all society."[137] The charade he was to publish in Eliot's *Criterion* before it appeared in book form is the il-lustration of that viewpoint.

Paid on Both Sides is Auden's first portrait of an entire culture since "'Lead's the Best'" from 1926. The collectivist code of the Germanic *comitatus,* or war band, whose ferocious ethos is celebrated in Anglo-Saxon poems such as *The Battle of Maldon* and *Beowulf,* is one Auden redescribes in contemporary terms. The *comitatus* stressed physical and spiritual loyalty over cerebral analysis or individual endeavor, as *Paid on Both Sides* does too. As in contemporary gangster films, members of the ethnocentric group have a full identity only when in contact with the other members of the family or extended circle, and what happens to one is deemed to have happened to all. These values are disturbing, and the charade itself has a fevered, paranoid quality.

This is striking because the pastiche of Old English style in which characters and the Chorus in *Paid on Both Sides* regularly speak is so evidently a mode of speech that depends on close similarities of expectation between speaker and listener (or writer and reader). The participants talk in a way that reflects the communal nature of their experiences: a frequent feature of the verse is the omission of definite or indefinite articles, as in the Chorus's opening evocation of "trouble, pressure on men | Born all the time, brought forward into light | For warm dark moan" or in John's later reference to "boy's voice among dishonoured portraits | To dockside barmaid speaking | Sorry through wires, pretended speech" (8, 17). The lack of articles implies an absoluteness, a lack of qualification. The context for such clipped speech is typically one in which the speaker can assume that listeners, sharing expectations with the speaker, will understand the phrase's exact meaning without having it spelled out for them. It is not just the characters in the play who are doomed. This is implied to be a fate that the play's audience shares, in the same way that they share the social and linguistic coordinates that allow them to understand terse stylized comments.

But although assumptions and knowledge are shared by the charade's warring groups, *Paid on Both Sides* makes the culture's fate seem largely outside human control. Almost all the human beings in the work are doomed to miscalculate or misconstrue. The society portrayed in *Paid on Both Sides* in its systematic violence and irrationality is pathological, in that everyone in it is doomed: "I have seen | The just and the unjust die in the day, | All, willing or not, and some were willing" (11).

But fatalism coexists with a pervasive uncertainty. The charade begins with a question, a question about a reported death: "You've only just heard?" (7) And, in fact, there are many questions in just the brief opening scene, six in all, including, "How did they get him? . . . Has Joan been told yet?" (7). These mundane queries help to set the tone of enigma, surprise, and bafflement that hangs over the whole work. The incomplete awareness of the situation implicit in that initial question—the lack of knowledge shown by Walter, a member of the Nower clan, about George Nower's death—is followed up by Walter's remark that the reason he did not hear immediately about the death was because of a "break-down at the Mill needing attention" (7). Lack of knowledge in humans is figuratively reflected in the fallibility of their machines.

At the end of the first scene, when the Doctor withdraws for his drink with Walter and Trudy into an adjoining room, the curtains suddenly and surprisingly open to reveal John Nower's mother holding her recently born son in her arms, with her dead husband stretched by her side. In contrast to the prosaic dialogue used earlier by Trudy, Walter, and the Doctor, Joan speaks in a gnomic, poetic idiom:

> Unforgetting is not to-day's forgetting
> For yesterday, not bedrid scorning,
> But a new beginning
> An unforgiving morning. (7)

Her speech compounds the sense of unsettlement by declaring an absolute break between the experience of this world and of the next: "not from this life is any | To keep; sleep, day and play would not help there" (7). Moreover, as she speaks her bleak, largely monosyllabic lines, the previous uncertainty of the characters asking questions becomes, because of the rapid change of idiom, the uncertainty of the audience struggling to follow charged and elliptical utterances in a changing register.

The play's language, which shifts back and forth from prose dialogue to poetic reflection and lament and which will soon (after the first twenty years of John Nower's life have suddenly elapsed) turn back again to prose dialogue, emphasizes the sense of discontinuity and unpredictability.[138] If the momentum and inner consistency of a text are a representation of its sense of how history moves or of how human understanding progresses, then *Paid on Both Sides* offers an image of the world as a radically unstable and never reliably knowable place but also one in which the outcomes are somehow foreordained.

During the charade, readers experience a society full of disruption and enigma. Although the feud has an utterly simple and ruthless "logic" to its development, it generates a world of ominous, irrationally charged portents like a "boy born fanged like a weasel" and of dire, riddling prophecies such as the one Seth Shaw delivers to his mother, that "much will come of this, chiefly harm" (11, 23). There are plotting "whisperers," thieves of "stolen news," and, conversely, bit players who, "muzzed with drink and lateness," give away secrets (22, 7, 9). Understanding is elusive; characters are often baffled by what they perceive or are ruined by what they do not see. Men are "Doubtful" and look for a reliable sign, but instead they find "surprise," "misfortune," and yet another "trap," in a society where events are "misunderstood" and "no remedy | Is to be thought of" (10–15).

Misinterpretations or mischaracterizations of the world abound. Sometimes this happens on a comic level, as in the traditional Mummers' pratfalls of the Doctor and his boy (16). (Even here in this comic section of the work, there is a ghostly echo of war. The author of the book from which Auden took his details about the Mummers' play was R. J. E. Tiddy, a lecturer in classics and English literature at Oxford, a friend of E. M. Forster, and a man who had collected folk songs and folk dances with the musicologist Cecil Sharp before the war. As his book on the Mummers makes explicit, serving with the Oxfordshire and Buckinghamshire Light Infantry, Tiddy had been killed in action at the Somme in August 1916. The first sentence of the book's preface identifies his as one of those "lives cut short by the War."[139]) But the Doctor's fumbling with words is a particular symptom of a larger linguistic uncertainty, of "rumour," "excuse," "erring sign . . . guessed-at wonders" (14–19). Characters feel unprepared by their education for the dilemmas that they must suddenly face:

> Always the following wind of history
> Of others' wisdom makes a buoyant air
> Till we come suddenly on pockets where
> Is nothing loud but us; where voices seem
> Abrupt, untrained, competing with no lie
> Our fathers shouted once. They taught us war,
> To scamper after darlings, to climb hills,
> To emigrate from weakness, find ourselves
> The easy conquerors of empty bays:
> But never told us this. (12–13)

Small wonder, then, that the rival families exist in a symbiotic relationship of "pursuit, rebellion and eclipse" (17). A baby's birth is precipitated by a death; his arrival means "pangs" for the mother and presages the "crying out" of his future victims before his own death occurs (7). In this feud culture, no one is able to know the world accurately for the "proudest into traps | Have fallen" (13).

But no mechanism, not even a trap, ever works perfectly in Auden's primitive but complex world; nothing is clean, definitive, or clear. Although the play ends with one "trap" and a blaze of gunfire, the murder cannot eradicate the future metastasizing growth of the feud. Nower is killed in the struggle, but so is a member of the opposing clan, Aaron Shaw. And some of Nower's men "got away, fetching help, will attack in an hour" (24). We are back where we began, with a new turn in the vicious cycle and with another woman mourning over a dead man's body. At the opening of *Paid on Both Sides,* Joan had grieved over her husband's corpse, but she was comforted by the baby she had just given birth to. Now, things are much worse. The baby we saw at the start has become the cadaver in the final tableau. And at the end, Anne has no child to symbolize (in counterpoint to the finality of death) the possible renewal of life. There is only some vague "hope from less noble men" (24).

The play ends with a vision of something like total defeat, embodied in a final reference to the lack of cognitive clarity. Anything positive that Anne remembers having clearly seen in the past is contrasted with the murky desolation of "now," as the Chorus declares:

> Though he believe it, no man is strong.
> He thinks to be called the fortunate,
> To bring home a wife, to live long.
>
> But he is defeated; let the son
> Sell the farm lest the mountain fall;
> His mother and her mother won.
>
> His fields are used up where the moles visit,
> The contours worn flat; if there show
> Passage for water he will miss it. (24)

Beliefs, ambitions, and thoughts are based on a misperception about the nature of reality. Even if there are possibilities ("Passage for water") for a man to seize on, "he will miss it." For the present, there is only the possibility of frustration, caused above all by women: "His mother and her mother won" (24).

Paid on Both Sides might seem to end firmly in key with the misogynistic interpretations and adaptations of saga literature that were common in the nineteenth century. The literary historian Andrew Wawn has remarked that "Victorian readers could have been forgiven for thinking that in saga literature, for every admirable Frithiof or Vagn, there seemed always to be two doomed Grettirs, or Gíslis, or Gunnarrs, or Njálls, or Gunnlaugrs, or Kjartans, or Sigurðs—all destroyed in the prime of life with women prominent amongst the engines of destruction. For every saintly Gudruda or stout-hearted Auðr, there seemed always to be an unfathomable Swanhild, or Hallgerðr, or Brynhildr."[140] Dr. Auden himself sounded this hostile saga note quite vehemently. In his 1929 article on "the difficult maladjusted child," written around the same time that his son finally finished *Paid on Both Sides,* he paused to cite examples from ancient times of the perceived phenomenon of women destroying men, including in his list "Hallgerda, the evil genius of the Njal Saga," whose "perverse wickedness . . . caused so much of the best blood in Iceland to flow in the tenth century."[141]

Such, at least, appears to be the message of what John Fuller calls the charade's final "Sophoclean chorus."[142] In 1926, about a year before Auden began *Paid on Both Sides,* Dr. Auden had published an essay lauding Sophocles in Arnoldian terms as one who "saw life steadily, and saw it whole."[143] The essence of Sophocles's excellence lies, for Dr. Auden, in his acute empathy for the suffering of others and for his diagnostic skill; he claims Sophocles as "one of the long line of physician poets."[144]

By borrowing the dispassionate Sophoclean note of the "physician poet" for this final chorus, Auden codes in a reference to his father's physiologically rooted ideas about disease and cure, ideas that were deeply anchored in the materialistic theories of the mind prevalent in the nineteenth century. The Chorus in effect interprets the events that have unfolded according to the attitudes of Auden's father's generation: "blame the women; they will always ruin the men." But such an interpretation does not stand up to a full scrutiny of the text. It was, after all, Anne who tried, albeit unsuccessfully, to break the feud cycle and John who refused:

A.   John, I have a car waiting. There is time to join Dick before the boat sails. We sleep in beds where men have died howling.

J.   You may be right, but we shall stay. (30)

John's stubbornness about "duty" is ultimately the cause of his death and the death of many of his followers. A woman tried to stop the violence. The "Sophoclean note" associated with Auden's father proves fallible and misleading. There is an ending to the charade but no resolution: the final, despairing words of the Chorus misapprehend this. The best solution would have been Anne's—departure.

In "I chose this lean country," Auden's speaker had remarked gnomically on "Margaret the brazen leech."[145] This was a reference to Margaret Marshall (as she was known at the time), whom Auden had met at Oxford through his Wadham friend Cecil Day Lewis. Though she was married, she and Day Lewis had had an affair. As Auden explained shortly afterward to Isherwood in a letter likely written in July 1927, "I am going to be psycho-analyzed probably next vac, by the Margaret referred to by your side [in "I chose this lean country"], one of those pleasant pornographic women."[146] (In his autobiography, Day Lewis adds his own derogatory comment about Marshall: "she had no tabus; her language could be, on occasion, as foul as mine." He suspected that "she secretly relished the disasters in which she was involved."[147]) Only a little later, Auden told his brother John, in a letter he wrote from Zagreb during his disastrous visit to Yugoslavia with their father: "I wish to improve my inferiority complex and to develop heterosexual traits." He suggested that Marshall might be helpful to John too if he undertook an analysis with her to cure his own misery: "I think you might make yourself happier."[148]

No one has yet been able to supply much convincing detail about the analysis Auden refers to. But it probably took place in fits and starts mainly in the Oxford vacations of late 1927 and the first half of 1928. Around Easter 1928, Auden told Isherwood, somewhat unconvincingly, "Had a most pleasant week with my analyst. Libido, it is proved, is towards women. The trouble is incest."[149] For the apparent next phase of the treatment, which occurred in July and August 1928, he traveled to the resort town of Spa in Belgium. It was the first time he had ever been for a stay in a French-speaking country. Soon afterward, he told his Christ Church friend David Ayerst that he had spent three weeks there: "staying with a psychologist." He added, "I find I am quite ambidextrous [bisexual] now."[150]

In the meantime, Auden had performed miserably in his schools examinations at Oxford. After the Anglo-Saxon paper, William McElwee went to see Auden in his rooms at Christ Church and found him weeping.[151] In June 1928, he was awarded an ignominious Third Class degree in English.[152] (It must have hurt that one of the Oxford examiners supervising the marking of finals in the summer of 1928 was Tolkien.[153]) And, to compound this disaster, Auden seems somehow to have been hoping that the McElwees—the siblings, children, and surviving elders of Auden's Oxford love, Bill McElwee—living at the relatively modest family home at Tapscott in Somerset, would perform his charade.[154] He had planned to travel there in September 1928 for that purpose; but in August this blew up too, and he had to report to Isherwood: "They refuse to do the play, as they say the village won't stand it."[155] Nor did Auden's bad luck end there. Shortly after leaving Oxford, he got engaged to Sheilah Richardson, a woman who lived in the same Birmingham suburb as the Audens and was training as a nurse at the Birmingham Children's Hospital where Dr. Auden was a consultant. There is a strong whiff of the parental intervention to this episode—and it proved as effective as most such interventions do. Either Auden or Richardson (sources differ) broke off the arrangement in the following year.[156]

While Auden was away in Belgium, half convincing himself that he was "quite ambidextrous," his university friend Stephen Spender was struggling to hand print a pamphlet of Auden's poems, his first, on a small press at the Spenders' house in Hampstead. A poem that Auden wrote in Spa, and even managed to squeeze into the copy for the little book, starts by insisting that it is possible simply to depart from unbearable personal and social history: "To throw away the key and walk away | . . . Learns more than maps upon the whitewashed wall," the poem begins. When someone does throw away the key and walk away, it claims, "All pasts | Are single old past now," and one can make a new beginning. Simply by leaving everything behind, the subject will undergo evolutionary change telescoped into a single lifetime: "with prolonged drowning shall develop gills." But in a second verse paragraph, Auden wonders what that change will feel like and imagines it will be lonely and exhausting: "Too tired to hear except the pulse strum," as the traveler enters a forbidding new landscape with "Rocks shutting out the sky, the old life done."[157] Neither going nor staying is easy.

Even as "To throw away the key and walk away" explores the possibility that sloughing off the past might be the right thing to do, the poem signals formally that the past could not easily be left behind.

This lyric, written while Auden was being psychoanalyzed, is one of the first in which he extensively imitates Wilfred Owen's pararhyming style. (The *OED* defines a "pararhyme" as a "half-rhyme in which there is vowel variation within the same consonant pattern," as, for example, in red/road or soon/seen.) Most famously used in the Owen poem "Strange Meeting," this pararhyming technique, which in a sense involves a strange (that is, oddly unexpected and clashing) meeting of two sounds, was an imitation of *proest*, an ancient Welsh technique of partial rhyming. Thus, in Auden's poem, his way of suggesting the inescapable weight of history on the present is doubled: Auden is imitating Owen imitating an ancient Welsh poetic device. He conjures up both a long-distant literary tradition and, more immediately, a dead poet's voice inside his own. Owen and the war poets are still haunting the field in Auden's poetry, like Longstaff's ghost-soldiers milling outside the Menin Gate.[158]

In the end, Spender's machine in Hampstead could not cope with the complexities of the printing job and broke down. With the long vacation concluding, Spender employed the Holywell Press in Oxford to finish the edition for him professionally.[159] The small volume they produced is bound with a reddish-orange paper wrapper and contains 20 poems. When Spender sent Auden his copies in October 1928, he parcelled them up and posted them to the foreign city where Auden was now living. As Auden remembered it, "The first personal choice I can remember making was my decision, when my father offered me a year abroad after I had gone down from Oxford, to spend it in Berlin."[160] After Spa, unlike John Nower, Auden had "walked away," just as his poem envisages. However, in doing that, he was traveling not toward the future but toward a further encounter with the past and its specters.

5   STRANGE MEETINGS
ENGLISH IN GERMANY, 1928–1929

*Every generation of Englishmen has its own "snobist" country. Before
1914 it was Italy; in the early 20s it was France; my generation swung
off to Germany.*

—W. H. AUDEN (1941)

IN WILFRED OWEN'S POEM "Strange Meeting," written in early 1918, a British
soldier who has escaped from battle down "some profound dull tunnel"
extending far beneath the conflict finds a group of "sleepers" slumped
on the ground. Are they dead or alive? He shakes and "probe[s]" them
with an extended arm, until suddenly one, a German he bayoneted to
death the day before, springs up and addresses him with "piteous recognition in fixed eyes."[1]

Eric J. Leed wrote of the "strangeness" of meeting an enemy soldier
during the war: "The invisibility of the enemy stripped him of any co-
herent shape. . . . To encounter, face to face, that which had been made
strange by propaganda and countless frustrated attacks, and to realize
they were 'like us' was an uncanny experience."[2] Desperately seeking
peace with this "Strange friend" in Owen's poem, the British soldier tries
to console his victim. The Tommy speaks just one bland, self-exculpating
line, saying: "here is no cause to mourn." In a response that lasts for
roughly thirty of the poem's forty-four lines, thus greatly outspanning his
killer's comment, the German soldier disputes the banality of the British
soldier's thought, describing the waste, the loss, and the opportunities to
better the world that his death means he will have to forgo. Then, speaking
to his "friend" (he uses the same word his killer had used to describe him
earlier), he recalls the trauma of his death: as the British infantryman
"jabbed," the German "parried": "but my hands were loath and cold."[3]

The gestures described throughout the poem are a dance of hands—
in this strange, underground world that Owen describes, hands are as
expressive as voices. While he is speaking, the dead German, as if reen-
acting his last earthly actions but with a different purpose, has been
"Lifting distressful hands" toward the Englishman, "as if to bless."[4] The
scenario is a little Whitmanesque, recalling "Reconciliation," in which
the poet bends downs to his enemy's corpse and "touch[es] lightly with
my lips the white face in the coffin."[5] And it is a little Dantesque: what
seems to be a living man with some special dispensation walks through
hell. Or is Owen's British soldier perhaps dead too?

The experience is so uncanny that Owen's poem breaks off, as if
unable to imagine how the reconciliation between killer and victim will
actually take place; the dead man's hands, lifted "as if to bless" at the
start of the poem, prove as ineffectual as they had a day earlier when
the Englishman plunged his bayonet into the German's body:

> I knew you in this dark: for so you frowned
> Yesterday through me as you jabbed and killed.
> I parried; but my hands were loath and cold.[6]

"Strange Meeting" ends with the German suggesting: "Let us sleep
now. . . ."[7] After setting up the moral victory over convention by allowing the German to have by far the greater part of the dialogue in this
English poem, Owen also gives him the last word. The ellipsis in the
German's final statement leaves us to ponder the concluding, splintered
half line, much as a reader might speculate on the lost words from the
fragment of a love poem by Sappho. "Let us sleep now. . . ." Owen would
be killed in battle a week before the war ended.

Until around 1926, Paris had been the cynosure city for Britons and
Americans involved with the arts. "Depuis plusieurs années," T. S. Eliot
wrote later, describing his frame of mind in 1910, "la France représen-
tait surtout, à mes yeux, la *poésie*" (From a few years before, France
stood above all, in my eyes, for *poetry*).[8] But, from about 1926 onward,
the countercult of northern literatures was starting to take hold, even
in enclaves like Oxford. And Berlin began to replace the French capital
as the most significant interwar venue for British and American visitors to Europe.[9] Owen's dream of peacemaking, of absolving "meetings"

between former enemies, had passed into the imaginations of many Britons of a younger generation: once they had been children who had suffered in wartime but who were also sensitized to German achievements by the middle-class world they had grown up in.

The formation of Auden's sensibility was deeply related to his awareness of German culture. His musical education was structured around a Germanic canon. When he first traveled abroad, it was with his father to attend the 1925 Salzburg Festival, held at one of the great centers of German-Austrian musical culture. Auden also connected Dr. Auden with Germany through the latter's absence at the war, through his queer uncle Harold (Dr. Auden's brother), who had studied in Germany, and through the unconventional scientific and medical texts, written by Germans, that Dr. Auden pored over.

As seen earlier, during the war Auden had even been accused at his prep school of wanting "the Huns to win," an experience that established, he said, "an unconscious bias" in his thoughts, associating Germany with "forbidden pleasures."[10] It was around the time of this incident at St. Edmund's that Christopher Isherwood remembered Auden confiding that he had "discovered, very early in life, the key to the bookcase which contained anatomical manuals with coloured German plates." These "German plates" he showed his classmates during the last years of the First World War, disclosing to them "the first naughty stupendous breath-taking hints about the facts of sex."[11]

What was in Auden's mind in 1928, when his parents offered him a post-university year abroad and he chose to spend it in Berlin? He had already made a few verbal allusions to Owen's poems since he started reading them around 1926.[12] But, as the end of Chapter 4 showed, until the summer of 1928 he had not yet tried to go any deeper and to absorb into his own poetry the meaning in the style of Owen's work, especially the meaning of pararhymes in a sequence of pentameters that are indelibly associated with "Strange Meeting." He had not ventured any deeper until now, that is, in the summer of 1928 when he was undergoing some form of psychoanalysis in Belgium and considering where to spend his next year. Suddenly, Auden started using Owenesque pararhymes with pentameters for the first time. In fact, he used them for two substantial poems in a single month.[13] It is a signal moment in his writing. Auden's thinking is artistic, not abstract—the forms that his poems take express his motivations as a poet. In early to mid-October 1928, after twice, in poems for *Paid on Both Sides,* evoking in his poetry memories of Owen's British soldier who meets his former adversary underground and wants to reconcile with him, Auden moved to Berlin.

At the time, he did not consciously understand why he had chosen to settle in the German capital. And Owen's poems did not *cause* him to live in the city, of course. But Auden's adoption, just before he went to Germany, of a technique almost uniquely tied to Owen, and to "Strange Meeting" in particular, provides the best vantage point from which to understand his reasons for subsequently going to Berlin. The desire in "Strange Meeting" for a reconciliation after shared historical traumas is mirrored formally in the pararhymes—with their unconventional fits between rhyme words, reaching out for a nonstandard connection with each other like the soldiers' hands in Owen's poem. (Pararhymes, with their deliberately mismatched vowels, almost *sound* as if they come from the voice of a nonnative speaker trying hard to pronounce English correctly and imperfectly succeeding.)

Much later, Auden told an interviewer that he did not "really realize why I went to Germany until after I'd done it."[14] But his stylistic choice to write in a style evocative of Owen in the poems "To throw away the key and walk away" and "The spring unsettles sleeping partnerships" lays bare some decisive if unconscious reasoning: Germany, long prohibited morally and therefore fascinating, could also be a place in which to enact a symbolic healing in the psyche of the war's wounds.[15]

Auden stayed in Germany from October 1928 to July 1929. During that time, he lived not only near Berlin's high-bourgeois Wannsee district but also in the city slum of Hallesches Tor and finally in the small town of Rothehütte in the Harz Mountains.[16] His time in Germany was a key period not just in his personal life but also in the evolution of his aesthetic ideals and his poetry. But the main result of this first sustained period of living and writing outside England is a paradox: in broadening his cultural and poetic horizons, it also confirmed, and narrowed, his identity as a self-consciously "English" poet. Auden continued to visit friends in Germany (principally Isherwood) enthusiastically on and off for shorter periods until the midwinter of 1932–1933. But whatever Auden's intentions were, his poetry from this period, like the soldier's hands that reach out and yet never quite grasp the enemy's in "Strange Meeting," tells the pessimistic story of a troubling divide that it was impossible to overcome—or, perhaps, of a divide that, unconsciously at least, Auden felt it was artistically essential to maintain.

Although landlocked, Berlin is a kind of island. This cosmopolitan metropolis, transected by the rivers Havel and Spree, sits on a vast plain formed during the last ice age. The early twentieth-century city contrasted with the natural world that surrounded it as an island does with the surrounding water. The philosopher Ernst Bloch wrote: "Here, it's especially easy for life to become new. The people have little else behind them to call a place of origin. . . . The city appears to have come into being in an empty land—completely fresh and bearing no relation to anything."[17] Berlin, with a nightlife and cultural life (and political strife) unlike anywhere else in Germany, was encircled by a conservative rustic population.[18] "All around Berlin," one right-wing intellectual wrote, "there still lie broad stretches of barbarian territory filled with German peasants and upright citizens, with villages and old princely seats."[19] The city's main gay monthly when Auden lived there, perhaps alluding to the idea of Berlin as a haven free from the hostility of the German population as a whole, was called *Die Insel* (The island).[20]

Within the city, though, there were, in effect, two interwar Berlins, related by antithesis. One was defined by the well-publicized, sunlit Apollonian Weimar atmosphere of advanced, hygienic, sophisticated modernity, of progressive social, technical, and cultural achievements, a place whose imaginative antecedent was classical Greece.[21] This was the Germany that a contemporary journalist described as having revived the "worship of the sun-god," a cult that by the early 1930s was "full-grown."[22] The other was a darkened, Dionysian city of total human degradation and exploitation, of violence, poverty, cruelty, cynicism, and bitterness, whose imaginative antecedent was like somewhere evil in a grim Nordic myth.

The country had been traumatized by the defeat in the First World War: 1.5 million Germans returned permanently disabled to a starving and bankrupt society; about 80,000 of these ex-servicemen were amputees.[23] Three hundred and fifty thousand Berliners had died in the war; the average nutrition level in the city in the years immediately after the conflict amounted to a mere 1,000 calories a day. In Berlin even in the later 1920s, when Auden arrived there, there were "innumerable war cripples lining the streets."[24] "It was a time of great misery," one observer wrote, "with legless war veterans riding the sidewalks on rolling planks, with a nation that seemed to consist of nothing but beggars, whores, invalids and fat-necked speculators."[25]

In these desperate circumstances, the country had been convulsed by an array of violent events: rebellions in the armed forces; the abdication of Kaiser Wilhelm II; the Spartacist uprising in Berlin in 1919; the creation of a short-lived Bavarian Soviet Republic in Munich, also in 1919 and briefly led as head of state by the playwright Ernst Toller (whom Auden was to meet and collaborate with some years later); the disastrous right-wing Kapp Putsch in Berlin in 1920; and rebellions in the Ruhr, in Saxony, and in Hamburg. In 1921 right-wing extremists killed Matthias Erzberger, the centrist politician who had signed the Armistice on Germany's behalf in 1918; the first chancellor of the Weimar Republic, Philipp Scheidemann, was attacked in 1919 with prussic acid; and in 1922, antisemitic, right-wing terrorists, former members of the Imperial Army, assassinated the foreign minister, Walter Rathenau, with machine guns.[26]

By 1923, the year of the Beer Hall Putsch in Munich, hyperinflation had swamped the German economy. It was a period when, as Hitler said, the "revolt of the starving billionaires" seemed possible.[27] Lawyers fumbled in the gutters for scraps; there were murderous fights over a rotten potato; Berlin had become the "suicide capital of Europe," with people withdrawing their life savings from banks to purchase a stamp for the letter they would post before they killed themselves.[28] Recalling those times, Hannah Arendt wrote: "George Grosz's cartoons seemed to us not satires but realistic reportage: we knew those types, they were all around us."[29] The greatest of Berlin's *feuilletonistes,* Joseph Roth, described the city as "so heartless in its bustle, so cold in its evident urge to utility, and so often teetering on the edge of kitsch where it would be sensitive" and as "grisly" with its "asphalt streets, grayshaded parks, and blue canals [where] death lurks with revolver, chloroform, and gag," amid the "anonymous misery."[30]

When Auden came to what he called "the much grimmer and [more] disturbing . . . but, at least uncartesian world of Berlin" in 1928, violence and social disruption were still endemic.[31] (By saying that Berlin was "uncartesian," Auden was contrasting it with the dry, abstract intellectualism of the affluent Oxford world he had become used to, and his adjective meant something like "with no assumption that the mind's existence was separate from the body's," with added shades of "ambiguous" and "multisided.") In January 1927, from a total population of about 4.3 million, there were some 284,000 unemployed; by October 1929, when Auden was back in England, almost 500,000 Berliners were without work.[32] Grosz's cartoon "Civil War," drawn in 1928, the year Auden arrived in the city, shows a cloth-capped worker with a rifle sitting on a can and smoking as he waits for the impending conflict. At his feet is a pile of stamped-out butts, like a heap of little victims.[33]

There were at least sixty-two organized Mafia-like gangs, known as *Ringvereine* (ring clubs, after the rings their members wore), in Berlin, controlling the thriving industries of drugs, gambling, car theft, child prostitution, blackmail, and racketeering.[34] Auden wrote approvingly to William McElwee's fiancée, Patience Kennington, that there were "170 male brothels under police control."[35] Political fights continued between members of the right-wing Der Stahlhelm (the Steel Helmet) and the left-wing Rotfrontkämpferbund (the Red Front-Fighters' League) paramilitary groups, made up largely of ex-servicemen. The cultural theorist Siegfried Kracauer wrote in 1931:

> Life has recently become cheap. . . . All things that go without saying are dying out one by one; our ethical foundations are being shaken along with the economic, and new points of stability are in the meantime wanting. . . . The suppression of binding social obligations is also intensified by the neutrality of important public expressions of opinion. . . . The exceptional degree of this insecurity is what characterizes the overwhelming process of social transformation that has been our lot since the end of the world war. Until the new contours have become solidified, our path will continue to be marked by blood and tears.[36]

The "suppression of binding social obligations" led many observers to sense a profound instability in the structure of the city's life, as though, morally speaking, it were sinking into the equivalent of the swamp on which the actual metropolis was built. Currency values altered constantly, as did the law. The "multiplicity of daily changing laws at that time," Grosz wrote, "was such that everybody would break one or the other unintentionally, or even unknowingly."[37] Auden would later say: "I remember how odd it was, on my first trip to Berlin after Oxford. It was the first time I felt the ground shaking under my feet."[38]

For Bloch, who worked as an editor and then a journalist in Berlin in the 1920s, contemporary Germany had become a country stalked by the ghosts of earlier times and mentalities because its uneven development meant that there was still "a particularly large amount of pre-capitalist material." Next to the most technologically and economically advanced developments, he noted, older "types of being thus occur right in the city, older ways of thinking and objects of hate as well."[39] The city encompassed peasant-like, feudal mindsets alongside radicalized industrial workers and a vast, alienated body of middle-class employees struggling to survive the recent economic catastrophes. Here was a place in which the most violent contrasts, fractures, and contradictions burst through not only in its everyday social life but in its art— evident, for example, in the endless stylistic metamorphosing of a Berlin musician such as Kurt Weill or in the mixture of scientific sobriety and ghoulish sadism in the paintings of George Grosz.

Weimar Germany's newspaper readers were obsessed with murder, the bloodier or more repellent the better.[40] And Berlin pornography of the 1920s placed an "unusual emphasis on body worship, extreme fetishism, scatology, dark roleplay, . . . ritualized gender struggle, . . . [and] eroticized violence."[41] In this material, men and women flogged and scarified each other while onlookers ogled; youth administered enemas to their chained-up elderly victims (or vice versa); the participants brutalized their own bodies with nails, straps, and paddles or played out games in which love could only appear as its enemy, wearing the mask of hate. The Berlin sexologist Magnus Hirschfeld related much of this to historical traumas, concluding that, as far as the cauldron of Berlin was concerned, the "Great War was the greatest sexual catastrophe that has ever befallen civilized man."[42] Berlin produced images of women riding, whipping, or otherwise humiliating a ready supply of battered and submissive men, making it clear that the Germany where Auden settled was a nation in which some significant fraction of the country's sexual imagination was drawn to stylized representations of defeated soldiers being punished by agonized widows.

At his parents' urging, Auden first stayed with the Muthesius family as their paying guest until sometime in December 1928. The family patriarch, Hermann Muthesius, had been a well-known German architect and architectural critic with significant Anglophilic sympathies for late-Victorian ideas about craft, functionality, and restraint (like those espoused by Auden's parents). He had been killed in a road accident in 1927. His family stayed on in the large and frigidly stylish Haus Muthesius, which was a showpiece for Muthesius's Arts and Crafts–influenced aesthetic, at Potsdamer Chausee 49 in Nikolassee, near Wannsee, a "lakeside colony of middle-class villas to the south-west of the city."[43]

Hermann Muthesius's widow, Anna, herself an author, was the head of this household. She took in lodgers like Auden in order to make ends meet and also to speak some English, a fact that gave Auden a pretext to move out and live on his own, since he could honestly say he was not improving his German much while he stayed there. Relatively little is known about his life during the time he stayed with Anna Muthesius, but he was working hard on the second version of *Paid on Both Sides*. (Oddly, given that there were so many enthusiastic photographers among his friends in the city, there are very few images of Auden from the months of his stay in Germany.) He composed another nine poems for the "charade"—or "the play," as he had started to call it sometimes—in the first few months of his stay: "I am doing quite a lot of work," he told McElwee's fiancée, Patience, at the end of 1928.[44]

The poem beginning "Can speak of trouble, pressure on men" was probably the first he wrote in the city, in October 1928. It is a plain, laconic, but elevated lyric for the charade's Chorus. The poem contains intense, gnomic phrases describing psychological confusion ("heart fears all heart cries for") and ends with an almost religious intuition about, and a longing for, radical change:

> O watcher in the dark, you wake
> Our dream of waking, we feel
> Your finger on the flesh that has been skinned,
> By your bright day
> See clear what we were doing, that we were vile.
> Your sudden hand
> Shall humble great
> Pride, break it, wear down to stumps old systems which await
> The last transgression of the sea.[45]

Most striking is the fact that this crisis-bound poem feels at once completely of its moment in Berlin and yet also as if it exists in a tragic, lyric space outside time with no recognizably contemporary scenery or characters. Like Berlin itself, where hypermodern and feudal mentalities were adjacent, the poem's style reads as both new and archaic. God is an impoverished night watchman and an all-seeing "watcher in the dark."

Earlier in 1928, when Auden chose to go to the German capital, his parents appear to have displayed relative equanimity about the prospect, although unease with his sexuality must have meant that his decision was not an easy one for them to acquiesce in. Berlin, once a Prussian military garrison, had a long-established reputation as the homosexual capital of Europe. Auden's father seems to have been concerned with discretion, avoidance of scandal, and the preservation of respectability, while Auden's mother by this stage may have just given up the struggle, exhausted. And in Berlin, Auden was living a life that involved a lot of poetry but also a lot of sex or at least a lot of thinking about sex.

Long before the end of the 1920s, when a flood of titillated foreigners descended on the city, Berlin, a "Babylon-am-Spree," was known as a European city of vice. And this status had been consolidated as the country fell apart after the First World War. "The collapse of moral structures gave people freedom," a historian writes. "Depravity was one consequence, an extraordinary flowering of art and sciences was another."[46] Moreover, the police and the judiciary, besides in some cases being discreet but essential stakeholders in the sex trade, had been instructed by the government to ignore most violations of the Criminal Code as it related to homosexuality.[47] This meant that one of Berlin's most famous tourist attractions was its array of gay sex businesses (and the related trafficking in drugs).[48]

The implosion of the German economy, compounded by Berlin's uninhibited traditions and its relative isolation, meant that Berlin was "by far the most immoral city in Europe," according to the actor Walter Slezak.[49] "Geld macht sinnlich" (Money makes you sexy), Fatty the Pimp sings in Weill and Brecht's *Aufstieg und Fall der Stadt Mahagonny* (*The Rise and Fall of the City of Mahagonny*), written in Berlin between 1927 and 1929. Wyndham Lewis called it the "Perverts' Paradise, the Mecca of both Lesb and So."[50] By the mid-1920s, more than 150,000 Berliners were involved in one way or another in the sex trade.[51] There were about

100,000 female prostitutes in 1926, including many "Half-Silks," amateurs who had other employment but who made extra money by prostituting themselves occasionally.[52] Then there were 35,000 male prostitutes in addition.[53] Out of over 4 million Berliners, 350,000 people were estimated to be homosexuals by 1930.[54] Estimates for the number of lesbians in the city at the time range from "85,000 to 400,000," depending on the source.[55] Berlin had at least thirty lesbian clubs and was second only to Paris as an enclave for lesbians.[56] Scholars have suggested there were somewhere between sixty-five and 160 gay *Dielen* or "lounges" in the city.[57] (As noted earlier, Auden thought there were 170 male brothels.) Linguistic imports from American English into German in the 1920s included "jazz," "cocktail," "dancing," "flirt," and "sex appeal."

Berlin's discourse on sexuality was remarkably open, calm, and rational. This frankness was one reason why Magnus Hirschfeld's Institut für Sexualwissenschaft (Institute for Sexual Science), at the corner of In den Zelten and Beethovenstraße, near the Tiergarten, opened in 1919.[58] Hirschfeld, "the Einstein of Sex," as the Berlin newspapers called him, created an institution unique in its scope and influence.[59] The splendidly appointed buildings housed his huge library of books on sexual matters, medical, psychological, iconographic, and pornographic. Embellished by wall plaques with delphic inscriptions such as "Justice through Science" and "What the World Calls the Soul, We Call the Endocrine System!" the institute was open to the public (including classes of schoolchildren), attracting many famous guests, and visits from some 1,100 doctors each year, who attended panels, workshops, lectures, and film screenings there. It was Germany's first "Marriage Bureau," where clients could obtain suggestions for partners or get advice on their relationships, as well as being a type of laboratory, "a hospital [in which abortions were carried out] and a free university under one roof."[60]

The museum-like "Gallery of Derangements of the Sexual Instincts" at the institute was especially popular. Special docents and assistants solemnly led visitors past displays containing "Sanskrit sex manuals, miniature shoes worn by foot-bound Chinese courtesans, medieval chastity belts, . . . antique steam-driven vibrators, . . . [and] lacy panties found on the corpses of von Hindenburg's heroic officers." There were also "free-standing sex machines and masturbation devices of every shape and variety."[61] Hirschfeld manufactured and marketed aphrodisiacs of various kinds, including one brand called "Titus Pills," as a way of making money and keeping the institute's name before the public. Auden saw and claimed that he was sturdily unimpressed by all this. On a visit to the institute in March 1929 with Isherwood, he was dismissive: "We waited in an eighteenth-century drawing room with elderly ladies and adhesive trouser boys. Why was this so obscene? . . . Lets have nothing of this pornography for science. A eunuch's pleasure."[62] But the public visibility of organizations like the Institut für Sexualwissenschaft and the flourishing underground world of bars and brothels that Auden reveled in were symbiotic phenomena, equally characteristic of Berlin.

Mainstream, respectable guidebooks for tourists looked the other way as far as Berlin's sex businesses were concerned. The reliable but lacunae-filled volumes produced by such firms as Baedeker, Michelin, and Thomas Cook created a market for "alternatives to the bestselling and most broadly appealing guides."[63] For instance, niche volumes concentrated on innocuous matters such as places to shop at and coffeehouses to visit but also, to varying degrees, on sites for sexual tourists and adventurers. Other guidebooks went further. In 1927, the journalist Eugen Szatmari published *Das Buch von Berlin* (The book of Berlin), the first in the "Was nicht im 'Baedeker' steht" (What is not in "Baedeker") series.[64] Another famous tourist guide was by Curt Moreck (the pen name of Konrad Haemmerling): *Ein Führer durch das "lasterhafte" Berlin* (A guide to "depraved" Berlin), published in 1931, which devotes a very substantial section to "Stammlokale des männlichen Eros" (Favorite haunts of the male Eros).[65]

Around the same time, and enabled in part by the examples of sexual straightforwardness in modernist works by D. H. Lawrence and James Joyce, some German novels began to appear in the mid-1920s that moved further into the previously occluded world of Berlin's gay life. Chief among them are Klaus Mann's *Der fromme Tanz* (*The Pious Dance,* 1925) and John Henry Mackay's *Der Puppenjunge* (*The Hustler,* 1926). Andreas Magnus, Mann's hero, is a confused young man, a child of the "great all-consuming upheaval" of the war, for whom the revolutionary atmosphere of 1914 had, without him understanding it, "stamped itself on his soul only as a kind of great uprising, a clanking, booming noise, a vague period after which everything had to be different from what it was before."[66] He comes to Berlin, falls into friendships with more experienced inhabitants of the city, and tours (and performs in) Berlin's night world.

Mann describes, in lightly camouflaged form, real clubs and bars, giving them such false but plausible names as the "Little Garden of Eden" and "Saint Margaret's Cellar." The latter evokes the mood of Auden and Isherwood's favorite haunt, the "Cosy Corner," and that of other bars in the southeastern part of the city that they visited, such as the "Adonis-Diele" on the Alexandrinenstraße. Mann writes of one such place: "The heartiness was more hollow, less effervescent, not so buoyantly maintained as up west. The room, down a couple of steps, was cramped and the air was so thick that it was hard to breathe. The deaf, stocky landlord with the drooping white moustache would walk back and forth, stroking the boys' hair with morose affection when they pleased him, swatting them when they annoyed him."[67]

Mackay's *Der Puppenjunge* describes a doomed love affair between two young men of different classes who arrive almost simultaneously in Berlin from different parts of the country. ("Always there remained a barrier between them, which they were never allowed to cross."[68]) The scenario is mainly a pretext for Mackay to furnish the reader with reportage about places such as the "Passage" (the Linden-Passage, a 400 foot long and forty foot high, glass-covered arcade between Unter den Linden and the Friedrichstraße), "the notorious . . . meeting place of a certain segment of the Berlin population at all times of day and night," and "Uncle Paul's saloon," with its "hustler table," situated near the Friedrichstraße train station.[69] (Auden knew the Passage and visited it more than once.) Mackay also offers detailed descriptions of the "Adonis-Diele," which had a heavy curtain at the entrance, like the "Cosy Corner." Inside, "gentlemen danced with the boys, some boys danced among themselves, and two aunties in women's clothing, with wigs and gigantic feather hats, danced like crazy."[70]

Auden went to the Adonis-Diele a number of times to find boys willing to have sex for tiny amounts of money. For example, on 26 April 1929, he recorded in his journal that he "Picked up Herbert in Adonis Diele. For two hours of every position [illegible] gave him 2 M[arks]."[71] Another hangout for Auden, and later Isherwood, was "Bei Voo-Doo" ("Voo-Doo's"), as it was unofficially known, the club at Skalitzerstraße 7 in Kreuzberg where Auden notes in his journal that he once had a not very happy sexual encounter. This was an establishment run by the famous dancer Willi Pape, often described in the press as a "transvestite," who appeared onstage under the name of "Voo-Doo," and by Pape's friend Emil Schmidt.[72]

But Auden's preferred bar, and Isherwood's after Auden had introduced him, was the low-key "Cosy Corner" on Zossenerstraße in the Kreuzberg district. Isherwood wrote:

> Such places depended on their regular customers. They were small and hard to find and couldn't afford to advertise themselves, so casual visitors were few. . . . Nothing could have looked less decadent than the Cosy Corner. It was plain and homely and unpretentious. Its only decorations were a few photographs of boxers and racing cyclists, pinned up above the bar. It was heated by a big old-fashioned iron stove. Partly because of the great heat of this stove, partly because they knew it excited their clients (*die Stubben*), the boys stripped off their sweaters or leather jackets and sat around with their shirts unbuttoned to the navel and their sleeves rolled up to their armpits.
>
> They were all working class and nearly all out of work. If you chose to describe them as male prostitutes (*Pup[p]enjungen*) you had to add that they were mostly rank amateurs, compared with the more professional boys of the West End. They were greedy but not calculating, temperamentally unable to take thought for the morrow.[73]

In bars like the "Cosy Corner," there may have been as much sitting around and chatting in broken German as coupling. Auden would later recall "our Berlin" to Isherwood as "that wonderful old atmosphere of sex and boredom."[74]

The lack of information about Auden's early months in the city in part reflects the life that he was leading there, with its fleeting connections and illicit meetings. Some of his sex partners were mysteries to him. With mock bravado, he claimed to Patience Kennington, McElwee's fiancée, that Berlin was "the bugger's daydream."[75] But the not particularly lengthy list of "Boys had" that he jotted down in 1929 toward the end of his stay (nine names in about as many months) has entries for "Unknown from Passage," "Unknown from Zum Kleinen Raimund" (presumably the name of a small gay dive), "Unknown in Köln," and "Unknown from Scarlitzer 7" (the "Bei Voo-Doo" in Skalitzerstraße). Other entries on the list are "Pieps," "Cully," "Gerhart," "Herbert," and "Otto." Of these, "Gerhart" is Gerhart Meyer, a sailor, and "Otto" refers to Otto Küsel. Cully may have been a nickname for a boy named Kurt Groote. But for six out of the nine people on the list, we know next to nothing—their own dates and life stories are largely enigmas now, as are Auden's relations with them.[76] Underneath his list, he noted his restricted boldness with honesty: "I regret the Scarlitzer [Skalitzer] one. He was not nice and was very dirty; i.e. Pure lust on my part. All the others were nice people."[77] Auden admitted to himself in his journal that he had "often thought I would go brothel crawling but I can't do it. I become attached to someone, and enter on a relationship at once."[78]

However, in the table Auden made in another notebook much later, around May 1947, commemorating what Edward Mendelson calls "the emotional milestones" who were "the sexual loves that had had the greatest effect on his life and work," he included none of these German boys.[79] Unlike Isherwood, who became deeply and lengthily enmeshed with his German lovers' lives, Auden's German acquaintances were people to have flings (at best) with, not affairs—and this dynamic of foiled or brief encounters (partly outside Auden's control but also perhaps partly within it) is a clue to the deeper meanings of many of the poems he wrote in Germany.

In Berlin in the autumn and early winter months of 1928, Auden's poetry was almost exclusively composed for the final version of *Paid on Both Sides.* After "O watcher in the dark," the other lyric from his early months in Berlin that commands attention is "Because I'm come it does not mean to hold," which he wrote in November of that year, for the second version of *the charade.* The poem, possibly a bit self-indicting, is spoken by an Expressionist-style "Man-Woman," a character whom Auden would probably not have conceived of or been able to write for until he was in Berlin. The Man-Woman appears "as a prisoner of war behind barbed wire, in the snow," delivers an accusatory poem on behalf of the repressed power of love, and then disappears:

> Love was not love for you but episodes,
> Traffic in memoirs, views from different sides;
> You thought oaths of comparison a bond,
> And though you had your orders to disband,
> Refused to listen, but remained in woods

Poorly concealed your profits under wads.
Nothing was any use; therefore I went
Hearing you call for what you did not want.[80]

Again, the style is taken from Owen's weary, melancholic pararhyming. The Man-Woman, significantly, is a "a prisoner of war." In Auden's Berlin poetry, war is not so much a metaphor for love, nor love for war: rather, the two subjects are to be taken literally and bound up with each other as inextricable. And, again, both love and war are treated with resignation and pessimism. After delivering the speech, the Man-Woman disappears, and John Nower, the doomed central figure in *Paid on Both Sides,* continues the cycle of bloodshed by having a captured spy from the Shaw family shot.

Auden was reading Marcel Proust in Germany, and the Man-Woman must owe something to Proust's discussions of "les hommes-femmes" in *Sodome et Gomorrhe* (1921–1922). But, more significantly, this ambiguously gendered figure appears in *Paid on Both Sides* as an obvious outgrowth of Auden's immersion in Berlin's artistic and sexual freedoms—he took advantage of the city's emancipated cultural atmosphere, seeing, for example, an early performance of Brecht and Weill's sensational *Die Dreigroschenoper* (*The Threepenny Opera*) at the Theater am Schiffbauerdamm, probably in the first few months of his stay.[81] For a useful contrast of artistic modes and ambitions, it is worth remembering that one of the biggest hits on the London stage at the same time in late 1928 was R. C. Sheriff's *Journey's End,* a well-made realist play about four British junior officers stuck together in a dugout in 1918.

During Auden's early months in Berlin, he was often in the company of other visitors to Germany, above all, of his fellow English. That is because his fascination with German culture was widely shared and was part of a broad mood among those who were too young to have fought against Germany in the First World War. On a visit to Robert Medley's family home, Colby Hall in Wensleydale, in the summer of 1928, just before he left for Berlin, Auden dismissed Eliot's beloved city of culture, Paris, saying: "it was overly fashionable and suited only to intellectual snobs."[82] This offhand comment is representative of currents of thought and feeling in artistic circles. In the later 1920s, a youthful section of the British intelligentsia was becoming very sympathetic to contemporary German culture. For instance, the photographer Barbara Ker-Seymer, who briefly worked on visual projects with Auden's friend Brian Howard, said essentially the same thing as Auden when she recalled her influences and interests during the later 1920s and early 1930s: "We were passionately interested in everything German."[83] George Orwell's *Down and Out in Paris and London* (1933), his account of life as a *plongeur* in 1929 in the capital of high modernism, is dramatically disenchanting. Paris was over as a literary city, Orwell's work signaled; it was now only a place where young writers scraped the grease off dirty plates. (Eliot, the previous literary generation's greatest enthusiast for Paris, rejected Orwell's book for Faber and Faber in 1932.)

Germany was therefore positioned in a historical situation in which it could fulfill a dramatic role for English imaginations in the postwar years. First a despised (and feared) enemy nation and then a defeated, chaotic, violent, pathos-ridden country in the 1920s, the "pariah of European politics," it stood for everything repressed, dangerous, alluring, libidinal. As a result, for varying individual reasons but with a common outcome, a certain intellectual stratum of young, artistic England flocked to the country in the second half of the 1920s.[84] Late-1920s books of disenchantment about the First World War by Graves, Blunden, and others—books that often contained sympathy for the troops in the opposing trenches—were being published at a time when a new generation of artists was experiencing the very opposite of Germanophobia. And, suggesting the two cultures were in synchrony, in Germany, there was a rising fascination with British culture: in 1929–1930 there was a "war books" boom there too, which included memoirs and novels that expressed fellow feeling for British suffering.[85]

Auden passed substantial amounts of his main stay in 1928 to 1929 in the company both of Isherwood and of Stephen Spender, who, according to one biographer who follows Spender's own self-mythologizing, was half German.[86] But Isherwood and Spender were not the only members of Auden's loose circle of friends to visit Berlin in this period. Others, such as Edward Upward, Brian Howard, and John Lehmann, also spent time there, and this group itself formed just a small part of the tourist and refugee waves that washed through the city in the late 1920s.[87]

Some English people even went to Germany for academic reasons. David Haden Guest spent a couple of terms at Cambridge during the period from 1929 to 1930 studying with Ludwig Wittgenstein before lodging for a year at the University of Göttingen reading German philosophy. Haden Guest was radicalized and politicized during his stay (he participated in an Easter Sunday 1931 Communist demonstration at which he was arrested), and when he returned to Cambridge later in 1931, he quickly became one of the key figures in the Cambridge cell of Communists.[88]

Stephen Spender's younger brother, Humphrey, had studied architecture and art history at Freiburg from 1927 to 1928, and he returned to Berlin at the end of the 1920s, where he developed his gifts as a photographer.[89] The camera that Humphrey used was a Leica, recommended to him by his brother Michael, who had also been in Berlin, working for the Leitz Company, which made Leicas. In 1927, Francis Bacon, then an interior decorator, had spent a few luxurious weeks at the Adlon Hotel in the German capital with his lover, the diplomat Sir Percy Loraine, before Loraine abandoned him in the city. Bacon's early paintings were interpreted as deriving from contemporary, hard-edged German models. Alfred Hitchcock's earliest films as a director were made in Germany in the mid-1920s, and Hitchcock was often in Berlin. In 1927, Hans Prinzhorn briefly and ineffectually psychoanalyzed Auden's Oxford friend Brian Howard in Frankfurt.[90] Other English-speaking intellectuals to visit Berlin included the novelist Malcolm Lowry and the left-wing composer and pianist Alan Bush. Berlin, the "reddest city outside Russia," according to Hitler, was such a popular venue by the start of the 1930s that there were 150,000 foreigners among its population of 4.3 million.[91]

In fact, the German capital now became a kind of London-on-Spree. The socialist Felix Stössinger complained in an August 1929 article, "The Anglicization of Germany": "Germany actually is adopting more and more of the manners and external appearances of a newly won English colony."[92] During this short-lived Germanophilic vogue among the English, Berlin even fascinated an established modernist English writer of an older generation. In his contemporary polemic, *Hitler,* published in 1931, Wyndham Lewis, the self-declared "Enemy" of Parisian chic, cited with approval the comment that Germany was now "the political and economic hub of Europe." He announced that "the german destiny is bound up with ours much more than is that, for instance, of

cosmopolitan France."[93] Going to Germany was a way to encounter a
different culture but also to meet like-minded Englishmen—John Layard, a key member of the Auden circle in Berlin, estimated, a bit ex-
travagantly, that by the end of the 1920s, half of the boy bars in the city
(the "Cosy Corner," for example) had English names.[94]

Much of the critical commentary on Auden's time in Berlin has focused
on the impact on Auden of Layard's exposition of ideas about "Love"
held by the renegade American psychoanalyst Homer Lane. Layard
had been a patient of Lane's in London in the early 1920s and felt that
Lane (who, after sex scandals pushed him out of Britain, died in Paris
in 1925) had "in about three months transformed me from a broken
down almost paralytic puritanical prig, to its opposite—a live person."[95]
But Layard himself was to have at least as much influence on Auden's
life and thought as Lane did indirectly.

Layard was a brilliant but highly disturbed individual who had accompanied W. H. R. Rivers to the New Hebrides, had lost a younger
brother in the Great War, and had fallen in love with Rivers around 1917
while the latter was analyzing him, leading his mentor to reject him.[96]
His career began as an anthropologist, though he later became an eminent psychoanalyst. He arrived in Berlin around 1926 to be analyzed by
Freud's pupil Fritz Wittels, one of many well-known psychoanalysts
whom Layard consulted during his turbulent and, ultimately, very successful life.[97] Auden and Layard met through an intervention by their
mutual friend David Ayerst, who had been at Christ Church with Auden.
Ayerst went on a hiking holiday in Germany in 1927 with Rolf Gardiner,
the ecological activist and campaigner for closer ties between England and
Germany. There he met Layard, who was also a member of the walking
party. They struck up a friendship, and at the end of November 1928
Ayerst wrote to Layard suggesting he contact Auden in Berlin.

When they spoke on the phone, Layard, who was more than fifteen
years older than Auden, was intimidated by Auden's "very pronounced
Oxford accent," but he recorded that at their first meeting, he was
struck by Auden's "absolutely smooth and angelic face" and that he "fell
for him like a ninepin."[98] And Auden was deeply moved by Layard's conversation "about Lane and love": he put into the mouth of the central

character in the play "The Fronny," which he wrote in 1930, his gratitude to Layard for "having largely raised me from the dead."[99] Layard
imparted to Auden Lane's tenets about the psychosomatic origins of
disease and about the overwhelming importance of acting from love
and the promptings of the unconscious. He also discussed his own anthropological expertise as a member of the now largely forgotten diffusionist school and his experiences with Rivers, whose books had already proved so significant to Auden.[100] Auden notes in early April 1929
that "During my first few meetings with John I felt his existence and his
explanation of Lane [had] made a great difference to me."[101]

However, relations with Layard quickly became complicated, as
Auden also writes in his journal: "Going to bed with him at first . . . was a
mistake which lasts. I felt guilty about it. It was so dreary and compulsion-
istic and I didn't get any sleep."[102] Nonetheless, Layard played a significant
role in Auden's life in Berlin as well as afterward. (In 1934 Auden became
godfather to Richard Layard, the newly born son of Layard and his then-
lover, and later wife, Doris Dingwall, and Layard was the person who in
1938 recorded Auden's 1927 dream in Yugoslavia about Maurice Bowra.[103])

Auden was fascinated by stories Layard told him about Homer
Lane, but it would seem that Lane's main ideas, mediated through Layard, did not make a deep impact on Auden's poetry. Perhaps that is
because, at least in Layard's description, Lane knew little psychoanalytic theory and worked primarily through personal immediacy as a
charismatic, empathetic healer, trusting to "direct action between two
people," as Layard put it.[104] Lane's dogmas, abstractly stated, did not
transfer easily. For all Layard's testimony about Lane's theories, Layard's
importance in Auden's story lies mainly in the effects of his own genuine, open-minded intellectual brilliance, his wide acquaintance, and
his personal participation in Auden's Berlin life and in the expatriate,
English-speaking culture that was so strong in the city.

"The German proletariat are fine," Auden told Patience Kennington. "I
spend most of my time with Juvenile Delinquents."[105] Somewhere during the period when he sent *Paid on Both Sides* off to Eliot from Berlin
at the end of 1928, Auden moved out of the upper-middle-class Muthesius household and went to live in a slum, at Fürbringerstraße 8, near
the Hallesches Tor in the Kreuzberg district, on a street that intersected

with Zossenerstraße, where the "Cosy Corner," Auden's favorite seedy
Berlin boy bar, was located.

Kreuzberg was an area dominated by huge, late nineteenth-century
apartment buildings for the poor, known as *Mietskasernen* (rent bar-
racks); it was one of the most overcrowded and squalid parts of the city.
Stephen Spender wrote that these "sordid tenements," encrusted with
concrete "eagles, helmets, shields and prodigious buttocks of armoured
babies," emanated a "peculiar all-pervading smell of hopeless decay
(rather like the smell of the inside of an old cardboard box)."[106] It was
here in one of these festering edifices, not long after Auden had finished his charade, with its themes of endless feuding, death, and the
impossibility of bringing an end to the bloodletting, that he read one of
the greatest literary meditations on exactly these subjects. "My coldest
memory is of the Christmas week of 1928 in Berlin," Auden later reminisced. "I had spent my month's allowance and the friends from whom
I might have borrowed were all out of town, so that I could not afford
to leave the house and passed the days with my feet up on the very inadequate tiled stove, reading *War and Peace* for the first time, cold,
hungry and very happy."[107]

While Auden read Tolstoy's nineteenth-century masterpiece about
suffering and Napoleonic conflict, the aftershocks of the last war continued to be felt everywhere in Germany, along with the new social
possibilities that the war had also generated. One of the best early
poems by Auden's Oxford friend Stephen Spender is called "Written
Whilst Walking Down the Rhine." Composed in August 1929, it describes a walking tour with a group down the banks of the Rhine:

> A whim of Time, the general arbiter,
> Proclaims the love instead of death of friends.
> Under the domed sky and athletic sun
> The three stand naked: the new, bronzed German,
> The young communist, and myself, being English.

This is an evocation of the contemporary world that someone, "being
English," wants to celebrate: international solidarity and friendship, often
with an obvious sexual dimension. Only a short while before, it would
have been utterly different, Spender remembers: "Yet to unwind the trav-
elled sphere twelve years | Then two take arms, spring to a ghostly pos-
ture." Walking with Germans along the edge of the Rhine inevitably

recalls memories of the brutal meetings of young men of the two nations at different rivers, such as the Somme and the Ancre, twelve years before. Those who would have tried to kill each other twelve years ago, are in Spender's poem in 1929, full of "love instead of death."[108]

The "heavy leather door curtain" of the "Cosy Corner" that Isherwood recalls Auden pushing back in order to lead his friend inside, reads like a totemic reminder of the gas curtains that covered the entrances to dugouts filled with troops during the First World War.[109] But here the English enter to find friends, not enemies. Auden imagines a similar reversal in his uncompleted "epic," now referred to routinely as "In the year of my youth when yoyos came in," written between 1932 and 1933. There, Auden and his guide Sampson are confronted by a maddened British woman who has lost her two sons to German bullets during the war. Like Spender, she too links, by reversal, what happened then and what is happening now. Fear has turned into comradeship. Her sons fought Germans, but now she complains that "the up-to-date young men" are "waiting | Impatient in the crowd to catch a train | And shake a German gently by the hand."[110]

Isherwood makes a related point when he describes the symbolic reconciliation that he feels he is able to make through love with the world that his father's killers had belonged to: by embracing his German lover, "Christopher could hold in his arms the whole mystery-magic of foreignness, Germanness. By means of [his lover], he could fall in love with and possess the entire nation."[111] In the psyche of a generation, the heroic older brothers and fathers who had died in Flanders found living substitutes in "the Romantic friends who took their place in survivors' affections."[112]

The English taste for German culture and German sex partners was a historically shaped phenomenon: every strange or secret meeting, every illicit connection, was, symbolically, a small act of peacemaking, whether the participants were conscious of it or not. One of Auden's own favorite sexual scenarios involved a mild kind of juvenile fight with his partner that ended in clinches. Layard commented, "Wystan liked being beaten up a bit. This happened once in my room, when they were all there. It would start with pillow fights and end up with blows and then they would go to bed together."[113] Auden told Patience Kennington in December 1928, when he wrote to her about his love life in Berlin, "I am a mass of bruises."[114] The ritualized passage from struggle

to embraces is the allegory of a collective longing to heal the wounds of
war with acts of love.

However, these international encounters were as often foiled as successful.
As an example, take an incident that happened, or did not happen, on 23
April 1929. Auden went alone on an outing into the countryside, traveling
by rail to the small town of Hangelsberg about fourteen miles southeast of
Berlin and close to the Fürstenwalde forest. As he started back to the capital in the late afternoon, he was sitting in the train: "In the compartment
of the last train was a worker with a paralyzed right hand. We looked at
each other both I think wanting to speak. I wished to offer him some to-
bacco and of course didn't, but the contact was there. In the electric suburban trains business men shaking hands, chimneys of the steel works
against an indigo sky, factory windows catching the sun."[115]
    This vignette is suggestive because the rural worker with the wounded
hand (a war veteran perhaps?) belongs to an almost archaic world, a
world in which two strangers meet and then draw away from each other,
though "the contact was there." The moment is a frustrated reconciliation, a spot of time in which peaceful intimacy might have emerged
between strangers or antagonists, of the kind that dominated Auden's
and Isherwood's imaginations, as it had earlier dominated the imaginations of war poets such as Owen and Sassoon.
    Owen's dead German had raised "distressful hands, as if to bless."
But symbolic gestures of forgiveness, and perhaps more, between
Auden and the "worker with a paralyzed right hand" are foreclosed.
The moment of possibility fades, and the two remain strangers in a
new, modern world, symbolized by the "electric suburban" train, the
steel works, the glinting factory windows, and the indigo sky. It is a
picturesque but suggestively unsatisfying passage—the afternoon sunlight shines off glass instead of allowing a view into the interior of the
building; the sky's indigo contrasts with the muted colors of the steel
works. In "To Germany," a war poem Auden admired, the young
English soldier poet C. H. Sorley had imagined a future when Britain
and Germany had "Grown more loving-kind and warm" and when
both sides would "grasp firm hands and laugh at the old pain."[116] But
now, in 1929, though "the contact was there," Auden sits silently opposite the worker, instead of reaching out a hand. Meanwhile, the new,

self-confident "business men" of the Weimar Republic form a closed
group, shutting out Auden and "shaking hands" among themselves.
With the sinking sun, the light of clarity and the possibility of cross-
cultural empathy that afternoon are also slowly fading into the darkness
of the night world.

Paid on Both Sides ends with the knowledge that a synthesis and reconciliation is not possible, at least (in Anne Shaw's words) "Now not."[117] In
the charade, the image of a world in which people from different nations, classes, or political camps cannot presently be reconciled is part
of a dialectical movement toward a future when such a reconciliation
might be possible. For the moment, though, the world is a broken
place. It is a truth that "Under boughs between our tentative endearments, how should we hear," a gnomic poem Auden wrote in Berlin a
few months after finishing *Paid on Both Sides,* fatalistically concludes
has to be accepted:

> Let each one share our pity, hard to withhold and hard to bear.
> None knows of the next day if it be less or more, the sorrow:
>> Escaping cannot try;
>> Must wait though it destroy.[118]

When Isherwood came to Germany to visit Auden in March 1929,
in the same month that Auden wrote "Under boughs," Auden took his
friend to the "Cosy Corner," where Isherwood soon made the acquaintance of a German-speaking Czech youth whose nickname was "Bubi"
and whose real name was Berthold Szczesny, "a pretty, smooth-skinned,
blue-eyed, blond-haired and demanding young man, who was frequently
in trouble with the police."[119] Auden wrote a poem, perhaps slightly
envious but also pessimistic, about the apparent closeness of an
Englishman and a German; Isherwood called it "a beautiful poem about
Bubi."[120] It is Auden's dystopian version of Spender's "Written While Walking Down the Rhine":

> Before this loved one
> Was that one and that one
> A family
> And history

And ghost's adversity
Whose pleasing name
Was neighbourly shame.
Before this last one
Was much to be done,
Frontiers to cross
As clothes grew worse
And coins to pass
In a cheaper house
Before this last one
Before this loved one.

Face that the sun
Is supple on
May stir but here
Is no new year;
This gratitude for gifts is less
Than the old loss;
Touching is shaking hands
On mortgaged lands;
And smiling of
This gracious greeting
"Good day. Good luck"
Is no real meeting
But instinctive look
A backward love.[121]

The rhetorical character of this slender, terse poem is usually traced back to the influence of the poet Laura Riding, whose work Auden admired and whose pamphlets and books, such as *The Close Chaplet* (1926) and *Love as Love, Death as Death* (1928), he was buying. But the poem's theme is Auden's own. The pared-down language and the tiny, nervous lines with their rocking, anxious rhythms, give the lyric a sense of unease and awkwardness. This awkwardness is brilliantly amplified by the irregularities in line length, rhythm, syntax, and rhyme. For example, full rhymes ("Touching is shaking hands | On mortgaged lands") are mixed with Owenesque pararhymes ("The gratitude for gifts is less | Than the old loss") and pure verbal repetitions ("Before this loved one | Was that one and that one").

There is so much artistic sophistication displayed in "Before this loved one," but one of its subtlest features is a slight top-heaviness. The first verse paragraph, which explains the history that has led up to the present love affair and is thus couched in the past tense, has fifteen lines, while the second, which is concerned exclusively with the present, has fourteen. Auden is using form to suggest meaning—the weight of the past (stanza 1) is slightly greater than the temporary exhilaration of the present (stanza 2): there can be "no real meeting" between the eras, as there is none between lovers. The fact that the second stanza is a single sentence, or moment, while the first is made from two sentences, puts further emphasis on the differences between the first and second parts of the poem. The past counts for more than the present.

The poem also displays an enigmatic and intriguing degree of sound and syllable patterning, most prominently in the combinations of the "b" and "l" sounds. The first line of the poem establishes the pattern: "Before this loved one." This recurs in the middle of the stanza in "Before this last one," and then this combination returns in the last two lines of stanza 1: "Before this last one | Before this loved one." In the final two lines of the second stanza, we see the pattern reappearing in lightly camouflaged form: "But instinctive look | A backward love."[122] Thus, formally, the poem itself enacts a "backward love" since at the very end, it cannot rid itself of this sonic pattern with which it started. It "looks backward" to its own beginning. (Incidentally, the *b / l* combination occurs nowhere else in the poem within a single line, and an *l / b* combination within a single line is entirely absent.)

How to interpret this *b / l* pattern? Because of Auden's fascination with alliterative meter, his poetic ear was by now highly attuned to the patterning of syllables by line or word. At a conscious or an unconscious level (it does not matter which), the use of this pattern gestures toward the place in which Auden wrote the poem: *Ber*lin. One may also wonder if the pattern is at the same time a cipher of "*Ber*thold," the first name of Isherwood's *belo*ved immediately in question. Secretive, small-scale verbal designs like these are almost never included in the catalogue of Auden's strengths as a poet, but they appear in some of his most significant poems, like a spy's important message hidden in an apparently innocuous letter of greeting.

One of the poem's central ideas is that a new love is not a new beginning, is "no new year" and "no real meeting," but instead is the repetition of a recurrent situation. In Berlin at around the time he was writing this poem, Auden was reading Trigant Burrow, an unorthodox Freudian who saw neuroses as being collective and not personal in origin. Recall that Auden noted in his journal Burrow's criticism of Freud: while Freud argued that the neurosis was limited "to the individual," Burrow maintained that in fact the "neurosis involves all society."[123] Auden had also written down Burrow's complaint that Freud assumed, in relation to his patients and readers, an "authoritative attitude. You are neurotic. I am not."[124] Burrow's work is highly relevant to much of Auden's Berlin writing and beyond.

One reason for this now largely forgotten psychoanalyst's appeal to Auden may have been his nonjudgmental attitudes about sexuality. But Burrow's ideas about the social origins of individual neurosis are important for an understanding of Auden's Berlin poems. For example, "Before this loved one" dramatizes Burrow's suggestion that what seem to be an individual's pathologies are in fact representative of social pathology. Isherwood assumed this poem was "about" him and Bubi, but it is in fact a more general statement about the rupture between lover and beloved, a rupture that is based on a suprapersonal foundation: "A family | And history| And ghost's adversity."[125]

Auden recorded in his journal that he felt left out, turned into a third wheel, by Isherwood's apparent success with Bubi. For example, he described an outing with them: "I remember Christopher and Bubi playing ping-pong. The sense of bare flesh, the blue sky through the glass and the general sexy atmosphere made me feel like a participant in a fertility rite. . . . In the pine wood [where Isherwood and Bubi were making love] I felt like the third baboon and a public school one."[126] But Auden himself was as susceptible to the idealizing of German boys as Isherwood was. He wrote about a *Puppenjunge,* Pieps, in the journal he was keeping in Berlin in 1929: "He seems to belong to another world and might go up in smoke any moment. . . . Love is the two worlds. I, physically negligible, intellectually potent—He, mentally negligible, physically potent. The two types of acrobats. The brain, and the work-worn hands."[127] "Before this loved one" is as much about Auden's own habits of mind and emotions as it is about Isherwood's; the clinical, diagnostic tone is a defensive tactic against too direct a self-incrimination. The poem recognizes an illusion that both Auden and Isherwood were prey to in their personal lives: idealization of their lovers and neglect of the desperation that had driven many German men into life as full-time or part-time hustlers.

The identity of "this loved one" in this poem is deliberately indefinite (as, to an even greater degree, is the lover's); the lover is a little like an "Unknown from Passage." Auden keeps his protagonists shadowy, withholding specificities rather than, as a camera would, confirming them. The "Face that the sun | Is supple on" is a screen onto which a fantasy of love is projected, a fantasy that has been experienced many times before. In order for this most recent love affair to occur, many others had to take place first, "ones" that were essentially no different in kind from "this . . . one." But the present is the product of the past in a much broader sense than is implied simply by a list of the lover's previous affairs. A "family" produced the characteristics and temperament of the lover. And that family was itself part of a wider society, a product indeed of a "history." Bearing down on the "Touching" of the lovers in Auden's poem is the vast weight of all the factors out of which the past shapes the present.

Even so, still more was necessary before this affair could occur: "Was much to be done, | Frontiers to cross | As clothes grew worse | And coins to pass | In a cheaper house." The "frontiers" the lover had to cross before he could encounter "this loved one" seem at first to be national frontiers, in this case the British and German frontiers, and the shabbier "clothes" that the lover donned (Isherwood recalled that Auden wore a "workman's cap, with a shiny black peak" in Berlin) and the "cheaper house" where he lodged in the bankrupt, defeated nation.[128] But the financial connotation of "coins" and "cheaper" also raise the possibility that the "frontiers," while containing the wartime connotations of "front," are those of social class as well.

Again, in the second verse paragraph, Auden begins with an attempt to reach across national divisions. But the effort seems unsuccessful: "This gratitude for gifts is less | Than the old loss." The little presents from the comparatively well-off and privileged Englishman to the impoverished German boy are mere tokens compared with the "loss" that the boy and by extension his country have undergone a decade earlier at British and French hands. Seen in this light, the "Touching" of lovers' hands and bodies is no more than a financial transaction like "shaking hands | On mortgaged lands." The negotiations are concluded with a show of friendship that conceals the profit that the lender of the money will make from the owner of the "mort-gaged lands."

The reparations demanded of the Germans by the Treaty of Versailles were massive. The subsequent Dawes Plan of 1924 eased the scale of Germany's payments and offered the country huge loans but in return for highly advantageous access to its markets. In this context, Germany was certainly one of the "mortgaged lands"—for instance, an American loan (effectively a mortgage) of some 800 million Rentenmarks was guaranteed by vast slices of German industry. But the rise in the second paragraph of the financial metaphor from within the initial national metaphor ("the old loss . . . mortgaged lands"), paralleling the rise of the same in the first paragraph ("Frontiers to cross . . . And coins to pass"), shows how tightly interwoven issues of nationality are with issues of class for Auden. The lover comes from a richer country and a superior social milieu to "this loved one." Indeed, when Auden explained the lines "This gracious greeting | 'Good day, good luck'" to his French translator, he commented that "I want something suggesting the seigneur here."[129] The differences of nationality and class are what make the "love" possible but also temporary.

The presence of pararhymes in this poem about the unreal "meeting" between an Englishman and a German suggests, first, that "Before this loved one" is another devastating supplement to Owen's "Strange Meeting." Indeed, perhaps many of Auden's and Spender's Berlin poems (such as Spender's "Written Whilst Walking Down the Rhine") can be read as responses to Owen's overwhelmingly powerful poem. Spender's poem suggests that the flood of English youth to Germany in the later 1920s unconsciously re-created wartime "uncanny experience[s]" in a Utopian key. But Auden's poem, which in its vagueness of detail preserves a sense of the mystery of encountering someone from what was often called simply "the other side," concludes that the violent meetings between members of the two opposed nations in some "profound dull tunnel" in wartime cannot be reenacted and brought to more satisfactory endings in the present's dives. The "meetings" (a crucial, talismanic word present in both Owen's and Auden's poems) between lovers from countries of the former enemy states, occurring eleven years later in dark clubs on Zossenerstraße and environs, are still unequal and subtly estranged ones.

In this sense, "Before this loved one" confirms the despairing tenor (or "tragic situation," as William Empson called it) of Paid on Both Sides.[130]

The war was still going on; reconciliation was not yet possible, though there might be a benign will to reconcile on both sides: "Before the evil and the good | How insufficient is | The endearment and the look."[131] Just how present the war was for Auden shows in his choice of a birthday gift for himself. At the end of February 1929, he briefly returned from Berlin to stay with Cecil Day Lewis at Helensburgh Academy in Scotland. While he was there, he seems to have given himself a twenty-second birthday present. He wrote: "W.H.A. 21.2.29" on the endleaf of a copy of Wilfred Owen's *Poems*.[132] "Under boughs between our tentative endearments, how should we hear," the poem Auden wrote in the same month as "Before this loved one," puts it in another burst of Owenesque pararhyme:

> Sharers of our own day, thought smiling of, but nothing known,
> What industries decline, what chances are of revolution,
>   What murders flash
>   Under composed flesh.[133]

Some critics have read the final lines of "Before this loved one," in which Auden attributes this failure of the lovers to meet on equal terms as being the result of a "backward love," to mean that the problem is the homosexual disposition of the lovers. With Auden's habitual "bad conscience" (Robert Medley's phrase) about his sexuality in mind, perhaps "Backward" suggests the conventional Freudian idea that the homosexual falls narcissistically in love with an image of himself at an earlier stage in his sexual development. Auden jotted down in his journal around the time of writing the poem, "One falls in love with people of that age at which one was most unhappy."[134]

But the phrase about a "backward love," in this context, means far more than this. Its failure is not only the result of an individual disposition but, as Burrow taught Auden, of a social problem, showing that a looking back to the First World War, and a determining to make reparations for history's horror, could never be successful. *Paid on Both Sides* was Auden's last major retrospective "war poem," complemented by final, riddling lyrics such as "Before this loved one" in the spring of 1929. (Later, of course, there would be plenty of Auden poems generated by the new catastrophe, the Second World War.) This was perhaps partly because the subject of the Great War had suddenly become almost too easy to write about. The cascade of contemporary books on the subject—*Good-Bye to All That, Undertones of War,* and *Im Westen nichts Neues,* among others—showed this. The war was losing its symbolic richness by becoming a subject that could be tackled directly. In addition, though, Auden's Berlin poems declare that, indirectly or directly, one cannot redeem the past. Rather, one must abandon it and try something new. "The real 'life-wish,'" he wrote in his journal, "is the desire for separation, from family, from one's literary predecessors."[135] But is that true either?

Auden's most important love relationship in Berlin was a short-lived one with a beefy sailor named Gerhart Meyer. They met on 31 March 1929, Easter Sunday that year, at a gay dive in the Alte Jakobstraße in the working-class district of Kreuzberg, near where Auden was living. Alte Jakobstraße at the end of the 1920s was packed with bars and meeting places. That day, Auden had failed to get in to see Joe May's thriller *Asphalt* at the Ufa-Palast on the Alexanderplatz, and so he wandered round to the bar at Alte Jakobstraße 49 instead. Meyer was introduced to him there as someone who spoke English. In a comedy of cross-national communication, Auden spoke to Meyer in broken German, and Meyer replied in broken English: "Give me ten marks and I sleep with to-night."[136]

In any such relationship, there was more than just a personal connection between two people involved. Auden wrote while in Berlin that homosexuality had a symbolic quality, being a "Revolt against Authority. . . . The social ban makes buggery exciting."[137] Thus he enjoyed the frisson of kissing Meyer on the winding steps inside the massive Siegessäule (Tower of Victory), a monument to the German triumph in the Franco-Prussian War, on the Königsplatz in front of the Reichstag.[138] They went on a trip to Hamburg together (after seeing images of the city in an Emelka-Wochenschau newsreel at a Berlin cinema), had a row there, and returned to Berlin separately. Auden was exhilarated by Meyer's "extraordinary power": "he laid his hand on my knee and switched on the current, an amazing sensation."[139]

But this affair unfolded at the same time as dire developments were taking place in John Layard's sad, brilliant, chaotic life. Amid the turmoil of confrontations in the Berlin streets between rival factions, political murders, and gang wars over territory, the mood of violence permeated every corner of the city's culture. Georg Grosz noted bleakly: "you yourself are infected, you cannot keep aloof and you become a greedy beetle just like everybody else."[140] At the start of April 1929,

Layard, spurned by Auden, was in despair and meditating suicide. Auden wrote in his journal that, shockingly, he had "tried to persuade [Layard] to kill himself."[141] Later the same day, Layard sneaked Gerhart Meyer, whom he knew to be Auden's new lover, home and tried to have sex with him. (Layard could not climax—he found he was impotent.) It was a deeply personal humiliation besides being a "complete betrayal" of Auden, as Layard admitted.[142]

Layard had suffered from suicidal thoughts for a number of years and on one occasion in England had even written final letters to friends. Now, on 3 April 1929, in his sordid Berlin room, he dismissed Gerhart Meyer and shot himself in the head with a small pistol he had bought in case he ever needed "a means of dispatching myself." When he fired, the bullet went up his nasal cavity, damaging his olfactory nerve, and lodged in his forehead. But he did not die. Dazed and bleeding from the mouth, Layard took a taxi through the darkness and snow. After he arrived at Auden's lodgings, he was helped up the stairs by another young Englishman in Berlin, the archaeologist Francis Turville-Petre, to Auden's room. Auden had been having a party with some German boys.

Layard recalled later that, weeping, he had hoped Auden would complete the job "out of friendship." Auden corroborated this in his journal, writing that Layard "wanted me to finish him off." Layard recalled Auden responding with a kind of clumsy tact: "I'm terribly sorry, I know you want this, but I can't do it, because I might be hanged if I did. And I don't want to be hanged. Lie down on the divan." When Layard vomited blood, Auden retched. He felt obligated to kiss (with distaste) the distraught and wounded man, and then Layard passed out.[143]

Auden had Layard taken to hospital, where he was given morphine, patched up, and then deposited by Auden in a hotel.[144] (Auden would not witness anything like this level of violence again until he visited Spain in 1937 and remarked to a friend on the "stench of dead bodies."[145]) While Layard was recovering, Meyer moved into Auden's room in the Hallesches Tor slum on around 9 April, and then, on the afternoon of 16 April 1929, Auden came back from a lunch with John Layard's mother, now in attendance on her son, to find a note from Meyer telling him goodbye. Meyer had taken with him Auden's dressing gown and the gun that Layard had used to try to commit suicide.[146]

Auden soon found another lover, Otto Küsel, whom he met in Berlin at the start of May 1929. They were together for a couple of months, which included a trip to the tiny resort of Rothehütte in the Harz. Isherwood, who came to stay with them there, remembered that Auden beguiled the villagers: "He entertained them by thumping out German popular songs and English hymn tunes on a piano in the refreshment room of the railway station and intrigued them by wrestling naked with his friend in a nearby meadow."[147]

Auden wrote at least two poems inspired by Küsel.[148] The first, probably dating from June 1929, tersely expresses in loosely rhyming triplets doubts about the depth and solidity of the relationship:

> Upon this line between adventure
> Prolong the meeting out of good nature
> Obvious in each agreeable feature.
>
> Calling of each other by name
> Smiling, taking a willing arm
> Has the companionship of a game.
>
> But should the walk do more than this
> Out of bravado or drunkenness
> Forward or back are menaces.
>
> On neither side let foot slip over
> Invading Always, exploring Never,
> For this is hate and this is fear.
>
> On narrowness stand, for sunlight is
> Brightest only on surfaces;
> No anger, no traitor, but peace.

Here again, Auden uses that profound word, "meeting," to meditate on the equivocal, temporary nature of sexual friendships. He suggests that the people involved might only see each other as symbols of something else. Or, as D. H. Lawrence had insisted in his review of Trigant Burrow's book, "If you are quite normal, you don't have any true self, which 'seeketh not her own, is not puffed up.' The true self, in sex, would seek a *meeting*, would seek to meet the other. This would be the true flow. . . . But today, all is image consciousness. Sex does not exist, there is only sexuality. Selfseeking is the real motive of sexuality."[149]

While it is good, Auden's lines say, to take "a willing arm," this is just the "companionship of a game." Anything more in this cross-cultural and cross-class connection is dangerous and filled with "menaces" (Auden surely intends us to hear the pun on "men" in this word). "Sunlight is | Brightest only on surfaces," the poem concludes in lines that seem almost tautologous, suggesting that anything more than a concentration on surfaces is likely to prove disturbing or less than beautiful. The goal of the meeting is not discovery of otherness, the poem says, but using another resonant word, "peace." Auden's poem is both tender and fatalistic, perhaps partly as a result of the social constraints within which men like Auden and Küsel conducted their love lives, figuratively as well as literally, watched and gossiped over by dozens of eyes as they wrestled in a meadow.

For Auden, the spring and early summer of 1929 in Rothehütte was more a time of partings than of meetings with "a good nature." Isherwood had returned to the village from Berlin, where he had been searching fruitlessly for Bubi, Berthold Szczesny. The police were searching for the Czech too. In July 1929, failing to find him in the little town where Auden was staying, they instead arrested Otto Küsel as a fugitive from a reformatory. (Within a few years, after repeat offenses, Küsel would be a prisoner at the Sachsenhausen concentration camp.[150]) In the Harz Mountains, Auden passed Isherwood a letter from Bubi saying that he was in Amsterdam (illegally) and about to board a ship for a voyage as a deckhand to South America. On the spur of the moment, Auden and Isherwood decided to go to the Dutch capital to see Bubi off. They did so, and, after this strange farewell, the next day they toured the city's canals on a tourist launch. In the boat's guestbook, next to their names Auden justly added a quotation from the Soviet writer Ilya Ehrenburg's poem "The Sons of Our Sons" (1919): "Read about us and marvel! | You did not live in our time—be sorry!"[151]

The most important poem that Auden wrote in 1929 is a sequence in four parts—it is a beautiful and mysterious piece, the working out poetically of a moment of significant change in his writing and life.[152] In *Poems* (1930), the book in which this sequence was first collected, Auden marks it for readers as a pivotal poem. Of the thirty-one poems in the volume (counting *Paid on Both Sides* as one poem), he made this sequence the fulcrum, since it is the sixteenth poem, placed right at the book's center. In addition, it is by far the longest poem in the nondramatic section of *Poems* (1930) and is the only poem divided into parts. This sequence is also the only poem in Auden's 1930 book to use the pronoun "I" systematically; that pronoun appears prominently in each of the four parts. (Elsewhere in the volume, there are some glancing uses of the first-person singular in the poems "From the very first coming down" and "The strings' excitement, the applauding drum," but neither poem is comprehensively structured as an autobiographical narrative, and neither is nearly as extended or ambitious at this sequence.[153])

All these characteristics signal the sequence's significance. Auden wrote the first two parts in Germany and the second two parts after he had returned to England toward the end of July 1929. At its deepest, this is a work about foiled aspirations; it is Auden's valediction, for the time being, to the idea of a "strange meeting" of reconciliation that might grow from the effort to cross the boundaries of class and nation.

On 4 April 1929, the day after Layard had tried to kill himself, Auden retained enough sangfroid in the midst of the emotional chaos to send Eliot the last changes he wanted to make in *Paid on Both Sides*. The charade was finished. Not long after, Auden's brief, intense affair with Gerhart Meyer ended on 16 April 1929, when Meyer left for Hamburg with Layard's revolver. Two important components of Auden's Berlin life (one literary, one personal) were now over. But, almost immediately, something new began to grow. Less than two days after Meyer departed, Auden (with the innate hardiness of the artist who goes on creating, no matter what) had an auspicious dream. In a journal entry written just before he started composing the first part of what became this four-part poetic sequence, Auden scribbled down: "Had a good dream last night [17–18 April 1929]. Setting out in a new model submarine with sights like a rifle. Only one mistake on its first voyage. Captain like Captain [Cooper?] but not him. I said 'I know who you are.' Dad was there and his top hat box was part of my luggage. Evidently I feel hopeful."[154]

Dreams are always significant for the young Auden's poetry. Here, in this one, is a premonition of a more autobiographical type of poem, based on a personal narrative, that was a "new model" for him. And the submarine's journey beneath the waves represents the dive into the underworld that the hero, or poet, must undertake in order to be successful. Water, the medium in which a submarine moves, will be a significant element in the poem that Auden is now "setting out" to write. Although the dream does not show Auden in charge of the submarine, he is pleasantly familiar with the vessel's captain and happy with the dive, with

"Only one mistake." He is accompanied by his father (just as he was accompanied by Dr. Auden on his "first voyage" abroad to Salzburg). The socially accredited patriarch is there, for once (but in a dream), to support his son. Perhaps most significantly, Dr. Auden's "top hat box" has become part of the dreamer's luggage. The fancy headwear here symbolizes patriarchal privilege; the old-fashioned object endows its owner, or borrower in this case, with a commanding potency. (Auden would later describe all hats as "insignia of power."[155]) The son, inheritor of the inky-black headpiece, is for now in the position of authority. Later in the same journal entry, Auden, while berating himself for laziness and feebleness of mind, also wrote: "I want to do something on a larger scale." The outcome was, eventually, this enigmatic but powerful sequence that ends with an acceptance of reimmersion in a familiar world.[156]

Toward the end of April 1929 in Berlin, not long after he had the dream, Auden started writing the sequence's first part. This was during the tense run-up to the May Day riots of that year when, after battles between communists and the city's police, dozens of Berliners were left dead and the Weimar government's legitimacy was further undermined. He completed the last part of the sequence in October 1929, the month of "Black Thursday" (24 October 1929) and the Wall Street Crash, by which time he was lodging briefly in Kensington, a fashionable part of London, and working as a private tutor. A poetic sequence, which Auden began at a moment of political crisis in the slums near the Hallesches Tor in the German capital, was finished at a moment of economic crisis in an affluent section of the British capital. Underwritten by these facts about its compositional history, the sequence reads as the bridge across which Auden's work returns home from working-class Germany to middle-class England, the country and social world whose decayed condition, moral entanglements, and possible regeneration would be the deep subjects of his poetry for the next half decade.

The first part's first line, fittingly, situates the speaker at a recognizable moment of symbolic death and rebirth: "It was Easter as I walked in the public gardens" (36–37; from now on, I will refer to this part of the sequence as "It was Easter"). This is indeed a poem of a literary Easter within Auden's career, as it tells the story of the death of an ideal about cross-national and cross-class understanding and the reemergence of Auden as a self-consciously English poet. Turning back from his foray into a foreign life among the German unemployed, Auden, in part 4, looks ahead to the "death" of his earlier hopes for escape from England and to a revival in his original social and national settings— schools, England, and the middle class. Relentlessly, the four-part sequence begins to track a regress from a cautiously optimistic spring beginning in Germany to a fatalistic, almost eschatological, but somehow also sublime, autumnal conclusion in England, a conclusion that it suggests is terrifying, necessary, and generative.

The seasonal organization (moving from spring to autumn with a glimpse forward to winter) in Auden's sequence correlates with its roughly symmetrical formal structure. Thus, the sequence's two outer parts (1 and 4) are set in cities (Berlin and London) while the two inner parts take place predominantly in the countryside (first in Germany and then in England). Moreover, the poem's total of 166 lines are divided thus: the first and fourth parts (the metropolitan parts) both contain three verse paragraphs, and each runs for a total of thirty-three lines. (These are numbers that in a poetic context may suggest some literary symbolism.) Based on these identical formal dimensions and their thematic similarities, there are many correspondences or symmetries between the first and last parts of the sequence. The inner sections of the poem, parts 2 and 3, mapping onto late spring and midsummer, are more irregular and organic and less symmetrical.[157]

This intricate formal structure serves many purposes, one of which is to dramatize the acting out of an argument about the inevitability of a return to within the national fold. The firm, propositional opening, characterized by a driving urgency, is succeeded by two fluid and complex, binational middle parts. These middle parts are the acting out of the mind trying to make sense of a problem: "Coming out of me living is always thinking, | Thinking changing and changing living" (37). Then, a fourth part, as clear and definite in form as part 1 (and virtually identical structurally to its opposite), represents the sequence's arriving at both a formal end and a thematic conclusion.

In a Yeatsian style, Auden's sequence-poem constructs an apparently autobiographical narrative, placing the "I" in a number of different locations that Auden had actually visited, and it makes clear references to real people. There is no frame of irony or distancing that allows readers to construe this "I" as anything other than a representation of the poet speaking in the first person. One impetus for this tone of autobiographical candor—which, so far, is relatively unusual in Auden's published writing—may have to do with the work of Trigant Burrow, whom Auden had started reading in Berlin and who is the dominant intellectual influence on the sequence. In Burrow's 1927 book *The Social Basis of Consciousness,* he argued that a scientific examination into the "basis of consciousness" needed to begin with introspection and self-analysis because "we are ourselves the primary elements of our own inquiry."[158] Burrow insisted that all exploration of the outer world must be founded on our understanding of our own psyches because the mind structures whatever we experience outside ourselves. But Burrow's insistence on self-inspection only complements a process that is traditional in lyric poetry. In the way that lyric almost always does, Auden's poem gambles everything on the conviction that looking inward opens onto a vision of external realities.

Here is the opening of the sequence's first part:

> It was Easter as I walked in the public gardens
> Hearing the frogs exhaling from the pond,
> Watching traffic of magnificent cloud
> Moving without anxiety on open sky—
> Season when lovers and writers find
> An altering speech for altering things,
> An emphasis on new names, on the arm
> A fresh hand with fresh power. (36)

Moving rapidly (there is only one caesura in the first eight lines), Auden begins his description of the scene by locating his "I" in "the public gardens" and by stressing that I's movement through space by "walk[ing]." This part of the sequence is constructed in three blocks: first, a recounting of Auden's walk "in the public gardens" with "on the arm | A fresh hand with fresh power," during which he comes upon a desperate man "weeping on a bench." In the second block, the sight of the weeping man prompts thoughts about "all of those whose death | Is necessary condition of the season's setting forth" but with the "success of others for comparison." The third block draws to an eerie conclusion: as a shower of rain falls at the end of the day over "fallen bicycles like huddled corpses," a "choice" about whether to commit to the dead or to the living seems "a necessary error" (36–37).

In historical terms, Auden is writing another episode in English and Irish poetry's tradition of the meditative walk. Examples go back to John

Gay's *Trivia* (1716) as well as Wordsworth's many walking poems, including "Lines Composed a Few Miles above Tintern Abbey" (1798) and the multiple versions of *The Prelude*. In the twentieth century, the genre becomes more overtly politicized in works such as Yeats's "Easter, 1916," where the deeply ego-centered Yeats begins outside, in the street, recounting how, as he strolled, he met the future Irish revolutionaries "at close of day | Coming with vivid faces": "I have passed [them] with a nod of the head | Or polite meaningless words."[159] (The Easter setting of Yeats's poem makes it a significant reference point for Auden's "It was Easter.")

Outside and walking, Auden indicates the subjective mood that Burrow recommended as essential to "inquiry": he introduces his speaker "hearing" the frogs exhaling (rather than, for example, saying more impersonally that "the frogs were exhaling from the pond") and uses affective rather than strictly descriptive adjectives. The world is shown not as it objectively is but as it is perceived. Just as the poem's protagonist "hears" the frogs, he "watch[es]" what is happening in the sky. Rather than simply offering the reader a declarative statement about the heavens, he is "Watching traffic of magnificent cloud | Moving without anxiety on open sky." The clouds "moving without anxiety" suggest that the speaker's state—in contrast to that of the clouds—*is* an anxious one. (This, in itself, is another quietly significant moment: it is the first time that the word "anxiety," which will be repeated in the sequence's second part, enters Auden's poetry. Auden, the future author of the long work *The Age of Anxiety* [1944–1947], would eventually come to be known as the defining poet of that psychological state.[160]) The sequence thus begins in a mood of deep subjectivity complemented by a glut of present participles in the perfect continuous tense: hearing, exhaling, watching, moving, altering, thinking. These participle forms suggest an initial incompleteness and openness at the start of the poem's autobiographical story.

The first part then goes on to explore a set of recollected and foreseen experiences—a sublimation, or stylization, of what Auden in another poem from April 1929 called "living origins" because:

> Out of the common incidents of life
> And individual strength or weakness
> With general commentary upon their nature
> A work of art must have its genesis.[161]

In this case, the "living origins" of part 1 include the happiness of "my friend Kurt Groote" and Auden's meeting with Gerhart Meyer (who is mentioned by name) on 31 March, Easter Sunday 1929. It also redeploys some details of the despairing Layard's attempted suicide and a chance meeting with Layard that Auden had in Berlin on 6 April 1929. After the latter occasion, Auden noted in his journal that Layard, with his self-inflicted injury, "looked awful, like an embryo chicken."[162] In the poem, the speaker makes a similar observation:

> thinking so I came at once
> Where solitary man sat weeping on a bench,
> Hanging his head down, with his mouth distorted
> Helpless and ugly as an embryo chicken. (37)

The "fresh hand with fresh power" and the "Absence of fear in Gerhart Meyer | From the sea, the truly strong man" are contrasted with the pathos of the unnamed, Layard-derived "solitary man . . . weeping on a bench." In his journal, Auden wrote up the history of his dealings with Meyer and Layard together, as though the brief but inspiring appearance in his life of Meyer and the foiled self-destruction of Layard were in some way organically related. Auden's relevant heading in the journal joins the two events in a single clause: "Meeting Gerhart and John's attempted suicide."[163]

Meyer, the man "From the sea" with "fresh power," is counterpointed with floundering, nameless figures, who are associated with liquidity and weakness: the "solitary man . . . weeping on a bench" and those "Who sorry in this time look only back | . . . Fading in silence, leaving them in tears" (36). Auden's infatuation with Meyer is matched by his narcissistic fascination with the Layard-like weeping man's weakness and failure.[164] This is made even clearer in one of Auden's drafts of this section. In the published text, Auden's speaker is moving buoyantly through the sunny springtime atmosphere in Berlin when he sees the unnamed "solitary man . . . weeping on a bench" (37). The published version continues, a little coldly: "So I remember all of those whose death | Is necessary condition of the season's setting forth" (37). That pseudo-argumentative "So" is hard to interpret. In his draft, Auden frames his confrontation with this abject figure rather differently: "So forced by *the feeling of identification* | I must remember all those whose death | Is necessary condition of the season's setting forth."[165] With his not-infrequent combination of drive and masochistic self-criticism, Auden indicates that he was prey to feelings that he himself, like Layard, was someone who had to be left behind by the new season's growth: the "weeping man" is more central imaginatively, more like an "embryo" to the poem's expanding emotions than the "truly strong" one. The sequence as a whole will develop this idea further.

Layard's troubles reappear in coded form a few lines later. Auden recalls, with a brilliant double entendre on the word "analysis" (Layard was well-versed in psychoanalytic theory): "A friend's *analysis* of his own failure, | Listened to at intervals throughout the winter | At different hours and in different rooms" (37; emphasis added). If his loving admiration is for Meyer, his "feeling of identification" is with the weak Layard figure, a man of his own class and nation. Moreover, in this Easter poem, these references to a "truly strong man" and a man weeping alone on a wooden bench bring a mystical note into the poem's background through biblical allusions to John's account of Christ's death on the cross. Like Auden's man "Hanging his head down," in John's gospel Christ "bowed his head, and gave up the ghost." It is as if Meyer were like the risen Christ seen in the "garden" and Layard were like the abjected Christ on the cross who had to sacrifice himself for a new birth.[166] (It may not be an accident that the religiously aware Auden shadows his account of his friend John's misery with allusions to the account of Christ's suffering, given by the apostle with the same name.) For now, though, the sequence insists that the new season requires the abandonment of the past and its victims, "all of those whose death | Is necessary condition of the season's setting forth."

This part ends with a separate verse paragraph formed by a series of lines in a more elliptical, more image-freighted and less discursive register:

> A 'bus ran home then, on the public ground
> Lay fallen bicycles like huddled corpses:
> No chattering valves of laughter emphasised
> Nor the swept gown ends of a gesture stirred
> The sessile hush; until a sudden shower
> Fell willing into grass and closed the day,
> Making choice seem a necessary error. (37)

The passage is oracular, mysterious. The scene clears of human presences ("A 'bus ran home"), leaving an unfamiliar "sessile hush" ("sessile" means immobile or fixed) and a heavily symbolic shower of rain that "closed the [poetic] day." This suggests that the Audenesque speaker feels faced suddenly with the need to make decisions about how to live and whether, or how, to escape from the fate of "those whose death | Is necessary condition of the season's setting forth" (37). At the end of part 1, making a choice between the living (represented by the "fresh hand" of Meyer) and the dying (represented by the hanging head of the Layard figure) "seem[s] a necessary error." It appears to commit Auden to siding with life against death, Germany against England, foreigners from a different class against compatriots from his own social milieu. The opening part ends with foreboding: no choice is good, a choice must be made, and error is connected with the old secondary meaning of "erring"— that is, wandering through a strange, usually foreign, landscape. But, for all its apparent rightness, the wish to commit to the Homeric-sounding man "From the sea" will turn out to be misplaced; the identification with the "solitary man . . . weeping" will prove stronger.

Part 2 of the sequence, which begins "Coming out of me living is always thinking" (from now on, "Coming out of me living"), is longer than part 1. Written in lines of irregular length, it folds in moments from a number of different times and places. These include the May Day riots and Berlin street fighting from 1 to 3 May 1929, during which some thirty-three demonstrators were killed.[167] It also takes in details from Auden's trip with someone now known only by the first name "Dan," or alternatively as "the Dutchman," to Rothehütte in the Harz Mountains between Hannover and Leipzig. Auden's overnight stays in the small town of Gudensberg (which he spells "Gutensberg") between Kassel and Marburg, and in Hesse (called "Hessen" in the poem), are also mentioned. These are places that Auden visited in the first half of May 1929 after leaving Berlin semipermanently.[168]

This part of the sequence begins with another volley of participles: "Coming out of me living is always thinking, | Thinking changing and changing living" (37). Auden is once again in the open, but this time by a "harbour" (perhaps in Hamburg, where Auden and Meyer went for a trip, but more likely in one of the four ports in or around Berlin since, although the city is far inland, a network of canals and rivers links it to the Baltic Sea, the North Sea, and the Rhine). There, the Auden-speaker is "leaning on harbour parapet | To watch a colony of duck below | Sit, preen, and doze" (37).[169]

The appearance of the ducks on the "flickering stream" at the start of part 2 rhymes thematically with the presence of the frogs in the pond at the start of part 1. This simple parallelism keys readers into one important way to understand the sequence's structure: beneath the poem's "argument" there exists a large web of images and ideas, often at odds with, or disconnected from, logic and the argumentative surface. Often by invoking similar motifs at different points in the sequence, this web expresses significant thoughts and emotions that are barely articulated explicitly. Although Auden's sequence looks relatively conventional in formal terms, it works through chastened, less efflorescent versions of some of the same strategies that Eliot had used earlier in the decade in *The Waste Land.*

In fact, Auden seems to go out of his way to signal the connections, and the distances, between his sequence and *The Waste Land.* Similarities between the two works are evident. Like "It was Easter," the opening lines of Eliot's poem, focused on the month of April, are rich with traditional Easter symbolism of death and rebirth: "breeding | Lilacs out of the dead land, mixing | Memory and desire, stirring | Dull roots with spring rain."[170] This part of *The Waste Land,* like the first part of Auden's sequence, is also Germanic in its cultural references. Thus the "Hofgarten" in Munich in *The Waste Land* is echoed by Berlin's "public gardens" in "It was Easter," just as Eliot's scenic Starnbergersee (a huge freshwater lake in southern Germany) is the foil for Auden's mundane but fecund northern German "pond" with its burping frogs. And Auden plays off Eliot's evocation of a decadent aristocratic world by introducing his own proletarian affiliations. *The Waste Land*'s elegant "sled" has its counterpoint in the workers' "fallen bicycles" in Auden's poem. As one crosses from Eliot's ruined world into Auden's anxious, conflictual one, the older poet's vision slowly turns into a fresh but equally fraught panorama in the younger poet's lines. One writer's crisis-ridden waste land of the early 1920s is being supplanted by another writer's no-man's-land at the end of the decade.

Eliot claimed that the interweaving technique of imagistic fore-shadowing and recollection, in which *The Waste Land* abounds, was expressive and precise. The "suppression of 'links in the chain,' of explanatory and connecting matter" in a poem has "nothing chaotic about it," he argued in 1930, articulating in prose a point that was already clear from poems of his such as *The Waste Land*. "There is a logic of the imagination as well as a logic of concepts."[171] The "logic of the imagination" is clearly operative in Auden's sequence too. As in so many of Auden's important poems, and especially those thematically connected to England, feathered creatures appear insistently either as metaphors or as naturalistic elements of the poetic scene. Birds function here as visible "links in the chain," appearing as leitmotifs in each of the sequence's four parts: "an embryo chicken" (part 1), a "colony of duck" (part 2), a "jay" and "frozen buzzard" (part 3), and simply "birds" (part 4). The nature-loving country boy was still alive inside this now very sophisticated young man, who was taking his cues from advanced poetic techniques. More importantly, Auden's sequence, like Eliot's poem, is filled with constellations of ideas and images centered around the concept of "liquid." There is the link between the "pond" in the public gardens at the start of part 1 and the "harbour" in part 2. But many other references to water can be found throughout: "weeping," "tears," "the sea," "a sudden shower," "flickering stream," "baby, warm in mother," "drunkenness," "the weir," "that savage coast," "the storms," the "flooded football ground," and so on (36–40).

Why is water so important to the meaning of Auden's sequence? Because water (and its antitype, drought) symbolism is pervasive in so much poetry as a means of connecting a local scene with larger historical processes. *The Waste Land,* so concerned to diagnose the sickness of Western civilization, is filled with references to rain, rivers, and tears. In that, it draws on a vast and ancient tradition of poets using apocalyptic floods and great, quasi-biblical, all-destroying tides to represent through metaphor historical catastrophes or changes. Other contemporaries, besides Eliot, continued to use this symbolism. For example, in Yeats's "The Second Coming" (1919), the "blood-dimmed tide is loosed, and everywhere | The ceremony of innocence is drowned." This poem, like *The Waste Land,* is in the immediate background of Auden's sequence.[172]

By the 1920s, the metaphors of flood and tide had also become common elements of revolutionary rhetoric. For example, in 1927 a triumphant Stalin—having just defeated his enemies Trotsky and Zinoviev and expelled them from the Communist Party—announced in Moscow to the 15th Congress that "a new wave of revolution" was expected because "the tide has turned towards the revolutionary flood on which the U.S.S.R. is moving for the working-class of Europe and the oppressed colonials."[173] The "dangerous flood" of history (Auden's phrase in a poem from 1935) was an especially charged metaphor for catastrophe or revolutionary change not only in directly political discourse but also in plays and poems well into the 1920s and 1930s. In 1922, Yeats wrote about a flood in *The Player Queen*, while around 1926 Brecht attempted to compose a play updating the Noah story about a great flood, called variously *Die Sintflut* (The flood) or *Untergang der Paradiesstadt Miami* (The sinking of the paradisal city of Miami).[174] To accompany the Group Theatre's performance of Auden's play *The Dance of Death* in London in February 1934, Auden chose *The Deluge*, a medieval version of the story of Noah from the Chester Mystery Cycle. And in Brecht's mid-1930s poem "To Those Born Later," a desperate political refugee addresses one of those "who will emerge from the flood | In which we have gone under."[175] Auden himself would write many politically charged poems containing imagery of floods, ungovernable oceans, or unstoppable bodies of moving water.

Water imagery has a political and cultural vision implicit, and Auden's four-part sequence from 1929 has a fund of imagery evoking historical process by likening it to moving water. But the sequence also carries a metacommentary on the way that an individual's experience finds formal embodiment in poetry. Bodies of moving water have a longstanding connection not only with political upheaval, but also with literary creativity and with myths about inspired poetry—from the Castalian Spring at Delphi, regarded by Greek and Roman poets as the source of lyric poetry, even down to the sluggish, solid, but, to Eliot, ironically inspiring waters of the Thames in *The Waste Land*. In his pivotal 1927 poem "Who stands, the crux left of the watershed," Auden had situated himself at the origin of many of the major rivers of northern England.[176] The imagery of sudden spurts or movements of gurgling water has associations with political destruction, but also with literary creativity. In *The Prelude*, besides referring to the French Revolution as a "deluge," Wordsworth can report how he began his own poem "like a torrent":

> I sang
> Aloud in dithyrambic fervour, deep
> But short-lived uproar, like a torrent sent
> Out of the bowels of a bursting cloud
> Down Scawfell or Blencathara's rugged sides,
> A waterspout from heaven.[177]

Blencathra with its steep, "rugged sides" is one of the most northerly mountains in the Lake District. It is a six-topped peak, the highest of which is Hallsfell Top, looming up directly behind the place where the Audens had their holiday cottage, Wesco, in the village of Threlkeld. The plunging "torrent" that Wordsworth uses as an image of his literary creativity is probably the swollen state of either Gate Gill or Doddick Gill, the two streams that run down the sides of Hallsfell Top's spur and that are visible from below in Threlkeld. As a young poet, Auden must have seen them often, sometimes in spate. Wherever there is water, at least in verse, there are associations with revolution, creativity, and hints of death.

In part 2 of the 1929 sequence, the watery opening, with Auden watching the colony of ducks from a parapet, emphasizes the height of the human speaker above the subject. The scene symbolizes his assumption of intellectual superiority over them, even as, at the same time, he envies their happy unselfconsciousness:

> Those find sun's luxury enough,
> Shadow know not of homesick foreigner
> Nor restlessness of intercepted growth. (37)

As he surveys the ducks, Auden dramatizes himself in a foreign port meditating on a difference between humanity and harmless (and nationless) creatures living a natural existence.

Throughout his 1929 journal, Auden insisted again and again that humanity's evolutionary development is in a direction away from the physical body, from animals, and from the natural world. In different places in the text, he referred to "man's journey away from nature" and postulated that "the development of the mind is one more and more of differentiation, individualistic, away from nature."[178] The very term that

Auden chose "journey," shows how this idea about evolution is closely correlated with his own travels away from home. At one point he warned himself: "Young men. Travel abroad but go alone. To travel with one's family is a contradiction in terms."[179] But while Auden's prose ego insisted on the necessary "weaning" of humanity from nature, his poetic id was far more intent on immersion in the natural world and—as the narrative drift of the 1929 sequence shows—returning to "home," the "place | Where no tax is levied for being there" (39).

Auden's speaker in part 2, emphasizing the gap between the human and the creaturely, imagines that the ducks do not know the anxiety of "homesick foreigner | Nor restlessness of intercepted growth" (37). The word "homesick" reflects Auden's ambivalence about "home." Within the poem, where double meanings can abound, he contrives to have the word carry both its conventional sense of "longing for home" and an almost antithetical meaning of "made sick by home." Indeed, part of this work's achievement is to dramatize the pathology of a representative speaker who has been sickened by home and who is, at the same time, like an addict, longing for what has made them suffer. (The phrase "restlessness of intercepted growth" in part 2 is taken directly from Burrow's book *The Social Basis of Consciousness*. There, Burrow writes: "Seen clearly, man's restlessness to-day is, after all, the restlessness of intercepted growth.")[180]

Another reason for the prominence of water in the sequence is that Burrow too was attracted to liquid imagery. For Burrow, life's "course is one of quiet flow," and "in its incipient rapport with the world of objectivity, life maintains still a fluid, undifferentiated, confluent mode."[181] The watery metaphors, drifting sentences, and fluent turns of phrase that sustain Burrow's writing epitomize his sense of the fluidity of the boundaries between inner and outer worlds. Life is a continuum rather than a series of discrete, cellular aggregations or boundaries between mind and body, self and other: "the unconscious reactions of the social mind about oneself are reflected unconsciously within oneself, the individual being but an element in our common consciousness."[182] We are in need, Burrow insists, of "a more conscious realisation of the social involvement of our personal separateness."[183] It is a key remark for understanding Auden's ambitions in his sequence: if this is an autobiographical work, it is one that uses personal narrative to explore collective social and historical pathologies.

Burrow's ideas provided Auden with an even broader framework for thinking about the relation of the individual to society. The psychoanalyst's arch-Romantic conclusion is that "in its very birth conscious-ness embodies a biological recoil—an organic impaction. Its very un-folding is an infolding, its begetting a misbegetting. For the rudiment of consciousness is self-consciousness. In its origin it is self-reflexive, self-relational. That is, consciousness in its inception entails the fallacy of *a self as over against other selves.* It is in this inevitable *faux pas* of man's earliest awareness . . . that consists the error or lapse in the process of his evolution."[184] These ideas appear in poetic form in part 2 of Auden's sequence, where for the poet "living is always thinking" (37). This phrase, while it may sound positive, carries a negative con-notation of existing with an excessively cerebral relation to the world.

Like Wordsworth's *Prelude,* Auden's narrative of the progressive il-lumination of the poet's mind is set against revolutionary turmoil—in this case, the clashes that began in Berlin on 1 May 1929 after the Berlin police chief, Karl Zörgiebel, banned public demonstrations on May Day. When the Communist Party defied the ban, the police launched a carefully planned attack on the marchers. After observing the ducks in the harbor, Auden's speaker recounts a conversation about the violence with a politically involved friend. He writes that:

> All this time was anxiety at night,
> Shooting and barricade in street.
> Walking home late I listened to a friend
> Talking excitedly of final war
> Of proletariat against police—
> That one shot girl of nineteen through the knees
> They threw that one down concrete stair—
> Till I was angry, said I was pleased. (37–38)

The notion that one could expect such a thing as a "final war" to cure the world's ills, or that one should be "excited" by such a prospect, would appear deeply wrongheaded to anyone who credited Burrow's theories. For, according to Burrow, "the settlement of war is properly the concern not of politics but of psychiatry."[185] The theorizing intelli-gence of Auden's speaker purports to be "pleased" by this hastening of a final apocalyptic confrontation, but the speaker's conscience is pri-vately angered by the political tactic of escalating violence in a crisis that should be solved by psychiatry. Just as Auden found a gap between humanity and the natural world, represented in part 2 by the ducks, so he now describes a rift between himself and his friend, as well as between his own private thinking and his outward expressions.

Burrow's antagonism to differentiation, dialectic, or opposition—visible, for instance, in his hostility to the "fallacy *of a self as over against other selves*"—is at the very base of his wholesale critique of modern society and the "the present self-conscious phase of [humanity's] mental evolution."[186] In this phase, we experience "the delusion of separateness" from one another and from nature, much as Auden's speaker does looking down on the colony of ducks and feeling jealous that they "find sun's luxury enough" (37).[187] In its hostility to what Burrow calls the "societal neurosis," his argument extends beyond moral and political attitudes to enclose and indict the whole modern apparatus of logic and even of perception.[188] He insisted that "in constituting ourselves perceptual foci from which, according to our self-appointed terms, we look out as from a background upon the phenomena of life, we have unconsciously become artificially detached spectators of a merely static *aspect* of life."[189]

This is the argument concealed in part 2's contemplative scene in rural Germany that Auden describes immediately after his account of his own reaction to the prospect of "final war" in Berlin. Writing in his journal about the "view at Gutensberg," probably meaning the prospect from one of the small basalt hills, such as the Obervorschütz, surrounding Gudensberg, Auden remarks that "this perfection of nature would [be complete] with [a] perfect boy."[190] In the poem, the moment is redescribed with a Tintern Abbey–like contemplativeness:

> Time passes in Hessen, in Gutensberg,
> With hill-top and evening holds me up,
> Tiny observer of enormous world.
> Smoke rises from factory in field,
> Memory of fire: On all sides heard
> Vanishing music of isolated larks:
> From village square voices in hymn,
> Men's voices, an old use. (38)

Here, the journal's reflection on the desirability of a "perfect boy" has disappeared. The scene is now dominated by Auden's picturesque description of watching the smoke "from factory in field" while listening to "isolated larks" and the far-off voices of the men's choir, who follow the ancient custom by practicing their hymns in the square in front of the church of St. Margaret in Gudensberg.

Auden has left the antagonisms of the city and is now in the countryside. But has anything changed internally with the change of external scene? To be the "tiny observer" of an "enormous world" implies that one is not a part of that world. Burrow puts it like this: "To observe is to stand apart from and record the impressions reflected to us from the object observed."[191] A sequence that began with the speaker excitedly "Watching traffic of magnificent cloud | Moving without anxiety on open sky" and entertaining the rousing idea of evolving "new names" and an "altering speech for altering things" has now become preoccupied with the fading and indistinct sounds of a natural and collective life that is already out of reach and now almost out of hearing: "Vanishing music of isolated larks . . . voices in hymn, | Men's voices, an old use."

Auden's speaker, "above standing," now begins both to apprehend and to demonstrate the predicament that Burrow saw as intrinsic to modern self-consciousness: its alienation from life, its "saying in thinking" (38). When the protagonist gives a speech in part 2, it appears in quotation marks, which creates a strange but highly apposite doubling effect. It is as if the speaker is talking and at the same time listening, like another person, to himself talking. The speech is a potted history of the catastrophic advent of self-consciousness:

> "Is first baby, warm in mother,
> Before born and is still mother,
> Time passes and now is other,
> Is knowledge in him now of other,
> Cries in cold air, himself no friend.
> In grown man also, may see in face
> In his day-thinking and in his night-thinking
> Is wareness and is fear of other,
> Alone in flesh, himself no friend." (38)

At first, the child is "warm in mother" but soon "Is knowledge in him now of other" and, as an adult, "In his day-thinking and in his night-thinking | Is wareness and is fear of other."

The poem then seems to gesture toward the shadow of the Great War that is still lying across relations between the English and Germans:

"'He say "We must forgive and forget," | Forgetting saying but is unforgiving | And unforgiving is in his living'" (38). In this context of "unforgiving," acts of love are inadequate. Love, when denatured by self-consciousness, is a wholly insufficient attempt to create union:

> "Body reminds in him to loving,
> Reminds but takes no further part,
> Perfunctorily affectionate in hired room
> But takes no part and is unloving
> But loving death. May see in dead,
> In face of dead that loving wish,
> As one returns from Africa to wife
> And his ancestral property in Wales." (38)

In devastatingly satiric fashion, the simile about the colonial expatriate returning to an ancestral home suggests that modern humans, trapped in our own minds, desire death more than anything else. It implies that we see, in the face of the dead, the smug but enviable contentment of a colonial planter, returned after years abroad in Africa to his "ancestral property in Wales." The implication is that, after surviving through exploitation in the world of the living, the colonist longs to turn at last to his "ancestral property," the estate of death.

The second part of the sequence might appear to end on a relatively optimistic note as Auden's speaker remembers moments of happiness or satisfaction ("strict beauty of locomotive, | Completeness of gesture or unclouded eye") and is moved by "In me so absolute unity of evening | And field and distance" that he feels "at peace." He resolves:

> To love my life, not as other,
> Not as bird's life, not as child's,
> "Cannot", I said, "being no child now nor a bird." (39)[192]

But the stillness of "evening" and "distance" and "peace" recall one of the notes Auden made in his journal in Berlin while he was reading Freud's *Beyond the Pleasure Principle:* "The death wish is an entropy wish."[193] Stillness here is a closeness to death.

In the context of Burrow's thought, the speaker's resolution to "love my life" for what it is looks like a desperately selfish and self-isolated gesture. Burrow writes: "Captivated by the phylogenetically new and unwonted spectacle of his own image, it would seem that [the modern

human] has been irresistibly arrested before the mirror of his own likeness and that in the present self-conscious phase of his mental evolution he is still standing spell-bound before it."[194] Auden's speaker, in this
final scene set in Germany, is fascinated by his own condition of separateness. It is as if the world, stretching its arms toward him—like the
hands that the dead German soldier stretched out to the British Tommy
in Owen's "Strange Meeting"—were being met by someone more intent
on self-consciously watching himself react than on truly reciprocating
another being's reaching.

By the end of July 1929, Auden was back in England. At the end of that
month he saw Sheilah Richardson, the Birmingham nurse he was engaged
to. He had to give some bad news. Afterward he wrote in his diary: "Have
broken off my engagement. Never—Never—Never again. She is unhappy."[195] Perhaps his Berlin life had convinced him that a straight marriage would never work. (As we will see, though, the dream of an officially
sanctioned relationship with a woman would haunt Auden long afterward.
He even proposed to Hannah Arendt in the 1960s.) The rupture does not
appear in an explicit way in the third part of his sequence, written soon
after in August 1929. But references to the "frightened soul," "mourning,"
and a "forethought of death" perhaps are verbal residues of the painful moment he and Richardson had just been through together (39–40).

  The third part, beginning "Order to stewards and the study of time"
(from now on, "Order to stewards"), inaugurates the "English" half of
the poem, marking the transition from Germany to Auden's home
country and the speaker's temporary return to a "life of sheep and hay |
No longer his" (39). Whereas parts 1 and 2 begin with Auden's speaker
on foot, part 3 opens with him sitting in a train, a signal to readers
about the importance at this point in the poem of a movement between
places. This part is apparently set in the late summer of 1929, close to
the time of writing. Beginning on the train that brings Auden to his
family's holiday home in the Lake District, it then follows him on foot
to various places in that region. Here are the opening lines:

  Order to stewards and the study of time,
  Correct in books, was earlier than this

> But joined this by the wires I watched from train,
> Slackening of wire and posts' sharp reprimand,
> In month of August to a cottage coming. (39)

All of "this" had occurred earlier: the lunch order that the speaker gave to the stewards in the dining car as he traveled toward the "cottage" in the Lake District and his "study of time" in J. W. Dunne's cult book *An Experiment with Time* (1927), which he reads as he barrels northward. The train's journey is like an image of time conventionally conceived as a unidirectional progression.[196] But, in ways reminiscent of Burrow's mysticism, Dunne argued our wakeful experience of the world limits us to a restrictive, linear understanding of time, focused primarily on "now." However, as our consciousness relaxes, and especially in states of somnolence and dream, he claimed we can see more broadly into a time continuum that includes the future as well as the past. Here, Auden describes moments from the past that feel curiously similar, or "joined," to those the speaker is experiencing now as the repetitive sight of "Slackening of wire and posts' sharp reprimand" outside the train's windows lulls him into postprandial drowsiness. In a Dunne-like fashion, past and present begin to fuse in the speaker's half-asleep state.

The third section of the sequence admits to a rational confusion about humanity's destiny:

> he every hour
> Moves further from this and must so move,
> As child is weaned from his mother and leaves home
> But taking the first steps falters, is vexed. (39)

This fatalistic idea reflects the only partial success of Auden's movement away from "mother" and "home." Having left for Germany, his speaker has now returned, "vexed," to England and to a familiar "cottage," one primarily associated with Auden's mother. (Significantly, these lines echo the ending of "Who stands, the crux left of the watershed." There, toward the poem's end, the "stranger," having failed in his attempt to make contact with an alien world, is told to "Go home" and to "turn back again, frustrate and *vexed*."[197])

Most of the rest of this section is given to a set of ideas about love and human development that seem deliberately vapid in poetry but that closely match reflections in Auden's own journal from the time. The poem asserts that the "frightened soul" seeks security in love, but this

> gives less than he expects.
> He knows not if it be seed in time to display
> Luxuriantly in a wonderful fructification
> Or whether it be but a degenerate remnant
> Of something immense in the past but now
> Surviving only as the infectiousness of disease
> Or in the malicious caricature of drunkenness. (39)

When belief in love fails, the human subject tries to create independence and solitary invulnerability:

> Moving along the track which is himself,
> He loves what he hopes will last, which gone,
> Begins the difficult work of mourning,
> . . . .
> . . . so may the soul
> Be weaned at last to independent delight. (39)

The phrases here, rolling with an orotund emptiness, give the reader a hint to remain skeptical. Auden is a great enough poet that in his chosen artistic medium he can offer a critique of ideas that, in his personal life, he felt he believed in. As if the vagueness of the thoughts is matched by a vagueness in the scenario, the poem now reveals that at an undefined point the speaker has moved from the train or cottage into a wood. As the poem winds down, these lofty but unconvincing thoughts are dramatically undercut by the "violent laugh of jay."[198]

Recalled by the bird's "laugh" from his ruminations about destiny, the speaker goes "from wood." But Dunne's mystical ideas about time and apprehensions of what Burrow calls "a new and untrammelled consciousness" now return. While he was aware primarily of links between past and present at the start of this section, the speaker now embraces Dunne's ideas about a sense of connection with the future. A flood of images replaces the previous burst of insipid, overly abstract reasoning and discourse with a more irrational and emotive approach to truth:

> I went from wood, from crunch underfoot,
> Air between stems as under water;

As I shall leave the summer, see autumn come
Focusing stars more sharply in the sky,
See frozen buzzard flipped down the weir
And carried out to sea, leave autumn,
See winter, winter for earth and us,
A forethought of death that we may find ourselves at death
Not helplessly strange to the new conditions. (39–40)[199]

The "violent laugh of jay" by "water," which debunks the speaker's cerebral meditation, almost immediately leads by the logic of the imagination to the "frozen buzzard" whose corpse the speaker imagines he will observe floating out to sea. In a Dunne-like amalgam of past, present, and future, the "forethought" at this point also recalls the sequence's earlier parts in which thoughts about death are prominent and at the same time looks ahead to the concluding part in which death becomes omnipresent. Death has loomed in the sequence from the very beginning, where Auden reflects on it as a "necessary condition of the season's setting forth" (37). It reappears at the end of part 2 when he suggests that the "grown man" is in love with death, thinking of it as a possession or a home. Here, in part 3, the "winter" of death becomes unignorable, even in the midst of summertime: the speaker knows he will "See winter, winter for earth and us, | A forethought of death" (40).

Part 4, the sequence's last section, starting "It is time for the destruction of error" (from now on, "It is time"), was written in the economic crisis month of October 1929 (40). With its seasonal "falling leaves" and "flooded football ground," it is set in the early autumn of that year in London. This doom-laden but also future-conscious part is the "present" of the sequence, the temporal point from which the previous three sections are recalled:

The chairs are being brought in from the garden,
The summer talk stopped on that savage coast
Before the storms, after the guests and birds:
In sanatoriums they laugh less and less,
Less certain of cure: and the loud madman
Sinks now into a more terrible calm. (40)

In part 1, choice had seemed "a necessary error." In the final part, an oracular voice announces that it is now "time for the destruction of error." Burrow argued that "normality" was more pathological in character than a state of neurosis because "normality, in evading the issues of the unconscious, envisages less the processes of growth and a larger consciousness than the neurotic type of reaction, which, however blind its motivation, at least comes to grips with the actualities of the unconscious."[200] Burrow saw neurotics as more in touch with fundamental psychic processes and thus more sensitive to the realities of underlying disturbances in a society than the people whom society defines as normal. In "sanatoriums," Auden writes, "they laugh less and less, | Less certain of cure; and the loud madman | Sinks now into a more terrible calm" (38–39).

In 1927, Burrow predicted that "as overwhelming as is the catastrophe of the present war—and present it is—this catastrophe is but the detonator preceding the crash that is to come."[201] Accordingly, Auden's lines now summon a new, even more profound disaster than any that has recently occurred:

> The falling leaves know it, the children,
> At play on the fuming alkali-tip
> Or by the flooded football ground, know it—
> This is the dragon's day, the devourer's. (40)

Once again, love is inadequate. Returning to its opening ideas about death and rebirth, the sequence concludes with a vehement sense that collective death is now both inevitable and necessary before regeneration can begin. Here is the poem's ending:

> You whom I gladly walk with, touch,
> Or wait for as one certain of good,
> We know it, we know that love
> Needs more than the admiring excitement of union,
> More than the abrupt self-confident farewell,
> The heel on the finishing blade of grass,
> The self-confidence of the falling root,
> Death of the old gang; would leave them
> In sullen valley where is made no friend,
> The old gang to be forgotten in the spring,
> The hard bitch and the riding-master,

Stiff underground; deep in clear lake
The lolling bridegroom, beautiful, there. (40)

In these memorable final lines of the sequence, the deaths of the
"old gang" and of "us" culminate in the intensely personal image of
"deep in clear lake | The lolling bridegroom." At first, this might read
simply as a glance at the abandoned plans of Auden's engagement to
Richardson and the now-rejected idea of himself as a bridegroom (40).
But while this shade of meaning is present, so is much more. Profoundly,
as in a fantasy, the image of the drowned bridegroom, drifting or
"lolling" in the water, is overdetermined and multivalent (as well as
being reminiscent of course of the "drowned Phoenician Sailor" in *The
Waste Land*). Auden's sequence has been so deeply caught up by the
theme of water, and often by the idea of a watery death—from his initial
dream of a voyage in "a new model submarine" through the frogs in the
pond at the public gardens, the solitary man "weeping on a bench" and
the man "From the sea," the rain falling on bicycles, the ducks in the
harbor, the frozen buzzard, the storms and the "flooded football ground."
It is right aesthetically that it should end with a submerged figure.

In "It is time," the sequence's final image gathers all of these moments into a phrase of luminous portent and indeterminacy, showing
that the deaths needed to begin a new world will include a drowned
man: "deep in clear lake | The lolling bridegroom, beautiful, there" (40).
Into this image of the "lolling bridegroom," Auden folds the collapse of
his aspirations in Germany to be the suitor with "A fresh hand with
fresh power" on his arm, or the lover made whole by "the admiring excitement of union" (40). And the poem's two final, innocuous-seeming
words, "beautiful" and "there," are spectacular choices in this context.
The "lolling bridegroom, beautiful, there" offers a condensed, elegiac
recognition of Auden's own "beautiful," but somehow desultory, "lolling"
and his failed attempts to be the "bridegroom," to marry figuratively the
otherness of another cultural and social world in Germany. The image of
the corpse "there" in the "clear lake" also includes a sense that the attempt
at a new identity came in Germany, that country "there" (not "here"), as the
load-bearing last word indicates.

There is an enormous sadness in this ending. In one of the very
candid reviews that he published late in life, Auden would write: "Few,
if any, homosexuals can honestly boast that their sex-life has been

happy."[202] This image from 1929 hints at what he saw as a subjective truth about his own existence. But the image links the personal with a wider social context. Auden and Isherwood (and many others in their generation) saw a symbolic dimension to their private lives. Like the foiled attempts at embraces in Owen's "Strange Meeting," the end of Auden's 1929 sequence signals that reconciliation between the citizens of old enemy nations is not easily made. The drowning of those utopian hopes in a "clear lake" is part of what, once Auden has returned to England, a new direction in his poetry will require.

At the end of October 1929, in the same month that Auden finished the fourth part of his sequence, filled with apocalyptic imagery, the New York Stock Exchange suffered the "Wall Street Crash" and the onset of the Great Depression. Burrow's ideas from 1927 about an impending "crash that is to come—a crash that has been gathering momentum" look uncannily predictive in this context. "The tremors we are experiencing at this moment throughout the political and economic world undoubtedly owe their impulse to the awakening of a new order of consciousness," he wrote.[203]

What would that new order of consciousness feel like? One of the major impacts on Auden of living in Germany at the end of the 1920s was paradoxical. He went abroad to learn that, at least as a poet, he needed to be at home, among the similar and the like-minded. Germany, the vortex of contemporary European history, was gripped by a desire for collective belonging, for national coherence, for a gathering in of its resources into a unified whole. Germany seemed to be leading the countries of Europe into a phase in which self-enclosure and self-protection would become the paradigms of social and national organization. Wyndham Lewis wrote for his English audience that, in Germany, National Socialism "desires a *closer and closer* drawing together of the people of one race and culture, by means of bodily attraction. It must be a true bodily solidarity. Identical rhythms in the arteries and muscles, and in the effective neural instrument—that should provide us with a passionate *exclusiveness*, with a homogeneous social framework, within the brotherly bounds of which we could live secure from alien interference, and so proceed with our work and with our pleasures, whatever they may be."[204]

This, Lewis insisted, was "the big idea" behind contemporary political movements on the right in Germany.

Anyone who took this toxic ideal seriously was forced to acknowledge that life in "a passionate *exclusiveness*, with a homogeneous social framework" could probably only be achieved in one's own country. If unity is an absolute value, then the traveler must go home, must return to the gemeinschaft of their own tribe, must live within the comitatus of their own kind. Auden's poems from Germany dramatize, with great honesty and perhaps against his own conscious ambitions and wishes, their inability, at least for now, to cross the divide and effect a "real meeting" with the representatives of another culture. His four-part sequence traces at length this reluctant withdrawal from connection with difference.

Lewis's bald assertions illustrate what Auden's poems intuited in Berlin from the "brotherly" nationalism of the Germans: *he* could become national too "in a true bodily solidarity." But he could not do this abroad. This intuition closes one phase of Auden's writing and opens another, with morally challenging implications that are probably clearer to readers today than they were to Auden at the time. For Auden in 1929, the brotherly nationalism that seemed like a way of dissolving separateness, alienation, and individuality could only be found in England. It was to a reassertion of his identity as an English poet that he now moved. Symbolically, that had required, as the last line of his most important poem from 1929 insisted, an immersion, a death by water.

PART THREE   GARDEN

6   THE ENGLISH CELL
DREAMS AND VISIONS, 1929–1932

An artist who is not a mere entertainer and money-maker, or self-advertising gossip-star, must today be penetrated by a sense of the great discontinuity of our destiny. At every moment he is compelled to be aware of that different scene, coming as if by magic, behind all that has been familiar for so long to all the nations of the Aryan World. Nothing but a sort of Façade is left standing. . . . It is what is behind the Façade that alone can be of any interest in such a pantomime.

—WYNDHAM LEWIS (1934)

WHY DID THE IMAGE OF a body sunk deep in water suggest Auden's return to his origins as a poet? Late in his life, Auden reminisced that his very first poem in what would have been the spring of 1922 had been a "Wordsworthian sonnet" about a small lake, Blea Tarn, in the Lake District. It ended, he said, with the lines "and in the quiet | Oblivion of thy waters let them stay."[1] He could not remember who or what "they" were, but the "oblivion" of the waters where "they" now "stay" suggests that the poem concluded with thoughts about a drowning. The sonnet has been lost, and there is no record of Auden and his family visiting the Lake District between the summers of 1921 and 1922, by which latter time he had already been writing poetry for a few months. Perhaps he was slightly misremembering his early artistic history. Nonetheless, the recollected poem had symbolic value for him.

Blea Tarn is the site of the Poet's and the Wanderer's visit to the Solitary in books 2–5 of *The Excursion* (1814). It is a "beautiful abyss," Wordsworth writes of the lake, "By Nature destined from the birth of things | For quietness profound."[2] (Auden loved the purity of silence, and his lost poem appears to have shared Wordsworth's appreciation for the quietness of Blea Tarn.) Yet the main intertextual link between Auden's lost poem and Wordsworth's poetry is not *The Excursion*. Rather, that is book 5 of the 1805 version of *The Prelude,* one of Auden's favorite parts of that long poem and one he went back to repeatedly.[3] Book 5 has two emotional and verbal highpoints. The first is an episode about the so-called boy of Winander (Winander was an alternative name in the nineteenth century for Windermere and its lake), whom Wordsworth describes cupping his hands to blow protopoetic "mimic hootings" to the owls "by the glimmering lake," with the owls responding: "with quivering peals | And long halloos, and screams." Hints of a connection between death and water develop indirectly as Wordsworth wonders if the boy noticed how "that uncertain heaven, [was] received | Into the bosom of the steady lake." Then, the poet announces with a strange matter-of-factness: "This boy was taken from his mates, and died | In childhood ere he was full ten years old." He recalls that as a child himself, he passed the boy's burial spot and would spend "oftentimes | A full half-hour together" looking "Mute . . . at the grave in which he lies."[4]

Not long after this episode in *The Prelude* comes a twinned, though more ghoulish, anecdote in which Wordsworth recounts seeing through "the gloom" on the opposite shore of a nearby lake, Esthwaite Water, a "heap of garments, left as I supposed | By one who was there bathing." The clothes belonged to a man whose body was later pulled from the water with "grappling-irons and long poles." Wordsworth says that although he was only nine at the time, he had already read of such things among "the shining streams | Of fairyland," so that now the grisly scene seemed graced with "A dignity, a smoothness, like the words | Of Grecian art and purest poesy."[5] The links in Wordsworth between death, poetry and water, and the mood of dignity and calm imbued in these passages he recounts in *The Prelude* are echoed by Auden's Blea Tarn lines, with their resignation over the "quiet oblivion" of what might have been another body in a northern lake.

In October 1929, Auden's four-part sequence ended in a Wordsworthian fashion with the image of the "lolling bridegroom" who lies "deep in clear lake" and is "beautiful, there." This is an eerily radiant and peaceful moment in the natural world, where boundaries between inner and outer, self and other, seem annulled.[6] In concluding his 1929 poem with the image of a young man drowned in a lake, Auden reaches back, as if to begin again, to his own first recalled poem and, beyond that, to a seminal text by a poet who had made monumental the world and people in the English region where the Auden family had started to spend substantial parts of the year. Grasmere in the Lake District, where Wordsworth had lived, is a mere twelve or so miles south of the Audens' cottage in Threlkeld, where Auden had spent part of the summer of 1929. Water is where life originated; when Auden revisits his beginnings as a poet, he reaches for an image of death and rebirth in water, linking this search to a location where English Romanticism, which had come to define so much of what was modern in lyric poetry, arose at its source.

However, this drama of return has a complicated quality. In part, Auden wrote that the bridegroom's body was beautiful not "here" but "there"—because this Wordsworthian image was written not in the Lake District but in London. The same month that he wrote the poem, Auden took a temporary position in the capital as a live-in tutor for a wealthy family. The job was to teach a small Eton-bound boy named Peter Solomon (later Benenson) who lived with his parents on Hornton Street in Kensington. Peter's father, Lt.-Col. Harold Solomon, MC, was a career army officer and a prominent figure in Anglo-Jewish affairs, whose wealth came from his family's stockbroking business. Solomon had served with the British Mission to the Serbian Army during the war; a hunting accident in peacetime had left him in a wheelchair. (He was to die in July 1930, a few months after Auden left the tutoring role.) Flora Solomon, Harold Solomon's wife and Peter's mother, was a Russian heiress whose family had made a fortune in gold and oil, much of which disappeared during the 1917 Revolution. Grigori Benenson, her father, had re-amassed his wealth while living in exile in London.[7]

At Hornton Street, Auden lived in the nanny's old room at the top of the Solomons' large and expensive home. Just as philosophical coordinates and literary traditions can often explain how poetry evolves, the (usually sad) material conditions within which beautiful poetic language comes into being can also make their presence felt—imaginatively lingering like a fragrance in the house of art. In this case, Auden faced unpropitious circumstances: the city world, which he disliked, headstrong employers, unfamiliar surroundings, and daily duties performed with not much more than glorified servant status. And yet, while he squeezed into the quarters intended for domestics, Auden's poetry flowed like the streams rolling down the hillsides behind Wesco.

Auden's cultural status and his marginal socioeconomic condition were mismatched for many years. Like T. S. Eliot, Auden was a renter for much of his life. Although he co-owned a tiny seaside frame cottage at Cherry Grove on Fire Island for a time in the second half of the 1940s, the first property he owned by himself was a small house in Kirchstetten, Austria, that he purchased in 1958 when he was fifty-one and already a Pulitzer Prize winner and the professor of poetry at Oxford. He told Stephen Spender that in Kirchstetten, "sometimes he stood in the garden with tears of gratitude and surprise that he possessed a home of his own."[8]

But in 1929, those tears of gratitude and surprise lay far in the future. Until early 1930, while he tried to find something better to do, Auden stayed at his live-in job in Hornton Street. This period in London—a city that Auden, the proud provincial, felt uncomfortable in and mostly avoided—marked a disconsolate reentry to life in his home country. But it was the start of a signally important new phase in the continuing crystallization of his identity as an "English poet." Another dreamlike meaning in the image of the bridegroom in the lake suggests that the man is "marrying" the natural world.[9] What makes this London moment in Auden's work striking is that even in these very mundane personal circumstances, Auden wrote as a poet not just with observations and theories but with visions. There is something Blake-like about Auden in London. He was a poet of dreams and prophecies—and while some of these dreams and prophecies from the late 1920s and early 1930s are strange and intensely poetic, others are poetic and unsettling.

Two lyrics that Auden wrote as he was settling in at Hornton Street in October 1929 foreshadow important directions in his poetry in the coming couple of years. Both poems have a prophetic cast. The first is a loosely rhyming sonnet:

> Sir, no man's enemy, forgiving all
> But will his negative inversion, be prodigal:
> Send to us power and light, a sovereign touch
> Curing the intolerable neural itch,
> The exhaustion of weaning, the liar's quinsy,
> And the distortions of ingrown virginity.
> Prohibit sharply the rehearsed response

> And gradually correct the coward's stance;
> Cover in time with beams those in retreat
> That, spotted, they turn though the reverse were great;
> Publish each healer that in city lives
> Or country houses at the end of drives;
> Harrow the house of the dead; look shining at
> New styles of architecture, a change of heart.[10]

The poem, which is a kind of prayer or (as Auden later titled it) a "petition," borrows Gerard Manley Hopkins's mode of addressing, and arguing with, God as "Sir," and more distantly the poem recalls George Herbert's direct addresses to God as "Lord."[11] But, in the context of the English class system and of Auden's living arrangements, "Sir" also suggests an appeal to a social superior (and in this case an army officer).

Auden was not a practicing Christian at this stage in his life, but he was always imaginatively moved by concepts from religious, and especially Christian, thought. The poem chooses another striking way of referring to "Sir," the deity. It is not like Dante's positive circumlocution in the last line of the *Paradiso*, where he calls God "l'amor che move il sole e l'altre stelle" (the love that moves the sun and the other stars). Instead, Auden uses a poignant negative. For Auden in 1929, God is simply and astoundingly "no man's enemy," as if the most powerful facet of the divinity's otherness from the world of the English at the end of the 1920s is that he is not hostile to anyone. Sometimes, in poetry, simple "noes" and "yeses" carry unexpected weight.

Auden avoids traditional rhyme schemes for the sonnet and deploys a form of mostly half-rhyming or pararhyming couplets to indicate something awry. It is as if he wants readers to feel that he is making a strained and only partially successful effort to achieve the perfectly fitting rhymes of a classic sonnet—a task that is no longer easy in a modern world of linguistic (and social) decay. The poem's deliberate misshapenness in its rhymes also provides a verbal equivalent to the need for correction of "the distortions of ingrown virginity" and other manifestations of human fallenness and corruption in the world that the poem describes. What the fallenness consists of specifically is never defined, but words such as "inversion," "distortions," and "ingrown" overlap with the prejudicial terminology in use at the period to hint at a connection with Auden's own sexuality.

"Sir, no man's enemy, forgiving all" (from now on, "Sir, no man's enemy") has no political program and is not even really an argument—it is instead more like the repeated elaboration of a single thought: heal this sick country and us. What might do that is a power that comes from outside, a power with a religious force and mystery. The phrase that locks the poem in place at its conclusion epitomizes this idea. The sonnet ends with the hope for "New styles of architecture, a change of heart." With its rich vowel patternings, this line has a Tennysonian flavor (Tennyson was an unfashionable poet who mattered a lot to Auden at the end of the 1920s) mixed with the George Herbert of the sonnet "Prayer." "Prayer" (ca. 1630–1632?) ends with the line "The land of spices, something understood." The formula in the noun-centered last lines of Herbert's sonnet and of Auden's is the same: something concrete ("new styles of architecture") plus something abstract and cognitive ("a change of heart").[12]

A "change of heart" becomes a beautiful and deep phrase in itself when one remembers the more commonplace expression ("a change of mind") that it swerves away from. What is needed now, the poem says, is something more profound—"a change of heart." In later comments, Auden returned a number of times to his regrets about this poem's stylistic obscurities.[13] But its force came through strongly at the time—he places it last in his first commercially published book, *Poems,* issued by Faber and Faber in September 1930. So, his first book's final words, "a change of heart," are an epitome of Auden's entire, vaguely psychological program for renewal in a struggling country.

The need for change through moral and emotional regeneration is part of an important cluster of motifs in Auden's work after his return to England from Germany, as are two other facets of this poem that have received little attention. The first is the suggestion, audible through the surface exuberance in lines such as "Prohibit sharply the rehearsed response" and "Cover in time with beams those in retreat," that moral and psychological change will require some kind of coercive force to effect it. Second, there is the attempt to visualize the collective of "us," which is only a step from being able to speak for that collective. Here, Auden seeks to register comprehensively "each healer that in city lives | Or country houses at the end of drives." His attempts to widen his field of vision and to take in a more extensive spectrum of contemporary life in cities and the countryside are faltering and overblown as yet, but the

poem's ambition to include some of the breadth of the everyday world
is impressive. And the poem asks for a cure for the first-person plural:
Auden's vision is not just personal but social, communal.

The desire to achieve a representative vision is also clear in another
poem Auden wrote in October 1929. This one begins, "Which of you
waking early and watching daybreak," and is a long, incantatory, blank
verse speech (almost sounding like a speech from a play) about the
sense of hope and renewal that light brings as the sun comes up each
morning:

> Which of you waking early and watching daybreak
> Will not hasten in heart, handsome, aware of wonder
> At light unleashed, advancing, a leader of movement,
> Breaking like surf on turf, on road and roof,
> Or chasing shadow on downs like whippet racing.[14]

Again, as in "Sir, no man's enemy," there is a strong tilt here toward religious piety, even piousness. And once more, ungainly as the poem is,
Auden combines this tilt with a broader attempt to bring into language
the unglamorous world of contemporary England and especially of
town and city life. The "dawn of common day is a reminder of birth,"
and awareness that a new beginning can break in on mundane activities at any time:

> What man but is reminded? Whistling as he shuts
> His door behind him, travelling to work by tube
> Or walking through the park to it to ease the bowels,
> His morning mind illumined as the plane sea,
> No trace there of that midnight fleet of persecutors
> Gone down with all hands, will not guess at success,
> A fresh rendezvous or unexpected inheritance?[15]

Auden presents readers with a banal suburban landscape, inner and
outer, like the ones that in 1934 Eliot (who was by then being influenced
by this powerful younger poet) evokes in the choruses to his pageant play
The Rock as "the land of lobelias and tennis flannels."[16] Auden's description of how light transforms the (male) suburban mind is mildly satiric.
But, more significantly, it is a tender, if uncompleted, attempt to reach

beyond a narrow, literary field into the shared social world of work and life in a modern, bureaucratized, and increasingly denatured society.

At the time he was writing these two poems and performing his tutoring duties, Auden was also picking up extra money through a side job teaching Latin to the son of the writer and activist Naomi Mitchison, whom he had met earlier in 1929.[17] Mitchison was involved in plans for a magazine called *The Realist,* whose literary editor was to be the well-publicized mystic and broadcasting personality Gerald Heard. Alison Falby writes that Heard sought to "reconcile science and religion" within what he called a "third morality," which she sees reflecting "many of the intellectual currents of his day, including idealist philosophy, pacifism, modernist theology, eastern religious philosophy, and psychical research."[18] It was through Mitchison that Auden encountered Heard in London at the end of 1929, the year when Heard published one of his most influential books, *The Ascent of Humanity.* Theatrical but learned, worldly but sincere, sententious but ethereal, Heard was to rank with Layard as a personal friend and intellectual inspiration for Auden during the next few years.

Not long after meeting Heard, Auden left the Solomons in Hornton Street, probably sometime around the middle of January 1930. He stayed for a month with Manya Harari, Flora Solomon's sister, in a grand house on Cambridge Square just north of Hyde Park. Harari, highly cultured and already rich in her own right, was married to an immensely wealthy banker and art collector, Ralph Harari, who bought his otherworldly wife outfits from ultrafashionable couturiers such as Schiaparelli, Paul Poiret, and Balenciaga. It may have been now, while Auden was staying with her in the winter of early 1930, that he spent some time trying on Manya Harari's expensive clothes while she watched and laughed.[19] Perhaps, as Auden slipped into one luxurious Parisian dress after another, he thought about his father wearing his mother's clothing in 1914 or about the costume for his own performance as Shakespeare's Shrew at Gresham's in 1922.[20]

Not long after, though, he decided to leave this privileged London world, when he accepted the job being vacated by his Oxford friend C. Day Lewis at a down-at-heel boys' school called Larchfield Academy, in a town near Glasgow. However, before departing for Scotland, Auden had to undergo an operation for the painful but treatable condition of an anal fistula, about which he joked with some friends but not with others. The operation was conducted in early March 1930 at a nursing home in Harborne, the Birmingham suburb where his mother and father lived. The procedure was a qualified success: the underlying problem was cured, although the wound did not heal quickly.

Auden recuperated for a while at his parents' house. To Layard, who continued to play a significant role in Auden's life even though he remained in Berlin, Auden had written just before the operation, asking his friend to visit "to help me get better." He added: "John please come. The pain has been rather bad."[21] The comment is a strange reversal of psychological roles from the time a year or so earlier when Auden had written a cool survey of a figure based on Layard: a "solitary man ... weeping on a bench, | Hanging his head down, with his mouth distorted | Helpless and ugly as an embryo chicken."[22] Now Auden projected his own feeling of helplessness to Layard.

While Auden was in Birmingham, he wrote another poem that imagines a network uniting disparate people across the country into a whole. This time the collective is a dystopian grouping, but the ambition to synthesize a scattering of separate individuals remains similar to the mini-panoramas in "Sir, no man's enemy" and "Which of you waking early and watching daybreak." Poetic adaptations of film aesthetics are often visible in Auden's early poetry; and this new poem begins in cinematic style and with a volley of imperatives:

> Consider this and in our time
> As the hawk sees it or the helmeted airman:
> The clouds rift suddenly—look there
> At cigarette-end smouldering on a border
> At the first garden party of the year.[23]

When he composed this poem (from now on, "Consider this"), Auden was feeling debilitated after his operation. Perhaps readers are invited to sense that there is a faintly compensatory tone here, as if someone feeling weak were trying to disguise that vulnerability by barking orders. The earth seen from the air is familiar through Auden's love of Hardy's "hawk's vision." Here, it is present in the view of the poet's surrogate, the hawk-like "helmeted airman," and it emphasizes clarity of visual particulars: first, in this opening scene, with a zoomed-in shot of a "cigarette-end" and soon after with a long-shot "view of the massif" (52).

An emphasis on precision of seeing was one of the essential markers of modern poetry during the period in which Auden started writing. Images such as "fallen bicycles like huddled corpses" (to cite an example from the opening part of Auden's most ambitious Berlin poem) set his work within the paradigm of visual sharpness in modern poetry inaugurated by images like H.D.'s "pointed pines" of crashing ocean water in "Oread" and the glistening "petals" of Pound's "In a Station of the Metro."[24] The critic and poet Randall Jarrell noted in 1942 as one of his "general characteristics of modern poetry" a "great emphasis on details— on parts, not wholes. . . . Poetry exploits particulars."[25] This is clarifying in relation to Auden's lines here. But, beyond noting particularly vivid visual details, Auden's drive is toward a synthesis between parts and wholes. In his poem's opening section, he offers a view of what he calls the "insufficient units" (meaning, perhaps, various inadequate people or groups). These "units" are a set of private parties who are "constellated at reserved tables" in the "Sport Hotel" (52). "Constellated" pinpoints the members of the sinister group "in furs, in uniform" in the hotel like individual stars, but at the same time it unites them into a pattern, a constellation, with a greater meaning.

This synthesizing move is then repeated in a different manner as Auden transitions from a single scene to a wider view composed of specific people, geographically separate but still "constellated," now by technology. He does this by taking up the idea of a radio network bringing a dispersed audience of isolated people together as they collectively listen to the same musical performance by a "band" made up of individuals joined together for the collective endeavor of music making. The "insufficient units" are:

> Supplied with feelings by an efficient band
> Relayed elsewhere to farmers and their dogs
> Sitting in kitchens in the stormy fens. (52)

Like so many Auden poems, "Consider this" is composed in three parts, each organized into a verse paragraph. Already secreted within the particulars of the poem's opening scene is the germ of the next section. The "cigarette-end smouldering" is a brilliant flip of the normal word order (which would be a "smouldering cigarette-end"), that in

Auden's version puts the adjective next to the tip of the hyphenated noun, the "cigarette-end," that is doing the "smouldering" as if the word "smouldering" were like the ash about to flake off the lit cigarette. The ominous-sounding detail of the cigarette, along with the "Dangerous" units and the "stormy fens," hint at a coming crisis.

As the poem's second paragraph unfolds, the nature of that crisis becomes clearer. Auden again addresses a metaphysical presence in biblically heightened language, as he had in "Sir, no man's enemy." This time though, it is not God but the "supreme Antagonist," all humanity's enemy, so to speak, that the poem talks to. This is a figure that is easy to read as a version of Satan. (Satan's name in Hebrew means "adversary," and in the first book of *Paradise Lost* Milton refers to Satan as the "arch-enemy."[26]) The "Antagonist" has a network of the militantly diseased whom he can summon into action at the time of his choice:

> You talk to your admirers every day
> By silted harbours, derelict works,
> In strangled orchards, and the silent comb
> Where dogs have worried or a bird was shot.
> Order the ill that they attack at once:
> Visit the ports and, interrupting
> The leisurely conversation in the bar
> Within a stone's throw of the sunlit water,
> Beckon your chosen out. (52)

Once again, this world might appear just as a disparate collection of colorful pathologies haunting an entropic landscape of "silted harbours, derelict works, | . . . strangled orchards." But it acquires deeper meaning as it is revealed to be a world within which a secret army of Satanic followers are ready to begin an apocalyptic battle. On command, these angry recruits will do the Antagonist's work, "Scattering the people, as torn-up paper | Rags and utensils in a sudden gust, | Seized with immeasurable neurotic dread" (52).

The Antagonist's army forms an ironically unified whole that will rip apart the unwitting groups of the pseudo-healthy who are described in the third and final part of the poem. These are self-satisfied, wealthy, and placid people, those primly sheltered in colleges and ecclesiastical establishments, as well as various others, as a derisory phrase puts it, who are "seekers after happiness." Once the interior revolution breaks out, there will be no escape. The privileged are destined "After some haunted migratory years | To disintegrate on an instant" (53).

The exact scenario that this memorable poem—which often seems to be hovering somewhere on the border between bullying and camp—envisages is unclear. But it seems to be that, "in our time," the Antagonist's diseased followers are so committed and numerous that they will create an upheaval destroying the complacent middle class. However, more important than the details of this vaguely revolutionary scheme is the effort the poem makes to flesh out a surreal, religiously flavored vision. It imagines a vast collective world in which different parts are unknowingly related in a whole, just as the "Financier, . . . typist and . . . boy" all work within a system to make money that is spent elsewhere (53).

The vision described is one of disaster and collapse. In an ironic key, the poem presents a picture not of the moral adventures of a single individual but of a communal fate in which all are implicated. And the poem thinks through this perspective about a collective destiny not just thematically but stylistically. Auden, Spender, and Isherwood saw many newsreels during visits to Berlin cinemas during their days and nights in the city. Auden does not dramatize a clearly particularized speaker anywhere within his poem's setting, and the poem's political commitments seem morally ambiguous. But he does project to readers a strong presence in the poem. That speaker's presence has authority to point, remark, explain—it works something like the magisterial, disembodied voice in the darkness commenting calmly on the scenes of financial chaos being shown in newsreels at contemporary movie theaters in the wake of the economic catastrophe of the Wall Street Crash.

Such a voice, both in a newsreel and in a poem, seeks anonymously to establish its power to reveal the realities behind complex and contradictory phenomena, and it does so by naming, instructing, and reassuring its audience about the meaning of events. In doing this, the poetic voice brings momentarily into being a community with a shared understanding. The experience of reading a poem like this is not only of admiring literary style or learning about a poet's ideas but, through a process of manufactured consent, of becoming, for a while, part of a secular congregation of the like-minded. The poem is designed not just to convey content but to make readers experience a sense of belonging. Auden's poetry is not only describing an atomized, unhealthy society but also suggesting that through the right poetic language, it might be able to remake and unify that society too.

Throughout Auden's life, whether he was currently describing himself as agnostic or Christian, Easter, the mythological moment of death and rebirth, was a point in the year with special imaginative significance for him as a poet. Thus, the emotional awakening described in "It was Easter" is set, as the poem tells us, on Easter Day 1929. As Auden sought to recuperate further from his fistula operation a year later, in early April 1930, he went up to the family home in the Lake District. On Easter Sunday, 20 April 1930, in Wesco, still convalescing, he wrote the wild, preachy, demagogic poem beginning, "Get there if you can and see the land you once were proud to own" (from now on, "Get there if you can").[27] It is not just a poem written at Easter; it is an Easter poem.

Auden borrows the meter and the stanzaic form of Tennyson's two very idiosyncratic "Locksley Hall" poems: two "fifteener" lines of trochaic octameter (with the last, unstressed syllable omitted) in rhyming couplets that are set off as two-line stanzas.[28] Auden's imitation of Tennyson is virtuosic and ornate, and it has a relentless, driving regularity. This is the first significant moment in his writing life in which he uses a poetic form that goes beyond relatively commonplace set pieces such as the sonnet, a poem in quatrains, a poem in blank verse, or one of Hardy's convoluted but brief stanza forms. Auden's Easter 1929 poem from Berlin talks about those whose deaths are the "necessary condition of the season's setting forth" as a counterpoint to the emergence of the "fresh hand with fresh power."[29] Here, the following year, in a poem that is formally magisterial, the focus is almost exclusively on weakness, sickness, and the decayed condition of English society. The people with a positive vision of renewal are all dead. In their absence, "we" have to decide if we want to live, or "If we don't, it doesn't matter, but we'd better start to die" (46).

In what ways is this an Easter poem, if we disregard the possibility that it simply lingers ironically on the idea of death at a solemn moment of renewal? One way to answer that question is to see that Auden gives his readers the faintest glimmerings of a new vision, glimmerings also visible in the recently completed "Consider this." Here, he sketches another entropic panorama, suffused with feelings of trauma and rage:

> Smokeless chimneys, damaged bridges, rotting wharves and
>   choked canals,
> Tramlines buckled, smashed trucks lying on their side across
>   the rails;
>
> Powers-stations locked, deserted, since they drew the boiler fires;
> Pylons fallen or subsiding, trailing dead high-tension wires.
>
> Head-gears gaunt on grass-grown pit-banks, seams abandoned
>   years ago;
> Drop a stone and listen for its splash in flooded dark below.
>   (44–45)

The possible "splash" in the "flooded dark" is the tiny, enigmatic hint of poetic regeneration discernible beyond the surface of social wreckage.[30]

In the late winter of 1939, Auden wrote a letter to his father in which he responded to his parent's stated ambition for his son to be "the mouthpiece of an epoch." (Dr. Auden, who asked a lot of himself, also expected much from his sons.) Auden replied: "If he wishes to be the mouthpiece of his age, as every writer does, it must be the last thing he thinks about. Tennyson for example *was* the Victorian mouthpiece in *In Memoriam* when he was thinking about Hallam and his grief. When he decided to be the Victorian Bard and wrote *Idylls of the King,* he ceased to be a poet."[31] The letter shows that Auden understands a poet to be a "mouthpiece" for more than just one person; a poet needs social representativeness. The example from a different era that comes to Auden's mind, as he discusses this idea, is Tennyson. So "Get there if you can," written as a pseudo-Tennysonian pastiche, signals (like something that claims to be a joke but conveys a serious message) Auden's desire to be born, or to grow, as a writer with a voice that incorporates other voices and speaks on their behalf. But the letter from 1939 also shows that Auden believes writing as a representative voice does not mean writing what an audience thinks it wants to hear or what it might easily recognize as representative. "Truth always rests with the minority," Kierkegaard wrote.[32] Poets, for Auden, focus on what means most to them, however trivial or nonsensical it might seem—and they have faith that its "truth" connects with something bigger than their own personal wants and anxieties.

In both these senses, "Get there if you can" is a poem in which the work's overall "content" matters less than the sense of a new poetic voice coming into being. Easter marks the death of a god-human who is then reborn as humanity's redeemer. The idea of poetry with a transformational or redemptive power is a messianic fantasy that Auden embraces and reacts against throughout the period from 1929 to 1936.

A few months after Auden wrote "Get there if you can," he composed an apparently despairing little lyric for his play "The Fronny."[33] The lyric has survived the disappearance of much of the rest of the play's text. In this poem, a speaker bemoans at length the triviality and venality of the country's population: "I saw them lie by letter | I saw them hide their fears." Though simpler, livelier, and more dramatic, this catalogue of faults is similar to the scenes of decay described in "Get there if you can." And in "The Fronny" poem, Auden's speaker's response is exasperated and dismissive. The poem ends: "I saw them and I said as I took my hat | 'No doctor in England can cure all of that.'"[34] Someone other than a doctor, though, the poem's line of thought runs, perhaps some other type of healer, perhaps a poet, *might* be able to "cure all of that."

"Get there if you can" looks at one level like a return to the wrecked landscapes of Auden's earlier "battlefield poems," discussed in Chapter 4. But there is a difference. In this stirring, hortatory lyric, Auden uses again a phrase that he had used only once before. As he looks around for guides, he finds false leaders and martyrs:

> When we asked the way to Heaven, these directed us ahead
> To the padded room, the clinic and the hangman's little shed.
>
> Intimate as war-time prisoners in an isolation camp,
> Living month by month together, nervy, famished, lousy, damp.
>
> On the sopping esplanade or from our dingy lodgings we
> Stare out dully at the rain which falls for miles into the sea.
>
> Lawrence, Blake and Homer Lane, once healers in our English land;
> These are dead as iron for ever; these can never hold our hand. (45)

Here, Auden denounces the absence of healers in "our *English land*." As he does, he gives, by negation, one of the first glimpses of a new role he imagined for himself, that of a collective, regenerative voice, a new "healer" with a national focus. The emergence in Auden's poetry of the subject of England coincided with the very start of his writing. As seen earlier, the poem "California" imagines a relationship between the human and the divine or supernatural that is modeled on the closeness of "a man" to English nature: "A man could walk along that track | Fetch the moon and bring it back," the very young Auden writes. Or he could "gather stars up in his hand | Like strawberries on *English land*."[35]

After a long hiatus, England, or "English land," suddenly reappears in Auden's work in "Get there if you can" in 1930. The situation in the "land" that draws the poet's attention toward national questions is one of social crisis and entropy. More specifically, the poem laments the bourgeoisie's tragic hounding to death of the writers, or "healers": it is telling that when Auden imagines literature's social function he uses the medical term "healer" as an honorific label for some of his favorite writers. These "healers" might have regenerated the country through the energies that can be tapped from the unconscious and the irrational.

As the lines about the dead healers indicate, the poem sees the full advent of a rousing, mock-threatening, schoolmasterish voice that Auden has been playing with on and off in his poems for around six months. It is also sounded in earlier poems such as "It is time for the destruction of error," "Sir, no man's enemy," "Which of you waking early," and "Consider this."[36] But, more significantly, "Get there if you can" also functions as a significant milestone on Auden's poetic journey southward from his northern fastnesses toward a home-counties landscape of "tennis, . . . motor cars, . . . continental villas [and] cocktails" beside the "sopping esplanade" and the "dingy lodgings" of holiday towns (45). This southern world would feature very importantly in the landscape of his work in the next few years, but, paradoxically, he only reached that world imaginatively by a roundabout way, first going north to live and write in Scotland.

In April 1930, Auden arrived at Larchfield Academy, just west of Glasgow on the Firth of Clyde, the deepest stretch of coastal water in the United Kingdom. Humphrey Carpenter described the school, which had seen much better days, as a "preparatory establishment catering for boys between six and thirteen, with just a few older pupils.

The forty or so boys were taught in bleak, old-fashioned buildings lit by gas jets."[37] In the autumn of 1930, some months after he came to Larch-field Academy, Auden wrote a poem about what it meant to work in a setting like this. In the poem, the institution is brilliantly ambiguous, with overtones of somehow being at once a hotel, a barracks, an asylum, and a school. Auden begins buoyantly: "What siren zooming is sounding our coming."[38] But the poem tracks the way that absorption into institutional life leads inexorably to lowered horizons and the "slight despair | At what we are." Ultimately, its denizens

> In groups forgetting the gun in the drawer
> Need pray for no pardon, are proud till recalled
>> By music on water
>> To lack of stature
>> Saying Alas
>> To less and less. (120)

The poem is addressed to the writer Edward Upward, who, like Auden, had taken a job with "lack of stature" as a schoolmaster (in Upward's case, at the Boys' High School in Scarborough, a less-than-glamorous resort on the North Sea coast in Yorkshire).[39]

The unusual, bifurcated, T-shaped stanza form—almost resembling an architectural overhead diagram of a school floor plan—is rich with the ambivalent assonances and half rhymes that were becoming so characteristic of Auden's work by now. The poem describes the gradual draining away of initial energy and "ginger pluck" in those who work in a run-down place like a provincial school until, in a beautiful, final onomatopoeic image, the "pwffwungg of burner" or a gas jet being turned off in a school dormitory becomes a muted signal of "Accepting dearth | The shadow of death" (120). Death is the poem's last word, but the ode is also a beginning. As it turned out, this strange, melancholic, explicitly autobiographical poem about professional life, was the first element of a book-length work that Auden was to write in Helensburgh, mainly between February and November 1931, called *The Orators: An English Study.*

The completed version of *The Orators* is divided into three wildly surreal books or parts, with a prologue and an epilogue. Seeking to bring an order to the melancholic exuberance and beautiful chaos in Auden's book,

John Fuller has described the overarching theme as "the quest for social and spiritual health," while Edward Mendelson writes that it is "an account of everything a group ought not to be" as well as "a study of language, a transcript of the rhetorics that make a group coalesce and decay."[40] These are valuable summaries, but my feeling is that *The Orators* is a less abstract project than this and that, beneath the camouflage of the intellectual explanations that Auden typically and habitually provided to inquiring friends and admirers and that have been inherited by scholars, *The Orators* has more to do with his own life and his sense of inner disorder and futility than it does with impersonal themes. Once again, he takes his own idiosyncratic intuitions as representative, "Rummaging into his living," until he "fetches | The images out that hurt and connect."[41]

In books 1 and 2, *The Orators* is apparently the story of an attempted rebellion against the forces of a repressive regime that has a strong resemblance to bourgeois English society. The leader of this rebellion is a mysteriously nameless, dead "airman," and the first book, "The Initiates," was, Auden explained to a friend, about "the development of the influence of the Hero (who never appears at all)," tracing the formation of a group around memories of the airman's charismatic personality.[42] It is wholly in keeping with Auden's continuing, haunted fascination with the aftermath of the First World War that he should structure this book around the impact on others of a military figure's death. The second book, titled "Journal of an Airman," is like a diary discovered in a drawer after the hero who wrote it dies. It is the airman's own version of his extraordinarily eccentric (batty might be a better word) attempt at a rebellion, ending, apparently, with his departure on a suicidal mission that he has decided is his only way of defeating the Enemy.

Auden at first intended to complete *The Orators* with these two books. But sometime in the autumn of 1931, he gathered together five odes he had written in the previous months, including "What siren zooming is sounding our coming," composed one more ode, and added them all together as what he told Eliot was "the third and last part" of *The Orators*.[43] This last book is the only one of the three to be made up entirely of poetry.

Even as its frantic, jump-cutting, surrealist energies made it difficult for contemporary readers to interpret, *The Orators* was quickly recognized as a significant poetic achievement when it was published in 1932. In the spring of 1926, Auden and Tom Driberg had read *The Waste Land* together with "growing awe."[44] Little more than six years later, in October 1932, the bibliophile and critic John Hayward (who had been at Gresham's with Auden) wrote a review of *The Orators* in the *Criterion*, linking it to the impact of the First World War and to what had happened to English poetry in the wake of Eliot: "The generation, for whom the last war is a confused memory of darkened windows, margarine and fearful visions in the pages of the 'Illustrated London News'; of fathers and elder brothers returning on leave with bits of shrapnel and pressed wild flowers; of drawing-rooms littered with cretonne bags and skeins of wool; that generation has grown up since the publication of 'The Waste Land', ten years ago." And he called Auden's book "the most valuable contribution to English poetry" since Eliot's landmark poem.[45] His statement, published in the *Criterion*, suggested that his view carried Eliot's imprimatur: besides being the *Criterion*'s editor, Eliot was the publisher of the book under review.

Subsequently, *The Orators* has attracted a large amount of attention from literary critics and scholars—as mentioned, Mendelson and Fuller have intricately plotted the many intellectual sources for *The Orators* and most specifically the sources for books 1 and 2, which are mostly in prose. Critical analyses have usefully linked these books to an anthropological paper that John Layard published in the second half of 1930 on the results of the research that he undertook on his trip to Vanuatu (then called the New Hebrides), initially with W. H. R. Rivers and A. C. Haddon, where he lived on the tiny island of Atchin off Malakula from 1914 to 1915. Mendelson calls this paper, which deals with epilepsy and trickster rituals, the "hidden key" to *The Orators*.[46] But another key, if there is such a thing, might be found in *The Orators* itself. And that key lies in the transition between books 2 and 3, between the fictional airman's journal (largely in prose) in the second part and the third part's largely personal poetic odes that Auden wrote about his and his friends' lives.

The first five of the six odes in book 3 have a strongly autobiographical tenor and are addressed to pupils, colleagues, and friends. As described already, in a strictly chronological sense the whole work began in October 1930 with the composition of Ode III, "What siren zooming is sounding our coming," which is about life as a schoolteacher, the profession that Auden had now adopted. Ode I, the second piece of *The Orators* to be completed (in January 1931) before Auden had written much of books 1 and 2, carries even more significance for understanding of the work as a whole. In *The Orators'* final form, the placing of Ode I after the wild fictional scenario developed in books 1 and 2 suggests that Auden intends the story of the airman's revolt against the Enemy to be seen as a fantasy dramatization of his own divided and ambivalent experiences.

In the winter and spring of 1931, Auden was writing Ode I and just starting on book 1 of *The Orators,* in which he projects his own voice into different fictional characters, as if he were trying on a set of literary costumes. At the same time, he was doing a more literal version of the same thing, taking part in rehearsals for a production of J. M. Barrie's *A Kiss for Cinderella* (1916), which the local amateur theatrical company was putting on. He had three small roles in the play, including one as a lame, one-eyed war veteran, Danny.[47]

Because composition of *The Orators* had begun with book 3's poetic autobiographies, with the elaborate fictional scenarios of books 1 and 2 developing after that, the first two books function a bit like the stylistically anomalous dream sequence reflecting John Nower's divided psyche in *Paid on Both Sides* where the fantasy is a projection of actual events in the charade's world. In *The Orators,* the link between the autobiographical real world and the fantasy world of the airman's attempted revolution is made in the transition between books 2 and 3. The final words of the "Journal of an Airman" in book 2 are the airman's notations of conditions inner and outer as he takes off before dawn on his final, fatal journey.

> 3.40 a.m. Pulses and reflexes, normal.
> Barometric reading, 30.6.
> Mean temperature, 34° F.,
> Fair. Some cumulus cloud at 10,000 feet. Wind easterly
> and moderate.
> Hands in perfect order. (113)[48]

The words immediately following this are the opening lines of Ode I in book 3, where "in middle night," Auden converts the obvious meaning of "plane" (as in the airman's aircraft) to another meaning (a flat surface in space), as he recalls spending the last days of 1930 and the start of 1931 in Berlin on a holiday visit:

> Watching in three planes from a room overlooking the
> courtyard
> That year decaying,
> Stub-end of year that smoulders to ash of winter,
> The last day dropping;
> Lo, a dream met me in middle night, I saw in a vision
> Life pass as a gull, as a spy, as a dog-hated dustman:
> Heard a voice saying—"Wystan, Stephen, Christopher, all of
> you,
> Read of your losses". (114–115)

This is a New Year poem—Auden gave it the title of "January 1, 1931" in a later collection.[49] At the end of Ode I, readers learn that the courtyard is "far below" Auden's room in the city, thus establishing height (besides "plane") as another shared property of the situation in which the airman's final words in book 2 occur and the very different location of the opening words of the "I" who speaks this poem in book 3.[50] The airman is aloft, and so is the ode's speaker: there is a clear rhyme between the books right at the moment of transition. Other similarities connect the last glimpse of the airman at the end of book 2 and the awakening "Auden" in Ode I at the start of book 3. These include the mention of "Pulses and reflexes" in the airman's last entry in his "Journal," which is echoed in Ode I's recollection of a "Lent scene," a few lines later, when Auden remembers a visit by the night nurse to check on his condition as he was coming round from the "morphia" after his operation in Birmingham in March 1930.

To solidify the links between the story of the airman and the story of the poet, at the end of Ode I, Auden returns to the scene in the Berlin courtyard above which he is waking up. It is a beautiful, plausible ending to the poem—urgent, mysterious, and yet mundane. Sleep itself, as well as drowsing off and waking, are among Auden's favorite poetic states, because he is a writer deeply at home in the shadowlands where thought and intuition merge. At the very start of the fictional story of the airman's revolt in book 1 in *The Orators*, a fantastical speaker at a school prize day had launched a volley of questions ("What does it mean? What does it mean? . . . What does it mean to us, here now? It's a facer, isn't it, boys?") (77). And at the end of the first ode in book 3, through his drowsy consciousness, Auden hears a beggar shouting in the courtyard.

The man's voice seems in a dreamlike way to be asking another volley of questions, this time about ancient Greek history:

> "Won't you speak louder?
> Have you heard of someone swifter than Syrian horses?
> Has he thrown the bully of Corinth in the sanded circle?
> Has he crossed the Isthmus already? is he seeking brilliant
>   Athens and us?" (115)[51]

In retrospect, readers begin to suspect that everything happening in books 1 and 2 is a fevered fit or fantasy projection, both surreal and revelatory, of the underlying realities of the life that the speaker of the poems in book 3 is leading in contemporary Berlin and Scotland. Only something that looks bizarre, as the description of the airman's revolt in books 1 and 2 does, can measure up to the chaos of the school world, and more broadly, English social and economic life, that Auden so vividly and self-implicatingly describes in book 3.

For most of Ode I, the speaker, half awake and half asleep, casts the bulk of the poem in the form of a dream-vision filled with details about his own life and the activities of his friends, including Spender and Isherwood, as he looks back on the events of 1930. Some of these vignettes are autobiographical and personal, while some he views as "general but in sorrow" as he wistfully realizes that "Neither in the bed nor on the arête was there shown me | One with power" (115). The dream culminates when the "voice" (the voice of the beggar in the courtyard whose words keep breaking into the dream) reacts to the panorama of social and psychological misery:

> "Save me!" the voice commanded, but as I paused hesitant
>   A troop rushed forward
> Of all the healers, granny in mittens, the Mop, the white
>   surgeon,
> And loony Layard. (115)[52]

As the call for help rings out, the hesitation that overcomes Auden allows a troop of pseudo-healers and cranks (unlike the real but dead healers from "Get there if you can"), including "loony Layard," Auden's friend, to burst forward and take up the redemptive task. And then Auden wakes to hear the beggar, whose voice was speaking in ciphered form through the dream, crying in the street below. *The Orators* as a whole is that "hesitant," confused, half-real, and half-unreal moment before Auden was to respond in his own way to what he interpreted as the country's call for salvation.

After Ode I, the following poems, or odes, contain some of the work's most charged content both politically and erotically. They also waver back and forth between an optimistic but bullying energy and an elegiac pessimism (the latter being the note that I would say is closer to Auden's poetic soul). In Ode II, dedicated to William McElwee, Auden celebrates the triumph of a Sedbergh School rugby team in a parody of Hopkins's homoerotic exultations in poems such as "To what serves mortal beauty." In Ode III, as already seen, Auden writes to Upward about the gradual draining of spirit attendant on work in an institution such as a school. Ode IV celebrates John Warner, the infant son of Frances Warner and his Oxford friend Rex Warner, in terms that, as Auden explained in 1965, show "all the sentiments with which his followers hailed the advent of Hitler, but these are rendered, I hope, innocuous by the fact that the Führer so hailed is a new-born baby and the son of a friend."[53]

These oscillations between optimism and fatalism, hectoring and vulnerability, mirror social realities both in the later part of 1931, when Auden was writing many of the odes for *The Orators,* and also in much of the earlier part of the year, when he was writing the work's first two books. Contemporary history in Britain was swinging wildly from one crisis to another. In an April 1931 "Commentary," Eliot felt compelled to admit that "the present system not only does not work well now but will probably never work well again. . . . The present time may well be as critical, or more critical, than the war."[54] After a budgetary crisis for the country, there followed the collapse of the Labour government in August 1931, the departure of Britain from the gold standard in September, and the near eradication of the Labour Party in the October 1931 general election. Britain confronted what seemed an unprecedented situation, generating an interlocking web of political, economic, and social problems.

Writing at this time, the historian Arnold Toynbee described 1931 as the "*annus terribilis,*" when "men and women all over the world were seriously contemplating and frankly discussing the possibility that the Western system of society might break down and cease to work."[55]

D. S. Mirsky, a Russian critic and literary historian who had emigrated to Britain in 1921, was a combative and acute witness to these events. Mirsky explained that the British intelligentsia's renewal of interest in politics in 1931 increased its "need for a world view, for a system." And he added: "The purpose of this system was to save an intellectual from being isolated, to provide him with a group, to enable him to feel part of some greater whole, to elaborate a system of arguments to justify the aims of the whole, and in short to provide him with a key to the chaos."[56] Auden's faith in this period is, precisely, in what Mirsky called the "group." And, for Auden, that group's life had a very specific, localized form, too: it is an "English" group.

In October 1931, the month of the general election that would usher in a National Government, Auden told Isherwood in a letter: "I've had a most important vision about groups which is going to destroy the Church."[57] Auden's comment about a "vision" could be taken as just a flip, self-deprecatory remark. But I think it should be treated almost literally. Auden's poetry from these years (Ode I in *The Orators* is an obvious example) is filled with dreams, prophecies, intuitions. Books and ideas are an important part of Auden's inspiration, but in my estimation, all kinds of nonrational movements of consciousness matter as much, or more, to him as an artist. Ode I, centered on a dream, is a litmus test of exactly how readers prefer to interpret Auden's work. Given his emerging sense of himself as poetic prophet in a crisis atmosphere, Auden genuinely believed he was subject to significant visions. At this period, his friend Margaret Gardiner once had Auden staying with her in Cambridgeshire, where she had taken up work as a schoolteacher. She was shocked and feared a scandal with her landlady when, early one morning, Auden walked into Gardiner's room in his pajamas, oblivious, or indifferent, to gendered social niceties, and "sat down on the end of my bed." Then, he announced, "I've had the most extraordinary dream."[58] This is Auden in the late 1920s and early 1930s— an enraptured dreamer-poet.

The vision that Auden mentions in his letter to Isherwood probably appears in camouflaged, ironized form in Ode IV, a poem he wrote in the same month, October 1931, as he sent the letter to his friend. Ode IV asks: "Who will save? Who will teach us how to behave?" The Messiah who would "save John Bull" was the little baby John Warner. He is "Our gadget, our pride, | Our steel-piercing bullet, our burglar-proof

FIG. 5 *Auden in a dressing gown, in a portrait probably taken around 1931, by a Helensburgh friend and fellow schoolteacher, Anne Bristow. Auden wrote on the print a joking quotation about a man's rapid loss of innocence and morals: "Utopian youth grown old Italian," a line from John Donne's poem "To Sir Henry Wotton" (ca. 1597).*

safe" (124). Having "march[ed] on London" and "undone" his enemies, the infant savior will usher in a new order, a totalitarian one:

> The gauche and the lonely he will introduce of course
> To the smaller group, the right field of force;
> The few shall be taught who want to understand,
> Most of the rest shall live upon the land;
> Living in one place with a satisfied face
> All of the women and most of the men
> Shall work with their hands and not think again. (125)[59]

The lonely and the "gauche" (with connotations both of clumsy and leftist) will surely include Auden himself, who was believed in literary circles to have left-wing sympathies, although, as this book has been exploring, that was a far-from-simple, or even accurate, characterization. Auden's assertion that the "gauche" will be introduced to the "smaller group, the right field of force," apparently without any choice in the matter, is a strange, perhaps disturbing moment. But this is what, in *The Orators,* "the season of the change of heart, | . . . The official re-marriage of the whole and the part," means (125). The "change of heart" (the same phrase that appears at the end of "Sir, no man's enemy") is perhaps as much a matter of the writer's political position as it is of the altered morale of the country as a whole. Gone "the tension, over the alarms, | The falling wage, and the flight from the pound" (125). And now John Warner:

> On English earth
> Restores, restore will, has restored
> To England's story
> The directed calm, the actual glory. (126)

Ode IV works hard to present its vision of a redeemer who will correct the chaos in England as an exercise in a slapstick mode. But its lengthily enthusiastic presentation of the idea that a strongman, both terrifying and necessary, has arrived to solve the problems of the democratic state has an unsettling undercurrent.

In Ode V, Auden, the schoolmaster, speaks in despairing, pessimistic terms to his pupils, a scenario that recalls the old boy speaking to the school assembly in the first part of book 1. In the poem, the pupils and masters are conscripts to a struggle between opposing, ambiguously defined forces but that, for them, involves enlistment on the side of the forces of repression. The struggle has become perpetual and meaningless: "Boy," the speaker says, "the quarrel was before your time, the aggressor | No one you know" (127). A final ode, VI, cast as a parody of the Scottish Psalter, also acknowledges that "we" are on the wrong side and are doomed to fail: "Not, Father, further do prolong | Our necessary defeat" (130). This sense of deadlock and resignation is accentuated in the "Epilogue," where a parable about the importance of choice and action ends with an ill-defined feeling of impasse:

> "Out of this house"—said rider to reader
> "Yours never will"—said farer to fearer
> "They're looking for you"—said hearer to horror
> As he left them there, as he left them there. (131)

Although *The Orators* was the subject of critical praise like John Hayward's, within a year of its publication, it also became the subject of some of Auden's most caustic comments on his personal state of mind and his political affiliations. In late 1932, in a letter to an inquirer, Auden implausibly called the book "a stage in my conversion to Communism." But he more consistently associates *The Orators* with the opposite political extreme. For example, on 16 August 1932, just a few months after Faber and Faber issued *The Orators,* Auden told an American correspondent that the book "is far too obscure and equivocal. It is meant to be a critique of the fascist outlook, but from its reception among some of my contemporaries, and on rereading it myself, I see that it can, most of it, be interpreted as a favourable exposition."[60] Sometime later, his comments included calling the book "a catharsis of the author's personal fascism" and even remarking: "My name on the title-page seems a pseudonym for someone else, someone talented but near the border of sanity, who might well, in a year or two, become a Nazi."[61] These startlingly self-critical characterizations are oddly consistent and deserve serious thought. This is part of what, for Auden, it meant to be a national poet in 1931.

"Writing" is an article that Auden began shortly after *The Orators* was completed. He contributed it to an anthology of essays for children that his friend Naomi Mitchison was editing. In the piece, beneath the humane, schoolmasterly tone, there is a clear fascination with moments of force and terror.[62] For example, alluding to Freud's theories, in such works as *Totem and Taboo* (1913) and *Group Psychology and the Analysis of the Ego* (1921), about the birth of culture out of violence, Auden argues in his essay that speech originated in a desire to recover the collective excitement expressed in the "noises, grunts, howls, grimaces" made by a group of men, "when, say, the quarry was first sighted" or, as he puts it later, when "dancing round food or advancing together to attack."[63] Mendelson rightly points out that "a violent confrontation" was one of the "central features of Auden's imaginative world."[64]

Just how distinctively violent (and modern) Auden's scenario is can be calibrated by juxtaposing it with Yeats's ideas in his essay "The Symbolism of Poetry" from 1900, where sound—in contrast to being (as it was for Auden) a recollection of the group's chants during battle or the hunt—exists for the purpose of calling "down among us certain disembodied powers, whose footsteps over our hearts we call emotions." For Yeats, "It is only those things which seem useless or very feeble, that have any power."[65] By the start of the 1930s, Auden has traveled far from the ideas of one of his main poetic models: now those verbal moments of collective life have power to recall the onset of killing.

If we set aside, in *The Orators,* the political valences of hero worship, obscure conspiracies, and a diffuse atmosphere of force, the continuities between that book and Auden's other poems from this period are obvious. "Consider this" and "Get there if you can" offer no practical (or even ideal) solutions to the social and psychological decay they expose. Similarly, there are no resolutions in *The Orators.* But, at the same time, the book does represent a remarkable deepening of Auden's ability to bring a hugely variegated and interconnected world into focus. The volume feels a little like the work produced by the "picked body of angels" whom the speaker at the prize day in book 1 imagines setting off in all directions across Britain: "one to the furnace-crowded Midlands, another to the plum-rich red-earth valley of the Severn, another to the curious delta-like area round King's Lynn," and so on. Then, with "every inch of the ground . . . carefully gone over, every house inspected," they return to collaborate on a "complete report" on the country's moral health (77). *The Orators* is Auden's version of that complete report—a comprehensive and disturbing picture of a nation in crisis.

The encyclopedic drive of Auden's writing in books 1 and 2 demands comparison with Walt Whitman's enormous catalogues of discrete activity among a vast nation of freeholders, slaves, and laborers in *Song of Myself.* In Auden, the catalogues have a surreal and slightly antic quality that is missing from Whitman. But no poem comes closer in an English context than *The Orators* to evoking a massive, Whitman-esque beehive of independent yet interconnected national activity: "One in a red-brick villa makes designs for a bridge, creates beauty for a purpose. One is eloquent, persuades committees of the value of spending: one announces weddings in a solemn voice. One is told secrets at night, can stop a young girl biting her nails. One can extirpate a goitre with little risk. One can foretell the migrations of mackerel; one can distinguish the eggs of sea-birds" (85). Although the airman notes in his "Journal" that "Much more research [is] needed into the crucial problem—group organisation (the real parts)," the book in which he appears marks a decisive advance in Auden's ability to write on behalf of a "group" or a nation (109). It is just that, for now, in the writing of *The Orators,* Auden's ability to portray collectivity is ironically generated by his feeling for a group's pathology, for the widespread penetration of aberrancy, moral failure, aggression, and emotional stuntedness into English life. Within a short span of time, though, this negative vision was to change into something more positive.

In the wake of the political and economic crisis in Britain in 1931, the main year of *The Orators'* writing, many young British authors became self-consciously radicalized and political. Upward, the most committed writer in Auden's circle of acquaintances, had started working for the Communist Party during 1931 and had been on a visit to the Soviet Union during the summer of the same year. Upward's taking up party work had seemed at first "an extraordinary action" to Spender and Isherwood, but they rapidly became greatly affected by it.[66] After meeting Upward in Berlin in August 1931, Spender wrote to John Lehmann that "I think we have all become communists."[67] And by December of the same year, Spender was telling Vita Sackville-West that his friends were "almost exclusively . . . young communists."[68]

However, in the 1930s, dissident ideological energy and intense criticism of the current social order were as likely to emanate from the right as from the left, as the examples of Eliot and Lewis show. In his April 1931 *Criterion* "Commentary," Eliot insisted (praising "some germs of intelligence" in a pamphlet outlining Oswald Mosley's political program) that "the nineteenth century is over, and . . . a thorough reorganisation of industry and of agriculture is essential."[69] Isherwood had recognized in himself at Cambridge a temptation to "homosexual romanticism," centering on a daydream of a career as "an austere young prefect" in which, having triumphed over all obstacles, he would emerge "a Man." The "rulers of Fascist states . . . profoundly understand and make use of such phantasies and longings," Isherwood later wrote. "I wonder how, at this period, I should have reacted to the preaching of an English fascist leader clever enough to serve up his 'message' in a suitably disguised and palatable form? He would have converted me, I think, inside half an hour."[70] Auden, in such close creative symbiosis with Isherwood throughout the 1930s, and so sensitive to the danger of his own "personal fascism," saw in himself similar aspirations and weaknesses. Talking to Spender in Oxford around 1928, Auden said cryptically that "at heart, the poet's sympathies are always with the enemy."[71]

In Auden's case, the nature of the political resolutions that he imagined to the crisis of the time is coded into the frequent use of the language of nationhood, which recurs in a set of important poems from this period: as when, for example, he writes about "our English land" (from "Get there if you can") or "English earth" (from *The Orators,* which is subtitled an "English study").[72]

In some of these important "English" poems, Auden is striving to represent not just the world of literary coteries but a broader expanse of the English middle classes. That is made clear in a letter he wrote in December of the *annus terribilis,* 1931, to the poet and anthologist Michael Roberts, who had asked Auden to work on a magazine with him. Behind the youthful, self-mocking swagger, there seems to be a tone of seriousness in Auden's response: "About this magazine. What are [you] really out to do? Discuss Economics or cause a Revolution? If the former I'm not interested. If the latter, good, but have you the money. We want cyclostyled satires dropped by aeroplanes and all that."[73] He alludes to the doomed, heroic gesture of the Italian antifascist and amateur aviator Lauro De Bosis, who, on 3 October 1931, after dropping hundreds of thousands of political leaflets into the skies over Rome, was killed when his plane crashed. But in a way that only Auden (and not Roberts) would have recognized prior to publication of *The Orators,* Auden is also referring in this letter to his own quasi-fascist airman's plan to have "10,000 Cyclostyle copies" of his poem "Beethameer, Beethameer, bully of Britain," written in rhyme royal, made "for aerial distribution" (105). (This poem in *The Orators* marks the first use of the rhyme royal stanza form in Auden's work.[74]) After Auden's airman has taken off on his fatal, final journey, he will scatter copies of "Beethameer, Beethameer" in a dream-parallel to the scattering, through publication and distribution, of *The Orators* itself.

Auden continues, only half flippantly, in his reply to Roberts: "Secondly, if you are out for propaganda, who do you want to reach? I cannot state too clearly that no paper which does not set out to preach to the vicarages and golf-clubs and Badminton courts, is of the slightest interest to me."[75] In the wake of finishing *The Orators*, Auden soon attempts, in a simplified style, to create pictures of English society as a whole that at least aspire to reach toward a constituency in the "vicarages and golf-clubs and Badminton courts." Indeed, all three settings appear in his two-part poem "A Happy New Year," written within a couple of months of this pronouncement to Roberts.[76] And this poem also includes a vignette of a pilot in a "Bristol Fighter" who, like the earlier crazed airman, "threw down a paper which fell at [the speaker's] feet."[77]

Motifs and phrases from the syncretic, mystical historian and pundit Gerald Heard's two major books on human evolution, *The Ascent of Humanity*, published in 1929, and *Social Substance of Religion*, published two years later, in 1931, begin to appear in clusters in Auden's writing around the end of 1931 and the start of 1932.[78] In "A Happy New Year," which is a key poem, though Auden published it in its entirety only once, in the anthology *New Country* in 1933, there is one of the first directly traceable influences of Heard's ideas on Auden's poetry. The poem is also the first of Auden's ambitious attempts, in the wake of completing *The Orators*, to project again an "English" totality. "A Happy New Year," dedicated to Heard, is a perfect example of the way in which Auden's work was moving, under Heard's guidance, from *Orators*-like obscurity to lucidity and to a kind of subtle hopefulness. Indeed, the Janus-faced structure of this two-part poem is built around a thematic contrast between disorder and order and a stylistic contrast between verbal overload and poetic simplicity.

Part 1 of "A Happy New Year," written in February 1932 in Helensburgh, revisits the surreal anarchy of *The Orators*, including another use of rhyme royal for the central dream-vision in this part of the poem. The airman in *The Orators* had provided the first use of this stanza form in Auden's work in "Beethameer, Beethameer, bully of Britain." This is the poem that was to be dropped in a shower of cyclo-styled copies from the airman's plane. In a symbolic sense, the rhyme royal form floats down out of *The Orators* into a new poetic place here in "A Happy New Year." In a letter to Isherwood, Auden referred to the new poem, "A Happy New Year," as "a Helensburgh Vision."[79]

Liberated from school duties by the end-of-term examination period, Auden's speaker ascends the moorland above Helensburgh, and there, at a moment of silence and stillness, the "secret-bearing sensitive taut line | Which south into alluvial England ran" begins vibrating, precipitating in Auden an auditory vision that seems to be calling him back toward his home country: "The age of migrations is over and gone. . . . I show you a cooled soil, fertile for grain, | A land of rivers, a maternal plain." It urges him—using the story of Moses and the biblical phrase for the territory promised to the Israelites—to "Look down, look down at your promised land" (137–138). It is as if, as Fuller remarks, "from such a height, even though in Scotland, he can see the whole of England."[80] This is an acute observation. The poem dramatizes Auden's poetic self calling him back to England, away from the chaos that is associated (unreasonably, it goes without saying) with Scotland and with political turmoil. In the wake of hearing this message in the "sensitive taut line" in part 1, the second part of the poem will draw Auden further toward his England and to a kind of private order built around the small groups of people, praised as an ideal by Heard.

But, for a moment, this idea is postponed. Moved, in part 1 of "A Happy New Year," into a visionary mood by the sounds he imagines he hears in the telephone wire, Auden begins to see a huge, ragtag "army recruited there" emerging in front of him on the moor: "The English in all sorts and sizes come" (138). They assemble in an ill-coordinated, tawdry, self-obsessed grouping, composed overwhelmingly of the psychologically maimed:

> So much stammering over easy words
> So much laughter spasmodic and queer
> So much speech that resembled a bird's
> So much drawling concealing a fear

So much effort to sound sincere
So much talk which was aimed at the floor
Was never heard in one place before. (140)

The group includes quacks, tycoons, and politicians: Ramsay MacDonald, Stanley Baldwin, Viscount Snowden, Winston Churchill, Oswald
Mosley, the press barons Viscount Rothermere and Lord Beaverbrook,
and so on.[81] Celebrities and the famously frivolous are there as well.
This huge and motley public gathering—which also features musicians,
dispatch riders, poets, and many others besides—is a chaos, an impression enforced on the reader by the plentiful use of a language of mess,
disorder, and irregular movement: "untidy rooms," "Boats on a bay like
toys on a floor," a back wheel that "juddered," drawers that are "constantly
slipping," "laughter spasmodic and queer," and so forth (137–143). The
Edwardian patriarch of English prosody, George Saintsbury, explained
the fit of Auden's stanzaic form here to this kind of subject matter when
he wrote that rhyme royal "can do several things well, and one thing,
the expression of clangorous cry, it can do supremely."[82] In this sense,
the rhyme royal form is an apt choice for the clangor of the first part of
"A Happy New Year."

Part 1's orchestrated chaos arises in part from the separateness of
the poem's speaker. His aloneness is emphasized from the start of the
poem. Liberated on a frosty December day from a social existence in
the school where he teaches, "I stepped and passed | Outside the win-
dows" at a time when "the day [is] my own" (137). The speaker is also
released from a private erotic relation as his worker-lover has returned
to a factory: "Hands miles away were laid on iron | That rested lately in
the dark on us" (137). If this is based on a real person, it must refer to a
now-unknown partner of Auden's in Helensburgh. One of Auden's
other, better-documented lovers in the town was Derek Wedgwood,
but Wedgwood, who does not appear to have had literary interests,
came from an upper-crust local family and had attended public school
at Shrewsbury (where Auden's brother Bernard went) before returning
to Helensburgh. He was unlikely to have been working in a factory, as
the detail of "Hands miles away . . . laid on iron" suggests.[83]

The speaker's self-concern, shading over sometimes into ego-
tism, is touched on in the accumulation of first-person actions: "I
stepped," "I climbed," "I walked," "I stood," "I saw" (137). Inevitably, this

self-isolation returns at the end of the poem as the vision of the mad crowd of "English in all sorts and sizes" disappears. The verse form abandons visionary rhyme royal for a more conventional eight-line stanza, and the speaker is alone again:

> Stillness was total; everyone had gone
> I stared into the road; the snow fell on
> Soundlessly closing on the winter day
> All other feelings died away
> Absorbed in its enormous slight sensation
> Leaving the mind to moralise
> Upon these blurring images
> Of the dingy difficult life of our generation. (144)

The entire first part of "A Happy New Year" dramatizes the perceptions of one who has, as part 2 will put it, "fallen apart | Into the isolated personal life" (145). In terms that seem reminiscent of Trigant Burrow's ideas, Heard insists in *The Ascent of Humanity* that "Man's first consciousness was pre-individual, a group consciousness, [but] is now mainly individual, and is becoming super-individual."[84] For Heard, the "first human unit is the group, not the individual," and our ancestors had a tribal sense that precluded "any consciousness of individual separateness" from the group.[85]

The speaker's isolation in part 1 of Auden's poem reflects Heard's commonplace diagnosis of the problems of modern egotism and individualism. But equally important, and in fact in a symbiotic relation to the speaker's individualism, is the enormous but unsatisfactory attempted collectivization of the poem. This takes the form of a grouping of people on the Scottish moor who can never come into a coordinated whole but instead lurch about, bumping off one another anarchically like the molecules of a gas. Heard's "beloved community," on the other hand, is formed "when two or three are gathered together in the spirit of the future." When that happens, a new consciousness "begins to dominate them, to break down their isolation, to confer new powers, and finally to deliver them into a new unity as real as their former separation."[86] Heard argues that for such a release from imprisoning individualism to take place, people must come together: "It is essential that the 'field,' the group, be kept the right size. Probably the dozen gives the best results."[87] In the large, disordered world that Auden describes outside on the Scottish moor in the first part of "A Happy New Year," no kind of meaningful personal contact is possible: "When eyes met they darted sideways on shame | Or braved it out in an awkward stare" (139).

In reaction, Auden has returned in part 2 of "A Happy New Year" to the more delimited world inside the boarding school's buildings. Part 1 has shown him moving away from his pupils, up onto a remote landscape, alone. Now in part 2, the speaker has come back to his responsibilities and, more importantly, to a shared world, a field, a group.

Wider issues than just personal satisfaction are involved. The dual structure of "A Happy New Year" dramatizes a movement away from formal anarchy, surrealism, irrationalism—all qualities that could be, at least in caricature, associated with the modernism of the 1920s and the politics of the early 1930s (and with the recently completed *The Orators*, where the wild disorder of books 1 and 2 is succeeded by the more formal and personal, albeit still exuberantly eccentric, odes of book 3). The second part of Auden's new poem, "A Happy New Year," gravitates toward restraint and legible form, a kind of stylistic conservatism that was to set the tone for much poetry in the coming decade. Auden's Oxford friend John Betjeman was announcing at the end of 1931 (the moment when Auden's poem is set) that modernism had died as an artistic movement.[88] Betjeman's claims crystallize a transition that plays out much more subtly in Auden's new poem, as it moves from disorder to peace and order. But, for all his hyperbole, Betjeman was identifying an extreme version of a development that was becoming more widespread in much English poetry at the start of the 1930s: a shift away from the fractured, improvisatory poetic forms associated with modernism, toward a new poetics that emphasized more traditional verse patterns and the use of other obvious formal structures.

The bounded world of the school, which Auden returns to in part 2 of "A Happy New Year," reflects Heard's belief that everyone has had in their own life an experience of group unity and unity with the world, the conditions that preceded the evolution of modern individuality and self-consciousness. (This was a variant of the idea, commonplace at the time and deriving from the nineteenth-century German naturalist Ernst Haeckel, that phylogeny repeats ontogeny, or that the stages in the embryonic development of a single organism recapitulate the evolutionary developments undergone by that organism's ancestors.) Heard's belief is that this experience of group unity comes in childhood, when young people "who have yet to become acutely self-conscious and individual enjoy that sense of peace and are really aware only of an eternal present."[89] Childhood, then, "is the best clue we have to the state of the pre-civilised psyche."[90] (Heard's views, with which Auden was now so taken, are the exact opposite of those of Dr. Auden, who saw childish individualism as being the more primitive, anarchic state and group consciousness as being the later, more mature, social, and civilized one.[91])

Auden's connection with schools had not been widely noticed until about 1932. The publication of *The Orators* in May of that year serves as a benchmark against which to measure the growth of commentary linking Auden and his places of work. For example, in late 1932, the novelist Graham Greene spoke of the book's "slight smell of school-changing rooms."[92] And the critical success that *The Orators* obtained also led to aggressive linkages between Auden's school world and homosexuality. Hugh Gordon Porteus, a follower of Wyndham Lewis, in February 1933 worried that it "is impossible not to remark Mr. Auden's curious obsession. More than half his imagery, it is little exaggeration to say, is drawn from the rugger field, the labs, and the OTC." And Porteus jibed, with no concern about camouflaging homophobic stereotypes, that Auden's poetry "continues to insist, in a most disquieting manner, on its unimpeachable schoolboy complexion."[93]

Auden's interest in schools and children has a distinct content, not to be confined or reduced to his needing a job as a schoolmaster or to his sexuality, which some reviewers were now beginning to allude to, using bullying code words of the time, such as "adolescent" or "immature." Auden's own prose solidifies the connection that critics saw between his work and the world of school. His first school-associated essay, "Writing," was published in September 1932, the same month that *Scrutiny* published the first in a number of reviews and essays Auden wrote on schools, teaching, and education.[94] A month or so later, his first review for the *New Statesman* was a piece titled "Problems of Education."[95] This turn toward the experiences of childhood and school came in the context of Auden's belief, at least in part adopted from Heard, that the child's world offered access to the pre-individualistic stage of early civilization—a glimpse of the past that could also augur a better future.

Following Heard, Auden was looking for something substantial and precious, something with a distinct social import, that could be found in the world of the school. As he was to write in his letter to his father in 1939, a poet stands a chance of becoming representative, a "mouthpiece of an epoch," only when that poet ignores normative estimations of importance and decorum and focuses instead on their own obsessions.[96] Auden's own work, from its obsession with mines to its immersion in the world of schools, shows him as a writer acting again and again on that conviction.

Here are the opening lines of part 2 of "A Happy New Year:"

> Now from my window-sill I watch the night
> The church clock's yellow face, the green pier light
> Burn for a new imprudent year;
> The silence buzzes in my ear;
> The jets in both the dormitories are out.[97]

Whereas the poem's anarchic first part is narrated in the past tense, the insistent present tense of part 2 mirrors the "eternal present" of Heardian childhood. The public names of celebrated but empty figures in part 1—the politicians mentioned earlier, as well as Lawrence of Arabia, Sir Thomas Horder, Dr. Norman Haire, and others—are modulated in part 2 into the more intimate first names of boys and masters: Favel, Holland, Alexis.[98] The geographical features earlier viewed alone by the Auden-speaker of part 1 on the moors—the Clyde, Glen Fruin, Loch Lomond, and so on—are now played off against the chosen names of private houses in Helensburgh: The Lindens, Ferntower, Westoe, and "this pen" (146).[99] The "frost came at last" in part 1 of the poem, but now, with the year having turned, part 2 is set "in this season when the ice is loosened" (137, 145).

In place of the jaunty, baggy, all-inclusive, and elastic rhyme royal of part 1, Auden now tightens and chastens his stanza form, as if he were drawing the verbal world of his poem into a more shaped and coordinated circle by using an unusual five-line, loosely rhyming stanza. Auden has used the cinquain (a five-line stanza) much earlier, in poems such as "The Dying House," to write about social decay.[100] Here he uses it in a poem about social renewal. The five-line stanza closely correlates at a formal level with the atmosphere described in the poem: the emotional intensity and sense of closeness that come from people sitting around a table to drink tea in a small group, or what Auden calls in the poem the "field of five or six," like the lines of each stanza clustered into groups of five (146). One reason why Auden finds himself writing in five-line stanzas about a unique time and place, and pupils at a boys' school gathered together there, is because he envisaged a link between this closed stanzaic "group" of poetic language and the limited "group" of an ideal society envisaged by Heard. In the "Writing" essay, Auden asserts that "the feeling as it were excites the words and makes them fall into a definite group going through definite dance movements, just as feeling excite[s] the different members of a crowd and makes them act together."[101] His words in this part of "A Happy New Year" form a "definite" stanzaic grouping, reflecting the uniqueness and specificity of the group life portrayed in the poem.

Heard traced the origin of speech and art to a "proto-human circle that thrilled, gesticulated, grunted and hopped while the leaders effected some common purpose."[102] For him, humans needed to recapture a "community sense," a feeling of being part of a group, and one central method that we, as a species, have evolved to do that comes from religious rites and ritual "chant-dances."[103] Once "they are all 'in time,' and in step everyone can sink into the rhythm which expresses urgency," Heard wrote. "The rhythm will thus end by becoming itself an end. The group will find that it enjoys ritual for its own sake, that there is a sense of strange import, worth and well-being in the chant-dance."[104] Because Heard viewed modern cities as vast agglomerations of largely uncoordinated individuals, much of his writing is anti-metropolitan; correspondingly, Auden's "A Happy New Year" is set in a small provincial town where a group enjoys the small ritual of drinking tea together.

Auden's scenario does not involve a dance as such, but the gathering together after a game. In a time of social crisis, he writes tenderly about life in an enclave in the far North:

> At the end of my corridor are boys who dream
> Of a new bicycle or winning team;
> On their behalf guard all the more
> This late-maturing Northern shore,
> Who to their serious season must shortly come. (146)

The tone resonates closely with parts of Yeats's "The Tower," and the line length and rhyme scheme evoke other Yeats poems like "In Memory of Major Robert Gregory." In the latter poem, the first five lines in Yeats's adapted eight-line stanza often take the same form that Auden uses here. (Yeats borrowed the eight-line stanza from Abraham Cowley's seventeenth-century elegy for his friend William Hervey.[105]) There is also a Coleridgean mood present in Auden's poem, evoking the quiet, nighttime atmosphere of that poet's "Frost at Midnight" and "that solitude, which suits | Abstruser musings."[106]

Shortly before he started writing this poem, Auden had talked to Rolf Gardiner, a neo-Lawrentian activist with decidedly right-wing views, who campaigned for rural arts and organic farming practices and worked to promote closer links between German and English cultures. (Rolf was Margaret Gardiner's brother.) Rolf Gardiner believed "in the 'kinship' of German and English youth, compared with the 'Mediterranean peoples.'"[107] In an example of how intriguing Auden could be to some figures on the right, Gardiner came on a visit to see Auden in Helensburgh. During one of their conversations, Gardiner praised the extroverted, militant character of German nationalism, but Auden demurred and contrasted it with English passivity and peaceable rootedness. He defended the English by saying they were "so much older than the G[ermans]" and added that "this hatred of soldierliness, [of] romantic moving about[,] was fundamental to the modern English."[108] In the light of this comment about English quietism, it is clear that the stillness, peace, and contemplativeness in the second part of the "A Happy New Year" poem have a subtly national tenor to them. The serenity and balance in the poem's lines are expressions of Auden's temporarily held ideas about what is characteristic for the nonmilitant, "modern English." In another remark to Rolf Gardiner, this one in a letter of 4 March 1932, he elaborated on what he saw as an English love for a kind of organic slowness: "Remember in England we live on small plots of land; and dawdle. Nothing worth much in personal relations take place in a rush, I think."[109] The gentleness of part 2 of "A Happy New Year," its predictable rhythms and consistent stanzas (so different from the hectoring onrush characteristic of the odes in *The Orators* and from part 1 of "A Happy New Year"), all create a mood of contemplative, slowly unfolding calm that arises, in Auden's belief, from the people and the culture it describes.

However, after setting the meditative scene at his windowsill, representing the boundary between inner and outer worlds, Auden immediately adds, as a contrast, that the "Great Bear | Hangs as a portent over Helensburgh" (145). The Ursa Major constellation is seen as a symbol of impending violent revolution, animating the looming threat of the Soviet "Bear." But the poem is braced to distance itself for as long as possible from such international perspectives and threats, to be "deaf to prophecy or China's drum" (145).

The central drive of the poem is to create a haven or enclave, free, at least for now, from the pressures of contemporary international politics and modern, mercantile civilization. It is fitting, then, that the "Lords of Limit," from Auden's private mythological pantheon, should preside over this schoolboy world. They take the form here of a pair of mythical Super-teachers, "training dark and light" and "Oldest of masters, . . . erratic examiners" (145).[110] Although the Lords of Limit are mysterious, invisible, volatile creatures, Auden begs for indulgence from them for himself and his schoolboy charges: "Look not too closely, be not over quick; | We have no invitation, but we are sick" (145). He pleads with the Lords to preserve the beautiful atmosphere of "swimming-bath and tennis-club" and to be "very very patient, gentlemen," with his pupils. These boys, he writes, "to their serious season must shortly come," in a passage that culminates with a stark self-indictment of poets' characters, requesting that the Lords of Limit:

> Give [the pupils] spontaneous skill at holding rein,
> At twisting dial, or at making fun,
> That these may never need our craft,
> Who, awkward, pasty, feeling the draught,
> Have health and skill and beauty on the brain. (146)

Robert Gregory was a "Soldier, scholar, horseman" in Yeats's poem: "where was it | He rode a race without a bit? | And yet his mind outran the horses' feet."[111] As he implies, Auden, "awkward, pasty, feeling the draught," was one of those who lack "spontaneous skill at holding rein." It must have bothered him. Auden told his brother John that he had agreed to contribute his essay to Naomi Mitchison's anthology so he could learn that skill: "In order to have riding lessons I've sold myself to the devil by undertaking to do the article on Writing."[112]

Lacking those aristocratic skills (and attitudes), in part 2 of "A Happy New Year" Auden writes passionately about this provincial, unglamorous setting:

> Permit our town here to continue small,
> What city's vast emotional cartel
> Could our few acres satisfy
> Or rival in intensity
> The field of five or six, the English cell? (146)

In part 1, Auden seems to have been able to see all England from a particular vantage point in Scotland. Here, the narrowed perspective of the "field of five or six, the English cell" in a Scottish school is intended to serve as the paradigm of a reintegrated social order, albeit with a strangely off-key national character, given that the setting for this "English cell" is not England.

Containment and the desire to stay within limits: these are major underlying themes of the poem. Auden wishes for the middle-class verbal and social counterpoints of "spontaneous skill at holding rein": a small circle of people, linked together by love and described in a circumscribed and unusual poetic shape. That circle is about to find form and be completed within the time of the poem as the boys arrive for conversation. Auden comments, in what feels like an almost maternal tone, that "the tea is on the stove" as "up the stair come voices that I love" (146). In a poem filled with intimacy-producing deictic markers (such as "my," "there," "our," "them," and "this"), the circle will form round "this table" in a touchingly mundane but blissful re-creation of Heard's agapic paradigm: "The small group of about a dozen leant over the cushion of the pulvinus or sigma, and so formed an inward-looking group, perhaps a ring. There was a great cry of Sursum Corda (probably the oldest part of the Eucharist). It was the outbreak of exultation as the worshippers realized they were in the formed psychic field. Then there was the kiss of peace, the manifestation of psycho-physical tenderness, the love that is an intensity of serenity."[113] The raising of the mugs of tea at "this table" parallels the transubstantiated bread and wine on the altar. And the desired satisfaction of the bodily needs of hunger and thirst in this quiet tea ceremony contrasts with the mad prophecy of "the starving visionary" whom Auden imagines outside the school walls (146).

It is important that Auden sets the moment of group-formation outside "school hours" (as the poem, with its careful attention to time, insists) because Heard's agapic ring was structured not by authority or hierarchy but by equality. In a letter of July 1932 to the writer and old Greshamian John Pudney, Auden wrote that "There are some, poets are generally such, who will always be a little outside the group, critical, but they need the group to feel a little out of just as much as the rest need it to be at home in."[114] The liminality of the space where the poem originated, at "the window-sill" in a flat that was situated in the grounds of Auden's place of work, preserves the equivocal nature of Auden's membership of the formed group. Auden, by virtue of his different age and greater experience, is a little outside the shared world of the other youthful members of this group, who "dream | Of a new bicycle or winning team," while, by training, background, and gender, he remains closely related to the others around him in "the English cell" (146).

The word "cell," in the phrase "the English cell," seems to sum up Auden's idea of a poet as someone inside and outside a group. Expressing the full spectrum of his hopes and fears about this group-based model of social integration, the "English *cell*" has the biological flavor of an organically unified living thing. It has the social flavor of a tightly limited and intense political group or faction united in the face of an enemy by a common belief. And it has the administrative flavor of a place of confinement. "Cell" itself is a "little outside" a stable meaning. "English" too has a spectrum of meanings for Auden, but his conception of a group, or cell, is intimately linked to the fact of what he imagines is its redemptive Englishness.

It is noticeable that Auden does not describe in any detail the members of the circle of tea drinkers around the table in part 2, although their presences indicate a bringing into order of the anarchic world of part 1. In a literary world, in which plentiful amounts of innuendo were already starting to circulate—in print and by word of mouth—about Auden's life as a teacher, perhaps caution is a factor in his choice not to give too many specifics about the group assembled there, and certainly there is no analogy in the poem to Heard's "kiss of peace." But more significant as a factor in this well-judged vagueness is Auden's artistic finesse. The particular characters or appearances of the individuals are not important—the group can be formed anywhere and does not depend on the participation of unique members but on immersion of everyone present in a type of ritual. In his essay on writing, Auden wonders if "small groups" of the kind that he finds desirable can only exist at present as "short-lived oddities" and if, for their continuing existence, it will take "a one-class state where the distribution of money and leisure is more or less equal, and where industries [have] become decentralised." If that were to be so, then cities would presumably dissolve into smaller social groupings, and we would no longer be "compelled to herd together in unmanageable masses."[115] The small group or cell, by contrast, is bounded, "managcable," knowable, and loveable. The amorphous disorder of part 1 has become the defined unit, the "real whole," of part 2, all the more precious and poignant because it will be "short-lived."

Auden had written other poems before that imagined a collective world, but that world was imagined in negative terms as a society bound together by sickness: the Adversary's army of the malevolent and diseased in "Consider this," for example. The second part of "A Happy New Year" is one of the first poems in which Auden's poetic sensitivity to circled limits, to enclosures and sheltered spaces, becomes manifest as a positive quality. Indeed, "happy," the adjective in the poem's title, is not just an element in a pat phrase but one that has deep meaning for Auden (as "happy" did too for John Milton, a poet whom Auden often seems close to). In pronouncing the title, the stress should fall more heavily on "Happy" rather than "Year." For Auden, "happy" means something stronger and warmer than just "content"; it means being something like "fortunate" and "fulfilled" (and, with the accidental echo of "happenstance," it connotes a state that is often experienced by chance or good fortune). Within these blessedly narrow limits, a new clarity and definition is possible; the world becomes intimate, representable, and can be fitted into a genuine totality or a gestalt of ordered parts. The moment and the place represent the very temporary overcoming at an emotional level of the centrifugal, violent, psyche-destroying anarchy of nearly twenty years of political, economic, and military history. For Auden, after experiencing the Great War within the confines of school, a school is now the place where a kind of peace is restored.

But the subtle shadow of the First World War still haunts this temporarily happy world. The notion of small collectivities as a cure for the huge, amorphous, atomized "societies" of the contemporary world was a fashionable one at the time among British intellectuals. It seems possible that this interest in the early 1930s in small units of people living and co-operating together was partly stimulated by the flood of war memoirs in the late 1920s, in which it was often clear that the most intense loyalty and concern felt by soldiers was not for abstract symbols such as "The Crown" or for concepts such as "honour" or "glory" but for the other members of their small unit (or "section," in the jargon of the British Army) on whom they depended for survival. What had worked in wartime might work equally well in the economic maelstrom of peacetime crisis.

Auden's evolving interest in circled limits, enclaves, and enclosed spaces reflects a new sense of the power of poetry written inside closed poetic forms. One of the final events of the agapic celebration described by Heard in *The Ascent of Humanity* was a moment of inspiration. Heard quotes Canon Pearcy Dearmer (quoting the historian Louis Duchesne—Heard is happy to include lengthy quotations from others to pad out his books) on the "spiritual exercises" that succeeded the "kiss of peace, the manifestation of psycho-physical tenderness." Following that moment, "inspired persons began to speak and to manifest before the assembly the presence of the Spirit that animates them. Prophets, ecstatics, the speakers with tongues, the interpreters, *les médecins surnaturels* now take up the attention of the faithful," Heard wrote. The forming into a group leads, at the rite's culmination, to inspired speech and an intense closeness between speaker and audience: "The inspiration can be felt; it thrills the organs of some privileged person; but the whole congregation is moved, edified, and even ravished to a greater or less extent, and is transported into the divine sphere of the Paraclete [Holy Spirit]." The formation of the group becomes a stimulus to an ecstatic speaking, an inspired poetry that leaves the participants "moved, ... and even ravished."[116] Auden's poem leads up to this moment in part 2 but does not actually include it—he is not ready, at least not yet ready, to end a poem either with an epiphany or with a celebration of poetry itself.

And just as the poem contains beautiful but not ravishing speech, the tiny "English cell," sealed gracefully into these elegant stanzas, is nonetheless threatened and provisional.[117] Indeed, the Lords of Limit themselves "endear | Our peace to us with a perpetual threat" (145). With the threat in mind, the poem continues, "Deeper towards the summer the year moves on": a sense of impending danger hangs over the poem. This danger comes not only from the looming threat of foreign influences, symbolized by "the Great Bear" and "China's drum," but more locally from the "serious season" of sex and work that growing schoolboys must soon enter and from the possibility of internal political turmoil (146). That note had been introduced at the start of the poem, where Auden writes that the "lilac bush like a conspirator | Shams dead upon the lawn" (144).

The note of foreboding returns in more explicit fashion at the poem's end, when Auden imagines "a starving visionary" who has "seen | The carnival within our gates, | Your bodies kicked about the streets" (146). But the ultimate threat is simpler and more urgent: that without the Lords of Limit, the charmed circle may dissolve:

> We need your power still: use it, that none
>
> O from this table break uncontrollably away
> Lunging, insensible to injury,
> Dangerous in the room or out wild-
> -ly spinning like a top in the field,
> Mopping and mowing through the sleepless day. (146–147)

This powerful vision of dissolution seems to guarantee that at some point the dissolution will actually take place. Auden dramatizes the process of breakup in Hopkinsian ways: he leaves the word "none" suspended, vertiginously isolated at the end of the penultimate stanza (it is the only stanza in the poem to run on into the next). And then, unusually, having violated a stanza break, Auden fractures a word between lines with the "wild- | -ly spinning" boy (strongly evoking the charging youth who, with a "trickle of blood from a bullet smear" showing under his cap, "zig-zag[s] shrieking down the road" [143] near the end of part 1), linking him to present participles of incomplete action ("Lunging," "spinning"). Tender though the poem is, it ends by reluctantly imagining the probable fading of the magic closeness in the group as one "from this table break[s] uncontrollably away | . . . Mopping and mowing through the sleepless day" (146–147). The anguish of the moment is registered in the way that the earlier, cherished "unexpected beauty of speech or face" will be threatened by the prospect of someone "mopping and mowing," that is, making grotesque faces or grimaces, as they rush away.

A couple of months later, Auden tried again to write about a vision of togetherness with social implications. In "The chimneys are smoking, the crocus is out in the border," a daringly frank poem about a "desire" that cannot move along a "straight" route but is "crooked," he imagines an erotic relationship between himself and his lover that, "though it hide underground," can transmit spiritual rightness to those around them:

> And since our desire cannot take that route which is straightest,
> Let us choose the crooked, so implicating these acres,
> These millions in whom already the wish to be one
>> Like a burglar is stealthily moving,
>> That these, on the new façade of a bank
>> Employed, or conferring at health resort,
>> May, by circumstance linked,
>> More clearly act our thought.

Although Auden claims to desire that people in the everyday world "act our thought," the poem ends with whimsy and a fanciful note as he calls on "the boatmen, virgins, camera-men and us" to dance "Round goal-post, wind-gauge, pylon or bobbing buoy" with the "bird-like sucking tread | Of the quick dancer."[118]

In "Prologue," written shortly after, in May 1932 (the same month that, as noted earlier, Faber and Faber published *The Orators*), Auden reaches for a new, more ambitious social vision and a deeper, more rapturous poetic tone.[119] Like so many of his works, "Prologue" has a fundamentally tripartite structure, reflected here in its use of tercets as the stanza form. "[W]axing and waning as our hope" (as Auden puts it in another poem, composed a little later), "Prologue" has a tidal in-out-in movement that starts with aspiration and a lost dream of unity, moves into despondency, and ends with the hope of a ship approaching, hope restored, and a new dream of collective rebirth that might soon begin.[120] The poem also takes up again the symbolism of water, recalling the drowned but beautiful bridegroom in "clear lake" from the 1929 sequence as well as moments from numerous other poems Auden wrote in the early 1930s: the "Boats on a bay like toys on floor" in part 1 of "A Happy New Year," for example, or the "green pier light" that Auden says he can see from his window in part 2 of the same poem. (One local friend, Arnold Snodgrass, believed that Auden was exaggerating for poetic effect and could not really glimpse the Firth of Clyde's water from

his room at Larchfield Academy: he just wanted to write that he could.)
Water is a crucial element, too, in "The chimneys are smoking, the
crocus is out in the border"—composed the month before "Prologue"—
which mentions a buoy and a "cruiser."[121] All this poetry, almost instinctively oriented toward life's interactions with water, reaches a high point
in "Prologue," another of Auden's many dream-visions written in the
early 1930s. Here the inspired language ends with a memorable account
of a mythic sea voyage across the Atlantic Ocean that will bring the hope
of renewal to England's "impoverished constricting acres."[122]

Just as he had tried to do in "A Happy New Year," here Auden sets
out with the ambition to write another prophetic, redemptive work. But
this time, heightening the literary stakes, he invokes the most visionary
of all European poets, Dante. The poem, which is one of Auden's
weirdest and most beautiful, offers a panoramic survey of England's
plight. In it, he tries to bring together the chaotic social present and the
dream of a redeemed future—to hold, as Yeats said, "in a single thought
reality and justice."[123] Here is the opening:

> O love, the interest itself in thoughtless Heaven,
> Make simpler daily the beating of man's heart; within,
> There in the ring where name and image meet,
>
> Inspire them with such a longing as will make his thought
> Alive like patterns a murmuration of starlings
> Rising in joy over wolds unwittingly weave;
>
> Here too on our little reef display your power,
> This fortress perched on the edge of the Atlantic scarp,
> The mole between all Europe and the exile-crowded sea;
>
> And make us as Newton was, who in his garden watching
> The apple falling towards England, became aware
> Between himself and her of an eternal tie.
>
> For now that dream which so long has contented our will,
> I mean, of uniting the dead into a splendid empire,
> Under whose fertilising flood the Lancashire moss
>
> Sprouted up chimneys, and Glamorgan hid a life
> Grim as a tidal rock-pool's in its glove-shaped valleys,
> Is already retreating into her maternal shadow;

Leaving the furnaces gasping in the impossible air,
The flotsam at which Dumbarton gapes and hungers;
While upon wind-loved Rowley no hammer shakes

The cluster of mounds like a midget golf course, graves
Of some who created these intelligible dangerous marvels;
Affectionate people, but crude their sense of glory. (183)[124]

In an indirect way, this great poem may have emerged from a "vision" Auden had of the subatomic world. Early in 1932, he observes near the start of his "Writing" essay that the smallest "whole thing" in the universe is constituted by "the negative electrons of the atom which run round its positive central nucleus, already a group."[125] The most minuscule and basic thing in nature, in other words, is a kind of material micro-version of a human group: even here, multiple entities are naturally arranged in a coordinated and interdependent pattern. One point of departure for "Prologue" appears to have been a feeling for this basic unit of the universe. The poem's first line, "O love, the interest itself in thoughtless heaven" (183), takes off from an abandoned line in "The chimneys are smoking, the crocus is out in the border." There, Auden had offered a similar address to "Love": "O Love, sustainer of the unbreakable atomic ring."[126] (We, to our loss, know, as Auden could not, that certain atomic rings are not unbreakable.) With his interest in science, Auden had used the imagery of subatomic particles as early as 1926 in a Donne-like lyric, "Song."[127] But here, in 1932, the image of the "unbreakable atomic ring" has an imaginative, Heardian quality. It was probably inspired by Auden's conversations with Gerald Heard during the "very interesting holiday" the pair took together in Devon from late March until early April 1932, including a visit to Dartmoor, presumably to look at ancient menhirs and stone circles.[128]

On the holiday that Auden and Heard spent mostly in Devon, they added a stop-off with William McElwee, Auden's old Oxford love, at Tapscott in Somerset. The trip also featured a visit to Dartington Hall in Devon at the start of April. The Hall, a 1,000-acre estate near Totnes, had been established in the late fourteenth century. It was purchased in ramshackle condition in 1925 by Dorothy and Leonard Elmhirst (both scions of wealthy families, she, especially, as a daughter of the American financier W. C. Whitney) as a venue at which to try out their ideas on education, rural regeneration, and the arts. Alongside a small school run according to progressive educational theories, the estate boasted two separate farms, a commercial orchard, a poultry business, a large forest, a small building firm, and a sawmill.[129] Dorothy Elmhirst had a strong involvement with literature and music, and she attracted to Dartington many well-known visitors from the world of the arts.

Gerald Heard may have become interested in Dartington because of his intimate knowledge of earlier attempts to revivify or reform country life. Born in Ireland, he had been a private secretary to the Irish agrarian reformer Sir Horace Plunkett from 1919 to around 1929. Heard apparently first visited Dartington in June 1929, but he saw Dorothy Elmhirst particularly often in 1932 and 1933. He stayed at the Hall eleven times in 1932 and thirteen times in 1933. Heard also had contacts in the Society for Psychical Research, and for the rest of their lives he and Dorothy Elmhirst remained close friends, united by a shared fascination with mysticism.[130]

Commentators usually see Auden's April 1932 visit to Dartington as an example of his interest in education.[131] Dartington Hall School, which had opened in 1926, had around a hundred pupils (girls and boys) at the time of Auden's visit. The academy was run by a disciple of the philosopher Bertrand Russell, W. B. Curry, whom the Elmhirsts had hired in 1930 after questions had been raised about lax standards. Curry was careful to keep the school at arm's length from its rich owners and from the activities on the rest of the Dartington estate. But his experimental approach fitted the ethos of Dartington as a whole: by the lights of the period, he was a progressive educationist, stressing cooperation, coeducation, an agnostic attitude to religion, no corporal punishment, and only a relatively small number of rules.[132]

Auden was in general enthusiastic about what he observed at Dartington, but he told his brother John that the "snag is the school. Co-ed and all that, a little factory for neuters."[133] However, in May, shortly after his and Heard's holiday, he seems to have written to the school inquiring about a position there.[134] Behind the progressive facade, the institution, predictably, remained quite conservative socially. On the day Auden visited, he had declared the complicated nature of his political sympathies by wearing a pink shirt, which at the time may have suggested to his cautious hosts someone who was left of center (but less so than a "red").[135] More likely though is that the shirt set off alarm bells because, although pink triangles were not introduced as the identifying symbol for homosexuals in German concentration and labor camps until 1937, the color already seems to have carried gay associations in the early 1930s. Having caused doubts in the minds of the school's theoretically forward-looking but still exceedingly formal and scandal-wary authorities, the shirt's color seems to have lost Auden any chance of a job as a Dartington teacher.[136]

Much more than the school, however, it was the world of the estate—a loosely knit community where rural industry, farming crafts, and arts were all practiced in close proximity—that was important to Auden. Writing a bread-and-butter letter to Dorothy Elmhirst after the visit, Auden says: "I had a nice comfortable journey going over in my mind everything I saw. It seems that the Mayflower has returned at last. Believe me, it makes a little Englander, like myself, a little ashamed but very happy. I shall not easily forget either Dartington or your beautiful hospitality."[137] What Auden is thinking about in his comment to Dorothy Elmhirst emerges from his awareness that Dartington in Devon is only about twenty-five miles east of Plymouth, the port the Puritans departed from in 1620 to sail to America and found a community based on love, living beyond the power of the state. Auden now fancifully imagines a later incarnation of that dissenting, religiously inspired, self-reliant group sending a representative—in the shape of the rich American reformer Dorothy Elmhirst—back on a return voyage from Massachusetts to the point of origin to provide the English with a model—in a closely knit, vibrant, self-sufficient rural community—of a viable future life here at home. When Auden wrote this elaborate, flattering compliment to Elmhirst, he may also have been vaguely thinking about another American reformer who had been in the general area, one whom he had learned about from Layard in Berlin: Homer Lane's Little Commonwealth had been located in not-far-distant Dorset until 1918.

In calling himself a "Little Englander" in his letter, Auden refers to a highly patriotic but anti-imperial, anti-militarist, anti-jingoist Liberal political tradition, which reached a peak of popularity at the time of the Second Boer War (1899–1902). The movement called for an end to foreign entanglements and mercantile expansion overseas and for the dis-

mantling of the Empire, and instead for a reengagement with the resources of "England" alone. It promoted a kind of "Radical insularism,"
as one historian put it.[138] Little Englandism continued to be a significant
source of political meaning for a number of intellectuals like Auden in
the 1930s because the genteel dissidence of its anticapitalist, anti-
imperial energies could somehow be blended with a patriotic commitment to a middle-class version of rural English life. Whenever Auden
writes about his politics explicitly, as he does here in his words to Dorothy Elmhirst, his views sound more emotional than practical.

Shortly after this visit to Dartington, Auden, in a letter to his brother
John, who was in India, changed the vector of outside influence. There,
he suggested—perhaps partly to please his left-leaning sibling—that
the Soviet Union, rather than the United States, provided the right external analogue and model for Dartington. He said "I've just been down
to what seems to me the most remarkable thing in England; An estate
in Devonshire run on real community lines. It smells quite genuine;
and seems the right English variant on Russia." Once again, "English"
concerns are prominent in Auden's language. And he insists that John
should see the community of which the school was a part: "When you
return to England you must go and have a look at it."[139] In this letter, the
godless Soviet system has replaced the theological community from
the *Mayflower*. But the point is still the same: a nucleus of people with a
vibrant faith and a strong sense of collective care for one another, originating elsewhere, offer a model of communal renewal for "a Little Englander like myself."

With his experiences in the provincial atmosphere at Helensburgh in
mind, Auden—like Eliot—was now becoming increasingly interested in
the idea of small parochial communities or "circles," such as schools,
living an intense group life in rural or semirural isolation. In the *Criterion* for October 1931, Eliot had asserted that "agricultural life is capable
of being the best life for the majority of any people." Auden, like most
other ambitious young literary persons of the time, would have read the
magazine carefully. (He had extra reason to study that issue of the periodical because it included his own "Address for a Prize-Day" from *The
Orators*.) Eliot went on: "it is hardly too much to say that only in a primarily agricultural society, in which people have local attachments to

their small domains and small communities, and remain, generation after generation, in the same place, is genuine patriotism possible."[140] In Ode IV of *The Orators*, composed in the same month, Auden gives a sexist précis in doggerel of these ideas:

> Most of the rest shall live upon the land;
> Living in one place with a satisfied face
> All of the women and most of the men
> Shall work with their hands and not think again. (125)

Or, as he puts it in "Writing": "Towns must be smaller. I am inclined to think we read far too much; that if literature is to survive, most of us will have to stop learning to read and write, stop moving from place to place, and let literature start again by oral tradition." He adds: "One thing is quite certain. We shall do absolutely nothing without some sort of faith either religious like Catholicism or political like Communism."[141] In prose, Auden's "faith" sounds a bit threadbare and even cruel. In poetry, it is something else. There, his "faith" at this stage turns out to be neither exactly religious nor political in any obvious sense: "make us," he implores "love" in "Prologue," "as Newton was who in his garden watching | The apple falling towards England became aware | Between himself and her of an eternal tie" (183).[142] This antic vignette maps natural phenomena like gravitation onto social values like patriotism. It is brilliant, odd, and a bit disturbing. And, ultimately, it shows that in 1932 Auden's own poetic "faith" is not really programmatic or practical, but national, emotional, and Anglophilic.

Auden's point in the image of Newton is that "we" do not any longer believe easily in an "eternal tie" with England—and that this is a failing. For this reason, just as he does in "Sir, no man's enemy," Auden here sighs for a terrifying, enlivening "change of heart." He envisages a solution not only for himself but for an entire country, once unified but now atomized—or, as he puts it in "A Happy New Year," "fallen apart" into "the isolated personal life" (145). As he thinks of this possible regeneration, he consolidates the connection between his own poetry and a vision of a revitalized and reintegrated "England." And "Prologue," for all its idealistic literary language, is deeply embedded in the contemporary historical moment. Auden's references to the economic recession in Britain, which lasted from 1929 until 1933, are stylized, but only lightly: "Now that dream which so long has contented our will," he writes: "Is already retreating into [England's] maternal shadow; || Leaving the furnaces gasping in the impossible air" (183). His reference to those who "inertly wait" in "bar, in netted chicken-farm, in lighthouse" (183) points to the widespread appearance of the kind of smallholdings in the countryside, known as "plotlands," that were often sold to returning soldiers. Settling on these meager pieces of ground, veterans, when not in "bar[s]," tried to scrape together a living in diminished circumstances from raising pigs or chicken farming.

These topical, contemporary images are balanced against a "timeless" florid literary language. The phrasing and ideas in the poem's first half profusely evoke Shakespeare or, rather, a particular moment in Shakespeare: John of Gaunt's dying speech in *Richard II*, perhaps the most famous and most heavily plundered piece of island rhetoric in the language. Recall that, by a curious coincidence, Auden's maternal grandmother Selina Acton Bicknell, who was an enthusiastic student of her own ancestry, claimed to be descended from John of Gaunt. This claim, if true (and perhaps Auden believed it was), would have meant that Auden too was remotely descended from the famous fourteenth-century patriot immortalized by Shakespeare.[143]

In his deathly murmurs, Shakespeare's Gaunt, who is despairing over the state of the nation he is leaving, bends nostalgically toward an idea of the "scepter'd isle" as organically rounded, referring to it as the "other Eden" (the Garden of Eden was usually represented in art as being circular in shape), the "fortress" (Auden borrows this word in his poem), the "little world," the "precious stone," the "earth," and the "teeming womb":

> This royal throne of kings, this sceptered isle,
> This earth of majesty, this seat of Mars,
> This other Eden, demi-paradise,
> This fortress built by Nature for herself
> Against infection and the hand of war,
> This happy breed of men, this little world,
> This precious stone set in the silver sea,
> Which serves it in the office of a wall
> Or as a moat defensive to a house

Against the envy of less happier lands,
This blessed plot, this earth, this realm, this England,
This nurse, this teeming womb of royal kings,
Feared by their breed and famous by their birth,
Renowned for their deeds as far from home,
For Christian service and true chivalry.[144]

Gaunt's speech reflects a mythos that grew partly from the physical fact that England is situated on an archipelago. The mythos proposed the nation's geographical isolation had allowed a unique culture and political system to evolve, with traditions of independence, individualism, and emancipation. In Auden's poem, echoing Gaunt's description of the nation, England is "our little reef . . . | This fortress perched on the edge of the Atlantic scarp, | The mole between all Europe and the exile-crowded sea" (183).[145] Here Gaunt's "fortress" recurs, while Auden's "our little reef" simply rephrases in a more attenuated, precarious language the old, dying patriot's "little world."

Gathering up these Shakespearean images into its vision of a unified and revitalized country, "Prologue" also draws on Auden's October 1931 "vision about groups" just as it absorbs his reading and his conversations with Gerald Heard about the importance of group life and communal rituals. And—so much feeds into this landmark work— Dante is as vital to the poem as Shakespeare, although ironically, and a bit oddly, Auden deploys the Italian Dante—as he does Shakespeare— in the service of a special kind of eccentric and idealistic English patriotism. In combining the forces of Dante and Shakespeare, he seeks to situate himself against the two classic authors with the greatest stature in English literary circles at the time. "Dante and Shakespeare divide the modern world between them," Eliot proclaimed in his 1929 "Dante" essay, "there is no third."[146] Auden attempts to fold both poets into his poem, but just as he focuses on one mythic moment in Shakespeare, so he adapts a very particular version of Dante: T. S. Eliot's.

Eliot's long "Dante" essay was first printed as a booklet in Faber and Faber's "The Poets on the Poets" series. Since "Prologue" is based on Auden's version of Eliot's version of Dante, it might fit equally well in a series titled "The Poets on the Poets on the Poets." For Auden, Dante was "*the* greatest poet," and in this he was closely following Eliot's own influential views.[147] For Eliot, Dante was the poet of "*simplification,*" by which he meant that Dante's poetry "simplifies the diction, and makes clear and precise the images" and that it clarifies the logic behind the "complete scale of the depths and heights of human emotion."[148] Dante looms over the tercets of "Prologue," which visually recall his *terza rima*, especially when Auden asks a Dantesque principle of "love" to "Make simpler daily the beating of man's heart" (183). He also petitions the personified "love" to reunite the fractured pieces of language and the world:

> There in the ring where name and image meet,
>
> Inspire them with such a longing as will make his thought
> Alive like patterns a murmuration of starlings
> Rising in joy over wolds unwittingly weave. (183)

This dynamic image of the "murmuration of starlings," although deploying the relatively common medieval phrase about a "murmeracion of stares," strongly evokes another passage in Eliot's "Dante" essay. There, Eliot discusses the moment in canto 5 of the *Inferno* when the lustful lovers are likened to starlings borne along on autumnal winds.[149] For Eliot, Dante employed this kind of immediately visual simile "solely to make us see *more definitely* the scene."[150]

Throughout his essay, Eliot largely ignores the intense factional struggles that saw Dante exiled from his home city of Florence. Instead, he strives to make his readers believe that the poet lived during a time of intellectual unity in Europe. As he does, Eliot plays with the relationship of the "visual" to the "visionary." "Dante's is a *visual* imagination," he asserts.[151] One effect of that intellectual unity, Eliot posits, is Dante's ability to write in a clear, visual manner—a competency that became difficult to achieve after "the process of disintegration" in the political world that set in "soon after Dante's time." This left poets with "an opacity, or inspissation of poetic style throughout Europe." Eliot diagnoses the Victorian poet A. C. Swinburne as Dante's antitype and the greatest (and most damnable) exponent of this inferior, murky style.[152]

Unlike Swinburne, Eliot claims, Dante is a great poet because he uses language in "a healthy state" (playing on "state" as meaning both a "condition" and a "body politic"). This is partly because he sustained a vision of political union and lived in what Eliot saw as a spiritually united world. In such a world, "language" and "object" are all but inseparable.[153] Inspired by the idea of language and objects once having been joined together, in Auden's poem he wishes that "name and image" will be inspired with such "longing" for each other that, merged, they will again produce sharply etched, almost tangible images. Indeed, language itself will become something like the thing it refers to. With his habitual feeling for the significance of birds, Auden materially represents the idea of the starlings rising into the sky by a "murmuration" of words: the vast scatter of tiny black ink curves and straights on a plain sheet of paper are like the sight of the wheeling, energized birds set against the background of a pale sky. Piercing visual clarity will be granted to the poet as a result of the (re)joining within "the ring" of name and image—and that clarity will point to a newly discovered and "healthy" political unity among the English in which the rifts of class and culture might heal.

Joining name and image together, "love" will "Inspire" (how often beautiful are Auden's line openings, which allow him to capitalize specially important words!) poetic thought, just as it will make "us" aware again of the "eternal tie" with England. The result is the poem's spectacular clarity of vision, evoked in the image of English children "looking to Moel Fammau [in north Wales] to decide | On picnics by the clearness or withdrawal of her treeless crown" (184). In *The Changing Face of England* (1926), a book Auden loved, Anthony Collett, the natural historian and journalist (and war veteran), and from whom Auden borrows this image, described the "glorious views" from the border-country hills and the prospects "expand in the translucent intervals of wet weather to almost incredible distances."[154] Auden's heroic simile using Moel Fammau compares the "possible dream" of national renewal with the childish excitement generated by the thought of a picnic expedition at a spot in the Clywd Hills. In the poem, the relative clarity of Moel Fammau's peak is a kind of natural rain gauge to far-off observers, as the hill's degree of visibility depends on the amount of vapor in the air. The idea comes from Collett: "Chester knows Moel Fammau, the mother mountain of the little hills of the border, and divines the coming weather by the clearness or withdrawal of her bare crown."[155]

But, in a poem that has so many "influences," it is important to remember Auden's own abundant, freely originating creativity is in play as well. He does not simply copy out the language that he takes from Collett. He embellishes it: for instance, he turns the naturalist's phrase "bare crown" into the more elegant and mysterious "treeless crown," in a great instance of Auden's poetic love for the subtleties of the negative.

The "treeless crown" evokes both the absence of trees at Moel Fammau's summit and also the tree-covered lower slopes out of which the hill's bare crown emerges. And it is Auden's feeling for emotional drama, triggered by Collett's idea of a "mother mountain," that produced the singular idea of children looking from Cheshire in England across the Welsh border toward Moel Fammau for a sign, as if watching for a signal of assent from some distant female deity, at once "foreign" and unknowable. ("Fammau" means motherly or maternal in Welsh.)

"Prologue" is enlivened by such acts of elated seeing. And, in Eliotic fashion, seeing clearly in this poem is associated with having visions. "Prologue" is a Dantesque visionary poem, structured around two dreams. The first dream, now vanished, is the dream of "uniting the dead into a splendid empire" (183). It is the dream lying behind national expansion, the Industrial Revolution, and capitalism, underwritten by a progressive notion of history in which the successes of the near present ("the splendid empire") have evolved seamlessly from the achievements of the past ("the dead"). Under the "fertilising flood" of the "splendid empire," the "Lancashire moss || Sprouted up chimneys," the Welsh coalfields around Glamorgan thrived, the furnaces in the shipbuilding yards at Dumbarton roared, and the hammers pounded in the great iron foundries at Rowley Regis (in the Black Country, very near Auden's home in Birmingham, and the site of his great-grandfather John Auden's house and his mine-leasing business). The "Affectionate people" who created these "intelligible dangerous marvels" expected the "splendid empire" to continue forever into the future. But it did not: "the seed in their loins were hostile, though afraid of their pride" (183).

That first dream has retreated into England's "maternal shadow," leaving the English "too much alone" and afflicted with a "hopeless sigh." Now the inhabitants are, as Auden puts it in language of haunting tawdriness:

> In bar, in netted chicken-farm, in lighthouse,
> Standing on these impoverished constricting acres,
> The ladies and gentlemen apart, too much alone. (183)

The expression of aloneness in this, the shortest sentence in the whole poem, is halting, staccato. Here, the poem reaches the present state of crisis, the "now" when one dream has withdrawn, another has yet to appear, and in the interval the populace can only "inertly wait." And so they "Consider the years of the measured world begun, | The barren spiritual marriage of stone and water" as the poem's linguistic momentum falters. Two sentences cover less than three tercets. At this low ebb of poetic energy, the language is also at its least sustaining and expansive. The prim, segregating regime of the comma rules the sentence structure.

Then the third and longest part of the poem begins, and verbal energy gathers again, like a rolling wave building up power, as Auden hopes for the realization of a new "possible dream" (183). The poem launches out on its longest and most complex sentence. It is the concluding one. As Auden evokes the idea of the dream being born, or reborn, from the past, the poem regains the poetic intensity and the hope that is visible in its first part, and the vocative "O" appears just as it had at the poem's beginning:

> Yet, O, at this very moment of our hopeless sigh
>
> When inland they are thinking their thoughts but are watching
>   these islands,
> As children in Chester look to Moel Fammau to decide
> On picnics by the clearness or withdrawal of her treeless crown,
>
> Some possible dream, long coiled in the ammonite's slumber
> Is uncurling, prepared to lay on our talk and kindness
> Its military silence, its surgeon's idea of pain;
>
> And out of the Future into actual History,
> As when Merlin, tamer of horses, and his lords to whom
> Stonehenge was still a thought, the Pillars passed
>
> And into the undared ocean swung north their prow,
> Drives through the night and star-concealing dawn
> For the virgin roadsteads of our hearts an unwavering keel.
>   (183–184)

What was alive and then dead and fossilized is now alive again. This is a dream "long coiled in the ammonite's slumber," which, "uncurling," is "prepared to lay on our talk and kindness | Its military silence, its surgeon's idea of pain" (184).[156] The "talk and kindness" are the private, personal values of bourgeois liberalism, which the poem says, in shadowy, threatening lines, must be transcended by a new more rational public order that will require both force ("military silence") and technical expertise (the "surgeon's idea of pain").

In "O love, the interest itself in thoughtless Heaven," Auden imagines that the regenerating "dream" will arrive like that (completely fictional) moment when, heading for prehistoric England, "Merlin, tamer of horses, and his lords to whom | Stonehenge was still a thought, the Pillars passed || And into the undared ocean swung north their prow" (184). The poem's language now is magical, pseudo-Homeric, and mythical: the phrase "Merlin, tamer of horses" assigns to Merlin the epithet that Homer uses for the Trojan prince Hector in the *Iliad*. This is memorable and mysterious, but Auden is drawing on some of the most eccentric ideas in the British branch of the "diffusionist" school of anthropologists, with whose work he was greatly taken during the later 1920s and early 1930s.[157] Of special relevance among the diffusionists' writings is the once-influential H. J. Massingham's book *Fee, Fi, Fo, Fum: or, The Giants in England* (1926). Massingham there rehearses some of the diffusionist school's main hypotheses, arguing that civilization spread around the world from its original center in Egypt through a series of maritime expeditions made by men whom he calls the "Ancient Mariners." In his book, Massingham goes on to summon up one of Auden's longest-standing fascinations, arguing that these mariners were also miners. This, he claims, was one of the primary motivations for these expeditions: to search for "metals, pearl-shell, and other precious things" that the Mariners regarded as "life-givers" likely to ensure immortality.[158] Auden's connections of the British wizard Merlin with ancient culture, with the building of Stonehenge ("to whom Stonehenge was still a thought"), and with a sea voyage out of the Mediterranean ("the Pillars passed || And into the undared ocean swung north their prow") are all ideas that appear in Massingham's *Fee, Fi, Fo, Fum*.[159]

The correspondences between Massingham's book and Auden's poem are thus very pointed. To take just one more example, Auden draws on one of Massingham's epigraphs for the heroic language that he uses to describe the poem's fantasy of a redemptive nautical voyage: specifically, he uses a passage from H. M. Tomlinson's *Tidemarks* (1923), with which

Massingham introduces his chapter on the Ancient Mariners' voyages to the Isles of the Blest. There, Tomlinson praises the "dauntless men" who "pulled galleys westward through the Pillars [of Hercules] for the first time, and then turned northward towards the top of the world."[160]

Massingham supplies the reason for the Mariners' journey north, drawing on a common idea among the diffusionists, that the reason for these expeditions was the desire for precious metals and shells. Dorset is the county where Anthony Collett described an "unearthly fresco" of fossilized ammonites.[161] The diffusionist anthropologists were especially attracted to the belief in the ancient world that stones and shells were places where the dead could survive and from which they could ultimately return to life. (In his *Naturalis Historia,* Pliny the Elder linked ammonites to the sacred Egyptian horns of Ammon, which he suggested could stimulate prophetic dreams.) For the ancients, the diffusionists maintained, a shell is a symbol of rebirth or of the progress of one generation rising from the death of another.[162] The conjoining of Collett's descriptive, emotive language for describing ammonites and Massingham's assertion that another mollusk's shell, the cowrie, was a bearer of immortality explains why Auden suggests that the "dream," which will "perhaps" awaken England, is "coiled in the ammonite's slumber."[163] For many readers of poetry, these ideas will seem both wildly eccentric and deeply suggestive: Auden has founded a magnificent piece of writing on the most speculative, some might say the shakiest, of intellectual foundations.[164] But the strengths of Auden's poetry consistently emerge from metaphors, dreams, introspection, an acute social sensitivity, and the works of peculiar, marginal thinkers, rather than from well-grounded scholarship. Existing in an almost antithetical relationship to its fantastical sources, "Prologue" is one of the English Auden's most solid, intense, and memorable early poems.

In April 1932, Auden had told Dorothy Elmhirst that at Darington Hall: "It seems that the Mayflower has returned at last." It may have seemed like a throwaway compliment, but there was a creative thought behind it. Now, at the end of "Prologue," written in May (an apt month for a poem that has in its background the idea of a new *May-flower* "return[ing] at last"), Auden envisages salvation arriving like a ship plowing through salt water toward the island's virgin anchorage, where its crew will inaugurate the new and better life. This ending to "Prologue," as the "possible dream," interwoven verbally with the fantasy of Merlin's ship, moves "through the night and star-concealing dawn" and "drives | For the virgin roadsteads of our hearts an unwavering keel" (184), is the culmination of the visual and the visionary strains that have existed interdependently since the opening of the poem.

As noted, "Prologue" is replete with appeals to the visual imagination, starting with the image of "the murmuration of starlings" weaving patterns over wolds and moving to ideas of "watching" and "looking." Newton watches the apple, as do the inland inhabitants who are "watching these islands." The "Affectionate people" who started the Industrial Revolution were "Far-sighted" and "looked down another future," while "children in Chester look to Moel Fammau." These obvious references to seeing are supplemented by subtler appeals to the sense of sight: the image of "glove-shaped valleys," for example, or, at the very end of the poem, the sense-enhancing sequence of "night" followed by a Tennysonian "star-concealing dawn," where the speaker, like a visionary, somehow continues to see in his mind's eye the stars that the dawn light is slowly concealing from ordinary sight (183–184).

As the poem sees far, so it dreams deeply. "Prologue" imagines "an eternal tie" between writer and land, just as it dreams of a country whose disparate social and geographical parts are bound together by love. The poem is a prologue in the sense that it looks forward to the moment when society has been reintegrated, but it is written at a moment before this occurs. When that reintegration does happen, the black specks of Auden's starling-thoughts, woven unwittingly into a beautifully patterned order by the reunification of name and image, will evoke not just a restored visual shapeliness in poetry but an ideal, unified social order too. Pound implied something similar when he wrote that: "If you clap a strong magnet beneath a plateful of iron filings, the energies of the magnet will proceed to organise form. . . . The design in the magnetised iron filings expresses a confluence of energy."[165] Auden imagines a moment of revolutionary change unlike anything that has come before, since it will, if it arrives, anchor "in the virgin roadsteads of hearts" (184). And yet, the dream of the future is also the rebirth of something very old, something that is secreted in a fossil, an ammonite, but that can still be reborn in the present.

A new clarity comes into focus in Auden's writing with a new world of beliefs and events. And that clarity, for Auden, is not just an epistemological gift: it is also a means of producing national unity. Eliot commented in his essay that Dante "lived in an age in which men still saw visions." By contrast, he lamented that "we have nothing but dreams, and we have forgotten that seeing visions . . . was once a more significant, interesting, and disciplined kind of dreaming."[166] Auden's vision of a "possible dream" is one in which the prospect glimmers of a new social unity in England being the product of a mystical invasion arriving from outside our perceptions of the everyday world.

The vision of a country drawn into a unified gestalt is enacted in the very form and language in the poem. It begins with an invocation, "O," which is also an image of self-completeness, a letter equivalent of the ring that Heard so enthusiastically promoted as the ideal social grouping. Meanwhile, the poem's ending curves around to turn in on itself, to complete a lyric circle. Consider, for instance, how the first part of the poem is echoed sonically, visually, and verbally in the third part. The "O love" (183) in the first movement of the poem is matched by the "O, at this very moment" (184) that initiates the third part. "Thoughtless" is mirrored by "treeless," and "heart" in line 2 echoes "hearts" in the final line; the images of circles and spheres at the start of the poem ("apple," "ring") recur near the end (the "ammonite" and its "coil"). The poem's drive to connect disparate parts of the poem is matched to the idea of the mariners' keel driving toward an anchorage within "our hearts."

"Prologue"'s two proper names are also balanced against each other, paired and contrasted. They occur in the first and third parts of the poem where, respectively, Newton is watching an apple (183) and Merlin sees the Pillars of Hercules disappear as he sits gazing into the "night and star-concealing dawn" (184). It is a sign of just how rapturous and inspired as a poet Auden could allow himself to be that Newton, the scientist, is locked into an earlier part of the poem while the mythical magician and mariner Merlin presides over the poem's final, crowning images. Auden thus elevates magic and prophecy and largeness of aim, represented by Merlin, over the rational methods of science with their detailed empirical focus, represented by Newton.

These mirroring links across the poem are crucial to its meaning as it looks for forms of connection and completion. Perhaps, while he was writing, Auden even felt he had gone too far in the pursuit of this web of parallels and that he had occasionally become artistically heavy-handed in spelling out his meaning. There is a significant change that he made from draft to finished work in the opening line of the poem's third-to-last stanza. The published version of the line reads: "Some possible dream, long coiled in the ammonite's slumber" (184). The draft, however, reads: "Some dream, say yes, long coiled in the ammonite's slumber."[167] In the earlier version of the line, Auden addresses love directly again ("say yes"), just as he does at the start of the poem. Moreover, "say yes" has an almost perfect palindromic verbal structure, imitating in miniature the palindromic, or tidal in-out-in, movement of the poem as a whole. Auden dialed back his ceaseless ingenuity by revising the line and avoiding making his pattern-finding seem like an artistic tic. But, and once again, the intricate ingenuity of this young poet's beautiful scrimshandering takes the breath away.

In 1929, "Sir, no man's enemy" can only imagine England in negative terms, and the poem defines God simply by a "no," an absence of hatred. In 1932, Auden ends a phase in his poetic development with a work that, at least for a moment, says "yes" and envisions the country on the brink of an almost ecstatic transformation. Around the end of June 1932, about a month or so after he completed "Prologue," with its final epic images of voyaging mariners inspired by mystical knowledge sailing toward England, Auden left his job in Helensburgh and went south.[168] And when the summer was over, he started in a new position at a school in Colwall at the foot of the Malverns Hills, deep in rural Herefordshire. Yet even in the English countryside, Auden and his art were not far from water. Colwall is only about forty miles from the point where the River Severn feeds out into an estuary and then a channel that leads to the "undared" Atlantic Ocean that Auden imagines in "Prologue." But, closer to home, Colwall itself has associations with water, and hence with poetry. It was reputed to be the location for the beginning of one of the most famous medieval works in English, *Piers Plowman*—a poem that opens with a man falling asleep and having a vision next to a flowing spring named Primeswell.

7   THE FLOOD

FEAR AND LOVE, 1932–1935

Never, perhaps, in the memorable and spacious story of this island's history has the land beyond the city offered so fair an inheritance to the children of its people, as to-day, under the visible shadow of the end.

—C. F. G. MASTERMAN (1909)

AUDEN WROTE THE POEM that begins, "O love, the interest itself in thoughtless heaven" in May 1932, just before he left Helensburgh for good. By early summer that year, he had given it the title "Prologue." Initially, he was probably thinking simply about the idea that the poem would form the prologue to a play he had an idea for (but never got round to writing). Then, a bit later, he thought of it as a prologue to a long, unfinished "epic" he worked on intensively in 1932–1933 before abandoning un-completed; that big poetic fragment is usually known by its first line, "In the year of my youth when yoyos came in." Even when he set aside "In the year of my youth," the title of what would have been its prefatory poem stuck. Eventually, "O love, the interest itself in thoughtless heaven" would form the "prologue" to the book of poems that Auden published in Britain in 1936 and in the United States in 1937.[1]

Although he imagined placing it before a variety of texts, Auden always envisioned "Prologue" as a poem describing the start of something new, something that lay outside its own frame. In a straightforward sense, the poem does imagine a prologue: a vision in which a "possible dream" of regeneration for English culture might be about to emerge, as if brought from the world beyond English shores by Merlin and his mariner companions and now on the brink of entering "actual History."[2]

But the poem, structured around two dreams, is a prophetic work living in (to borrow Shakespeare's words) "the brightest heaven of in-

372

vention."[3] Like all prophecies, therefore, it contains a wealth of messages, some of them perhaps unforeseen by its maker-medium. There is one deeper connotation to the concept of a prologue, not so far discussed. In his autobiography, John Layard—an anthropological diffusionist along with all his other interests—remarked that "Homer Lane . . . pointed out to me that sailing was one of the great homosexual symbols."[4] It is quite possible that Layard shared this odd but suggestive comment with Auden. (Does Auden even secrete a clue about this in the strange epithet "tamer of horses," applied here to the sailing Merlin but borrowed from "Homer"?) Lane's idea might account for some of the rapturous, sensuous feeling at the end of Auden's poem as the ship of adventurers "Drives through the night and star-concealing dawn | For the virgin roadsteads of our hearts an unwavering keel."[5] More importantly, it illuminates another of the possible meanings of the title: in the light of what would happen to Auden in the next few years, this poem comes to look like a "prologue" to love.

"Prologue" was only the second time in his poetry that Auden directly addressed a personified presence, "love"—the first was in a poem written in December 1931 (but not published until the summer of 1933) that begins, "Enter with him | These legends, Love."[6] Although Auden was to become known as a great love poet, he wrote very few poems that can easily be described as "love poems" until around the end of 1931. There are memorable or interesting poems written before this date that feel as if they have love somewhere inside them. But it remains hidden or baffled or inexpressible. There are poems that express awe over physical presence but that are not love poems, such as the extraordinarily delicate "This lunar beauty" from April or May 1930.[7] Then, rather than as love poetry, some early poems might be better described as "brief encounter" poems, such as "That night when joy began" from November 1931.[8] There are also a few buoyant, semipublic, almost virtuosic set-piece poems, such as "What's in your mind, my dove, my coney" from November 1930, that purport to address a lover but do so in a fashion that seems curiously unintimate.[9] Both "That night when joy began" and "What's in your mind, my dove, my coney" are associated with Auden's on-again, off-again, uppercrust lover in Helensburgh, Derek Wedgwood.[10]

With understandable wariness, Auden later in life claimed that he did not "think the sources in life which suggest a poem to its author are really relevant." But, earlier, he had privately marked lovers' initials (including Wedgwood's) next to several poems in copies of his books owned by close friends.[11] Although, in conventional terms, Wedgwood was apparently not a glamorous or magnetic young man, he does seem to have played a significant part in enabling Auden to expand the range of emotions in his poems, including overt expressions of love, however temporary. In 1934, Auden would write a poem beginning, "A shilling life will give you all the facts," about a Hercules-like hero of whom "Some of the last researchers even write | Love made him weep his pints like you and me." The person who owns the hero's heart is one (gender carefully unspecified) who might have reminded Auden's friends of Wedgwood:

> Who, say astonished critics, lived at home;
> Did little jobs about the house with skill
> And nothing else; could whistle; would sit still
> Or potter round the garden.[12]

More often than not, though, Auden's poems from the late 1920s and early 1930s are quite cynical about the possibilities of lasting love. In "Before this loved one," from March 1929, Auden declares that being with a lover is "no real meeting | But instinctive look | A backward love."[13] Another instance comes in the ode addressed to his Helensburgh pupils from November 1931 (the same month as he wrote "That night when joy began"):

> Do you think that because you have heard that on Christmas
>   Eve
> In a quiet sector they walked about on the skyline,
> Exchanged cigarettes, both learning the words for "I love you"
>   In either language:
> You can stroll across for a smoke and a chat any evening?
>   Try it and see.[14]

The first time that Auden in his canonical poetry, speaking in something like his own voice, directly writes the words "I love" about anything relating to another human being only comes in part 2 of "A Happy New Year," composed in February 1932, when the speaker says of his schoolboy charges and colleagues:

> The clocks strike ten: the tea is on the stove;
> And up the stair come voices that I love.

Love, satisfaction, force, delight,
To these players of Badminton to-night,
To Favel, Holland, sprightly Alexis give.[15]

The word "love" is modulated from a first-person verb to a (capitalized) noun at the start of the next line, meaning that the word is skillfully repeated for emphasis. Auden told John Pudney in July 1932 that "poets . . . need the group to feel a little out of just as much as the rest need it to be at home in."[16] Through its mention of "voices that I love," Auden's "A Happy New Year" poem of the same year subtly gestures toward his feelings of connection with, and outsideness from, this group of younger people. That the speaker can say he loves their voices exactly calibrates the complicated balance of discretion and daring that Auden works with. Yet, although this is apparently not a poem of romantic love, and although the specifics are in any case veiled, "I love. | Love" suggests an opening out to emotional experiences that Auden poems have usually hitherto addressed more circumspectly or ironically.

His next poem after that, beginning, "The chimneys are smoking, the crocus is out in the border," is a love poem of sorts too, referring to the departure, perhaps, on a short trip, of "my magnet, my pomp, my beauty | More telling to heart than the sea." The poem is extraordinarily candid about the indirection and subterfuge necessary for gay lovers in a town like Helensburgh in the 1930s. However, in part because of that constraint, love is not addressed directly in the poem. Instead, it is seen only as part of something larger, a bit like an element of evolutionary development, a "game" that "is in progress which tends to become like a war, | The contest of the Whites with the Reds for the carried thing | Divided in secret among us."[17] In the last year or so of the poems Auden wrote in Scotland, he was touching on the subject of love with increasing frequency and intensity but still always with some level of ambiguity, irony, or distancing.

"Prologue," one of Auden's last poems written in Scotland, fits within this frame. In addition to all the other meanings that it has, this is a prophetic poem concerning its maker's own life and writing, but with emotional renewal still somewhere outside or beyond the poem's ending. However, the "love," addressed here as an impersonal force, in a poem culminating in "one of the great homosexual symbols," is soon to become a central subject in Auden's personal experience, in his poetry, and in his search for a redeemed English world. That will be a sea change.

Although Auden left Larchfield Academy in the summer of 1932, he did not begin his new job at the Downs School in Colwall, Herefordshire, until around the end of September of that year. Oddly, given his move to a position at a prep school in a predominantly rural, agricultural world in the southern half of England, one of the first poems he wrote after he departed from Helensburgh was titled "A Communist to Others." He completed this in August 1932 in the setting (unlikely, given the subject matter) of the Auden family's holiday home, Wesco, in the Lake District. The poem in its original 1932 version, begins:

> Comrades who when the sirens roar
> From office, shop and factory pour
>   'Neath evening sky;
> By cops directed to the fug
> Of talkie-houses for a drug
> Or down canals to find a hug
>   Until you die.[18]

The poem's breezy formal virtuosity shows a lingering attachment to Scottish modes, or to English versions of Scottish modes, even after Auden has left the country. In twenty-two stanzas written in a Scottish eighteenth-century flyting form, the poem, which is spoken by a voice that never uses the first-person singular, spends five stanzas (four at the start and one at the end) talking to, or at, the "Comrades," who are clearly working class.[19] The rest of the poem, the greater part, harangues various representatives of Auden's own socioeconomic milieu, the middle and upper-middle classes. In spite of its title, which suggests that the poem is going to be one communist addressing others of the same mind, the poem is much more centered on the bourgeoisie than it is on the working class.

"A Communist to Others" was widely noticed among poetry readers when it appeared in a periodical called *Twentieth Century* and then in the *New Country* anthology in 1933. For example, the writer Julian Symons, the radical founder of *Twentieth Century*, saw it as "straight forward: an appeal to join the Party," never doubting that "the poet was himself a Party member."[20] Auden later cut and revised the poem extensively (just a few years later he replaced the word "Comrades" at the start with the vaguer "Brothers," for example) before printing it in his next collection of poems in 1936. The poem is a confusing mixture of dictions, filled with invective. But it ends with a more authentically Audenesque note, not with a rational conclusion but an expression of emotional intensity and longing. After addressing again the "Comrades to whom our thoughts return," the supposedly revolutionary speaker turns from comments about the inadequacies of the middle class to feelings of love. He explains, daringly, that he is addressing the group now as "Brothers for whom our bowels yearn | When words are over," adding that "Love outside our own election | Holds us in unseen connection."[21]

In the end, "A Communist to Others," more than it is a politically involved poem, reads as one more type of indirect love poem about a mysterious "unseen connection" between "Others" who are "Brothers." This ending hardly offers a straightforward Marxist understanding of social struggle: instead of mounting a political rallying cry, the poem finishes with yearning. Auden did publicly allude at least once at the time to a personal alignment with leftist politics, telling an American correspondent at the end of 1932 that *The Orators* had been "a stage in my conversion to Communism."[22] But by the second half of 1932, his poems were traveling in a very different direction than the one he was describing to others in letters such as this one: his poetry is never militant about class conflict, and it is much more concerned with emotional healing. If one were needed, this is another clear sign of how different the voice of Auden's poetry often is from the personal, prose voice he used in talking about his work. In his poems, "Love outside our own election" would soon truly hold him "in unseen connection."

The world that Auden entered in 1932 when he went to live and work in Colwall, at the foot of the Malvern Hills, is the context for many of the poems that he would collect in a book in 1936. It is a recognizably southern and rural "English" landscape. Colwall lies iconographically in the "South Country" (a term coined by the Catholic writer Hilaire Belloc). This was idealized as a world of gentle, cultivated landscapes, hedgerows, small villages, organic and supposedly harmonious social arrangements, downland and coast, a natural repository of the mythic wealth and values not of Britishness but of Englishness: moderation, reasonableness, expertise, natural bounty, and social cohesion.[23] Broadly speaking, it is part of what the influential interwar ruralist (and *Criterion* contributor) H. J. Massingham, whose work had played such an important role in "Prologue," would call "the Holy Land of England."[24] The move Auden made to the Malvern Hills had an element of choice rather than simple economic necessity to it. As seen in Chapter 6, he had already tried to get a job at a school in the South-West, Dartington School in Devon, earlier in 1932. Auden himself had had a country childhood, and the Downs was a workplace but also a rural home.[25]

The Malvern Hills and Colwall, where Auden now went to live and which are the scene over the next few years of such poems as "Out on the lawn I lie in bed" and "Here on the cropped grass of the narrow ridge I stand," are not, in geographical terms, in the South of England at all. Rather they are in the middle of the country (the Midlands), the nearest big city being Auden's hometown of Birmingham. But in terms of its perceived characteristics, the pastoral world of Worcestershire and Herefordshire was grafted onto the "South Country." As one historian notes, the real existence of the geographically defined South Country became occluded behind "a set of yardsticks of 'rurality' by which the observer judged the landscape." This meant, for example, that Shropshire, with its "half-timbering, village greens, and hedgerows," could become part of the South Country, whereas Cornwall, further south, never could.[26] Using such yardsticks, the Malverns and surroundings qualify as part of what the historian Patrick Wright calls "deep England": an idealized southern world of villages and mellow landscapes, whose "heaths and cliffs have achieved totemic status in the national imagination," often serving an ideological purpose as the "thought of its green hills has been carried around the globe, and into the most terrible military engagements, by generations of armoured soldiers."[27]

The 1937 edition of Baedeker's guide to Great Britain notes only a "racecourse and the Schweppes mineral water factory" in the town of Colwall.[28] The Downs itself was a privately run preparatory school for boys from the ages of eight to thirteen years. It was very "English," very rural, very upper-middle-class. Founded by Quakers in 1900, it was still owned by Friends at the time when Auden arrived. One pupil from Auden's time there as a teacher remembered it as set in "lovely countryside: lush, green, gentle, rolling fields, farms" and thus as "a very out-doors sort of school."[29]

Auden had already identified very strongly with the Midlands region, part of the old kingdom of Mercia, which included the site of Colwall. The Midlands had been the center of what scholars called the "alliterative revival" in the second half of the fourteenth century, producing such works as William Langland's huge, alliterative poem *Piers Plowman* and the anonymous *Sir Gawain and the Green Knight*.[30] Auden had connected imaginatively to alliterative poetry in Anglo-Saxon and Middle English through his student years at Oxford: and that literary tradition courses through his poetry at the end of the 1920s. These poetic interests compounded his attraction to the area in which he now found himself. The Malvern Hills are an important cultural site, associated with Langland and his visionary poem, which begins by naming the place where a pilgrim-dreamer falls asleep "on a May morwenynge on Maluerne Hilles."[31] Auden's interest in Langland, the most revolutionary and dissident of major medieval writers in England, was now linked to his lifeworld at the foot of these very hills.

He even began to discern an organic relationship between Langland, alliteration as a poetic form, and the landscape he was now living in. His friend Naomi Mitchison, the writer and editor who had introduced him to Gerald Heard, remembered that "While he was teaching at Malvern we walked once in the Malvern hills and he compared their contours with the rhythms of 'Piers Plowman' in an extremely convincing way; even the moving cloud shadows seemed to come in on his side."[32] It is natural that, in returning to his "promised land" (the phrase from part 1 of "A Happy New Year"), Auden should have taken a cue from *Piers Plowman* and begun writing a poem in an alliterative style, the mode, according to scholars such as Tolkien and C. S. Lewis, that was one of the most distinctively "English" of metrical forms.[33]

The literary critic Lucy S. McDiarmid has suggested that claims from *New Light on "Piers Plowman,"* an academic book on Langland published in 1928—if Auden had read it—might have made him recognize that the Downs School was situated very near to the spot where that book argues Langland's protagonist drowsed next to a flowing natural water source called Primeswell Spring. (In 1927, Schweppes purchased the rights to use this spring for its "Malvern Water" product.)

Primeswell Spring, the starting point for Langland's vision, is only about a mile and a half from the Downs School.[34]

There was more, besides the Langland connection, to strengthen the "English" associations of Colwall and nearby Great Malvern for Auden. Reminders of the area's patriotic heritage were strongly increased in the 1920s and 1930s by the link, which the musically informed Auden was probably well aware of, to the music of Edward Elgar, composer of the oratorio *The Dream of Gerontius* and of the 1901–1902 patriotic anthem "Land of Hope and Glory." Elgar had been born in a small village in the Malvern Hills and had lived in various houses around Malvern for many years. His wife was buried in a churchyard in nearby Little Malvern in 1920 (and Elgar would be buried next to her in 1934). When Auden arrived in Colwall, Elgar was holder of the royal position of "Master of the King's Musick," essentially the musical equivalent of the poet laureateship. In *The Music Student* in August 1916, Percy Scholes had insisted that "If this country had a 'Musician Laureat' it would be to Elgar that the laurel would be offered. For he, of all our musicians, is the one to whom we turn in times of national feeling to provide us with the musical expression for which our spirits crave."[35]

In sum, Colwall and Malvern had strong symbolic links to the myth of a magical wellhead of pure, unspoiled, rural Englishness. Aside from Auden's simply needing a job and this position at the Downs School being on offer, the region's cultural reputation was something that he could capitalize on for his poetry.

In "A Happy New Year," Auden's speaker sees the telephone wire above his head, which "south into alluvial England ran." "Alluvial" is a revealingly self-referential adjective for Auden to attach to his vision of England: it refers to the deposits made in a stream or riverbed or on a floodplain by sediments that have been washed away from one place and deposited in another by the action of running water. Auden too was now being washed from higher ground to lower. The wire in the air (the wire has a voice in his dream-vision) asks him if he sees "the halt for the narrow-gauge motor train? | Take it. It's yours. Descend to your plain."[36]

With Auden having heard the injunction to take the train south, that mode of transportation, the direction of the journey, and the poetic style closely associated with the Malvern Hills are combined in the first major literary effort he made after leaving Scotland, a work that begins on a train leaving Glasgow. This is the loosely alliterative poem in cantos "In the year of my youth when yoyos came in" (from now on, "In the year of my youth"), which Auden started around July or August in 1932, wrote through the autumn (when he zestfully began referring to it in letters to friends as an "epic"), into the winter and early spring, and then abandoned sometime around March or April 1933.[37]

A yo-yo craze in England peaked in 1932, the time when the poem was started—it was the year when a trademark for the toy was issued and when the first yo-yo world championship took place in London. For the ever-verbally sensitive Auden, the yo-yo fad allows him to use the device as a little heraldic motif for his poem—the out-and-return action of the yo-yo (with its attractively alliterating name) captures the starts and arbitrary ending movements of lines of poetry, spinning around the repeated consonant sounds as they unspool and stop, return, and unspool again. More covertly, the yo-yo gives a clue to the back-and-forth, momentum-driven oscillations of Auden's ideological positions at the period. This was a truth about his political viewpoint that he was more able to acknowledge through the artistic medium of poetry than he was as a young man writing didactic letters to admirers.

The first scene in the poem opens with Auden's speaker drowsing in a train as it runs along near the flowing waters of the River Clyde (just as Langland's speaker falls asleep next to the gurgling of a spring):

> In the year of my youth when yoyos came in
> The carriage was sunny and the Clyde was bright
> As I hastened from Helensburgh in the height of summer
> Leaving for home in a lounge suit.

Departing from Scotland and traveling south is going "home" for Auden. The country he is returning to is in a parlous state, but Auden contrasts his own private relaxation with the public tensions:

> The stokers were seasick on the ship of state
> For the decks were dipping though MacDonald was steering.
> Rumours were rife about the Reinmuth object
> And Stiffkey was sued by the See of Norwich
> For poking his parishioners in their private parts.

Between our vans and the vision the valves were closed.
I sat in my still corner while the country ran
Listening to the lulling low of the lines,
And a shadow-train flitted foreshortened through fields
Of the English counties one after another
Day wore on. I dozed and dreamed.[38]

In the dream-vision that takes place as he sleeps in the railway carriage, the train pulls into a city vaguely like London, where the poem turns into an amalgam of the visionary Langland now crossed with the visionary Dante, already so present in Auden's poetry from the moment of "Prologue." In the city, Auden meets a figure named Sampson, who is his analogue for Virgil in Dante's *Inferno* and *Purgatorio*. Sampson bears a loose but clear resemblance to Gerald Heard, having plenty of Heard's personal primness and volubility as well as his dreamy pet theories.

Together Auden and Sampson drive to a club, where over dinner they discuss history and contemporary events. As they do, a waiter stages a protest, calls out to his "Comrades," and jumps through a window (either to his death or to a rendezvous with other workers). "What you have just been witnessing, has become | Quite common this year," Sampson comments matter-of-factly, "in this country town | As combines totter, credits freeze" (471–472). Sampson and Auden then receive a discreet invitation to visit an enigmatic pair, Titt and Tool, the "Lords of Limit" whom Auden has already brought up in "A Happy New Year" as part of his personal mythological system.[39] But before they do so, they tour a dream version of London, observing scenes of desperate poverty as well as the magnificence of the city's cathedral.

They take a tram to the "Cattle Market" stop, disembark, and there find Titt and Tool's smart caravan parked. Entering, they talk to the wizened "Lords of Limit" about themselves and others until the pair sing them a monitory song that warns the listeners to "be careful what you say | Or do. | Be clean be tidy, oil the lock, | Trim the garden, wind the clock" (482–486).[40] Auden and Sampson leave, chastened, and return to their hotel where, after swearing an undying friendship, the canto ends as they fall asleep (in the same bed).

The following morning, Sampson is up early, and after Auden has performed his morning ablutions, they drive out into the countryside to a Deanery, where a set of establishment figures are to gather for a manhunt of workers who, like the previous evening's waiter, have absconded to join a guerrilla army of "Comrades" hiding in the area. Just as the privileged company assembles, the poem peters out, unfinished. Suggestively, in the work's uncompleted state, the figure representing Auden never wakes from the dream-vision. (Likewise, a scholarly debate about whether or not *Piers Plowman* is a finished poem was already well underway by the 1930s and continues to this day.)

"In the year of my youth" is Auden's most ambitious piece of writing since *Paid on Both Sides*. Such commentary as exists on this uncompleted work has focused mainly either on the poem's unsatisfactory and ultimately broken narrative conception as the reason why Auden was unable to progress beyond the initial stages of canto 2 or on Auden's borrowings from Heard's books.[41] Both approaches are valuable, but they do the poetry an injustice and miss so much that is extraordinary in this largely unprecedented, eccentric fragment.

Of deeper interest than sources or story are the intensely important discoveries (verbal and conceptual) that Auden made while writing the poem. Although he never published it in its original form, he returned to it again and again, cannibalizing phrases, schemas, and even whole sections that he printed separately. (In parallel to this, the poem also contains the first appearance in verse of Auden's long-lasting historical blueprint of the "Three Ages" of the Christian world, reused on several occasions in the 1930s.[42]) Although Auden never published the totality of what he had written, "In the year of my youth" is a significant poem in Auden's career because it is so profoundly, thought-provokingly descriptive and circumstantial. Earlier poems, such as the four-part sequence written in Germany and England in 1929, include autobiographical details and description, but no poem Auden had written before this is so filled with close observation of the appearances of objects and people. It signals a new emphasis on quasi-realistic settings for his poems in his writing of this period. "Find the mortal world enough," Auden touchingly says to a sleeping figure in one of his great love lyrics from the mid-1930s.[43] "In the year of my youth" finds the whole spectrum of the mortal world more than enough for poetry.

As the opening lines show, the poem is freighted with references to political and social events. Once again, as so often in Auden, memories of the last war abound, though here they are seen in the context of the present economic crisis. For example, Sampson warns Auden in canto

1 that "the seed of a hatred" is now "germinating in tenement and gas-lit cellar" (the pun on "German" in "germinating" is obvious) and will soon "shake the world in a war to which | The filling with the killed for four years of a furrow | From the North Sea to the Alps was only a manœuvre" (471). This is a postwar world in which "Business shivers in a banker's winter" (472). A little later on, Auden learns that the lead and silver industries in the place he is visiting have been destroyed by a deal the government made in 1919, the "year of grace when the German fleet | Scuttled itself at Scapa Flow" (475).[44]

Edward Mendelson has a nice phrase to describe a division between two kinds of poem by Auden: those that seem located in a timeless, place-less, and unspecific universe and others, dubbed by Mendelson as "up-to-date poems," that are circumstantial and full of modern objects and people.[45] There were flashes of this up-to-date mode in earlier poems—in *Paid on Both Sides,* for example, or in the cigarette ends, plate-glass win-dows, cocktails, and gumboots of "Consider this" and "Get there if you can."[46] *The Orators* was up-to-date as well, being, for example, the first poetic work in English to mention one of the twentieth century's most momentous and recent inventions: "images cast on the screen of a *television set.*"[47] Thus, Auden had already shown, on occasion, an intense re-sponsiveness to the embodied, incarnated, tangible, object-filled nature of modern existence. (This characteristic in Auden reminds me of the physicality so pervasive in the poems of the Romantic poet John Keats.) Now, like the string hooking the yo-yo toy to a finger and transmitting pulses back and forth between human mind and object, Auden's attune-ment as a poet to the thingscapes and appearances of the contemporary world suddenly takes a leap of kind, not degree, into specificity and con-creteness from the very first line of "In the year of my youth."

Medieval alliterative verse, perhaps because it tends to draw two nouns into a balancing pair within a line—to take a couple of examples from Langland: "I schop me in a *shroud* as I a *scheep* were" or "Undur a brod *banke* bi a *bourne* side"—is often filled with a profusion of things and people. That is true of Auden's poem as well. For instance, the de-scription of the start of Auden and Sampson's dinner together carefully limns both objects and persons:

> "Here's mud in your eye," he murmured, lifting a glass
> Blown on the Danube, beautiful here,

And unfolded a napkin, fuller's delight.
And we sipped a wine of such a flavour
Now as I write I also thirst.
Silver and cutlery shimmered on linen
Stamped with the mark of that sombre town
Which fouls the Don still fresh from the moor.
Waiters scuttled from side to side
Of the vast hall feeding the valuable people,
Or as goldfish come to the glass of their tank
For a second then vanish with a flick of their tails. (469)

Or take, as just one other example, the line about a pair of dead soldiers and "Their bibles, watches, badges, waders"—a whole unembellished verse that just lists things (478).[48] There are so many objects, literally, in Auden's poem—perhaps no poem has been as beautifully cluttered since Alexander Pope's *The Rape of the Lock,* written over 200 years earlier. Profuse, too, as if it were a little primer to the object-filled richness of the whole work, is the elaborate description Auden gives of the figures on a stone frieze, a "quarried curtain covered with carving," on the side of a cathedral, rife with exempla:

A virgin creeping like a cat from a desert,
A happy king with hawks and hounds,
A ploughing peasant with my father's features,
Boys playing leapfrog and blowing trumpets,
Angels flying and usurers boiling;
Ran dragons, badgers, birds and oxen
In the sky above us from south to north
Like a flooded road on the rim of the space
Studding the Milky Way for millions of miles. (476–477)

In an unexpected side comment on the inhibiting individualism and self-consciousness of modern artists and, by extension, modern poets, Auden explains this fantastical profusion of ornate carving as the work of "men unknown by name and deed" who "Casually casting into the creating sea, | Had fished such treasures from its teeming fathoms | As move to despair any modern dredger" (476).

Auden touches and tastes in this poem, but the copious world of objects that he writes about in "In the year of my youth" is most often captured visually. For Auden, seeing is uniquely intense in this work, going even beyond the ubiquitous acts of sighting that he described in "Prologue." Seeing is more than noticing and more than a simple naming of things: it is a careful, powerful registering of appearances. Light is everywhere in Auden's poem, as if the "epic" (Auden's term) were criss-crossed by verbal searchlight beams illuminating things that had previously stood largely in the darkness beyond poetic representation.

Because of the light that Auden's poem casts onto the world, "In the year of my youth" is full of subtle effects, where all kinds of illumination, natural and artificial, play off, highlight, alter, and obscure a variety of surfaces. Auden had advanced some way into this visual territory in slightly earlier poems such as "Prologue" (with its "star-concealing dawn"), intended at one time as a prologue to "In the year of my youth."[49] But, from the very start of this new poem, he displays an unprecedented concern with the look of light on objects.

No other work of his is so sustainedly hungry for the poetry of lit-up surfaces and places, from the "sunny" carriage at the very beginning, and on through dozens of light details, such as (I pick out just a few, though enough to suggest the pervasiveness of light, and hence *vision,* in the poem) a "shadow where giglamps guttered and winked," "light from the shops [that] | Lit up the leaves on their undersides," old men's "reflections in glass," a dining room where "in the shaded light of standard lamps | Clever and sad looked the simplest face," the "spurt of flame" from a match, a tram with its "lights flickering, | The cable above it crackling with sparks | Like a knife being ground," a road "dotted with red lamps," and so on. For a supposedly intellectual poet, this is a very carnal, materialistic poem. Inside Titt and Tool's caravan base are "Tube lights let into the tunnel roof," while outside, a man waits "with an electric torch" (466–486). The poem's obsession with light is Dantesque, but it also evinces an attempt by Auden to create a poetic version of the effects of realism and circumstantiality usually associated with novels.[50] Moreover, because seeing and naming are often the precondition for knowing, the extreme visibility of the world in Auden's poem is a manifestation of his reborn sense of connection with a shared, familiar, English realm as he stages his journey "home" and the world there becomes cognitively mapped and known again.

The sustained focus on effects of lighting is epitomized by the magnificent image at the start of canto 2:

Dawn was a glimmer, like a great lamp
With the switch at the first resistance stuck,
Descrying furniture cold in room. (488)

Naturally, then, in such a poetic landscape, colors are ubiquitous: "sun browned," "gilded," "grey," "Pickle-red," "wort-blue," "silver," and "spat coloured" (467–495). And elsewhere, many nouns imply a color strongly but indirectly: "coffee," "pewter," "paper," "Irish linen," "teak," and "make-up matching the morning" (472–495). A poem this full of hues highlights how limited a role color normally plays in Auden's poetry.

These remarkable descriptions of varying light phenomena depend on the many vignettes of everyday actions, objects, and scenes that the poem brings into view. Look, for example, at the technical specifications of a modern internal combustion engine powering the car that Sampson and Auden drive out to the Deanery in canto 2. Most of the engine's technical specifications are plausible. It is a "compact four cylinder unit, | O-h-v with forced lubrication | And a Claudel down draught carburettor" (490).[51] Other examples of the seemingly infinite variety of the things and people of the world appearing, as if by magic, include the "half coconut | And morsels of mutton fat moving on string" arranged for the birds at the Deanery and the very "out" character whom Auden and Sampson meet after their arrival there, the offspring of General Gorse, "Who created many widows in the World War," and his wife. This is the man Auden calls "Christopher their son with the shishi walk" (493, 494).

Commenting on his translation of Homer's *Odyssey*, Pope wrote that there "is a real beauty in an easy, pure, perspicuous description even of a *low action*."[52] (By "low," Pope means commonplace or ordinary.) Auden's own "epic" is full of everyday, familiar actions, some "low," and of people and things described with real beauty. The poem lingers in its descriptions on many everyday objects, as if they were new and mysterious inventions being seen for the first time. At the start of canto 2, Sampson hands the drowsy Auden an electric shaver, a device that was just starting to be marketed in the early 1930s:

Produced from his dressing gown pocket,
Attached to a coil of twisted flex,
An object the size of an infant's fist,
Pear shaped, broad at the base for a grip

But flattened out to a serrated edge
Like a barber's clipper at the business end.

The magical new machine or "engine" produces a highly sensual and intimate piece of poetry, when, shaving, Auden "soft as insect palps | Felt the pulsating blade sweeping my face" (489).

The poem's focus on the things and the people of this world, along with its keen temporal awareness (clocks and watches abound), dramatize a new power in Auden's writing to visualize, understand, and "fix" a knowable contemporary English scene. So much "world" suddenly comes into this poem just as the yo-yo suddenly came into fashion in society at the same time. And the thing-filledness and -seenness of this English world carry an almost patriotic phenomenological message of integration, familiarity, and concord between poet and surroundings.

Incidentally, Auden makes visible too some socially subterranean milieux of the time, not least the queer world of the 1930s. Christopher "with the shishi walk" is one example of this effort, but Auden mentions as well that, when he and Sampson got off the tram at the "Cattle Market" stop on their journey to see Titt and Tool, he notices in the "very centre" an "underground cottage frequented by the queer" (479). That night Sampson and Auden will fall asleep together in a moment full of tender feeling. Then, rather daringly—and in a way that (had the poem been published) would surely have been interpreted at the time as "effeminate"—when Auden gets up in the morning, in another moment of bodily frankness, he describes how, still in his pajamas, he gives himself a quick sponge bath: "Then [I] tugged at the girdle which sustains trousers | Letting them slip to leave me naked | Thoroughly sponged the parts at the fork" (489). (By this point in canto 2, readers have noticed that the commitment to a strict alliterative style has weakened considerably.) Auden's demythologized version of the poetic self stands silently at a mirror with no clothes on, seeing in a still faintly alliterative poem an alliterating image of the "white flesh" of his own body in the mirror, while he cleans himself off.[53]

However, there is always more to the question of a poem's contemporaneity than simple historical references or allusions. This is a poem of material presence summoned by language. "A sentence uttered makes a world appear" is the beautiful opening line to one of Auden's later poems.[54] As the sentences of "In the year of my youth" unspool and we hear in our heads the "lulling low" of the poem's alliterating lines while Auden is "leaving for home," a visible and tangible world does begin to appear. After modernism's fracturings, among so much else this is a manifesto-like piecing back together of a knowable world in 1930s poetry. Auden may not have finished his "epic" poem's narrative, but the rich worldliness and descriptiveness of the passages that he did write suggest that one of the primary purposes of "In the year of my youth" was fully achieved or, to use a better word, realized. A world came into focus, and it was recognizably an "English" one.

At almost the very moment when he was beginning the most lit-up, referential poem he ever composed, Auden told his brother that he was "ashamed of [*The Orators'*] obscurity." He related the "obscurity" to "swank," by which he seems to have meant a kind of hammed-up version of artistic individualism.[55] After the verbal saturnalia and "obscurity" (originally a term denoting darkness or invisibility) of *The Orators* and the "blurring images" of the first part of "A Happy New Year," the linguistic world of "In the year of my youth" is extraordinarily *clear* and *full.* That clarity and fullness feel solid and yet, at the same time, because of the Langland pastiche Auden uses, made up, as if the world were both there and somehow not quite there. At a time of historical crisis, the poem gives the world back to the reader with a slightly different texture than its actual one. But here, in poetry, is a stabilized and clarified form of physical existence, creating a kind of bond, or a community, of shared understanding between readers and text.

This gesture is generous from one viewpoint. From another, though, it is also exclusionary—only some readers will identify with the English world and the community in the poem. "Nationalism fails not because the nation is too small a group but because it is too large," Auden commented in a review published in October 1932, when he was a few months into writing "In the year of my youth." He seems to imply that true national feeling can only exist in smaller and more cohesive groups than a vast modern nation-state.[56] As one poem from this period put it, every individual needs a small "group where for his hour | Loved and loving he may flower."[57]

A small group or tribe can only exist in relation to a larger body that is not inside the charmed circle: this is one of the moral dilemmas Auden struggles with as a poet, working in a profound but relatively niche artistic medium, in the 1930s and beyond. It is perhaps a dilemma that every poet faces—no poem can ever be about only one person's experience nor can it be about everyone's. The beauty of Auden's poetic cosmos (like those of other poets as well) is dependent in mysterious and morally fascinating ways on its semi-closed character, to which only some readers can fully relate.

In September 1932, during the early stages of composing "In the year of my youth," Auden wrote to his geologist brother John, who was now in India, thanking him for the return of some money Auden had loaned. Auden told his brother that he did not need what John Auden had sent and that he had therefore taken part of it and donated it to the "Lancashire strikers," that is, to the more than 150,000 workers in the cotton-manufacturing industry in the North East who were then taking industrial action (unsuccessfully) to maintain wage levels.[58] (It would be interesting to know how many other established poets in the 1930s ever contributed to a strike fund.)

The poem Auden was writing at the time of this incident does not hold back from denunciations of a class-based, exploitative society. Auden, accompanied by Sampson, witnesses scenes of poverty and dehumanization that cause him to cry out:

> O human pity in the English heart
> Wincing at sight of surgeon's lancet,
> Gripped by the crying of a captured bird,
> Shudder indeed at what I saw and tell.
> Weep now, howl, till your eyes are full,
> That life on one littoral lucky to be
> Can make its tittle of eternity so cruel. (474)

Only a few lines further on, he insists that there are pains that cannot be assuaged by a cult of private happiness: "Here I made certain of a sorrow," he writes, "not | To be forgotten even in the act of love" (475).[59] As a person, Auden remained on the side of labor and was aware of the plight of the poor throughout the crisis years of the early 1930s. While he and Sampson walk through backstreets on their way to see the Lords of Limit, they pass scenes of painful immiseration:

> Some sitting like sacks, some slackly standing,
> Their faces in the glimmering gaslight grey,

Their eyeballs drugged as a dead rabbit's
Or child I saw at a window by want so fretted
His face had assumed the features of a tortoise. (475)

Yet, in the same letter to his brother in which he informs John about the donation to striking cloth workers, Auden sounds a slightly different note as he comments on the crises gripping the country. With an elegiac flourish, he tells his brother that he felt "the approaching end to our little world."[60] (As Chapter 6 showed, a "little world" was one of John of Gaunt's descriptions of England in *Richard II*.) Many poems he was soon to write were not about socialist comrades but about "our little world" of privilege and comfort and its possible "end." In a review Auden published the following month, he described how communism's "increasing attraction for the bourgeois lies in its demand for self-surrender for those individuals who, isolated, feel themselves emotionally at sea."[61] When a friend wrote after seeing the review, Auden told him, "No. I am a bourgeois. I shall not join the C.P."[62]

Auden's allegiances at the time are hard to pin down; they seem to shift continuously between the poles of anticapitalist critique and a lingering attachment to "our little world" of insular, upper-middle-class professional life and romantic love in sheltered corners of the rural world. Take another example. In December 1932, as already noted, Auden wrote to an American critic, calling *The Orators* "a stage in my conversion to Communism." But in the same letter he almost immediately reverts to a patriotic argument with references to the desperate fluctuations in military fortune for the British Army in the last year of the Great War: "England will get worse and worse till there is [the prospect of] an utter defeat," Auden says, "and then it's possible I think that as we have often done before we shall stand the winner."[63]

By the time he made the declaration in this letter, Auden was probably composing the final sections of canto 1 of "In the year of my youth." Earlier in the poem, Sampson has explained that disgruntled or alienated workers are "Slipping away without warning or reason; | In twos and threes they have taken to the hills" to join what sounds like a guerrilla army, an army that the establishment forces were to have hunted down in the sections of the poem Auden never drafted (472).

In December 1932, Auden wrote a passage about the mysterious destiny that Titt and Tool are concocting for his own poetic avatar.

Auden in the poem is jobless (in reality, he was already working at the Downs School). Yet Titt and Tool reassure him that things will work out: "You'll find yourself | Among *hills* again," they tell him, referring to the new position at the Downs School they have planned for him (480; emphasis added). Yet at the same time they make a connection between his own future and the communists who in a different but related way "have taken to the *hills*" (472; emphasis added). The nature of this connection between Auden's life among hills and the communists in the hills is never spelled out. Titt and Tool immediately add approvingly, as if they were mirroring the shifts in Auden's own politics, that these hills are "the oldest in England" (480). The exact ideological tenor of Auden's move into rural Herefordshire is uncertain: it is both an advance and a retreat.

Then, at the start of canto 2 of the poem, Auden slips on a "red shirt." The implication is that a "red" identity is not an immutable fact but one that can be put on and taken off at will like a garment. Auden also hints that the shirt he wears is only "loose-fitting." While it is made of the warm, comforting material "light flannel," he chooses a word that means both a kind of cotton or woolen fabric but also verbal nonsense or blather. Moreover, although the shirt's dye is distilled from "coal-tar," it is not natural. The "exact shade" is "Calculated in a notebook"—that is, the red is self-consciously created by a set of sickly men ("to whom thermometers are more than women") whose function is to write things down—formulas or, by extension, poems (489).

To the red shirt, Auden adds a tie, an expensive tweed suit, fine climber's boots, and, perhaps rather ominously, since they sound as they might come from a military outfitter, some "spiral khaki puttees" (489–490). There is no solid record of Auden wearing a red shirt in real life at this period. But recall that on the occasion of his visit to Dartington earlier in 1932, he wore a pink one (with all that might have connoted at the time about the wearer's leftism and homosexuality) and suffered the consequences. Auden's clothing in canto 2 could just be treated as trivial description. But, in Auden's career as a whole, clothes often make the man or reveal something in the man that had until now been occluded. Here, the costume of his poetic representative—like a complex emblem—articulates a deep ambivalence: one article is "red"; some, being costly, are beyond the purchasing power of a laborer; and some, like the khaki puttees, might belong to a person on the right side of the political spectrum.

When Auden wrote to his brother about donating money to the "Lancashire strikers" and sensing the "end to our little world," he added: "I'm just going off to a quaker school at Colwall, to teach culture to those who can afford it. Its difficult to know what we ought to do. Its wicked to try and keep the ship going; its conceited to join the 'We're doomed' gang, and cowardly to jump into the sea."[64] The Downs was his morally ambiguous solution to the problem of what to do, born partly out of necessity and partly out of inclination. "Wonderful buildings, and food," Auden announced, describing his new "working place" to his friend Iris Sinkinson in Helensburgh: "Open air dormitories etc. 84 boys. The assistant masters who are unmarried (there are 9 staff, 6 ♂ and 3 ♀) live in our own house and have dinner there. The headmaster I believe to be a great man, in spite of religion. (We are quakers here.) . . . The atmosphere I find a little intense. I suppose it's what the Communist state will be like; one feels it isn't done not to be enthusiastic about everything. The place is run on scout lines, with packs and leaders."[65] More informally, Auden told Gabriel Carritt, "This place is quite incredible," adding that the atmosphere is a "cross between The Plumed Serpent and the Church Lads Brigade."[66] By referring to the Downs in this way, Auden seems to have meant that this prep school had a mixture of the highly charged sexual and irrationalist atmosphere of Lawrence's 1926 novel *The Plumed Serpent* (centered on the "ancient phallic mystery" powering a revolution in Mexico) and a pious, Anglican organization for youths, complete with its own uniform and quasi-military messaging, founded at the end of the nineteenth century to promote knowledge of religion in recreational and educational contexts.

The Downs combined a serious, unconventional moral ethos with a striking informality.[67] The ethical seriousness stemmed principally from the school's Quaker background. The Downs was supported by money from one of the most prominent Quaker mercantile dynasties in the Midlands. "Our money comes from chocolate," Auden told Naomi Mitchison. Geoffrey Hoyland, a Quaker, the school's headmaster and owner, was married to Dorothea Hoyland: "Mrs. Head is a Cadbury."[68]

While Geoffrey Hoyland was the public face of the Downs, Dorothea Hoyland, a member of the Board of Governors, was "the sympathetic, very human liaison" between her charismatic but aloof husband and many of the pupils and the people working at the school.[69]

Several prominent Quaker families had sent their children to the Downs, finding it a place that cherished the principles of the Society of Friends. In absolute contrast to the majority of prep and public schools, the Downs School during the First World War had been staffed by conscientious objectors, and the boys had, as Peter Parker puts it, been kept "isolated . . . from the prevailing war psychosis." The school's headmaster at the time, Herbert Jones, used to intone the proverb "Pax melior bellum" (Peace is better than war) in Latin lessons rather than Horace's "Dulce et decorum est pro patria mori" (It is sweet and fitting to die for one's country).[70]

On the other hand, as Carpenter explains, "emphasis was put on hobbies; music and painting were much encouraged, and there was an outdoor swimming pool and even a model steam railway."[71] Auden soon became a particular friend of the school's art master, Maurice Feild, and his wife, Alexandra Feild. Maurice Feild, a conservative painter who was devoted to Impressionism and especially to the work of Camille Pissarro, was an excellent teacher. Andrew Forge, a pupil in the 1930s and later a distinguished painter and critic, remembered that Feild had "a mind like Ruskin's, [and] emphasized really looking and learning to look."[72] (Perhaps coincidentally, Auden started his very visual, light-filled poem "In the year of my youth" around the later summer of 1932 and arrived at Colwall by early October before he had got very far into it.[73]) As an example of the success this all-boys establishment at its best had as an educational enterprise, Feild nurtured a remarkable number of young talents who later went on to successful careers as mainly traditional painters in the British art world, including Forge, Anthony Fry, Patrick George, Lawrence Gowing, Anthony Hill, Francis Hoyland, and Kenneth Rowntree. Into this creative microcosm, Auden fitted easily; Fry remembered him as "an inspired teacher, . . . young, crazy, completely original."[74]

Auden probably abandoned, or at least put aside, "In the year of my youth" around April 1933. After so much effort expended on the poem for eight or nine months when he had written relatively little else, it must have felt like a considerable setback. On his twenty-sixth birthday, 21 February 1933, as he tried to maintain some vestige of progress on the poem, he wrote to a Scottish friend, Arnold Snodgrass, "I am living miserably like a hen scratching for food."[75] A month or so later, he told Geoffrey Grigson, the editor of *New Verse,* toward the end of March 1933 that he had no new work to share because a "narrative poem sucks everything in."[76] While composing "In the year of my youth," Auden had often turned to maritime imagery in his prose and letters. In September 1932, he had commented to his brother that "Its wicked to try and keep the ship going; its conceited to join the 'We're doomed' gang, and cowardly to jump into the sea."[77] And, in October of that year, he wrote in the *New Statesman* about communism's appeal "for those individuals who, isolated, feel themselves emotionally at sea."[78]

It is no surprise, then, that a few months later, in April 1933, when he wrote another dream-vision poem, this one private and almost certainly never intended for publication, he should describe it in terms of water and a sailing vessel. In the poem, Auden pictures himself falling asleep "in a deck-chair" in Oxford. The dream he then has allegorizes his artistic situation: this bird lover temporarily becomes a seagull looking down on a "ship | Evidently in motion," for which the "name painted on her bows | Was Wystan Auden Esquire." Ominously, the ship is laboring through a storm at sea.[79] The seagull notices that the ship the *Wystan Auden Esquire* is "flying the Union Jack"—a detail that once again ties Auden's sense of his poetry in the early 1930s to his sense of a national identity (497).

Given its fugitive nature, it is not surprising that this poem is composed in a (for Auden) unpolished style, but it has delicate touches that show his emotional investment in the story: the scene-setting "*deck*-chair" where he falls asleep leads to the dream content of a ship's tale that begins on the *deck;* the *ship* becomes a vehicle for Auden to meditate on his poetic *craft,* and when he wakes from the dream, the detail with which he chooses to end the poem is that the "table was laid for *tea,*" hinting, not very convincingly, that the whole dream has been just a storm in a *tea*cup (497, 502; emphases added).

The *Wystan Auden Esquire,* which is "looking for land" but runs into a gale, is commanded by a "thin as a biscuit" female captain who bears a sharp resemblance to Auden's vehement mother. The kindly but ineffectual "first mate" who brings her cups of tea and meekly endures her criticisms seems curiously similar to Auden's father. There is an array of other crew members, including an engineer, a Duke who is flirting with a cabin boy, and an obsessed Professor with a strong similarity to Auden's Oxford acquaintance, the scholar of Greek R. M. Dawkins, who is completely absorbed in making string figures no matter what happens to the ship (498–500). With the exception of the Duke and the cabin boy, the ship's crew and command do not seem to serve a shared purpose. No one seems interested in, or adept at, what they are doing, aside from the Professor, whose involvement with complex formal questions related to constructions of lines of string suggests Auden's fascination with technical issues in poetic form.[80]

Having berated the crew while "the gale whirled shriller and colder," the ship's maddened captain starts firing her musket in all directions before she turns, hisses at the seagull, calling it "Saboteur, spy," and shoots (502). (In New York, more than a decade later, discussing Mrs. Auden's spectacular temper, Auden told an acquaintance that "There were times when I was sure that my mother would kill me."[81]) As the captain fires at the gull, there is "a sudden flash, | A roar in my ears," and Auden wakes up (502).

The shooting of the bird that brings the dream to an end constitutes another suddenly truncated story, reminiscent of the planned but never completed hunt with guns for traitors in "In the year of my youth." We do not know whether the vessel *Wystan Auden Esquire* is supposed to be foundering, but the dream tells us that the dreamer is a vessel in distress and feeling lost.

Although Auden rarely presented his poems in the order of their composition in his books, they form their own story when read chronologically: one moment leads to, even produces, another. In May 1933, a month or so after the mad voyage described in "The month was April," Auden composed a poem that makes a crucial reference to Gerard Manley Hopkins's shipwreck meditation "The Wreck of the Deutschland," written between 1875 and 1876. This new poem, which begins, "Hearing of harvests rotting in the valleys," is one of the twentieth century's classic examples of the sestina. It is not Auden's first attempt at this newly fashionable form (an earlier one is included in *The Orators*).

The sestina's resurgence as a viable poetic option is often tied to William Empson's discussion in *Seven Types of Ambiguity* (1930) of Philip Sidney's double sestina opening, "Ye goatherd-gods, that love the grassy mountains," from *The Countess of Pembroke's Arcadia* (1593).[82]

In *Seven Types of Ambiguity*, Empson describes the sestina in a very specific way, one that shaped the understandings of poets like Auden as they were beginning to experiment with this form. Empson sees the sestina—which is usually traced back by historians to roots in troubadour love poetry—as freakish. Musing on Sidney's ornate double sestina, he calls it "so curiously foreign to the normal modes or later developments of the language." And he remarks that Sidney's "lovelorn" poem "beats, however rich its orchestration, with a wailing and immovable monotony, for ever upon the same doors in vain." It has, in a phrase strikingly relevant to Auden's current imaginative world, "something of the aimless multitudinous beating of the sea on a rock." For Empson, Sidney's poem is not so much a philosophical or allegorical meditation as it is a complaint about frustrated love, and it works not as a set of sequential propositions or an argument but rather as "a unit of sustained feeling."[83] "Hearing of harvests rotting in the valleys," Auden's claustrophobic, dreamlike poem, which shares two of its six end words (valleys and mountains) with Sidney's, is similarly unified and plaintive. And, like the end words in Sidney's poem, all of Auden's end words are drooping, softly landing trochees.

"Hearing of harvests rotting in the valleys" uses the slow, tidal repetitions of the sestina form to evoke a mood of frustrated longing for whatever world we do not have:

> Hearing of harvests rotting in the valleys,
> Seeing at end of street the barren mountains,
> Round corners coming suddenly on water,
> Knowing them shipwrecked who were launched for islands,
> We honour founders of these starving cities,
> Whose honour is the image of our sorrow.[84]

The end words suggest the poem's basic emotional scheme: a catalogue of five varying place words—valleys, mountains, water, islands, cities—and one human constant: sorrow. The stark, old Germanic word "sorrow" is beautifully chosen: it has a strongly Shakespearean aroma—think, for instance, of Sonnet 120: "how hard true sorrow hits," or *Richard II:*

"Write sorrow on the bosom of the earth." "Sorrow" is a word that Auden comes back to unusually frequently in his poems: "Love shall not near | The sweetness here | Nor sorrow take | His endless look" and "None knows of the next day if it be less or more, the sorrow" are just two examples, out of many, written at this period.[85] The sestina, with its long, looping recurrences, is a form with an aura of fatalism; by the time we have read the first stanza, we know what all the key elements are, and we have a feeling for at least some of how they will interact for the rest of the poem. In this case, the formal fatalism is even more pronounced because all the end words are nouns (again, like those in Sidney's poem), not verbs: the end words are things of a fixed nature; that is, none of them are actions that might bring change.

The first line suggests a contemporary predicament, as if this is to be another of those "up-to-date" poems. This turns out to be not exactly the case, but Auden presents a diffuse, dreamlike picture of social want and disappointment that recalls some of the passages in "In the year of my youth." Here, "So many, careless, dived and drowned in water; | So many, wretched, would not leave their valleys" (190). But the key to this vague, haunted world comes close to the poem's center in stanza 3: "at night the water | Running past windows comforted their sorrow; | Each in his little bed conceived of islands" (189). Islands are beloved, inspiring, and entrapping: Auden's ambivalence about them (including, of course, the mythic "island" of England) is dramatized here in the varying shades of meaning with which each end word returns. Islands in this poem are places of isolation and disaster about which nonetheless humans continue to dream and to "conceive" of, just as they do of a place where "love was innocent, being far from cities" (189).[86] The sorrow at night in the lonely "little bed," comforted only by the sound of running water, is the bleak reality. It is a fantasy to imagine a life where "love was innocent."

"Love" is the counterpoint to "sorrow," but as the poem's formal rules demand, "sorrow" appears seven times (six in the emphatic position of a line end), and "love," poignantly, only once, midline, surrounded—and almost occluded—by other words. By its solitariness and by its promise of happiness, though, "love" catches the reader's eye:

> every day was dancing in the valleys,
> And all the year trees blossomed on the mountains,
> Where love was innocent, being far from cities. (189)

All sestinas must conclude, or merely stop, in a single three-line stanza that incorporates all six end words and that is usually called the "envoi," though for Auden's poem the alternate (originally Occitan) term "tornada," or "return," seems more fitting. Here is Auden's tornada:

> It is the sorrow; shall it melt? Ah, water
> Would *gush, flush, green* these mountains and these valleys,
> And we rebuild our cities, not dream of islands. (190; emphasis
>   added)

"Shall it melt?" These words form the first question to appear in the entire poem, as if a sense of deadlock were beginning to thaw. Although Auden never explains what might cause the melting of sorrow, he does imagine the outcome: the world would change. And he looses a trio cascade of verbs to dramatize that change: "gush, flush, green." This line contains a clear allusion to "The Wreck of the Deutschland," in which Hopkins compares the revelation of the meaning of Christ's sacrifice bursting in on a sinner's mind to the flood of bitter and intense physical sensations that a bitten sloe suddenly unleashes in the mouth:

> How a lush-kept plush-capped sloe
>   Will, mouthed to flesh-burst,
> *Gush!—flush* the man, the being with it, sour or sweet
> Brim, in a flásh, fúll![87]

The connotations of a sudden flood of gushing, flushing, greening, conjoined with Hopkins's erotic description of a moment of religious release, together suggest that Auden's ostensibly public poem about social discontent is actually, at a deeper level, the "lovelorn" (Empson's word) private expression of a longing for connection.

In mid-June 1933, just two months after Auden had written his private vision of a beleaguered ship bearing his name and lost at sea, a belated review of his book *Poems* (1930) appeared in *The Listener* in a group notice. The reviewer was one of London's leading literary journalists, Bonamy Dobrée, an acquaintance of T. S. Eliot and of Auden.[88] In his piece, Dobrée wrote about the new "school of which W. H. Auden is leader, round whom are grouped in particular Stephen Spender and C. Day Lewis." And he went on to characterize these writers by giving a rather oxymoronic definition of their writing. "They are, on the whole, communists," Dobrée said, gesturing toward their professed contempt for tradition, for the class structure of British society, and for the suffocating pieties of monarchy and empire. (He was also hinting at the unwelcome "foreignness" with which such political views were conventionally associated in Britain at the time.) But, Dobrée added, twisting his initial thought in an unexpected direction, they are "communists with an intense love of England."[89] This is reminiscent of Auden writing to his brother with his comments that oscillate within a few lines from a remark about contributing to the Lancashire strikers and then foreseeing the "end to our little world," a world that is at least in part based, as Auden was well aware, on exploitation of other people's labor.

The writer who was the main subject of Dobrée's acute review was intensely conscious of his "intense love of England" ("Prologue" alone shows that) and of the way his imagination leaned toward national settings and themes. A few days after Dobrée's piece appeared, Auden, from his home at a boys' school in one of the deepest and lushest parts of the English countryside, wrote to his fellow poet Stephen Spender. Spender had contacted Auden complaining about the way that another reviewer, Charles Madge, had drawn Auden to his side during an attack on Spender. Much of Auden's letter is diplomatic and backpedaling as he tried to assuage Spender's anger about the Madge piece and the burst of criticism it had evidently generated from Spender about Auden's parochialism. "I must say at once that I had nothing whatever to do with Madge's article," Auden protested when he wrote back. As if to lessen the offense, he noted for Spender at the end of the letter that "You got a lovely puff from Dobrée in the Listener." (He tactfully refrained from mentioning the praise that Dobrée heaped on Auden himself in the same review or from commenting on the idea that Spender was merely a member of the "school"—perhaps a deliberately catty choice of noun in this context—of which Auden was the "leader.")

In the heart of this 1933 letter to Spender, though, Auden went on to lay out one of his clearest explanations of how he understood the connection between his poetry and what he called here "national emblems":

I entirely agree with you about my tendency to National Socialism, and its dangers. It is difficult to be otherwise when ones surroundings, and emotional symbols are of necessity national emblems.

I'm no more of a communist than you are but to acheive the kind of society I think we both wish for, it is fatal to ignore the national psychological factor. The number of the completely disinterested is never quite large enough.

The success of fascism seems to show that if people have any share; even only a cultural one, (eg the secondary school clerk,) He responds to the national call and if the right appeal is not made, the wrong one will be.

Personally I think that the more internationally you can think and feel, the more I admire you.

For myself, I know my temperament and necessity, force me to work in a small field.[90]

Indirectly responding to Dobrée's idea that they were "communists with an intense love of England," Auden declared, "I'm no more of a communist than you are." (This alone would have grated on Spender, since he identified strongly with socialist causes at this time.) Auden could have stopped there. In fact, though, he went much deeper. He sympathized, he said, with Spender's avowals of internationalism. But he could not share them. Quite the contrary. Referring to what were evidently some criticisms by Spender of Auden's narrower perspective, Auden spelled something out. "I entirely agree with you," he wrote "about my tendency to National Socialism, and its dangers."[91]

Even after reading Auden's self-critiques of the ambiguous politics in *The Orators,* including his diagnosis of the book as "a catharsis of the author's personal fascism," the phrase in his letter to Spender about his "tendency to National Socialism" comes as a surprise, perhaps as a shock.[92] Auden could be picking up here on Dobrée's description, suggestive in the political context of 1933, of himself as a "leader." (By as early as 1922, true believers had been calling Mussolini "il Duce" and Hitler "der Führer."[93]) In confessing his ideologically dangerous "tendency" as a writer to Spender and, with eye-opening frankness, by labeling that danger as "National Socialism," Auden seems to have had in mind the idea that his poems were underwritten by an anti-metropolitan celebration of an ideal of organic, egalitarian, communal rootedness, sharing resources, located in a country environment, nationalist by implication and feeling, and perhaps having some vaguely cult-like elements.

But it is not easy to separate that more idiosyncratic and humane meaning from the conventional connotations of "National Socialism." Auden had seen plenty of "National Socialists" during his visits to Berlin in previous years. Even if there is no facile equation to be made between Auden's own politics and the contemporary meanings of the term, he would have known that it was provocative, at the least, for a supposedly left-wing writer to describe himself in 1933 as having a "tendency to National Socialism." Auden was obviously not a Nazi, but he sees a "tendency" in himself toward an extreme political position. Mendelson remarks that what Auden says here "suggests fighting fire with fire, using the psychological methods of fascism to serve fascism's enemies."[94] There is something to that: Auden tells Spender, a bit weakly, that he uses national symbols to promote "the kind of society I think we both wish for." But my inclination is to take Auden more literally: with self-awareness, he points to the tie between his poetry and an alluring, and dangerous, mythology about the nation.

The weight of Auden's letter is significant, and it clearly connects with the sense of Englishness that he has been grappling with in his poetry in the 1930s. For Auden, Englishness invokes an infinitely complicated mixture of beauty, eroticism, poetic apprehension, personal comfort, toxic historical legacies, personal guilt, and socially learned self-hatred. To take him at face value when he describes his "tendency to National Socialism" is, as nonjudgmentally as possible, to recognize that the aesthetic power of Auden's poetry in the early 1930s is inseparable from ethical quandaries about some of its underlying values. (In a poem addressed to Eliot in the 1940s, in which he reflects on Eliot's own political transgressions, on poets' lives more generally, and perhaps also on the lives of poetry readers, Auden asks, alluding to *Hamlet*: "which of us shall escape whipping?"[95]) As we will see at the end of this book, Auden himself would eventually come to understand this quandary and its limiting effect on his poetry.

Continuing his remarks in the 1933 letter about "my tendency to National Socialism, and its dangers," Auden observed to Spender that it "is difficult to be otherwise, when ones surroundings, and emotional symbols are of necessity national emblems." This shifts the moral burden a little, making it seem that the rural landscape where he happens to be living is in some way to blame. But his concluding remark on the subject moves back toward taking some responsibility, even if it also seems like a rather too casual shrug of the shoulders: "I know my temperament and necessity, force me to work in a small field."

A "small field" (a phrase with connotations of the rural world but also evoking the Heardian idea of a psychic "field") recalls other Auden phrases, public and private, already encountered: for example, the wish from part 2 of "A Happy New Year" that "our town here" may "continue small" so that emotional "intensity" can persist within the "field of five or six, the English cell"; or "our little reef" of England in "Prologue": "This fortress perched on the edge of the Atlantic scarp, | The mole between all Europe and the exile-crowded sea." Auden's comment about working in a "small field" also recalls his letter to his brother, expressing regret over the end of "our little world."[96] The letter to Spender integrates cleanly with many other comments in poems and letters that Auden made around this time, and it crystallizes Auden's realization about the values and range of his poetic mind. Scarred by war and by English culture, he was wrestling with the imagination he had, not the imagination he might have liked: "For myself, I know my temperament and necessity, force me to work in a small field."

In 1933, Auden was recognizing the poet in himself who was inspired by groups of like-minded people living in an English rural setting, as he did at the Downs School. And, as such, he believed that the map of his own creative and emotional world in a mysterious but real way corresponded to the map of a whole culture's mythological and iconographic imagination. This belief might explain why he was already evoking such positive responses in an influential, and often conservative, English readership, represented most prominently by his Faber and Faber editor T. S. Eliot, "classicist in literature, royalist in politics, and Anglo-Catholic in religion."[97] However, at the same time, although Auden's and Eliot's views about rootedness and community occasionally seemed very close in this period, Auden was capable of challenging Eliot directly about the political valences in his work. In late February 1934, Eliot published *After Strange Gods: A Primer of Modern Heresy,* a vehemently prejudicial meditation on cultural politics. It contains some of his most notorious, conservative comments, including a passage where he insists that the "population should be homogeneous; where two or more cultures exist in the same place they are likely either to be fiercely self-conscious or both to become adulterate. What is still more important is unity of religious background; and reasons of race and religion combine to make any large number of free-thinking Jews undesirable. There must be a proper balance between urban and rural, industrial and agricultural development. And a spirit of excessive tolerance is to be deprecated."[98]

Eliot seems to have sent Auden a copy of *After Strange Gods*. After an interval, Auden wrote back to his patron, editor, and poetic model about the book: "Some of the general remarks, if you will forgive me saying so, rather shocked me, because if they are put into a political scale, and it seems quite likely [they will be?], would produce a world in which neither I nor you I think would like to live."[99] Auden's own distance from the practical "political scale" is clear. Although there are obvious ideological reverberations in his poems and letters, to extrapolate a specific program of action from his poetry is impossible, and he found Eliot's attempts to recommend particular, severely constraining cultural programs shocking.

For a prolific writer, Auden had had a relatively fallow time poetically since arriving at the Downs School in the second half of 1932. His major creative effort, "In the year of my youth," had been abandoned. But either at the time when he wrote to Spender or shortly before, Auden produced a poem, beginning "Out on the lawn I lie in bed" (from now on, "Out on the lawn"), that became one of his most iconic and that, as much as any other, was to define him as an English poet, crystallizing a sense of connection to his English identity and surroundings through the experience of well-being and love of all kinds.

Auden's letter about his "tendency to National Socialism" and his imaginative investment in "national emblems" was written closer in time to this great poem than any other piece of writing by him that we know of. The poem, which is the first he set clearly at the Downs School, is important and beautiful and central enough to Auden's work—more so than ever in light of the unsettling letter to Spender—to merit printing in its entirety (stanza numbers have been added to aid with the subsequent discussion):

> Out on the lawn I lie in bed   1
> Vega conspicuous overhead
>   In the windless nights of June;

Forests of green have done complete
The day's activity; my feet
   Point to the rising moon.

Lucky, this point in time and space   2
Is chosen as my working place;
   Where the sexy airs of summer,
The bathing hours and the bare arms,
The leisured drives through a land of farms,
   Are good to the newcomer.

Equal with colleagues in a ring   3
I sit on each calm evening,
   Enchanted as the flowers
The opening light draws out of hiding
From leaves with all its dove-like pleading
   Its logic and its powers.

That later we, though parted then   4
May still recall these evenings when
   Fear gave his watch no look;
The lion griefs loped from the shade
And on our knees their muzzles laid,
   And Death put down his book.

Moreover, eyes in which I learn   5
That I am glad to look, return
   My glances every day;
And when the birds and rising sun
Waken me, I shall speak with one
   Who has not gone away.

Now North and South and East and West   6
Those I love lie down to rest;
   The moon looks on them all:
The healers and the brilliant talkers,
The eccentrics and the silent walkers,
   The dumpy and the tall.

She climbs the European sky;   7
Churches and power stations lie

Alike among earth's fixtures:
Into the galleries she peers,
And blankly as an orphan stares
Upon the marvellous pictures.

To gravity attentive, she   8
Can notice nothing here; though we
Whom hunger cannot move,
From gardens where we feel secure
Look up, and with a sigh endure
The tyrannies of love:

And, gentle, do not care to know,   9
Where Poland draws her Eastern bow,
What violence is done;
Nor ask what doubtful act allows
Our freedom in this English house,
Our picnics in the sun.

The creepered wall stands up to hide   10
The gathering multitudes outside
Whose glances hunger worsens;
Concealing from their wretchedness
Our metaphysical distress,
Our kindness to ten persons.

And now no path on which we move   11
But shows already traces of
Intentions not our own,
Thoroughly able to achieve
What our excitement could conceive,
But our hands left alone.

For what by nature and by training   12
We loved, has little strength remaining:
Though we would gladly give
The Oxford colleges, Big Ben,
And all the birds in Wicken Fen,
It has no wish to live.

Soon through the dykes of our content   13
The crumpling flood will force a rent,
    And, taller than a tree,
Hold sudden death before our eyes
Whose river-dreams long hid the size
    And vigours of the sea.

But when the waters make retreat   14
And through the black mud first the wheat
    In shy green stalks appears;
When stranded monsters gasping lie,
And sounds of riveting terrify
    Their whorled unsubtle ears:

May this for which we dread to lose   15
Our privacy, need no excuse
    But to that strength belong;
As through a child's rash happy cries
The drowned voices of his parents rise
    In unlamenting song.

After discharges of alarm,   16
All unpredicted may it calm
    The pulse of nervous nations;
Forgive the murderer in his glass,
Tough in its patience to surpass
    The tigress her swift motions.[100]

This extraordinarily rich, mellow lyric draws from the deep well of Auden's primal sources of inspiration, as is evident from his double-mentions of "the *birds* and rising sun" that "Waken" him and "all the *birds* in Wicken Fen," a famous nature preserve of unspoiled fenland in Cambridgeshire (186; emphasis added). The poem, sixteen stanzas in length, pivots just at its center between the eighth and ninth stanzas. The last word in the poem's first half is the talismanic noun "love," so recently relegated to midline obscurity in "Hearing of harvests rotting in the valleys." (And the adjective "gentle" is the first substantive word in the poem's second part.) "Love," used twice here, once as a verb and once as a noun, is this masterpiece's hinge point and keyword.

The poem's first part is centered on a beautiful but privileged world, albeit one that is shadowed from outside by class unrest. "What comes may be better for society," Auden once told a journalist, "but what is lost is most of what one has loved as an individual. . . . What one loves is often evil. How difficult it will be to change."[101] There is cosmic and personal harmony in this spot where a poet looks upward into the darkness and sees Vega, one of the brightest stars in the sky, which usually appears in summer in the Northern Hemisphere sometime after midnight (its name derives from a loose transliteration of an Arabic word meaning "falling"). Vega is a special star for a poet because it forms part of the Lyra constellation, the pattern of stars thought since ancient times to resemble Orpheus's lyre. When Auden looks up at the night sky, he glancingly sees a sign that seems meant for him: Vega shining down is a Dantesque affirmation of his own poetic role in the universe. Yet the private, middle-class world in this lyric's first half is focused not primarily by a star but by the moon, to which Auden's feet (physical and poetic) "point" at the end of the first stanza. Taking attention subtly away from Vega, the moon is the goddess that queens over the opening stanzas.

The poem's first half is centered on relaxation, conversation, love, sleep, work, friends, and harmonious continuities with nature. This private world of material and emotional satisfactions begins to crumble in the eighth stanza, exactly at the moment when the poem transitions from the private, image-filled world of sensual and personal celebration to doubts about the validity of life in the "gardens where we feel secure" and "our picnics in the sun." A troubled polis of "violence," the "doubtful act," and hungry "multitudes" now enters the poem (185). This shift is brilliantly managed. Auden begins the pivot near the center of the poem, with a new sentence, the subject of which is the moon, "she," who "Can notice nothing here." He ends the same sentence after two stanzas with a new presiding celestial witness, the "sun," which is related here to the world of historical struggle and endings (185).

Emotionally, the poem's first half is full of pleasure and calm while the second is dominated by fear and guilt, and then by glimmerings of hope. This second half is more abstract and argumentative, less scenic, and more violent than the first. It is illuminated by the "public" world of the sun that pushes up the "shy green stalks" after the revolutionary "crumpling flood" and sets the scene for the workmanly noise of "riveting" as what has suggestions of a new postrevolutionary socialist world is being built (185–186). The detail about riveting (not a common subject in poetry in English) in stanza 14 is designed to sound like it might have been taken from a Soviet newsreel about heroic labor.

The private moon-world of the poem's first half is passive and, literally, supine: Auden's speaker sits or lies on his back (as, slightly later, do all his friends), sleeps, has a point in time and space that "is chosen" for him rather than being one of his choosing; and "sighs" over the mild "tyrannies of love" (185). (That this place is *chosen* recalls Auden's comment in the almost contemporaneous letter to Spender that "my temperament and necessity, *force me* to work in a small field." Imaginatively at least, some part of Auden the poet believes that a larger power makes decisions about his life and art.) An antithesis in the fifth line of the first stanza brilliantly encapsulates the speaker's passivity: the "Forests of green" have completed their day's activity, whereas the speaker lounges on the grass; he has no parallel *feat* to proffer, only his upturned "feet." In light of these subtle clues about inaction, it is not surprising that this world, though idyllic, "has little strength remaining," and its inhabitants are moving on paths that show "already traces of | Intentions not our own" (185).

By contrast, the sun-centered second half of the poem is filled with images of action. There is an uncanny force even in the "creepered wall [that] stands up" as if it had a will of its own, especially when juxtaposed with the poet's loved ones who "lie down." And as the poem unfolds, Auden imagines that a flood, brutally powerful, will "force a rent, | And, taller than a tree, | Hold sudden death before our eyes" with all the "vigours of the sea" (186). The second half is, as Auden puts it, a world of "strength," destructive, inexorable, and renewing.

Until the exact middle point, Auden gives little more than a hint that there is anything troubling about the English scene being celebrated. The moon rising in "the European sky" obliquely gestures toward Continental political realities (to be encapsulated in a later poem as the "sixteen skies of Europe").[102] But Auden temporarily forestalls those ideas here: at first the moon is simply a part of the natural world that takes no more interest in "marvellous pictures" than it does in "Churches and power stations" that "lie | Alike among earth's fixtures" (185).

However, the lofty, all-seeing perspective that an animate moon might have had—although really "she | Can notice nothing here"—prepares for the poem's developing view of a wider world into which the

English scene inescapably fits. The double movement of the poem emerges in Auden's pun at the very start of the second part in stanza 9: "And, gentle, [we] do not care to know, | Where Poland draws her Eastern bow" (185). Gentleness as a moral virtue sums up the soothing world that Auden has just sketched so lovingly. But "gentle"—Auden leaves the word floating suspended, pinpointed between two commas—also announces, through its other, class-based meaning of "well-born," the political and social perspectives that dominate the poem's second part. Not the least of these is the realization that this gentleness is not a universal given, like "gravity." Rather, as stanza 9 shows, it is selective, socially coded, and ultimately dependent on some very violent hierarchies and injustices to sustain "Our picnics in the sun" and "Our kindness to ten persons" (185).

It is at this moment, when political forces visibly enter the poem, that Auden introduces a key phrase: "this English house." Contrary to much that he had written in the past few years, the poem explores the feeling that England, at least here in this garden, is a place of temporary freedom, love, and peace, as well as of a beauty free of responsibility. Its inward-looking inhabitants show only faint interest in the violence, including imperial violence, beyond its borders, even though "Our freedom in this English house" is contingent on such unacknowledged "doubtful act[s]" (185).

Scholars have usually linked "Out on the lawn," this major poem set at the Downs, to what in later life the deeply Christian Auden would describe as a mystical "Vision of Agape." ("Agape" is a term, derived from a name for a celebratory communal meal held in a church, which in the Christian theological tradition came to symbolize a selfless love for God and for others, akin to another religious term, "charity." It is often contrasted with "eros," meaning sexual love.) The term "Vision of Agape" comes from an account that Auden gave of an agapic moment in his introduction to an anthology called *The Protestant Mystics*. Although Auden introduces this episode as if it might conceivably have happened to someone else, he is almost certainly recounting his own experience. He wrote the introduction in 1963, a full thirty years after the time described in the poem. Mendelson's explanation of what Auden describes, though not the first, is the most authoritative.[103] He writes that on a warm June evening in Colwall in 1933: "Auden experienced what he later called a mystical vision, probably the only such event in his life. He characterized it as a *vision of Agape,* one in which, for the first time, he knew what it meant to love his neighbor as himself. . . . Within a few days or weeks he celebrated its mood in the poem he later entitled 'A Summer Night.'"[104] The experience that Mendelson refers to involved Auden's sitting outside with three other teachers and feeling himself, in Auden's words, "invaded by a power which, though I consented to it, was irresistible and certainly not mine. For the first time in my life I knew exactly—because, thanks to the power I was doing it—what it means to love one's neighbour as oneself." Auden added that neither sexual interest in his companions nor alcohol were factors in what occurred.[105] His late-in-life account of the Vision of Agape, which (beyond this poem) he had never written about until then or, so far as is known, even mentioned to anyone, has come to structure most readings of this poem. And it is unquestionably an important part of understanding the emotional world of "Out on the lawn."

This interpretation, focused on an agapic experience, is sharpened by the poem's use of Gerald Heard's theories. Katherine Bucknell and others have argued that Auden's "ring" of colleagues in "Out on the lawn" evokes Heard's theories about the "Love Feast" or Agape, in which a "small group of about a dozen . . . formed an inward-looking group—perhaps a ring," with the resulting outbreak of "exultation . . . in the formed psychic field" and the appearance of the "love that is an intensity of serenity."[106] Heard was preoccupied and anguished by his homosexuality, and his theory that the central human need is for food rather than sex can be read as an expression of his desire to escape the unhappiness of a disappointing emotional life.[107] The move from sex to "agape" (at its base, a rite of eating and thus of self-satisfaction rather than giving to or connecting with another person through sex) as a central experience is thus one that the poem, as subtly and controllingly glossed by Auden in the 1960s, entertains.

But to focus too narrowly on Heard or on the Christian "Vision of Agape" is also to repress many other significant experiences that the poem describes. To begin with, the poem is not centered on a single epiphanic evening like the one its maker described in 1963. (Auden wrote that this Christian vision at its full intensity lasted only about two hours.[108]) In the poem, the lying out on the lawn for the *"nights* of June" is explicitly a repeated experience. Indeed, the fact that it is repeated night after night is part of what makes that experience so pleasurable. Likewise repeated is the experience of sitting in a ring with colleagues "on *each* calm evening" (184; emphasis added). On especially warm nights, it was a tradition at the Downs to let "senior" boys (i.e., thirteen-year-olds) sleep outside in "Paradise Row," part of a school field named Brock Meadow. Auden himself often seems to have slept in a bed manhandled out onto the lawn in front of the Master's Lodge, where "in the early morning he could be seen reclining in bed with an umbrella overhead and some geese underneath."[109] (In the 1930s, Auden and the Downs schoolboys were hardly alone in sleeping outside and gazing up with mystical pleasure at the stars. The author Llewellyn Powys, for example, used to do the same thing at his home at East Chaldon in Dorset.[110])

The text indicates that nothing special happens on any one occasion. It is the total accumulation of delights—social, visual, regional, mystical, and, yes, as we shall see, romantic—that the poem celebrates. Although the "agapic reading" lays great emphasis on Auden's description of sitting "Equal with colleagues in a ring," it is telling that this is not the first image in the poem and that, when it occurs, it does not occupy more than one (or perhaps two) of the poem's sixteen stanzas.

The poem begins "in bed" and "out on the lawn," and the first two adjectives that Auden uses to describe the world of the Downs School are erotic rather than agapic: "Lucky" and "sexy."

> Lucky, this point in time and space
> Is chosen as my working place;
>   Where the sexy airs of summer,
> The bathing hours and the bare arms,
> The leisured drives through a land of farms,
>   Are good to the newcomer. (184)

"Sexy" emerged as a word around 1925, in the middle of the flapper decade. This is probably the first appearance in a poem of what was still a relatively rare adjective. (It is also the one and only time that the supremely verbally sophisticated Auden uses the word in his poetry, indicating that there is a deep, non-accidental reason for its being here.[111]) Highly sensitive to new language, Auden not only incorporates the word; he also elaborates on what the "sexy airs of summer" consist of: "The bathing hours and the bare arms, | The leisured drives through a land of farms" (184). He has some beautiful and very similar lines in a poem about Helensburgh: "Make swimming-bath and tennis-club a place | Where almost any summer day | A visitor is carried away | By unexpected beauty of speech or face."[112] In "Out on the lawn," "sexy" is linked to "bathing and "bare" and "leisured." In E. J. Brown's book on the Downs School, *The First Five,* a photograph of the Downs's swimming pool, seemingly from the interwar period, shows the boys bathing nude, as was common at the time.[113]

When Auden published the poem in the *Listener* in 1934, he titled it "Summer Night," leaving it deliberately unclear whether he meant to refer to what night is like in summer or to *a* summer night in particular. Perhaps he intended an allusion to Matthew Arnold's poem "A Summer Night." Both Auden's and Arnold's poems share a relaxed, easy mood. But more relevant to the poem's ambitions is Arnold's touchstone phrase in his sonnet "To a Friend," about Sophocles, "Who saw life steadily, and saw it whole."[114] In Auden's poem, set in a "land of farms," he wants both to see the "whole" of England, "North and South and East and West," and to see it not just as regions but as a "whole." The spirit here closely resembles the thoughts that E. M. Forster attributes to one of his protagonists, Margaret Schlegel, in *Howards End:* "In these English farms, if anywhere, one might see life steadily and see it whole, group in one vision its transitoriness and its eternal youth, connect— connect without bitterness until all men are brothers."[115]

In *The Tempest,* Caliban describes his love for his island:

> The isle is full of noises,
> Sounds and sweet airs that give delight and hurt not.
> Sometimes a thousand twangling instruments
> Will hum about mine ears, and sometimes voices
> That, if I then had waked after long sleep,
> Will make me sleep again; and then, in dreaming,
> The clouds methought would open, and show riches
> Ready to drop upon me.[116]

It has not been easy to understand fully the riches that Auden felt dropping on him out of the clouds or night sky in rural Herefordshire. In particular, until recently it has been difficult to write candidly about some crucial aspects of Auden's life at the Downs, or to "see it whole." The main reason that this was a delicate task had to do with romantic and then erotic love, not with agapic connection. In 1935, Auden responded to a query from a friend about his poem "Easily, my dear, you move, easily your head." He explained: "The speaker is not necessarily you or me or anyone, rather it is all of us who find their emotional interests in their juniors."[117] Auden counted himself among those who "find their emotional interests in their juniors." But a necessary discretion was imposed on Auden scholars during the lifetime of the person whom Auden met at the Downs, taught English to, and was deeply in love with from around the summer of 1933 until around 1938, inspiring many famous poems including "Easily, my dear, you move, easily your head," "Let the florid music praise," "Dear, though the night is gone," "Lay your sleeping head, my love" and others.[118]

As Robert Lowell asks simply but powerfully about his own life in his late poem "Epilogue": "why not say what happened?"[119] Nearly a century on from these events, we can do the same for Auden and his world and just say what happened. Around June 1933, Auden fell in love with a Downs pupil. He was a brown-haired, slender boy named Michael Yates. When this emotional upheaval in Auden's life occurred in the early summer of 1933, Yates was a thirteen-year-old (he turned fourteen in mid-July) and Auden was a twenty-six-year-old Downs master. Yates was interested in art and spent a lot of time in the art room, where he was taught, and painted, by Auden's friend Maurice Feild. (Eventually, Yates, while continuing to paint and sketch, became more interested in drama and stage design; Auden would help him get into the Yale Drama School in 1938.) Auden's intense feelings about Yates were almost certainly alive in 1933 by the time when he wrote "Out on the lawn."[120] His love for Yates eventually evolved into a romantic relationship that lasted until around 1938. Neither seems to have subsequently expressed any regret at all over the episode, and they remained close friends for the rest of Auden's life.

In his "National Socialism" letter to Spender, written at the time when, or shortly after, he composed "Out on the lawn," Auden included a picture of the young Michael Yates, saying: "I am wildly in love with the enclosed, who is going to be a good painter."[121] In the context of the letter to Spender, it is reasonable to suppose that Auden's love for Yates was closely bound up with his recognition of his own gravitation toward "emotional symbols" that were "national emblems" and his need to "work in a small field," which is the main subject of the letter. A

FIG. 6 *The Downs School annual photo from the early summer of 1933. Auden, in a bow tie, sits on the far right of the staff row, next to the school gardener Peter Roger, who, like the boys, wears an open-necked shirt. (Roger and Auden had an affair while Auden was at the Downs School.) The bespectacled man with a child on his knee in the middle of the same row is the closeted headmaster, Geoffrey Hoyland. His wife, Dorothea Cadbury Hoyland, sits on his left. Auden's friend, the art master Maurice Feild, is third from the left in the staff row. In the row behind and directly to the left of Hoyland stands Michael Yates, with whom Auden had fallen in love. This photograph must have been taken within weeks, perhaps even days, of Auden writing a masterpiece about love of many kinds, the poem beginning, "Out on the lawn I lie in bed."*

poem written a short while later, set on a Malverns hilltop and also probably referring to Yates, puts it like this:

> When last I stood here I was not alone; happy
> Each thought the other, thinking of a crime,
> And England to our meditations seemed
>   The perfect setting.[122]

"Thinking of a crime" is a phrase that arrests the attention. It could mean something innocuous like "fantasizing about a crime," and it could mean "remembering a crime"—Auden skillfully leaves both options open. His courage, or recklessness, has a confrontational quality that coexists with his suavity: he suggests that the lovers were thinking about not just about a moral infraction, but about a "crime." And while they did so, "England to our meditations seemed | The perfect setting," as if there were a link between the beauty of the place and the lovers' connection—as if, Auden seems to be saying, deep down there is for him something "English" about queerness and vice versa. That feeling is present as well in "Out on the lawn."

Isherwood believed when he was embracing his friend Bubi that he "could hold in his arms the whole mystery-magic of foreignness, Germanness. By means of Bubi, he could fall in love with and possess the entire nation."[123] Auden too felt that there was a magical, symbolic quality to the way that same-sex lovers view each other and behave.[124] In the same letter in which Auden admits to Spender his "tendency to National Socialism," attributing it to the influence of "ones surroundings, and emotional symbols" functioning as "national emblems," he connects Yates with these "emblems" by sending the young man's picture as an enclosure. Auden's love for Yates, like Isherwood's for Bubi, has a symbolic valence. It is as if in falling in love with Yates, Auden also felt imaginatively that he was falling in love with and possessing or "enclosing" a symbol of an entire English culture. An embrace was a way of grasping history, or, as one poem inspired by Yates from this very year, 1933, puts it: the lover "within his arms a world was holding."[125]

Certainly, by the summer of 1933, gossip about Auden's attachment to Yates was beginning to do the rounds in literary circles, fueled in no small part by Stephen Spender (in whom Auden had confided). For example, the American editor and writer Lincoln Kirstein—who did not then know Auden personally, but would later befriend him when Auden moved to New York at the end of the 1930s—recorded in his diary on 2 August 1933 that Spender had told him how "Auden has fallen in love with a 13 yr. old pupil at his school—and how his verse sounds more & more as if it were written for school-boys."[126] Notwithstanding Spender's own complicated love life, his indiscretion reflects the gathering prurience and censoriousness that Auden was starting to attract in England.

Unless further evidence emerges, no one can ever say with certainty when Auden and Yates began to have sex with each other. To judge from the very incomplete record, it seems likely to me that although Auden fell in love with Yates in 1933, their relationship probably became a sexual one only in the second half of 1934, when Yates was fifteen, or in the first half of 1935. Yates left the Downs in the summer of 1933, when in the normal way he graduated from the prep school and moved on to Bryanston School in Dorset, an institution that had close connections with the Downs. At the time a relatively new boarding establishment, housed in a palatial, neo-Georgian edifice designed at the end of the nineteenth century by Norman Shaw, Bryanston is over eighty miles south of Colwall, but Auden and Yates continued to see each other from time to time. The second half of 1934 seems a likely date for the onset of the sexual phase of their relationship, if some parts of "Easily, my dear, you move, easily your head," a poem that Auden wrote in November 1934, are to be taken literally. While not definitive, phrases in that poem do seem to hint that some kind of sexual relationship is happening. "Looking and loving our behaviours pass," Auden says at one point in the poem. At another, he states: "You stand now before me, flesh and bone."[127] By the time this poem was written, Yates had been away from the Downs for over a year.

To complicate matters, probably by the spring or summer of 1934, Auden was also in a relationship at the Downs with a man closer to his own age, Peter Roger, who had been a pupil at the school in the 1920s and had returned to work as a gardener in the 1930s. The onset of Auden's affair with Roger may have been predicated on the fact that after the summer of 1933 Yates was no longer at the Downs. Roger and Auden, along with another Downs master, Austin Wright, had started living at a property belonging to a neighboring estate in Colwall. In a show of campy bravado, Auden christened the house "Lawrence Villa," probably in homage to D. H. Lawrence's well-known hostility to sexual repression and prudishness.[128] A Downs pupil who visited remembered the house as "rather like undergraduate rooms, piles and piles of books, filled ashtrays, cups of cold coffee, and half-peeled oranges."[129]

In the summer of 1934, Auden, Yates, and Roger (that is, Auden and two people he loved) embarked on a madcap journey through central Europe to visit a stretch of the Carpathian Mountains in what is now Slovakia, a region that is the setting for Bram Stoker's vampire novel *Dracula* (1897). Long after, in his poem "Prologue at Sixty," Auden describes Poprad, a city they visited in 1934, as one of the places made sacred in his imagination "by something read there, | a lunch, a good lay, or sheer lightness of heart."[130] No doubt, all these experiences were part of the "Dracula" trip. But in November 1934, in the wake of this journey

FIG. 7 *Auden* (middle) *with his two loves of the time, Peter Roger* (left) *and Michael Yates* (right). *There is no way to be sure exactly when or where this picture was taken or who took it. But the year is likely to be 1934, and it may relate to the "Dracula trip" that the trio made to the Carpathian Mountains that summer. If this date is right, Roger is around twenty-three, Auden twenty-seven, and Yates fifteen. As a mark of this picture's significance, Christopher Isherwood gave it pride of place on the inside cover of one of his meticulously curated photo albums from the 1930s.*

through Europe, Auden, writing about the trip (in "Easily, my dear, you move, easily your head"), recalls "the night's delights."[131] One cannot be sure now who was involved in those "delights." But the internally rhyming phrase, linking two similar-sounding words right next to each other, might be intended very obliquely to mirror the joining of two similar, though not identical, bodies through the rhyme of love.

Auden's love for Yates has to be seen in the context of the historical codes and assumptions operating in English culture in the 1930s. Sex between masters and pupils was rife at single-sex public schools in Britain during the early twentieth century, as it had been in the nineteenth century. In 1920, the school chaplain at St. Edmund's had sex with the thirteen-year-old Auden. Auden's own affair with Yates, assuming it started in 1934, would be condemned by many were it to happen today, but it may not have been so exceptional at the Downs at that point in its history. Auden once "remarked casually" to a pupil in one of his classes, apparently towards the end of his time at the school, that the "masters had been judging the boys in a beauty contest, and that the winner was a certain boy, X."[132] Stephen Spender—never the most reliable source of information, but not the least reliable either, and in any case someone in a unique position to know much otherwise unrecorded history of the Auden circle—claimed that Geoffrey Hoyland, the Downs's headmaster (and owner) and the man to whom Auden eventually dedicated "Out on the lawn" when it was collected in book form, was himself having an affair with a Downs pupil of Yates's age, Michael Paget Jones.[133]

Hoyland was a Quaker, a pacifist, a hymn writer, a visionary educator and, for many observers at the time, a convincing leader of the Downs.[134] It is hard to know what the dedication of "Out on the lawn" connotes, but there is at least an open question about whether it contains more than simple collegial admiration. Hoyland was almost certainly aware of Auden's love for Yates, and Auden was very likely to have known about Hoyland's own heart-flutters. The art historian Andrew Forge, who was a pupil at the Downs in the 1930s and was taught by Auden, believed that Geoffrey Hoyland long oscillated in and out of the closet. Forge remembered waking in the school dormitory to see Hoyland "walking silently between rows of beds, stark naked, [his] erection glistening in the moonlight."[135] Was Auden, in dedicating the poem to Hoyland, inviting the headmaster (and others beyond him) to identify with the unspoken meanings included in this account of Auden's own experiences?

Late in life, Spender claimed, perhaps maliciously, that Auden was lucky to get away from the Downs School in 1935 without a scandal blowing up.[136] But the Downs may have been a place where Auden felt sheltered under Hoyland's wealthy and understanding wing. Forge thought that at the Downs, Auden "was outrageously what would nowadays be called 'gay' in his demeanour, and was always camping it up and playing around, [but] he was absolutely in control of himself."[137] John Catlin, the son of the feminist author and activist Vera Brittain, also reported gossip about Auden's time at the school. Catlin had been a pupil at the Downs between 1937 and 1940, after Auden had largely departed from Colwall. But, apparently in 1938, he heard Auden give a talk at the school about his recent visit to China with Isherwood. Long afterward, Catlin remembered being told at the time that the young Auden had "liked boys to put buttercups in his mouth while he lay in the long grass, and that he was asked to leave the school because he used to wander naked round the school grounds in summer. Once, inadvertently, he strayed too far and had been apprehended by Colwall's one and only policeman."[138] Gossip attaches to those who are a focus of attention, desire, even envy, and it is impossible to determine now the accuracy of Spender's and Catlin's stories. They do indicate, though, that rumors about Auden's time at the Downs School were circulating not long after he left.

Shielded by the protection of its "creepered wall," the Downs was undoubtedly a "lucky" point in time and space, where Auden could be assured that "when the birds and rising sun | Waken me, I shall speak with one | Who has not gone away" (185). There is a brilliant verbal indefiniteness to this touching scene: Auden's language indicates that he will be sleeping (outside) with one "Who has not gone away," a statement that could refer simply to the fact that masters and boys slept collectively, like a human constellation, under the stars. Yet also obliquely but definitely it suggests something like an intimate romantic feeling. Auden's description of "eyes in which I learn | That I am glad to look, return | My glances every day" also seems to reflect the discovery of a personal love, but they could also be taken as a simple statement of affection (185). Auden's poetry is written on a knife edge of provocative subtlety. Composed at a time when he was in love with Yates but when they were probably not yet lovers, the poem also finds other ways to express its many meanings. "Out on the lawn" features two indented and rhyming lines in each of its six-line stanzas. Visually, this structure evokes a situation of two connected people who are attached to each other by an irrational bond (love / rhyming) but who, because of social proprieties, have to lie close but apart (separated by other people / lines).

"Lucky" is a word that, as a poet, Auden seems to have idiosyncratically cherished, associating it in his mind with the unforeseen and with love.[139] The importance of the word "lucky"—linked to "sexy" in stanza 2 of "Out on the lawn"—strongly suggests that at least a part of what "this for which we dread to lose | Our privacy" is to be taken as the blessed good fortune of love for another person of the same sex.[140] And, later on in the poem, the "it" that may "unpredicted" (or fortuitously) eventually "calm" the postrevolutionary world of the future in the final stages of "Out on the lawn" carries, again in part at least, the same meaning. This is not all that the poem is about, of course. But Auden's brilliance in the first half of "Out on the lawn" lies less in his description of a monolithic feeling of agapic charity and more in his integration of a whole ecosystem of human experiences: harmonies with the landscape and the cosmos, the "windless nights," the sights brought by "opening light," the "Enchanted" flowers, the farms, the birds, the peace of "these evenings when | Fear gave his watch no look," the trees, the swimmers, the healers, the dumpy, the drives and the rising suns. And among all these, there is also a feeling for the rightness of personal, same-sex love that is blossoming in this poet in beautiful ways in "this English house" (184–185).

Auden had not been ready to use the phrase "I love" in his poetry until only recently, but "love" was now becoming as much a keyword for Auden in 1933 as it had been earlier for Walt Whitman. The moment, the position, and the mood evoked in "Out on the lawn" are strikingly similar to Whitman's summer vision of universal love and interconnectedness in *Leaves of Grass* (1855). There, Whitman describes lying on the grass on a June morning with a lover:

> I mind how we lay in June, such a transparent summer
>   morning; . . .
> Swiftly arose and spread around me the peace and joy and
>   knowledge that pass all the art and argument of the earth;
> And I know that the hand of God is the elderhand of my own,
> And I know that the spirit of God is the eldest brother of my own,
> And that all the men ever born are also my brothers . . . and the
>   women my sisters and lovers,
> And that a kelson of the creation is love.[141]

It is unclear whether Auden knew Whitman's work at this stage. But just like Whitman's speaker, Auden wakes on a June morning in the grass, where he experiences a vision of both personal emotional fulfillment and universal love. In Auden's poem, the erotic preoccupation with the "tyrannies of love" intersects with the limited but real agapic sympathy of "Our kindness to ten persons" (215).

The density and allusiveness of Auden's poem also link it to the work of another writer, a closer contemporary than Whitman. Auden's attempt to inscribe a happy same-sex love into the "land of farms" recalls Forster's effort to do something similar in his then-unpublished novel *Maurice*, which Forster had written around 1919 and then reworked intensively in 1932.[142] In the spring of 1933, Forster had shown the revised version of the novel in typescript to close friends of Auden, such as Christopher Isherwood and Stephen Spender. It is very likely that Auden read the book around the same time.[143] *Maurice* was so significant a work to Auden's closest friend, Isherwood, that when he talked about the book with Forster on 18 April 1933 in London, Isherwood wept.[144] Even if Auden did not read *Maurice*, the same paradigm of outcasts who are nonetheless a culture's true representatives appears widely in Forster's published work, including in *Howards End* (1910), which Auden had read.[145] Written just two months after Isherwood's intense experience of Forster's novel, "Out on the lawn" begins by cleverly literalizing the notion of the "outsider" as someone who sleeps *outside*. But that "outsider," as the poem goes on to show, is also paradoxically an "insider," someone who is *inside* the perimeter walls of the "English house." It is as if Auden seeks here to make a tribute to Forster's privileged outsiders or outcast insiders, or (putting it another way) to find a way of writing a publishable, poetic supplement to *Maurice*.

Auden's poem dramatizes his happy but guilty awareness of people like himself as outsiders on the inside who know that their loves are genuine expressions of a certain kind of idealistic Englishness but also know that these loves, not least because of social condemnation, are often doomed to end soon. When that end comes, the poem says, the people in this "English house" will be "parted," a past participle that leaves it unclear whether the friends will have chosen to separate or will have been forced apart (184). Forster's *Maurice* concludes with the lovers Alec and Maurice united as outcasts: "England belonged to them. That, besides companionship, was their reward. Her air and sky were theirs, not the timorous millions' who own stuffy little boxes, but never their own souls."[146] Alec and Maurice watch the *Normannia* sailing away at Southampton and turn back toward England together. Auden's poem also evokes a world of love and then in stanza 13 imagines its ending—although on a more isolated, and less optimistic, water note than Forster's. In Auden, a dream makes itself felt of a "crumpling flood" that will break through and "taller than a tree, | Hold sudden death before our eyes" (186). After this revolutionary moment imaged as a "crumpling flood" is over, Auden offers hopeful conditionals about a possible survival of the privileged English values and emotions in a changed world as the waters retreat and "shy green stalks" appear and "stranded monsters" lie gasping in the aftermath. In that world, Auden pleads that what we dread to lose our privacy for will "to that strength belong" (186).

As a counterpoint to the poem's vision in its last eight stanzas of eventual disappearance, separations, and the destruction of the "English house," technically the poem is a masterpiece of enduring construction, signaling through poetic form that something old will indeed persist past the moment of revolution. Each of the sixteen verses is perfectly sized, honed, and balanced, as though the magic of shaped poetic language was certain to survive and provide a kind of continuity with the new world. The stanza form itself, the one used by the eccentric eighteenth-century poet Christopher Smart for his "Song to David" (a deeply religious poem supposedly composed while Smart was behind the high walls of a London mental asylum in 1763), offers a paradigm of assuring repetition and self-completeness: six lines long, the rhyme scheme of the first three lines (*aab*), which are often very strongly enjambed, is mirrored and completed in the second three lines (*ccb*). Here, the imbalance between an opening rhyming couplet and a line that does not rhyme is "corrected" at the end of the stanza, as after a second couplet the third line picks up its verbal partner in the sixth.[147] Auden capitalizes on the involuted formal beauty of the stanza form, metaphorically perhaps equivalent to Heard's "inward-looking ring" of celebrants, to reinforce the poem's vision of harmonious interconnections.

In fact, Auden had drawn this equation between metrical forms and social groups himself in his 1932 essay "Writing": "When a poet is writing verse, the feeling as it were excites the words and makes them fall into a definite group going through definite dancing movements, just as feeling excites the different members of a crowd and makes them act together."[148] By fitting a single sentence—which can at least emblematically represent a single proposition—perfectly into, or onto, almost all of the stanzas in "Out on the lawn," Auden enacts a concordance of "form" (stanza) and "content" (sentence). Just two of the sixteen stanzas end in colons, with the sentence picking up in the following stanza. But, importantly, Auden's sentences never stop jarringly in the middle of a stanza. The symmetries and harmonies of near-perfect form make the poem not just an account of Auden's own happiness but a way for readers to experience happiness themselves, as craft and art, content and form, ethics and beauty, people and setting harmonize and "fit" for a moment.

The sense of pastoral bondedness to England and a trajectory toward the enclave of the heart and the enclave-heart of the country are so strong in "Out on the lawn" that their essence survives the vision of their destruction. Here, for a while, in this "windless" world are "gardens where we feel secure," protected behind a "creepered wall," as upper-middle-class citizens enjoy "Our freedom in this English house" (184–185). The sense of rootedness and completion rest mainly in the poem's first half as Auden describes the scene around him. But even its apparently apocalyptic ending moves from the dangerous flux of water back to the stability and security of soil where the poem began: "when the waters make retreat | And through the black mud first the wheat | In shy green stalks appears" (186). The sense of interconnection emerges at linguistic and grammatical levels as well. The stanza form is visually rounder and more tightly closed in on itself than the elongated, rhymeless tercets of "Prologue," the poem Auden placed immediately before "Out on the lawn" when he collected both poems in 1936.[149] (In retrospect, by making this back-to-back arrangement of the poems in his book, Auden indicates that he now sees "Prologue" as a prologue to his own new life, to a new kind of poetic shape in his work, and to a new centrality for personal love.) In each stanza of "Out on the lawn," the pattern is of two joined halves (like the two joined halves of the poem as a whole): as noted earlier, the first couplet is succeeded by a new rhyme sound, then another couplet, and then a sixth line that rhymes with the third. Each half of each stanza, in other words, perfectly mirrors the other half's movements.

The poem, like each individual stanza, also folds in on itself through a network of verbal parallels: the stranded monsters "lie" in the mud among "green stalks" at the end as Auden "lies" on the grass at the beginning, the tigress at the end matches up with the "lion griefs" at the start, the newly born child is "happy" where Auden is "lucky," and the parents' voices "rise" at the end just as the moon rises at the start of the poem. This ring-like structure is a verbal equivalent to the icon of the Ouroboros, the circled snake swallowing its own tail, an ancient image of eternity and peace.

The circling form also promotes a sense of community and related-ness that works in tandem with the poem's heavy use of deictic forms of various kinds. Deictics are linguistic markers that function to create an involuntary and subliminal sense of community, drawing the reader into the world of—in this case—the poem. Examples of various kinds of deictics in the poem include "*the* sexy airs of summer, | *The* bathing hours and *the* bare arms, | *The* leisured drives through a land of farms" (definite articles), "*this* point" (a demonstrative), "later *we,* though parted then | May still recall *these* evenings" (first-person plural pronoun and another demonstrative). The literary historian David Trotter notes that Auden's canny use of the definite article allows the reader to "identify the item in question from his own experience." These definite articles, Trotter argues, "encouraged [Auden's] own little set, and the larger 'set' which grew out of it, to supply information which only it could supply, and thus draw closer together." These small words are, he rightly concludes, "making a readership."[150]

If there is something to add here, it is that the deictics also create a sense of boundedness, of coherence and stability between text and world, writer and audience. Motifs of retreat, consolidation, circling, withdrawing, hiding, the centripetal movement away from water and toward land, the disposition toward contact with the soil—all these qualities glow in the poem and draw its readers together like a second circle around the "colleagues in a ring." The poem shows how, even in the face of eventual loss, all these characteristics of connection can come alive (in the words of Auden's letter to Spender) "in a small field" aptly named "Paradise Row."

However, the poem also recognizes that there is no simple dichotomy between a private and a public world: it is "doubtful act[s]" that allow individual "freedom" (185). As Auden's early works often do, "Out on the lawn" aims to destabilize or, at least, to erode stark divisions. Indeed, the first stanza provides a litany of interrelated contrasts: "out" / "in," "head" (from "overhead") / "feet," lying / "rising," "nights" / "day." A pervasive network of cross-connection and patterned contrasts also knits together the two halves of the poem. The "eyes in which I learn | That I am glad to look, return | My *glances*" in the first half are balanced against the "gathering multitudes outside | Whose *glances* hunger worsens"; the "lawn" and the "forests of green" return as the "shy green stalks" burgeoning in the mud; and the "birds" that will wake the speaker are counterpointed by "all the birds in Wicken Fen" that "we would gladly give" away if it made any difference to the fate of this lovely, ethically questionable, declining world.

These parallels and contrasts advance the argument of Auden's poem in extralogical terms. Whether they actually persuade us that Auden has found a real bridge to connect the poem's two halves, to link private fulfillment with historical change, is open to question. But the poem is a poignant, ambivalent plea for the beautiful, cherished privileges of the class-based, innocent but substantially queer world that Auden inhabits. This plea is powered here by his feeling for the naturalness of his intense love for Michael Yates, which is to be transferred to, and somehow to be redeemed in, a new, classless world that is coming into being. All the different varieties of love that the poem profoundly celebrates may "to that strength belong." The uncertainty and openness of the future that the poem can imagine is part of what makes "Out on the lawn" so moving—perhaps love of all kinds *will* finally find acceptance there. Perhaps it is *only* there, in a changed world, that they can all be accepted and openly spoken of.

So, through patterns and parallels, the world of the poem's first eight stanzas reappears in the last eight stanzas, even as these lines apparently describe a very different place. The "calm" of the evenings that the "colleagues" enjoy will survive to "calm | The pulse of nervous nations" in the new world. And the subtle, sophisticated poet who "lies" in the greenery in stanza 1 is playfully reincarnated in the postrevolutionary era as one of the "stranded monsters" who, like him, "lie" on the ground in stanza 14. Parallels and patterning are not the same as argument, though, and of course the differences between the worlds are enormous: a flood will wash away the old world, the walls that created the cherished privacy will be gone, there will be no "forests of green" but only "black mud," "shy green stalks" and the "sounds of riveting" (186). Tellingly, the future monsters' inhumanly "whorled unsubtle ears" will be unlike Auden's classically trained and disciplined poet's ear. (In *The Tempest*, Antonio talks of hearing a "din to fright a monster's ear," and "monster" is the term that Stephano and Trinculo use insistently for Caliban.[151]) But there are hints of strange similarities too: "gasping" in the mud, the monsters will be as much strangers to their new world as the poet now is a "newcomer" to the English bourgeois world of farms and gardens.

If that is the case, just as the all-encompassing loves "for which we dread to lose | Our privacy" (186) may survive into the new order, so may one of the most fundamental marks of identity in the modern world: the grouping of people into nations. Official socialism defined itself as "international," but Auden imagines a better world in which nationalities would nonetheless persist as if immutably. Human violence would still exist in the new world, but love would "Forgive the murderer in his glass." Predatory hungers would continue, but love would be "Tough in its patience to surpass | The tigress." And conflicts would still exist, but "after discharges of alarm," love would "calm | The pulse of nervous nations" (186; emphasis added).

This seems like a vision of a vaguely socialist future: as I described the references to a revolutionary flood followed by the growth of "wheat" and the industrial sounds of "riveting" deploy stock elements of Soviet propaganda. But this is clearly, as Auden says in his letter to Spender, a socialist future that is also somehow national. The poem does not try to harmonize contraries or settle ideological issues. Yet the virtuosic Auden is often at his strongest as a writer when he is on the shakiest intellectual ground, trying to reconcile conflicting emotions or to move beyond "reason." Written in the ecstatic glow of his new-found feelings about Michael Yates, "Out on the lawn" is one of the aesthetic high points of Auden's genteel poetic nationalism. But (like a love that, just when it flares up, is already foretelling its own eventual dimming) the poem is also the moment at which Auden's Edenic poetic conservatism begins, slowly at first, to break apart.

By the time that Auden fell in love with Michael Yates at the Downs School, he had written an enormous number of significant poems in a great variety of forms in only a few years. Yet he had not written a sonnet—that cherished and yet almost predictable form of expression for a formalist poet—since the tortured pleas and twisted pararhymes of "Sir, no man's enemy" from October 1929. There, his speaker is preoccupied with the pathological "exhaustion of weaning, the liar's quinsy, | And the distortions of ingrown virginity."[152]

Suddenly, in 1933 and 1934, Auden embarked on an ambitious cycle of poems, many of them love sonnets imbued with a Shakespearean fullness of utterance—and perhaps with hints, via the story of

Shakespeare and the "fair youth"—of homoerotic love, the "flood on which all move and wish to move."[153] It is evident that Auden had a Shakespearean poetic paradigm in mind for the situation with Yates: when he wrote to the author Frederic Prokosch about Yates in 1937, he referred to this young man, his love, as "my All."[154] That phrase is from the end of Sonnet 109 ("O! Never say that I was false of heart"): "For nothing this wide universe I call, | Save thou, my rose; in it thou art my all."[155]

The first of the sonnets in Auden's sequence of love poems appeared in *New Verse* as early as July 1933, meaning that it must have been written very soon after Auden fell in love. It features an attenuated variation of the deliberately awkward rhymes of "Sir, no man's enemy" and of many other Auden poems. And, again like "Sir, no man's enemy," it depicts a one-sided love met with indifference or unawareness from the other side. But now there is more wonder than frustration in the speaker's tone:

> But you are death this summer, we the hurt
> For whose profoundest sigh you give no penny
> Though, calmer than us all, you move our lives;
> Send back the writer howling to his art,
> And the mad driver pulling on his gloves
> Start in a snowstorm on his deadly journey.[156]

Yates did "Send back the writer howling to his art," continuing to provide Auden with intense creative inspiration in the wake of "Out on the lawn." The original version of another of these love poems opens with a first line that is strongly reminiscent of the beginning of Auden's slightly earlier masterpiece: "Sleep on beside me though I wake for you," the new poem begins.[157] Like many Whitman poems, these sonnets and other lyrics by Auden at times appear so frank as almost to be hiding their socially unacceptable messages in plain sight.

When he had completed a full sequence of sixteen love poems, twelve of them were sonnets. Auden sent them all to Isherwood as a group sometime in late 1934.[158] Although he eventually collected nine of the sixteen poems, two of them were never published, and the original idea of the love poems as a sequence was effectively blurred into invisibility in the public record.[159] Dating some of these poems is difficult now because of a lack of evidence. Two seem to derive from the time of Auden's affair with Derek Wedgwood in Helensburgh between

1930 and 1932, although they were developed further in Colwall.[160] It is likely that the other fourteen poems were all written after the romantic stage in Auden's feelings for Yates began in the summer of 1933. (It is unclear how long these feelings remained one-sided and only on Auden's part.) He continued to add to them after the sexual stage of their relationship began, probably in the second half of 1934.

Isherwood was the sharer of many of Auden's secrets, not least this one about the affair with Yates. But it is suggestive that Auden sent him the complete sequence of Yates-related love poems at a moment in their careers when he had stopped regularly sending Isherwood poetry in the way he had when they were younger. Showing the manuscript of the poems to Isherwood in this fashion, Auden perhaps intended his cycle of love poetry to be read as another private analogue (like "Out on the lawn") for the account of love in the unpublishable manuscript of Forster's *Maurice* that had moved Isherwood to tears when he read it in 1933. And—as was the case with the unpublished *Maurice*—awareness of the full depth of meaning within "Out on the lawn" and the sixteen-poem sequence was to remain for many years hidden from all but a few.

Newly and sincerely in love, Auden was (as one of the 1933 love sonnets puts it) able "Through sharpened senses [to] peer into my life | With insight and loathing."[161] As he did, his love poetry, predominantly in sonnet form, flowed like a river through the summer and autumn of 1933 and into the following year. Yet this period also gave rise in Auden to a frenzied burst of didacticism about grandiose topics such as humanity's destiny, usually couched either in abstract language or in scenarios where Auden's speaker is isolated. This was the flip side to the verbal ripeness and truthfulness of the very personal poems inspired by Yates. Somehow he also seems to have prompted the sudden appearance of these didactic poems too. Auden as a poet was a lover now, but he also remained a schoolmaster.

He managed to hold the two worlds of love and earnest prophecy together in "Out on the lawn." Some of the poems he wrote afterward seem to split the worlds apart. The summer of 1933 was the moment of a masterpiece, "Out on the lawn," and also of a daunting poem in tercets, beginning: "Friend, of the civil space by human love | Upon the unimaginative fields imposed." The latter poem is filled with circular arguments, implausible exhortations, and logical conflicts: Mendelson calls it, not unfairly, "the most problematic poem Auden ever wrote," characterizing it as "the unpublished poem in which he first stated his redemptive ambition" for England.[162]

The poem adjures an unnamed "Friend" who seems in fact to be another version of Auden and who therefore is somehow both speaker and listener in the poem, to reveal the disorder of the contemporary world to his audience with the aim of improving his readers' moral fitness. Auden instructs the Friend: "So write that reading is changing in their living, these | May save in time their generation and their race."[163] Aware of how preachy the poem is, Auden never tried to put it into print, but he did quarry the final section of the poem for a long, hortatory poem he wrote in the late summer or autumn of 1933. This poem, which has already been glanced at, begins:

> Here on the cropped grass of the narrow ridge I stand,
> A fathom of earth, alive in air,
> Aloof as an admiral on the old rocks,
>   England below me.[164]

The speaker is placed on the Malvern Hills, which run north-south just to the east of Colwall; toward the end of the poem, he hears the clock chiming the hour from Great Malvern Priory in the distance. The contrast between the settings of "Out on the lawn" and "Here on the cropped grass," though they were written close in time to each other, could not be more pointed. In the earlier poem's first line, the speaker "lies" on the grass; in the second's first line, he "stands" on a ridge with "England below me." In the earlier poem, Auden lies and sits among companions, "Equal with colleagues in a ring" (184); in the second, he is alone, "Aloof as an admiral on the old rocks" (201).

Part of that aloneness stems from the fact that Auden was facing a new school year separated from the person he loved and with whom he associated the Downs. "When last I stood here I was not alone," the poem says (202). Michael Yates had left in July 1933, only a month or two after Auden had fallen in love, to go to Bryanston, an institution that many Downs pupils enrolled at once they had finished their years in Colwall. Yates remained a pupil there until July 1937, meaning that from September 1933 onward, he and Auden probably mainly saw each other during the school holidays.

Again, as in "A Happy New Year" or "Prologue," in "Here on the cropped grass," Auden describes himself as one of Forster's spiritual inheritors of England who "have somehow seen her, seen the whole island at once."[165] Countering likely reality, Auden's perspective in the poem allows him to survey a vast stretch of landscape:

> Eastward across the Midland plains
> An express is leaving for a sailor's country;
>   Westward is Wales
> Where on clear evenings the retired and rich
> From the french windows of their sheltered mansions
> See the Sugarloaf standing, an upright sentinel
>   Over Abergavenny. (201–202)

"Eastward across the Midlands plains" is where an "express is leaving for a sailor's country" (one of the ports along the east coast of England all the way from Harwich to Hull). As so often in Auden's panoramic writing about England (as in "Prologue" or in the choruses to his and Isherwood's play *The Dog Beneath the Skin*), he momentarily tilts, in an act of private homage, to his favorite topographical source, Anthony Collett's highly patriotic book, *The Changing Face of England*. There, Collett records how "the heart leaps at the sight of the peaked Sugarloaf standing sentinel over Abergavenny."[166] Again, Auden embellishes: the details about "the retired and rich" and their "french windows" together with the Sugarloaf that is "upright" (that is, standing tall and somehow also morally strong) all come from Auden's imagination (201–202).

The lofted perspective, once more, is associated in Auden's mind with Hardy's long poem *The Dynasts* about the Napoleonic Wars, this time with the addition of Wilfred Owen's poems about the First World War intermixed. Owen read the Hardy poem during the last full winter of his life.[167] In his 1917–1918 poem "The Show," he attempts to re-create Hardy's vast downward-looking, visionary dispassionateness:

> My soul looked down from a vague height, with Death,
> As unremembering how I rose or why,
> And saw a sad land, weak with sweats of dearth,
> Grey, cratered like the moon with hollow woe.[168]

Auden carries on Owen's mode in "Now on the cropped grass." His socially motivated surveying of the landscape beneath him parallels and contrasts with the self-concerned gazing of "the retired and rich" from their mansions. What Auden sees is an "England" radically different from the compromised but idyllic space he had celebrated in "Out on the lawn." In the past, "England" had seemed the "perfect setting" for lovers' embraces (202). Now, when he is alone, England looks to Auden as if it

> has no innocence at all;
> It is the isolation and the fear,
>> The mood itself;
> It is the body of the absent lover,
> An image to the would-be hero of the soul,
> The little area we are willing to forgive
>> Upon conditions. (202)

Here is another of the poems in which the poet of England, the poet of the "small field," articulates an intense feeling of crisis in his culture and in himself: "These years have seen a boom in sorrow," Auden writes, using again the weighted word "sorrow," which had played such a key role in his sestina "Hearing of harvests rotting in the valleys" (202).[169]

From his (in every way) superior vantagepoint, Auden, with a self-parodying middle-class sense of superiority, surveys the mass society, "the crowd," which he had not yet managed to fit in realistic detail into his vision of England:

> I give
> The children at the open swimming pool
> Lithe in their first and little beauty
>> A closer look;
> Follow the cramped clerk crooked at his desk,
> The guide in shorts pursuing flowers
>> In their careers;
> A digit of the crowd, would like to know
> Them better whom the shops and trams are full of,
> The little men and their mothers, not plain but
>> Dreadfully ugly. (202)

The deliberate heterogeneity of the examples chosen reflects the disorganization and inorganic fecundity of the world that (in Auden's view)

England has become, an ill-sorted place of "lanterned gardens," "Gaumont theatres," and "cathedrals" (202–203).

The rest of the poem dramatizes the temptations that arise in Auden once he has moved out of the "small field" and confronts, or overlooks, this perceived disarray. The poem demonstrates the evident limitations of his ability, as yet, to make a gestalt or ordered shape out of a much wider cross-section of society. Having seen a world in which even people in groups are "self-absorbed," the solitary poet reflects in melodramatic fashion on the rise and fall of civilizations from the past, the "empires stiff in their brocaded glory" and the "intercalary ages of disorder" (203).

Such a vision generates an apocalyptic frisson of collapse, as "over the Cotswolds now the thunder mutters"—a moment out of *The Waste Land* but taking place in the "Holy Land of England." The thunder is an indictment of modern culture's evasiveness, never facing up to its real tasks but using instead "the common language of collective lying," and offering a warning of impending death (203). Then, somehow, "the bones of the war" insist that humans have been inadequate to the tasks imposed by the discoveries they have made and the machines they have built, although "Never higher than in our time were the vital advantages" (203–204). This cacophony of voices and the kaleidoscopic blur of images are designed to dramatize the ending of the poem.

In the poem's last part, Auden returns the focus to the point where he started: on a "narrow ridge" in the Malvern Hills. And now, instead of imposing an analytic order on nature, the human world tolls him back to his sole self. "The Priory clock chimes briefly and I recollect | I am expected to return alive | My will effective and my nerves in order" (204).[170] The speaker does not veer off into death but "returns alive" to his tasks at ground level, saying sententiously, "These moods give no permission to be idle, | For men are changed by what they do" (204).[171]

Auden's work, rooted in his life at the Downs School, continued in full spate with the components of his sequence of love poems blossoming repeatedly throughout the second half of 1933 and the first half of 1934. At some point, probably in this latter year, his love for Yates turned into an affair between them. At the same time, the Downs School drew on his energies as a charismatic teacher. In March 1934, at the traditional

Easter Sing-Song, the school staged a version of *The Deluge* from the Chester Mystery Cycle, a play chosen by Auden and testifying to his love of inundations, storms, and torrents as well as of the Middle Ages. The drama tells the story of Noah and the Ark during the flooding of the world, as described in Genesis. Junior boys draped themselves in bedsheets, rushing back and forth to represent the movement of waves, while Auden, offstage, in his plummy accent intoned (as perhaps every poet would occasionally like to) the voice of God.[172]

However, at the same time as Auden continued his employment as a schoolmaster, his social positioning was beginning to change. On 20 January 1934, he spoke on the radio for the first time when he took part in a discussion on the BBC Midland Regional Programme about the question: "Do we read too much and think too little?" In March 1934, he read out four of his poems (including "Out on the lawn") on the same network.[173] And, although it is not known when Auden first bought a car (he seems to have had the use of one, occasionally, while he was at Oxford), by the time he had settled in at the Downs, and perhaps as a result of the regular salary he was drawing, he owned a Morris-Cowley.[174]

Now an intermittent broadcaster and a car owner, in January 1935 Auden traveled in a plane for the first time. Using money that Faber and Faber had advanced him for the ticket, he flew to Copenhagen to consult with Isherwood on the play they were writing together. The trip was the occasion for a disconcerting moment for a novice air passenger (Auden probably caught the KLM morning flight from Croydon Aerodrome). T. S. Eliot reported to Emily Hale that "Auden left by air for Copenhagen this morning, and [Frank] Morley and I send [sic] him a cardboard box as a departing present—containing a celluloid ear."[175] At the time, Eliot was working on his play *Murder in the Cathedral* about the assassination of Thomas Becket, to be performed in Canterbury Cathedral in June of that year, but the "present" here alludes to another, but very different, murder story. Delighting in his own puerile but complicated and intense sense of humor, Eliot hinted to Hale that the fake ear Auden received out of the blue in a box was an allusion to Arthur Conan Doyle's crime of passion story "The Adventure of the Cardboard Box" (1893), in which Sherlock Holmes is called on to solve the mystery of a woman from Croydon (hence the amusement of sending a box to a passenger at Croydon Aerodrome) receiving a parcel containing two human ears packed in salt. Auden, perhaps out of a sense of tact, never seems to have mentioned the matter and he continued his journey without further incident.

Auden is obsessed with aerial perspectives in his poetry, but there is no direct record of his reaction to this first experience of flight. The play he worked on with Isherwood was published as *The Dog Beneath the Skin, or, Where Is Francis?* at the end of May 1935.[176] Its opening chorus, while borrowing many topographic details from the Auden favorite Anthony Collett, nonetheless has a panoramic beauty that feels as if it was inspired by a sunlit morning in the air over northern Europe:

> The Summer holds: upon its glittering lake
> Lie Europe and the islands; many rivers
> Wrinkling its surface like a ploughman's palm.
> Under the bellies of the grazing horses
> On the far side of posts and bridges
> The vigorous shadows dwindle; nothing wavers,
> Calm at this moment the Dutch sea so shallow
> That sunk St. Paul's would ever show its golden cross
> And still the deep water that divides us still from Norway.[177]

These memorable lines, sketching in the region of "Europe and the islands," also seem to foretell a new frame of reference for Auden: for the first time, he mentions the shallowness (literal and figurative) of the waters that divide England from the Continent, a geographical hint that Britain is not so fundamentally isolated as poetic myth maintains. And that wider frame of reference now takes on not just a poetic reality but a startling personal meaning as well. The story of Auden's life and poetry from 1932 to 1935 is extraordinary in its richness and complications. No episode from this period is—to write "is stranger" would be wrong because it assumes that there is any normality in the affairs of the heart—more unexpected or more thought-provoking than the final plot twist.

Christopher Isherwood, in the autumn of 1931, had become friendly with the novelist Thomas Mann's son, Klaus, and, through him, Isherwood had come to know other members of the Mann family. The Manns' eldest daughter, and Thomas's favorite child, Erika, had a politicized cabaret troupe, Die Pfeffermühle (The Pepper Mill), which was continuously plagued by Nazi agitators wherever it performed, even in Switzerland, where the Mann family had exiled themselves. Erika Mann (who was in a relationship with the actress Therese Giehse, one of the cofounders of Die Pfeffermühle) had become aware that the government in Germany intended to revoke her citizenship, making it impossible for her to travel or, even more importantly, to avoid a forced return to Germany.

In the first half of 1935, probably in May, Erika Mann asked Isherwood in an Amsterdam restaurant after a performance by Die Pfeffermühle if he would marry her so that she could obtain a British passport. For complicated, self-involved reasons, Isherwood declined. But he offered to introduce her to Auden. He wrote to his friend at the Downs School, explaining the situation. When Auden broke off his engagement to Sheilah Richardson in 1929, he wrote in his journal, "Never—Never—Never again."[178] But in May 1935, when he got Isherwood's letter asking if he was interested in helping Erika Mann by marrying her, he telegraphed back: "DELIGHTED."[179] Austin Wright, who was living with Auden and Peter Roger at Lawrence Villa, recalled: "Isherwood wrote saying that Erika Mann's life was constantly in danger. She was in political cabaret in Amsterdam. Shots fired in the theatre. She had to change her hotel every night. Would Auden marry her and provide a British passport? This, Wystan said, was a question you decided at once. And he did. But in no time he was full of worries about what his mother would think—staunch Anglo-Catholics. And what about Geoffrey Hoyland? 'We shall see the headmaster pacing the lawn.'"[180]

Wright implies that Auden, having decided to marry Mann, also feared that, with this decision, he was betraying someone or something important. Perhaps, at an unconscious level, he was. Michael Yates was now at Bryanston, but their ardent affair continued. Auden's understanding with Peter Roger seems to have been quite relaxed and casual. But it is too easy to say that Auden's decision to marry was purely a question of altruism, although concern for a persecuted stranger was surely one factor in what happened. As in his relationship with Yates, there was a symbolic dimension to this arrangement with Mann in Auden's emotional life. He wrote to Michael Yates's father, a solicitor who may have helped with some of the citizenship papers and who had evidently asked about the wedding: "You mustn't think my views about marriage are 'advanced.' When one marries by choice, I believe it is for better, for worse etc."[181]

FIG. 8 *Erika Mann and W. H. Auden in Colwall, photographed by Alec Bangham on or around the day of Mann and Auden's wedding, 15 June 1935. Bangham, thirteen at the time, was one of Auden's pupils at the Downs School. (He later became a distinguished medical researcher.)*

As anticipated, on 11 June 1935, the government in Berlin published its fourth "Ausbürgerungsliste des Deutschen Reichs" (Denationalization List of the German Reich), announcing that Erika Mann and thirty-seven others, including Bertolt Brecht, were no longer Germans. She had forfeited her German nationality, and her property was confiscated for offenses with Die Pfeffermühle that violated her "duty of loyalty to the Reich and the people."[182] Mann somehow managed to fly to London the next day.[183] She sent some photographs of herself ahead to the Downs School, then she arrived in Colwall. Erika Mann was now a stateless person inside the United Kingdom. Auden's profound feeling for the subjective importance of national belonging, and his sense of its connection to the kind of poetry he was able to write, now encountered the reality of a state's life-or-death authority over national status and thus its power to strip it away from, or bestow it on, any individual it chose.

When Auden started at Gresham's in 1920, he (like every other pupil) had been compelled to promise he would not smoke. In the intervening years, from at least his time at Helensburgh onward, whether in school or not, he had started carrying a carton of Player's cigarettes around under his arm in the fashion of a lady's handbag. Either shortly before or on the day of the wedding, Auden paid Alec Bangham, thirteen years old and one of the pupils in his Downs English class, five cigarettes to take a photograph of the couple at the school.[184]

It is an accomplished image of two people on the brink of an extraordinarily emotionally complicated moment for them both. On 15 June 1935, their wedding took place in the registry office in the tiny, sleepy town of Ledbury (the birthplace of the poet laureate John Masefield), about five miles southwest of Colwall. The witnesses who signed the register were Maurice Feild and Peter Roger. Auden and Mann then (presumably out of sight of the registrar) signed a document promising not to make any financial claims on each other.[185] Auden drove his wife back to the Abbey Hotel in Malvern, and he returned to teaching. "I didn't see her till the ceremony and perhaps I shall never see her again. But she is very nice," Auden wrote to Spender.[186] On the day following the ceremony, Thomas and Katia Mann, the bride's parents, who were in mid-Atlantic, on a liner laboring its way through the waves to New York, received a radio telegram from England. It read: "ALL LOVE FROM MRS. AUDEN."[187]

8 IMAGES IN THE DARK
PROPHECIES AND CHANGE, 1935–1936

You have no feeling for the fact that prophetic human beings are afflicted with a great deal of suffering; you merely suppose that they have been granted a beautiful "gift," and you would even like to have it yourself. But I shall express myself in a parable. How much may animals suffer from the electricity in the air and clouds! We see how some species have a prophetic faculty regarding the weather.... But we pay no heed that it is their pains *that make them prophets. When a strong positive electrical charge, under the influence of an approaching cloud that is as yet far from visible, suddenly turns into negative electricity and a change of the weather is impending, these animals behave as if an enemy were drawing near and prepare for defense or escape; most often they try to hide. They do not understand bad weather as a kind of weather but as an enemy whose hand they already* feel.

—FRIEDRICH NIETZSCHE (1887)

IN JUNE 1935, less than a decade after Auden had been writing hermetic poems that overlaid Great War battlefields and their brutal struggles on deserted northern English moors, he was the son-in-law of an eminent German family. He had lived in Germany; become a competent German speaker; had German lovers; driven across Europe (including through Germany, where in Eisenach, J. S. Bach's birthplace, he had "Sat in a café in the market square listening to Hitler shouting from Hamburg"); had traveled by air for the first time (being part of a generation of civilians for whom observing the earth from the sky was starting to become a slightly less rare experience), seeing beneath his plane "Europe and the islands; many rivers | Wrinkling its surface like a ploughman's palm";

439

married a German woman; had a play staged in London; and begun broadcasting his poems to a relatively large audience of unseen listeners.[1] His beloved, Michael Yates, was no longer a pupil at the Downs School, but Auden's relationship with him continued.

While these widened horizons opened in Auden's personal and creative lives, the British government was moving away from its policy of isolation, pulled into engagement with Europe by the turbulent politics on the Continent. Germany's disregard for the Treaty of Versailles was made plain in its announcement in early 1935 that it would begin to rearm. The British government showed its own flagrant cynicism about the provisions of the treaty when it consummated the Anglo-German Naval Agreement in June, three days after Auden and Erika Mann's wedding.

In this context, it became even harder for Auden to maintain an identity as the poet of the "small field." Writing is like mining: a "human activity," as Auden said, "that is by nature mortal." A poetic subject, just like a mineral deposit, can become exhausted.[2] His poetic veneration for the enclave of an English rural world had reached its zenith and was beginning its end. This shift took place by fits and starts, sometimes in bursts of grandiloquent, affirming language, sometimes in poems that express doubts about the country's moral foundation and its narrowed perspectives. The Downs, either directly or by implication, had been the setting for some of his most important poetry of the "English house."[3] In July 1935, whether voluntarily or under pressure, Auden left his job at the school.

Auden as a person loved routine, and, as an art, poetry—with its formal commitments to pattern and repetition and its endlessly recurring subject matter—has a stylized version of routineness structured into it. But, as if Auden wanted to codify the more uprooted and provisional qualities that were starting to take over his life, he set his next substantial poem in a guest room at a holiday boarding house and imagined it as a letter to a friend abroad. Here is the first stanza:

> August for the people and their favourite islands.
> Daily the steamers sidle up to meet
> The effusive welcome of the pier, and soon
> The luxuriant life of the steep stone valleys,
> The sallow oval faces of the city

Begot in passion or good-natured habit,
Are caught by waiting coaches, or laid bare
Beside the undiscriminating sea.[4]

"August for the people and their favourite islands" (from now on, "August for the people") was at first titled "To a Writer on His Birthday." It is an occasional poem, written to salute Christopher Isherwood's thirty-first birthday on 26 August 1935. The event was being celebrated in The Hague with a party of dubious propriety thrown by Gerald Hamilton, a genial but ruthlessly self-absorbed con man who had become a central figure in the Isherwood circle. Along with other guests of varying degrees of notoriety, E. M. Forster, Klaus Mann, and Stephen Spender attended.[5]

Auden, though, was absent. He could not be there because he was on holiday with Michael Yates and Yates's family on the Isle of Man, a small island in the Irish Sea with the odd status of a "crown dependency" of the United Kingdom. "August for the people" is the poem he sent from there to Isherwood in Holland. For two weeks in August 1935, Auden stayed with Yates and most, if not all, of the other Yateses at the Peveril, a boarding house in the resort town of Ramsey.[6] Given the depth of his personal and creative ties to Isherwood, it is a measure of how vital Yates (who had turned sixteen a month earlier) was to Auden that he chose the Isle of Man over The Hague, while other, more distant friends of Isherwood, including Auden's brother-in-law, Klaus, made the journey to the Dutch city.

Unknown to Auden and the Yates family, as they enjoyed a holiday in 1935, within a decade two of the boys would be dead, and two others, including Michael, would have endured terrifying combat experiences and harsh physical deprivation.[7] Is it only hindsight that makes intuitions about impending disaster visible in the poem that Auden wrote on the island in 1935?

Auden had sent Isherwood (and others) verse epistles before. His four-part poetic sequence from 1929, for instance, had begun as a cycle of verse letters to Isherwood.[8] But "August for the people" is still an unexpected gift because its strangeness and ambition are so marked and exceptional. Besides its power as a piece of writing, one significant circumstantial detail sets this poem apart in a completely different way. When Auden collected "August for the people" in *Look, Stranger!* in 1936, he gave Michael Yates a copy of the book and wrote next to this

poem: "Do you remember taking this down in the Peveril?"⁹ This is the
only poetic work that Auden is known to have dictated even in part to
a transcriber. And the transcriber there in the room, as the words came
to Auden, was Yates. That this happened is an unmistakable mark of
the pair's closeness and trust.

Auden's contribution from afar to the gathering in The Hague is a message of public affection for Isherwood's "squat spruce body and enormous head." At a time of political "crisis and dismay," it is also a tribute
to Isherwood's "strict and adult pen" and its power to "warn" and "reveal" through "insight" (215–216). Auden had always had his doubts
about the characters of poets—including, of course, his own. In part 2
of "A Happy New Year," he refers to poets as creatures who "awkward,
pasty, feeling the draught, | Have health and skill and beauty on the
brain."¹⁰ As a complement to that self-indictment, "August for the
people" brings into public view for one of the first times in Auden's
poems his complicated reverence for the art of the novel.¹¹

Isherwood was a determined fictionalizer of his own experiences,
and, as a form of tribute perhaps, Auden ensures that "August for the
people" is unusually full of autobiographical details. It is a personal
survey of the nine years since Auden and Isherwood had visited the Isle
of Wight together in the culturally pivotal year of 1926. This was the
visit, Isherwood's biographer Peter Parker suggests, when "it is probable that . . . [Auden and Isherwood] became lovers."¹² If this is true, it
accounts for the nostalgic look back in Auden's 1935 poem to the 1926
holiday, a reference that no other readers aside from Auden and Isherwood (and perhaps Yates) were likely to have understood fully. "August
for the people" also indirectly reflects more contemporary private feelings: Auden remembers the past moment when he and Isherwood—
"Half-boys" as the poem says—are likely to have sexualized their friendship, from within the present context of his love for Michael Yates, the
teenager silently taking dictation of at least some of this poem (215).

"August for the people" displays Auden's usual preference for
working with a division into three: in this case, visits to three holiday
resorts, two with Isherwood and one without him, punctuate the poem.
"Nine years ago," in July 1926, Auden and Isherwood visited the Isle of
Wight, "that southern island | Where the wild Tennyson became a

fossil" (215). Auden here refers to Tennyson's prolonged residence, starting in 1852, at his house Farringford, overlooking Freshwater Bay, the same bay where Auden and Isherwood's lodging house was situated.[13] Then, in July 1931, Auden had again visited Isherwood, this time at the little town of Sellin on the island of Rügen in the Baltic.[14]

On both islands, Auden and Isherwood had played self-indulgently with a favorite, master explanation of the world and with a role, built around it, that they jokingly assumed together. Auden remembers that in 1926, "Our hopes were set still on the spies' career, | Prizing the glasses and the old felt hat" (215). The first master explanation, the solution to everything, was, from behind the mundane disguise of binoculars and hat, to view the world around them as a spy would—as someone who looks innocuous but is in fact identifying a society's deepest secrets. But the attraction of that ludic role faded: "all the secrets we discovered were | Extraordinary and false" (215). Then, as in a film, "Five summers pass," and in 1931, under the influence of Homer Lane's doctrines:

> the word is love.
> Surely one fearless kiss would cure
> The million fevers, a stroking brush
> The insensitive refuse from the burning core.

Auden refers here to Lane's lessons, transmitted to him by Layard in 1928 to 1929, about trusting the unconscious to express itself freely and believing that love would cure any disease. The poem acknowledges that in the summer of 1931, Auden and Isherwood fancied these lessons would bring liberation. But they led only to "the no-subtler lure | To private joking in a panelled room, | The solitary vitality of tramps and madmen" (215).

Now, in 1935, fantasies of exposure or of psychological cure have been superseded: "the moulding images of growth | That made our interest and us, are gone" (215). Whatever their past usefulness as vehicles of artistic "growth," these ways of interpreting the world—and their potential to bring change—are at an end. And here Auden is on a third pleasure island, the Isle of Man, this time without Isherwood:

> All types that can intrigue the writer's fancy,
> Or sensuality approves, are here.
> And I, each meal-time with the families,
> The animal brother and his serious sister,

Or after breakfast on the urned steps watching
The defeated and disfigured marching by,
Have thought of you, Christopher, and wished beside me
Your squat spruce body and enormous head. (214–215)[15]

From among the damaged survivors of the First World War, the
"defeated and disfigured," Auden suggests that in 1935, the most important contribution a writer like Isherwood can make is to use their talents, "your strict and adult pen," to clarify the dangers and temptations
facing Europe (216). Is there a new master explanation that can diagnose Europe's sickness? Auden leaves this question unanswered in the
poem, suggesting that he does not see one and is certain only that this
is another moment of transition in his writing life.

If nothing else, "August for the people" demonstrates the continuing
iconic significance of islands in Auden's imagination. At one point, he
even seems to have called this poem, at least in his notes, "The Island."[16]
That private title is not just factual but also expressive: it refers to the
poem's physical setting, but also to Auden's feelings of loneliness in the
midst of these frolicking, middle-class families. For here, Auden is himself "the island" of the Isle of Man, with his awkward status in the household as the sixteen-year-old's considerably older "friend" and former
teacher, at a time when his world is in flux. And that title, "The Island,"
reflects another suggestion that drifts through the poem: life on an island, such as the one that Auden and the Yates family are on, can only be a
temporary blessing. The poem hints that there is something symbolically
important about Isherwood's residence in mainland Europe, which now
seems to fit better a writer's immediate task.

On the island, the poem positions Auden as an outsider among
both "the sallow oval faces of the city" and "the families" in Ramsey. In
this sense, the poem echoes the overall nature of Auden's relationship
with Yates once the latter left the Downs School at the end of the
summer term of 1933. They saw each other only intermittently in the
months afterward. In October 1933, Auden visited Yates at Bryanston
School in Dorset, where Yates had just started as a boarder. During the
Christmas holiday of that year, Auden spent a few days at the Yates's
home in Brooklands, an expensive part of the town of Sale, just outside
Manchester. This is the scene for the poem beginning, "The earth turns
over, our side feels the cold," where Auden glumly pictures himself

among "the holly and the gifts . . . | The carols on the piano, the glowing hearth." Again, he is a visitor, an outsider, "Son of a nurse and doctor, loaned a room, | Your would-be lover."[17]

Auden may have visited Bryanston again the following spring, before he, Yates, and Peter Roger went on their trip through Europe in August and early September 1934. In late 1934, Auden sent Isherwood his sixteen-poem sequence of love poems, many of them inspired by Yates.[18] It is as if Auden "met" Yates more often in his poetry than in life. Although the pair may possibly have seen each other again before August 1935, there is no record of any such meeting. And when they were with each other, as now, the occasion for Auden must have been a mixture of romantic fulfillment and a doubtless excruciating rigmarole of small talk and Yates family activities during which so much had to be camouflaged.

"August for the people" is rightly called an occasional work, a poem of the sort that, as Auden was to say in 1948, W. B. Yeats had "transformed . . . from being either an official performance of impersonal virtuosity or a trivial *vers de société* into a serious reflective poem of at once personal and public interest." In "new and important" poems such as "In Memory of Major Robert Gregory," Auden wrote, Yeats "never loses the personal note of a man speaking about his personal friends in a particular setting."[19] Auden's poetry from the 1929 four-part sequence onward is often at its strongest when it is "occasional" in this sense. But his work adds another shade of meaning to the term. Like Yeats, Auden is a poet who again and again rises to the "occasion," confronting and responding in a heightened way to significant moments of historical change. Here, in "August for the people," the moment is an intuition about eras—personal, artistic, and political—starting to end when: "In the houses | The little pianos are closed, and a clock strikes." As this happens, Auden writes, managing to reach something at a deeper, more impersonal level than surface appearances and private concerns, "all sway forward on the dangerous flood | Of history" (216).

Auden's comments about Yeats's occasional poems clearly apply to his own "August for the people," which (as he would have expected readers to notice) uses an unrhymed version of the eight-line stanza that Yeats had so characteristically deployed for the "In Memory of Major Robert Gregory" poem, about the shock of an Irish aviator's death in the First World War.[20] Following Yeats's model, "August for the people" works hard to establish a particularly "realistic" and credible setting: here, a modern world of annual holidays, mass-produced clothing, tourism, and rented seaside accommodations. There is also an obvious clue to Yeats's influence: Auden notes that in his and Isherwood's early years, "The enemy were sighted from the Norman tower," an allusion to the Norman origins of Yeats's famous home, his "tower" at Thoor Ballylee in County Galway (215). It is not surprising, given Auden's skill at ciphering unspoken meanings into his work, that in a poem tacitly featuring the listening presence of Michael Yates and with all the topics relating to him that cannot be mentioned, his almost-namesake Yeats should be such an obvious, even blatant, reference point.

In the introduction to *The Poet's Tongue*, the anthology that Auden compiled with John Garrett and that was published in June 1935 (not long before Auden left for the Isle of Man), he declared that poetry is a morally alert but nondidactic medium: "Poetry is not concerned with telling people what to do," he insisted, "but with extending our knowledge of good and evil, perhaps making the necessity for action more urgent and its nature more clear, but only leading us to the point where it is possible for us to make a rational and moral choice."[21] In "August for the people," Auden reuses the idea that the best writing does not tell readers what to do, as a piece of agitprop would, but reveals enough of the world to make a decision about action feasible. Using almost identical language, he transfers the role of "leading people to the point where it is possible . . . to make a rational and moral choice" from poetry to the novel. This is the basis for his praise of Isherwood's austere art:

> So in this hour of crisis and dismay,
> What better than your strict and adult pen
> Can warn us from the colours and the consolations,
> The showy arid works, reveal
> The squalid shadow of academy and garden,
> Make action urgent and its nature clear?
> Who give us nearer insight to resist
> The expanding fear, the savaging disaster? (216)

Oddly, the phrase "this hour of crisis and dismay" has a vague origin in the prose of Winston Churchill. It stems from a review that Auden had written of Churchill's *Thoughts and Adventures* in 1933, where he praises "the old humbug" Churchill's "extraordinary verbal sense," exemplified when he describes the scene before the German army's offensive in March 1918 as "an hour of intolerable majesty and crisis."[22] Once again, the long shadow of the First World War falls across Auden's poetic imagination, even in the middle of the 1930s.

But what the "hour of crisis and dismay" refers to here is deliberately ambiguous. It could be taken as a reference to political developments in Europe during 1935 that contributed to a sense of impending disaster. These now included the passage of the antisemitic Nuremberg Laws in Germany and the massing of Italian troops for the invasion of Abyssinia (the exonym used in Europe at the time for Ethiopia). This was a military operation long contemplated and threatened, that would actually begin in October 1935. However, the "hour of crisis" may also refer, more covertly, to Auden's sense of a vital change in his own life and work. In this context, a new note makes itself heard in the poem: Auden's idea that the writer's task is to "warn" a readership. This seems to be the first poem in which Auden associates the verb "to warn" with a writer's role. A writer does not insist on anything but advises, cautions, warns. Auden picks up here another perennial wartime presence in his writing of the 1930s: Wilfred Owen, who insisted in the preface to his poems drafted in 1918 that "All a poet can do today is warn."[23] The echoes of Yeats in this poem thus reverberate alongside the words of Owen, a poet whom the Irish writer affected to despise.

Auden issues no partisan appeal to action because, as he makes clear, Isherwood is showing what a writer, especially a novelist, should do: not incite struggle but warn and "give us nearer insight to resist | The expanding fear, the savaging disaster" (216). The poem's next and final stanza, recalling the nighttime view from the windowsill in part 2 of "A Happy New Year" (1932), is deliberately downbeat, quiet, almost passive:

> This then my birthday wish for you, as now
> From the narrow window of my fourth floor room
> I smoke into the night, and watch reflections
> Stretch in the harbour. In the houses
> The little pianos are closed, and a clock strikes.
> And all sway forward on the dangerous flood
> Of history, that never sleeps or dies,
> And, held one moment, burns the hand. (216)[24]

Auden's "birthday wish for you" refers doubly to the quietly heroic role he *wishes* for Isherwood's writing and to his own *wish* for Isherwood's presence "beside me" on the novelist's birthday. Families, lovers, and friends alike are adrift "on the dangerous flood of history," which, in a beautifully and massively mixed metaphor, "never sleeps or dies" but for a moment can be "held" (meaning either "grasped" or "stopped"), and somehow also "burns the hand" (216). These complexities and contradictions signal the speaker's inability to pin down or fix the vast and momentous reach of history, a crumpling "flood" that is so incomprehensible, so shapelessly sublime in scope, that it cannot be known, even indirectly, except through a cascade of figurative language.

If the poem recognizes that historical processes can be sensed but are at the same time mysterious and unknowable, just as importantly, it marks Auden's dawning recognition that no permanent "insulation" from politics and conflict is possible in a world where "history . . . never sleeps or dies" (216). This is the key to some of the poem's most striking characteristics, not least the way that Auden infuses the apparently carefree holiday scene with a sense of impending violence and terror. Notes of crisis and omen first emerge in his description of standing after breakfast on "the urned steps watching | The defeated and disfigured marching by" (214–215).

However, Auden also deploys a more speculative and unusual technique to create this fearful atmosphere. Critics often remark on Auden's strikingly personal description of Isherwood's "squat spruce body and enormous head" and his "strict and adult pen." The phrases are curiously specific, slightly grotesque, and they have a clumsily obvious, quasi-sexual tone. Considering how they seem to objectify Isherwood's body and his artist's mind ("your strict and adult pen"), the descriptions have an overtly fetishistic quality (216). But other *things* in the poem, besides Isherwood's head and pen, are also viewed with a kind of lingering, fascinated, fetishistic relish. In Auden's imagination objects on the island seem to be welling with a vital but obscurely coded importance.

The mention of an "adult pen" is a reminder that Freud claimed the "normal prototype of fetishes is a man's penis."[25] For Freud, the fetish is an everyday object, whether a nose, a foot, a piece of clothing (or a head or a pen), that acts as a substitute for the overwhelming threat of the mother's supposedly missing penis. In response to the perceived shocking absence of this crucially important body part, according to Freud the male child allows himself to believe it is somehow still there by transferring the idea of the missing penis to another, associated object or part of the body. That object replaces the "missing" body part, as Freud elsewhere remarks, by "a symbolic connection of thought, of which the person concerned is usually not conscious."[26]

The fetish, while never losing its own identity, thus comes for Freud to glow with the significance of something that is absent, something that it is not and that it cannot too obviously resemble because the absent object, seen directly, would inspire terror. (Thinking about these Freudian theories, I am reminded of what Proust says about love and am impressed by how truly his thought applies to many other psychic processes as well: "love, even in its humblest beginnings, is a striking example of how little reality means to us."[27]) Understood in a broader, more historical sense, Freud's idea of the fetish, and the horror that the fetish veils, explains the sheer proliferation of obtruding objects, besides Isherwood's head and pen, in "August for the people."

In Auden's poem, these verbally spotlit objects feel charged with a sinister significance: the "tigerish blazer and the dove-like shoe," for example, or the "little pianos" and "a clock" (214–216). This is not a case of Auden using the familiar modern technique of "symbolism," by finding objects or scenes that evoke something well matched that is not directly present or stated. Unlike a poetic symbol, the fetishistic image brings a strange quality of antitheticalness and a suppressed terror, fitting for a moment of crisis, with it. Auden uses these object images here to evoke something extremely unlike, and logically unconnected to, the idea or feeling being evoked. (This use of poetic language is the opposite as well of T. S. Eliot's famous concept of the "objective correlative," where an image is used to evoke a feeling to which it directly corresponds: "when the external facts, which must terminate in sensory experience, are given, the emotion is immediately evoked."[28]) The ominousness of images such as the "enormous head" and the "tigerish blazer" express the presence of a horrifying political world even on a "favourite" island where such things are supposed to be absent. Auden's poetic fetishism gives him a way of articulating how "history" can be felt by displacement even in a place like a holiday resort, which exists to shut out threatening realities. History from "there" is eerily present in its repression "here" on the Isle of Man, as something like a dissonant crackle within the resort world's banal objects and people.

At the end of the poem, Auden returns to his view of the island's harbor, a place of arrivals and departures, where the first stanza had begun with steamers sidling up to the pier. Now, though, Auden's speaker is apparently alone. He dramatizes his sense of social marginality both as a poet and as a queer man (writing to another queer man) in an enclave organized around the paradigm of straight family life. He situates himself in a less-than-impressive location, at the "narrow window of my fourth floor room." The darkness of night starts to hide activities that are coming to an end as lights are going out in the bourgeois resort. "In the houses | The little pianos are closed, and a clock strikes" (216).

As they do, Auden's poem "sway[s] forward on the dangerous flood" (216) toward a new understanding of the world, not yet fully revealed. By metonymic association, the "dangerous flood" calls implicit attention to what lies beyond the water: the British mainland, which is only about forty miles east of the Isle of Man, as well as the convulsed continent of Europe beyond. In October 1939, Hitler made a notorious speech in the Reichstag in which he declared that "this struggle unto destruction will not remain restricted to the continent. No, it will reach across the Sea. There are no more islands today."[29] In its forebodings about the "dangerous flood" on which "all sway forward," Auden's poem of August 1935 about the insubstantiality of "favourite islands" reflects a truth larger, more accurate, and more ominous than even its author probably knew.

That same year, 1935, the warden of New College, Oxford, H. A. L. Fisher, one of the most secure and establishment figures in contemporary Britain, used a metaphor like Auden's "flood" in the preface to his *History of Europe* when he compared contemporary history to "waves": "Men wiser and more learned than I have discerned in history a plot, a rhythm, a predetermined pattern. These harmonies are concealed from me. I can see only one emergency following upon another, as wave follows upon wave, only one great fact with respect to which, since it is unique, there can be no generalizations, only one safe rule for the historian: that he should recognize in the development of human destinies the play of the contingent and the unforeseen."[30]

As these "waves" broke on the world and the storm clouds gathered, sometime in or around the middle of 1935, Auden's conscience, or his poetic gift, was beginning to insist that he had to change his poetry. John Fuller identifies "August for the people" as the poem that "consciously, even programmatically, [divides] early Auden from the Auden of the later 1930s."[31] Perhaps what the nature of the change was did not yet seem clear to Auden, but, judging by this poem, it has to do with a need for direct knowledge of a wider world of historical events and with a new sense of urgency about a world in crisis. And, because Auden's poetry was always in a close, organic relation to his personal and historical experiences (as the very autobiographical details of "August for the people" alone suffice to show), this also meant he had to change his life.

In this context, Auden's wedding in June 1935 with Erika Mann cannot be seen simply as a goodwill gesture. It was an act freighted with symbolic weight and formed part of an urge in Auden to grow and change, perhaps also to shelter. Auden might have talked flippantly to some of his friends about his marriage. But this tie with Mann meant more to him than he let on. Like many queer men at the time, Auden idealized marriage. He sought to keep up good relations with Mann (and she with him), even after the Second World War was over and the Reich that had denationalized her was destroyed. They never divorced.

The marriage also deepened Auden's long, evolving relationship with German culture, rooted in the personal and national traumas of the First World War and now inflected by the very real prospect of another conflict between Britain and Germany. From 1935, these concerns were deepened because Auden had German family connections. What did that mean to him? When in 1939 he wrote an epithalamion for Erika Mann's sister, Elisabeth, and the dissident Italian author she was marrying in exile, he claimed that "this quiet wedding" may have seen the start of "Hostile kingdoms of the truth, | Fighting fragments of content" being "reconciled by love."[32] Consciously or unconsciously, Auden had perhaps already seen symbolism like this in his own quiet marriage in the summer of 1935. Auden's poetry about German boys in 1929 had been pessimistic about the chances of a "real meeting," but the union with Erika Mann, because superficially it seemed so obviously a pragmatic rather than romantic arrangement, might be a meaningful sign of "Hostile kingdoms of the truth" being "reconciled." Auden's marriage was one symptom of change in his life, but only one. Change, as yet intermittently, was also coming into his poetry.[33]

As all sway forward "on the dangerous flood | Of history" in that year, Auden infuses more than a simple surface meaning in the line: "The little pianos are closed, and a clock strikes" (216). The music of the "small field" (Auden's phrase in his 1933 letter to Spender) and the "little pianos" are ending as, at the conclusion of "August for the people," a clock (an object associated with the worlds of necessity and work) signals not just the finish of one hour and the start of a new one but the start of a new time in Auden's poems. The "little pianos" are an emblem of Auden's continuing concern about his limited artistic ambitions, about the adequacy (or the ethics) of producing entertainment for a small circle of friends. Seamus Heaney described the social dimension of Auden's imagination: Auden "was eager to make a connection between the big picture that was happening outside in Europe and England and the small one which was being shown inside himself: he sensed the crisis in a public world poised for renewal or catastrophe as analogous to an impending private crisis of action and choice in his own life."[34] Leaving a job, agreeing to a marriage, picking out for poetry the moment when the lid on the "little pianos" of an artistry of restricted scope closes and a clock strikes the hour—these are signs of a private crisis that is at the same time a reaction to crisis in the public world.

It is not known when or why Auden realized he would be ending his position at the Downs School, but it happened around the time that he and Erika Mann were married. Whether he reached the end of his contract and wanted a change, or there was no money to renew his employment, or (as Spender once flippantly hinted) there were whispers of scandal, is not recorded. He had started to think about leaving the Downs in 1934, during the school year following Michael Yates's departure from Colwall. After a half-baked aspiration to teach in the Soviet Union crumbled away, Auden applied for a position at Bryanston, the public school where his love and a number of other Downs pupils were studying. That prospect evaporated in the spring of 1935.[35]

Auden then pondered whether to get a job in a secondary (that is, state) school or to look for "a B.B.C. job connected with education." Perhaps the idea of working in broadcasting led to the notion of a job in a form of mass entertainment. In May or early June 1935, Auden wrote from Colwall to an acquaintance named Basil Wright about a position at the GPO (General Post Office) Film Unit.[36] Since 1933, Wright had been working for the dour film impresario John Grierson at the Unit, a small, poorly funded, governmental organization, attached to the Post Office, tasked with making documentary films about life in Britain.[37] Almost immediately Auden was offered a job (at a greatly reduced salary from his Downs pay) officially starting in September 1935. In July of that year, he told a Helensburgh friend, "I'm leaving teaching pro tem at any rate to work for Grierson at the G. P. O. Film Unit."[38]

Why Auden chose documentary film is a mystery. It may have been connected with his awareness of the limited nature of his social experience or with a desire for a more direct engagement with the contemporary world. In "Here on the cropped grass," written in mid-1933, he had expressed (with a dose of self-parodying campness) a desire to cross the gulf of class and learn more about working people's lives:

> A digit of the crowd, [I] would like to know
> Them better whom the shops and trams are full of,
> The little men and their mothers, not plain but
>   Dreadfully ugly.[39]

Change often includes recapitulation, and the first piece of writing Auden did for the GPO Film Unit, for a film eventually called *Coal Face,* took him back into the bleak landscapes of his earliest poetry and down into the subterranean worlds of the mine and the working class. The Unit had been planning for at least two films, *Coal Face* and another called *Night Mail,* by the time Auden received his offer letter in June 1935. The Unit wanted to include his words in these films as soon as possible, so Auden was asked to write his contributions and collaborate with others involved in the productions immediately, while he was still employed in the final weeks of his job as a schoolteacher. The first result of this work was the beautiful, highly stylized lyric beginning "O lurcher loving collier black as night" that he contributed to *Coal Face.*[40] (Auden soon titled the poem "Madrigal," which is how I will refer to it here.)

"Madrigal" dramatizes the meeting at the end of the working day of an unnamed miner surfacing from underground and his wife or lover, Kate. In a strange way, this haunting poem was prefigured in a knockabout drag performance that Auden had given at the Downs, six or so months earlier, in December 1934, during an elaborate "Revue" for an audience of masters' families and pupils as well as local citizens. Toward the end of the evening, Auden rode a bicycle onstage wearing a dress and a wig and then sang (probably in a falsetto voice) a piece he had written called "Rhondda Moon." In the persona of a miner's wife or girlfriend, and in something like an early version of "Kate" in "Madrigal," he warbled:

> On the Rhondda
> My time I squander
> Waiting for my miner boy.
> He may be rough and tough
> But be sure he is hot stuff.
> He is slender, to me tender,
> He's my only joy.
> Lovers' meeting,
> Lovers' greeting,
> O his arms will be about me soon.[41]

Once more, Auden, in a stage costume or playing someone else, was revealing a hidden aspect of his imaginative life. Hannah Arendt's profound recognition of Auden's "necessary secretiveness" gently implies that, sometimes, as here, the secrets might momentarily and unwittingly be displayed.[42] "Rhondda Moon" is about waiting for a lover, while "Madrigal" is about meeting a lover. But "Rhondda Moon" shows that the emotional and dramatic seeds of "Madrigal" were already germinating in the poetic soil by the winter of 1934.

Auden apparently wrote his new poem, to be sung by a female chorus, in June 1935, during the month of his marriage. Alongside many other things, "Madrigal," with its central theme of the meeting of male and female, "black" and "white," is a covert reflection on Auden's marital union with someone so different from himself. And perhaps the poem also conceals a thought about the possibility of marrying poetry to the alien medium of film (the black and white imagery in the poem suggests a reference to films).[43]

Much of the film *Coal Face,* which Auden apparently had almost no overall role in shaping, is taken up with establishing an informed, sober, and didactic perspective on mining. As such, it can stand as representative of the GPO Film Unit's documentary methods as a whole: the style involved both sophisticated camera work and sound recording, combined with, or conflicting with, an earnest, and highly verbal, commitment to social commentary from a middle-class perspective. The title of the film was originally going to be, simply, *Miners*.[44] But the change to *Coal Face* allows for a much greater richness of meaning. *Coal Face*, of course, literally refers to the physical center of mining activity, the place where coal is being hewn out of the surrounding rock. It could refer as well to a person's begrimed appearance, and, more figuratively, it can also point toward the socially and artistically advanced films that the Unit's leaders believed they were creating under challenging conditions at the furthest point of advance yet made by documentary filmmakers.

Toward the end of *Coal Face*, after an solemn, educational commentary on the mining industry, there is a montage section put together from close-up shots of different parts of the winches and engines that are drawing the miners—and the film's viewers—back to the earth's surface at the end of the shift and the film. As the miners emerge from the cage, their work done, Auden's poem suddenly begins. The film changes gear: a managerial narrator's male voice disappears, to be replaced by those of female singers; and the dry, factual discourse is replaced by a poetic register of language. Just as significantly, the poem switches the film's focus from the underground world of work to the world of the surface, of women as well as men, and of feelings and leisure. Auden's poetic contribution in *Coal Face*, unlike the rest of the film, comes on a Saturday evening when the hill is for a while "smokeless," the lamp is "out," and the "cages [are] still," the moment when work has stopped temporarily and something else begins. Here is the poem:

> O lurcher loving collier black as night,
> Follow your love across the smokeless hill.
> Your lamp is out and all your cages still.
> Course for her heart and do not miss
> And Kate fly not so fast,
> For Sunday soon is past,
> And Monday comes when none may kiss.
> Be marble to his soot and to his black be white.[45]

Leaving aside considerations about punctuation for a moment, the eight-line poem divides neatly into two halves that are formal analogues of the thematic dichotomies the poem explores. Just as the miners in the film are never named, the first four lines in the poem are addressed to the nameless "lurcher loving collier," while the second four lines apostrophize "Kate" and deliver the injunction to each that they are to come together as a pair of lovers, his "black" like night, mating with and complementing her "white" like marble.

Auden calls his poem "Madrigal" to evoke part-song, or nonsacred choral music, but also to play off a formal feature of madrigals, especially from the Renaissance: the use of strong counterpointing in which there are two separate musical lines, independent of each other but also interacting and interdependent (like the lovers in the poem). The Renaissance background is relevant too because of the poem's heavy emphasis on the symbolically contrasting qualities of blackness and whiteness. This makes it feel like a pastiche of familiar schemas in plays and lyrics from the Elizabethan and Jacobean periods, such as Iago's lurid, hallucinatory diagram in the first scene of *Othello*, where he warns Brabantio that "Even now, now, very now, an old black ram | Is tupping your white ewe."[46] In Shakespeare's play, the black/white metaphor is a contrast primarily rooted in a racial divide between a Black man and a white woman, the racial divide being mirrored by the parallel divides between genders and between ages. Such resonances survived of course into the 1930s, as in Nancy Cunard's pamphlet *Black Man and White Ladyship: An Anniversary* (1931), about her relationship with Henry Crowder.[47] But here, in Auden's poem of the summer of 1935, race seems less overtly at stake than are class and gender.

There are multiple antitheses, explicit or implicit, in the poem: the blackness of the man and the whiteness of the women correspond to the opposition of day and night. The blackness of the miner originates in the daytime world of work, whereas, paradoxically, the whiteness of the woman belongs in the world he comes up to as darkness falls. But this contrast also relates to the stillness of the pits, opposed to the "fly[ing]" and "cours[ing]" movements of the lovers; the softness of "soot" and the hardness of "marble" (the soft is unconventionally mapped onto the male and the hard onto the female); the weekday work world of "Monday" versus Saturday evening and Sunday, which is the time of leisure and the chance for love. The contrast patterns even link to the limestone in "marble" and the carbon of coal. But the basic oppositions are between male and female and, just as importantly, between black and white, as Auden's final line, which gets very close to being a tautology, makes clear: "Be marble to his soot and to his black be white."[48]

The poem ends with a double injunction to "Kate" simply to "be." As such, it epitomizes what has come before, because the whole of "Madrigal" is written as a set of instructions to the lovers: "Follow," "course," "do not miss," "fly not," "Be," "be." This scenario makes the language of the poem (written in the month of Auden's marriage) reminiscent of the directions to participants in a ceremony such as the marriage service from the 1662 Book of Common Prayer, with the poet's role like that of the minister: "The Minister, receiving the Woman at her father's or friend's hands, shall cause the Man with his right hand to take the Woman by her right hand, and to say after him as followeth." The terms of the amatory encounter in *Coal Face* are likewise dictated by a learned, middle-class, educated voice, in this case a poetic one, who is eager as much to form an aesthetically pleasing pattern out of male and female, black and white—as though he were leading them through a kind of dance or ceremony—as he is to encourage their pleasure. As with the role played by a minister in the marriage service, the schema in the poem makes the poet stand subtly, disinterestedly outside the sphere of active heterosexual love.

In this respect, the resolutions of the antitheses and contrasts that are such a prominent feature of the poem compound the ambitions of official documentary film to act as an integrating, civic-minded, consensus- and consent-creating medium. Opposites are conjoined and synthesized, male balances female, as black balances white, and middle-class voice (and audience) balances working-class bodies, forming them frictionlessly into a paradigm of the greater whole that does not allow space on their parts for decision, for agreeing or disagreeing or for withdrawal. The poem is a lyric masterpiece, but as in other poems Auden wrote in the mid-1930s, there is something strangely prescriptive, even at moments overbearing, or perhaps schoolmasterly, in the surface message. It is as though his poems were trying to organize or stabilize a scene not completely under their control and for which, therefore, some subtly emphatic instructions were required.

That Auden should have started his work in films in June 1935 with such a short but verbally grandiose piece of language might at first glance seem odd, given the highly visual nature of the film medium. In films, words usually have a secondary status, but here that hierarchy is subverted. However, Auden was as aware as anyone of the conventions, genres, and expectations of film because these were a familiar part of his world. He might only now have started to work in the industry, but films were already part of his existence, as they were of almost everyone else's in the 1930s. Like most of his literary friends, Auden was an enthusiastic consumer of the culture industry's products. To return one last time to the poem "Here on the cropped grass," Auden there enacts a fashionable highbrow attitude, looking down toward the everyday world and deploring "Gaumont theatres | Where fancy plays on hunger to produce | The noble robber, ideal of boys."[49] But in fact, as a young man like millions of other people, Auden went frequently to the cinema with romantic partners and with friends like Isherwood and the painter William Coldstream.[50]

Films were an extremely popular and cheap source of entertainment. Cinema audiences in Britain throughout the 1930s averaged around 18–19 million per week out of a total population of around 45 million, and most viewers paid less than a shilling for a seat. Abroad was little different. In his "1929 Journal," started in Berlin, Auden ends the first entry with a note about a visit to a cinema there with John Layard.[51] Elsewhere in the journal, Auden notes down regular episodes of cinema-going. In April 1929, he writes, for instance, that he and Gerhart Meyer had been to "Kino in afternoon" and had seen the latest edition of the *Emelka-Wochenschau* newsreel.[52] (While he was in Germany on and off in the period between 1928 and 1932, Auden had probably seen at least one of many films featuring Erika Mann's former husband, Gustaf Gründgens: the most famous of Gründgens's roles now is "Der Schränker" (The safecracker) in Fritz Lang's *M* from 1931. In the same year, Erika Mann herself appeared in the uncredited role of Fräulein von Atems in the lesbian-themed *Mädchen in Uniform* (*Girls in Uniform*), directed by Leontine Sagan. Auden saw that film, so he first laid eyes on his future wife when she was on-screen in a film about female-female eroticism.) Back in Britain, Auden and the novelist William Plomer went to see a Garbo film together in 1932 and sniggered loudly, to the annoyance of others in the audience.[53]

Christopher Isherwood had been a hardened filmgoer since his preteenage years. In *Lions and Shadows* he describes himself as a "born film-fan," and as a young writer Isherwood found that even "the stupidest film may be full of astonishing revelations about the tempo and dynamics of everyday life."[54] He collected publicity stills, cut out photographs from fanzines such as *Photoplay,* and kept a scrapbook with his cuttings and opinions carefully preserved and ordered.[55] When he went up to Cambridge, Isherwood soon became a member of the recently founded University Film Society, idly contemplated a career in films (something that he eventually achieved), and, in the interim, as Peter Parker says, "spent much of his time at the cinema."[56] Isherwood's cinema-going continued in Berlin. On his first visit to the city in 1929, he took his friend "Bubi" (Berthold Szczesny), picked up at the "Cosy Corner," to films: they saw, Isherwood writes, "Pudovkin's *Storm over Asia* and Pabst's Wedekind film, *Pandora's Box.*"[57] In Berlin during the next few years, Isherwood also saw other classic films such as Josef von Sternberg's *Der blaue Engel* (*The Blue Angel*), Fritz Lang's *M*, and G. W. Pabst's *Kameradschaft* (*Comradeship*).[58]

If "Berlin meant Boys" to Isherwood and his friends, including Auden, it also meant images, cameras, films (and boys on film and on camera). "Weston [i.e., Auden] returned from Germany to spend Christmas at home," Isherwood writes in *Lions and Shadows* in 1938, looking back to 1928, explaining how he himself came to visit the city through listening to Auden's descriptions. "He was full of stories of Berlin, that astonishingly vicious yet fundamentally so respectable city, where the night-life had a cosy domestic quality and where the films were the most interesting in Europe."[59]

Auden arrived in Berlin just as a new slew of Russian films for the huge émigré colony there was arriving too. These had a decisive impact on him, as they did on Isherwood and on Spender during their own stays in the city. An example of the influence of the avant-garde Russian aesthetic on these writers is Spender's early poem "The Express." With its imagery of the engine lunging in "luminous self-possession" and that "like a comet through flame, . . . moves entranced," it is based on the imagery in *Turksib*, Viktor Turin's 1929 film about the construction of a railroad from Turkestan to Siberia.[60] (*Turksib* was a film beloved by the GPO Film Unit's boss, John Grierson.) If Auden only began working in films in 1935, his imagination, like those of most of the other writers in his circle, was already saturated by cinematic ways of seeing.

Coal Face was labeled on the credits as an "Empo" film, Grierson's brand name for projects of a nonstandard nature.[61] Basil Wright commented that *Coal Face* was "a highly experimental film which was sort of a tryout, or a test-tube thing, if you like, which eventually came true in *Night Mail* the following year."[62] As was the nature of Grierson's partially collaborative system at the Film Unit (ultimately, there was only one person in charge), many people contributed in a number of guises to *Coal Face*. For example, Auden wrote the verse for the chorus near the end of the film, and Montagu Slater, the communist author and coeditor of *Left Review*, wrote the film's prose narration.[63] By early June 1935 the artist William Coldstream, who is listed in the on-screen credits as "editor" of the film, and Benjamin Britten, who is credited with the music, were also gathering material for the soundtrack of *Coal Face* without as yet being involved directly with Auden.

Miners were figures of enormous symbolic significance, not just to Auden and not simply to those in Auden's circle. Miners were a vital part of the larger image bank of 1930s Britain. As such, *Coal Face* was one of an increasing number of works from the mid-1930s in which the mines and representations of miners play an important role. In literary terms, much of the impetus for the increased representation of industrial experience was given by J. B. Priestley's account of his visit to the North in *English Journey* (1934).[64] Awareness of social unrest, industrial action, and widespread deprivation, all covered by Priestley, are the main drivers of the emergence of interest in mining across different media in the mid-1930s. But it might be said as well that the spate of war books from the late 1920s and early 1930s was succeeded by a profusion of works about mining because the subject of an often-subterranean war had gone underground again as a subject and was present disguised in the broader cultural obsession with mines.

In addition, there is a hermetic, self-conscious dimension to Auden's "Madrigal" in the context of *Coal Face* itself. This is a dimension that goes beyond poetry's functional role as aesthetic embellishment of the film's didactic message. To read or hear the poem's final words—"to his black be white"—crystallizes what has already been at play in a less explicit fashion throughout. Auden's lyric is about bringing contraries and oppositions into a managed order. But it is also a deeply visual poem, trading in the primary visual opposition of darkness and light, black and white. Inescapably, then, the text matches itself to the visual drama of the film, which trades in strong image contrasts between black and white: for instance, the darkened steel skeletons of the pit headgear outlined starkly against the blankness of the clouded sky.

Grierson had a strong preference for films shot on location because he believed that this conveyed a greater degree of realism than could ever be achieved by films that were shot in a studio.[65] Sometimes, and especially in the case of a film being made in difficult conditions, this could lead to problems. Auden remembered, much later, that *Coal Face* had been "shot in total darkness."[66] *Coal Face*'s codirector, Harry Watt, had a practical rationale or excuse for this, explaining that *Coal Face* "was partly shot underground, [and] the camerawork, to put it mildly, didn't come up to what was expected." Watt added: "It was bloody dark. Despite the efforts of the laboratory to get the brightest and clearest prints they could, in certain shots there was very little to be seen at all. And Grierson brilliantly converted this into a purposeful thing. . . . We wanted it to be as dark as this in order to give the impression of the dreadfulness and the difficulties of working underground."[67] As this comment suggests, the people working at the GPO Film Unit around Auden were able, as he was, after the fact to attribute symbolic qualities to lighting and the lack of lighting in this film. But Watt's cynicism can only carry so far. Darkness is integral to the meanings of the entire film, and in that sense, Auden's poem is like a signpost to the film's most important values.

The idea of the camera lighting up and capturing a once-hidden reality is a metaphoric enactment of documentary film's drive to widen the awareness of the national community and to bring different classes together. In spite of the obvious differences between the fully clothed people sitting comfortably in paid-for cinema seats and the crew of half-dressed miners hacking away in dangerous conditions in the bowels of the earth, the fact of the darkened cinema brilliantly folds the two groups together. The audience in its pitch-black world watches a screen on which people work in another pitch-black world. For as long

as the film lasts, workers and watchers alike are in the darkness together, bonded by a shared focus on the mine. Figuratively, at least, the
film briefly abolishes the gap between observers and observed and,
again figuratively, the distance between classes.

Because Auden began contributing to the GPO Film Unit in June 1935
while he was still employed at the Downs School, Basil Wright and Benjamin Britten visited him in Colwall on 5 July 1935 to discuss work.[68] Although, like Auden, Britten had attended Gresham's, they had not coincided there; this meeting in Herefordshire was the first time they had
encountered each other. (Wright, who was the same age as Auden, remembered that they both found the twenty-two-year-old Britten to be
"extremely young."[69]) That day at the Downs School, they apparently discussed Coal Face as well as another planned production by the GPO Film
Unit, Night Mail, which would again feature work going on in the dark.

The early-July 1935 meeting with Britten is another marker of
change in Auden's life. It led to one of his most important artistic partnerships during the second half of the 1930s and beyond. In the immediate context, their acquaintance developed into a guarded friendship
that took them to musical events together and generated correspondence. For instance, Auden remembered going with Britten to a memorial concert for the composer Alban Berg on 1 May 1936 at Broadcasting
House in London and throwing up in the street because of a "tummy
upset."[70] Britten's sensitivity to words and Auden's sensitivity to music
bound them together, as did their shared social background and their
experiences as gay men in a time when utmost bigotry was widespread.
Over the longer term, Auden's schoolmasterly meddlesomeness and
Britten's almost diaphanously thin skin made their relationship unstable. But their creative symbiosis while they were both employed by
the GPO Film Unit meant that they worked on poetry and music for
three films in 1935 and another in 1936. Meanwhile, Auden arranged
the text and provided a new poem, "The Creatures," for a song cycle,
"Our Hunting Fathers," that Britten composed during 1936.[71]

In spite of their mother's love of calligraphy and embroidery, the Auden
children had grown up in a home that was intensely, actively musical

and not very visual. One of the sons (almost certainly John Auden) told their father's official obituarist that neither of his parents "had any appreciation of the visual arts, as illustrated by the absense [sic] of a picture of real merit in the house."[72] Even so, Auden's involvement with visual culture, painting, and film was intricate and sustained. When Auden made his list of the "great emotional milestones of his life" in around May 1947, there were no musicians on it, but two of the five names (those of Robert Medley and Michael Yates) were painters, while another (that of Christopher Isherwood) had a commitment to a visual aesthetic that can be summed up in the literary credo that opens *Goodbye to Berlin* (1939): "I am a camera with its shutter open, quite passive, recording, not thinking."[73]

After Gresham's, Auden never lost touch with his first love, Robert Medley, while Medley studied art in London and then in Paris. Auden visited him and his lover, the dancer and theater director Rupert Doone, in London in the late 1920s. And while Medley was establishing his reputation as a painter in the capital during the 1930s, they became close again through their work for the Group Theatre collective. The Group Theatre itself moved Auden further into the world of art in other ways too. For instance, *The Dance of Death*, Auden's first drama to receive a performance, was staged by the Group Theatre on 25 February 1934 in a production including a mask designed for the central figure by the young sculptor Henry Moore.[74]

By the time, almost two years later, on 12 January 1936, when the Group Theatre produced Auden and Isherwood's play *The Dog Beneath the Skin* (containing the chorus that begins: "The Summer holds: upon its glittering lake | Lie Europe and the islands," as well as a version of "Rhondda Moon"), Auden had become even more strongly involved with people in the art and film worlds.[75]

His increasing interest in visual culture from 1934 onward is related to his friendship with Maurice Feild, the arts master at the Downs School. Feild and his wife, Alexandra, were Auden's closest friends among the staff there. And, at the Downs, Auden's interest in art deepened through the activities of Michael Yates, who was an enthusiastic student painter at the school. In 1934, Auden decided in a review that the art that truly appeals to the child's mind between the ages of "nine and fourteen" is not poetry: "Painting is much more the art of this period." (Michael Yates was fourteen at the time Auden wrote the review.[76]) Yates begins to be associated with the motif of visual images in Auden's work in late 1933 and then even more so during 1934, as if thoughts about Yates and about painting were bound up in Auden's poetic mind.

One other name that Auden at first included on his "emotional milestones" list but that he later crossed out (probably because, while there was love on Auden's part, they had no sexual involvement) was that of the painter William Coldstream. Next to Coldstream's name was the date "1935."[77] Coldstream and Auden had become friendly a decade earlier. They were introduced in London by a journalist mentor of Auden's named Michael Davidson.[78] Coldstream remembered that Davidson "talked a lot" about Auden and wanted the two of them to meet.[79] They did, apparently in the autumn of 1925, when Davidson and the painter Felicia Browne (later the first British volunteer to be killed in the Spanish Civil War) took the two young men to a performance of Leon Gordon's hit melodrama *White Cargo* (1923), a "play of the primitive" about strange goings-on in a rubber merchant's bungalow in West Africa.[80] Auden apparently tried, very gently, to seduce Coldstream and was rebuffed. But they remained friends, and Coldstream may well have visited the Auden family home in Birmingham. The painter later told Stephen Spender that Auden's pockets "were always stuffed with papers on which there were poems." He remembered a line from one poem, now probably lost: "The midwife seen against the curtain."[81]

However, Auden and Coldstream apparently did not stay in close touch in succeeding years, though they must have known something of each other. Auden had been involved with the Group Theatre since the summer of 1932. (His first finished piece of writing for the Group, aside from a prospectus, was a prologue used in a performance of songs, dance, and a play that the company performed in Croydon in July 1933.[82]) William and Nancy Coldstream are both listed as "members" of (that is, subscribers to) the Group Theatre as early as April of the same year.[83] Nonetheless, it was not until in the summer of 1935 when Auden began working at the GPO Film Unit, where Coldstream was also employed, that he and Coldstream became close.[84]

Britten's connection with the Film Unit had come about through Coldstream. William and Nancy Coldstream had moved to a ground-floor maisonette at 38 Upper Park Road in Belsize Park, London, and in the spring of 1935 the painters Claude Rogers and Elsie Few (who were married not long afterward) came to dinner at the Coldstreams' home.

During the evening, William Coldstream asked Few whether her sister, the pianist Margerie Few, who was studying at the Royal College of Music, might know anyone who could compose a score for film. As a result, Coldstream was told about Britten, who had graduated from the Royal College at the end of 1933 and was already one of its most visible former students.[85]

The head of the GPO Film Unit, John Grierson, held a strongly anti-individualistic, austerely responsible film aesthetic, an aesthetic that was largely determined by his admiration for polemical, avant-garde Soviet cinema. Such was the moribund state of British public film culture in the 1930s that some of Grierson's favorite films were proscribed from public display in the country at the time. For example, Sergei Eisenstein's *Battleship Potemkin* (1925), *Strike* (1925), and *October* (1928) were all banned by the British Board of Film Censors and could only be shown in film clubs.[86] For Grierson, writing in 1932, what avant-garde Soviet films from the 1920s, made by directors such as Eisenstein, Viktor Turin, and Vsevolod Pudovkin, offered was an "emphasis not on the personal life but on the mass life, their continuous attempt to dramatize the relation of a man to his community."[87]

For all his love of Soviet films, Grierson's values were stereotypical. One critic writes that, in the later 1920s, Grierson praised the "manly" virtues of "strength, simplicity, energy, directness, hardness, decency, courage, duty, upstanding power" and attacked any hint of effeminacy or the feminine: "sophistication, sentimentality, lounge-lizards, excessive sexuality, homosexuality, nostalgia, bohemianism, status-seeking and social climbing."[88] This led inexorably to an emphasis on the heroic, male worker, a cliché idealized, rather than a person who was idiosyncratic and real. Films made under Grierson's aegis returned again and again to manual workers and to the largely male world of physically arduous working experience—Auden's "Madrigal," sung by women at the end of *Coal Face,* is like a relieving reprieve from Grierson's controlling patriarchal hand.

In spite of the apparent sympathy for, and interest in, the working class, at least when the workers were viewed through a camera lens, Grierson and the Film Unit have been accused by critics of paternalism and social conservatism. Some of this is unquestionably justified. But, as

Ian Aitken writes, in "a period when only middle-class experience was considered to be worthy of representation in novels and films, positive representations of working-class experience in the arts were often considered to be 'left-wing propaganda.'"[89] Simply to put the worker on film at all implied a kind of daring: the communist Montagu Slater, also in the orbit of the Film Unit and, as seen earlier, a contributor to *Coal Face*, argued that "to describe things as they are is a revolutionary act in itself."[90]

Carl Jung wrote that a physician who wanted to grow should put away their books and "wander with human heart throughout the world." There "in the horrors of prisons, lunatic asylums and hospitals, in drab suburban pubs, in brothels and gambling-hells, in the salons of the elegant, the Stock Exchanges, Socialist meetings, churches, revivalist gatherings and ecstatic sects, through love and hate, through the experience of passion in every form in his own body," the physician would discover "richer stores of knowledge than text-books a foot thick could give."[91] Perhaps some similar motivations, albeit realized in much more decorous contexts than most of Jung's examples, underlie Auden's participation in films like *Coal Face* and *Night Mail*. They took Auden out of his "English house" and beyond the "creepered wall" sheltering the privileged, child-filled world of the Downs.

After *Coal Face*, Auden, Britten, and Coldstream were involved in another "Empo" production: *Night Mail*. This shows the operations of the nightly postal train taking mail from London to Scotland. Auden started his contribution not long after he finished the *Coal Face* madrigal. He began drafting words for the film in July 1935 while he was still living in Colwall: "I'm writing ... choruses for a film about the Night Mail to Scotland," he told a friend in a letter, and, perhaps reflecting Grierson's chauvinistic wishes, he added: "Have to get in all the Scotch place names I can find."[92] (In the event, the poem he wrote is not particularly overloaded with such place-names.)

It is likely that the film's directors, Harry Watt and Auden's acquaintance Basil Wright, were responsible for the opening sections of the film, which strongly evoke the film culture of Berlin in the late 1920s.[93] In particular, the shots of shining rails making semiliquid, quasi-abstract patterns on the screen as they run in parallel, cross each other, merge, and glide apart while the mail train moves out of the station are borrowed from, indeed are an explicit homage to, the famous images in Walter Ruttmann's classic nonnarrative film *Berlin: Die Sinfonie der Großstadt (Berlin: The Great City's Symphony*, 1927).[94]

The British film is a conceptual "negative" of the German film, reversing its trajectory. In Ruttmann's *Berlin*, the shots of rails and wheels are parts of the evocation of a train arriving at daybreak in the German capital from the countryside. As Grierson put it: "In smooth and finely tempo'd visuals, a train swung through suburban mornings into Berlin. Wheels, rails, details of engines, telegraph wires, landscapes and other simple images flowed along in procession."[95] In *Night Mail*, the train is leaving the British capital as night falls and heads into the countryside and the darkness. But the homage to *Berlin: Die Sinfonie der Großstadt* shows that German models of filmmaking, like Soviet ones, were reference points within British visual culture in the mid-1930s, and especially in Auden's place of work.

Like *Coal Face, Night Mail* is a film set in a world of semi-darkness, in this case at night inside and outside a mail train, rather than in the gloomy chasms of a mine. After the initial evocation of Ruttmann's style, the film becomes a domesticated and deheroicized Griersonian version of Turin's railway drama *Turksib*, in which a chirpy, British, get-on-with-the-job, official pragmatism replaces wild Soviet ideology and fevered engineering heroics.

Auden's poem for *Night Mail* is more extensive and ambitious, and much more varied, than his poem for *Coal Face*. But, again, in one sense it is at odds with the main "educational" parts of the film. That may be because Auden's poetic coda was not an integral part of its conception but was something added later. The codirector Basil Wright recounted watching an initial rough-cut version of the film with his colleagues Alberto Cavalcanti and Grierson. Wright remembered that after they had watched it: "somebody, probably Grierson, said, 'There's something missing.'"[96] As a result, Auden's poem was added. It starts like this:

> This is the night mail crossing the border,
> Bringing the cheque and the postal order,
> Letters for the rich, letters for the poor,
> The shop at the corner and the girl next door,
> Pulling up Beattock, a steady climb—
> The gradient's against her but she's on time.

Past cotton grass and moorland boulder,
Shovelling white steam over her shoulder,
Snorting noisily as she passes
Silent miles of wind-bent grasses;
Birds turn their heads as she approaches,
Stare from the bushes at her blank-faced coaches;
Sheepdogs cannot turn her course
They slumber on with paws across,
In the farm she passes no one wakes
But a jug in a bedroom gently shakes.[97]

Arthur Elton, a fellow member of the GPO Film Unit, wrote at the time that the commentary used in *Night Mail* was not there "as pedantic description, but as a poetic means of giving perspective and background reference."[98] Dramatic in its contrasts between a speeding train and a sleeping world through which the train passes, the poem alternates between moods of tension and momentum and moods of relief and stillness. It is constructed from two different formal patterns: passages of predominantly rhyming couplets, associated with the hurtling locomotive filled with letters, and sections of unrhymed free verse, associated with the letters' destinations and the reactions of their recipients:

Dawn freshens, the climb is done.
Down towards Glasgow she descends
Towards the steam tugs, yelping down the glade of cranes
Towards the fields of apparatus, the furnaces
Set on the dark plain like gigantic chessmen.
All Scotland waits for her;
In the dark glens, beside the pale-green sea lochs
Men long for news. (422)

Auden's poem is more focused on the meaning of the letters being distributed than it is on the mechanisms of distribution—mobile sorting cars, high-speed, seamless loading and unloading of the mail sacks, the expertise of the sorters, and so on—that the rest of the film is largely concerned with and fascinated by (and eager to persuade its audience they should find fascinating too).

As in *Coal Face*, Auden's method is again to imagine disparate entities and then reconcile them verbally. The opening lines provide an obvious instance: "Bringing the cheque and the post order" contrasts the form of money sent from a private bank account with the form of money sent by someone too young or too poor for a bank account. "Letters for the rich, letters for the poor," the next line, simply replays this contrast in more obvious terms. "The shop at the corner and the girl next door" offers another contrast: the public and commercial versus the private and individual (422). The intent is not simply to set up an opposition but to suggest opposing entities that are being joined together into a larger whole, in this case simply by that mystificatory but all-powerful conjunction "and."

Further contrasts follow in the next few lines: grass and stone, steam and steel, (light) birds and (heavy) coaches. The massive thundering onrush of the engine's "course," which cannot be turned aside, is juxtaposed (and connected) with the gentle shaking of a jug in a farmhouse bedroom (422). Contrasts abound as well in later stages: "Letters of thanks, letters from banks, | Letters of joy from the girl and boy, | . . . News circumstantial, news financial. . . . | Clever, stupid, short and long, | The typed and the printed and the spelt all wrong" (422–423). Even possible dreams in this rhetorical world became balanced, antithetical, and conjunct: they are either of "terrifying monsters | Or a friendly tea beside the band" (423).

On the face of it, though, in spite of this repeating mode of opposites reconciled, Auden allows for much more variety in his subject matter here than he had in "Madrigal." The binary contrast of male and female, black and white, becomes in "Night Mail" something more like a world of many different emotions, colors, and styles:

> Written on paper of every hue
> The pink, the violet, the white and the blue
> The chatty, the catty, the boring, adoring,
> The cold and official and the heart's outpouring. (423)

But the centripetal, unifying drive, the desire to bring disparate parts together into a holistic group, is in fact even stronger in "Night Mail" than in "Madrigal," and this reflects not just the public-spirited ethos of Grierson and the Film Unit but Auden's own obsessive fascination with what in a 1931 poem he had called the "official re-marriage of the whole and part."[99] The Postal Service makes it possible to reach every corner of the British Isles with writing. And the letters knit together the country:

the sleeping citizens will "wake soon and long for letters" (423). The film suggests that the ideal society would be one in which everyone was tied into the system of national communication, with no one left out (or allowed to stand aside). As the end of the poem puts it, in some of Auden's simplest and yet most memorable lines: "none will hear the postman's knock | Without a quickening of the heart | For who can bear to feel himself forgotten?" (423).

As he was working on his contribution to *Night Mail*, Auden measured out the duration of line lengths with a stopwatch since the footage had already been shot to which his words had to fit. "He kept bringing it, and—the cheek of us, in a way we turned down so much. He'd say, 'Alright. That's quite all right. Just roll it up and throw it away.' The most magnificent verse was thrown away, and in that situation, with all that noise going on and being harassed and used, he turned out the very, very famous lines of *Night Mail*."[100] Most of these lines would eventually be recorded for the soundtrack by the young filmmaker Stuart Legg, but the last lines, expressing the GPO Film Unit's ethos of the civic need to bind individuals into a community, were recorded by "the Chief" himself, John Grierson. That suggestion that writing will be the means of tying the nation together (with the Post Office, which was paying for the film, seen as indispensable in achieving that goal) recalls the sentiments in Auden's crucial "National Socialism" letter to Spender from the summer of 1933. In Auden's talk of "the national psychological factor" and "national emblems," it is easy to miss that Auden and Spender share an assumption that writing, and specifically their poetry, has a role to play in the drive "to achieve the kind of society I think we both wish for."[101] "Night Mail" is underwritten by the same modestly grandiose viewpoint.

Both "Madrigal" and "Night Mail" were important auguries of the new, or new and old, directions that Auden's poetry would take in the next few years. Auden had moved from teaching into film, from the world of a provincial school into the London-based world of documentary cinema: it is emblematic that the first line of the second poem he wrote for the Film Unit describes a train, like a stand-in for Auden's poetry, "crossing the border" ("Night Mail," 423). "Madrigal" is a cryptic, hermetic work, perhaps partly because of its mildly subversive playing with gender roles. As such, the poem is economical, suggestive, laconic, all characteristics it shares with many poems in Auden's early poetic style. Conversely, "Night Mail" points toward poems that, as a result of the experience of writing for a film audience, would open Auden's poetry up, making it simpler and more direct.

The fascination of "Night Mail" with communication by letter rather than face to face, complementing "August for the people," written just a few weeks later and originally framed as a letter poem (titled "To a Writer on His Birthday"), shows how important the idea of a poem as an epistolary communication was becoming for Auden. In 1937, he explained to an unidentified correspondent: "Try to think of each poem as a letter written to a friend, not always the same friend. But this letter is going to be opened by the postal authorities, and if they do not understand anything, or find it difficult to wade through, then the poem fails."[102] Although the poem-letter has to be clear, this model is a lonelier, more mediated form of artistic communication than the ideal of in-person speech. The paradoxical undertow of "Night Mail," amid the explosion of writing—"The chatty, the catty, the boring, adoring, | The cold and official and the heart's outpouring"—is a feeling of latent isolation in which "men long for news" and no one can "bear to feel himself forgotten" (423). That isolation can only be assuaged or held at bay by the relentless delivery of letters or the panting enunciation of lines of poetry—as if Auden saw the production of language as having a purpose a little like Scheherazade's in *One Thousand and One Nights*, where death is postponed as long as one keeps spinning stories or poems.

Although Auden wrote so extensively about England in the first half of the 1930s, the wider frame of Britain's empire has a curiously occluded presence in his early work. In the period between the First and Second World Wars, the British Empire—now at its largest extent ever—had at least notional control over roughly one quarter of the earth's land mass, included within its boundaries some 460 million "subject peoples," and, along with the monarchy, constituted a crucial element in many British citizens' sense of national identity.[103] Auden's poems from the first half of the 1930s rarely acknowledge the vast expanse of these imperial possessions directly, although the empire, like the war, is often a shadow on the landscape. But his vision of English identity during these years is frequently insular, most commonly focused on "the island." It

is as if Auden's poetic imagination at the time were somehow disconnected from the truth that the England of his poems was built through
and dependent on the exploitation of its colonial holdings. Occasionally, though, glimpses of the wider world do break through. In "Out on
the lawn," couching his language in careful negatives, Auden writes
about how "we": "gentle, *do not care* to know, | . . . What violence is
done; | *Nor*" do we ask: "what doubtful act allows | Our freedom in this
English house, | Our picnics in the sun."[104] The word "picnics" artfully
suggests the consumption of sugar, fruits, and spices that probably did
not originate in the fields around Colwall. In the mid-1930s, Auden's
writings, including his poems, do—fitfully—begin to register some
glimpses of the imperial world that he would explore more fully in the
second half of the decade.

For example, later on, in *Journey to a War*, the travel book that
Auden and Isherwood wrote about their experiences reporting on the
Sino-Japanese War in 1938, they repeatedly notice that however far
away from Britain they travel, they always seem to find its presence in
front of them. In Auden's sonnet, "Hongkong," he observes the imperial colony and sees how: "Ten thousand miles from home and What's-
her-name, | The bugle on the Late Victorian hill | Puts out the soldier's
light," while "off-stage, a war || Thuds like the slamming of a distant
door."[105] On the same journey, they attend a lunch in the luxurious
Shanghai Club in the city's International Settlement, with an Englishman of their own age, John Keswick (one of the hereditary heads of the
vast British trading firm Jardine, Matheson), and four Japanese interlocutors. There is an awkward moment as the Japanese guests explain
that Japan invaded China to "save her from herself, to protect her from
the Soviets." Auden and Isherwood draw a breath, turn aside, and
watch as "through the window which overlooked the [Huangpu] river,
the gun turrets of H.M.S. *Birmingham* slid quietly into view, moving
upstream."[106] The appearance of the British warship (coincidentally
named after Auden's hometown) sailing up a Chinese river reveals the
profound British stake in the struggle between imperial powers taking
place on the other side of the world.

Auden's slightly earlier work in cinema in the mid-1930s provides a
striking prefiguration of this eventual, more concerted engagement
with wider political and cultural realities. Interwar cinema in both
Britain and the United States was heavily involved in efforts to legiti-

mize and normalize imperial dominance, through a welter of "feature films, newsreels, and documentaries that depicted Britain's role, and control, in the empire."[107] Yet toward the end of 1935, Auden wrote a script for a short film, to be called "Negroes," that attempted to examine colonial violence in a more critical way. Apparently conceived by Auden, Britten, and Basil Wright together in the early autumn of 1935, "Negroes" was planned as an exploration of the slave trade. Coldstream was also heavily involved with their work, as Britten's diary entries show.[108] "Negroes" was never released in the form that Auden and his collaborators envisaged, but the script constitutes a striking and little-explored moment in his writing.[109]

Although it is hard to know how much specifically about Auden can legitimately be read into a collective project, the film does fit a pattern developing in his work in which he began to write about parts of the world beyond his habitual settings in England and Scotland. Coldstream recalled that they were intending to use West African wooden figures from the British Museum in part of the film, and Britten's diaries record working with Auden in early September 1935 "in bookshops, gramophone shops (Levy—Whitechapel) & elsewhere," looking for primary material.[110] The script they produced has no real plot but is more like a selective historical survey, interspersing the recitation of facts with brief lyric interludes.

In Night Mail and Coal Face, working-class life had been treated mainly as the pretext for voice-over commentary by middle-class filmmakers. One difference between "Negroes" and these earlier GPO Film Unit productions in which Auden had taken part is that here, for the first time, speeches were to be given to the "subjects" of the film. The primary voice in the new script is still a middle-class, presumably white, representative, as in earlier GPO Film Unit productions. This is the "Tenor Solo," whose task is to introduce information impartially and to explain history as it was clearly understood by the professionals making the film. But there is also a countervoice, the "Negro Commentator," who speaks directly to the audience, briefly describing the appalling experiences of Africans as the slave traders arrived on the continent: "Out of every hundred Negroes shipped from Africa, | Only fifty lived to be effective labourers" (425). However, much remains uncertain about the vision for the film: there do not appear to be surviving notes about who was actually to play the role of the "Negro Commentator" in the production, or even whether any Black performers were to be involved at all.

The "Tenor Solo" intones various facts and statistics and is then joined by a "Soprano Solo" (425–426), who, among other things, delivers more historical details and sings a verse from Blake's poem "The Little Black Boy." Later, a "Female Voice" sounds out. "To-day nearly all manual work in the West Indies is done by Negroes," she explains, noting that "in the coffee industry women are largely employed" (426, 427). The content of the sections spoken or sung by women does not seem to differ significantly from the content in the speeches by men. But these female voices constitute another departure from the GPO Film Unit's habitual emphasis on the all-male world of work, as does a section featuring calypso music.

The motif of mercantile distribution and interconnection visible in *Night Mail* is retained in "Negroes," although now what is being distributed, unforgivably, is a human commodity. Another link between earlier films and the script that Auden produced for this planned film appears in the theme of Blackness that leads from the miners of *Coal Face* to the dark nightworld of *Night Mail* to now the "black slaves" of "Negroes" (424). The script also highlights, retrospectively, the narrow national circumscription of *Night Mail*. There, Auden had been asked to "get in all the Scotch place names I can find."[111] Here, the topography is much farther flung. His script includes references to three continents—Africa, Europe, and North America—and is filled with African place-names likely to have been far less familiar to an insular British audience than the names of a few towns in Scotland. These place-names include a number of African rivers that Auden, given his fascination with rivers, must have relished: "the Senegal, the Nune and the Sassandra, | The Komoe and the white Bandama | . . . the Tano and the Volta," "the long Niger," "Sanaga and Ogowe," "Kom," "Mwibu and Chiloango," and "Congo" (425).[112]

In a commentary for which Auden was at least partially responsible, the script asserts at the start that the "Middle Ages" is a point when "there was no contact between Europe and Africa" (424). That sealed-off condition changed when the Portuguese began "to voyage in every direction in search of adventure, of ivory and gold" (424). The film script subsequently traces a trajectory from closure to openness, although it does not associate this trajectory with progress, since the opening of civilizations to each other inaugurates the slave trade. Subsequently, "Negroes" attempts to erode ideas of national or racial differences in an assertion of universal concerns, as the Commentator declares that "in sleeping car, in hotel, in dock, in factory, in the fields or on the stage, in the hospital or the law court, in each of us, stronger than our will or the accidents of our lives, something of Africa lives on"—a statement that would not have been likely to be popular in Britain at the time (428).

The goal of this uncompleted film seems to have been a critique of empire and slavery, although it deals heavily in stereotypes about Europeans and Africans that undermine the strength of the message. The original concept, along with the title, reflect the racism and exoticization that were almost ubiquitous in European portrayals of African peoples and history during this period. Filmgoers in Britain rarely encountered accounts of African experience framed in sympathetic terms, and—had the film been made as Auden and Britten designed it—there would probably have been very few people of color in the audience to watch their effort. Even though Britain's overseas possessions were huge, in the 1930s the country itself was extraordinarily racially homogenous: the number of people from Africa, India, and the Middle East living in Britain totaled only between 20,000 and 30,000 out of a population of about 45 million.[113]

"Negroes" was a flawed and contradictory project in very many ways. However, within the constraints of the ideological universe that Auden and his collaborators inhabited, it does read as an effort to bring into view and explore the evils of the trade in enslaved people and the long history of colonial violence, highlighting realms of experience that most of the GPO Film Unit's audience probably preferred to ignore. The possibility that it would not have been well received by this paying audience may have been part of the reason why the project was abandoned; the film's concept was too ambitious and discomforting to fit within the narrow imaginative and political limits acceptable in an English cinema in 1935. Nonetheless, more profoundly, the text itself hints that the project might have started to seem too challenging to its makers.

Auden had planned to end the film with a sonorous chorus that announces:

> Acts of injustice done
> Between the setting and the rising sun
> In history lie like bones, each one.

Memory sees them down there,
Paces alive beside his fear,
That's slow to die and still here.

The future hard to mark
Of a world turning in the dark
Where ghosts are walking and dogs bark.

But between the day and night
The choice is free to all; and light
Falls equally on black and white. (428)[114]

The cliché light-white final rhyme clinches the chorus's would-be dispassionate assertion that "light | Falls equally on black and white." As it does, the ending marks an aesthetic withdrawal from the ethical recognition of the coercion and violence that shape some people's lives more than others'. As if pulling a curtain across a window, these last lines shut out the theme of racial injustice that the brief film was to have highlighted. But, in the midst of ideological ambiguities like these, in the coming years and with increasing energy Auden would continue to circle, approach, withdraw from, and reengage with the imperial expanse beyond the island.

While Britten, Coldstream, and Auden worked on "Negroes," Auden was sensing his own life touched, very tangentially, and ultimately inconsequentially, by a contemporary iteration of the colonial practices that drove the project of enslaving and selling human beings. This development was the Italian invasion of Abyssinia. Another follow-up to *Night Mail,* titled "Air Mail to Australia," was in the planning stage, with the Film Unit choosing Auden as a codirector. The project was to have used the transportation of letters between continents by plane as a pretext for exploring the cultures over which the letter-carrying aircraft flew.[115] Auden had planned to travel by air with a film crew from Europe to Australia, and he seems to have taken advantage of a Swiss layover on the initial stage of his trip to make a weekend visit to his new in-laws, Thomas and Katia Mann.

Since 1933, the Manns had been living in exile in Küsnacht, at that time something of an artistic colony, on the edge of Lake Zurich. Auden

arrived in mid-October" 1935, took his meals with the Manns, presumably speaking in German, a language he was by now quite competent in after his stays in Berlin. It is hard to imagine what the visit must
have been like—the Manns' family life was extraordinarily complex,
even as they lived under the shadow of mortal threats from the German
government. Did the arrival of a queer English son-in-law married to a
lesbian daughter in the home of a closeted patriarch of Nobel Prize–
winning fame become the topic of any conversations? Or was the obvious unusualness of the occasion passed over in silence or treated like
a game? The only clue to an answer lies in the fact that after Auden had
left, as a thank-you gift he sent Thomas Mann a copy of a book about
the uniting (or "marriage") of contraries: Blake's *The Marriage of Heaven
and Hell,* in which Mann could have read of Blake's idea that there are
no moral absolutes, that nothing is divinely forbidden, and that "All
deities reside in the human breast."[116]

On his departure from Küsnacht, instead of proceeding on to Australia as he had planned, Auden was forced to cancel the rest of his
journey because the Italian invasion of Abyssinia had begun. This devastating colonial war led to disruptions of civilian passenger air routes
across the Middle East and North Africa. Auden returned to London in
mid-October 1935. The filmmakers, including Auden, may have started
to understand by now the contradictory positions they were forced into
by trying to make a government-funded film about the slave trade that
would be unchallenging enough to reach a wide audience. And it may
also be that the decision shortly afterward to discontinue the work on
"Negroes" was accelerated by this latest violent European foray into Africa. The start of the invasion, which had been long in the making, took
place at the beginning of October 1935. Britten wrote in his diary: "Abyssinia is to-day attacked by Italy. Great indignation & excitement in
London. . . . Go up to Soho Square in morning & work with Auden &
Coldstream on Negroes."[117] Not long after, the project was no more.

Auden's artistic language had often been visual and image based, even
before it began to move within the gravitational field of film, a predominantly visual medium. But sometimes his words went beyond
what film could absorb. Basil Wright remembered that, in the editing of
Night Mail, the Film Unit "cut some of the stanzas [that Auden wrote]

from it, planning it with his agreement. He tended sometimes to make verbal images which were too violent for the pictorial content. He described the Cheviots [hills in Northumberland] as 'uplands heaped like slaughtered horses'; no picture we put on the screen could be as strong as that."[118]

When Auden moved to London in the autumn of 1935, "pro tem," and began work with the GPO Film Unit, he left behind the secluded, genteel, and rural world of the Downs School, Lawrence Villa, the unofficial beauty contests, the "bathing hours and the bare arms," and the sitting "Equal with colleagues in a ring | . . . on each calm evening."[119] He now had to live in Britain's capital city, a place he disliked, and he found himself in a chaotic, free-form work world where, according to Watt, he was put in a narrow corridor at the back of the Unit's premises in Soho Square among Post Office messenger boys, "fifteen year-old Cockney kids, wild as hell, [as] they made their tea and whistled and played cards up at one end. The only place we could find for Auden was at the other end of this passage—say, twenty yards from them. There, on that old Post Office table, he wrote the most beautiful verse."[120]

At first, in the autumn of 1935, Auden lodged in Highgate, in North London, with Basil Wright, the person who had secured him a job with the Unit in the spring of that year.[121] Wright had plenty of money and lived in Highpoint I, an ultra-fashionable block of flats designed in the modernist International Style by Tecton's Berthold Lubetkin. The building was prominently set on Highgate Hill and had been finished earlier in 1935.[122] (Lubetkin had also designed and constructed the modernist Penguin Pool in Regent's Park Zoo the year before.)

With its pared-down, purist aesthetic, Highpoint I itself was hardly likely to be to Auden's taste. According to Humphrey Carpenter, there were as well tensions over Auden's cavalier treatment of Wright's expensive piano, which Auden liked to play before breakfast. If so, they were perhaps tensions that had been waiting to emerge from the moment Auden arrived in the building. Wright and Auden also argued when a film for which Auden was the production manager, *Calendar of the Year*, ran over budget and Auden, "in reply, burst into a tirade against the whole Unit and its working methods."[123] He decided to move out, and at the end of 1935 or the start of 1936, he went to live as a lodger with William and Nancy Coldstream in Belsize Park.[124] By the time Auden left Wright's precious little flat in the winter of 1935–1936 and settled in

with the Coldstreams, from a creative point of view his brief time with
the Film Unit was effectively over. Most of the projects that he worked
on in the latter part of 1935 (*Calendar of the Year,* "Air Mail to Australia," and "Negroes") fizzled, died, or, if completed, did not reach the
aesthetic level of *Coal Face* and *Night Mail.* Auden later described the
GPO Film Unit as an "odd organisation" and commented, "Personally I
loathed my job, but enjoyed the company enormously."[125] In "Letter to
William Coldstream, Esq.," written in mid-1936, Auden recalls his stint
with Coldstream in the Film Unit's headquarters in

> Soho Square and that winter in horrible London
> When we sat in the back passage pretending to work
> While the camera boys told dirty stories
> And George capped them all with his one of the major in India
> Who went to a ball with dysentery
>   told it in action
> Till we sneaked out for coffee and discussed our colleagues
> And were suspected, quite rightly, of being disloyal.
> Especially you, whose tongue is the most malicious I know.[126]

At a more fundamental level, though, Auden had begun to doubt
the solidity of the whole project of documentary film, as he makes clear
in his review of the filmmaker and cinema historian Paul Rotha's book
Documentary Film. Auden published the piece in the *Listener* in mid-
February 1936, at about the time when he had taken a judiciously timed
two-month leave from the Film Unit.[127] The review was unsigned, but
Auden's authorship was an open secret in the London film world.

For Auden in his review of Rotha's book, the fact that the documentary movement concentrated on people in society and at work, to
the exclusion of explorations of their inner lives, which he claimed the
movement considered "unimportant," had produced films "which had
many excellent qualities, but to the ordinary film-goer were finally and
fatally dull."[128] His analysis of the practical problems involved in making
documentary films is acute—his main assertions are that that because
filmmaking is so expensive, there is never enough time for directors to
assimilate and understand the material properly before they are obliged
to churn out their product; that the middle-class vantage point of "most
British documentary film directors" means that they can only deal "superficially" with working-class characters; and finally that the sponsors

of documentary films, "large-scale industries and government departments," will never countenance paying for "an exact" and truthful "picture of the human life within their enormous buildings."[129] All these criticisms were relevant to the constraints the GPO Film Unit faced when making some of the films that Auden himself had worked on, including *Coal Face, Night Mail*, and "Negroes."

However, more interesting than the Rotha review in relation to Auden's poetry is the report of the lecture on "Poetry and Film" that Auden gave to the North London Film Society at a YMCA in Tottenham Court Road in February 1936, at around the same time as he was writing his *Listener* account of Rotha's book. There are clear points of connection between the lecture and the review.[130] But, revealingly, the lecture is less polemical about documentary filmmaking than the review is, and it is more concerned with the relationship of visual culture—both film and painting—to poetry. It represents an early instance of what would become the central focus of Auden's involvement with visual and musical cultures: the effort to define the nature of poetry through its similarities to and differences from other arts. For Auden, film (and by extension photography) was an overwhelmingly truthful recorder of particularity. He declared in his lecture that "film's essential factor is its power to concentrate on detail. . . . The film gives the concrete visual fact." Capable, beyond any other medium, of assimilating the real, it was anchored (and trapped) in "the immediate present." Film was able to deal in depth with "the material that contemporary life offers."[131]

For many people in the mid-1930s, the documentary film had become the paradigm of what a new art, in any medium, should strive for: direct records of daily life, with as little intrusion, commentary, or artistic embellishment as possible. But Auden's emphasis on film's indiscriminate particularizing power also led him to point in his lecture to a rift between verbal and visual languages. The "relation of visual images to word images," he argued, is not a close one, for the "visual image is a definite one, whereas verbal images are not sharp; they have auras of meaning. A visual image cannot be made to mean a number of things, nor can a word image be confined to one thing."[132] Language, and especially poetic language, is ambiguous, layered, and suggestive, in a way that (for Auden) film never could be.

In the context of Auden's thinking about film's specificity as a medium, it is clear how much weight he invested in "August for the people" in the notion that Isherwood's camera-like art "reveals" things, makes them "clear," and supplies "nearer insight"—the film and the photograph are, then, both an aspiration and a warning.[133] They are an aspiration because Auden was determined that the poet should assimilate as much of the "real" and the "immediate" as possible. Films were a warning because it is a fantasy to believe that poetry could ever become as sharp and specific as the camera or prose, such as Isherwood's, with aspirations modeled on the camera's eye.[134] Auden's absence from The Hague was not just a practical matter—it also had symbolic substance. While Auden, as a friend, in the poem is praising Isherwood's art on the birthday of his closest associate, as a poet he is also gently distancing himself from Isherwood's prose of clear definition. If Auden lauds Isherwood's sharp, needle-like power to "warn us from the colours and the consolations" ("August for the people," 216), the poem is also a private caution to Auden himself about staying true to his own artistic medium, because "a word image [cannot] be confined to one thing."

However, if Auden delivered warnings to others about the need not to confuse the nature of film with the nature of poetry, he did not always take his own advice. Around the time in November 1935 that work on the international and historical perspectives of "Negroes" was abandoned, Auden retrenched poetically with a sublime lyric that zoomed in on the English coastline and recommitted to the mythic currency of islands. This is the poem beginning, "Look, stranger, at this island now" (from now on, "Look, stranger"). Auden gave it a landscape-like title, calling it "Seaside," when he published it in periodical form at the end of 1935.[135] The wider poetic lenses used in "August for the people" and "Negroes" are discarded almost completely, and, as they are, this seems to lead naturally to the reemergence of another dazzling piece of lyrical nationalism in "Seaside."

Although the poem celebrates a brilliant, sunlit moment on the English coastline in the middle of "summer," it was written in London in the cold depths of the autumn of 1935. It was thus anything but a direct response to experience. Indeed, one might conjecture that Auden sat in the dark and watched film footage of summers at the seaside in order to produce his poem about the sunlit coastal scene. This reflects the fact that the poem started life as a contribution to another of the

mildly paternalistic films that he worked on at the GPO Film Unit—
Beside the Seaside, released in December 1935.[136] One of Auden's
greatest island poems, and at the same time one of his final efforts in
this subgenre, it celebrates in spellbinding language the peaceful, haven-
like quality of England, the "jewel set in a silver sea"—and yet it was
probably a response to some film clips from a commercial job, albeit a
gem of a job, to be projected on the silver screen.

Benedict Anderson, the greatest modern theorist of nationalism,
remarked that a primary function of the idea of the nation is to coun-
teract the destabilizing, atomizing, differentiating forces of modernity
by finding ways to unify large groups of people. It does this in part by
imbuing them with a set of shared characteristics, ceremonies, and beliefs. This is part of what Auden describes in his 1933 letter to Spender
as "the national psychological factor."[137] National myths, Anderson explained, bind people who do not know one another into a vast collective whole, stranger identifying with neighbor and with stranger, as
nationality brings together an anonymous community of individuals in
"deep, horizontal comradeship"—an image that in this context feels
strangely evocative of row after tightly packed row of cinemagoers sitting together in the darkness.[138] On a more modest scale, Auden's seaside poem creates exactly such a moment of identity-giving solidarity
among strangers as those described by Anderson.

In the second part of "A Happy New Year" in 1932, Auden begs that
the Lords of Limit

> Permit our town here to continue *small,*
> What city's vast emotional cartel
> Could our few acres satisfy
> Or rival in intensity
> The *field* of five or six, the English cell?[139]

There, in solution (spotlit by my emphasis), is the phrase "small field" that
in the following year, 1933, Auden uses to define, in the letter to Spender,
the enclave-like arena within which he believes he makes his poetry: "my
temperament and necessity, force me to work in a small field."[140] The pas-
toralizing "few acres," in line 3 of the stanza from "A Happy New Year"
cited here, act like a stepping-stone to get the reader down and across the
verse from "small" in line 1 to "field" in line 5. Here is the connection of a
privileged, highly charged space to "the English cell," a metonymic exten-

sion of intense local unity and shared beliefs to the point where it comes to stand in for the ideal of an integrated national whole.

Auden comes back to the phrase "small field," which is secreted inside "A Happy New Year" and which he uses in the letter to Spender, in November 1935, in a line from "Look, stranger": "Here at the small field's ending pause." This famous lyric is infused with what John Fuller identifies as a "rediscovered sense of Englishness."[141] Significantly, the poem with this intense sense of "Englishness" shares an identical phrase with Auden's "national emblems" letter of 1933. And putting that letter about Auden's tendency to "National Socialism" and his use of "national emblems" next to "Look, stranger" makes visible the social and political stakes that are in play in the 1935 poem, stakes that are very high.

The new poem has three parts like a poetical England, Scotland, and Wales, neatly divided into three stanzas as so many of Auden's best lyrics are:

> Look, stranger, at this island now
> The leaping light for your delight discovers,
> Stand stable here
> And silent be,
> That through the channels of the ear
> May wander like a river
> The swaying sound of the sea.
>
> Here at the small field's ending pause
> Where the chalk wall falls to the foam, and its tall ledges
> Oppose the pluck
> And knock of the tide,
> And the shingle scrambles after the suck-
> ing surf, and the gull lodges
> A moment on its sheer side.
>
> Far off like floating seeds the ships
> Diverge on urgent voluntary errands;
> And the full view
> Indeed may enter
> And move in memory as now these clouds do,
> That pass the harbour mirror
> And all the summer through the water saunter. (187–188)[142]

The sonorous surge of heightened language does not fully begin until stanza 2, but in stanza 1, the "stranger" is immediately instructed what to do by the speaker. And implicitly, the stranger obeys. "Stand stable here | And silent be," the poem enjoins, gently but firmly. Stanza 2 of the poem says to the stranger, "Here at the *small field*'s ending pause" (188; emphasis added). It is almost as if this person, the reader's avatar inside the poem, with their eyes closed, is being moved gently about by the shoulders and every so often told to open their eyes and admire the natural beauty. These injunctions are the aesthetically pleasing residues of the paternalistic, explanatory middle-class voice that provided commentary and instruction in GPO Film Unit productions while images flashed before the audience's gaze.

In ways that are reminiscent of the injunctive orchestration of the collier and Kate in "Madrigal," in "Look, stranger," Auden's poetic voice, like the film commentator's, acts to bind the audience into a specific way of viewing and knowing: "Look," "stand," "[be] silent," "pause." And the instructions about what to "see" vary through the poem continuously: a long shot of "this island," a medium shot of a particular spot "here," a panorama of the sea, the image of a field dropping away "to the foam," the tide beating against the rocks, a close-up of the shingle being dragged rolling back into the water, then cut to a gull perched on the side of the cliff, then a pullback to a long shot of the horizon with ships far off enough to look like floating seeds, a pan into the idyllic, patriotic emptiness and purity of the sky and the clouds, and finally the reflection of the clouds on the surface of the calm "harbour mirror," registering the scene above as faithfully and minutely as images thrown by the sun-like projector onto the flat surface of a cinema screen (188).

Auden's kino-eye is always in motion, much as, according to the contemporary critic Erwin Panofsky, the camera in a film forces the "aesthetic subject" in the audience always to identify with the "lens of the camera which permanently shifts in distance and direction." If spectators want to watch a film, they have no choice about where to look. The movie, Panofsky says, dynamizes space and, "as space becomes charged with time, time becomes, naturally, bound to space."[143] Through a similar dynamism, Auden becomes the "director" of the reader's attention in this highly charged, symbolically rich poem. He provides instances of the way that space is charged with time, as in the line about the reflections that "all the summer [time] through the water [space] saunter," and of the way in which time is bound to space, as in the glimpse of the gull that "lodges [space] | A moment [time]" on the cliff side. The fusing of space and time in this fashion makes the poem "cinematic," but it also implicates Auden's lyricism—moving us here, as readers, and then moving us there—in a didactic program that is not fully separate from the GPO Film Unit's, a charge to assist with the task of weaving the country's citizens into a collective and compliant whole.

Nowhere does a camera appear in "Look, stranger," any more than we glimpse a lens as we watch a film. (By contrast, in later poems Auden sometimes draws attention to the presence of the seeing device: as in these lines from 1949: "The eyes of the crow and the eye of the camera open | Onto Homer's world, not ours."[144]) But at a deeper level, this brilliant poem is formed in a way that positions it close to the dynamics of 1930s public cinema, the modern means of mass persuasion and consensus building. In an influential pamphlet published in 1932, Sir Stephen Tallents, one of Britain's pioneers of public relations techniques, argued for the cinema's participation in promoting national identity, as if it were the analogue to a commercial brand: "no civilized country can to-day afford either to neglect the projection of its national personality, or to resign its projection to others."[145] Although composed at an entirely different artistic level from the one occupied by workaday documentary and public information films, Auden's poem was initially written for what was, in effect, a piece of advertising on behalf of the country's travel industry. "Look, stranger," or "Seaside," provides the ultimate use of the "camera-aesthetic" in poetry to produce a vision of a holistic, integrated, and contented island nation. It is a vision in which images of a shared landscape of high symbolic value—the relentlessly mythologized white cliffs of the southern coastline of England, where "the chalk wall falls to the foam," with Europe only a short distance away—can stand in for a common set of beliefs or desires (188). Attentiveness to geology and space becomes a kind of patriotism.

The poem is obviously mesmerizing, but this beautiful piece of language also has something faintly but chillingly coercive about it. Auden's poetry is now like an authoritative voice, dispensing shimmering lyric language and images yet at the same time "directing" his reader's views. There is a managerial tone underneath the beauty, something infantilizing in the way the poem refuses to allow the reader's mind to "stand stable" for more than a moment. In 1940, Auden wrote that "The Devil . . . is the father of Poetry, for poetry might be defined as the clear expression of mixed feelings."[146] Reading these great works by Auden, written only a few years earlier, one may wonder if poetry criticism, mirroring its subject, must also be an expression of mixed feelings.

"Here" in the "small field" on this island—the locating, fixing word "here" is used insistently in both stanzas 1 and 2—Auden's poetics of boundedness and national insularity reach their fullest expression, and here the most expansive sense of Auden's play with the "national emblems" of his imagination is visible. In 1934, Cyril Connolly had written that in the new iconography of the period (he was reviewing an exhibition of posters commissioned by Shell-Mex), "England is merry again." And so "farewell romantic caves and peaks, welcome the bracing glories of our clouds, the cirrhus and the cumulus, and the cold pastoral of the chalk."[147] In Auden's poem, written a year or so later, all the key elements are present: a scene of Englishness, nature, an enclave, "national emblems" (the chalk cliffs, the sea, the sky, the island itself), a moment of timeless, isolated plenitude and peace, and—in lines like "through the channels of the ear | May wander like a river | The swaying sound of the sea"—a sense of a close, perhaps even mildly erotic relation between individuals (187–188).

In this Edenic moment in a beautiful, and heavily ideological, rural English setting, someone who is a stranger—Auden's figure for the reader whose responses he manipulates with such expert verbal tenderness—consents to be guided through a sensuous experience by a commanding but warm, well-wishing, and yet remote voice who must, logically, be a stranger to this stranger.[148] The beautifully faceless nature of the poem's voice, its intimate anonymity—very different from the modernist tone of analytic impersonality—is accentuated by the lack of a title for the poem when Auden collected it in 1936.[149] The poem is stripped of the frame that a title would give it; instead, it is just warmly, starkly there, like an unexpected object in the world.

In "A Happy New Year," Auden writes about the way that "the silence buzzes in my ear," as if the silence that is in reality outside him is nonetheless felt as being inside him, silently buzzing.[150] Here, in "Look, stranger," the stranger is encouraged in language of extraordinary plasticity to let the sounds of the land-, air-, and seascapes gratifyingly invade the body's interior spaces in "the channels of the ear" as "the shingle scrambles after the suck- | ing surf" (187–188).[151] Time feels as if it is distending or slowing down as the "suck-" of the surf stops for a second and the "gull lodges" as if frozen in space. It is like a moment in the myth of Orpheus when the singer charms nature to still itself into silence and listen to him.

The lyric's theme of a complete, autonomous world, an important component in the ideological figure of the "island," is reinforced formally. The poem has a rich verbal density of interconnection and reflection within itself, coalescing around patterns and echoes. Readers are alerted to this web of subtly meaningful interrelatedness by the way that the poem's first stanza focuses on, and sensitizes us to, the experience of hearing the world (and, by extension, the poem) as it exists in the "channels of the ear." Rhymes and half rhymes are the most obvious and conventional formal instances of this phenomenon of sounding self-involution: each stanza of seven lines has three rhymes or half rhymes—only the stanzas' first lines stand alone, like verbal promontories, without rhyming partners. But the process of the language folding in on itself to suggest internal harmony also reappears in the heavy use of alliteration ("leaping light," "Stand stable," "swaying sound of the sea," and "the shingle scrambles after the suck- | ing surf" are just a few examples). There is also plentiful assonance ("Stand stable," "chalk wall," "Diverge on urgent," and "water saunter"), repetition and internal rhyme ("light . . . delight," "small . . . | wall falls . . . tall"), and internal half rhyme ("wander . . . river," "harbour mirror," "summer . . . water saunter"). In the final line, "summer" and "saunter" also wrap the poem in on itself, phonically recalling the "stranger" of line 1. This is a stunning fantasy, at the verbal level, of endless insular self-completeness, of ceaseless inner joining (187–188).

Finally, though, Auden's poem has an understated but important dimension that cuts against the idea of complete isolation. This is easiest to detect in the way that, like a glimpse or prophecy of a future life, "Far off like floating seeds the ships | Diverge on urgent voluntary errands" (188). Set in a particularly numinous and mythologized part of the English landscape, the chalk cliffs of the southern coast evoke political tensions. At a period of heightened international anxiety in Britain and Europe, the chalk cliffs (sounding a little like John of Gaunt, Auden calls them a "wall") project directly out into the English Channel and so toward

Europe. The ships are like "floating seeds"—marginal but noticeable, they are the tiny beginnings of the future entering into the poem's view. Perhaps we are meant to pick up the hint of a diaspora, a word that has its root in the action of dispersing or scattering "seeds." "Look, stranger" is an Orphic poem of incantatory, spellbinding power, a poem that responds ambitiously to the elevated cultural role assigned to poetry in 1930s England. As if it knows more than its creator does, or as if it was saying something that was not accessible to Auden's conscious mind, when he invokes "the small field" in this 1935 poem, he does so in a phrase that talked about the field's "ending" (188). This was Auden's last great "cinematic" poem and one of his finest "island" poems. After "Look, stranger," the "full view" does indeed begin to enter his writing, and Auden never uses the phrase "small field" in his poems again.

After completing "Look, stranger," Auden seems to have written little or no poetry at the end of 1935 or at the start of 1936. The demands and frustrations of slow-moving film projects may have got in his way. One of those film projects, for which he was serving as a not-very-effective production manager, is a short piece titled *Calendar of the Year* (the film whose budget he and Basil Wright had a row about). The character of Father Christmas appears in *Paid on Both Sides,* in a scene written in 1928 in Berlin. There, at the center of the charade, Father Christmas, the traditional personification of the holiday in English culture, acts as a kind of master of ceremonies, presiding over John Nower's fevered dream of death and revival, featuring the Man-Woman.[152] Probably in December 1935, not long after the writing of "Look, stranger," Auden put on a Father Christmas costume for a small scene needed for the Film Unit's shooting of *Calendar of the Year,* directed by Evelyn Spice. (For unknown reasons, the film was largely completed by 1936 but not released until 1937.) In the words of one critic, *Calendar of the Year* dutifully showcases "the many aspects of British life impacted by the GPO's network of telephone, telegraph and postal services" and suggests how "the nation . . . is held together" by these networks.[153]

In the Father Christmas scene, which occurs near the end of the film, Auden is standing in a department store in London with a group of children around him. His face is obscured by Father Christmas's fur-edged hood, but his voice is immediately recognizable. He stoops

FIG. 9 *Auden's appearances disguised in dramatic costumes, whether as Caliban or here as Father Christmas, are always revelatory. This is a still from the documentary film* Calendar of the Year, *released in 1937. For a very short scene, toward the film's end and apparently shot around December 1935, Auden dressed up for the role in a London department store. In an unconscious parody of his role as a poet, he pulls parcels out of a sack and hands them to children gathered round him.*

toward the children and asks the girl in front of him, "And what would you like for Christmas?" She replies, "Um, a doll's house." "And what would you like inside it?" Auden asks as he proffers a wrapped present. "I don't know," she says, taking the present. Two other children then take gifts from him.

The Father Christmas clip, with Auden in costume, is a tiny moment, both in *Calendar of the Year* and, more broadly, in Auden's life as a poet. But, in the immediate wake of writing "Look, stranger," this vignette reads as an ironical miniature epilogue to Auden's poem and to what that poem so brilliantly dramatizes about his increasingly prominent and stylized role in English culture. The intricate, dollhouse-like magic of construction contracted to a small scale in the poem, the sudden gift of one more beautiful poem, as if pulled out of a genius's sack and bestowed on a passive audience, the hooded enigma of a personal presence in disguise as Auden plays a traditional lyric role—all of these valences are there in the department store with Auden dressed up and with the awkward circle of young people gathered around this mythical figure. The little scene lights up some of the artistic dilemmas in writing poetry like "Look, stranger." *Calendar of the Year* is another Wildean moment of masked truthfulness, an epiphany in black and white revealing the mesmerizing but subtly overbearing poetic part that Auden, trading exquisitely in old stories and myths, was in danger of assuming. In a flash of harmless playacting, and no doubt completely unintentionally, the scene evokes the kind of seigneurial relationship Auden was hardening into with an English audience gathered expectantly around him.

Auden's dry spell as a poet lasted from the end of 1935 into the start of 1936. In February 1936, though, he provided Britten with "The Creatures," a psalmically cadenced prologue for "Our Hunting Fathers," the song cycle that the composer was writing:

> They are our past and our future: the poles between which our
>   desire unceasingly is discharged.
> A desire in which love and hatred so perfectly oppose them-
>   selves that we cannot voluntarily move; but await the
>   extraordinary compulsion of the deluge and the earthquake.
> Their affections and indifferences have been a guide to all
>   reformers and tyrants.
> Their appearances amid our dreams of machinery have brought
>   a vision of nude and fabulous epochs.
> O Pride so hostile to our Charity.
> But what their pride has retained, we may by charity more
>   generously recover.[154]

The Bible and Blake's *The Marriage of Heaven and Hell* (Auden's gift to Thomas and Katia Mann), with its oracular "proverbs," lie in the background to this mysterious prose poem. The intellectual side of the text can be understood as an analysis of the ways in which throughout history human beings have used animals symbolically for our own self-interested ends, either to recall an Edenic world or to foreshadow a future Utopia. Understood in this way, the poem shares some of the commanding, grandiloquent style of Auden's prose commentaries for the GPO Film Unit productions.

Understood more expressively, however, the second line, which easily exceeds in length all the other lines in the poem (and any other line anywhere in Auden's poetry, past, present or future), seems to call out to the reader for special attention. Just as "love," though only mentioned once, was the keyword in the midst of "Hearing of harvests rotting in the valleys," so here "love," though used only once, is at the core of this vast line: "A desire in which love and hatred so perfectly oppose themselves that we cannot voluntarily move; but await the extraordinary compulsion of the deluge and the earthquake." The line is so long that it generates a feeling of anxiety in the reader: hatred and love are so balanced that they generate an immobility that can only be broken by an external force; and the poetic line itself seems unable to break off while it awaits that moment. The metaphor of the spark gap across which, only when the conducting capacities of two electrodes are sufficiently separated, a spark can leap is an image of almost unbearable emotional tension. The potential for the crack and flash of the spark is sensed before it exists, and then suddenly electricity jumps between the conductors. It is as if Auden, thinking about animals, senses an analogy between the absence of electrical discharges and his own immobilized creative drives. The stasis seems like it will not end. But then, after writing "The Creatures," his imagination leaps back into life. After a period of artistic deadlock at the turn of the year, at the start of 1936, suddenly Auden's inspiration sparks. In the next three months, as if a deluge or an earthquake had occurred inside him, he wrote at least six major love poems (all with lapidary, short lines).[155]

It is hard to be certain about the order in which this burst of love poems from the late winter and early spring of 1936 was written. All of them are at the far end of the spectrum from Auden's "up-to-date" mode, the mode in which poems are filled with circumstantiality and references to events and contemporary products or scenes.[156] These poems instead seem to have a ciphered, introspective quality—as perhaps was to be expected in a world in general still so deeply hostile to same-sex love.

There is an almost Elizabethan mood of formal clarity and aloofness in some of them. They seem like they are floating outside time and beyond censure. In them all, Auden manages with dexterity to write about love without using a single gender-specific pronoun. (Of course, that very avoidance of specificity was itself an obvious and recognizable way of expressing tacitly what cannot be said explicitly.)

Most of the poems relate in some way to Auden's love for Michael Yates—and several seem to raise doubts about the true closeness between lovers and about the durability of love, or they explore states of hesitation and guilt. For example, "Let the florid music praise," which was probably the earliest of the set to be written and which was composed in the Coldstreams' flat in Belsize Park, ponders the beauty of the beloved's outward appearance and the inner vulnerability that allows the "unloved" to bring "the weeping and striking." The speaker even foresees how "my vows [will] break" before death takes "his look" at the handsome lover.[157]

Perhaps the next in the sequence, and one of the most memorable, begins: "Dear, though the night is gone, | The dream still haunts today."[158] The opening of the poem is resonant because dreams haunt so much of the day throughout Auden's early poetry; and dreams are often where he feels his poetry comes from. (This is another point of cross-century closeness between Auden and John Milton.) Dream poems from these years include the redemptive prospect offered by "some possible dream" that might be even now emerging into the "Actual History" of present-day England.[159] Elsewhere the dream is central to the poetry written by an "author, stand[ing] between these dreams."[160] There are the citizens "Dreaming of evening walks," the boys "who dream | Of a new bicycle or a winning team," and the deluded poet's salvationary "dream" that he is the "physician, bridegroom and incendiary" whose words others need.[161] In a sense, even the "Look, stranger" poem, with its trance-like slowing of time, could be called a kind of waking dream, a fantasy coming from the dream factory of filmmaking. And these examples are only a small selection from the dream poetry written in Auden's first few years as a published poet.

The young Auden offers abundant testimony to the fact that he saw the sources of poetry beginning in a preconscious world; for instance, he told Spender in a letter in 1934 that the world of the unconscious is "collective, creative and purposive."[162] Small wonder, then, that in his love poetry, which almost always belongs to the night world, Auden's imagination lays emphasis on dreams. "Dear, though the night is gone" is another poem about a dream (it was at one stage in its composition titled "The Dream"), and the poem is based, with significant alterations, on a real dream Auden had shortly before the time of composition. Here is the poem:

> Dear, though the night is gone,
> The dream still haunts to-day
> That brought us to a room,
> Cavernous, lofty as
> A railway terminus,
> And crowded in that gloom
> Were beds, and we in one
> In a far corner lay.
>
> Our whisper woke no clocks,
> We kissed and I was glad
> At everything you did,
> Indifferent to those
> Who sat with hostile eyes
> In pairs on every bed,
> Arms round each other's necks,
> Inert and vaguely sad.
>
> Oh but what worm of guilt
> Or what malignant doubt
> Am I the victim of;
> That you then, unabashed,
> Did what I never wished,
> Confessed another love;
> And I, submissive, felt
> Unwanted and went out?[163]

In the first two of its three stanzas, "Dear, though the night is gone" tells the story of a dream that "still haunts to-day." In the poem's dream, the speaker finds himself and his lover in a "room, | Cavernous, lofty as

| A railway terminus." They lie in a bed there and make love, "Indifferent to those | Who sat with hostile eyes | In pairs on every bed." The poem and dream change direction radically in the third stanza, in which the speaker wonders "what worm of guilt | Or what malignant doubt" he is the "victim" of that, after they made love, caused the dream lover to do "what I never wished, | Confessed another love." As the poem ends, the speaker says that a "worm of guilt" in his own conscience caused the other's confession, which made the dreamer feel "submissive" and "Unwanted" so that he did what he actually wanted and "went out."

Here is the account Auden made of the dream on which the poem is based:

Dream (Feb 1936)

It was a large dormitory. My bed was on the same side as the door, ie., on the left-hand side as you came in. At the door end [and?] along the wall were BOWES and others. Apparently, there was one bed too few so that M had to share mine. We made love. No turns, mostly kissing. M was warmer and freer than he has ever been. He said something like: "I feel this is what I need. It's alright, don't you think?" I was very happy but, as the dream continued, it became obvious that – & Co at the other end of the room knew what was happening. There was a great deal of talking, but I don't remember being serious[ly] upset—only bothered by their interruptions. Then some one said it was unfair that I should behave like this after what I'd said about others and produced what seemed to be a cablegram form which was a recommendation that some people—I know there were three names but can only remember the names FO and GY, both of which had homeric epithets attached to them—ought to be put to sleep in a far off dormitory. I did not take this very seriously, but was a little puzzled as I did not remember having written it. Then I was back in bed, suggesting to M that he should come and stay with me in April. He said: "Well, I don't think I shall want to leave flat country." I don't remember if he actually said so, but I knew that "flat co[u]ntry" meant Chester and Liverpool, and that he was in love with someone there. I was upset, but hid my feelings and was determined to be sane and sympathetic. He told me that his love (I think I was surprised at the sex being male) was sixteen years

old and then some more about him which I don't remember, except
that, in a later dream, I learned he was effeminate and used to wear
a bodice at one time but had given it up. I knew that he was attractive and that M was seriously in love with him. I next found myself
in the changing-room alone with my sponge-bag and feeling very
lonely. I went back to the dormitory to speak to M and found everybody seated at benches round the wall—the room now reminded
me of a laboratory—working at lathes. M looked up in the distance
and said that they were communists and busy. I knew I wasn't
wanted and left.[164]

The prose account of the dream contains some quite radical differences from the version re-created and reworked in the poem: necessarily, the full narrative scope of the dream is truncated in the published, poetic version. (One detail that the poem omits but that draws
attention in the prose version is the comment that "M," the Yates figure
in the dream, is "warmer and freer than he has ever been.") The poem
also extends past the actual narrative of the dream into the field of interpretation, something that is conspicuously missing from the prose
version of the dream, which just records the dream contents. In the
prose account, "left" is a key word, occurring very near the start and
again at the very end. The dreamer and "M" find themselves in a "large
dormitory" on the "left-hand side." That is, they are both on the homosexual end of the sexual spectrum ("left" often means gay in Auden's
work) and on the liberal or socialist side of the social group. In the
dream, the news of "M's" new "effeminate" lover does not immediately
trigger the speaker's departure. Instead, the speaker finds himself in the
"changing-room" and then wanders forlornly back to the dormitory to
find everyone working, in orthodox Soviet style, "at lathes."

"M" looks up, and Auden omits from the poem the politically
charged moment when in the dream "M" says that he and his fellow
lathe workers are "communists and busy." In the final sentence of the
prose account, the speaker comments that he "wasn't wanted and left,"
returning to the symbolism of the "left-hand side" foregrounded at the
start of the dream. But the juxtaposition of "left" with "communists,"
used in the sentence before, creates an important ambiguity. The
speaker knows that he is unwanted, and so he leaves the room; but he

also knows that he is unwanted because he is not "left[-wing]": "I knew I wasn't wanted and left."

Part of the subject matter of the dream is not simply Auden's relationship with Michael Yates but, more broadly, Auden's place as a poet within a community. The "terminus" at the start of the poem not only prepares for the idea at the end that the relationship is *terminating* but also evokes the railway-station world of *Night Mail.* That linkage is not there in the same way in the actual dream, but the dream does have the detail about everyone sitting "at benches round the wall": "the room now reminded me of a laboratory—working at lathes." The idea of a laboratory where, by definition, something *experimental* is taking place, coupled with the fact that all are occupied with lathes (a lathe is a tool, usually rounded, that rotates about a central axis, an image that brings it very close to the image of a reel of film turning on a spindle), suggests that Auden's looming doubts about his place in the GPO Film Unit are present in the dream as well.

In this context, it helps to remember that, in a very delicate way, Michael Yates had first covertly entered Auden's poetry in the summer of 1933 in "Out on the lawn." In that poem, Auden and Yates were among a group that had been lying together outside on a lawn at night. There, unlike here in the dormitory dream, Auden will wake in the morning to "speak with one | Who has not gone away." Crucially, that poem consolidated Auden's sense of working "in a small field" with "national emblems," writing, literally and figuratively, from "this English house."[165] The "creepered wall" encircling and protecting the idyllic space of the school world in that poem return here in more claustrophobic form in the enclosed spaces of the "dormitory" and, later, "laboratory," where in the dream Auden lies in bed with Yates, amid a group of envious, gossiping schoolboys. That this space is, indeed, also a version of the Downs School is indicated by the presence of not only Yates but also other Downs pupils such as John Bowes.

The fault line in the dream is the moment when the audience of "– & Co." complain that it is unfair that Auden is indulging in favoritism toward Yates when he has recommended that others, FO and GY (conveniently spelling, when merged, "FOGY"—that is, a person with old-fashioned or conservative ideas) and one other, ought, in a slightly ominous phrase, "to be put to sleep in a far off dormitory." Someone produces a "cablegram form" composed by Auden with names and "homeric epithets" on it. This can only be a reference to Auden's own poetry, which contained "homeric epithets" (like the "tamer of horses" tag applied to Merlin in "Prologue") and which critics had likened a number of times to a cablegram or telegram. The way that "homeric epithets" are attached to schoolboy names (with a suggestion that "homeric" is also the unconscious's code for "homoerotic") suggests a ciphered reference to Auden's school-dominated poetic world and perhaps to such things as the beauty contests for pupils that the Downs masters were said to have held.[166]

Primarily, then, the dream is about group life and Auden's sense of shaky integration into a group world, which has also come to stand as a microcosm of the national community. The resolution of the dream comes when Auden leaves the group; it is a distancing from the group (herded together as "communists") by the I who "wasn't . . . left." Someone who is not "left" is, presumably, *right,* not in the political sense necessarily but in the sense of someone who has justice on their side. The prose version of the dream, spoken by an "I," seems in greater sympathy with the dreamer than with those who are in his dream. In the poetic version of the dream, the speaker is harder on himself in questioning why he should have dreamed that he was not "wanted."

In the poem's final stanza, Auden attributes the departure not simply to the dream's apparent message, that his lover has found another partner—"Confessed another love"—but to the fact that in coded form, the relationship has induced a "worm of guilt" in him or a "malignant doubt." The language of the metaphors ("worm" and "malignant") seems suggestively internal, as if these feelings were known in the "gut" but not in the mind, which apparently "wishes" for something else. In both the prose account and in the poem, though, in spite of differences, the message is the same: the dreamer has lost faith in his connection to a lover and to the world around the lover. In the dream, he might seem as though he is being driven out, but the third stanza of the poem suggests that Auden has realized that this development is not something imposed on him but something he wants. The "worm of guilt" or the "malignant doubt" are what produce the confession that prompts the dreamer-speaker, feeling victimized and therefore blameless, to leave. Probably unknowingly, one further emotional step—in a dream and in a poem—has been taken on Auden's journey away from the world of schools, countryside, island iconography, and England.

The likely next poem in the informal sequence of spring 1936 is "Night covers up the rigid land," another poem of doubt, faithlessness, and fatalism. After night has fallen over "the rigid land" (perhaps a covert reference to England and English culture), the wakened sleeper listens:

> The wounded pride for which I weep
>   You cannot staunch, nor I
> Control the movements of your sleep,
>   Nor hear the name you cry.[167]

It is intrinsic to poetry that some powerful residue of enigma remains, even after a poem has become familiar. In the lecture Auden gave in February 1936, right in the middle of the time when he was writing this extraordinary cascade of love poetry, he insisted that poetry has "auras of meaning" and cannot be "confined to [meaning] one thing."[168] All these mysterious poems show that, but most seem to return quite consistently to ideas about the fragility and temporariness of love, to betrayal and disappointment.

The fourth lyric in the sequence of love poems that Auden wrote as he moved away from his involvement with documentary film begins: "Fish in the unruffled lakes."[169] This too is likely to have been written at the Coldstreams', and it is a different kind of poem than others in the set. How is it different? The note of doubt has vanished, and instead there are feelings of something more like happiness and satisfaction. The poem, again a three-stanza lyric, sets up a contrast, as Auden has done so recently in "The Creatures," between animals and humans. Animals have an unconscious beauty: "Swans in the winter air | A white perfection have." But humans carry anxiety and self-consciousness: we "till shadowed days are done, | We must weep and sing." The two worlds of animals and humans are tied together in the third stanza:

> Sighs for folly said and done
> Twist our narrow days;
> But I must bless, I must praise
> That you, my swan, who have

All gifts that to the swan
Impulsive Nature gave,
The majesty and pride,
Last night should add
Your voluntary love.[170]

"Voluntary love" is the human addition that augments the natural beauty that has "All gifts that to the swan | Impulsive Nature gave" with the uniqueness of a personal choice to love. That is where the poem ends, so this is a poem about one who, at least so far, "has not gone away."

It would be naive to link any of these poems too directly to specific events in Auden's life (although, of course, also naive to pretend there were no connections). The "necessary secretiveness of the great poet," to quote again Arendt's profound phrase about Auden, is compounded by so much that, for reasons of discretion, could never be revealed or explained or even simply recorded at the time, as it almost certainly would have been in the life of a straight writer from this same period.[171] Sometimes, all there is to go on is a clue in the biographical record akin to the momentary, submerged flash of light as the sun reflects off a fish's scales and is noticed only as the creature itself vanishes.

Around 1943, Auden (always one of nature's list-makers) made a list of sixteen people he had fallen in love with or perhaps simply had sex with. On the same page in his notebook he wrote another list, derived from the first, in which next to five of those sixteen names he tallied up what was probably the number of poems he had written about each person.[172] Next to the name "David," in that second list, is the number "1." While he was working in London, Auden went back and forth to and from his parents' house in the Birmingham suburb of Harborne. It must have been in Birmingham that Auden met, or remet, "David" in early 1936. This is David Impey, a former Downs School pupil, whose family lived fairly near the Audens in another suburb, Kings Norton.[173] The Impeys had Quaker connections, and David's father was a partner in a firm that manufactured business stationery and supplies. Auden and David Impey had an affair while Auden and Michael Yates were still in some form of relationship, even though they were living apart, and the "1" poem that Auden wrote that was inspired by Impey is probably the serene "Fish in the unruffled lakes." In a notebook, Auden called the poem

"The Swan"—as if this lover were like a great, beautiful bird that had suddenly glided into view from nowhere.[174]

Since the middle of 1935, Auden had got ten married, given up two jobs, moved at least twice, continued at least one affair and started at least one new one, composed poems that indicated many doubts about the viability of his relationship with Michael Yates (though the relationship lasted in some form into 1938), written for the new medium of film, and met a composer who would ardently set his poetry to music.

This was already a changed life, with many small clues in it about changed attitudes to the world he lived in and the poetry he was writing. But Auden's first intuitions about his fracturing relationship with English culture, which are only implicit, for example, in his dream about "M" and the "school dormitory" and the "changing room alone" from February 1936, became obvious to him during the writing he and Isherwood did on their new play, *The Ascent of F6*. Auden took a leave from the Film Unit to work in Portugal with Isherwood on the play.

While he was there, just as Britten was converting his part-time position at the Film Unit to a full-time one, Auden sent in a resignation letter, realizing that something more than just a job was over. At the very moment when Auden was starting to understand, at first only subliminally, that he had to leave England and relinquish his increasingly prominent position within English literary culture, he wrote a poem about a dream in which he feels a "worm of guilt" or a "malignant doubt" about a beloved person, Yates, and as a result believes he is "Unwanted and went out."[175] From the spring of 1936, the time of the haunting dream of disconnection beginning in a "railway terminus," where long journeys end and new departures start from, Auden's poetic affair with England and Englishness deteriorated fast as if, in his unconscious mind or in his artistic spirit, he had already begun to leave.

Since December 1935, Isherwood had been living in Sintra, an ancient Portuguese town, dotted with crumbling palaces, not far from Lisbon. He and his lover Heinz Neddermeyer, along with Stephen Spender and his lover Tony Hyndman, had leased the Villa Alecrim do Norte in the suburb of São Pedro, perched on the slopes of the Sintra hills. (Alecrim do Norte is the Portuguese name for northern rosemary, a medicinal plant said to lessen sexual desire.) Spender and Hyndman left shortly before Auden arrived there on a steamer on 16 March 1936.

Almost immediately, Auden and Isherwood began their new play, which was to be about an ambitious mountaineer, Michael Ransom, who leads a party to attempt the conquest of a mountain named F6 on the border between British and Ostnian "Sudoland" for the purposes of imperial propaganda. All of Ransom's companions, bar an avuncular Doctor, perish as Ransom drives the expedition toward the summit. At the peak, Ransom encounters the Demon who rules over the mountain. At first shrouded, the Demon later reveals herself to be Ransom's mother, and Ransom melodramatically dies in her arms.

Auden and Isherwood dithered over the ending to the play, producing at least two versions. The ending of the second edition of the play privatizes and psychologizes Ransom's downfall, attributing it above all to his pride. But the first published edition, essentially the one composed by Auden and Isherwood in Portugal in the spring of 1936, ends within a more public and mythic resolution.[176] In this version, the reason for Ransom's doom is not private and internal but cultural and public: Ransom is the heroic victim that the nation needs to establish English control of the mythical mountain. A group of representatives from English society gather reverently to eulogize him. Lord Stagmantle, a newspaper magnate, mourns one of England's "greatest sons." The word "son" ties together the maternal bond and the citizen's national bond with the mother country. Ransom, who has died in his mother's arms on the mountaintop, has therefore also died in the embrace of England.

This was something that W. B. Yeats recognized after seeing the play performed at the Mercury Theatre in early April 1937. In letters to Rupert Doone, the play's producer, Yeats praised parts of *The Ascent of F6* as "magnificent." But he suggested that it would be "good theatre" if Ransom's mother should be revealed on the mountaintop as "Britannia from the penny." He explained to Doone: "Remember the English expedition is racing that of another country because the one who gets first to the top will, the natives believe, rule them for a thousand years; remember also what the Abbot said about will and about government. Britannia is the mother."[177] Yeats was, in effect, following up, in not particularly subtle terms, on the hints Auden and Isherwood planted in the text of the play. In the satiric closing moments of the play's first version, Lord Stagmantle concludes, as if he were taking part in a service of memorial for the fallen in the Great War, by saying that "Their names are the latest but not the least on that long roll of heroes who gave their lives for the honour of this country." The word "country" triggers the appearance of a tableau, a plain obelisk with "Ransom" engraved on it, around which a group of other characters—Isabel, James, the General, Stagmantle, and an Ostnian climber, Monsieur Blavek—stand reverently. "They died for England," the General says sententiously of the climbing party, leaving the audience to understand that England, needing martyrs, leads heroes to their deaths.

> James. Honour—
> Stagmantle. Service—
> General. Duty—
> Isabel. Sacrifice—
> Stagmantle. England—
> Blavek. Ostnia—
> The Others. England! England! England![178]

Like "Negroes," *The Ascent of F6* is another fitful turn from Auden toward broader international themes connected to Britain's empire and its role in world politics. At the same time, as if now there were no chance of turning back again, the play also links a commitment to English glory with inevitable death. Much later, Auden told an interviewer about his decision to quit England: "Yes. F-6 was the end. I knew I must leave when I wrote it."[179]

In early April, while they were working on the play, Auden and Isherwood spent some time in the company of the celebrated German dramatist and socialist activist Ernst Toller and his wife, the actress Christiane Grautoff. Toller and Grautoff were visiting Sintra as part of a long tour through France, Spain, and Portugal. Toller, accompanied by Grautoff, had been exiled from Germany in 1933; his books had been burned, as had the books of Thomas Mann. (Auden's father-in-law had defended Toller when Toller was on trial for his life in 1919 for his participation in the short-lived Bavarian Soviet Republic.[180]) Although rootless, Toller and Grautoff lived mainly in London in the mid-1930s, and they were married there in May 1935. It is conceivable that they made this trip to Sintra specifically to see Isherwood and Auden. In her autobiography, Grautoff remembered Auden in Portugal as looking "young and nice" with a "special face, smiling and laughing," and paying elaborate attention to her before suddenly switching to discussing politics and literature with Toller and Isherwood.[181]

Isherwood liked Toller. He wrote in his diary that when they "talked about Hitler, he simply couldn't bring himself to utter the words *Mein Kampf.* First he said, 'Mein Krampf,' and then, 'His book.'"[182] Auden must have enjoyed the famous playwright as well because he almost immediately set to work to help with adaptations of the lyrics for the English version of Toller's play *Nie wieder Friede!* (*No More Peace!*). The play went into rehearsal only about a month after Auden and Isherwood met Toller in Portugal. With Christiane Grautoff making her London debut in the role of Rachel, the play was first performed, to lukewarm reviews, at the Gate Theatre on 11 June 1936. In the next few years, Auden also provided some adapted translations of lyrics for Toller's play *Pastor Hall.*[183] And they collaborated on a monologue for Erika Mann's Pfeffermühle cabaret, which was performed in New York in January 1937.[184]

These distinguished figures all met in Sintra in the spring of 1936 at a moment when Auden, like Isherwood, like Toller and Grautoff, itinerant people in a world falling apart, were on the brink of momentous artistic and personal changes. Auden and Isherwood were about to embark on a period of far-flung wandering before they put down roots in the United States in 1939. And Toller and Grautoff as well would spend much of the later 1930s in the United States under great psychological and financial strain. Eventually they separated. In May 1939, in the Mayflower Hotel in Manhattan, Toller would be found hanging from the hook on the back of his bathroom door.[185]

The last holiday resort that Auden had been in before Sintra in March 1936 was Ramsey on the Isle of Man in August 1935. There, he wrote about "the dangerous flood | Of history, that never sleeps or dies, | And, held one moment, burns the hand" ("August for the people," 216). When one thinks about Toller's haunting journey toward death, and about Auden reaching the final stages in his exploration of the meaning of belonging and of Englishness, and when one reflects on the poetry he made of that exploration, other meanings of the word "resort" bubble to the surface: "resort" as an expedient (often desperate), as a recourse, as the action of traveling somewhere. While Auden struggled to understand his place within the English literary world, those associations of "resort" are all relevant to assessing this moment in his work and life.

In 1939, as Germany and Britain were on the brink of another war, Auden, in a kind of exile or expatriation of his own in New York, would write Toller's elegy. When he did, he may have remembered standing next to this charismatic German, smiling in Portugal only three years earlier, in 1936. Perhaps as Auden composed the poem for Toller, he managed to enfold some feelings about his own lost or abandoned world, so far off in 1936, back across a huge emotional chasm of not much time at all. Here is how Auden's Toller elegy ends:

> We are lived by powers we pretend to understand:
> They arrange our loves; it is they who direct at the end
> The enemy bullet, the sickness, or even our hand.
>
> It is their to-morrow hangs over the earth of the living
> And all that we wish for our friends: but existence is believing
> We know for whom we mourn and who is grieving.[186]

In a mysterious line, Auden writes that "We are lived by powers we pretend to understand." And then he adds—as if he were reflecting almost brutally on the method of Toller's end by his own "hand," as well as thinking back on his own history and on his own state of unknowing in Portugal in 1936, a time just before the extraordinary journey he was about to embark on—"They [the "powers"] arrange our loves; it is they who direct at the end | The enemy bullet, the sickness, or even our hand." His delphic thoughts conclude: "It is their tomorrow hangs over the earth of the living," as if the future were already in existence, looming over the present just as the past also does. Around the time when Auden met Toller and Grautoff in Sintra in 1936, and with a shadowed tomorrow hanging over the whole group, Auden knew that a book of poetry was almost finished.

EPILOGUE

THE ISLAND'S CALIBAN

All things Begin & End in Albions Ancient Druid Rocky Shore.

—WILLIAM BLAKE (1804–1820)

FROM 1933 ONWARD, while Auden had been writing love poetry inspired by Michael Yates, the poet whose last name was a homonym of his lover's haunted his mind. One day, while he and Isherwood were working on *The Ascent of F6* during Auden's visit to Portugal in the spring of 1936, they happened to be sitting together on a sofa in their rented house, Villa Alecrim do Norte. Isherwood's lover, Heinz Neddermeyer, was looking at them through his camera lens, getting ready to take a picture. Snapping his own (verbal) image of the moment, Auden murmured, "both | Beautiful, one a gazelle."[1]

The camp joke turns on a phrase from W. B. Yeats's "In Memory of Eva Gore-Booth and Con Markievicz," a poem about two iconic sisters. Yeats had included it in his most recent book, *The Winding Stair* (1933). Auden probably expected Isherwood, but doubtless not Neddermeyer, to remember the full phrase in the poem: "Two girls in silk kimonos, both | Beautiful, one a gazelle."[2] Beyond the seriocomic idea of Auden and Isherwood as "sisters," the point was that Yeats's poem elegized two mesmerizing figures from his youth who were "beautiful" but whom Yeats believed had been destroyed psychologically and physically by their involvement in politics. Constance "drags out lonely years | Conspiring among the ignorant," while Eva, "withered old and skeleton-gaunt," dreams of "Some vague Utopia."[3] As Auden posed for that (now lost) photo in Portugal, he was also saying that he wondered about his and his "sister's" fates as writers in a world making intense political demands on them and that he pondered if they were both too deeply in the grip of fantasies about the significance of their roles as artists. Auden's quotation was asking: How will we survive all this?

The chronological order, or even the exact number, of the handful of freestanding new poems Auden wrote in Sintra in 1936 alongside the work he did with Isherwood on *The Ascent of F6* is not known. There were perhaps four or five lyrics that came out of his time there.[4] One of these was prompted by a visit the little group made on 30 April 1936 to the casino at Estoril, not far south of Sintra, to show Auden what Isherwood described as "the horrible old afternoon gamblers."[5] When Auden collected this poem later in the year, it was the only lyric in his book that he gave a title to, aside from a few generic "Songs" and the poems called "Prologue" and "Epilogue." With a poet like Auden, no word, and no formal characteristic, is meaningless—the fact of there being a title gives the clue that there is something unique about the poem. With its focus on hands, the parts of any artist's body most intimately involved with the act of making, this is a self-portrait.

Casino

Only the hands are living; to the wheel attracted,
Are moved, as deer trek desperately towards a creek
    Through the dust and scrub of the desert, or gently
    As sunflowers turn to the light.

And as the night takes up the cries of feverish children,
The cravings of lions in dens, the loves of dons,
    Gathers them all and remains the night, the
    Great room is full of their prayers.

To the last feast of isolation, self-invited,
They flock, and in the rite of disbelief are joined;
    From numbers all their stars are recreated,
    The enchanted, the world, the sad.

Without, the rivers flow among the wholly living,
Quite near their trysts; and the mountains part them; and the
    bird,

Deep in the greens and moistures of summer,
Sings towards their work.

But here no nymph comes naked to the youngest shepherd,
The fountain is deserted, the laurel will not grow;
    The labyrinth is safe but endless, and broken
    Is Ariadne's thread.

As deeper in these hands is grooved their fortune: "Lucky
Were few, and it is possible that none were loved;
    And what was godlike in this generation
    Was never to be born."[6]

Very few people write about "Casino," partly because it is not seen as typical of Auden's poetry, having a kind of mystical greenness, a simplicity, and a flow of film-like images. For example, the part about the deer trekking "towards a creek | Through the dust and scrub of the desert" almost reads as if it were the verbal equivalent of a scene from a wildlife documentary (211). And, besides, the poem sounds a little like something composed by the young Stephen Spender (who had been in Sintra just before Auden arrived). I love "Casino," though, and consider it a revelatory poem. It is symptomatic of Auden's sensitivity as a writer that he converted the sight of "the horrible old afternoon gamblers" and lounge lizards in in a dusty, dark building in Estoril into a poetic picture expressing his own inner desperation and uncertainty as an artist, "To the last feast of isolation, self-invited." These are the same feelings that had underlain the affectionate, playful, but serious quotation from Yeats he had recalled as he sat next to Isherwood.

In a journal Auden started in late August 1939 as war was about to break out again in Europe, he wrote (for his eyes only): "I realise now that for the last four years a part of me at least has been wanting to die."[7] The timeline puts the start of this unconscious desire for death in the period from 1935 to 1936 when Auden left the Downs School, was employed for a while with the GPO Film Unit, and wrote *The Ascent of F6* with Isherwood. It was during the work on *The Ascent of F6* that Auden realized that he had to leave England.[8] This dating also puts "Casino" squarely within the onset of this mysterious, tormented period that Auden himself did not understand until later.

In the poem's first stanza, the image of the roulette wheel (doubling as Fortune's wheel), which attracts "the hands" of those who are alive only in the activity of placing bets and gambling, has a dreamlike quality. The opening lines, scrambling normal word order, look as if they are expressing more than a simple surface meaning. And the self-indicting subtext here is an idea about artists, parts of whom are emotionally or intellectually dead, artists who have given up desire for anything except the compulsive interaction with the wheel of their medium. From "numbers" (an ancient synonym for poetry), Auden writes in "Casino," "all their stars are recreated" (211). "Casino" posits an identification between the person making the poem and the half-people bending over the gambler's wheel with flickers of vitality only discernible in their bet-making hands.[9] And if this reading is correct, then, alongside Auden's sense of the addictive nature of artistic making (or gambling), he is also giving voice to a feeling about how much of an aesthetic "win" is actually due to chance or to factors beyond an artist's conscious control, and how little it has to do with virtue or intelligence.

Outside the darkened cave of the casino's "great room," life goes on: "the rivers flow among the wholly living," and events happen as they should and must: "the bird, | Deep in the greens and moistures of summer, | Sings towards [humans'] work" (212). Then, in the fifth of the six stanzas, Auden changes the poem's key, suddenly, seamlessly, introducing Greek mythology into an almost documentary scene, as if there were no clear distinction between things happening on an eternal plane and things going on in a real but tawdry place, like this casino, on earth. Both worlds are sites of entropy and despair: the "fountain is deserted, the laurel will not grow." And in the "safe but endless" labyrinth of compulsive activity, "broken | Is Ariadne's thread," which would have enabled an escape from the infinite maze (212).

No one has so far discovered whether the words in quotation marks in the poem's last stanza were taken by Auden from an earlier source or whether he pastiched their bleak, fatalistic, and faintly Anglo-Saxon-sounding message in his darkened room at the Villa Alecrim do Norte (where, as at Oxford, he wrote "with the curtains drawn," according to Isherwood).[10] But, in a world of rationalized and instrumentalized language, part of why readers, and perhaps poets too, go to poetry is to rediscover the oracular there. The poem's last lines—"what was godlike in this generation | Was never to be born"—seem uncannily to know more than their maker does. In an enigmatic way, the words in the final stanza, coming out of nowhere like a voice in a vision, quietly declare the message that Auden as a person was not yet ready to say to himself: "a part of me at least has been wanting to die."

What did Auden mean by that stark statement in his 1939 journal? What was that part of himself he referred to? No answer can be definitive. On a personal level, the crisis perhaps made itself felt as a combination of a sense of loneliness, an exhaustion with the demands of a politicized audience, and a fear of being closed in artistically. Perhaps it also seemed like poetic successes were getting too easy in England? The same year that Auden admitted to himself that "part of me at least has been wanting to die," he had told his father that "Basically the writer's problem is that of everyone, how to go on growing the whole of his life, because to stop growing is to die."[11]

Another poem that Auden wrote in Sintra during the rainy spring of 1936, beginning, "As it is, plenty," is a portrait of a businessman, a hollow winner, who has given up his deepest needs in return for the "plenty" of worldly status and material reward: cars, a conventionally picture-perfect family, money. All that visible, valuable shallowness is substituted for deeper and more morally ambiguous gratifications:

> but love
> And the rough future
> Of an intransigent nature
> And the betraying smile,
> Betraying, but a smile:
> That that is not, is not;
> Forget, Forget.[12]

The poem suggests it is better for this unnamed man to delude himself about his happiness by continuing to "praise | . . . his spacious days; | Yes, and the success" and better to lie to himself about the moral compromises and denial of authentic selfhood that he makes. For if he were really to face the reality of his life "as it is," then he would recognize: "The loss as major | And final, final."[13]

It is not hard to see that, in the midst of the seeming unlikeness of a young author and a self-deluded, successful businessman, the poem is another self-portrait, a little akin in feeling to the closeness Auden posited between an artist and the despairing gamblers in "Casino." Here, the thought-provoking flips are to see an artist as a person in business and to imagine a queer poet as a family patriarch.[14] The shared characteristics common to both the portrait and its maker may be a sense of loss and a deep degree of bad faith. To read the poem in this way is to open up two further interpretations.

The first is that, superficially at least, this poem tries to persuade its reader to believe something wrong: that illusions about ourselves might be worth sustaining if the truth is too painful. This effort, which we are meant to understand is misplaced, implies doubts on Auden's part about the status of poems: Do they reveal truth or (as here) affirm lies? The second point flows out of the poem's insistent verbal repetitions: "the car, the car," "Give thanks, give thanks," "But love, but love," "Forget, Forget," "Let him bless, let him bless," "Final, final."[15] The poem repeats itself in a way that could be blandly understood merely as Auden indulging in lyrical insistence. But, more plausibly, the verbal doublings can be taken as a signal that Auden feels his poems are cycling back on themselves or, to put it more directly, they are repeating. There are further clues to a fear in Auden around now about artistic repetition. This poem recalls one of his earlier signature poetic formulas: elliptical, short-lined poems with sporadic pararhyme.[16] The examples are legion but could include the 1929 poems "From scars where kestrels hover" and "Before this loved one."[17] Those formulas are used again here. Auden is ambiguously trying to move ahead by going back to an old style.

Other poems that Auden wrote at the start of 1936 show that this phenomenon of circling round to his beginnings as a poet is less incidental than it is systematic. For instance, the song beginning, "Underneath the abject willow," probably also written in Sintra, borrows its first line from a line in "I chose this lean country," written in 1927. A poem beginning, "Night covers up the rigid land," borrows lines from a rough-hewn sonnet called "Lacrimae Rerum" (Tears at the heart of things) that Auden wrote in German around September 1930. John Fuller notes that, taken as a whole, "Night covers up the rigid land" returns to Auden's "Housman manner of 10 years earlier."[18] Auden's poetry in more traditional forms, forms in which he had once written with success and feeling, is now playing on "repeat."

That is true in a suggestive fashion of another lyric Auden wrote in Sintra, this one for his and Isherwood's play. In a phantasmagoric scene in *The Ascent of F6*, after the hero's brother, James Ransom, dies, two characters sing a dirge that begins:

> Stop all the clocks, cut off the telephone,
> Prevent the dog from barking with a juicy bone,
> Silence the pianos and with muffled drum
> Bring out the coffin, let the mourners come.
>
> Let aeroplanes circle moaning overhead
> Scribbling on the sky the message: He is dead.
> Put crepe bows round the white necks of the public doves.
> Let the traffic policemen wear black cotton gloves.[19]

The next three stanzas of the version used in the play describe the actions of characters caught up in the mourning for James Ransom. But Auden would come back to the poem in the early summer of 1937, rewriting its second half to strip away the tacked-on dramatic references and to turn it back instead into what it had perhaps originally been in disguised form: a personal poem about the death or disappearance of a lover.[20] When he cut back the circumstantial trappings needed for the play, he laid bare the core experience the poem describes: loss. That experience seems to pertain more genuinely to his own predicament as an artist than it does to the loss of a made-up character in a fever dream inside a play. Here is how the revised—and what one might call "truer"—version of the poem, which Auden eventually titled "Funeral Blues," concludes:

> He was my North, my South, my East and West,
> My working week and my Sunday rest,
> My noon, my midnight, my talk, my song;
> I thought that love would last for ever: I was wrong.
>
> The stars are not wanted now; put out every one,
> Pack up the moon and dismantle the sun,
> Pour away the ocean and sweep up the wood;
> For nothing now can ever come to any good.[21]

In place of the three stanzas describing how other characters should mourn the death of the play's James Ransom, the two new stanzas convert the poem into a lament for the speaker's own suffering. By the end, the new version of the poem has not moved far emotionally from where it starts: the elaborate imagery says essentially the same thing over and over again. But there is change of a kind in the poem—and the change takes the form of another recursion. In "Out on the lawn" in 1933, Auden extends his gaze and imagines how: "North and South and East and West | Those I love lie down to rest." The cardinal compass points and the West / rest rhyme reappear in "Funeral Blues," as do the stars, the moon, and the sun from the earlier poem, and the charmed "Forests of green" there have become a mere "wood" here that can be swept up and coldly disposed of.[22] Christopher Smart's mystical "Song to David" stanza from "Out on the lawn" has been replaced by a (not very faithful) imitation of a tragic, non-English form with very different cultural associations: the blues. The deeper motivation in "Funeral Blues" seems not to be to form a lament for James Ransom in a strained dramatic situation but to allow Auden, among other things, to sing a covert self-elegy for a phase in his artistic life.

Amid these lyric cyclings and recyclings, even for Auden to be writing poems outside Britain was itself a recursion to an early phase in his poetic career. When he arrived in Sintra in 1936, Auden had had an enormously productive half decade or more during which he had published scores of poems, had two plays produced, and had written copious amounts of prose. In addition, during the same period, he had traveled repeatedly to Germany as well as visiting Switzerland, middle Europe, Denmark, and Belgium. But in spite of that literary activity and his frequent movements, Auden had apparently not written a poem outside England since June 1929, when he was in Rothehütte in Germany and composed "Sentries against inner and outer."[23] It is as if, whenever Auden wrote poems in Sintra, whenever he found himself performing artful repetitions based on earlier work, he was looking at Rilke's archaic torso of Apollo, and the stone god of poetry was saying back to him implacably: to grow as an artist, "You must change your life."[24]

Besides composing poetry in Sintra and collaborating with Isherwood on *The Ascent of F6*, Auden was now also busy assembling a volume of his poems to send to Faber and Faber. Knowing the backstory of Auden's affair with Michael Yates (and probably of those with Peter Roger and

David Impey too) and aware how many poems were inspired by Auden's love for Yates, Isherwood feebly joked in a letter to Spender on 29 March 1936: "While I am typing out the play, Wystan will be collating his new volume of poems, which will be entitled: 'The Passions of a Pedagogue.'"[25]

There is no record of Faber and Faber suggesting a book to Auden or asking him for one—this is, rather, a moment when Auden felt he had completed the artistic chapter that any collection of poetry represents. He set to work to give that chapter a form. His books of poetry were never randomly sequenced accumulations of individual lyrics, nor were they simply arranged in chronological order of composition.[26] Instead, he habitually created a planned and yet organic literary structure, one that was not dependent on pure historical sequence (though not entirely independent of it either) and was not a volume amounting merely to the sum of its poetic parts. This is the process that Isherwood was referring to when he wrote that Auden was "collating" his new book.

Like a set of small mirrors set up at slight angles in a ring, light bounces from one lyric to another in Auden's collections, as separate images and lines in different poems illuminate and reflect. He juxtaposed poems on similar themes, counterpointing one approach against another, drawing attention to formal and verbal parallels, constructing narrative and tonal progressions. When Auden was putting his new book together in 1936, he created many examples of this holistic organization of disparate materials. To repeat one instance of this phenomenon mentioned earlier, immediately after the book's "Prologue," pleading with "love" to make its presence felt in England, Auden placed "Out on the lawn," in which love for one special person, love for colleagues and friends, love for the cosmos and for the immediate English setting, are all blended together in fulfillment, as if the book were saying that the god of Love was moved and the request in "Prologue" had been granted in "Out on the lawn."[27]

It is not only that Auden's poems as units are organized into meaningful sequences. Individual images and motifs also cross-connect between poems. To mention just a few examples, the apple that falls vertically always and forever toward Newton's Lincolnshire garden and "towards England" in the book's "Prologue" is echoed by the tiny ivory ball near the collection's end, bobbling around unpredictably in the horizontal roulette wheel in the casino at Estoril.[28] The communion of English colleagues equal in a ring in "Out on the lawn" at the start of the book returns transformed as the desperate circle of European gamblers bound to the wheel who come "To the last feast of isolation, self-invited" in "Casino." The "lion griefs" that in "Out on the lawn" tamely "loped from the shade" are contrasted with the menacing and powerful constellation "Leo," which is in charge of humanity's fate in the "Epilogue."[29] As these examples suggest, the surrounding architectonics are part of the total meaning of any individual poem. To a greater degree than was the case in Auden's earlier book of lyrics, *Poems* (1930), none of the poems he collated in 1936 was intended to exist in isolation.

A particularly strong example of the interdependence of different poems comes in the opening and closing lyrics of the volume Auden now arranged. The book begins with the "Prologue" envisioning the transmission by "love" of a regenerative "possible dream" that might be driving toward "the virgin roadsteads of our hearts."[30] The movement of the poem is centripetal, and the center is England. "Epilogue" (the poem that begins, "Certainly our city—with the byres of poverty down to | The river's edge") contrasts the England-focused "possible dream" of "Prologue" with a waking urban nightmare of the present:

> Certainly our city—with the byres of poverty down to
> The river's edge, the cathedral, the engines, the dogs;
>   Here is the cosmopolitan cooking
>   And the light alloys and the glass.
>
> Built by the conscience-stricken, the weapon-making,
> By us. The rumours woo and terrify the crowd,
>   Woo us. The betrayers thunder at, blackmail
>   Us. But where now are They
>
> Who without reproaches shewed us what our vanity has chosen,
> Who pursued understanding with patience like a sex, had
>   unlearnt
>   Our hatred, and towards the really better
>   World had turned their face?
>
> There was Nansen in the north, in the hot south Schweitzer, and
>   the neat man
> To their east who ordered Gorki to be electrified;
>   There were Freud and Groddeck at their candid studies
>   Of the mind and body of man.

Nor was every author both a comforter and a liar;
Lawrence revealed the sensations hidden by shame,
 The sense of guilt was recorded by Kafka,
 There was Proust on the self-regard.

Who knows? The peaked and violent faces are exalted,
The feverish prejudiced lives do not care, and lost
 Their voice in the flutter of bunting, the glittering
 Brass of the great retreat,

And the malice of death. For the wicked card is dealt, and
The sinister tall-hatted botanist stoops at the spring
 With his insignificant phial, and looses
 The plague on the ignorant town.

Under their shadows the pitiful subalterns are sleeping;
The moon is usual; the necessary lovers touch:
 The river is alone and the trampled flower,
 And through years of absolute cold

The planets rush towards Lyra in the lion's charge. Can
Hate so securely bind? Are They dead here? Yes.
 And the wish to wound has the power. And tomorrow
 Comes. It's a world. It's a way.[31]

This is a contemporary scene where, amid "the light alloys and the glass," the "peaked and violent faces are exalted," and the healers who "pursued understanding with patience like a sex" are gone. It is not hard to map the poem's despairing phrases onto the political events of the mid-1930s. This last poem in Auden's book, written in Sintra, broadens out toward a pessimistic, planetary view: "Can | Hate so securely bind? Are They dead here? Yes. | And the wish to wound has the power" (217). "Prologue" is dominated by the power of love and a "possible dream." In "Epilogue," "Hate" and the "planets" have bound the world into conflict. "Vega," effulgent in "Out on the lawn," the poem of love, is part of the constellation "Lyra." In the volume's final poem, the planets menacingly "rush towards Lyra in the lion's charge" (217).

Every book of poetry tells a story—this one is no exception. A central part of what Auden meant about something in him that had "been wanting to die" in 1935–1936 concerns the dissolution of a whole poetic vision of the world. The somber "Epilogue" points out of Auden's book and toward his poetic future. It does not summarize or conclude what has come before. Instead, as "The Hollow Men" looked beyond Eliot's completed work in *Poems: 1909–1925* (1925), "Epilogue" here looks beyond the volume that it is collected in, and it does so with trepidation.[32]

"Epilogue" ends with an allusion to phrases by the German Romantic poet Friedrich Hölderlin. Auden's pessimistic concluding words, "It's a world. It's a way," are, as he later told Chester Kallman, "a misheard crib from Stephen's translation of a poem of Hölderlin's."[33] The mishearing in question was of Spender's translation of a line from "Die Kürze" (published as "The Short Poems" in *New Writing* in the spring of 1936). In the original, German version, the text reads, "hinweg ists! und die Erd' ist kalt," which Spender rendered as "It's away, and the earth is cold."[34] He must have been working on the translation when he was in Sintra slightly before Auden arrived, and either he had left a manuscript of it behind or Isherwood or Heinz Neddermeyer quoted the lines to Auden from memory.[35] Auden seizes on Spender's words, which suited exactly his current purposes, choosing to write his poem in the "Hölderlin stanza" (a quatrain combining various patterns of two longer lines, followed by two shorter lines), which he also uses for another Spender-like poem, "Casino."[36]

In thinking about the perennial topic of the influences on Auden's poetry, I am struck not by the conventional idea that Auden trawled alone in some vast abstract sea of encyclopedic learning but rather by the way that tiny circles of personally connected enthusiasts, friends, and colleagues were the seedbeds from which his intellectual and artistic enthusiasms grew. It is remarkable how much came to him from small worlds. Auden's learning and influences are to a significant degree constrained, serendipitous, and historically channeled—it was his extraordinary sensitivity that lifted these often forgotten or discredited bodies of knowledge or writing into an artistic form that gives them imaginative force.

This was true, for example, of the way that Auden's interest in psychoanalytic ideas came not directly from Freud's works but from his father and his father's links to a small circle of British-based doctors, such as Rivers, who "englished" Freud in the 1910s and 1920s. Layard gave Auden a fascination with the forgotten but inspiring anthropologists of the diffusionist school. And in Sintra in 1936, Auden's deep interest in poets like Hölderlin and Rilke emerged in part through the influence of his family connection with the Manns and in part through Spender's enthusiasm for German poetry. However comical or exasperating Auden and Isherwood may have found the ardent, gossipy, blundering Spender as a person, Auden capitalized with great receptiveness on his friend's literary passions.[37]

In a sense, Auden's burgeoning interests in Hölderlin and Rilke are conjoined and became visible at almost the same time. Literary history often works like this: new translations are an index of the needs of a cultural moment, and it was in the mid-1930s that British culture began to "need" a new, purer kind of lyricism. Auden and Spender are a part of this trend, but other writers, such as the Scottish poet Edwin Muir, also moved in a similar direction. These two German poets, Hölderlin and Rilke, represented introspective, private, apolitical qualities that Auden, at least, was intuitively aspiring to—if only to swerve away from the fate that Yeats had tendentiously seen incarnated in Eva Gore-Booth and Con Markievicz: from youthful beauty and hope into physical decrepitude and embittered political disappointment. The story of Rilke and Auden is for another place. Auden first referred to Rilke (only in passing) in a review he wrote, probably in Sintra, of Herbert Read's *In Defence of Shelley*.[38] And by the summer of 1936, references to Rilke and Rilkean poetic strategies began to surface frequently. But the meaning of Hölderlin hit Auden first and is more crucial to the artistic narrative I am describing here.

With borrowings such as the one from Hölderlin in the last line of "Epilogue," the Nordic or Germanic theme, which recurs like a leitmotif throughout Auden's life and poetry, is audible again. From Auden's father's cult of the North and his familiarity with Germanic culture, as well as later his interest in German medical science, to Dr. Auden's long absence from 1914 to 1919 as a result of the war with Germany, through their trip together in 1925 to Austria, where Auden began to learn German, to Auden's early experiments with Anglo-Saxon at Oxford, his visits to Berlin in the late 1920s and early 1930s, and his marriage to Erika Mann in 1935, Germany and its people are always at least in the background of the work Auden produced and of the life he chose. It "is a German Age," Auden wrote to a friend in 1943, during the depths of the Second World War, "and the chances are, I have a suspicion, that after the war, it will continue to be."[39]

Germany and German literature became of crucial importance to Auden's generation in Britain, and perhaps especially to Auden, in the mid-1930s. It is within that cultural frame, looking away from England to an international world, that "Epilogue" belongs. The poet Louis MacNeice commented that however activist and political the writing of a poet such as Auden became, it was always balanced by a sense of the unique means and position of poetry, which could never be identified simply with a class attitude or a political slogan. Some "at least of these poets" from the 1930s, MacNeice wrote, thinking particularly of Auden and Spender, "always recognized the truth of Thomas Mann's dictum: 'Karl Marx must read Friedrich Hölderlin.'"[40]

Seeking to explain the appeal of German writers such as Hölderlin to his generation of writers, Isherwood claimed (as noted in the Prologue): "It was natural for us, the members of the immediate post-war generation, to be the first to react from the blind chauvinism of the war years."[41] Comments like these show just how sensitive a small section of the British intelligentsia was in the mid- to later 1930s to currents within contemporary German thought and feeling. The British interest in Hölderlin even tracks strikingly closely with the German philosopher Martin Heidegger's sudden engagement in the mid-1930s with Hölderlin's work. Seeking to enter more deeply and "poetically" into the nature of poetic language, Heidegger (with swastika pin affixed in his lapel) delivered his first public lecture on Hölderlin in Rome in April 1936, published as "Hölderlin und das Wesen der Dichtung" ("Hölderlin and the Essence of Poetry")—the lecture was given at exactly the moment when Auden was in Sintra working on Hölderlinian poems and Spender was publishing his translations in *New Writing*.

"Prologue" and "Epilogue" balance each other at either end of the collection that Auden was assembling in Sintra. This collection, as it took form, begins with a poem about "our little reef... | This fortress perched on the edge of the Atlantic scarp, | The mole between all Europe and the exile-crowded sea."[42] It ends, at the "water front," with the "cosmopolitan cooking" of a lyric composed as a counterweight in

Portugal in the company of exiles and with allusions to German poets. And the "foreign" nature of "Epilogue," written by a poet who not long before had invested so deeply in the idea of the "English cell," is intensified by another allusion.[43] Auden inquires of the whereabouts in the crisis-wracked present of those who "unlearnt | Our hatred, and towards the really better | World had turned their face?" (217).[44]

Auden is borrowing here from another German Romantic poet, Novalis, the pen name used by Freiherr Georg Friedrich Philipp von Hardenberg, and his comment in *Das Allgemeine Brouillon* (*The General Rough Draft* is perhaps the best of all the English translations of the untranslatable title). This is a collection of notes and essays that Novalis made for an encyclopedia. The ambitious project was never completed, but the gathering of notes, a mélange of philosophical aphorisms and reflections, was published posthumously. In one entry, during a meditation on religion, Novalis refers to the future as "this really better world, this is the core Christianity's behests."[45]

In all likelihood, Auden had not read *Das Allgemeine Brouillon*. In another example of the ways in which serendipity and casual reading played a significant role in his creativity, Auden became inspired by Novalis's phrase about the "really better world" while perusing the July 1933 *Criterion*. Thomas Mann published a long essay (written in 1929) there on the ultimately progressive and liberatory nature of Freud's work, titled "Freud's Position in the History of Modern Thought."[46] In his piece, Mann refers to the "revolutionary principle [that] is simply the will towards the future, which Novalis called 'the really better world.' It is the principle of consciousness and recognition, leading to higher levels."[47] Auden had read Mann's *Der Tod in Venedig* (*Death in Venice*) in German as early as 1927.[48] But he first refers in print to Mann only in late 1933 in a footnote to his essay "The Group Movement and the Middle Classes," where he drew attention to Mann's essay on Freud. And in Colwall a few months later, in March 1934, he wrote a poem, never published in his lifetime (John Lehmann rejected it for *New Writing*, and then Eliot rejected it for the *Criterion*) in which, using the Novalis phrase, he asks about healers who "rooted in life and loving in their lives, towards | The really better world have turned their faces."[49]

Unwilling to let the idea of the "really better world" disappear when he could not get his poem published, Auden picked up the phrase again in his 1936 poem about those who "towards the really better | World had turned their face." (Auden changed "faces" in 1934 to "face" in 1936, perhaps partly for reasons having to do with syllable count but also to suggest that all these healers had a shared vision, a single perspective, and thus, figuratively, a shared face.) When he did this, Auden was not simply borrowing from Novalis. He was borrowing Thomas Mann's recounting of Novalis's phrase, as if compressing two references or allusions into one.

The "really better | World" to which Auden gestures desperately in his 1936 poem is a German-flavored, or at least a non-English, idea. It is a familial one too, since Auden is here citing his father-in-law citing a poet. Through his language, Auden is suddenly, firmly integrating himself, at least at a linguistic level, into a circle of non-English writers and European concerns. Toward the end of the First World War, when Auden was in the dining room at his prep school in Surrey and reached for an extra slice of bread and margarine, a master had said bitterly in a quiet-loud voice before the assembled boys, "I see, Auden, you want the Huns to win."[50] Two decades later, there is an ironic fulfillment of that statement—Auden, married into a German family, and staying in Portugal among Germans, is now basing some of the ethical and artistic fundamentals of his poetry, and his vision of a possible future, on German culture. In the mid-1930s, Auden *did* want the (good) Germans to win—or at least to become ethical and artistic reference points for his version of English culture. As another war loomed over Europe, the First World War's shadow is still lying across Auden's world.

Now, he invoked Thomas Mann at a moment when Mann had just made an important, and very political, gesture. Since 1933, the Manns had lived outside Germany, and for most of those three years, Thomas Mann was under pressure from German exiles and opponents of the Nazi regime to go on the record with his criticisms of the Reich. From within his own family, the demand was intense, especially from his more politically committed children, Erika and Klaus. Erika Mann, in particular, was vehement about what she viewed as her father's equivocations and his complicities with the Nazis.[51]

In January 1936, a polemic sprang up between Leopold Schwarzschild, the editor of the Paris-based *Das Neue Tage-Buch,* an émigré journal, Thomas Mann, and Edouard Korrodi, the feature editor of the *Neue Zürcher Zeitung.* Schwarzschild in the *Neue Tage-Buch* first attacked Mann's publisher, S. Fischer Verlag, which continued to publish unimpeded in Germany even though its owner, Gottfried Bermann Fischer, was Jewish. Mann and others defended Bermann Fischer in a letter to the *Neue Zürcher Zeitung*, after which Schwarzschild returned to the attack, maintaining that almost all the major figures in German literature had now emigrated. Korrodi in the *Neue Zürcher Zeitung* counterpunched with heavy bias by arguing that Schwarzschild failed to make a distinction between German and Jewish literature. He also pointed out that Thomas Mann's work was still being issued in Germany. As one biographer puts it, this "brief *feuilleton*" landed like a bombshell among the German émigrés. For Mann, "Korrodi's denigration of the *émigrés*, and his open attempt to separate [Mann] from their company, came as nothing less than a challenge to declare where he stood."[52] Urged on by his children, notably Erika, who forecast a split with her father if he did nothing, Thomas Mann replied in "A Letter from Thomas Mann," published in the *Neue Zürcher Zeitung* on 3 February 1936.[53]

In his slow-paced but stringently precise response, Auden's father-in-law began by complicating the notion of what was and was not part of the national canon: "The line between émigré and non-émigré German literature is not easily drawn. It doesn't just coincide, mentally speaking, with the borders of the Reich."[54] While insisting (with what seems like an odd vehemence) on his own and his brother Heinrich's non-Jewishness, Mann declared that the "'international' component of the Jew is his Central European component—and this is at the same time German. Without it Germanism wouldn't be Germanism, but a sluggishness of no use to the world."[55] And Mann insisted that: "One is not German by being 'voelkisch.' German anti-semitism, however, or that of the German rulers, is aimed, spiritually regarded, not at the Jews at all or not at them exclusively. It is aimed at Europe and at all the higher Germanism itself. . . . [It is an attempt] to effect a fearful, an evil-laden estrangement between the country of Goethe and the rest of the world."[56]

Having sent off the letter to the *Neue Zürcher Zeitung*, Mann congratulated himself in his diary on 31 January 1936: "After three years of wavering [or hesitation], I have let my conscience and my firm conviction speak. My word(s) will not fail to make an impression."[57] He was right: the Nazi regime alluded to this letter published in February 1936, with its "violent insults to the Reich," in early December 1936 when they tried to justify their decision to deprive Mann of his German citizenship.[58] (The move was juridically meaningless since Thomas and Katia Mann had accepted Czech citizenship on 19 November 1936.)

Mann's February 1936 letter was ecstatically welcomed in beleaguered émigré circles. It marked him as a representative of the new ethical respectability of exile. A few days after Mann had been deprived of his German citizenship, the Marxist critic Ernst Bloch wrote at the start of December 1936, referring both to Mann's public letter and his denationalization: "if the noblest public figure of German culture rises against the Germany of today; if the prize for all this Germanness (the Nazi Nobel Prize, so to speak) consists in expatriation, then Germany lies elsewhere."[59] Now, Bloch announced: "expatriation has become a sign of honour, the only one that the Nazis are able to bestow. . . . The society of expatriates is becoming more and more synonymous with the true German character."[60]

When Auden uses the phrase the "really better |World" in "Epilogue," he is alluding not only to Novalis and not only to Thomas Mann. More specifically, he is referring to a Thomas Mann who in the *Neue Zürcher Zeitung* has just publicly pledged his allegiance to the "society of expatriates" in a world where the true representatives of a culture's highest spirit were no longer to be found within that culture's borders. Auden asks about the healers who "shewed us what our vanity has chosen"—and his stark question is: "where now are They?" (217). (This comes in one of only two entirely monosyllabic lines in "Epilogue.") An answer to Auden's question, the poem implies, is: "They" are in exile.

The context of these very public arguments, involving Auden's father-in-law, about the location of a true German culture require us to take the spatial implications of Auden's question seriously: "*where* now are They?" Where is true culture located? Within a bounded political space such as the nation? Or scattered outside the nation's frontiers? In the late 1920s and at the start of the 1930s, Auden's poetry has been based on a sense of disconnection from international modernism's cosmopolitan coordinates and a reembedding of poetry within national space. Now, in Portugal, in "Epilogue," Auden makes use of a "German," Hölderlinian form for an English poem, puts copious allusions to German culture (including phrases by Hölderlin and Novalis) into his English lines, and for a moment adopts the voice of Thomas Mann, a family member for whom "expatriation has become a sign of honour."

The implication for Auden and his readers is that by 1936 the authentic English poem is no longer necessarily one written within England's borders or one secured in its representativeness by references to English (or American) culture.

But Auden's new version of the English poem that matches the historical moment is an impure one with a melancholic, exilic status. The despair with which the poem ends—"Can | Hate so securely bind? Are They dead here? Yes" (217)—should be read not only in relation to Auden's pessimism about the advent of the "really better | World" but also as a displaced expression of the struggle that the poem makes as it anxiously wrenches itself free of its familiar moorings in English culture. "Epilogue" has profound stakes. Auden dreamed in February 1936 that "I knew I wasn't wanted and left." Not only was "a part of me at least . . . wanting to die" that spring of the same year, but it was also as if, in "Epilogue," Auden was trying to put a part of his old, "English" poetic self to death.[61]

As Auden did so, with infinite artistry he wrote in a poetic language that gives the appearance of being on the edge of falling apart. "Epilogue" has a pronounced use of the linguistic device of parataxis (as opposed to hypotaxis), emblematized by a line that both begins and ends with "and": "And the malice of death. For the wicked card is dealt, and" (217). In place of a hypotactic subordination and hierarchization of language, enforced by a complex syntax, Auden's poem works by accretion. Words from very disparate linguistic worlds can abut ("city" and "byre" in the first line is an obvious example). Instead of driving forward uninterruptedly, the poem often hesitates (as in the repetition of "us" at the start of three lines in a row in stanza 2).

Cunningly, Auden also uses grammar to suggest changes of mind in midstream. Thus, "Here is the cosmopolitan cooking" in line 3 hints, by its use of a singular noun and verb form, that a sentence is about to come to an end. But the next line, as if to indicate that Auden's speaker has suddenly decided to add further examples of the heterogeneous dreck in the modern world, inserts two more nouns—"And the light alloys and the glass"—thus rendering the singular form of the verb earlier in the sentence, strictly speaking, ungrammatical, while making the passage sound more plausibly like someone actually talking. These stylistic touches suggest to the reader that separate fragments cannot simply cohere into an organic, unified whole. This artfully patched-together awkwardness signals an inability to control the poetic world fully: the staging of a crisis in the language of Auden's poetry is mirroring a crisis in the wider world.

In "Prologue" from 1932, the magnificent thirteen-line-long concluding sentence sounds a note of expansive, controlling verbal confidence and mastery. And indeed, through most of the book that Auden was now collating, his craft skill in accomplishing such things as matching his sentences with the shapes of traditional stanza forms is remarkable. A regular pulsing beat is set up by the exact coincidence, time after time, of sentence with stanza. But an interesting faltering rhythm enters the book in the penultimate poem, "August for the people," where in the final stanza Auden suddenly contracts the length of his sentences so that there is now no presumptive fit between the poem's stanza form and its assertions:

> I smoke into the night, and watch reflections
> Stretch in the harbour. In the houses
> The little pianos are closed, and a clock strikes.[62]

Two sentences in three lines, one of them stopping, like a broken-down car, in the middle of a formally weak line, where the "in the" prepositional formula, repeated twice ("in the harbour. In the houses") in immediate proximity, sounds a bit like an expiring stutter.

"Epilogue," placed immediately after this poem in the volume that Auden put together in Sintra, takes this formal fracturing much further. The last poem's final stanza has a volley of minuscule sentences (one is only one word long). And, even when a sentence is longer, it seems to break too soon or too late to correspond to the "natural" dimensions of line and stanza.

> The planets rush towards Lyra in the lion's charge. Can
> Hate so securely bind? Are They dead here? Yes.
> And the wish to wound has the power. And tomorrow
> Comes. It's a world. It's a way. (217)

Auden squeezes eight sentences into four lines (including three in the last line and a half), with two being weakly tied to the next by the flabby, accretive sinew of repeated paratactic "ands." The closing note of his great book about England reveals a deep skepticism about the myths that his own poems have done so much to reinvigorate. It as if Auden were now finding formal patterns to dramatize the feeling of ideological certainties falling apart.

"Prologue" is replete with British place-names—Lancashire, Glamorgan, Dumbarton, Rowley, Chester, Moel Fammau—all of which serve to stabilize and locate the reader in relation to a specific set of knowable places on the map. However, in "Epilogue," the naming is not of places—there are no place-names here apart from that of the Soviet city of Gorki (now Nizhny Novgorod). Instead, there are generic or indefinite settings (the city, "the north," the "hot south") and lists of (for the English) foreign people. In "Epilogue," Auden writes an internationalized poem about an internationalized culture of "light alloys," of "cosmopolitan cooking," and foreign figures. (This is the first time he used the word "cosmopolitan" in his poetry, and then he used it again shortly afterward in July 1936 in another poem written outside England.[63])

Despairing, "Epilogue" looks around for healers. With a single exception, all the examples of people whom Auden names are not English: individuals such as Nansen, Schweitzer, Freud, Kafka, and Proust. Half of Auden's healers and redeemers in the poem are German-speaking, and no other nation or linguistic group contributes more than one sage each to the list. The sole English name on the list is that of D. H. Lawrence, whose works were banned and censored in his homeland and who had been driven into exile by his hatred of the country's amoral atmosphere. Lawrence fits in this international company because he was expatriated from England, a person who abandoned entirely what he saw as the constrictions of the nation's culture.

The note of meaningful foreignness in the list of names does not end there. The inclusion of Nansen is significant for Auden's approach to a (for him) new, international poetic language. Fridtjof Nansen had great achievements as an explorer of the Arctic and as a diplomat, but his most important claim to be one who, as Auden's poem puts it, has "unlearnt our hatred" was his role after the First World War as the League of Nations High Commissioner for Refugees. During that time, he was responsible for the creation of the "Nansen passport," first issued in 1922, which gave a stateless but internationally recognized passport to refugees. It is fitting that Nansen, as a protector of refugees, of the denationalized, and of exiles, should become a guardian figure watching over the development of Auden's new, stateless poetic style.[64] The last words in the poem developing this style to its fullest, the last words in Auden's book, are: "It's a way." It *is* a "way" of living, a "way" of writing. But, in reading or hearing the words, the reader also understands that, like the refugees Nansen worked for, the poem and Auden are "away."

Auden left Sintra in mid-April 1936 and sailed home with a typescript of *The Ascent of F6* and a tentative ordering of the poems in his new collection. Two things remained incomplete in relation to the latter: a title and a dedication. After he arrived in England, he seems to have spent some time at his parents' home in the Birmingham suburbs. A stay in Birmingham also meant a chance to visit David Impey in nearby Kings Norton. Then, in early May 1936, Auden took a boat from Harwich to Antwerp in order to see Erika Mann. Part of the motivation was to help with the details of another wedding between a queer English writer and a famous German queer woman, like the one in 1935 that Auden and Mann had performed in Herefordshire. Therese Giehse (the stage name for Therese Gift) was an exiled film star and cabaret performer who had cofounded the Pfeffermühle troupe with Erika Mann and the composer Magnus Henning. Mann and Giehse were lovers. Probably through Birmingham connections, Auden had arranged a ceremony with the author John Hampson (pseudonym of John Simpson). Before Simpson began writing, he had taken a succession of ignominious jobs, had been in Wormwood Scrubs for stealing books, and had spent time in Germany. He had written an unpublishable gay narrative in the late 1920s but enjoyed success in 1931 with a novel called *Saturday Night at the Greyhound,* issued by the Hogarth Press. His publisher dropped him in 1933 when he submitted "Foreign English," a book about a three-way love triangle in Berlin.[65] Having left prison and finding he could not earn enough from his pen, Simpson had taken a live-in job with a wealthy family of grocers in Dorridge, just outside Birmingham, who employed him to look after a young son, Ronald Wilson, suffering from Down syndrome. All in all, Simpson no doubt seemed an eminently suitable husband for Giehse, and he had generously agreed to the proposal.

Mann and Giehse arrived in England about a week before the marriage, and it was probably now that Erika Mann was introduced to Auden's parents as their daughter-in-law. Auden seems to have demanded a lot of his wife during this trip, which does not match expectations if this marriage is understood as being simply something done from expediency. While she was in London in May 1936, Erika Mann reported to her mother that "Mein Mann ist ein Tyrann" (my husband is a tyrant). She went on to explain that it gave Auden "great pleasure to introduce his wife," and she complained that she was expected to travel back the following day to the "ugliest" city of Birmingham, where her in-laws, Dr. and Mrs. Auden, were expecting her.[66] Klaus Mann recorded in his diary that after one trip, his sister returned from England talking about "her Wystan."[67] Another brother, Golo felt that within a few years, the relationship became a "serious friendship with even— believe it or not—a slight erotical touch."[68]

John Simpson, who was tiny, with brown hair and brown eyes, wore only brown clothes, and wrote mainly in brown ink, was mismatched physically with his bride, who was well built, charismatic, and imposing and who often wore masculine styles of clothing. (In the 1920s, when Giehse, who was Jewish, performed at the Munich Kammerspiele, Hitler and other Nazis had been among her biggest fans.) Both bride and groom were carrying large bouquets of flowers when they met at the train station in Solihull, a Birmingham suburb.[69] Dressed in a tweed suit, Giehse was married to the brown-clad Simpson in a registry office on 20 May 1936 (a low-traffic Wednesday morning), with Auden bustling around dealing with logistics, bringing the ring, supervising the guests, and helping Giehse with her English answers to the registrar's questions. Auden wore striped trousers for the occasion and had a carnation in his buttonhole. The writer Walter Allen recalled: "The clerk said to John: 'Shall I send the marriage lines to you at Four Ashes, Dorridge, Mr Simpson?' 'Yes, please,' said John. 'No, no, no,' said Wystan impatiently. 'They are to go to the bride at the Plough and Harrow Hotel, Hagley Road, Birmingham.'"[70] Afterward, the party adjourned to the nearby Barley Mow pub to celebrate. Auden ordered "large brandies all round," eventually explaining: "It's all on Thomas Mann."[71]

There followed a strange episode when Auden insisted on playing the pub's piano, only to be told that the room where it stood had been

FIG. 10 *Early in* The Tempest, *Prospero calls Caliban "thou earth." Here, Auden lies on the grass with a cigarette and a cup of coffee. The photographer is unknown but was perhaps Christopher Isherwood, and the setting is likely to be the Downs School in Herefordshire. The picture was probably taken in the period between 1935 and 1937, but its feeling is timeless—a metaphor for the experience of reading a lyric poem: a poet, stretched out on the ground, makes eye contact with their readers.*

locked. Probably the worse for wear by now, Auden demanded to be let in. When he and his guests were granted entry, they found themselves looking at a billiard table on which there rested an occupied coffin. The scene might have struck Auden as uncannily like a dream in which his subconscious urgently tried to communicate with him. In this possible dream, woozy from spirits, an artist, with what he would later identify as a death wish, wants to play the little piano in a locked room. When he perseveres and the door is opened, in front of him he sees a dead body in a box, like an image of a former poetic self, stretched out on a field of grass-green baize, waiting for its departure to a final resting place.

A meal for the wedding party, which included Erika Mann, the poet Louis MacNeice, and Allen, was followed by a "honeymoon" in the Futurist Cinema on John Bright Street, the first cinema in Birmingham to have shown talkies. Afterward, with this unusual day now almost over, Simpson went off to the station, carrying the gift of a bottle of whisky that his famous bride had presented to him, and took the train back to his job as a suburban caregiver.[72]

It was probably around this time that Auden settled on the question of the dedication for his new book. With collections of poetry, this was never an insignificant matter for him. In 1930, Auden's first book had been dedicated to his closest friend and literary confidant, Isherwood. In 1940, his third collection was dedicated to Chester Kallman, the American man whom by then Auden had started to consider himself married to. For his second collection, in 1936, he chose to dedicate the volume to his wife, Erika, with whom he had just now been spending time while she was in England for the Giehse-Simpson wedding. And he added a beautiful but mystifying prefatory quatrain, built around half rhymes that might be intended to express the complicated, awkwardly fitting / not-fitting nature of the relationship between himself and Mann:

> Since the external disorder, and extravagant lies,
> The baroque frontiers, the surrealist police;
> What can truth treasure, or heart bless,
> But a narrow strictness?[73]

The poem inscribes a contrast between "external disorder" and "lies," associated with the artistic styles of the baroque and of surrealism, which Auden probably intended to be understood as foreign to England. On the other side is a "narrow strictness" that, in the terms created, must stand for England and its artistic virtues. ("Strictness" calls back to mind earlier poems in which Auden, who evidently favored the word, had used variants of it: "strict beauty of locomotive," for example, or

Isherwood's "strict and adult pen."[74]) The German word for "narrow" is
eng. Perhaps, in invoking a "narrow strictness," Auden was playing on
the idea of an Eng-land. In any event, the poem is not an especially
good characterization of the collection that it opens. The poems in the
volume are often extravagant and sometimes baroque, while hardly
ever "narrow." By the end, in "Epilogue," they are open and porous and
(thankfully) the opposite of "strict."

After the book was published, Auden gave a copy to Michael Yates,
who might be imagined as the impossible-to-name-publicly co-dedicatee
with Mann. Auden signed the book "with love," and he wrote out the
second stanza of Hölderlin's poem "Sokrates und Alcibiades" (ca. 1798),
which ends with lines that Auden would refer to and cite many times.
They must have meant a great deal to him. In Hölderlin's poem, a voice
has asked: "Holy Socrates, why always with deference | Do you treat this
young man? Don't you know greater things? | Why so lovingly, raptly, |
As on gods, do you gaze on him?" The stanza that Auden wrote out for
Yates is the reply given by Socrates, the outcast, condemned for corrupting
Athenian youth. It says that: "Hohe Jugend versteht, wer in die Welt
geblikt | Und es neigen die Weisen | Oft am Ende zu Schönem sich"
("Wide experience may well turn to what's best in youth, | And the wise
in the end will | Often bow to the beautiful."[75]) Like someone balancing
worlds, Auden's quatrain of public dedication to the German Mann
was in English; his matching private inscription of a quatrain of loving
tribute for the English Yates was in German.

There remained for Auden's new book only the question of a title. It
evidently gave him some trouble, and when he handed in his typescript
to Faber and Faber, probably at the start of June 1936, the title page
read simply, "Thirty-One Poems."[76] (It perhaps did not help that, even
excluding the dedicatory quatrain to Mann, there are thirty-two poems
in the book.) Shortly afterward, someone, probably in house at the
publisher but following Auden's instructions, crossed out the first title
and wrote in, "*Poems. 1936.*" And on the title page of the same typescript, someone else scribbled "*?Title.*"

T. S. Eliot wrote to Auden on 18 June 1936, saying that the Faber
sales manager "takes grave exception to the title Poems 1936. . . . Will
you put your mind to work and let me have suggestions as soon as you
can, because the catalogue is in press?"[77] Auden had departed on a trip

to Iceland by this time, and Eliot's letter took a while to reach him; but he replied on a postcard postmarked 7 July 1936: "The titles I can think of are '*It's a Way*' or '*The Island*' but if you can think of a better please do."[78]

As things turned out, Faber and Faber ignored Auden's wishes, had some crossed wires in their office, or (Auden had given Eliot an invitation to do this) decided they could come up with something better. They issued the book under the title *Look, Stranger!* (adapting from the first words of the poem "Look, stranger," with the crude addition of an exclamation mark) in October 1936. Auden was very disappointed. The same month that the English version appeared, he wrote to his publishers in New York and asked them to call the American edition *On This Island* (another adaptation, with a changed preposition, of some of the first words of the same poem), which in February 1937, they did.[79]

The uncertainty about what to call the book points to a question about the collection's overarching meaning both in Auden's mind and in the minds of its first readers, his publishers. There is no better indication of the book's depth than that it resisted the simple generic label of "Poems" just as it defied easy summation in the form of an obvious title. But, on looking at this bibliographical history, it seems obvious in retrospect that both Auden's and Faber's main ideas centered around the volume's island imagery, as captured in the eventual titles of the book on both sides of the Atlantic.

If we set aside *It's a Way*, which went nowhere in subsequent discussions, Auden's response when pressed by Eliot comes closest to seeming right: he suggested the collection be called *The Island* because that phrase evokes the whole range of experiences that his early poems explore. *The Island* summons up the ghostly, cut-off strangeness of the abandoned worlds his poems found in the North of England, it alludes to the disturbingly parochial and schizophrenic institutions where Auden set some of his most surreal poetry, it brings to mind the Shakespearean enchantment of an enclave in the rural world where Auden found romance, it registers the confining narrowness of English middle-class life, and it hints at the loneliness of his own existence as a poet, subtly out of place among both his contemporaries and the people he loved. More broadly, of course, *The Island* is simply a central component of England's national iconography: it is a story that altered the world, a fiction on which an immense and violent empire was built.

Poetry was deep feeling-thinking for Auden. And, like many great lyric writers, he used "I" as the pronoun for the first-person plural. Even though he recognized his outsider status, he based his poetry on a faith that his experiences were particular but representative. At the start of this book, I noted that when Auden pictures to himself what a poet does, he produces the idea that by rummaging into the accidents and chaos of their own "living," a poet "fetches | The images out that hurt and connect" with the lives of a readership, with the state of a culture.[80] In Auden's case, one vital part of that "connection" comes from his struggle to understand what an identity is compounded of and to come to terms with the fact that, for better or worse, a modern identity is bound up with a sense—by turns anguished, relieved, consoling, and guilty—of national belonging. There is no good way round the exultations and qualms Auden found in his identity as an English poet.

Perhaps poets are a bit like spies: they have an acceptable cover story that they tell about themselves, but their real work goes on unacknowledged, with a necessary secretiveness, in the dark. Here is Auden's real work, happening underneath his very public theorizing and poetic volubility. All cultures are founded on acts of violence, and Auden's version of English culture is a haunted one, filled with ghosts from long cycles of war, especially, in his case, the living horror of the First World War, but populated too with memories of bitter social struggles like the enormous strikes of industrial workers throughout the interwar years and of communal losses like the entrenched poverty in cities like Birmingham and the injustices visited on men and women whose sexuality did not fit within conventional expectations. Of course, Auden's Anglophilic picture of English culture in the 1930s also includes worlds of natural and cultural beauty, a beauty that can be harsh or mellow. And it includes, as well, the beauty of people like Michael Yates whom Auden loved, a beauty that was bound up with Yates's and others' embodiment of a certain version of innocent, romantic Englishness. In the end, many of the core issues about the nature of Auden's writing come back to questions about what Englishness was—or is.

Auden did have messianic fantasies about his ability to act as the "indifferent redeemer" of English culture, as the poet, albeit with a tendency to "National Socialism," whose surroundings and emotional symbols were "national emblems." He believed he could make the "national call" and thought of himself as the writer who could perhaps be the "mouthpiece of an epoch."[81] There is a disturbing side to Auden's fluctuating but intense belief in his poetry's capacity to represent, diagnose, and rectify. But his work went deeper into a collective English psyche than even he was probably aware of. Auden's ambivalences about island life dramatize profound aspects of English history. To understand his broader significance, one final example will suffice. The year 1936, the same year that Auden completed his collection of poems, R. W. Seton-Watson, the great contemporary scholar of British foreign policy, was finishing a book as well. In it, Seton-Watson wrote: "Perhaps the real secret of foreign misunderstanding is the hesitation which has time after time asserted itself and led to Britain's temporary withdrawal [from European engagement], thereby deranging every balance and every calculation—a hesitation probably due to the vague feeling that Britain is of Europe, and yet not of it. The desire for isolation, the knowledge that it is impossible—these are the two poles between which the needle of the British compass continues to waver."[82] There could be no clearer or stronger historical illustration of that compass needle—still wavering today—than Auden's poetry.

Part of what makes the story of Auden's poetry in the first half of the 1930s sobering and thought-provoking is that the myths about England that he summoned in poems full of unforgettable literary grandiloquence, such as "Prologue," myths about English identity, English history, English sociability, seem so enduring but somehow also so fragile. The arc traced in his 1936 collection is long and in so many ways rich, but it bends toward emptiness—as if, after hundreds of years of lyrical rhetoric, Auden's end point in "Epilogue" is that there was something exhausted and terminal about the myths underwriting English traditions and values. If Auden deserves the title of a prophet, as perhaps he sometimes hoped he did, then this was a large part of what his prophecy said.

"Genius," as Stephen Spender once remarked, was a carefully hoarded, semisacred word in cultural circles in the 1930s. The term held together two important concepts. The first was the familiar Romantic meaning, referring to an individual of exalted artistic or intellectual talent. But "genius" also invoked the older sense, associated with a collectivity, of, in the *OED*'s definition, "a person or thing fit to be taken as an embodied type" of an abstract idea. ("Genius" comes from *genus,* meaning "type.") This second meaning of genius still survives in the formulation "genius loci" ("the spirit of the place"). In 1937, the year after Auden's collection of poetry, now titled *Look, Stranger!,* was published in Britain, three important figures of varying political persuasions all referred to Auden using the word "genius," seeing in him the embodiment of "the natural national form of expression"—a writer of singular talent who was also representative of something much larger than himself.

John Masefield, the poet laureate, told I. A. Richards that he thought Auden was "a man of genius." In a special November 1937 "Double Number" of *New Verse* entirely given over to celebrations of Auden's work, the poet Edwin Muir wrote that "such direct control of language and boldness of imagination are given only to poets of genius." And at Christmas 1937, the economist and arts patron John Maynard Keynes, albeit offended by Auden's standards of personal hygiene, told Virginia Woolf that Auden was "very dirty but a genius."[83] It was in line with these estimations that, in the same year, Wyndham Lewis only semi-ironically pinpointed Auden's sudden centrality in English culture when he called Auden a "national institution."[84] In 1925, Auden had chosen for himself, and begun acting out, the role of the demi-devil Caliban. One could imagine that now, in 1937, Auden might have recognized that he was being turned into a poetic Ariel and was even in danger, a few years down the road, of becoming something like Prospero, an old master.

Writing in the *Criterion* in October 1937, T. S. Eliot said he believed a poet had to be "representative of a particular people" and an art had to "represent a particular civilisation."[85] It was as if Auden, as much as Eliot, had now achieved that status, as if Lewis's perception was correct: he, like Eliot, was indeed a "national institution." This status was underlined by a ceremony that took place on 23 November 1937. In late February 1937, a committee consisting of ultra-establishment poetic mandarins, Masefield, I. A. Richards, Gilbert Murray, Walter de la Mare, and Laurence Binyon (author of "For the Fallen," one of the Great War's most famous poems), had decided to award Auden the King's Gold Medal for Poetry for his "Island" book, *Look, Stranger!* Now, in November, in a break with precedent, the new monarch, George VI, decided to present the medal to Auden personally. (The poet had to borrow a top hat and a set of tails from his friend, the critic Cyril Connolly, for his visit to the palace.)

In 1916, Masefield had published a whole book seeking to justify the debacle of the Gallipoli campaign that Auden's father had served in and barely survived. And, on the basis of that book's success, Masefield had then been officially commissioned to try to find a purpose in the Battle of the Somme. He was frustrated by the army bureaucracy that stymied his efforts to gain access to official documents, but he still wrote a volume called *The Old Front Line* about the landscape and geography of the battlefield. Masefield wanted to believe that nature would cleanse the wounds of modern, industrialized warfare and that the lethal "paths to glory" would soon fade from sight just as the war's trauma would soon ease in the mind. "When the trenches are filled in," he wrote in the book, which was published in 1917,

> and the plough has gone over them, the ground will not long keep the look of war. One summer with its flowers will cover most of the ruin that man can make, and then these places, from which the driving back of the enemy began, will be hard indeed to trace, even with maps. It is said that even now in some places the wire has been removed, the explosive salved, the trenches filled, and the ground ploughed with tractors. In a few years' time, when this war is a romance in memory, the soldier looking for his battlefield will find his marks gone. Centre Way, Peel Trench, Munster Alley, and these other paths to glory will be deep under the corn, and gleaners will sing at Dead Mule Corner.[86]

So it was that, in 1937, a man who believed that the earth's battle scars would vanish led a man whose poetry saw ghost trenches running through the English landscape into a room in Buckingham Palace. Auden told the *News Chronicle* immediately afterward: "The whole ceremony took only three minutes and there were only three people present. The Poet Laureate presented me to the King, and the King presented me with the medal."[87]

A month or so later, Auden traveled to Wesco in the Lake District to spend the holiday at his family's home there. While Auden was in the North, the poet and editor Geoffrey Grigson observed that around Christmas in London, an anonymously submitted object was delivered to the *Surrealist Objects and Poems* exhibition on view at the London

Gallery in the West End. The object was "a glass witch ball" (*OED:* a "hollow ball of . . . glass, formerly displayed in a house as a charm against witchcraft and now for decorative purposes). "Pointed, smart moustaches of various colours" were glued to the ball, and it was topped by a paper frill "encircling a trotter which held a cigarette between its nails." It was never known who sent in the object, but it must have been someone who hated what Auden was becoming. A newspaper cutting attached to the witch ball read: "Auden Receives Royal Medal."[88]

"Let me bring thee where crabs grow, | And I with my long nails will dig thee pig-nuts," Caliban proposes to Stephano and Trinculo as he looks for new masters.[89] Was Auden now looking for a new master? That Christmas in 1937—the Christmas of the Gold Medal, the witch ball, and the Lake District holiday he spent with his parents—would be the last that Auden, now thirty years old, would spend in England for the next thirty-five years.[90] By 1939, by way of wars witnessed in Spain and China and with intervals of intense poetic production at various cities on the margins of Europe, Auden would be in New York. The later Auden's poetry would have many other phases and valences, but it would never return to the hauntingly insular English poetry that he wrote until the middle of the 1930s.

In Shakespeare's play, Caliban stays on the island, but Prospero leaves it. Prospero sails away. In terms of the values and expectations of Shakespearean philosophical comedy, that is the conventional, order-restoring thing that a character like Prospero would do: he returns to civilization, to his home in Milan. Auden sailed away from his island, but by contrast, the journey was not a homecoming but a departure for elsewhere. Not knowing exactly where he was going and not reaching his destination in a single voyage, he too left. But Auden's departure settled nothing. Instead, it opened up a new poetic space. And Auden left for the opposite reason to Prospero. He left in another "protest against the honour system," Robert Medley's words about the regime enforced at Gresham's that Auden had railed against in the role of Caliban. A "protest against the honour system" was also a phrase applicable now to the patronage mechanisms operative in ceremonies like the conferring of the King's Gold Medal.[91] Auden left the island precisely to continue being a Caliban within English culture, a figure whose actions provoked, and provoke, outrage, bafflement, fascination, censoriousness, admiration, dismissal, and even calls for retribution.

The Tempest ends with an "Epilogue" spoken by the actor who is cast as Prospero. On behalf of the writer who made the play that Prospero finds himself in, he asks the audience: "As you from crimes would pardoned be, | Let your indulgence set me free."[92] (As the actor says this, we understand that Prospero all along has been as much a captive in his role as Caliban.) These words gently pleading for forgiveness and understanding resonate in many contexts. But they seem especially relevant here to Auden's copious and exquisite lyrics, so freighted with moral and political ambiguities, and at the same time so virtuosic, frank, and beautiful. Auden's life and work are an amalgam of the greatest artistic gifts, of privilege, courage, wrong turns, brilliant choices, vulnerability, and suffering. Work and life together raise many difficult questions about the tangled complexities and contradictions of the culture that formed Auden and many of his readers. But let our indulgence set him free.

From 1936 onward, swaying "forward on the dangerous flood | Of history," Auden was to exist and to write away from the place that he had once aspired to remake imaginatively as a different, better, more Edenic version of England.[93] "Turning" is an old term for writing with skill as well as art. In his memorial verses for Shakespeare, Ben Jonson praises the playwright's poetry for lines that are "well-turnéd."[94] Auden too was a master of the craft, endlessly capable of making well-turned lines. But in his case, "well-turning" has a further resonance. Auden's turning well from the "small field" of England, as it was in the middle of the 1930s, has a parabolic meaning. It does not seem to have been a fully worked out, programmatic decision but something more like an intuition or an instinctive reaction. Nonetheless, his turn away was a gesture freighted with implications about poetry's historical connections with representativeness and nationality, and with perceptions, at the beginning of the end of Empire, about the meaning and limits of Englishness as an identity. By turning elsewhere—to continental Europe, then briefly to China, and finally to the United States—Auden was suggesting something profound and elegiac about what lay behind him, about the exhaustion of the old poetic seams in this island's mine. Leaving was a form of commitment, one that completed an episode in his artistic life. With wandering steps, Auden slowly took his solitary way toward what would be for him, as a person and as a poet, the new world.

EXPLANATION OF AUDEN'S
TEXTS AND EDITIONS

If you go into a library or a bookshop or, better yet, into a poetry lover's home, you might see on the shelves one or more volumes of Auden's writing. If the collection is substantial enough, these volumes may have lots of different jacket colors and sizes, while the styles of the typography will vary by decade and place of production. Hardcover and paperback editions of the same book might look quite dissimilar. What are essentially the same volumes might have been published in different editions, and occasionally with different titles, on either side of the Atlantic. To give you a feeling for how big such a collection, if it were truly comprehensive, would be, I can note that (by my count) from October 1930 through until Auden's death in September 1973, he published twenty-two individual volumes, pamphlets, collections, and selections of his poetry in the United Kingdom with Faber and Faber alone, as well as four plays, one translation, two travel books, and six volumes of prose. *Thank You, Fog,* a collection of new poems that he had been working on at the time he died, was published posthumously in 1974. And those are just the British editions of Auden's own books, without regard to the anthologies he edited or contributed to.

This multiplicity is complicated still further by the fact that, in addition to being a hugely prolific author, Auden (like Wordsworth, W. B. Yeats, and Marianne Moore) was a poet who, in spite of manifesting a strong evolutionary urge as a writer, was never able to let go of his old work. Prey to a habit that formed in the mid-1930s but that, like many habits, grew stronger over time, Auden revised (by cutting, extending, retitling, rewording, cannibalizing, and repunctuating) his poems throughout his career. This often happened several times to the same book, and sometimes to the same poem, and when he was doing this,

Auden had varying goals, depending on his literary preoccupations at the point when he was revising. Sometimes he reused poems in different contexts, occasionally to give them quite different meanings. In a few famous cases he cut entire poems, though even this ultimate-seeming step could be a subtly ambiguous process. For example, in the early 1960s, at the same time as he was contemplating removing *Spain* and "September 1, 1939" from a future "Collected Poems," he allowed both poems to remain in print outside his official canon by granting the editor Robin Skelton permission to use them in a popular Penguin anthology, *Poetry of the Thirties* (1964).[1] In other words, Auden got rid of the poems but made sure they were kept around. In *Collected Shorter Poems: 1927–1957* (1966), the volume in which he cut *Spain* and "September 1, 1939" from his own works, he also made alterations to wording and punctuation in virtually every one of the hundreds of poems he did reprint.[2] In sum, Auden's literary prodigality, combined with his anxious unwillingness to leave his poems in the state in which they had first appeared, created a situation of great complexity and some confusion for his readers.

Edward Mendelson, Auden's literary executor and his editor, created an initial state of order by issuing, first, an edition of *Collected Poems* in 1976, largely in a form that he and Auden had planned together before Auden's death. This book contains "all the poems that W. H. Auden wished to preserve, in a text that honors his finals intentions," Mendelson wrote in his preface.[3] (It formed the basis for corrected and reset second and third editions with the same title, issued in 1991 and 2007.)

However, Mendelson recognized that Auden had not brought a good number of his longtime readers with him in his "final intentions" and that many did not assent to Auden's harsh decisions about some of his early poems. Thus, in 1977, to stand alongside the *Collected Poems*, Mendelson tactfully issued an edited volume he called *The English Auden: Poems, Essays and Dramatic Writings: 1927–1939*, which printed the poems from the earlier part of Auden's career almost always in the form in which Auden had first published them. With these two books, Mendelson recognized both the poet's wishes and the sometimes conflicting wishes of many of the poet's readers. In 1979, he added another important volume, *Selected Poems*, that was not merely a culling of masterpieces from his two earlier editions. In it, for example, he also included one of Auden's greatest works (though Auden later called it "trash"), the poem "Spain," in the form in which Auden had first published it with Faber and Faber as a pamphlet in 1937.[4]

Two other factors deserve mention in any consideration of the complexity of Auden's canon; both contributed to a massive proliferation in the number of places where one could read an Auden poem. The first factor concerns anthologies. A previously published Auden poem was reprinted in an anthology for the first time when "Portrait" appeared in a book called *The Best Poems of 1926* at a point when Auden was just nineteen.[5] In the decades that followed, his poetry has been included in countless anthologies and textbooks, a phenomenon that accelerated after the Second World War, when the higher-education boom in the United States led to a great demand for anthologies that could be used in college courses.

The second factor leading to widespread dissemination of Auden's poetry is more recent. It is one that was not even a thought when Mendelson's editions of the *Collected Poems, The English Auden,* and *Selected Poetry* were first published, but it has since enormously multiplied the ways of encountering Auden's poetry. That factor is the internet. On social media platforms, the web has led to an explosion of fan postings of images and transcriptions of Auden poems, some of the latter like the letters that Auden describes in "Night Mail," his poem about the delivery of overnight mail: the "typed and the printed and the spelt all wrong."[6]

In the face of this overwhelming profusion, a book like this one needs a single, consistent protocol for citations and references. Fortunately, there is now an easy choice. Edward Mendelson's further editorial work on Auden's writing has been consolidated into the (to date) ten volumes of the *Complete Works of W. H. Auden,* including his plays, film scripts, libretti, travel books, essays, poems, and sundry other material. These volumes were published between 1988 and 2022. The edition as a whole (to pick up Mendelson's prefatory comment from the first volume of *Poems*) contains all the works that Auden "published or submitted for publication," printed "in their original form, with only minor corrections that he marked in friends' copies at the time," while also giving descriptions of later revisions in the voluminous notes provided at the back of each volume.[7]

The *Complete Works* has transformed knowledge of Auden's achievement. Not only has it made readily available in a readable format a mass of material originally published in little poetry magazines, now-out-of-print anthologies, obscure theological journals, and the like; it has also established reliable, corrected texts of those works. In addition, Mendelson has distilled a lifetime's scholarship on Auden's writing into sets of detailed notes. Whenever a poem or other Auden text is included in Mendelson's edition of the *Complete Works,* I have cited here from the version given there.

If a poem is not included in the *Complete Works,* as is the case, for example, with the copious juvenilia that Auden wrote but never submitted for professional publication, then I have used the most reliable source available. With respect to Auden's earliest poems, that is Katherine Bucknell's edition of *Juvenilia: Poems: 1922–1928* (revised edition, 2003).

One small complication remains to be noted. In a few cases, the same poems or other materials are included more than once in the *Complete Works* in different volumes. This duplication usually happens because Auden printed a poem in a book that included substantial amounts of other content by him as well, and he later extracted the poem alone to use in one of his poetry collections. For example, the poem "Night Mail," quoted earlier, was first used for the soundtrack of a documentary film Auden worked on with the same title: *Night Mail* (1936). It was then submitted to (and withdrawn from) a magazine as a freestanding poem, issued as a contemporaneous broadside, and eventually collected in a volume of poetry by Auden only thirty years later in *Collected Shorter Poems: 1927–1957* (1966). "Night Mail" is thus included both in the volume of the *Complete Works* that prints Auden's work for the theater and cinema along with other dramatic writings (abbreviated here as *Plays*) and in the first of the two volumes of Auden's poems (abbreviated here as *Poems1*).

To cite one more instance of this phenomenon: the inclusion of the poem "Letter to Lord Byron" in the travel miscellany that Auden and Louis MacNeice published as *Letters from Iceland* (1937) and that Auden then printed as a separate poem in his *Collected Longer Poems* (1968) prompted Mendelson's sensible decision to include the poem both in the volume of Auden's travel books (abbreviated here as *Prose1*) and in the first volume dedicated to his poems (*Poems1*). In this and in a very few other similar cases, I have primarily cited the texts of these Auden poems in the edited volume that puts them in their original published context. Thus, with "Night Mail," my main reference is to *Plays*, but for convenience I also give a reference to *Poems1* in square brackets. Similarly, with "Letter to Lord Byron," I give the main reference to *Prose1*, but I also include the corresponding reference to *Poems1* in square brackets. My hope is that this system will be useful for readers who prefer to focus their attention on a single volume of writing by Auden.

ABBREVIATIONS

BOOKS BY AUDEN

J
Juvenilia: Poems 1922–1928, ed. Katherine Bucknell, rev. ed. (1994; Princeton: Princeton UP, 2003)

Libretti
[With Chester Kallman] *Libretti and Other Dramatic Writings by W. H. Auden: 1939–1973,* ed. Edward Mendelson (Princeton: Princeton UP, 1993)

Plays
[With Christopher Isherwood] *Plays and Other Dramatic Writings by W. H. Auden: 1928–1938,* ed. Edward Mendelson (Princeton: Princeton UP / London: Faber and Faber, 1988 / 1989)

Poems1
Poems, vol. 1: *1927–1939,* ed. Edward Mendelson (Princeton: Princeton UP, 2022)

Poems2
Poems, vol. 2: *1940–1973,* ed. Edward Mendelson (Princeton: Princeton UP, 2022)

Prose1
[With Louis MacNeice and Christopher Isherwood] *Prose and Travel Books in Prose and Verse,* vol. 1: *1926–1938,* ed. Edward Mendelson (Princeton: Princeton UP / London: Faber and Faber, 1996)

Prose2
Prose, vol. 2: *1939–1948,* ed. Edward Mendelson (Princeton: Princeton UP / London: Faber and Faber, 2002)

Prose3
Prose, vol. 3: *1949–1955,* ed. Edward Mendelson (Princeton: Princeton UP / London: Faber and Faber, 2008)

Prose4
Prose, vol. 4: *1956–1962,* ed. Edward Mendelson (Princeton: Princeton UP, 2010)

Prose5
Prose, vol. 5: *1963–1968,* ed. Edward Mendelson (Princeton: Princeton UP, 2015)

Prose6
Prose, vol. 6: *1969–1973,* ed. Edward Mendelson (Princeton: Princeton UP, 2015)

BOOKS AND ESSAYS BY OTHERS, AND PERIODICALS

Anderson, *Imagined*	Benedict Anderson, *Imagined Communities: Reflections on the Origin and Spread of Nationalism,* rev. ed. (London: Verso, 1991)
Ansen, *Table-Talk*	Alan Ansen, *The Table-Talk of W. H. Auden,* ed. Nicholas Jenkins (London: Faber and Faber, 1991)
AS1	Katherine Bucknell and Nicholas Jenkins, eds., *W. H. Auden: "The Map of All My Youth"; Early Works, Friends, and Influences,* Auden Studies, vol. 1 (Oxford: Clarendon P, 1990)
AS2	Katherine Bucknell and Nicholas Jenkins, eds., *W. H. Auden: "The Language of Learning and the Language of Love"; Uncollected Writings, New Interpretations,* Auden Studies, vol. 2 (Oxford: Clarendon P, 1994)
AS3	Katherine Bucknell and Nicholas Jenkins, eds., *W. H. Auden: "In Solitude, for Company"; Unpublished Prose and Recent Criticism,* Auden Studies, vol. 3 (Oxford: Clarendon P, 1995)
Auden Bibliography	B. C. Bloomfield and Edward Mendelson, *W. H. Auden: A Bibliography 1924–1969,* 2nd ed. (Charlottesville: UP of Virginia, 1972)
Auden in Context	Tony Sharpe, ed., *W. H. Auden in Context* (Cambridge: Cambridge UP, 2013)
Blunden, *Overtones*	Edmund Blunden, *Overtones of War: Poems of the First World War,* ed. Martin Taylor (London: Duckworth, 1996)
Bourke, *Dismembering*	Joanna Bourke, *Dismembering the Male: Men's Bodies, Britain and the Great War* (London: Reaktion, 1996)
Britten, *LFL*	Benjamin Britten, *Letters from a Life: The Selected Letters and Diaries of Benjamin Britten 1913–1976,* ed. Donald Mitchell, Philip Reed, et al., 2 vols. (London: Faber and Faber, 1991)
Brown, *First Five*	E. J. Brown, *The First Five: The Story of a School* (Colwall: n.p., 1987)
Burrow, *Social*	Trigant Burrow, *The Social Basis of Consciousness: A Study in Organic Psychology Based upon a Synthetic and Societal Concept of the Neuroses* (London: Kegan Paul, Trench, Trubner, 1927)

Carpenter, *Auden*	Humphrey Carpenter, *W. H. Auden: A Biography* (Boston: Houghton Mifflin, 1981)
Collett, *Changing*	Anthony Collett, *The Changing Face of England* (1926; London: Jonathan Cape, 1932)
Cork, *Bitter*	Richard Cork, *A Bitter Truth: Avant-Garde Art and the Great War* (New Haven: Yale UP, 1994)
Crawford, *Eliot*	Robert Crawford, *Eliot after* The Waste Land (New York: Farrar, Straus and Giroux, 2022)
Cunningham, *British*	Valentine Cunningham, *British Writers of the Thirties* (Oxford: Oxford UP, 1988)
Day Lewis, *Buried*	C. Day Lewis, *The Buried Day* (London: Chatto and Windus, 1960)
D-H, *Auden*	Richard Davenport-Hines, *Auden* (New York: Pantheon, 1995)
Eksteins, *Rites*	Modris Eksteins, *Rites of Spring: The Great War and the Birth of the Modern Age* (Boston: Houghton Mifflin, 1989)
Eliot, *Poems*	T. S. Eliot, *The Poems of T. S. Eliot*, vol. 1: *Collected and Uncollected Poems,* ed. Christopher Ricks and Jim McCue (London: Faber and Faber, 2015)
Eliot, *Prose,* vol. 1	T. S. Eliot, *The Complete Prose of T. S. Eliot: The Critical Edition,* vol. 1: *Apprentice Years, 1905–1918,* ed. Jewel Spears Brooker and Ronald Schuchard (Baltimore: Johns Hopkins UP, 2014)
Eliot, *Prose,* vol. 2	T. S. Eliot, *The Complete Prose of T. S. Eliot: The Critical Edition,* vol. 2: *The Perfect Critic, 1919–1926,* ed. Anthony Cuda and Ronald Schuchard (Baltimore: Johns Hopkins UP, 2014)
Eliot, *Prose,* vol. 3	T. S. Eliot, *The Complete Prose of T. S. Eliot: The Critical Edition,* vol. 3: *Literature, Politics, Belief, 1927–1929,* ed. Frances Dickey, Jennifer Formicelli, and Ronald Schuchard (Baltimore: Johns Hopkins UP, 2015)
Eliot, *Prose,* vol. 4	T. S. Eliot, *The Complete Prose of T. S. Eliot: The Critical Edition,* vol. 4: *English Lion, 1930–1933,* ed. Jason Harding and Ronald Schuchard (Baltimore: Johns Hopkins UP, 2015)
Eliot, *Prose,* vol. 5	T. S. Eliot, *The Complete Prose of T. S. Eliot: The Critical Edition,* vol. 5: *Tradition and Orthodoxy, 1934–1939,* ed.

Iman Javadi, Ronald Schuchard, and Jayme Stayer (Baltimore: Johns Hopkins UP, 2017)

Farnan, *Auden* Dorothy J. Farnan, *Auden in Love* (New York: Simon and Schuster, 1984)

Frost, *Poetry* Robert Frost, *The Poetry of Robert Frost: The Collected Poems, Complete and Unabridged,* ed. Edward Connery Lathem (1969; New York: Henry Holt, 1979)

Fuller, *Commentary* John Fuller, *W. H. Auden: A Commentary* (London: Faber and Faber, 1998)

Fussell, *Abroad* Paul Fussell, *Abroad: British Literary Travelling between the Wars* (New York: Oxford UP, 1980)

Fussell, *GW* Paul Fussell, *The Great War and Modern Memory* (New York: Oxford UP, 1975)

Gardiner, *Scatter* Margaret Gardiner, *A Scatter of Memories* (London: Free Association, 1988)

Garth, *Tolkien* John Garth, *Tolkien and the Great War: The Threshold of Middle-earth* (London: HarperCollins, 2003)

G. Auden, "Biological" G. A. Auden, "The Biological Factors in Mental Defect," *Psyche: A Quarterly Review of Psychology,* n.s., 3.3 (Jan. 1923), 240–256

G. Auden, "Difficult" G. A. Auden, "The Difficult Child," *Journal of the Royal Sanitary Institute,* 50 (Sept. 1929), 157–164

G. Auden, "Endogenous" George A. Auden, "On Endogenous and Exogenous Factors in Character Formation," *Journal of Mental Science,* 72 (Jan. 1926), 1–25

G. Auden, "Unusual" G. A. Auden, "An Unusual Form of Suicide," *Journal of Mental Science,* 73 (July 1927), 428–430

Gordon, *Voluptuous* Mel Gordon, *Voluptuous Panic: The Erotic World of Weimar Berlin* (Venice, CA: Feral House, 2000)

Graves, *Good-Bye* Robert Graves, *Good-Bye to All That: An Autobiography* (1929), ed. Richard Perceval Graves (Providence: Berghahn, 1995)

Graves, *Unreason* Robert Graves, *Poetic Unreason and Other Studies* (London: Cecil Palmer, 1925)

Haffenden, *Heritage* John Haffenden, ed., *W. H. Auden: The Critical Heritage* (London: Routledge and Kegan Paul, 1983)

Hansen, *Unknown*	Neil Hansen, *Unknown Soldiers: The Story of the Missing of the First World War* (New York: Knopf, 2006)
Hardy, *Works*	*The Complete Poetical Works of Thomas Hardy,* ed. Samuel Hynes, 5 vols. (Oxford: Clarendon P, 1982–1995)
Heard, *Ascent*	Gerald Heard, *The Ascent of Humanity: An Essay on the Evolution of Civilization from Group Consciousness through Individuality to Super-Consciousness* (London: Jonathan Cape, 1929)
Heard, *Social*	Gerald Heard, *Social Substance of Religion: An Essay on the Evolution of Religion* (London: George Allen and Unwin, 1931)
Howkins, "Discovery"	Alun Howkins, "The Discovery of Rural England," in Robert Colls and Philip Dodd, eds., *Englishness: Politics and Culture 1880–1920* (Beckenham: Croom Helm, 1986), 62–88
Hynes, *Auden Gen*	Samuel Hynes, *The Auden Generation: Literature and Politics in England in the 1930s* (New York: Viking, 1976)
Isherwood, *C&HK*	Christopher Isherwood, *Christopher and His Kind* (New York: Farrar, Straus and Giroux, 1976)
Isherwood, *Lions*	Christopher Isherwood, *Lions and Shadows: An Education in the Twenties* (London: Hogarth P, 1938)
Jünger, *Storm*	Ernst Jünger, *The Storm of Steel: From the Diary of a German Storm-Troop Officer on the Western Front,* trans. Basil Creighton (Garden City: Doubleday, Doran, 1929)
Leed, *No Man's*	Eric J. Leed, *No Man's Land: Combat and Identity in World War 1* (Cambridge: Cambridge UP, 1979)
Lewis, *Hitler*	Wyndham Lewis, *Hitler* (London: Chatto and Windus, 1931)
Lewis, *Rehabilitations*	C. S. Lewis, *Rehabilitations and Other Essays* (London: Oxford UP, 1939)
Medley, *Drawn*	Robert Medley, *Drawn from the Life: A Memoir* (London: Faber and Faber, 1983)
Mendelson, *EALA*	Edward Mendelson, *Early Auden, Later Auden: A Critical Biography* (Princeton: Princeton UP, 2017)
Milton, *PL*	John Milton, *Paradise Lost* (1674), ed. David Scott Kastan (Indianapolis: Hackett, 2005)

Osborne, *Auden*   Charles Osborne, *W. H. Auden: The Life of a Poet* (London: Eyre Methuen, 1979)

Owen, *Poems*   Wilfred Owen, *The Poems of Wilfred Owen,* ed. Jon Stallworthy (New York: Norton, 1986)

Parker, *Isherwood*   Peter Parker, *Isherwood: A Life* (London: Picador, 2004)

Parker, *Old Lie*   Peter Parker, *The Old Lie: The Great War and the Public-School Ethos* (London: Constable, 1987)

Pugh, *Danced*   Martin Pugh, *"We Danced All Night": A Social History of Britain between the Wars* (London: Bodley Head, 2008)

Rewald, *Glitter*   Sabine Rewald et al., *Glitter and Doom: German Portraits from the 1920s* (New York / New Haven: Metropolitan Museum of Art / Yale UP, 2006)

Richards, *Memories*   J. M. Richards, *Memories of an Unjust Fella* (London: Weidenfeld and Nicolson, 1980)

Rivers, *Conflict*   W. H. R. Rivers, *Conflict and Dream* (London: Kegan Paul, Trench, Trubner, 1923)

Rivers, *Instinct*   W. H. R. Rivers, *Instinct and the Unconscious: A Contribution to a Biological Theory of the Psycho-Neuroses* (Cambridge: Cambridge UP, 1920)

Sassoon, *Poems*   Siegfried Sassoon, *Collected Poems: 1908–1956* (London: Faber and Faber, 1961)

SE   Sigmund Freud, *The Standard Edition of the Complete Psychological Works of Sigmund Freud,* 26 vols., trans. and ed. James Strachey et al. (London: Hogarth P, 1953–1974)

Sidnell, *Dances*   Michael J. Sidnell, *Dances of Death: The Group Theatre of London in the Thirties* (London: Faber and Faber, 1984)

Simpson, *Howson*   J. H. Simpson, *Howson of Holt: A Study in School Life* (London: Sidgwick and Jackson, 1925)

Smart, *Heroes*   Sue Smart, *When Heroes Die: A Forgotten Archive Reveals the Last Days of the Schoolfriends Who Died for Britain* (Derby: Breedon, 2001)

Spender, *WwW*   Stephen Spender, *World within World: The Autobiography of Stephen Spender* (1951; New York: Modern Library, 2001)

Steedman, *Poetry*   Carolyn Steedman, *Poetry for Historians: or, W. H. Auden and History* (Manchester: Manchester UP, 2018)

Sussex, *Rise*	Elizabeth Sussex, *The Rise and Fall of British Documentary: The Story of the Film Movement Founded by John Grierson* (Berkeley: U of California P, 1975)
Swann, *Citizen*	J. C. Swann, *The Citizen Soldiers of Buckinghamshire: 1795–1926* (London: Hazell, Watson and Viney, 1930)
Thomas, *Poems*	Edward Thomas, *The Annotated Collected Poems,* ed. Edna Longley (Tarset: Bloodaxe Books, 2008)
Tribute	Stephen Spender, ed., *W. H. Auden: A Tribute* (London: Weidenfeld and Nicolson, 1975)
Weimar Sourcebook	Anton Kaes, Martin Jay, and Edward Dimendberg, eds., *The Weimar Republic Sourcebook* (Berkeley: U of California P, 1994)
WHASN	*W. H. Auden Society Newsletter*
Wiener, *English*	Martin J. Wiener, *English Culture and the Decline of the Industrial Spirit, 1850–1980* (Cambridge: Cambridge UP, 1981)
Winter, *Great War*	J. M. Winter, *The Great War and the British People* (Basingstoke: Macmillan, 1985)
Winter, *Sites*	Jay Winter, *Sites of Memory, Sites of Mourning: The Great War in European Cultural History* (Cambridge: Cambridge UP, 1995)
Wordsworth, *Poems*	William Wordsworth, *The Poems,* ed. John O. Hayden, 2 vols. (New Haven: Yale UP, 1981)
Wordsworth, *Prelude*	William Wordsworth, *The Prelude: 1799, 1805, 1850,* ed. Jonathan Wordsworth, M. H. Abrams, and Stephen Gill (New York: Norton, 1979)
Wright, *Village*	Patrick Wright, *The Village That Died for England: The Strange Story of Tyneham,* rev. ed. (1995; London: Faber and Faber, 2002)
Yeats, *Poems*	W. B. Yeats, *The Poems,* ed. Richard Finneran, rev. ed. (New York: Macmillan, 1990)

LIBRARIES AND ARCHIVES

BL	Department of Manuscripts and Archives, British Library, London
Bodleian	Department of Special Collections and Western Manuscripts, Bodleian Library, Oxford University

Columbia	Rare Books and Manuscripts Room, Butler Library, Columbia University, New York
Dartington	Archives of Dartington Hall Trust, Devon Heritage Centre, Exeter
Huntington	The Huntington Library, San Marino, California
Los Angeles	Library Special Collections, Charles E. Young Research Library, University of California, Los Angeles
NYPL	The Henry W. and Albert A. Berg Collection of English and American Literature, New York Public Library (Astor, Lenox and Tilden Foundations)
San Diego	John Willoughby Layard Papers, MSS 84, Special Collections and Archives, University of California, San Diego Library
Texas	The Harry Ransom Humanities Research Center, University of Texas at Austin

DESCRIPTIONS OF CORRESPONDENCE

ALS	Autograph letter signed
APCS	Autograph postcard signed
TL	Typed letter
TLS	Typed letter signed

NOTES

In the following notes, I give references to all of Auden's works, as well to other sources after a first mention, in shortened form. For full details, consult the Abbreviations list. Much valuable material concerning Auden is now online, but no URLs are included here because their rates of obsolescence and change are so high as to make such printed links generally unreliable. Instead, I include brief but sufficient indications about the website where the information was found. For Auden's family, friends and acquaintances, as well as for lesser-known figures in the literary and other worlds of the time, I provide birth and death dates wherever possible, usually at the first opportune moment.

FRONTMATTER

Epigraph: In the original, with emphasis by Novalis: "Jeder Engländer ist eine *Insel.*" Novalis, *Das Allgemeine Brouillon* [*The General Rough Draft*] (1798–1799), in *Werke, Tagebücher und Briefe Friedrich von Hardenbergs,* vol. 2: *Das philosophisch-theoretische Werk,* ed. Hans-Joachim Mähl (Munich: C. Hanser Verlag, 1978), 707.

PROLOGUE

Epigraph: W. L. George, "The Price of Nationality," *English Review,* 20 (May 1915), 184.

    1. Shakespeare, *The Tempest,* 2.1 (all references to Shakespeare's plays, where needed, are by act and scene).

    2. There is a photograph of a performance of *Love's Labour's Lost* taking place in 1913 in the Gresham's amphitheater (where Auden would act) in Sue Smart, *When Heroes Die: A Forgotten Archive Reveals the Last Days of the Schoolfriends Who Died for Britain* (Derby: Breedon, 2001), 92 (from now on, cited as Smart, *Heroes*). The audience at *The Tempest,* the *Times* reported approvingly, was "seated, as in the ancient amphitheatre, on ground rising gently in tiers, half circling the stage." See "School Speech Days. . . . Open Air Play at Gresham's School," *Times,* 9 July 1925, p. 11. See also J. M. Richards, *Memories of an Unjust*

Fella (London: Weidenfeld and Nicolson, 1980), 35 (from now on, cited as Richards, *Memories*).

3. J. H. Simpson, *Howson of Holt: A Study in School Life* (London: Sidgwick and Jackson, 1925), 22 (from now on, cited as Simpson, *Howson*). Auden mentions the annual Shakespeare play in "The Liberal Fascist [Honour]" (1934), in W. H. Auden, Louis MacNeice, and Christopher Isherwood, *Prose and Travel Books in Prose and Verse*, vol. 1: *1926–1938*, ed. Edward Mendelson (Princeton: Princeton UP / London: Faber and Faber, 1996), 56 (from now on, cited as *Prose1*).

4. See Robert Medley, "Gresham's School, Holt," in Stephen Spender, ed., *W. H. Auden: A Tribute* (London: Weidenfeld and Nicolson, 1975), 41 (from now on, cited as *Tribute*).

5. Shakespeare, *The Tempest*, 5.1; Robert Medley, *Drawn from the Life: A Memoir* (London: Faber and Faber, 1983), 60 (from now on, cited as Medley, *Drawn*). The link between Prospero's servants and Auden's miners is made explicit in his 1926 poem "'Lead's the Best'" about lead mining, discussed in Chapter 3. There, Auden cites, slightly inaccurately, Prospero's line from *The Tempest* (1.2) about Ariel, who "do[es] me business in the veins o' th' Earth." W. H. Auden, *Poems*, vol. 1: *1927–1939*, ed. Edward Mendelson (Princeton: Princeton UP, 2022), 408 (from now on, cited as *Poems1*).

6. Medley, "Gresham's School, Holt," 41. For more on the "Honour system," see Chapter 1 and the Epilogue.

7. Shakespeare, *The Tempest*, 1.2.

8. *Darwin's Finches* (Cambridge: Cambridge UP, 1947) by David Lack (1910–1973) is about the bird specimens from the Galápagos Islands that Darwin made a central part of his meditations on natural selection.

9. Shakespeare, *The Tempest*, "Dramatis Personae," 1.2.

10. For more on this incident, see Chapter 1.

11. Shakespeare, *The Tempest*, 5.1.

12. Simpson, *Howson*, 12–13, 88.

13. *Ibid.*, 22. Howson died of heart disease in Jan. 1919. On Howson's later years, marred by the sadness and guilt of so regularly having to go into Sunday chapel from 1914 to 1918 to discuss the life and character of yet another Old Greshamian who had recently been killed at the front, see Smart, *Heroes*, 163–166.

14. Cockerell (1910–1999), Strachey (1916–1975), Kearley (1904–1989), Nicholson (1904–1948), Shaw (1905–1994), Britten (1913–1976), Maclean (1913–1983). See Chapter 1 for more details.

15. "The Liberal Fascist [Honour]" (1934), *Prose1*, 59.

16. Hannah Arendt, "Remembering Wystan H. Auden . . . ," *New Yorker*, 50.48 (20 Jan. 1975), 39.

17. "Squares and Oblongs" (1947), in W. H. Auden, *Prose*, vol. 2: *1939–1948*, ed. Edward Mendelson (Princeton: Princeton UP / London: Faber and Faber, 2002), 345 (from now on, cited as *Prose2*); and "Address to the Indian

Congress for Cultural Freedom" (1951), in W. H. Auden, *Prose,* vol. 3: *1949–1955,* ed. Edward Mendelson (Princeton: Princeton UP / London: Faber and Faber, 2008), 247 (from now on, cited as *Prose3*); see also "Squares and Oblongs" (1957), in W. H. Auden, *Prose,* vol. 4: *1956–1962,* ed. Edward Mendelson (Princeton: Princeton UP, 2010), 66 (from now on, cited as *Prose4*).

18. "The Composer" (1938), *Poems1,* 339; emphasis added.

19. "On Lyric Poetry and Society" (1957), in Theodor Adorno, *Notes to Literature,* vol. 1, ed. Rolf Tiedemann, trans. Shierry Weber Nicholsen (New York: Columbia UP, 1991), 45.

20. I am remembering a comment by Randall Jarrell: "A good poet is someone who manages, in a lifetime of standing out in thunderstorms, to be struck by lightning five or six times; a dozen or two dozen times and he is great." "Reflections on Wallace Stevens," in Jarrell, *Poetry and the Age,* rev. ed. (1953; Gainesville: UP of Florida, 2001), 148.

21. To take one distinguished example, Edward Mendelson, the most influential of Auden's critics, writes about a mythological contest that takes place in Aristophanes's *The Frogs* between "two kinds of poet," the civic and the vatic (represented by the Greek dramatists Aeschylus and Euripides): "Aeschylus prays to the traditional gods, invokes the ancient tradition of the poet as moral teacher, and condemns the self-centeredness encouraged by his rival." In *The Frogs,* the judge decides in favor of Aeschylus. And, Mendelson writes, "So, in effect, did Auden." Mendelson, *Early Auden, Later Auden: A Critical Biography* (Princeton: Princeton UP, 2017), 5–6 (from now on, cited as Mendelson, *EALA*). Mendelson's book is a one-volume, updated, and slightly expanded version of his earlier studies: *Early Auden* (New York: Viking, 1981) and *Later Auden* (New York: Farrar, Straus and Giroux, 1999).

22. "Wystan Auden," in James Schuyler, *The Morning of the Poem* (New York: Farrar, Straus and Giroux, 1980), 29.

23. For more details on Auden's movements, see Nicholas Jenkins, "The Traveling Auden," *W. H. Auden Society Newsletter,* 24 (July 2004), 7–14 (from now on, this journal is cited as *WHASN*).

24. "Cultural Criticism and Society," in Theodor Adorno, *Prisms,* trans. Samuel Weber and Shierry Weber (Cambridge, MA: MIT P, 1981), 34; "The Cave of Making" (1964), in W. H. Auden, *Poems,* vol. 2: *1940–1973,* ed. Edward Mendelson (Princeton: Princeton UP, 2022), 509 (from now on, cited as *Poems2*).

25. "Address on Henry James" (1946), *Prose2,* 302.

26. See his contribution to [A Symposium on W. H. Auden's "A Change of Air"] (1963), in W. H. Auden, *Prose,* vol. 5: *1963–1968,* ed. Edward Mendelson (Princeton: Princeton UP, 2015), 75 (from now on, cited as *Prose5*). (A title of an Auden prose piece placed within square brackets indicates that this title or heading was chosen by the editor of his *Complete Works* in the absence of a title given by Auden himself.) By "historical," Auden does not necessarily mean something momentous, just something that actually occurred in the shared, social world of material facts and happenings.

27. "Letter to Lord Byron" (1936), *Prose1*, 328 [also *Poems1*, 251]. For discussion of citations like this one with a double reference, see the "Explanation of Auden's Texts and Editions" earlier in this book.

28. Forge's remark comes in an interview with Cathy Courtney, available as a recording for the National Life Stories Collection posted at the British Library's "Sounds" webpage.

29. Marcel Proust, *La Prisonnière* (1923): "Y avait-il dans l'art une réalité plus profonde où notre personnalité veritable trouve une expression que ne lui donnent pas les actions de la vie?" Proust, *The Captive; The Fugitive* (vol. 5 of *In Search of Lost Time*), trans. C. K. Scott Moncrieff, Terence Kilmartin, and D. J. Enright (New York: Modern Library, 2003), 204–205.

30. One recent work that moves in a similar direction is Carolyn Steedman's *Poetry for Historians: or, W. H. Auden and History* (Manchester: Manchester UP, 2018) (from now on, cited as Steedman, *Poetry*).

31. Sigmund Freud, "Negation" (1925), in *The Standard Edition of the Complete Psychological Works of Sigmund Freud*, 26 vols., trans. and ed. James Strachey et al. (London: Hogarth P, 1953–1974), 19:235–236 (from now on, cited as *SE*); emphasis in original.

32. "Smile, Smile, Smile," in Wilfred Owen, *The Poems of Wilfred Owen*, ed. Jon Stallworthy (New York: Norton, 1986), 167 (from now on, cited as Owen, *Poems*).

33. Henry Williamson, *The Patriot's Progress: Being the Vicissitudes of Pte. John Bullock* (London: Geoffrey Bles, 1930), 194.

34. See T. W. Bagshore, "How 'Runners' Got a Living from the Land," *Folklore*, 66.4 (Dec. 1955), 415.

35. W. H. Auden, "Friendship" (1925), in *Juvenilia: Poems 1922–1928*, ed. Katherine Bucknell, rev. ed. (1994; Princeton: Princeton UP, 2003), 97 (from now on cited as *J*).

36. Eric J. Leed, *No Man's Land: Combat and Identity in World War 1* (Cambridge: Cambridge UP, 1979), 195 (from now on, cited as Leed, *No Man's*).

37. "A Saint-Simon of Our Time" (1972), in W. H. Auden, *Prose*, vol. 6: *1969–1973*, ed. Edward Mendelson (Princeton: Princeton UP, 2015), 533 (from now on, cited as *Prose6*). See also, for example, "As It Seemed to Us" (1964), *Prose5*, 144; remarks on the subject to journalists include Don Chapman, "The Poetic Life—Out of a Suitcase," *Oxford Mail*, 1 Nov. 1972, p. 8; and Sharon Griffiths, "Auden: New Yorker in an Oxford Fog," *Radio Times*, 25 Jan. 1973, p. 12. For someone who felt that the First World War was irrelevant to him personally, Auden talked about it in public quite often in later life.

38. Wyndham Lewis, *Blasting and Bombardiering* (London: Eyre and Spottiswoode, 1937), 1.

39. Samuel Hynes, *The Auden Generation: Literature and Politics in England in the 1930s* (London: Bodley Head, 1976), 17 (from now on, cited as Hynes, *Auden Gen*).

40. John Connell (1909–1965), "Writing about Soldiers," *Journal of the Royal United Service Institution,* 110.639 (Aug. 1965), 221.

41. For more on Dr. Auden's war service and its meaning for his youngest son, see Chapter 1.

42. "As It Seemed to Us" (1964), *Prose5,* 141. This is not exactly true—Auden saw his father at least once during the war, but the occasion was a disturbing one for the family. See Chapter 1.

43. "Letter to Lord Byron" (1936), *Prose1,* 332 [also *Poems1,* 254]. On the "seafronts," the family is singing William Whiting's "Eternal Father, Strong to Save" (1861), a hymn often associated with the Royal Navy.

44. Jon Bradshaw, "Holding to Schedule with W. H. Auden," *Esquire,* 73.1 (434) (Jan. 1970), 26–28.

45. "As It Seemed to Us" (1964), *Prose5,* 143; "The Storyteller: Reflections on the Works of Nikolai Leskov" (1936), in Walter Benjamin, *Illuminations,* ed. Hannah Arendt, trans. Harry Zohn (New York: Schocken, 1969), 84. One glimpse of the fact that Auden did know some details about his father's time at Gallipoli (although Auden hardly ever mentioned it directly) comes in *The Orators* (1930–1932). In Ode IV ["Roar Gloucestershire, do yourself proud"], some manuscript drafts of the poem had a line asking, "Where is [T. S.] Eliot?" In the published version, the line reads, "Where is Moxon?" (*Poems1,* 125). Isherwood (1904–1986) explained that Reynard Moxon was a sinister character in the Mortmere fantasy universe that he and Edward Upward had invented. Isherwood, *Lions and Shadows: An Education in the Twenties* (London: Hogarth P, 1938), 104 (from now on, cited as Isherwood, *Lions*). But in *The Orators,* the use of the rare name Moxon was probably a private reference to Capt. H[arold] R[ichard] Moxon (1887–1937), who served in the RAMC with Dr. Auden at Suvla Bay in 1915. Another possible allusion to Dr. Auden's army service comes in the mention of "Captain Edward Gervase Luce" in Norfolk in "The Fronny" (1930), in W. H. Auden and Christopher Isherwood, *Plays and Other Dramatic Writings by W. H. Auden: 1928–1938,* ed. Edward Mendelson (Princeton: Princeton UP / London: Faber and Faber, 1988 / 1989), 479 (from now on, cited as *Plays*). Maj.-Gen. Sir Richard Luce (1867–1952) was the RAMC's assistant director for medical services for the Second Mounted Brigade (Dr. Auden's brigade) in 1914–1915, when Dr. Auden was in camp with his Field Ambulance unit in Norfolk. Luce and Dr. Auden almost certainly met there, and Luce, like Dr. Auden, later served with the RAMC at Gallipoli in 1915.

46. "In Memory of Sigmund Freud" (1939), *Poems1,* 782.

47. "A Household" (1948), *Poems2,* 381.

48. ALS from Christopher Isherwood to Humphrey Carpenter, 23 Sept. 1979, Rare Books and Manuscripts Room, Butler Library, Columbia University, New York (from now on, referred to as Columbia). There was a mass of homophobic innuendo about Auden in reviews and articles published during his lifetime and after. The pioneering academic study that discusses his poetry and

sexuality constructively is Richard R. Bozorth, *Auden's Games of Knowledge: Poetry and the Meanings of Homosexuality* (New York: Columbia UP, 2001).

49. ALS from W. H. Auden to Rosamund Harcourt-Smith, [late Feb. 1940?], private collection. Harcourt-Smith (1900–1987) was an author and society figure. Auden travelled to Germany with her husband, the diplomat and writer Simon Harcourt-Smith (1906–1982), in quest of information about Isherwood's lover Heinz Neddermeyer (1914–1984). For Neddermeyer, see also the Epilogue.

50. Mendelson gives some details of this aborted project in *Prose2*, 506.

51. "A Literary Transference" (1939 or 1940?), *Prose2*, 44; "As It Seemed to Us" (1964), *Prose5*, 141.

52. "New Year Letter" (1940), *Poems2*, 36.

53. "Are the English Europeans?: The Island and the Continent" (1962), *Prose4*, 430.

54. Alan Ansen, *The Table-Talk of W. H. Auden*, ed. Nicholas Jenkins (London: Faber and Faber, 1991) 17 (from now on, cited as Ansen, *Table-Talk*).

55. *Ibid.*, 26.

56. Auden gives two slightly different dates for when this Wagnerian scene happened—either when he was six (around 1913) or when he was eight (around 1915): see a 30 July 1942 ALS to James Stern, printed in "Some Letters from Auden to James Stern," ed. Nicholas Jenkins, in Katherine Bucknell and Nicholas Jenkins, eds., *W. H. Auden: "In Solitude, for Company"; Unpublished Prose and Recent Criticism*, Auden Studies, vol. 3 (Oxford: Clarendon P, 1995), 83 (from now on, cited as *AS3*); and "As It Seemed to Us" (1964), *Prose5*, 141. See also Ansen, *Table-Talk*, 24. Rhyme is a form of nonrational, subterranean connection between two words or names: Auden points out the rhyme of his first name and the name of the hero in the "Liebestod" scene in a clerihew probably written around 1970. See *Poems2*, 631: "*My first name, Wystan, | Rhymes with Tristan*" (emphasis in original).

57. "Are the English Europeans?" (1962), *Prose4*, 431 (see also *Prose4*, 442). Auden tells a version of the same story in "As It Seemed to Us" (1964), *Prose5*, 144–145. The incident probably took place in later 1917 or in 1918, when the British government was urging citizens to eat less bread as a patriotic duty. See also Chapters 3, 5, and the Epilogue.

58. See also Dorothy J. Farnan, *Auden in Love* (New York: Simon and Schuster, 1984), 114 (from now on, cited as Farnan, *Auden*).

59. The first words of German in Auden come in the title "Maria hat geholfen" (1925), *J*, 107; in "Ballad" (written in the winter of 1926–1927), there is a quotation of a public notice in German (*J*, 170). Then Auden seems to allude to the German version of Thomas Mann's *Death in Venice* in "The crowing of the cock," written in Sept. 1927 (*J*, 222–223). Six of Auden's German poems written in Berlin at the end of the 1920s are printed, with translations by David Constantine, in Katherine Bucknell and Nicholas Jenkins, eds., *W. H. Auden:*

"The Map of All My Youth": Early Works, Friends, and Influences, Auden Studies, vol. 1 (Oxford: Clarendon P, 1990), 4–15 (from now on, cited as *AS1*). In 1930, Auden inscribed two copies of his *Poems* (1930) to Isherwood with dedications in German. See Conor Leahy, "Some Copies of *Poems* (1930)," *WHASN,* 41 (Feb. 2023), 17.

Petzold (b. 1891?) proved to be an important figure in Auden's life—Auden stayed in touch during the early 1930s, and then, after a period of distance, he renewed their acquaintance and visited her in Kitzbühel multiple times in the 1950s. It was her daughter, Christa Eders, who found the home Auden bought in Kirchstetten, Austria, in the early autumn of 1957. Auden had just shut up this cottage for the winter when he died in Vienna during the night of 28–29 Sept. 1973. In effect, meeting Petzold in 1925 on his first trip abroad was the first stage of the journey that led to Auden dying in Austria nearly fifty years later in 1973.

60. Chapter 5 describes the appeal of Germany, and of Berlin in particular, for members of Auden's generation. But the myth about the special significance of Berlin for Auden and his friends was founded on the contents of two memoirs by Christopher Isherwood, *Lions and Shadows: An Education in the Twenties* (1938) and *Christopher and His Kind* (1976), as well as by Isherwood's book of stories, *Goodbye to Berlin* (1939). Academic studies include Norman Page, *Auden and Isherwood: The Berlin Years* (New York: St. Martin's P, 1998).

61. Christopher Isherwood, "German Literature in England," *New Republic,* 98.1270 (5 April 1939), 254.

62. Thomas Hardy, "The Pity of It" (1915), in *The Complete Poetical Works of Thomas Hardy,* ed. Samuel Hynes, 5 vols. (Oxford: Clarendon P, 1982–1995), 2:294 (from now on, cited as Hardy, *Works*); "Strange Meeting" (1918), Owen, *Poems,* 125–126.

63. Wyndham Lewis, "Editorial Notes," *The Enemy: A Review of Art and Literature,* 2 (Sept. 1927), xxvii–xxviii; emphasis in original.

64. "Out on the lawn I lie in bed" (1933), *Poems1,* 185.

65. Stanza from the original version of "Now from my window-sill I watch the night" (1932), part 2 of "A Happy New Year," *Poems1,* 146.

66. "Get there if you can and see the land you once were proud to own" (1930), *Poems1,* 45; *The Orators* (1930–1932), *Poems1,* 126, 73; "In the year of my youth when yoyos came in" (1932–1933), *Poems1,* 474; "A Happy New Year" (1932), part 2, *Poems1,* 146.

67. Benedict Anderson, *Imagined Communities: Reflections on the Origin and Spread of Nationalism,* rev. ed. (London: Verso, 1991), 145 (from now on, cited as Anderson, *Imagined*).

68. T. S. Eliot, "The Social Function of Poetry" (1943), in *The Complete Prose of T. S. Eliot: The Critical Edition,* vol. 6: *The War Years, 1940–1946,* ed. David E. Chinitz and Ronald Schuchard (Baltimore: Johns Hopkins UP, 2017), 439. Part of this paragraph is adapted from Nicholas Jenkins, "Auden in America," in Stan Smith, ed., *The Cambridge Companion to W. H. Auden* (Cambridge: Cambridge UP, 2005), 39–40.

69. Cited in Jacqueline Rose, *States of Fantasy* (Oxford: Clarendon P, 1996), 57.

70. David Mellor, "British Art in the 1930s: Some Economic, Political and Cultural Structures," in Frank Gloversmith, ed., *Class, Culture and Social Change: A New View of the 1930s* (Brighton: Harvester, 1980), 186.

71. Isaiah Berlin to John Hilton, [Oct. 1935], in Berlin, *Flourishing: Letters 1928–1946*, ed. Henry Hardy (London: Chatto and Windus, 2004), 138.

72. Foreword (1965) to the 3rd ed. of *The Orators* (1966), *Poems1*, 589; see also Chapter 6.

73. ALS from W. H. Auden to Stephen Spender [late June–early July 1933?], The Henry W. and Albert A. Berg Collection of English and American Literature, New York Public Library (Astor, Lenox and Tilden Foundations) (from now on, referred to as NYPL); see "Eleven Letters from Auden to Stephen Spender," ed. Nicholas Jenkins, *AS1*, 62; "Prologue" ["O love, the interest itself in thoughtless Heaven"] (1932), *Poems1*, 183.

74. Alison Light, *Forever England: Femininity, Literature and Conservatism between the Wars* (London: Routledge, 1991), 8.

75. H. M. Tomlinson, "War Books," *Criterion,* 9.36 (April 1930), 404. Auden read and remembered Tomlinson's striking phrase about the war, reusing it in his 1934 poem that begins "Our hunting fathers," *Poems1*, 186.

76. Bill Schwarz, "The Language of Constitutionalism: Baldwinite Conservatism," in *Formations of Nation and People* (London: Routledge and Kegan Paul, 1984), 2.

77. The phrase "Men of 1914" comes from Wyndham Lewis, *Blasting and Bombardiering* (London: Eyre and Spottiswoode, 1937), 251–252.

78. *Ibid.*, 1. See also Chapter 4.

79. The date of 23 Nov. 1925 is given in Donald C. Gallup, *T. S. Eliot: A Bibliography,* rev. ed. (New York: Harcourt, Brace and World, 1969), 33. However, *The English Catalogue,* one of the main official records of publication dates for books in Britain, lists the book as appearing in Jan. 1926.

80. T. S. Eliot to Ezra Pound, 13 Oct. 1925, in Eliot, *The Letters of T. S. Eliot,* vol. 2: *1923–1925,* ed. Valerie Eliot and Hugh Haughton (London: Faber and Faber, 2009), 758.

81. T. S. Eliot, *The Poems of T. S. Eliot,* vol. 1: *Collected and Uncollected Poems,* ed. Christopher Ricks and Jim McCue (London: Faber and Faber, 2015), 71 (from now on, cited as Eliot, *Poems*).

82. "The Hollow Men," Eliot, *Poems,* 84; emphasis in original.

83. Shakespeare, *The Tempest,* epilogue.

84. T. S. Eliot, "Last Words" (1938), in *The Complete Prose of T. S. Eliot: The Critical Edition,* vol. 5: *Tradition and Orthodoxy, 1934–1939,* ed. Iman Javadi, Ronald Schuchard, and Jayme Stayer (Baltimore: Johns Hopkins UP, 2017), 660 (from now on, cited as Eliot, *Prose,* vol. 5).

85. *Ibid.*, 661.

86. Robert Crawford, *Eliot after* The Waste Land (New York: Farrar, Straus and Giroux, 2022), 100–101 (from now on, cited as Crawford, *Eliot*).

87. T. S. Eliot, preface to *For Lancelot Andrewes: Essays on Style and Order* (1928), in *The Complete Prose of T. S. Eliot: The Critical Edition*, vol. 3: *Literature, Politics, Belief, 1927–1929*, ed. Frances Dickey, Jennifer Formicelli, and Ronald Schuchard (Baltimore: Johns Hopkins UP, 2015), 513 (from now on, cited as Eliot, *Prose*, vol. 3). *For Lancelot Andrewes* was published in Nov. 1928. See Chapter 3, note 83, and Chapter 7, note 97.

88. See Chapter 3.

89. Vera Brittain, *Testament of Youth: An Autobiographical Study of the Years 1900–1925* (1933; London: Penguin 2005), 9.

90. ALS from W. H. Auden to Dorothy Elmhirst, 3 April 1932, Archives of Dartington Hall Trust, Devon Heritage Centre, Exeter (from now on, referred to as Dartington).

91. Leed, *No Man's*, 117.

92. Alfred, Lord Tennyson, "Ode on the Death of the Duke of Wellington" (1852), in *Tennyson: A Selected Edition Incorporating the Trinity College Manuscripts*, ed. Christopher Ricks (Berkeley: U of California P, 1989), 497.

93. As early as 1930 and for the rest of the decade at least, the Foreign Department of the USSR (its spy agency) used "THE ISLAND" as its code name for Great Britain in its overseas messages. See Nigel West and Oleg Tsarev, *The Crown Jewels: The British Secrets at the Heart of the KGB Archives* (London: HarperCollins, 1998), 45. The "Hotel's weak activity against us and Tony's about the absence of Hut's work against us on the Island are suspicious" is an example of a coded Soviet message that Miranda Carter cites in her landmark biography, *Anthony Blunt: His Lives* (New York: Farrar, Straus and Giroux, 2001), 291.

94. Raphael Samuel, *Island Stories: Unravelling Britain*, vol. 2 of *Theatres of Memory*, ed. Alison Light, Sally Alexander, and Gareth Stedman Jones (London: Verso, 1998), 82.

95. The Campaign for the Preservation of Rural England was organized around the publication of the planner and preservationist Patrick Abercrombie's *The Preservation of Rural England: The Control of Development by Means of Rural Planning* (Liverpool: Liverpool UP, 1926), repr. from *Town Planning Review*, May 1926. For a very substantial survey of literary and artistic engagement with a "whole concerted project of national self-discovery" in England in the interwar period, see Alexandra Harris, *Romantic Moderns: English Writers, Artists and the Imagination from Virginia Woolf to John Piper* (New York: Thames and Hudson, 2010), 10.

96. See, for example, Christopher Hussey, *The Fairy Land of England* (London: Country Life, 1924); J. W. Robertson Scott, *England's Green and Pleasant Land* (London: Jonathan Cape, 1925); Anthony Collett, *The Changing*

Face of England (1926; London: Jonathan Cape, 1932). For Auden's fascination with Collett's writing, see Chapters 6–8.

97. H. V. Morton, *In Search of England* (London: Methuen, 1927). See also Harris, *Romantic Moderns,* 207.

98. Alex Potts, "'Constable Country' between the Wars," in Raphael Samuel, ed., *Patriotism: The Making and Unmaking of British National Identity,* vol. 3: *National Fictions* (London: Routledge, 1989), 167.

99. Unsigned review [F. R. Leavis], *Times Literary Supplement,* 22 June 1932, in John Haffenden, ed., *W. H. Auden: The Critical Heritage* (London: Routledge and Kegan Paul, 1983), 100–101 (from now on, cited as Haffenden, *Heritage*).

100. "Musée des Beaux Arts" (1938), *Poems1,* 339.

101. "Prologue" ["O love, the interest itself in thoughtless heaven"] (1932), *Poems1,* 183; "Atlantis" (1941), *Poems2,* 233.

102. "Among School Children" (1926), in W. B. Yeats, *The Poems,* ed. Richard Finneran, rev. ed. (New York: Macmillan, 1990), 216–217 (from now on, cited as Yeats, *Poems*).

103. "The Cave of Nakedness" (1963), *Poems2,* 527.

104. "Lay your sleeping head, my love" (1937), *Poems1,* 336–337; see also *Poems1,* 741. (Auden gave the poem the title "Lullaby" only in the later 1950s.) The person who persuaded Auden not to drop the poem was his longtime American partner, Chester Kallman (1921–1975).

105. "Making, Knowing and Judging" (1956), *Prose4,* 492.

106. "As It Seemed to Us" (1964), *Prose5,* 147; Humphrey Carpenter, *W. H. Auden: A Biography* (Boston: Houghton Mifflin, 1981), 31 (from now on, cited as Carpenter, *Auden*).

107. Edward Mendelson's edition of Auden's *Complete Works* has dramatically transformed understanding of the scope and focus of Auden's writing. The volumes published in the edition up to the time of my writing are W. H. Auden and Christopher Isherwood, *Plays and Other Dramatic Writings by W. H. Auden: 1928–1938* (1988 / 1989); W. H. Auden and Chester Kallman, *Libretti and Other Dramatic Writings by W. H. Auden: 1939–1973* (Princeton: Princeton UP, 1993) (from now on, cited as *Libretti*); W. H. Auden, Louis MacNeice, and Christopher Isherwood, *Prose and Travel Books in Prose and Verse, Prose,* vol. 1: *1926–1938* (1996); *Prose,* vol. 2: *1939–1948* (2002); *Prose,* vol. 3: *1949–1955* (2008); *Prose,* vol. 4: *1956–1962* (2010); *Prose,* vol. 5: *1963–1968* (2015); *Prose,* vol. 6: *1969–1973* (2015); *Poems,* vol. 1: *1927–1939* (2022); and *Poems,* vol. 2: *1940–1973* (2022). All these volumes are edited by Mendelson and published by Princeton UP and (through vol. 3 of Auden's prose) by Faber and Faber. The *Complete Works* is supplemented by volumes in the *W. H. Auden: Critical Editions* series: *Juvenilia: Poems 1922–1928,* ed. Katherine Bucknell, rev. ed. (1994; 2003); *Lectures on Shakespeare,* ed. Arthur Kirsch (2000); *The Sea and the Mirror,* ed. Arthur Kirsch (2003); *The Age of Anxiety: A Baroque Eclogue,* ed. Alan Jacobs (2011); and *For the Time Being:*

A Christmas Oratorio, ed. Alan Jacobs (2013). The *Juvenilia* and *Lectures on Shakespeare* were published by both Princeton UP and Faber and Faber; subsequent volumes in the *Critical Editions* series have been published by Princeton UP only.

The factual bedrock on which all critical writing about Auden's poetry rests is B. C. Bloomfield and Edward Mendelson, *W. H. Auden: A Bibliography 1924–1969*, 2nd ed. (Charlottesville: UP of Virginia, 1972) (from now on, cited as *Auden Bibliography*), supplemented by Mendelson's updates in *Auden Studies*, vols. 1–3. Indispensable too is Haffenden, *Heritage*. There are further bibliographical nuggets (including work by Mendelson) as well as a mass of anecdotal, factual, and essayistic material in the (to date) forty-one numbers of the *W. H. Auden Society Newsletter* (*WHASN*), which the society started publishing in 1988.

Many critical books focused only in part on Auden's work remain extremely useful, including Hynes, *Auden Gen*, as do many studies of the literature of the 1930s and of modern poetry generally that discuss his work in passing. Chief among them are Valentine Cunningham's *British Writers of the Thirties* (Oxford: Oxford UP, 1988) (from now on, cited as Cunningham, *British*); Steve Ellis's *The English Eliot: Design, Language and Landscape in* Four Quartets (London: Routledge, 1991); and Jed Esty's important study, *A Shrinking Island: Modernism and National Culture in England* (Princeton: Princeton UP, 2004).

There are many relatively recent works centered on Auden's poetry. I think in particular of John Fuller, *W. H. Auden: A Commentary* (London: Faber and Faber, 1998) (from now on, cited as Fuller, *Commentary*); and Mendelson, *EALA*. Among other notable studies of Auden's writing published in recent decades are Stan Smith, *W. H. Auden* (Oxford: Basil Blackwell, 1985); Lucy McDiarmid, *Auden's Apologies for Poetry* (Princeton: Princeton UP, 1990); John R. Boly, *Reading Auden: The Returns of Caliban* (Ithaca: Cornell UP, 1991); Michael O'Neill and Gareth Reeves, *Auden, MacNeice, Spender: The Thirties Poetry* (New York: St. Martin's P, 1992); Anthony Hecht, *The Hidden Law: The Poetry of W. H. Auden* (Cambridge, MA: Harvard UP, 1993); Stan Smith, *W. H. Auden* (Plymouth: Northcote House, 1997); Marsha Bryant, *Auden and Documentary in the 1930s* (Charlottesville: UP of Virginia, 1997); Alan Jacobs, *What Became of Wystan: Changes and Continuity in Auden's Poetry* (Fayetteville: U of Arkansas P, 1998); Page, *Auden and Isherwood*; Rainer Emig, *W. H. Auden: Towards a Postmodern Poetics* (Basingstoke: Macmillan, 2000); Bozorth, *Auden's Games of Knowledge*; Peter Firchow, *W. H. Auden: Contexts for Poetry* (Newark: U of Delaware P, 2002); Susannah Young-ah Gottlieb, *Regions of Sorrow: Anxiety and Messianism in Hannah Arendt and W. H. Auden* (Stanford: Stanford UP, 2003); Arthur C. Kirsch, *Auden and Christianity* (New Haven: Yale UP, 2005); Tony Sharpe, *W. H. Auden* (New York: Routledge, 2007); Rachel Wetzsteon, *Influential Ghosts: A Study of W. H. Auden's Sources* (New York: Routledge, 2007); Aidan Wasley, *The Age of*

Auden: Postwar Poetry and the American Scene (Princeton: Princeton UP, 2011); Alexander McCall Smith, *What W. H. Auden Can Do for You* (Princeton: Princeton UP, 2013); Stephen J. Schuler, *The Augustinian Theology of W. H. Auden* (Columbia: U of South Carolina P, 2013); Piotr K. Gwiazda, *James Merrill and W. H. Auden: Homosexuality and Poetic Influence* (London: Palgrave Macmillan, 2016); Bonnie Costello, *The Plural of Us: Poetry and Community in Auden and Others* (Princeton: Princeton UP, 2017); Steedman, *Poetry for Historians*; Richard Hillyer, *Auden's Syllabic Verse* (Lanham: Lexington, 2019); Ian Sansom, *September 1, 1939: W. H. Auden and the Afterlife of a Poem* (London: Fourth Estate, 2020); Ladislav Vít, *The Landscapes of W. H. Auden's Interwar Poetry: Roots and Routes* (New York: Routledge, 2022); and Susannah Young-ah Gottlieb, *Auden and the Muse of History* (Stanford: Stanford UP, 2022).

Also important to thinking about Auden is Katherine Bucknell's introduction to Auden's *Juvenilia*. Other significant essays can be found in the three volumes of the Auden Studies series, coedited by Katherine Bucknell and Nicholas Jenkins: *W. H. Auden: "The Map of All My Youth": Early Works, Friends, and Influences*, AS1 (Oxford: Clarendon P, 1990); *W. H. Auden: "The Language of Learning and the Language of Love": Uncollected Writings, New Interpretations*, Auden Studies, vol. 2 (Oxford: Clarendon P, 1994); and *W. H. Auden: "In Solitude, for Company": Unpublished Prose and Recent Criticism*, AS3 (Oxford: Clarendon P, 1995); as well as in Stan Smith, ed., *The Cambridge Companion to W. H. Auden* (Cambridge: Cambridge UP, 2004); Tony Sharpe, ed., *W. H. Auden in Context* (Cambridge: Cambridge UP, 2013) (from now on, cited as *Auden in Context*); and Bonnie Costello and Rachel Galvin, eds., *Auden at Work* (London: Palgrave Macmillan, 2016). In addition to these texts, there are now innumerable essays and book chapters in more broadly construed works that illuminate Auden's writing from many critical vantage points. I have learned gratefully from almost everything I have read, but the books I have turned to most often while working on this one are those by Fuller and Mendelson, complemented by Bucknell's work and by Peter Parker's brilliant biography of Auden's key collaborator, *Isherwood: A Life* (London: Picador, 2004) (from now on, cited as Parker, *Isherwood*).

108. There have been two informative, full-scale biographies of Auden so far: the one mentioned earlier, Carpenter, *Auden;* and Richard Davenport-Hines, *Auden* (New York: Pantheon, 1995) (from now on, cited as D-H, *Auden*). Another is Charles Osborne, *W. H. Auden: The Life of a Poet* (London: Eyre Methuen, 1979) (from now on, cited as Osborne, *Auden*). Ansen, *Table-Talk*, is a record of many illuminating comments made by Auden to a friend in the 1940s. Numerous other studies contain biographical information; these are cited whenever needed, as are, at relevant points, details in memoirs by Charles H. Miller, Dorothy J. Farnan, and Thekla Clark.

109. Anthony D. Smith, *Nationalism and Modernism: A Critical Survey of Recent Theories of Nations and Nationalism* (London: Routledge, 1998), 1.

110. "The Metropolis and Mental Life" (1903), in Georg Simmel, *On Individuality and Social Forms,* ed. Donald N. Levine (Chicago: U of Chicago P, 1971), 339.

111. One reviewer commented: "Why did Caliban come in first munching? . . . However it was a happy thought, at his second entrance, to bring him on with the Elves. And later on, in spite of difficulties of voice, the actor gave us enthralling action; when he got—what Shakespeare gave him—the bottle, and lumbered about right brutishly." C.H.T., "The Tempest," *Gresham,* 11.6 (25 July 1925), 101. Another member of the audience felt diametrically different about his performance: "Auden should be given a further word of praise for his grasp of 'Caliban' apart from the roystering scenes." This is from a review by T.B.H., originally printed in the *Times* and cited here from C.H.T., "Tempest," 101. This review must have appeared in early editions of the *Times* because there were only different, and briefer, reports on the school performance in the final editions of the *Times* (the ones that are preserved in archives for posterity): "School Speech Days. Gresham's School, Holt," *Times,* 7 July 1925, p. 13; and "School Speech Days. . . . Open Air Play at Gresham's School," *Times,* 9 July 1925, p. 11.

112. The poems are: "To E. T." (1925), *J,* 100; "Friendship" (1925), *J,* 97; and "The Dying House" (1925), *J,* 96–97. See earlier in the Prologue and in Chapter 2.

113. Shakespeare, *The Tempest,* 1.2.

1. THE HISTORICAL CHILD

Epigraph: Sigmund Freud, "Thoughts for the Times on War and Death" (1915), *SE,* 14:275.

1. *A Certain World* (1968–1969), *Prose6,* 326.

2. "Reveries over Childhood and Youth" (1916), repr. in William Butler Yeats, *Autobiographies,* ed. William H. O'Donnell and Douglas N. Archibald (New York: Scribner, 1999), 45.

3. "As It Seemed to Us" (1964), *Prose5,* 151.

4. G. A. Auden, "The Maladjusted Child," *British Journal of Educational Psychology,* 1 (1931), 269.

5. "Poetry, Poets, and Taste" (1936), *Prose1,* 163.

6. "Easily, my dear, you move, easily your head" (1934), *Poems1,* 208.

7. Aside from remarks in numerous interviews, Auden's main prose statements about his childhood and his early years as a poet come in "The Liberal Fascist [Honour]" (1934), *Prose1,* 55–61; part 1 of "The Prolific and the Devourer" (1939), *Prose2,* 411–423; "A Literary Transference" (1939 or 1940?), *Prose2,* 42–49; "Making, Knowing and Judging" (1956), *Prose4,* 478–484; "As It Seemed to Us" (1964), *Prose5,* 134–160; and "Phantasy and Reality in Poetry" (1971), *Prose6,* 704–723. Readers in search of a conventional, comprehensive

account of Auden's youthful biography can consult the two main efforts so far published: Carpenter, *Auden;* and D-H, *Auden.* Another indispensable source of work on Auden's early life is Katherine Bucknell's scholarship, especially in her introduction and notes to *J.*

8. Auden refers to himself (in German in the original) as a "serpent born under Pisces" ("die fischgeborene Schlange") in a message he sent to Robert Graves in 1961. Cited in Mendelson, introduction to *Prose4*, xxxii. In "Many Happy Returns" (1942), Auden calls himself "a doubtful Fish" (*Poems2*, 239); see also "To Stephen Spender on his Sixtieth Birthday: Greetings from Auden" (1969), *Prose6*, 359.

9. Auden's comment and Mendelson's response to it are in *EALA*, 534–535.

10. John Auden, "A Brother's Viewpoint," *Tribute*, 26. During the earliest stages of Dr. Auden's career, he had had an appointment at Lambeth's General Lying-In Hospital, one of the oldest maternity hospitals in Britain.

11. "As It Seemed to Us" (1964), *Prose5*, 152.

12. A "large village," Carpenter, *Auden*, 5. The phrase "earth privies . . . open space" is from "As It Seemed to Us" (1964), *Prose5*, 159.

13. "Letter to William Coldstream" (1936), *Prose1*, 345 [also *Poems1*, 267]. See Chapters 6 and 8 for more details of these stays in London.

14. "Letter to Lord Byron" (1936), *Prose1*, 333 [also *Poems1*, 255].

15. Cited in T. G. Foote, "W. H. Auden—Interview III" (1963), unpublished typescript.

16. "The Mill (Hempstead)" (1925), *J*, 87.

17. James Day, *Vaughan Williams*, 3rd ed. (Oxford: Oxford UP, 1998), 27.

18. The book's title page claims it was published in 1900 but it actually appeared a few months earlier, in 1899.

19. Bernard's legal first name was George, and his second chosen name Bernard. He appears to have been known as Bernard throughout his life. The birth and death dates of the Auden family are: George Auden (1872–1957), Constance (Bicknell) Auden (1869–1941), Bernard Auden (1900–1978), John Auden (1903–1991), and the shortest-lived, Wystan Auden (1907–1973).

20. David Cannadine, "The Context, Performance and Meaning of Ritual: The British Monarchy and the 'Invention of Tradition,' c. 1820–1977," in Eric Hobsbawm and Terence Ranger, eds., *The Invention of Tradition* (1983; repr., Cambridge: Cambridge UP, 1992), 125.

21. David Edgerton, *Warfare State: Britain, 1920–1970* (Cambridge: Cambridge UP, 2006), 1.

22. See Antoinette Burton, "Who Needs the Nation? Interrogating 'British' History," *Journal of Historical Sociology,* 10.3 (1997), 229.

23. ALS from W. H. Auden to Christopher Isherwood, 9 Jan. [1963], The Huntington Library, San Marino, California (from now on, referred to as Huntington).

24. Sveinn Haraldsson, "'The North Begins Inside': Auden, Ancestry and Iceland," in Andrew Wawn, ed., *Northern Antiquity: The Post-Medieval Reception of Edda and Saga* (Enfield Lock: Hisarlik P, 1994), 255.

25. Rev. Henry Birch (1820–1884); John Birch (1825–1897); Sir Arthur Birch (1837–1914); Dr. Harold A. Auden (1874–1960); Thomas Auden (1864–1936); John Auden (1758–1834). Auden mentioned that Rev. Birch lost his "thankless job" as tutor to the future Edward VII when "the Queen discovered that he had Puseyite sympathies." "As It Seemed to Us" (1964), *Prose5*, 139. Puseyites were adherents of the controversial nineteenth-century Oxford Movement that sought to bring the Anglican and Catholic churches closer together and to infuse some old Catholic practices and theology into Anglicanism.

26. Steedman, *Poetry*, 58–59. See also Adrian Caesar, "Auden and the Class System," in *Auden in Context*, 69–78. One quick way to get an immediate sense of Auden's class background is to listen to any of the numerous recordings of his voice available online and to register his startlingly posh Oxford accent.

27. "The Prolific and the Devourer" (1939), *Prose2*, 414. See also "Jane Hanly Remembers," *WHASN*, 13 (Oct. 1995), 2; and D-H, *Auden*, 354, n. to p. 15. Jane Hanly (1930–2016), daughter of Auden's oldest brother, Bernard, was thus Auden's niece. There are photographs showing the interior of some parts of the Audens' family home in Carpenter, *Auden* (photograph 1 [b]) and D-H, *Auden* (photograph 9).

28. Harold Llewellyn Smith, "At St. Edmund's 1915–1920," *Tribute*, 35.

29. D-H, *Auden*, 29.

30. "Ironworks and University" (1938), *Prose1*, 462.

31. Howard E. Smither, "Oratorio, §15: The 19th Century in England and America," *Grove Music Online* website.

32. *Spain* (1937), *Poems1*, 772.

33. See Rosamira Bulley, "A Prep School Reminiscence," *Tribute*, 31–33.

34. Steedman, *Poetry*, 57. Bucknell believes that Dr. Auden was "essentially agnostic" but, while possible, that seems overstated (introduction to *J*, xxxiii).

35. [Foreword to *The Flower of* Grass, by Emile Cammaerts] (1945), *Prose2*, 249. See also Auden's comments on his religious background in his 1955 contribution to *Modern Canterbury Pilgrims, Prose3*, 573–574.

36. Martin J. Wiener, *English Culture and the Decline of the Industrial Spirit, 1850–1980* (Cambridge: Cambridge UP, 1981), 22–23 (from now on, cited as Wiener, *English*).

37. "As It Seemed to Us" (1964), *Prose5*, 138.

38. "The Prolific and the Devourer" (1939), *Prose2*, 414. Some of Auden's mother's sisters and a brother had apartments in Brooke Street in London, and the Anglo-Catholic practices at nearby St. Alban the Martyr, Holborn, were the

demanding standard against which the Auden family measured other churches' doctrinal commitments: John B. Auden, "A Brother's Viewpoint," *Tribute*, 26.

39. Charles Bicknell (1820–1893). Bordighera was a fashionable watering hole for well-to-do Victorians on the "Italian Riviera," where a distant relation, Clarence Bicknell (1842–1918), was a prominent resident.

40. D-H, *Auden*, 7; "Jane Hanly Remembers," 2.

41. The maiden name of Selina Acton Bicknell (1829–1880) was Birch. Auden reports that one of his aunts told his mother at the time of her engagement: "If you marry this man, you know nobody will call on you" ("As It Seemed to Us" [1964], *Prose5*, 138). Selina Bicknell's claim about her ancestry is almost true. She was actually a direct descendant of Thomas of Woodstock, John of Gaunt's brother. Auden's grandmother and mother, and thus Auden, were therefore (at least notionally) directly descended from Edward III and every earlier Plantagenet king of England.

42. "Jane Hanly Remembers," 2. Expert, often highly ornamented calligraphy as well as illumination, illustration, and decoration of books were activities greatly valued in the Arts and Crafts movement. They were mainly taught to, and practiced by, women. Sewing and embroidery were other crafts associated with the female participants in the movement. May Morris (1862–1938), the designer, embroiderer, and craftsperson, taught periodically at the Birmingham School of Art at the end of the nineteenth century and the beginning of the twentieth century, contributing to the creation of an informed Arts and Crafts subculture in the city during the time when the Audens lived in the Birmingham suburbs.

43. Medley, *Drawn*, 44. Medley (1905–1994), a key figure in Auden's early life, started at Gresham's in 1919, was absent from the school for some time in 1921 while he recovered from a traffic accident, and left at the end of 1922 for the Byam Shaw School of Art in Kensington, London. He and Auden remained in close touch afterward, visiting each other at their families' homes and meeting in London. For some more details on Auden and Medley's friendship at Gresham's, see John Smart, "Gresham's Poems: John Hayward and W. H. Auden," *WHASN*, 26 (Dec. 2005), 9–11.

44. "1929 Journal" (1929), fo. [97], NYPL. Another version of this conversation is reported in a letter from Auden to John Layard, ca. 1929, cited in James Greene, "Introductory Note on John Layard," John Willoughby Layard Papers, MSS 84, Special Collections and Archives, University of California, San Diego Library (from now on, the location of the Layard archive is referred to as San Diego).

45. Reported in Farnan, *Auden*, 32.

46. See Mary Sandbach, letter to the editor, *Adam International Review*, 385–390 (1974–1975), 104.

47. "Jane Hanly Remembers," 1; John Auden, "A Brother's Viewpoint," *Tribute*, 27.

48. In the later 1940s (perhaps in Aug. 1948), Auden made a pilgrimage to Birmingham to collect his mother's crucifix. Natasha Spender (1919–2010)

remarked that "It was a terribly important almost ritualistic thing for him. It was as if he wanted her, or her bones." Cited in Bucknell, "Introduction: 'Freud's Not Quite O.K.,'" *AS3*, 174 and 174n97.

49. [Introduction to *Slick but Not Streamlined*] (1946), *Prose2*, 304.

50. Cannadine, "Context, Performance and Meaning," 131.

51. Pierre Nora, "Between Memory and History: *Les Lieux de mémoire*," *Representations*, 26 (Spring 1989), 8.

52. In the British context, the classic account of national or regional traditions manufactured during the nineteenth and twentieth centuries is still Hobsbawm and Ranger, *Invention of Tradition*.

53. Nora, "Between Memory and History," 12.

54. Anderson, *Imagined*, 7. When Anderson discusses modern rites of secular belonging, he borrows terms from religious practice to describe a nation coming into being, comparing tens of thousands of newspaper readers, largely unknown to one another, who privately open their copies of the paper at the same time on the same day and read the same stories, to a community of people at prayer. However private the action may seem, "each *communicant* is well aware that the *ceremony* he performs is being *replicated* simultaneously by thousands (or millions) of others" (*ibid.*, 35; emphasis added).

55. "Jane Hanly Remembers," 3; Medley, *Drawn*, 44.

56. In the year after W. H. Auden's birth, Dr. Auden published a translation of a guide to the prehistoric Danish artifacts in the National Museum of Denmark. See National Museum of Denmark, *The Danish Collection: Prehistoric Period: Guide for Visitors*, trans. G. A. Auden (Copenhagen: H. H. Thiele, 1908). He was elected a Fellow of the Society of Antiquaries of London in March 1909.

57. See Gillian Naylor, *The Arts and Crafts Movement: A Study of Its Sources, Ideals and Influence on Design Theory*, 2nd ed. (London: Trefoil, 1990), 157.

58. John Ruskin, "The Nature of Gothic," from vol. 2 of *The Stones of Venice* (1853), in *The Genius of Ruskin: Selections from His Writings*, ed. John D. Rosenberg, 2nd ed. (Charlottesville: UP of Virginia, 1998), 182.

59. There was competition for the post but, according to one writer, Dr. Auden's work at the York County Hospital and his membership of the city's school board secured his application's success. See "Obituary: George Augustus Auden," *Lancet*, 269 (11 May 1957), 999.

60. For example, in 1926 the Birmingham School Medical Service, of which Dr. Auden was head, reported that it oversaw the health of 143,456 children in elementary schools and 7,018 in secondary schools. See "Public Health Services," *Lancet*, 209 (14 May 1927), 1047. At this period (before the Butler Education Act of 1944), the majority of British children attended an "elementary school" until the age of fourteen, and only a small minority progressed from there to "secondary school," let alone to university. Auden talks

about this fundamental social division in "How Not to Be a Genius" (1939), *Prose2*, 19–20.

61. Dr. Auden's interest in "feeblemindedness" may have been stimulated by occurrences of the issue in both sides of his own family. His son explained: "I had an uncle on my father's side and an aunt on my mother's who were what is now euphemistically called 'mentally retarded.' Uncle Lewis [Frederick Lewis Auden, 1871–1948] was looked after by a house keeper, Aunt Daisy [Margaret Bicknell, 1866–1917?] by Anglican nuns" ("As It Seemed to Us" [1964], *Prose5*, 139). It has sometimes been hinted that Auden's eldest brother, Bernard Auden (1900–1978), may also have been a quiet and even slightly cognitively impaired person. Auden remarked to an interviewer that Bernard was "not good at books" (T. G. Foote, "W. H. Auden—Interview IV" [1963], unpublished typescript). Jane Hanly said of Mrs. Auden and Hanly's father, Bernard: "I know my father disappointed her; he didn't seem to achieve what she thought all her sons should have been capable of achieving" ("Jane Hanly Remembers," 3).

62. "The Art of Healing" (1969), *Poems2*, 651.

63. For example, see his comment in the "Viking Notes" column on a pagan superstition among fishermen and jet workers in Whitby: *Saga-Book of the Viking Club*, 5.1 (April 1907), 178; and his "Pre-Conquest Cross at Rolleston, Staffordshire," *The Reliquary and Illustrated Archaeology*, Jan. 1908.

64. "Obituary: George Augustus Auden," *Lancet*, 269 (11 May 1957), 999.

65. G. R. Searle, *Eugenics and Politics in Britain: 1900–1914* (Leyden: Noordhoff International, 1976), 28. "Tabid" means consumptive or wasted with disease.

66. Mark Jackson, *The Borderland of Imbecility: Medicine, Society and the Fabrication of the Feeble Mind in Late Victorian and Edwardian England* (Manchester: Manchester UP, 2000), 205.

67. See G. A. Auden et al., [Correspondence:] "Care of the Feeble-Minded," *Times*, 1 June 1910, p. 8; and "Feeble-Mindedness and Juvenile Crime," *Medical Officer*, 31, Dec. 1910. Pinsent (1866–1949) and her husband, the lawyer Hume Pinsent (1857–1920), moved from Birmingham in 1913, but she remained very involved with educational policy. See Anna Brown, "Ellen Pinsent: Including the 'Feebleminded' in Birmingham, 1900–1913," *History of Education*, 34.5 (Sept. 2005), 535–546. In 1908, Pinsent was instrumental in founding the Monyhull Colony near Kings Norton for feebleminded adults, and Dr. Auden was the medical adviser there (see TLS from Lucy Faithful to Humphrey Carpenter, 28 May 1979, Columbia). The Pinsents' son, David Hume Pinsent (1891–1918), is the dedicatee of Ludwig Wittgenstein's *Tractatus Logico-Philosophicus* (1921–1922). At the Downs School in the 1930s, Auden taught Christopher Pinsent (1922–2015), another member of this powerful philanthropic and legal dynasty in Birmingham. Pinsent (later Sir Christopher Pinsent) became a painter and at various stages studied with

Auden's artist friends Maurice Feild and William Coldstream; see Chapters 7 and 8.

68. The Eugenics Education Society had been founded at the national level in 1907–1908. The main, and most polemical, attack on Dr. Auden's involvement with eugenics comes in R. A. Lowe, "Eugenicists, Doctors and the Quest for National Efficiency: An Educational Crusade, 1900–1939," *History of Education,* 8.4 (1979), 293–306. Lowe's controversial essay apparently had wide circulation in educational circles at one time. He wrote: "It can be demonstrated that the mental measurement movement had its origins in concerns about racial purity and mental degeneracy. . . . A number of leading eugenicists and psychometrists were highly successful in securing positions of power in local authorities in the period before and after the First World War which enabled them to influence education and social policy: Raymond B. Cattell in Leicester; George Auden first as a member of the York School Board and then as School Medical Officer for Birmingham; Ellen Pinsent as a co-opted member of the Birmingham School Board; above all, Cyril Burt in London." However, while not commenting directly on Lowe's points about Dr. Auden, Gillian Sutherland sharply attacks Lowe's methods, credibility, and his "very selective and tendentious use of evidence" in his article in her book *Ability, Merit and Measurement: Mental Testing and English Education 1880–1940* (Oxford: Clarendon P, 1984), 86–89.

69. G. A. Auden, "On Endogenous and Exogenous Factors in Character Formation," *Journal of Mental Science,* 72 (Jan. 1926), 8 (from now on, cited as G. Auden, "Endogenous"). For another example of criticism, see Dr. Auden's "The Biological Factors in Mental Defect," *Psyche: A Quarterly Review of Psychology,* n.s., 3.3 (Jan. 1923), 256 (from now on, cited as G. Auden, "Biological").

70. "The Prolific and the Devourer" (1939), *Prose2,* 418.

71. Reported in "Loren Eiseley" (interviewed by John F. Baker), *Publishers Weekly,* 208.18 (3 Nov. 1975), 10. News of the sinking began to spread in Britain a bit more than a week after Easter 1912. Auden was almost certainly at his parents' home at Apsley, Lode Lane, Solihull, at the time he heard about the disaster. "The Convergence of the Twain" (1912), Hardy, *Works,* 2:13.

72. Adam Tooze, *The Deluge: The Great War, America and the Remaking of the Global Order, 1916–1931* (New York: Viking, 2014), 20.

73. Stan Smith, *Edward Thomas* (London: Faber and Faber, 1986), 40.

74. Samuel R. Williamson Jr., "The Origins of the War," in Hew Strachan, ed., *The Oxford Illustrated History of the First World War* (1998; Oxford: Oxford UP, 2000), 15.

75. Cited in "The King and the Conference," *Times,* 22 July 1914, p. 9.

76. For descriptions of the euphoric mood in the major cities of Europe after the news that war had been declared, see, among many other accounts, Modris Eksteins, *Rites of Spring: The Great War and the Birth of the Modern Age* (Boston: Houghton Mifflin, 1989), 90–94 (from now on, cited as Eksteins, *Rites*).

77. John Garth, *Tolkien and the Great War: The Threshold of Middle-Earth* (London: HarperCollins, 2003), 41 (from now on, cited as Garth, *Tolkien*).

78. J. M. Winter, *The Great War and the British People* (Basingstoke: Macmillan, 1985), 155 (from now on, cited as Winter, *Great War*).

79. Jon Bradshaw, "Holding to Schedule with W. H. Auden," *Esquire*, 73.1 (434) (Jan. 1970), 26–28. Carpenter comments that John B. Auden believed that this happened in 1912 not 1914 (*Auden*, 13).

80. Peter Parker, *The Old Lie: The Great War and the Public-School Ethos* (London: Constable, 1987), 163 (from now on, cited as Parker, *Old Lie*). Photograph 2 in *Tribute* (p. 17) shows Dr. Auden in military uniform.

81. Richards, *Memories*, 27.

82. "As It Seemed to Us" (1964), *Prose5*, 161. See also the Prologue. John Auden said that he too sang duets with their mother. See Thekla Clark, *Wystan and Chester: A Personal Memoir of W. H. Auden and Chester Kallman* (New York: Columbia UP, 1995), 73.

83. "The Happy Tree" (1926), *J*, 167. Ryde is a town on the Isle of Wight where Mrs. Auden and her sons spent part of their Easter holiday in April 1917.

84. In a letter to Hedwig Petzold, Auden recalls playing "an arrangement for four hands" of the Beethoven violin concerto in D major (op. 61) with her in the mid-1920s (ALS from W. H. Auden to Petzold, 28 April [1952], NYPL); and in "New Year Letter" (1940), Auden describes playing a Buxtehude duet with Elizabeth Mayer (1884–1970) (*Poems2*, 10). For more on Petzold, see the Prologue.

85. "1929 Journal" (1929), fo. [87], NYPL; "Psychology and Art To-day" (1934), *Prose1*, 95.

86. Auden briefly coincided at Oxford in the 1920s with Frank Pakenham (1905–2001), the Earl's second son and eventual successor, and he submitted a poem, "Cinders" (1926), to a university periodical that Pakenham had founded. See note in *Poems1*, 794. In the later 1930s, Auden also wrote some reviews for the Birmingham periodical the *Town Crier*, which Pakenham had recently bought: see Mendelson, introduction to *Prose1*, xxxiii. In the 1950s through to the 1980s, Pakenham, by this time the Seventh Earl of Longford, was one of the most influential campaigners in Britain for the decriminalization of homosexuality.

87. See "The Services," *Lancet*, 184 (14 Nov. 1914), 1163; see also "The London Gazette," *Times*, 19 Nov. 1914, p. 13. For a brief account of the Second South Midland Mounted Brigade Field Ambulance's service during the war, see J. C. Swann, *The Citizen Soldiers of Buckinghamshire: 1795–1926* (London: Hazell, Watson and Viney, 1930), 78–90 (from now on, cited as Swann, *Citizen*).

88. See "Jane Hanly Remembers," 4.

89. [A. W. Moore and H. F. Humphreys], *A Mounted Brigade Field Ambulance in Peace and War* ([Damascus, Syria?], 1919), 17. This account of the

activities of the Field Ambulance unit that Dr. Auden was attached to for the first half of the war was written by two of the unit's officers who served through the entire campaign.

90. Swann, *Citizen*, 81.

91. Richard R. Trail, "George Augustus Auden," in *Munk's Roll*, vol. 5: *1926–1965* (London: Royal College of Physicians, 1968), 16.

92. [Moore and Humphreys], *A Mounted Brigade Field Ambulance*, 17.

93. Swann, *Citizen*, 81.

94. Dr. Auden commented that "the wells, by which [the graves] were placed, came in for a good deal of daily shelling, and it was only safe to linger over them in the early morning or after sunset." Cited in C. A. Hutton, "Two Sepulchral Inscriptions from Suvla Bay," *Annual of the British School at Athens, 1914/1915–1915/1916*, 21 (1914–1916), 166.

95. Information related by John B. Auden to Edward Mendelson.

96. "The Services," *Lancet*, 186 (23 Oct. 1915), 938.

97. Form of 21 Jan. 1916, in the National Archives copy of the Armed Forces service record for "Captain George Augustus AUDEN. Royal Army Medical Corps [1916–1920]" (ref.: WO 374/2788).

98. Swann, *Citizen*, 81. On 21 Jan. 1916, a medical board, recommending two months of reduced activity, attributed his problems to "Exposure"; see National Archives copy of Armed Forces service record for "Captain George Augustus AUDEN."

99. "I: The Dream Time," from "Out," in *Wodwo* (1967), in Ted Hughes, *Collected Poems*, ed. Paul Keegan (London: Faber and Faber, 2003), 165.

100. "As It Seemed to Us" (1964), *Prose5*, 144. In 1915, Bernard Auden was already at his public school, Shrewsbury, when John and Wystan were sent to St. Edmund's.

101. "'Expatriate? I don't know what the word means,' he said. 'I more or less left the Midlands, where I was born, at seven, when I went to boarding school.'" Quoted in Polly Platt, "W. H. Auden," *American Scholar*, 36.2 (Spring 1967), 269.

102. Isherwood, *Lions*, 183. Photograph 8 in *Tribute* (pp. 20–21) shows Auden, his brother John, Isherwood, and Cyril Morgan-Brown at St. Edmund's in 1915.

103. "As It Seemed to Us" (1964), *Prose5*, 139.

104. Parker, *Old Lie*, 54.

105. *Ibid.*, 42.

106. "Mr. J. C. Morgan-Brown: Fifty Years a Schoolmaster," *Times*, 25 Feb. 1929, p. 17. Parker gives an excellent short sketch of Morgan-Brown (1856–1929) in *Isherwood*, 35. During Morgan-Brown's reign at the school, which he owned, he employed his sisters, Monica and Dora Morgan-Brown, and his daughters, Rosamira and Winnie. Morgan-Brown's wife had suffered a breakdown early in her life and was permanently institutionalized (Parker, *Isherwood*, 35–36).

107. Parker, *Isherwood,* 63–68.

108. Joanna Bourke, *Dismembering the Male: Men's Bodies, Britain and the Great War* (London: Reaktion, 1996), 140–144 (from now on, cited as Bourke, *Dismembering*); Parker, *Old Lie,* 129.

109. Peter Parker says that the building, "Blen-Cathra," designed by Charles Bridger in 1891, had previously been leased by George Bernard Shaw (*Isherwood,* 38–39). However, Ian Nairn, Nikolaus Pevsner, and Bridget Cherry claim that the school building was designed circa 1895 by Dudley Newman. See Nairn, Pevsner, and Cherry, *Surrey,* rev. ed. (London: Penguin, 1971), 598. The "conifer-and-ravine" phrase is from Nairn, Pevsner, and Cherry, *Surrey,* 313.

110. Parker, *Isherwood,* 38–39.

111. Nairn, Pevsner, and Cherry, *Surrey,* 313.

112. Parker, *Old Lie,* 63–65; Bourke, *Dismembering,* 180–183.

113. "As It Seemed to Us" (1964), *Prose5,* 144. See "Not in Baedeker" (1949): "sphagnum moss (in the Latin countries | Still used in the treatment of gunshot wounds)," *Poems2,* 373.

114. "The Prolific and the Devourer" (1939), *Prose2,* 415.

115. "Letter to Lord Byron" (1936), *Prose1,* 330 [also *Poems1,* 253].

116. Thomas Charles Henchman Birch (1815–1857), one of the poet's great-granduncles, and Frederick William Birch (1804–1857), a distant cousin, several times removed. Both were officers in the Bengal Army. Today, the "Mutiny" is more commonly known as the Indian Rebellion.

117. In a poem he wrote the year after Ciddy's death, Auden castigates him as one of the betrayers of youth in "Get there if you can and see the land you once were proud to own" (1930), *Poems1,* 45. During the 1914–1918 conflict, at the Quaker-associated Downs School in Colwall, where Auden would teach from 1932 to 1935 (see Chapter 7), the school's headmaster used to intone the proverb "Pax melior bellum" (Peace is better than war) in Latin lessons rather than asking boys to decline "bellum" or to parse Horace's "Dulce et decorum est pro patria mori" (It is sweet and fitting to die for one's country). See Parker, *Old Lie,* 269.

118. D. H. Lawrence, *Kangaroo* (1923), ed. Bruce Steele (Cambridge: Cambridge UP, 1994), 212; emphasis in original.

119. Robert Graves, *Good-Bye to All That: An Autobiography* (1929), ed. Richard Perceval Graves (Providence: Berghahn, 1995), 202 (from now on, cited as Graves, *Good-Bye*). See Neil Hansen, *Unknown Soldiers: The Story of the Missing of the First World War* (New York: Knopf, 2006), 150–151 (from now on cited as Hansen, *Unknown*), for further examples.

120. Geoffrey Gorer, *Death, Grief and Mourning in Contemporary Britain* (1965), cited in Hansen, *Unknown,* 229.

121. Bourke, *Dismembering,* 33–35, 58.

122. Philip Gibbs, *Realities of War* (London: William Heinemann, 1920), 447.

123. C. H. Sorley, "When you see millions of the mouthless dead," in *The Collected Poems of Charles Hamilton Sorley*, ed. Jean Moorcroft Wilson (London: Cecil Woolf, 1985), 91.

124. Cited in D-H, *Auden*, 35.

125. "Gems of Belgian Architecture" (1927?), in Christopher Isherwood, *Exhumations: Stories Articles Verses* (New York: Simon and Schuster, 1966), 176–177.

126. Graves had been bullied at Charterhouse in the prewar period (when considerable anti-German feeling already existed in Britain) because his middle name was "von Ranke." See Graves, *Good-Bye*, 42–43.

127. "Are the English Europeans?: The Island and the Continent" (1962), *Prose4*, 431. See also the Prologue. Auden tells another, very similar version of the story in "As It Seemed to Us" (1964), *Prose5*, 145. He wrote the latter, an important autobiographical essay, in the autumn of 1964 (it was finished in early Dec. of that year). It is fitting that Auden should have been in Berlin, in what was during the First World War the "Hun" capital, when he included this memory of being accused long ago of German sympathies. Auden lived in the city as a Ford Foundation artist in residence from Oct. 1964 to Feb. 1965.

128. "Letter to Lord Byron" (1936), *Prose1*, 330 [also *Poems1*, 253]. See also "Assistant masters, young and old, came and went, becoming more peculiar each year" ("As It Seemed to Us" (1964), *Prose5*, 144).

129. "Letter to Lord Byron" (1936), *Prose1*, 330–331 [also *Poems1*, 253]; "As It Seemed to Us" (1964), *Prose5*, 144. Capt. or 2nd Lt. (as mentioned, sources differ) Reginald Oscar Gartside Bagnall (1893–1978) had apparently served in the Royal Berkshire Regiment (Princess Charlotte of Wales's) during 1915–1916, after which he was invalided out for reasons unknown. He was a biologist, later noted (writing as Oscar Bagnall) as the author of a book in the field of auric research called *The Origin and Properties of the Human Aura* (London: Kegan Paul, Trench, Trubner, 1937), an investigation of the apparent phenomenon of human radiations.

130. Kathleen Bradshaw-Isherwood is cited in D-H, *Auden*, 35.

131. "As It Seemed to Us" (1964), *Prose5*, 144.

132. *St. Edmund's School Chronicle*, June 1917, cited in Carpenter, *Auden*, 18. Auden recalls participating in these kinds of drills in "As It Seemed to Us" (1964), *Prose5*, 144. Rosamira Bulley adds details of the "field day," organized by a "young man invalided from the army" who "with enormous zeal organized the school into a military force which seemed to have considerably more officers and NCOs than privates," in her "A Prep School Reminiscence," *Tribute*, 32. (Quite possibly, the young man was the highly irregular "Reggy." See earlier in this chapter.) For a recurrence of The Devil's Punchbowl in Auden's imaginative life, see Chapter 3.

133. Parker, *Isherwood*, 51.

134. C. Day Lewis, *The Buried Day* (London: Chatto and Windus, 1960), 84 (from now on cited as Day Lewis, *Buried*). See also Auden's reference in

Paid on Both Sides (1927–1929) to learning little from "maps upon whitewashed wall" (*Poems1*, 19).

135. Isherwood, *Lions*, 13.

136. *Ibid.*, 75.

137. For the date of Auden and Isherwood's first meeting, see Parker, *Isherwood*, 52–53.

138. Manuscript holiday diary made by W. H. Auden, cited in Carpenter, *Auden*, 20. Part of the relevant entry from the diary is reproduced in *Tribute*, photograph 10 (pp. 22–23). The atmosphere of war and emergency emerged again shortly afterward—the next entry in the Isle of Wight holiday diary notes that after the family had visited the fossil-rich Headon Hill geological formation, they went to what "looked like an old disused fort," which they found was in fact an "Isolation camp," and saw "two large muzzle-loaded guns there" (*Tribute*, 23).

139. Their activities are described in some detail in the communal diary (in fact largely written by Mrs. Auden) titled "Easter Holidays 1917 at Weston Bank (Mrs. Preece) Totland Bay I.W.," NYPL.

140. H. M. Tomlinson, "War Books," *Criterion*, 9.36 (April 1930), 404. See also the Prologue.

141. Harold Llewellyn Smith, "At St. Edmund's 1915–1920," *Tribute*, 34.

142. G. A. Auden, "The Difficult Child," *Journal of the Royal Sanitary Institute*, 50 (Sept. 1929), 157 (from now on, cited as G. Auden, "Difficult").

143. "The Liberal Fascist [Honour]," (1934), *Prose1*, 55.

144. See Parker, *Isherwood*, 44–45. Bradshaw-Isherwood (1869–1915) served with the York and Lancaster Regiment.

145. "Base Details," in Siegfried Sassoon, *Collected Poems: 1908–1956* (London: Faber and Faber, 1961), 75 (from now on, cited as Sassoon, *Poems*).

146. Cited in A. J. P. Taylor, *English History: 1914–1945* (New York: Oxford UP, 1965), 110.

147. Cadet Geoffrey Auden (1900–1918) was a son of one of Dr. Auden's older brothers, Rev. Alfred Auden (1865–1944).

148. John Betjeman, *Summoned by Bells,* new ed. (London: John Murray, 1976), 44. "Skipper" was the boys' nickname for the Dragon School headmaster, Charles Lynam (1858–1938).

149. Osborne, *Auden*, 18.

150. Winter, *Great War,* 84. For every nine men who went there, five were killed, wounded, or went missing.

151. *Ibid.,* 89.

152. *Ibid.,* 97–98. Because the upper- and upper-middle classes were such a small fraction of the total population, it is important to note that in terms of raw numbers, the total deaths of working-class men far exceeded the number for the socially privileged sectors of the population. See *ibid.,* 282.

153. The figures of thirty-seven deaths and fourteen new boys per year are taken from Rosamira Bulley's "A Prep School Reminiscence," *Tribute*, 33, 31.

154. Winter, *Great War,* 98. At the start of the First World War, Auden's next school, Gresham's, had 229 boys enrolled. During the war 501 old Greshamians served, and exactly 100 ex-pupils were among the "fallen." J. R. Eccles gave the figure; he is cited in "School Speech Days. Viscount Grey on Holidays," *Times,* 28 July 1919, p. 14. The casualty rates for St. Edmund's and Gresham's match quite closely the levels obtaining at other prep and public schools. See Parker, *Old Lie,* 20.

155. Jay Winter, *Sites of Memory, Sites of Mourning: The Great War in European Cultural History* (Cambridge: Cambridge UP, 1995), 44–45 (from now on, cited as Winter, *Sites*).

156. David Cannadine, "War and Death, Grief and Mourning in Modern Britain," in Joachim Whaley, ed., *Mirrors of Mortality: Studies in the Social History of Death* (New York: St. Martin's P, 1981), 232, 230, 233. See also p. 189.

157. In a third codicil to his will, dated 22 Jan. 1956, Dr. Auden bequeathed an unexplained "pecuniary legacy of Twenty pounds" to "Miss Ann Haverson" (the will is now stored by the British government's HM Courts and Tribunals Service).

158. Details in this and the following paragraphs come from unpublished biographical notes made by Edward Mendelson on a conversation with John B. Auden, as well as from two TLS of 27 July 1979 and 2 Aug. 1979 from John B. Auden to Humphrey Carpenter, both now at Columbia.

159. Bourke, *Dismembering,* 162–163.

160. "Jane Hanly Remembers," 3.

161. TL from G. A. Auden to the War Office, 10 Sept. 1917, in National Archives copy of Armed Forces service record for "Captain George Augustus AUDEN." Dr. Auden said in his letter that he had been away from home since August 1914. The extant records are incomplete and ambiguous, but it seems more likely that he volunteered slightly later, in early September 1914.

162. See note by Dr. Malcolm Allen in "Obituary: G. A. Auden . . . ," *British Medical Journal,* 18 May 1957, p. 1187.

163. After retirement, Dr. Auden lived at Wesco, the family's cottage in the Lake District, between 1945 and ca. 1949 (see Chapter 2), and then he moved back to his birthplace, Repton, where he died in 1957. He had wanted to sell Wesco against the wishes of Auden and his brother John, telling them he could more easily leave them money than a house, but John Auden told Mendelson that Dr. Auden resented Wesco because it had belonged to their mother—and because she was the one who had planned the additions there. In the end, the house was still in Dr. Auden's possession when he died.

164. Some details of Dr. Auden's service are drawn from Mendelson's notes on a conversation with John B. Auden. With the rank of acting major, Dr. Auden was seconded as deputy assistant director of medical services for the Eastern Command between March 1918 and July 1918 ("The London Gazette," *Times,* 8 March 1918, p. 2; "The London Gazette," *Times,* 12 July 1918, p. 4). However, he was dissatisfied with the inconsequential nature of the work

he was given, and by the early summer of 1918 he was trying to join the RAF as a medical officer. That effort failed, and he saw out the war as an army doctor, traveling between Britain and France, restored to the rank of captain.

165. For Dr. Auden's illness, see D-H, *Auden*, 23. Dr. Auden wrote and spoke frequently about encephalitis lethargica in the early 1920s, usually in relation to child patients. See, for example, G. A. Auden, "Behaviour Changes Supervening upon Encephalitis in Children," *Lancet*, 200 (28 Oct. 1922), 901–904; and "Medico-Psychological Association," *Lancet*, 206 (1 Aug. 1925), 221–222, a report on his paper delivered in Birmingham in July 1925, titled "Psychological Implications of Encephalitis Lethargica." The latter was soon published in full as "Encephalitis Lethargica—Its Psychological Implications," *Journal of Mental Science*, 71 (Oct. 1925), 647–658. See also G. A. Auden, [Correspondence:] "The Structure of Neurosis," *Lancet*, 217 (7 Feb. 1931), 321. In the 1920s, Dr. Auden became one of the country's leading authorities on the disease and was often cited on the subject by other researchers. In 1932, Dr. Auden diagnosed a Birmingham boy, Philip Leather (1920–2002), as suffering from the illness. Until his death, Mr. Leather was one of the very last surviving victims of the disease. See Nick Craven, "He Was a Child Prodigy and Brilliant Pianist . . . ," *Daily Mail*, 2 Jan. 2003, p. 34. One of the reasons why W. H. Auden was so moved by *Awakenings* (1973), the book by his New York physician friend Oliver Sacks (1933–2015) about the use of L-Dopa to rouse patients who had contracted encephalitis lethargica during the 1918–1926 epidemic, some of whom had then been in decades-long trances, may have been that Dr. Auden had suffered from the disease and had treated other victims. Perhaps these patients, some of them roughly Auden's contemporaries, cared for by his father, who had suffered from the same illness, licensed pleasant memories about his parent. Auden offered an enthusiastic encomium about Sacks's book in a letter that was used as publicity material (see *Prose6*, 732). Clearly, Auden and Sacks discussed the issues at stake because in the revised edition of the book—*Awakenings*, rev. ed. (Harmondsworth: Penguin, 1976), 35—Sacks comments of encephalitis that the "notion of a disease with a 'Dionysiac' potential was often discussed in the Auden household." Dr. Sacks explained to me that Auden "was intrigued . . . by the heightenings and unexpected powers which sometimes went with illness, especially illnesses of an excitatory (or 'hyperphysiological' sort). . . . He called this a 'Dionysiac' potential, and said that his father too had been intrigued by the emotional and intellectual 'releases' sometimes seen in children who developed encephalitis lethargica. This 'other side' of illness—at least of some illnesses, some conditions—has been a long preoccupation of my own, and one, I think, much influenced by Auden's interest" (TLS from Sacks to Nicholas Jenkins, 31 July 2006).

166. Daniel Halpern, "Interview with W. H. Auden," *Antaeus*, 5 (Spring 1972), 141.

167. "As It Seemed to Us" (1964), *Prose5*, 141.

168. "Letter to Lord Byron" (1936), *Prose1*, 329 [also *Poems1*, 252].

169. The University of Tübingen awarded Harold Auden (1874–1960) his doctorate in science in 1897. See Harold Auden, "Über einige neue Osazone" (On some new osazones) (PhD diss., Eberhard-Karls-Universität zu Tübingen, 1897). Carpenter mentions Harold Auden's collections of pictures: *Auden*, 10. Auden calls Harold Auden his "favourite uncle" in "Phantasy and Reality in Poetry" (1971), *Prose6*, 709. Harold Auden was a research chemist at the United Alkali Company; his main work is H. A. Auden, *Sulphuric Acid and Its Manufacture* (London: Longmans, Green, 1930). Harold Auden also had an interest in spiritualism and sedulously attended séances. See Chapter 2.

170. See Carpenter, *Auden*, 21 (his interlocutor was Alan Ansen [1922–2006]—this anecdote is not included in Ansen, *Table-Talk*).

171. See the Prologue.

172. Friedrich Nietzsche, *Beyond Good and Evil: Prelude to a Philosophy of the Future* (1886), trans. Walter Kaufmann (New York: Vintage, 1966), 81.

173. "Gabriel, full occupied in either," addressed to Gabriel Carritt and probably written in very early May 1930 for Carritt's birthday on 9 May, accompanying a gift of "this book, The | Castle by Kafka" (the manuscript is in a private collection). For more on Carritt, see Chapter 4.

174. "Symmetries and Asymmetries" (1963–1964), *Poems2*, 548; emphasis in original.

175. "Marginalia" (1965–1968), *Poems2*, 602.

176. Isherwood, *Lions*, 182.

177. Harold Llewellyn Smith, "At St. Edmund's 1915–1920," *Tribute*, 35.

178. Isherwood, *Lions*, 181–183. St. Edmund's was a relatively small place, and Auden and Isherwood probably "met" in a literal sense in the autumn of 1915 shortly after Auden arrived at the school. However, Isherwood's first reference in his scrupulously maintained school diary to anything like a budding friendship with Auden does not come until 25 Feb. 1917, a Sunday, when he "walked with Auden ii" (Isherwood's diary is cited in Parker, *Isherwood*, 53).

179. "Hic et Ille" (1956?), *Prose4*, 525. In "As It Seemed to Us" (1964), he dates the interests as running between "six and twelve" (*Prose5*, 142); see also *A Certain World* (1968–1969), *Prose6*, 326. And he gives other ages for this interest in different parts of his writing. For example, in "Letter to Lord Byron" (1936), he says it dated from "my sixth until my sixteenth year" (*Prose1*, 330 [also *Poems1*, 252]). He also writes in "The Prolific and the Devourer" (1939) that as a child, he was "interested almost exclusively in mines and their machinery": "From the age of four to thirteen I had a series of passionate affairs with pictures of, to me, particularly attractive water-turbines, winding-engines, roller-crushers, etc., and I was never so emotionally happy as when I was underground" (*Prose2*, 415). In "The Well of Narcissus" (ca. 1962?), he comments that "Between the ages of seven and twelve my fantasy life was centered around lead mines" (*Prose4*, 525). There are many other similar remarks that give varying ages for this interest. On balance, Auden seems most often to

date his fascination with mines from around 1914 to around 1919–1920, and I have accepted the "seven to twelve" periodization as best fitting the available facts and statements.

180. "A Literary Transference" (1939 or 1940?), *Prose2*, 42.

181. Alan Ansen, "Notebook 2" (undated but late 1946?), NYPL. Mendelson gives details about Auden's collection of books on mining in "A Note on Auden's 'Nursery Library,'" *WHASN*, 22 (Nov. 2001), 36–38; see, as well, Bucknell, "Appendix: Auden's Nursery Library," *AS3*, 197–206.

182. "As It Seemed to Us" (1964), *Prose5*, 142.

183. D-H, *Auden*, 18. MacDonald (1824–1905) may have been an acquaintance of Auden's mother; her relative Clarence Bicknell persuaded the novelist to spend many months at the Italian resort town of Bordighera, where she probably met MacDonald during a visit.

184. E. Henry Davies, *Machinery for Metalliferous Mines: A Practical Treatise for Mining Engineers, Metallurgists and Managers of Mines*, 2nd ed. (London: Crosby Lockwood, 1902).

185. D-H, *Auden*, 11; emphasis in original; "Prologue at Sixty" (1967), *Poems2*, 628.

186. See Osborne, *Auden*, where one image in the section of photographs following p. 64 shows Auden at Goathland in the North Riding in 1913.

187. Carpenter, *Auden*, 12.

188. Carpenter reproduces a photograph of W. H. Auden, aged seven, leaning over a rail at the waterworks in Rhayader (see photograph 2 [b]). Mrs. Auden and John B. Auden's diary of the summer 1913 holiday is cited in Carpenter, *Auden*, 12–13. Titled "Summer Holidays 1913," it is now in NYPL.

189. The diary of the holiday kept by Mrs. Auden and by John B. Auden notes that the family climbed the legendary Cadair Idris mountain in Snowdonia (W. H. Auden having to be carried part of the way). In Aug. of 1915 and 1916, Mrs. Auden returned to the area with her sons, staying at Dyffryn, a few miles up the coast from Fairbourne.

190. "Prologue at Sixty" (1967), *Poems2*, 628. Carpenter mentions the visit in *Auden*, 14. Auden's geologist brother, John, wrote: "Limestone landscapes became Wystan's chosen environment, a passion originating at the time we were at Bradwell." See John B. Auden, "A Brother's Viewpoint," *Tribute*, 27.

191. [Introduction to *Slick but Not Streamlined*, by John Betjeman] (1946), *Prose2*, 307.

192. For details of the tensions that surfaced between Dr. Auden and his wife on this holiday, see earlier in this chapter.

193. See "Amor Loci" (1965), *Poems2*, 584–585—Auden called this the "Rookhope poem" (Rookhope, pronounced RAY-cup, is about twenty miles due west of Durham): "Phantasy and Reality in Poetry" (1971), *Prose6*, 710. In "England: Six Unexpected Days" (1953?), *Prose3*, 434, Auden describes Rookhope as "the most wonderfully desolate of all the dales." See also "New Year Letter" (1940), *Poems2*, 36.

194. For Auden in 1917 at St. Edmund's, see D-H, *Auden*, photo facing p. 86.

195. "Letter to Lord Byron" (1936), *Prose1*, 209 [also *Poems1*, 209].

196. See Bucknell, "Introduction: 'Freud's Not Quite O.K.,'" *AS3* 174, referring to the *St. Edmund's School Chronicle*, Nov. 1919.

197. Rosamira Bulley, "A Prep School Reminiscence," *Tribute*, 33.

198. Cited in Charles H. Miller, *Auden: An American Friendship* (New York: Charles Scribner's Sons, 1983), 38. The intonation and phrasing do not sound exactly like Auden's own here, but there is no reason to doubt the gist of the conversation Miller recalled having with Auden in Ann Arbor, Michigan, in 1941.

199. Rev. G[eoffrey] G[unnel] Newman (1886–1970), who, in the first half of 1920, when these events transpired, would have been about thirty-four years old. Bucknell, drawing on the *St. Edmund's School Chronicle* for June 1920, describes his career in her introduction to *J*, xxxvii. Mendelson gives details of a list Auden compiled in around May 1947 of the "great emotional milestones of his life": Auden wrote down and then deleted "Mr. Newman" at the head of the list (*EALA*, 579). With the times and the morals being what they were, it seems implausible that Auden was the only pupil that Newman had sex with. It is possible that Newman was the master whom Auden describes in "Letter to Lord Byron" (1936) as having "to leave abruptly in a taxi"—a phrase that often implies the emergence of some kind of sexual scandal with the attendant departure of the perpetrator (*Prose1*, 330 [also *Poems1*, 253]). The line may even have been an in-joke for Auden's friends.

200. "As It Seemed to Us" (1964), *Prose5*, 154; Harold Llewellyn Smith, "At St. Edmund's 1915–1920," *Tribute*, 36.

201. [Contribution to *Modern Canterbury Pilgrims*] (1955), *Prose3*, 575.

202. John Smart, "Gresham's Poems: John Hayward and W. H. Auden," *WHASN*, 26 (Dec. 2005), 13.

203. See the Prologue. Auden's grandfather was Rev. R. H. Bicknell (1823–1869) of Wroxham, Norfolk.

204. Karl Baedeker, *Great Britain: Handbook for Travellers*, 9th rev. ed. (Leipzig: Baedeker, 1937), 344.

205. Michael Davidson, *The World, the Flesh and Myself* (London: Quality Book Club, 1962), 129.

206. Richards, *Memories*, 33.

207. Auden describes the primary belief in most English public schools of the period that "Character is more important than Intellect" in "How Not to Be a Genius" (1939), *Prose2*, 19.

208. "The Liberal Fascist [Honour]" (1934), *Prose1*, 56.

209. Simpson, *Howson*, 33; Robert Cecil, *A Divided Life: A Biography of Donald Maclean* (London: Bodley Head, 1988), 13.

210. The Jungian psychoanalyst Michael Fordham (1905–1995), a contemporary of Auden's at Gresham's, told Humphrey Carpenter about this incident (ALS from Fordham to Carpenter, 1 April 1980, Columbia). See

Carpenter, *Auden,* 51n1. Aside from anything else, this was hypocritical on Eccles's part. At a London conference in 1921, Eccles had condemned "corporal punishment of any kind" and noted that boys at his school were punished by being made to play cricket when they wanted to cycle or to tidy up rooms or sweep the fives court. See "To Cane or Not? Headmaster of Rugby's Views," *Times,* 19 March 1921, p. 7.

211. See "The Liberal Fascist [Honour]" (1934), *Prose1,* 55; Carpenter, *Auden,* 24.

212. "As It Seemed to Us" (1964), *Prose5,* 139.

213. For Auden's appreciative comments about Greatorex (1877–1949), see "The Liberal Fascist [Honour]" (1934), *Prose1,* 57; and "As It Seemed to Us" (1964), *Prose5,* 147. Greatorex (nicknamed "Gog") was director of music at Gresham's from 1911 until his retirement in 1949. He composed his best-known work, "Woodlands," in 1919. This is the music used in the Anglican hymn "Lift Up Your Hearts" (words by H. Montagu Butler). He also composed many other pieces of hymn and organic music and taught, besides Auden, Lenox Berkeley, and Benjamin Britten. Britten had a much lower opinion of "Gog's" musical talents than Auden did. See Benjamin Britten, *Letters from a Life: The Selected Letters and Diaries of Benjamin Britten 1913–1976,* ed. Donald Mitchell, Philip Reed, et al., 2 vols. (London: Faber and Faber, 1991), 2:96–97 and 2:97n1 (from now on, cited as Britten, *LFL*); and John Bridcut, *Britten's Children* (London: Faber and Faber, 2006), 15. Large in size, and with a Pickwickian face, Greatorex's other nickname was "Greatoxe." After leaving Gresham's, he moved to Bournemouth and was dead within a few months. He was a distant cousin of the organist and composer Thomas Greatorex (1758–1831).

214. "Saturday Music," *The Gresham,* 10.10 (5 April 1924), 150.

215. On Tyler, see "The Liberal Fascist [Honour]" (1934), *Prose1,* 57; and D-H, *Auden,* 39.

216. Simpson, *Howson,* 22.

217. "Gresham's School Play. Open-Air Performances," *Times,* 5 July 1922, p. 12. Auden played opposite the future professional actor Sebastian Shaw (1905–1994), who remembered Auden as an imperfect foil, not very adept at acting as a girl, "red wrists projecting from frilly sleeves and never knowing what to do with his hands"—quoted in Medley, "Gresham's School, Holt," *Tribute,* 39. Shaw became best known for playing the dying Anakin Skywalker in *Return of the Jedi* (1983).

218. Robertson (1874–1929) had seen Auden writing a poem during a homework session and had mocked him (alluding to Thomas Gray's "Elegy Written in a Country Churchyard"): "You shouldn't waste your sweetness on the desert air like this, Auden." Robertson died of cancer relatively young, but in 1934 Auden confessed: "even to-day I cannot think of him without wishing him evil" ("The Liberal Fascist [Honour]" (1934), *Prose1,* 57). Robertson's demise is mentioned in "It was Easter as I walked in the public gardens" (1929), *Poems1,* 37; see Chapter 5, note 165.

219. Carpenter, *Auden*, 25. J. M. Richards remembered Eccles as "opinionated and forceful and somewhat eccentric as an educationist" (*Memories*, 35). ("The Liberal Fascist," the title of Auden's essay, is drawn from a famous self-description by H. G. Wells.)

220. "The Liberal Fascist [Honour]" (1934), *Prose1*, 59. Medley gives a good account of his own "three promises" interview with Eccles in *Drawn*, 32.

221. Comment in Medley's interview with Andrew Lambirth, available as a recording for the National Life Stories Collection posted at the British Library's "Sounds" webpage.

222. "The Liberal Fascist [Honour]" (1934), *Prose1*, 59. Auden explains the "Honour System" in *Prose1*, 58-59.

223. There was a vein of significant political dissidents among early twentieth-century pupils. For example, both James Klugmann (1912-1977), the Communist Party of Great Britain's intellectual historian, and a likely Soviet mole and the future diplomat and spy, Donald Maclean (1913-1983), were at Gresham's at the same time in the second half of the 1920s. The military theorist and Communist Party activist Tom Wintringham (1898-1949) had been there earlier (1910-1916). (Although meetings between Auden and Wintringham are not recorded, in 1996 Adam Sisman discovered a holograph notebook, used by Auden for his poetry in the later part of 1923, among Wintringham's papers. See Bucknell, "Auden's Newly Discovered 1923 Notebook," *WHASN*, 15 [Nov. 1996], 1-10.) The sons of the Lancashire industrialist Ernest Simon (later Lord Simon of Wythenshawe), Roger Simon (1913-2002), a Labour Party researcher, and Brian Simon (1915-2002), an eminent professor of education, attended Gresham's; both were virtually lifelong members of the Communist Party. T. O. Garland (1903-1993), the head boy of Farfield, Auden's house at Gresham's, later became a Communist Party member and a doctor in the East End (for Auden's description of him under the pseudonym "Wreath," see "The Liberal Fascist [Honour]" [1934], *Prose1*, 57); Auden stayed in close touch with Garland and his wife, Margaret, during the mid-1930s. (See "Auden and MacNeice: Their Last Will and Testament" [1936], *Prose1*, 370 [also *Poems1*, 285].) Erskine Childers (1905-1974), a boy from an Irish nationalist family (his author father, also named Erskine Childers, was executed by an Irish firing squad in 1922) and a future president of Ireland, attended the school as well.

224. "The Liberal Fascist [Honour]" (1934), *Prose1*, 59.

225. Simpson, *Howson*, 40.

226. "The Liberal Fascist [Honour]" (1934), *Prose1*, 56-57.

227. "Out on the lawn I lie in bed" (1933), *Poems1*, 184. See Chapter 7.

228. "The Liberal Fascist [Honour]" (1934), *Prose1*, 59. In 1936, Auden mockingly bequeathed "three broken promises" to his old school. See "Auden and MacNeice: Their Last Will and Testament" (1936), *Prose1*, 362 [also *Poems1*, 277].

229. Making up for lost opportunities, at different points Auden slept with both of them after they had all left Gresham's.

230. Medley's comment comes in his interview with Andrew Lambirth, posted at the British Library's webpage for the National Life Stories Collection.

231. Simpson, *Howson*, 30; emphasis in original.

232. *Ibid.*, 84.

233. Cecil, *A Divided Life*, 15. See also D-H, *Auden*, 38; Simpson, *Howson*, 24.

234. John Lanchester, email to Nicholas Jenkins, 29 Aug. 2006. Logie Bruce Lockhart (1921–2020), the headmaster at Gresham's from around 1955 to 1982, shared this information with Lanchester. Davenport-Hines confirms that there were "no inter-school matches" at Gresham's (D-H, *Auden*, 37).

235. D-H, *Auden*, 37.

236. There is no reliable history of this school, which was founded in 1555 by Sir John Gresham and was still run in the early twentieth century under the aegis of the Fishmonger's Company, a London livery company formerly led by Gresham. In 1920, when Auden entered Gresham's, his mother's cousin, Wyndham Lindsay Birch (1874–1950), a career military officer, was the prime warden of the Fishmonger's Company, in effect the chair of the school's board of governors.

237. Medley, *Drawn*, 33.

238. Simpson, *Howson*, 19.

239. "The Liberal Fascist [Honour]" (1934), *Prose1*, 59.

240. Information from Logie Bruce Lockhart, reported in John Lanchester, email to Nicholas Jenkins, 14 July 2006.

241. "The Liberal Fascist [Honour]" (1934), *Prose1*, 55. See earlier in this chapter for the possible valence of the phrase "difficult child" for Auden.

242. Medley, *Drawn*, 60.

243. Michael Fordham (see earlier in this chapter) commented that in Auden's school study at Gresham's "were the Collected Works of Freud to whom I was first introduced by him" (ALS from Fordham to Humphrey Carpenter, 1 April 1980, Columbia).

244. Richard Read, *Art and Its Discontents: The Early Life of Adrian Stokes* (University Park: Pennsylvania State UP, 2002), 13, 15.

245. See Medley, "Gresham's School, Holt," *Tribute*, 42.

246. "A Literary Transference" (1939 or 1940?), *Prose2*, 43.

247. "The Liberal Fascist [Honour]" (1934), *Prose1*, 55.

248. John Pudney, *Home and Away: An Autobiographical Gambit* (London: Michael Joseph, 1960), 46.

249. "As It Seemed to Us" (1964), *Prose5*, 147.

250. Carpenter, *Auden*, 31. See the Prologue. In 1924, Auden wrote a poem called "November at Weybourne," which contemplates the "waste of cold dark-featured seas" (*J*, 26). Robert Medley identifies the naturalist who met Auden at Weybourne as Richard (Dick) Bagnall-Oakeley (1908–1974), "the school naturalist and a local scholar," and he says that this happened "several times" (Medley, "Gresham's School, Holt," *Tribute*, 41; see also *Plays*, 488–489).

251. "The Liberal Fascist [Honour]" (1934), *Prose1*, 55. Auden's poem "The Mill (Hempstead)" was written in 1925 (*J*, 87–88). Also possibly associated with Hempstead Mill is the poem "The Mill" (*J*, 37).

252. Eksteins, *Rites*, 255.

253. See Catherine Moriarty, "Christian Iconography and First World War Memorials," *Imperial War Museum Review*, 6 (1991), 63–75.

254. Richard Cork, *A Bitter Truth: Avant-Garde Art and the Great War* (New Haven: Yale UP, 1994), 261 (from now on, cited as Cork, *Bitter*).

255. See Nikolaus Pevsner and Bill Wilson, *Norfolk I: Norwich and North-East*, rev. ed. (London: Penguin, 1997), 556. The window was designed by Reginald Bell (1886–1950).

256. Cork, *Bitter*, 262. Most of the literature on the painting uses the title *Unveiling Cookham War Memorial*, but an alternative, sometimes given, is *Unveiling a War Memorial at Cookham*. The picture is in a private collection.

257. Winter, *Sites*, 98.

2. MINING THE COUNTRYSIDE

Epigraph: Comments from a letter written in Sept. 1918 while Sargent was touring the battlefields near Arras (where Edward Thomas had been killed the year before); cited in Cork, *Bitter*, 220.

1. "'And There Was a Great Calm'" (1918), Hardy, *Works*, 2:356–357. Hardy's title is from Matthew 8:26.

2. This comment comes in an interview conducted by Cathy Courtney and now available in the National Life Stories Collection posted at the British Library's "Sounds" webpage. For more on Forge, see the Prologue and Chapter 7.

3. "National Ghost" (1965), in Ted Hughes, *Winter Pollen: Occasional Prose*, ed. William Scammell (London: Faber and Faber, 1994), 70–71.

4. See Medley's interview with Andrew Lambirth, available at the National Life Stories Collection posted at the British Library's "Sounds" webpage. The visit to Howlett and White's Boot and Shoe Factory in Norwich took place on 22 March 1922. See Katherine Bucknell, "Auden's First Published Poem?," *WHASN*, 4 (Oct. 1989), n.p. The conversation with Medley about poetry probably took place on 26 March 1922.

5. Medley, *Drawn*, 39.

6. "Letter to Lord Byron" (1936), *Prose1*, 332–333 [also *Poems1*, 255]. He later described the scene in "As It Seemed to Us" (1964), *Prose5*, 155.

7. "California" (1922), *J*, 3. Bucknell prints this poem first in her edition of Auden's *Juvenilia*. For her reasoning, see the notes in *J*, 3. Auden claimed in the 1960s that "the first poem I ever wrote" was about "Blea Tarn in the Lake District," Auden himself remembered it as being a "Wordsworthian sonnet" ending with the lines: "and in the quiet | Oblivion of thy waters let them stay."

[Foreword to *W. H. Auden: A Bibliography*, by B. C. Bloomfield] (1963), *Prose5*, 80. He could not remember who or what "they" were. Perhaps this poem has been lost. Auden seems to have visited the Lake District in the summer of 1921, and he and his family did not return there again until the summer of 1922, when he had already been writing poetry for a few months. He may be misremembering: the later Auden was not a good chronicler of his own career, and he may not have been accurate in saying that this now-lost poem was his first. Scholarly debates on the issue include Bucknell, "Auden's First Published Poem?"; and John Smart, "Gresham's Poems: John Hayward and W. H. Auden," *WHASN*, 26 (Dec. 2005), 9–11. See also Chapter 6.

8. See "Woods in Rain" (1923), *J*, 20. It was printed in *Public School Verse: An Anthology*, vol. 4: *1923–1924* (London: William Heinemann, 1924).

9. See Wiener, *English*, 41–42; Alun Howkins, "The Discovery of Rural England," in Robert Colls and Philip Dodd, eds., *Englishness: Politics and Culture 1880–1920* (Beckenham: Croom Helm, 1986), 63 (from now on, cited as Howkins, "Discovery"). See also Paul Fussell, *The Great War and Modern Memory* (New York: Oxford UP, 1975), esp. 231–235 (from now on, cited as Fussell, *GW*). Five anthologies of *Georgian Poetry* were issued from 1912 to 1922; the name alludes to George V's reign as monarch, which began in 1910.

10. "One had to be versed in country things | Not to believe the phoebes wept." Robert Frost, "The Need of Being Versed in Country Things," from *New Hampshire* (1923), in *The Poetry of Robert Frost: The Collected Poems, Complete and Unabridged*, ed. Edward Connery Lathem (1969; New York: Henry Holt, 1979), 242 (from now on, cited as Frost, *Poetry*).

11. References are as follows: blackbird (*J*, 20, 47, 100, 103, 114, 117); buzzard (*J*, 64, 113); chicken (*J*, 98); chiffchaff (*J*, 134); coot (*J*, 87); cuckoo (*J*, 90, 93, 117, 132); dabchick (*J*, 87); finch (*J*, 65); greenfinch (*J*, 116); goldfinch (*J*, 125); hawk (*J*, 41, 116); jay (*J*, 93, 98); kestrel (*J*, 92); lark (*J*, 92, 104, 108, 110); linnet (*J*, 99); martin (*J*, 43, 96); missel-thrush (*J*, 86); nightingale (*J*, 14, 15, 132); owl (*J*, 50, 94); pheasant (*J*, 99); plover (*J*, 236); raven (*J*, 69); robin (*J*, 55, 86, 88, 118); rook (*J*, 60, 74, 83, 90, 108, 126, 134); rooster (*J*, 56); seagull (*J*, 85); sparrow (*J*, 33); sparrowhawk (*J*, 87); starling (*J*, 26, 88, 99, 112, 118, 131); stonechat (*J*, 32, 62, 90); swallow (*J*, 88, 93); swift (*J*, 65); thrush (*J*, 17, 31, 38, 43, 60, 86, 90, 97, 131); wagtail (*J*, 90); woodpecker (*J*, 93); wren (*J*, 22, 55); and wryneck (*J*, 90). For illustrations of, and information about, all these birds, see the Royal Society for the Protection of Birds' online "Find a Bird" guide.

12. See Bucknell's introduction to her edition of Auden's *Juvenilia* for a discussion of motifs in his early poetry (*J*, esp. xix–xlv).

13. "Doom is darker and deeper than any sea-dingle" (1930), *Poems1*, 26.

14. "Letter to Lord Byron" (1936), *Prose1*, 333 [also *Poems1*, 255].

15. "The Fronny" (1930), *Plays*, 479. Edward Mendelson describes what is known about "The Fronny" in *Plays*, 464–465. "Luce" may have been a pseudonym, perhaps for the Gresham's naturalist Richard Bagnall-Oakeley

(see Chapter 1). However, see also the Prologue: Luce was the last name of a senior doctor in the RAMC, Maj.-Gen. Sir Richard Luce, whom Dr. Auden knew quite well, and the "naval range-finder" seems to hint at a military flavor in the name "Luce" as it is used here. King's Lynn is a Norfolk port about thirty-five miles west of Gresham's.

16. In the original German, his comment was that weather and climate are: "viel wichtiger für ein Künstler, als die meisten wahrhaben wollen." Cited in Cornelia Jacobsen, "Ein halbes Jahr zu Gast in Berlin," *Die Zeit*, 20.17 (23 April 1965), 22.

17. See Bucknell's introduction to *J*, xxi–xxii.

18. See *J*, 87–88, 89n.

19. Huxley told him that some candidates had identified the bone as "the skull of an extinct reptile." See W. H. Auden, "The Art of Poetry XVII [interview with Michael Newman]," *Paris Review*, 57 (Spring 1974), 37.

20. "New Year Letter" (1940), *Poems2*, 14; emphasis added.

21. "A Literary Transference" (1939 or 1940?), *Prose2*, 45. Auden's mother, Constance Auden, loved French culture, and if she ever read this sentence, it must have stung her. See Chapter 1.

22. Margaret Gardiner, *A Scatter of Memories* (London: Free Association, 1988), 149 (from now on, cited as Gardiner, *Scatter*).

23. "California" (1922), *J*, 3.

24. *Ibid.*

25. The village got its name from an episode in 1848 when some gold coins were found there at the same time as the gold rush was beginning in the American West. In a sense, this background fits with the poem's description of being in a place where there might be magical riches to be had.

26. To mention just a few examples: part 2 of "A Happy New Year" (1932), *Poems1*, 144–147; "Out of the lawn I lie in bed" (1933), *Poems1*, 184–186; "Night Mail" (1935–1936), *Poems1*, 175–177; "Lay your sleeping head, my love" (1937), *Poems1*, 336–337; "Brussels in Winter" (1938), *Poems1*, 329–330; "September 1, 1939" (1939), *Poems1*, 375–377; "New Year Letter" (1940), *Poems2*, 9–49; *The Age of Anxiety* (1944–1947), *Poems2*, 263–338; and "A Walk After Dark" (1948), *Poems2*, 393–394.

27. "California" (1922), *J*, 3.

28. "Jane Hanly Remembers," *WHASN*, 13 (Oct. 1995), 1.

29. G. Auden, "Difficult," 158.

30. Etymologically, a poetic trope *is* a turning away since the word comes from the Greek τρόπος, a turn.

31. "March Winds" (1924), *J*, 37.

32. "The Gypsy Girl" (1925), *J*, 112.

33. Freud claimed that "the very recollection to which the patient gives precedence, which he relates first, with which he introduces the story of his life, proves to be the most important, the very one that holds the key to the

secret pages of his mind." See "A Childhood Recollection from *Dichtung und Wahrheit*" (1917), *SE*, 17:49.

34. Dominic Hibberd and John Onions, introduction to Hibberd and Onions, eds., *Poetry of the Great War: An Anthology* (Basingstoke: Macmillan, 1986), 13.

35. "A Literary Transference" (1939 or 1940?), *Prose2*, 44. The Wessex edition of Hardy's work was issued in twenty-four volumes by Macmillan mainly between 1912 and 1913 but with four later additions. The books were bound in maroon cloth with gold lettering on the covers. Bucknell believes that "Hardy's influence is most evident" in the poems Auden wrote during 1924 (introduction to *J*, xxi).

36. "There is so much that I can share with you" (1924), *J*, 65.

37. "Afterwards," in *Moments of Vision* (1917), in Hardy, *Works*, 2:308. On 11 June 1956, at the end of his inaugural lecture as professor of poetry at Oxford, Auden read out "Afterwards," remarking: "but for the man who wrote it, I should not be here now" (see Mendelson's note in *Prose4*, 951).

38. Auden's best-known comments about *The Dynasts* are in "A Literary Transference" (1939 or 1940?), *Prose2*, 46–47.

39. Auden continued to refer to *The Dynasts* in his own writing as late as *The Age of Anxiety* (1944–1947). For details, see Fuller, *Commentary*, 386.

40. This association is based on Auden's statement in "A Literary Transference" (1939 or 1940?), *Prose2*, 46. I suggested (see Chapter 1) that Auden's parents were Ruskinian in many of their social and aesthetic ideals. It may also be that Auden absorbed the immensely lofted perspective not only from Hardy but also from the famous passage in *The Stones of Venice* in which Ruskin tries to rise in his imagination even higher than the flight of the stork or hawk or swallow and to see "the Mediterranean lying beneath us like an irregular lake, and all its ancient promontories sleeping in the sun: here and there an angry spot of thunder, a grey stain of storm, moving upon the burning field; and here and there a fixed wreath of white volcano smoke, surrounded by its circle of ashes; but for the most part a great peacefulness of light, Syria and Greece, Italy and Spain, laid like pieces of a golden pavement into the sea-blue, chased, as we stoop nearer to them, with bossy beaten work of mountain chains" and so on. See John Ruskin, "The Nature of Gothic," from vol. 2 of *The Stones of Venice* (1853), in John D. Rosenberg, ed., *The Genius of Ruskin: Selections from His Writings*, 2nd ed. (Charlottesville: UP of Virginia, 1998), 173.

41. *The Dynasts*, Part Third, Scene Eight, in Hardy, *Works*, 5:203–204. In the original, these lines are printed in italics.

42. "To a Field-mouse" (1922 or 1923), *J*, 14.

43. *Ibid.*, 14; "After Reading Keats's Ode" (1922 or 1923), *J*, 15–16; "The Sower" (1922 or 1923), *J*, 22; "The Dragon-fly" (1922 or 1923), *J*, 25; "The Owl" (1923 or 1924), *J*, 50; "The Cat" (1924), *J*, 54; "The Robin" (1924), *J*, 55–56; "Buzzards" (1924), *J*, 64–65.

44. "But These Things Also" (1915), in Edward Thomas, *The Annotated Collected Poems*, ed. Edna Longley (Tarset: Bloodaxe Books, 2008), 67 (from now on, cited as Thomas, *Poems*).

45. T. S. Eliot, "Reflections on Contemporary Poetry, I," in *The Complete Prose of T. S. Eliot: The Critical Edition*, vol. 1: *Apprentice Years, 1905–1918*, ed. Jewel Spears Brooker and Ronald Schuchard (Baltimore: Johns Hopkins UP, 2014), 574 (from now on, cited as Eliot, *Prose*, vol. 1).

46. "Letter to Lord Byron" (1936), *Prose1*, 332 [also *Poems1*, 255].

47. "To a Field-mouse" (1922 or 1923), *J*, 14; "Ploughing" (1925 or 1926), *J*, 115.

48. "The Old Lead-mine" (1924), *J*, 30.

49. "Woods in Rain" (1923), *J*, 20. Again, Auden the naturalist knows that birds stop singing when it rains. See earlier in this chapter.

50. One of the standard accounts of the Georgian movement remains Robert H. Ross, *The Georgian Revolt, 1910–1922: Rise and Fall of a Poetic Ideal* (Carbondale: Southern Illinois UP, 1965).

51. "Reflections on Contemporary Poetry, I," Eliot, *Prose*, vol. 1, 576.

52. "Last Words" (1938), Eliot, *Prose*, vol. 5, 660. See also the Prologue.

53. Eliot, *Poems*, 201; emphasis added. The poem's title comes from the name of a village in Cambridgeshire.

54. Alun Howkins traces the emergence of this theme in English politics and culture to interlinked senses of urban, racial, and industrial crisis in Britain during the 1880s (Howkins, "Discovery," 63–67).

55. "Home" (1915), Thomas, *Poems*, 81.

56. The "English Spring is lovelier than we," "March Winds" (1924), *J*, 37; reused in "Elegy" (1924), *J*, 58; "Three hundred English seasons nearly," "Flowers and Stationmaster" (1925), *J*, 114.

57. See Chapter 1.

58. Hynes, *Auden Gen*, 20.

59. W. H. R. Rivers, "An Address on the Repression of War Experience," *Lancet*, 191 (2 Feb. 1918), 173. For more on Rivers and the Audens, see Chapters 3–5.

60. Sassoon's case is discussed under the pseudonym of patient "B" in Rivers's posthumously published *Conflict and Dream* (London: Kegan Paul, Trench, Trubner, 1923), 166–172 (from now on, cited as Rivers, *Conflict*). Robert Graves writes about Rivers briefly in *Good-Bye*, 233–234, and Sassoon describes his relations with him at length in *Sherston's Progress* (London: Faber and Faber, 1936). For a brilliant, more recent fictional portrait, see Pat Barker, *Regeneration* (London: Viking, 1991).

61. Isherwood, *Lions*, 185.

62. Bourke, *Dismembering*, 35.

63. Winter, *Great War*, 273. Eventually 350,000 children received benefits because their fathers had died during the war (*ibid.*). See also Juliet Nicholson,

The Great Silence: 1918–1920: Living in the Shadow of the Great War (London: John Murray, 2009), 25.

64. W. H. R. Rivers, *Instinct and the Unconscious: A Contribution to a Biological Theory of the Psycho-Neuroses* (Cambridge: Cambridge UP, 1920), 2 (from now on, cited as Rivers, *Instinct*).

65. Bourke, *Dismembering*, 109.

66. Leed, *No Man's*, 185.

67. This soldier was described by Sir Henry Head in his evidence to a postwar official committee on the "shell-shock" phenomenon. Head is cited in *Report of the War Office Committee of Enquiry into "Shell-Shock"* (1922; repr., London: Imperial War Museum, 2004), 69.

68. Ted Bogacz, "War Neurosis and Cultural Change in England, 1914–22: The Work of the War-Office Committee of Enquiry into 'Shell-Shock,'" *Journal of Contemporary History*, 24.2 (April 1989), 227; Bourke, *Dismembering*, 109.

69. Elaine Showalter, *The Female Malady: Women, Madness, and English Culture, 1830–1980* (New York: Pantheon, 1985), 190.

70. Isherwood, *Lions*, 253.

71. "For the Duration," in *Wolfwatching* (1989), repr. in Ted Hughes, *Collected Poems*, ed. Paul Keegan (London: Faber and Faber, 2003), 761.

72. "As It Seemed to Us" (1964), *Prose5*, 144. For more on Gartside Bagnall, see Chapter 1.

73. A[ndrew] Bruce Douglas (1897–1963) became housemaster of Farfield, Auden's former house, after Auden left, and he was acting headmaster at Gresham's on two occasions.

74. See Michael Davidson, *The World, the Flesh and Myself* (London: Quality Book Club, 1962), 83. Davidson (1897–1975) introduced Auden to the painter William Coldstream (1908–1987) in 1925: see Chapter 8. For a small part that Davidson claimed to have played in Auden's early career as a poet, see *Poems1*, 792; and *J*, 20–21n.

75. See Chapter 1.

76. Michael Kennedy, *The Works of Ralph Vaughan Williams*, 2nd ed. (London: Oxford UP, 1980), 150.

77. Fussell, *GW*, 235. Many poems, such as Ivor Gurney's "Mist on Meadows" (1920–1922?) or Edmund Blunden's "Zillebeke Brook" (1917) and "In Wiltshire" (1929?), which Blunden said was suggested "by points of similarity with the Somme country," compare the appearance of the French or Belgian countryside with the English countryside from which the soldiers had come or to which they had returned after combat; see Edmund Blunden, *Overtones of War: Poems of the First World War*, ed. Martin Taylor (London: Duckworth, 1996), 144 (from now on, cited as Blunden, *Overtones*).

78. "November at Weybourne" (1924, rev. 1924 or 1925?), *J*, 26.

79. Compare "The huddled clouds of lead" with Wilfred Owen's description from the front line of how "Dawn massing in the east her melancholy

army | Attacks once more in ranks on shivering ranks of grey" ("Exposure" [1917], Owen, *Poems*, 162).

80. "Night on the Convoy," Sassoon, *Poems*, 101.

81. The classic account of this phenomenon is Winter, *Sites*, 54–77.

82. "The Sower" (1922 or 1923), *J*, 22.

83. "Mental Cases" (1918), Owen, *Poems*, 146.

84. See Bucknell, introduction to *J*, xlv.

85. "As the team's head-brass" (1916), Thomas, *Poems*, 123–124.

86. *Ibid.*, 124.

87. For examples of the relative equanimity with which people accustomed to killing and death dealt with the war's daily reality of corpses and murdering, see Ernst Jünger on "how callous war had made" him, in *The Storm of Steel: From the Diary of a German Storm-Troop Officer on the Western Front*, trans. Basil Creighton (Garden City: Doubleday, Doran, 1929), 294 (from now on, cited as Jünger, *Storm*).

88. "September" (1923 or 1924), *J*, 34.

89. "The Owl" (1923 or 1924), *J*, 50. Compare "To a Field-mouse" (1922 or 1923), *J*, 14. Sassoon's poem was collected in *The Old Huntsman and Other Poems* (London: William Heinemann, 1917, 27–29), a volume dedicated to Hardy.

90. "The Owl" (1923 or 1924), *J*, 50.

91. For Dr. Auden's copies of ancient tomb inscriptions, see Chapter 1.

92. "On a Greek Tomb Relief" (1922 or 1923), *J*, 15.

93. "J. S. Bach" (1924), *J*, 68. Rachel weeps over her children's fates in Jeremiah 31:15.

94. "To a Field-mouse" (1922 or 1923), *J*, 14; "To a Toadstool" (1922 or 1923), *J*, 14; "The Dragon-fly" (1922 or 1923), *J*, 25; "The Cat" (1924), *J*, 54; "Ploughing" (1925 or 1926), *J*, 115; "To a Small Buddha" (1922 or 1923), *J*, 15.

95. Fyodor Dostoyevsky, *The Idiot* (1869), trans. David Magarshack (Harmondsworth: Penguin, 1955), 92.

96. See Chapter 1.

97. Roland Dorgelès, cited in Eksteins, *Rites*, 179.

98. "Ploughing" (1925 or 1926), *J*, 115.

99. "A Literary Transference" (1939 or 1940?), *Prose2*, 42.

100. "Arthur's Quoit, Dyffryn" (1923 or 1924), *J*, 44. This neolithic monument, Coetan Arthur, is not to be confused with the more famous burial chamber of the same name in Pembrokeshire.

101. "Punchard" (1925), *J*, 98–99.

102. *Ibid.*, 99. In "Letter to Lord Byron" (1936), Auden writes, not altogether happily, of Dr. Auden: "No gentler father ever lived" (*Prose1*, 329 [also *Poems1*, 252]).

103. For instance, in "Poem" ["'Sweet is it,' say the doomed, 'to be alive though wretched'"] (1934), Auden writes about scientists who were "kind fathers,

pillars of their churches, | Meaning to do no more than use their eyes" and yet "Each from his private angle, then sapped belief" (*Poems1*, 163).

104. "Punchard" (1925), *J*, 99.

105. "September," *J*, 34; "Arthur's Quoit, Dyffryn," *J*, 44. Bucknell dates both "September" and "Arthur's Quoit, Dyffryn" to either 1923 or 1924; my hunch is that they were written in 1923.

106. Hardy continued to publish new poetry during the years when Auden was first reading him: *Human Shows, Far Phantasies, Songs and Trifles* appeared in 1925, and *Winter Words in Various Moods and Metres* appeared posthumously in 1928, the year of Hardy's death.

107. "Heredity," in *Moments of Vision* (1917), Hardy, *Works*, 2:166–167. Another example is "One We Knew," in *Time's Laughingstocks* (1909), about Hardy's grandmother Mary Hardy (1772–1857); see Hardy, *Works*, 1:331–332.

108. "A Literary Transference" (1939 or 1940?), *Prose2*, 44. Each volume in the Wessex edition of Hardy's works (see earlier in this chapter) that Auden read at Gresham's has a photogravure portrait of Hardy as a frontispiece.

109. Edward Thomas, *Norse Tales* (Oxford: Clarendon P, 1912).

110. The book is now at the University of Texas at Austin.

111. "To E.T." (1925), *J*, 100.

112. "California" (1922), *J*, 3.

113. "'The Road's Your Place'" (1925) *J*, 95.

114. See *The Prelude* (1805), book first, ll. 372–476, in William Wordsworth, *The Prelude: 1799, 1805, 1850,* ed. Jonathan Wordsworth, M. H. Abrams, and Stephen Gill (New York: Norton, 1979), 48, 50 (from now on, cited as Wordsworth, *Prelude* [1805] with book and line numbers of the poem followed by the page number in the edition).

115. "Below me Ticknall lay but in the light" (1925), *J*, 94. Auden writes that the fern owl "Uttered his easeful note of victory," an odd echo of Keats's declaration in another bird poem, "Ode to a Nightingale" (1819), that "many a time | I have been half in love with easeful Death."

116. "Below me Ticknall lay but in the light" (1925), *J*, 94.

117. "The Dying House" (1925), *J*, 96–97. I follow Bucknell in not adding any extra punctuation to Auden's version. When Auden wrote the poem, probably during his last month at Gresham's, he had recently read Thomas's book on the Victorian naturalist Richard Jefferies, *Richard Jefferies: His Life and Work,* issued in 1909, as much because of his immersion in Thomas's writing as because of an interest in Jefferies's prose. See *J*, 92n. It was during the same summer of 1925 that Auden wrote the poem of tribute addressed directly to Thomas, "To E. T." (*J*, 100).

118. "Gone, Gone Again" (1916), Thomas, *Poems,* 132.

119. This narrative is now generally read in the form known as "The Ruined Cottage" (1797–1798), but Auden presumably knew it through the only version then generally available, the revised one published in book 1 of *The Excursion*

(1814). See William Wordsworth, *The Excursion,* 1:18–970 (from now on, cited as *The Excursion,* with book and line numbers of the poem), in *Poems,* ed. John O. Hayden, 2 vols. (New Haven: Yale UP, 1981), 2:41–67 (my quotations here are from 41, 66, 64) (from now on, cited as Wordsworth, *Poems*).

120. "The Sunshade," from *Moments of Vision* (1917), and "'And There Was a Great Calm,'" from *Late Lyrics and Earlier* (1922), Hardy, *Works,* 2:233, 2:355–357; "The Bridge" (1915), "It Rains" (1916), "The Sheiling" (1916), and "Out in the Dark" (1916), in Thomas, *Poems,* 66, 121, 137, 138–139.

121. Frost, *Poetry,* 5–6, 6–7, 15–16, 23–24.

122. Vera Brittain's "May Morning" (1916) also uses a stanza of five rhyming lines; see Vera M. Brittain, *Verses of a V.A.D.* (London: Erskine Macdonald, 1918), 25–27.

123. See Chapter 6.

124. Compare *The Excursion:* "The light extinguished of her lonely hut, | The hut itself abandoned to decay, | And she forgotten in the quiet grave" (*The Excursion,* 1:508–510, Wordsworth, *Poems,* 2:54).

125. "Richard Jefferies" (1925), *J,* 92.

126. "To E.T." (1925), *J,* 100.

127. See also a related poem about a decaying house and a woman giving birth (in this case, the mother, not the child, dies): "Motherhood" (1925–1926), *J,* 123.

128. Auden is probably remembering Thomas's poem "House and Man" (1915), in which a tree's branches have grown up so close to a house in the forest that the "boughs | . . . made the mossy tiles | Part of the squirrels' track" (Thomas, *Poems,* 60).

129. Genesis 21:16: "And she went, and sat her down over against him a good way off, as it were a bowshot: for she said, Let me not see the death of the child. And she sat over against him, and lifted up her voice, and wept." (The reason for all this, Hagar's liaison with Abraham and the birth of Ishmael, is recounted in Genesis 16:1–16.) Auden referred to the story of Hagar once more, later that year, in "The Gypsy Girl" (1925), *J,* 112. Again, the Hagar narrative is linked there with references to England.

130. Northrop Frye, *Anatomy of Criticism: Four Essays* (Princeton: Princeton UP, 1957), 271.

131. *The Excursion,* 1:53, Wordsworth, *Poems,* 2:55.

132. "Report on Experience" (1929?), Blunden, *Overtones,* 143.

133. Edmund Blunden, preface to *The Poems of Edmund Blunden: 1914–1930* (London: Cobden-Sanderson, 1930), vi–vii.

134. "The Midnight Skaters" (1925?), Blunden, *Overtones,* 138. For other examples of this theme in Blunden's postwar work, see "The Pike" (1919) and "The Estrangement" (1919), *ibid.,* 62, 63.

135. Edmund Blunden, *Masks of Time: A New Collection of Poems Principally Meditative* (Westminster: Beaumont P, 1925).

136. "Water Moment" (1923?), Blunden, *Overtones,* 90; emphasis added.

137. W. H. R. Rivers, "An Address on the Repression of War Experience," *Lancet*, 191 (2 Feb. 1918), 175.

138. Auden's first journey to the Continent did not occur until the summer of 1925, just after he left Gresham's, when he traveled with his father to the music festival in Salzburg. See the Prologue and Chapter 3.

139. Auden consistently claimed in later life that 1919 was the year he first encountered the Pennines, though there does not seem to be any surviving contemporary evidence about this stay. See also the Prologue and Chapter 1.

140. Keswick Public Library now possesses a book that Auden apparently bought in a local bookshop in Aug. 1921. See Alan Myers and Robert Forsythe, *W. H. Auden: Pennine Poet* (Nenthead: North Pennines Heritage Trust, 1999), 9. Keswick is near the northern tip of Derwentwater in the Lake District.

141. See *J*, 30n. In 1924, he wrote a poem titled "Rookhope (Weardale, Summer 1922)," *J*, 54.

142. "The Old Lead-mine" (1924), *J*, 29–30. See also the closely associated "The Old Mine" (1924 or 1925), *J*, 31. Other instances in which Auden writes about the dropping of a stone into disused mine workings come in "Get there if you can and see the land you once were proud to own" (1930), *Poems1*, 45 (see Chapter 6); and "New Year Letter" (1940), *Poems2*, 35–36.

143. "Appletreewick" (1923), *J*, 22.

144. ALS from W. H. Auden to James Stern, [30 July 1942], in "Some Letters from Auden to James and Tania Stern," ed. Nicholas Jenkins, *AS3*, 83. For more on the trip, see *AS3*, 83n16.

145. See TLS from John B. Auden to Humphrey Carpenter, 19 June 1980, Columbia.

146. Statement drafted by Auden in Berlin in the autumn of 1965 for commentary on a debate in the House of Lords on the decriminalization of homosexuality. Cited in D-H, *Auden*, 316.

147. "The Old Lead-mine" (1924), *J*, 29–30.

148. "Christ in Hades" (1923 or 1924), *J*, 46.

149. "Elegy" (1924), *J*, 58.

150. "Christ in Hades" (1923 or 1924), *J*, 46.

151. Examples include "To a Small Buddha" (1922 or 1923), *J*, 15; "Autumn" (1922 or 1923), *J*, 25; "November at Weybourne" (1924, rev. 1924 or 1925?), *J*, 26; "Stone Walls" (1923 or 1924), *J*, 46; "In the Nursery" (1923 or 1924), *J*, 49; "Before" (1924), *J*, 63; "Skyreholme Mill" (1925), *J*, 80; "Stone Walls" (1925), *J*, 81; "Below me Ticknall lay but in the light" (1925), *J*, 94; "Punchard" (1925), *J*, 99; "Maria hat geholfen" (1925), *J*, 107; "Autumn Evening" (1925), *J*, 108; "At the Maison Lyons" (1926), *J*, 125.

152. "Stone Walls" (1923 or 1924), *J*, 49.

153. "The Old Colliery" (1924), *J*, 59–60; "Allendale" (1924), *J*, 70.

154. "Rookhope (Weardale, Summer 1922)" (1924), *J*, 54.

155. "'Lead's the Best'" (1926), *Poems1*, 408.

156. "Phantasy and Reality in Poetry" (1971), *Prose6*, 711.

157. See TLS from John B. Auden to Humphrey Carpenter, 16 April 1980, Columbia: "I think therefore we must have acquired the first half of Wescoe [*sic*] either late 1924 or early 1925." It seems that the Audens eventually became sole owners of the property—and there is a suggestion that the title to the home belonged to Mrs. Auden (see Chapter 1). After her death in 1941, her ashes were scattered in St. Mary's churchyard in Threlkeld. The correct spelling of the house's name appears to be Wesco, but it is often given as Wescoe. The house and adjoining barns are now Grade II listed buildings, denoting structures that the British government considers "of special interest."

158. ALS from George A. Auden to Elizabeth Mayer, 10 March 1946, NYPL.

159. V. M. Allom says the car that Auden shared with another undergraduate while at Oxford was a D'Yrsan, an inexpensive, two-seater "cyclecar" manufactured in France between 1923 and 1928. See V. M. Allom, "W.H.A.: A Further Tribute" (1975), a photocopied manuscript of which is at Columbia; see also Chapter 7, note 174.

160. Stanley Smith, *Lead and Zinc Ores of Northumberland and Alston Moor* (London: H. M. Stationery Office, 1923), 11, pointed out by Mendelson in "A Note on Auden's 'Nursery Library,'" *WHASN*, 22 (Nov. 2001), 38. As discussed briefly in Chapter 1, Auden's father's family had some business connections with mining. In "Letter to Lord Byron," Auden, probably referring to his great-great-grandfather John Auden (1758–1834), writes that "My father's forebears were all Midland yeomen | Till royalties from coal mines did them good" ("Letter to Lord Byron" [1936], *Prose1*, 329 [also *Poems1*, 251]). John Auden and his family lived at Rowley Regis in Staffordshire. John Auden's father, William Auden (1726–1794), may also have had some coal interests in Rowley Regis.

161. Shakespeare, *Hamlet*, 1.2. Contemporary mythological studies, such as James Frazer's *The Golden Bough: A Study in Comparative Religion* (London: Macmillan, 1890), made similar connections between a kingdom's decay and a weakened or absent ruler.

162. "The Prolific and the Devourer" (1939), *Prose2*, 415.

163. "Like other men, when I go past" (1925), *J*, 82.

164. "Phantasy and Reality in Poetry" (1971), *Prose6*, 710–711; emphasis in original.

165. This is a connection made through the ligature of rhyme in the earlier "November at Weybourne" (1924, rev. 1924 or 1925?): The huddled clouds of *lead*, | . . . And the men that are *dead*." *J*, 26; emphasis added; see also earlier in this chapter.

166. See John Stevenson, *British Society 1914–45* (London: Allen Lane, 1984), 182–183; Winter, *Great War*, 35.

167. Miners were physically more impressive than most other workers. Even given the relatively generous criteria of fitness established for service in

the trenches during the First World War, doctors rejected large numbers of working-class men from frontline, or even home-front, service because they were such poor specimens physically. But miners were an exception who "produced an excellent type of recruit, hard, well-developed, and muscular." See Winter, *Great War,* 62, citing a report on physical examinations of conscripts issued by Parliament in 1919.

168. *St. Edmund's School Chronicle,* June 1917, cited in Carpenter, *Auden,* 18.

169. For example, Wilfred Owen writes about how on a soldier's body "the slow, stray blood came creeping | From the intruding lead" ("Asleep" [1917], Owen, *Poems,* 129).

170. See John Keegan, *The First World War* (New York: Knopf, 1999), 122–123, 175–186.

171. Leed, *No Man's,* 138.

172. *Ibid.,* 91.

173. Stills from the film are reproduced in Bryn Hammond, "Professionals and Specialists: Military Mining on the Western Front," *Imperial War Museum Review,* 6 (1991), 9. Auden's visit was to the Blue John Cavern in Derbyshire; see Chapter 1.

174. Cited in Leed, *No Man's,* 139. The word "troglodyte" was in use among troops by 1916 in references to their own circumstances: see Eksteins, *Rites,* 349n2.

175. Winter, *Sites,* 178. In 1916, the French painter Fernand Léger made drawings of sappers at work in the ground beneath Verdun.

176. H. M. Tomlinson, *All Our Yesterdays* (New York: Harper and Brothers, 1930), 277.

177. An infantryman's letter printed in Laurence Housman, ed., *War Letters of Fallen Englishmen* (London: Victor Gollancz, 1930), cited in Leed, *No Man's,* 20. "The retirement of the combatant into the soil," Leed said, "produced a landscape suffused with ambivalence. . . . The battlefield was 'empty of men' and yet it was saturated with men" (*No Man's,* 20).

178. "Rural Economy" (1917), Blunden, *Overtones,* 106.

179. Jünger, *Storm,* 197, 209.

180. From the German side, Jünger remembered that "It was only now and again that one caught sight of a brownish-yellow fleeting shadow against the desolate countryside that stretched on and on before one's eyes" (*ibid.,* x). From the British side, Blunden recalled that "Germans [were] seen as momentary shadows among wire hedges" (Edmund Blunden, *Undertones of War* [London: Cobden-Sanderson, 1928], 85).

181. Isherwood, *Lions,* 173.

182. Lewis Mumford, *Technics and Civilization* (New York: Harcourt, Brace, 1934), 73.

183. "The Old Colliery" (1924), *J,* 59.

184. "The Miner's Wife" (1924), *J,* 52.

185. Fussell, *GW,* 299.

186. "The Tarn" (1924), *J*, 62.
187. "Miners" (1918), Owen, *Poems*, 112–113.
188. Letter of 14 Feb. 1918, cited in Owen, *The Poems of Wilfred Owen*, ed. Edmund Blunden (London: Chatto and Windus, 1931), 125.
189. "The Rear-Guard," Sassoon, *Poems*, 69.
190. "Remorse," Sassoon, *Poems*, 91.
191. "The Traction-engine" (1924), *J*, 67.
192. "Though thy rafters are grown rotten" (1923 or 1924), *J*, 69.
193. "Allendale" (1924), *J*, 70.
194. Rookhope, which Auden visited first in 1922, is where one of the two families involved in the feud that drives the charade's plot lives. See *Paid on Both Sides* (1927–1929), *Plays*, 17, 29 [also *Poems1*, 9, 20], and Chapter 4.
195. *Paid on Both Sides* (1927–1929), *Plays*, 7, 19 [also *Poems1*, 43, 11].
196. "Bones wrenched, weak whimper . . ." (1927), *Poems1*, 61.
197. "The crowing of the cock" (1927), *Poems1*, 60.
198. In the mid-1940s, Auden commented that as a child, "your father is the person you think of as being all-wise, all-powerful, all-good and caring for you," with the implication that this changes later (Ansen, *Table-Talk*, 73).
199. "Letter to Lord Byron" (1936), *Prose1*, 213 [also *Poems1*, 239].
200. Compare Fuller: "Mining in the mother earth is symbolically presented as a male activity in the very early Auden, so that the abandoned workings can be seen as a dereliction of fatherhood (strangers and the fatherless are commonly associated in Deuteronomy, Psalms and Jeremiah)" (*Commentary*, 10).
201. "Letter to Lord Byron" (1936), *Prose1*, 209 [also *Poems1*, 235].
202. "Frost" (1925 or 1926), *J*, 113. I have left the punctuation (or absence of punctuation) as it stands in Bucknell's edition of *J*.
203. Auden had written about buzzards earlier in a love poem, "Buzzards" (1924), *J*, 64–65. Bucknell notes that Auden reused the image of the dead buzzard a number of times in subsequent works (*J*, 114n).
204. "The Estrangement" (1919), Blunden, *Overtones*, 63.
205. "Behind the Line" (1922?), Blunden, *Overtones*, 73.
206. Wootton is cited in Hansen, *Unknown*, 264–265.
207. Descents into the underworld are exemplified by Odysseus's descent in book 9 of Homer's *The Odyssey* and Aeneas's journey in book 6 of Virgil's *The Aeneid*. Auden's landscapes offer after-echoes of these classical paradigms.

3. THE RHINO AND THE CHILD

Epigraph: Robert Graves, *Poetic Unreason and Other Studies* (London: Cecil Palmer, 1925), 115.
1. "Last Words" (1938), Eliot, *Prose*, vol. 5, 660; see also the Prologue.
2. For an example of an important vision Auden had in 1933, see Chapter 7. Auden seems to show increasing skepticism about the relevance of

dreams only from the early 1960s. In "A Change of Air" (1961), for example, he warns against "the flashy errands of your dreams" (*Poems2*, 530). But this was a late attitude, and, before this, he set much greater store in the worth of dreaming.

3. Report of a dinner conversation in New York, 18 Feb. 1939, in the unpublished journal (1938–1943) of Selden Rodman, now in the Selden Rodman Papers (MS 871), Manuscripts and Archives, Yale University Library.

4. Conor Leahy has established that, for Auden's chosen degree, he is recorded as passing the required preliminary zoology examination in Trinity (spring) term 1925 before he officially entered the university. (Julian Huxley perhaps waved him through that as a result of his successful application interview; see Chapter 2.) He passed the parallel examination in botany during Michaelmas (autumn) term 1925. He then passed examinations in chemistry and holy scripture (the latter still mandatory for all at Oxford at this time) during Trinity term 1926. See also Carpenter, *Auden*, 52.

5. "The Carter's Funeral" (1925), *J*, 109. Auden added "Ch. Ch. J. C. R." at the foot of the holograph he made of the poem. See *J*, 109n.

6. *Ibid.*, 109.

7. "Raw provincial" is from "Letter to Lord Byron" (1936), *Prose1*, 333 [also *Poems1*, 255]; see Chapter 2.

8. "Rain" (1925), *J*, 110.

9. See "Flowers and Stationmaster" (1925 or 1926), *J*, 114; "Ploughing" (1925 or 1926), *J*, 115–116; "At last, down in the lane" (1925 or 1926), *J*, 117–118.

10. "'Lead's the Best'" (1926), *Poems1*, 407–409.

11. Carpenter, *Auden*, 53; D-H, *Auden*, 52–53. See also Chapter 2.

12. The Marx comment is from *The 18th Brumaire of Louis Bonaparte* (1852).

13. "'Lead's the Best'" (1926), *Poems1*, 407–408 (from now on, cited parenthetically in the main text). Earlier poems containing direct speech from others include "A Tale" (1923), *J*, 17–18; "The Miner's Wife" (1924), *J*, 52–53; and "The Engine House" (1924), *J*, 72. None of the interlocutors in these poems is clearly working class.

14. "Mr. Cook at Oxford," *Times*, 30 Jan. 1926, p. 12.

15. John Parker, "Oxford Politics in the Late Twenties," *Political Quarterly*, 45.2 (April–June 1974), 223.

16. D. G. O. Ayerst (1904–1992), a socialist who took a First in history at Oxford, was an active member of the Oxford University Labour Club who later became a *Guardian* journalist and author; Carpenter notes "The Child" as Ayerst's nickname for Auden (*Auden*, 47). Richard Crossman (1907–1974), with whom Auden had a brief sexual fling at Oxford and who stayed friendly with Auden afterward, became an Oxford don and remained active in Labour politics in the city; he was eventually a member of Parliament (MP) and then

a cabinet minister in the Labour governments of the 1960s. Tom Driberg (1905–1976), who left Oxford without a degree, worked as a journalist and wrote the "William Hickey" gossip column for the *Daily Express;* he was a long-serving Labour MP who never held high office (for obvious reasons) but was an influential figure in the party and may have been a mole for the Soviet Union.

17. The Cashwell mine, Bucknell notes, "is a lead-mine just below Cross-fell in Alston Moor" on the western side of the North Pennines across the Eden Valley from the Audens' cottage at Threlkeld in the Lake District (*J,* 129n). See also Chapter 2.

18. Auden's slight misquotation is from Prospero in Shakespeare, *The Tempest,* 1.2. See also the Prologue.

19. Bucknell points to the possible influence on this section of the poem of Gordon Bottomley's "Littleholme" (which appeared in *Georgian Poetry 1918–1919*), describing a "vanished community of weavers whose industry once connected them, like Auden's miners, to the larger world" (*J,* 129n).

20. Shakespeare, *The Tempest,* 1.2.

21. P. M. Oppenheimer, "Harrod, Sir (Henry) Roy Forbes (1900–1978)," *Oxford Dictionary of National Biography* online (Oxford: Oxford UP, 2004). See also Jennifer Wicke, "'Mrs. Dalloway' Goes to Market: Woolf, Keynes, and Modern Markets," *Novel,* 28.1 (Autumn 1994), 5–23.

22. In *J,* 129, Bucknell notes the influence of Blunden's "A Transcription" (ca. 1925?) from *Masks of Time* (1925) on the first two lines cited here.

23. Hodge derives from the common medieval pronunciation of Roger, a typical name for a peasant man. The mention of corrupt "Paris" is a momentary signaling of Auden's dislike of French culture.

24. "Who stands, the crux left of the watershed" (1927), *Poems1,* 34.

25. "What on earth does one say at a Gaudy" (1958?), *Poems2,* 540. Auden turned twenty in Feb. 1927.

26. Reported in Don Chapman, "The Poetic Life—Out of a Suitcase," *Oxford Mail,* 1 Nov. 1972, p. 8.

27. Recalled in T. G. Foote, "W. H. Auden—Interview IV" (1963), unpublished typescript.

28. "As It Seemed to Us" (1964), *Prose5,* 149.

29. Isherwood, *Lions,* 74.

30. "Letter to Lord Byron" (1936), *Prose1,* 333 [also *Poems1,* 256]. The meaning is obvious as it stands, but in using the term "glosses," Auden might have been hinting at specific sexual practices: the Greek word γλῶσσα, from which the English "gloss" derives, means "tongue." When writing "As It Seemed to Us" (1964), which is in part a review of Evelyn Waugh's *A Little Learning: An Autobiography* (Boston: Little, Brown, 1964), Auden told friends that he had decided to be charitable and stay silent about his knowledge of Waugh's homosexual life at Oxford, coverage of which Waugh (1903–1966) had carefully omitted from his book.

31. Isherwood, *Lions*, 179.

32. Yorke (1905–1973) is cited in C. S. Lewis's diary entry for 20 May 1926; see Lewis, *All My Road Before Me: The Diary of C. S. Lewis 1922–1927*, ed. Walter Hooper (San Diego: Harcourt Brace Jovanovich, 1991), 399.

33. The Trades Union Congress was the country's biggest union federation. John Betjeman (1906–1984), whom, like Driberg, Auden met in the spring of 1926, also drove a car for the TUC during the strike. During their Oxford careers, Auden at one point had to pay a bribe of £5 to silence a college servant who found Auden and Betjeman in bed together (D-H, *Auden*, 108). Auden commented later to friends that the experience had not been worth the money.

34. "As It Seemed to Us" (1964), *Prose5*, 151–152. Tawney (1880–1962) was a prominent socialist economic historian. He had served in the Twenty-Second Manchester Regiment during the First World War and had been wounded at the Somme in 1916.

35. ALS from W. H. Auden to Christopher Isherwood, [April or early May 1926], cited by Bucknell in *J*, 137n.

36. "'Fight for Right.' Sir H. Parry's Music for the Movement," *Times*, 29 March 1916, p. 11. See also Glenn Watkins, *Proof through the Night: Music and the Great War* (Berkeley: U of California P, 2003), 57. Parry's music had a major influence on later composers identified with a self-consciously "English" music, including Edward Elgar, Ralph Vaughan Williams, William Walton, and Gerald Finzi. C. S. Lewis attended a concert at the Sheldonian Theatre in Oxford on 12 Nov. 1922, the day after raucous Armistice Day celebrations in the city, and heard, among other pieces, Parry's "Jerusalem" and Vaughan Williams's setting of "For All the Saints," both of them, according to Lewis, "spoiled by the bad, sentimental practice of making the audience join in." See Lewis, *All My Road Before Me*, 135.

37. Isherwood, *Lions*, 75–77.

38. *Ibid.*, 76.

39. *Ibid.*, 77. Peter Parker gives a reconstruction of the novel's plot in *Isherwood*, 106–110. Isherwood and Auden met again in Dec. 1925 through Auden's vulturish Christ Church friend A. S. T. Fisher (1906–1989). Fisher was later ordained and became a poet, novelist, and historian of early church documents. He was chaplain at Bryanston School (1934–1935), a period that later formed the basis of a scandalous novel, published under the pseudonym Michael Scarrott and titled *Ambassador of Loss* (London: Fortune P, 1955). He was presiding over the school's religious life for part of the time when Auden's love, Michael Yates, was a pupil there (see Chapter 7).

40. "The Carter's Funeral" (1925), *J*, 109.

41. "My father brought me up on them [the Icelandic sagas]. His family originated in an area which once served as headquarters for the Viking army. . . . My mother came from Normandy—which means that she was half

Nordic." W. H. Auden, "The Art of Poetry XVII [interview with Michael Newman]," *Paris Review,* 57 (Spring 1974), 59.

42. Isherwood, *Lions,* 192.

43. Bryn Hammond, "Professionals and Specialists: Military Mining on the Western Front," *Imperial War Museum Review,* 6 (1991), 13.

44. Cited in Carpenter, *Auden,* 50.

45. ALS from Constance Auden to A. S. T. Fisher, 20 April 1926, cited in Bucknell's introduction to *J,* xxxii.

46. The phrase is from "A Literary Transference" (1939 or 1940?), *Prose2,* 44.

47. T. S. Eliot to E. J. H. Greene, cited in *Revue de littérature comparée,* July–Sept. 1948, p. 365.

48. T. S. Eliot, "The Metaphysical Poets," in *The Complete Prose of T. S. Eliot: The Critical Edition,* vol. 2: *The Perfect Critic, 1919–1926,* ed. Anthony Cuda and Ronald Schuchard (Baltimore: Johns Hopkins UP, 2014), 391 (from now on, cited as Eliot, *Prose,* vol. 2).

49. Edmund Wilson, *Letters on Literature and Politics, 1912–1972,* ed. Elena Wilson (New York: Farrar, Straus and Giroux, 1977), 97.

50. Ezra Pound to T. S. Eliot, [24 Jan.] 1922, printed by Christopher Ricks and Jim McCue in their "Commentary" in Eliot, *Poems,* 550.

51. See Bucknell's explanation in *J,* 138n. Examples of Sitwellian-sounding Auden poems written during the spring of 1926 include "Chloe to Daphnis in Hyde Park," *J,* 134–135; and "Cinders," *J,* 143–145.

52. Tom Driberg, *Ruling Passions* (London: Jonathan Cape, 1977), 58.

53. "Letter to Lord Byron" (1936), *Prose1,* 333 [also *Poems1,* 256].

54. "Thomas Prologizes" (1926), *Poems1,* 411. A sord is the name for a flock of mallards: bird language survives (just about) even in Auden's most unnatural poetry. He later decided that the lines about Isobel were among the most "ridiculous" he had ever written. [Foreword to *W. H. Auden: A Bibliography,* by B. C. Bloomfield] (1963), *Prose5,* 79. Whom the character of the poem's Thomas was intended to allude to is unclear: it could have been Driberg, T. S. Eliot (in this very Eliotic poem), St. Thomas, the disciple of Jesus, or St. Thomas Aquinas, whose works Auden was proudly referring to at the time.

55. "Thomas Epilogizes" (1926), *Poems1,* 416.

56. "Consequences" (1926), *Poems1,* 418–419; "Cinders" (1926), *Poems1,* 414–415.

57. Discussion of the links between Eliot's exceptional poetry and his ultraconservative, racist, classist, homophobic, and antisemitic attitudes has a long history. A landmark in the debate is Anthony Julius, *T. S. Eliot, Anti-Semitism, and Literary Form* (Cambridge: Cambridge UP, 1995). Further revelations, especially relating to Eliot's antisemitism and his love life, came through the 2020 release of 1,131 letters to Emily Hale (1891–1969), written between 1930 and 1957. An edition of the Eliot-Hale letters, compiled by John Haffenden, is now available online at the tseliot.com website. The Eliot scholar

Frances Dickey surveyed the letters to Hale and their connections to Eliot's poetry in "May the Record Speak: The Correspondence of T. S. Eliot and Emily Hale," *Twentieth-Century Literature*, 66.4 (Dec. 2020), 431–462.

58. Michael North, *The Political Aesthetic of Yeats, Eliot, and Pound* (Cambridge: Cambridge UP, 1991), 105.

59. The poet Allen Tate (1899–1979) later explained: "in those days a lot of people like Hart [Crane] had the delusion that Eliot was homosexual." Cited in *O My Land, My Friends: The Selected Letters of Hart Crane*, ed. Langdon Hammer and Brom Weber (New York: Four Walls Eight Windows, 1997), 90.

60. Included in the letter from Pound to Eliot of [24 Jan.] 1922, printed by Ricks and McCue in "Commentary," Eliot, *Poems*, 551n.

61. Virginia Woolf in a brilliant sentence from her diary for 12 Nov. 1934 described how Eliot "conveys an emotion, an atmosphere, . . . something peculiar to himself; sordid, emotional intense—a kind of Crippen in a mask: modernity & poetry locked together" (Virginia Woolf, *The Diary of Virginia Woolf*, vol. 4: *1931–1935*, ed. Anne Oliver Bell and Andrew McNeillie [London: Hogarth P, 1982], 260). Eliot had already told Alfred Kreymborg by 1925 that he wanted no biography, but his furtiveness and reticence—truly part of Eliot's desire to be what the critic Hugh Kenner would later call him, an "invisible poet"—only made fantasy, speculation, and curiosity more pervasive.

62. The Sitwell brothers had been to a dinner at Eliot's Charing Cross Road, London, hideaway, during which, so they believed, Eliot had worn pale-green face powder. Virginia Woolf thought so too, and in 1922 she also believed that he was painting his lips. Of Eliot, Osbert Sitwell said that there was "an ambience permeated with tragedy, tinged with comedy, and exhaling at times an air of mystification." See John Pearson, *Façades: Edith, Osbert, and Sacheverell Sitwell* (London: Macmillan, 1978), 239; Pearson is quoting from unpublished notes on Eliot by Osbert Sitwell.

63. Mark Ford covers some of these rumors in his essay "Hyacinth Boy," *London Review of Books*, 28.18 (21 Sept. 2006), 32–34.

64. Isherwood, *Lions*, 191; see Parker, *Isherwood*, 132. Isherwood hints very indirectly at the start of his and Auden's sexual relationship while on this holiday by recollecting Auden's comment during the stay that "laughter . . . is the first sign of sexual attraction" (*Lions*, 189).

65. "Ben Jonson" (1919), Eliot, *Prose*, vol. 2, 153. Other Eliot essays that use the word (for example, his 1917 *Egoist* essay on Turgenev or the short book *Ezra Pound: His Metric and His Poetry*, published in New York in 1917) are more fugitive, and Auden had probably not read them. In a poem addressed to Isherwood in 1935, Auden recalls this phase and again harks back to the word "austere": "Nine years ago [in 1926], upon that southern island [the Isle of Wight] | Where the wild Tennyson became a fossil, | Half-boys, we spoke of books and praised | The acid and austere, behind us only | The stuccoed suburb and expensive school," "August for the people and their favourite islands" (1935), *Poems1*, 215; see Chapter 8.

66. "Tradition and the Individual Talent," Eliot, *Prose*, vol. 2, 108.

67. Stephen Spender, *World within World: The Autobiography of Stephen Spender* (1951; New York: Modern Library, 2001), 57, 59 (from now on, cited as Spender, *WwW*).

68. The exception is the first part of "Lovers' Lane" (dating from around Aug. 1926): "Now England | Has conquered Wales, until eclipsing clouds | Pass" (*J*, 153).

69. Bucknell, introduction to *J*, xliii.

70. See *J*, 139. See also the important letter from Auden to Isherwood about Eliot's poems, Aug.–Sept. 1926, cited in *J*, 159n.

71. [June? or Dec.? 1927], cited in Bucknell, introduction to *J*, xxix.

72. John Betjeman, "Oxford," *Tribute*, 44. Auden moved from Meadow Building to Peckwater Quadrangle in Christ Church at the start of the Michaelmas (autumn) 1926 term.

73. Bevis Hillier, *Young Betjeman* (London: John Murray, 1988), 141.

74. Isherwood, *Lions*, 215; emphasis in original.

75. "Quique Amavit" (1927), *J*, 181. The title is taken from the late Latin poem *Pervigilium Veneris* and means "Whoever has loved." Auden's poem is dedicated in Shakespearean fashion to "the onlie begetter Mr W. L." (*J*, 182n). McElwee's initials were W. L. His is included in a list of eight names of early loves that Auden penciled in a notebook in 1942–1943. Also on the list is a younger brother, Patrick McElwee (1911–1963), whom Auden had a passion for as well. See *J*, xxxvii n56. William McElwee (1907–1978) was later a history tutor at Stowe School for nearly three decades and then head of modern studies at the Royal Military Academy Sandhurst. Patrick McElwee taught at Blundell's School in Devon. Auden writes briefly about the McElwee brothers in his "1929 Journal" (1929), fos. [103, 105], NYPL. It is possible that Auden had already been back to see Petzold in Austria in the winter of 1925–1926 with another Oxford friend, Harold Llewellyn Smith (1907?–1975), whom Auden had known at St. Edmund's and who was now at New College. However, details about this trip, and even whether it took place at all, are uncertain.

76. W. H. Auden to David Ayerst, [Jan. 1927?], cited in Carpenter, *Auden*, 69. Bucknell has comments on the Auden-McElwee friendship, hinting that she believes little or nothing sexual happened: see introduction to *J*, xxxvii.

77. W. H. Auden to William McElwee, [15 April 1927], cited in *J*, 187n; and [Easter vacation 1927], cited in *J*, 194n.

78. *J*, 197n. Parts of this poem would be recycled in "It was Easter as I walked in the public gardens" (1929), *Poems1*, 37. See Chapter 5.

79. "The Megalopsych" (1927), *J*, 202.

80. Roger Kojecky, *T. S. Eliot's Social Criticism* (New York: Farrar, Straus and Giroux, 1971), 219. The Action Française was a militant far-right monarchist organization, denounced by Pius XI in Dec. 1926. In a letter to the *Church Times* (24 Feb. 1928), Eliot styled himself "one of the few defenders of *L'Action*

Française in this country who cannot be accused of seizing upon this affair for the purpose of 'No Popery' or Protestant propaganda" (*Prose*, vol. 3, 351).

81. Eliot was baptized by W. F. Stead on 29 June 1927 and confirmed the next morning by Thomas Strong, the bishop of Oxford (Crawford, *Eliot*, 100–101). After a long process that moved in fits and starts, Eliot's naturalization finally took place in London on 3 Nov. 1927. See Elizabeth Joan Micaković, "T. S. Eliot's Voice: A Cultural History" (DPhil diss., U of Exeter, 2015), 83, 90, 93. Eliot's naturalization was even mentioned in news periodicals: "New Subject," *Time*, 10.22 (28 Nov. 1927), 14.

82. "Journey of the Magi," Eliot, *Poems*, 101–102. As a kind of parallel to "Journey of the Magi," Eliot had also started working in 1926 on another "journey poem," his translation of St. John Perse's *Anabase*, published in France in 1924 (and in Eliot's translation into English in 1930).

83. Preface to *For Lancelot Andrewes: Essays on Style and Order* (1928), Eliot, *Prose*, vol. 3, 513. See the Prologue, note 87, and Chapter 7, note 97.

84. Eliot made his confession on 21 Feb. 1928 (Shrove Tuesday) to Father Francis Underhill (1878–1943); he wrote the letter to Stead on 15 March 1928. See Crawford, *Eliot*, 115–116; and Eliot, *The Letters of T. S. Eliot*, vol. 4: *1928–1929*, ed. Valerie Eliot and John Haffenden (London: Faber and Faber 2013), 96. Stead (1884–1967) had been born in the United States but became an Anglican clergyman. At the time of Eliot's baptism, he was chaplain of Worcester College, Oxford.

85. "Marina," Eliot, *Poems*, 107. Eliot also uses the "island" motif with deliberate emphasis in another poem, begun in 1928 and published in 1930, *Ash-Wednesday*: "there is not enough silence | Not on the sea or on the islands" (*Poems*, 94).

86. "Last Words" (1938), Eliot, *Prose*, vol. 5, 660–661. See the Prologue.

87. Sacheverell Sitwell (1897–1988), who served in the Grenadier Guards during the First World War, had encouraged Auden to submit his poetry to Eliot. Although Auden's Oxford friend Tom Driberg knew the Sitwells quite well, it seems the story of how Auden came to submit his poems to Eliot at Faber and Gwyer (from 1929, Faber and Faber) in 1927 requires a reference back to the day of 4 July 1925, when Auden played Caliban in Norfolk, and it shows us a clear example of one of the upper-middle-class queer social networks into which the young Auden fitted. On 4 July 1925, at the Gresham's Prize Day, the Bloomsbury essayist, lawyer, and (by this point) largely retired Liberal politician Augustine Birrell (1850–1933) presented the prizes. Birrell was a great uncle of Auden's Gresham's friend Robert Medley: see "School Speech Days. Gresham's School, Holt," *Times*, 7 July 1925, p. 13; and Medley, *Drawn*, 22. After Gresham's, Medley remained an important figure in Auden's life. In Feb. 1927, Auden visited Medley and his lover Rupert Doone (1903–1966) in London, and through them he was then introduced to Augustine Birrell's son Francis Birrell (1889–1935). Francis Birrell was another writer in the Bloomsbury world, a "figure," and a lover of the writer and publisher David

Garnett. (Birrell and Garnett had worked together on the Friends' War Victims' Relief Committee during the Great War.) Francis Birrell, with whom Auden kept in contact during 1927, gave Auden an introduction to Sacheverell Sitwell, himself a poet and critic (Carpenter, *Auden,* 69–70). Although by this point Auden had got over an undergraduate fascination with Edith Sitwell's poems (see a letter to Isherwood of ca. 7 June 1927, cited in *J,* 191n), he met Sacheverell Sitwell for a meal in London in June 1927. It seems that, at that meeting, Sitwell, who knew Eliot through Bloomsbury circles, persuaded Auden to send his poems to Eliot, which Auden did shortly afterward. On 9 Sept. 1927, Eliot wrote back rejecting the collection but saying he would like to follow Auden's work (see *Poems1,* 547; and Chapter 4). Auden and Eliot met for the first time in London in mid-Oct. 1927. That Auden was more interested in Eliot than in simply being part of the Faber poetry list is clear from the fact that Eliot's latest biographer calls the state of the Faber list that Eliot was overseeing "unspectacular" (Crawford, *Eliot,* 106). One could fairly say that the chain of causality that eventually led to Faber and Faber being Auden's lifelong publisher began in a ploughed field in 1922 with Medley asking Auden if he wrote poetry and stretched through Auden's performance in Shakespeare's last play at Gresham's in 1925 and then, because of Medley, meetings with Francis Birrell and Sacheverell Sitwell and Eliot. Literary history is often made from contingencies and connections such as these.

88. ALS from W. H. Auden to William McElwee, 15 April 1927, cited in *J,* 198n. For more on McElwee's house, Tapscott, see Chapter 4.

89. "Out of sight assuredly, not out of mind" (1927), *J,* 195.

90. "Bones wrenched, weak whimper . . ." (1927), *Poems1,* 61. Bucknell dates the poem to May 1927 (*J,* 192). When Auden first wrote the poem he embellished it with an epigraph from his undergraduate course work—a quotation from an Eliot favorite, the Elizabethan / Jacobean playwright John Marston (1576–1634). The poem also makes an obvious allusion to *King Lear* (see Fuller, *Commentary,* 5).

91. Bucknell, introduction to *J,* xlvi.

92. See *Prose1,* 3–5.

93. ALS from W. H. Auden to William McElwee, [June 1927], Department of Manuscripts and Archives, British Library, London (from now on, referred to as BL).

94. "I chose this lean country" (1927), *Poems1,* 391–393 (from now on, cited parenthetically in the main text).

95. Cited in Bucknell, introduction to *J,* xlv. Auden and Day Lewis allude in their own preface to Wordsworth's preface to the second edition of his and Coleridge's *Lyrical Ballads* (1800); see *Prose1,* 4.

96. See "Hodge Looks toward London" (1927), *J,* 188–190.

97. G. Auden, "Difficult," 157.

98. Robert Graves, *Poetic Unreason and Other Studies* (London: Cecil Palmer, 1925), 265 (from now on, cited as Graves, *Unreason*). Graves is quoting

here his own earlier statement in *On English Poetry*... (London: William Heinemann, 1922).

99. ALS from W. H. Auden to Christopher Isherwood, [late May 1927], cited in Bucknell, introduction to *J*, xlv. See also Fuller, *Commentary*, 7. For the *Criterion* version of Yeats's poem, see W. B. Yeats, "The Tower," *The Monthly Criterion*, 5.3 (June 1927), 287–293.

100. "The Tower," Yeats, *Poems*, 199.

101. "Rocky Acres," in Robert Graves, *Complete Poems*, vol. 1, ed. Beryl Graves and Dunstan Ward (Manchester: Carcanet P, 1995), 83.

102. "Nineteen Hundred and Nineteen," Yeats, *Poems*, 210; "The Tower," Yeats, *Poems*, 194–196. Both poems are included in Yeats's collection *The Tower* (London: Macmillan, 1928). Edna Longley points out that both "Nineteen Hundred and Nineteen" and "Meditations in Time of Civil War" have many parallels with work by Wilfred Owen and that the brutal images of Yeats's poems "are marked by trench poetry" and "by the war generally": Edna Longley, "The Great War, History, and the English Lyric," in Vincent Sherry, ed., *The Cambridge Companion to the Literature of the First World War* (Cambridge: Cambridge UP, 2005), 76.

103. Graves, "Rocky Acres," *Complete Poems*, 83–84.

104. "The Tower," Yeats, *Poems*, 198.

105. Graves, "Rocky Acres," *Complete Poems*, 83.

106. See *J*, 213n.

107. For more on Margaret Marshall, who seems to have performed some form of psychoanalysis on Auden in 1927–1928, see Chapter 4.

108. This part of the poem, in which Auden's speaker-dreamer is "sucked down" into the "buried engine-room" of the unconscious mind, was considerably altered between 1927 and 1928, when the poem was published, but the essential points remain the same. Bucknell details the changes and revisions in her notes on the poem: *J*, 211–212n.

109. Auden reuses these lines in his poem "Underneath the abject willow" (1936), *Poems1*, 210. See the Epilogue.

110. For Ogilvie-Grant, see Betjeman, "Oxford," *Tribute*, 44. Ogilivie-Grant (1905–1969) later became a botanist and served in the Scots Guards during the Second World War, attached to a secret unit operating behind enemy lines in Greece before his capture. For "past the gas-works . . . ," see Day Lewis, *Buried*, 177. Auden's Oxford friend V. M. Allom (1904–1985), later a schoolmaster at Eastbourne College, wrote of Auden: "He would visit an area close to the railway where the town's rubbish was dumped and burnt, and which had as its background the city gas-works. Here he found his antidote to the architectural beauties of Christ Church, and we would brood together over flickering flames amid the acrid stench of the burning rubbish. At other times he would satisfy his need by visits to the low pubs in back streets frequented by the dregs of Oxford." See Allom's memoir, "W.H.A.: A Further Tribute" (1975), n.p., Columbia. For "in a darkened room," see Spender, *WwW*, 56 (Day Lewis also mentions the darkness

of Auden's rooms in *Buried,* 177); for "abject depression," see a letter from Auden
to William McElwee, Easter 1928, cited in Carpenter, *Auden,* 80; for two episodes of Auden as a man in his twenties bursting into tears, see *ibid.,* 50, 80.

111. For McElwee and Carritt, see Bucknell, introduction to *J,* xxxviii–
xxxix, and for more on Carritt, see Chapter 4.

112. John Betjeman, "Five," *Shenandoah,* 18.2 (Winter 1967), 47.

113. Betjeman, "Oxford," *Tribute,* 44. Betjeman means John B. Auden, not
his oldest brother, the quiet Bernard, whom Auden was never close to. See
Chapter 1.

114. "Argument" (1931), in *The Orators, Poems1,* 82.

115. Isherwood, *Lions,* 191.

116. G. Auden, "Endogenous," 22. Douglas Mao has drawn attention to
Dr. Auden and W. H. Auden's shared interest in Rivers. See Mao, "Auden and
Son: Environment, Evolution, Exhibition," *Paideuma,* 32.1–3 (Spring–Winter
2003), 312–315.

117. See earlier in this chapter.

118. Isherwood, *Lions,* 215; emphasis in original.

119. Certainly, Auden must have heard about Freud from his father before
1929. Dr. Auden mentions both Freud and Jung in passing in articles such as
his 1926 "Endogenous" essay (19–20). But this article, like many others by
Dr. Auden, is based primarily on the work of a circle of eclectic British psychiatrists centered on Rivers but also including his pupils Myers and William
McDougall. The joking reference to Freud, or his followers, comes in a letter
Auden wrote to William McElwee in 1927 in which he refers to Milton as "one
of the early Freudians" (ALS, [Easter 1927], BL).

120. "Get there if you can and see the land you once were proud to own"
(1930), *Poems1,* 45.

121. Carpenter, *Auden,* 9.

122. G. Auden, "The Biological Factors in Mental Defect," *Psyche: A Quarterly Review of Psychology,* n.s., 3.3 (Jan. 1923), 240–256 (from now on, cited as
G. Auden, "Biological").

123. G. Auden, "Endogenous," 12. In W. H. Auden's first review in the *Criterion,* he too refers to "the Rivers-Head experiments on protopathic and epicritic sensibility." [Review of *Instinct and Intuition,* by George Binney Dibblee]
(1930), *Prose1,* 5 (see also 6).

124. G. Auden, "Encephalitis Lethargica—Its Psychological Implications,"
Journal of Mental Science, 71 (Oct. 1925) 657, 656.

125. *Ibid.,* 649.

126. For more on Rivers's ideas about different strata in the nervous
system and the mind, see Chapter 4.

127. G. A. Auden, "An Unusual Form of Suicide," *Journal of Mental Science,* 73 (July 1927), 428–430 (from now on in this chapter's main discussion
of Dr. Auden's article, cited parenthetically in the text, and elsewhere as
G. Auden, "Unusual").

128. Ironically, this has proven to be one of Dr. Auden's longest-lived articles and is still sometimes cited in medical and psychiatric literature on the subject.

129. G. Auden, "Biological," 251, 250.

130. *Ibid.*, 248.

131. "As It Seemed to Us" (1964), *Prose5*, 141. See Chapter 1.

132. See Bucknell, introduction to *J*, xlix, quoting "As It Seemed to Us" (1964), *Prose5*, 141.

133. See Chapter 1.

134. "On the frontier at dawn getting down" (1927), *Poems1*, 394–395.

135. Graves, *Unreason*, 52–54.

136. See Paul Fussell, *Abroad: British Literary Travelling between the Wars* (New York: Oxford UP, 1980), 24–36 (from now on, cited as Fussell, *Abroad*).

137. [Introduction to *The Poet's Tongue*] (1935), *Prose1*, 105.

138. "Stiffens" carries the obvious double meaning of a body having an erection and a body hardening after death—states that were virtually superimposed in the case of X.Y.Z. The "feeling of identification" is a phrase Auden used in a draft of the poem beginning "It was Easter as I walked in the public gardens" (1929) in a passage about contemplating others' weaknesses and failures; see *Poems1*, 36–37, and Chapter 5.

139. "The Tower," Yeats, *Poems*, 200.

140. Keats, *Complete Poems*, ed. Jack Stillinger (Cambridge, MA: Belknap P of Harvard UP, 1982), 361.

141. "On the frontier at dawn getting down" (1927), *Poems1*, 395.

142. [Introduction to *The Poet's Tongue*] (1935), *Prose1*, 105.

143. G. Auden, "Unusual," 429. Dr. Auden's phrase "Daily fish sale round" has a sound close to "daily official round," the kind of round that Dr. Auden and other public servants were used to making.

144. "In Search of Dracula" (1934), *Prose1*, 72.

145. Bucknell, introduction to *J*, xlix.

146. See "1929 Journal" (1929), fo. [111], NYPL. See also later in this chapter. An indolent ulcer is one that is largely painless but often slow to heal.

147. Bucknell, introduction to *J*, xlix.

148. "Truly our fathers had the gout" (1927), *Poems1*, 445; "We, knowing the family history" (1927), *Poems1*, 445–446. Edward Mendelson says the second poem was written in Aug. 1927 at the Audens' home in Harborne just after the return from Yugoslavia (*Poems1*, 446). Auden used "indolent ulcer" again in his 1928 poem "Because sap fell away" (*Poems1*, 398).

149. "Truly our fathers had the gout" (1927), *Poems1*, 445. Mendelson notes that the poem was written in Split in Aug. 1927.

150. Pointed out by Mendelson in *Poems1*, 445.

151. For more on Layard (1891–1974), see Chapters 4–7.

152. *J*, 214–218, gives the poems that Auden is known to have written while in Yugoslavia with his father or shortly afterward. Bucknell offers some details and speculations about the trip in her introduction to *J*, xlviii–li.

153. See Day Lewis, *Buried*, 164–165.

154. Anthony Powell, *Infants of the Spring*, cited in Jeremy Lewis, *Cyril Connolly: A Life* (London: Jonathan Cape, 1997), 108. Bowra described himself to Isaiah Berlin as a member of the "the Immoral Front," cited in L. G. Mitchell, "Bowra, Sir (Cecil) Maurice (1898–1971)," *Oxford Dictionary of National Biography* online (Oxford: Oxford UP, 2004).

155. "A Don in the World" (1967), *Prose5*, 354.

156. Cited in Mitchell, "Bowra, Sir (Cecil) Maurice (1898–1971)."

157. "A Don in the World" (1967), *Prose5*, 354. The scare quotes around Bowra's name here are perhaps an awkward attempt to claim that the real person was not as formidable as his reputation suggested.

158. It seems likely that Bowra was one of the skeptics the thought of whom disturbed Auden when he was preparing his inaugural lecture as professor of poetry at Oxford in 1956. He wrote to Spender on 8 May that year, "I have been discovering surprising things about myself in relation to England and Oxford in particular while working on my inaugural lecture. Fits of real blind sweating panic during which a printed sentence makes no sense and I do not take in what people say to me. . . . Why are the English so terrifying?" (cited in Mendelson, introduction to *Prose4*, xiv).

159. Bowra was interested in epic poetry of the classical world, partly as a result of his study of Homer, and it seems likely that he was in Yugoslavia in connection with the research that scholars were then conducting in that country on oral poetic traditions, investigations that culminated in Milman Parry's two famous trips to Yugoslavia in 1933 and 1935.

160. From a typed transcript, apparently made by Layard, and with the note in pen at the top "W.H.A. Nov. 9th 1938," San Diego. The typist twice misspells Bowra's first name, Maurice. There might an allusion through "Morris" Bowra in this dream about Oxford to the biggest British car manufacturer at the time, Morris Motors, who produced its vehicles, including Morris Oxfords, at a large factory in Cowley, not far to the southeast of the city center.

161. Bucknell, introduction to *J*, xxix.

162. Cited in Carpenter, *Auden*, 50.

163. *St. Edmund's School Chronicle*, June 1917, cited in Carpenter, *Auden*, 18. See Chapter 1.

164. Charles Dickens, *The Life and Adventures of Nicholas Nickleby* (1839; Oxford: Oxford UP, 1950), 275.

165. Shakespeare, *The Tempest*, 5.1.

166. ALS from W. H. Auden to Theodore Spencer, [26 March 1944], Houghton Library, Harvard University. Auden was commenting on the speech he wrote for Caliban in his "commentary" on *The Tempest*, "The Sea and the Mirror" (1942–1944), which draws on some of the details from the Yugoslavia dream (see *Poems2*, 158).

167. See Chapter 1.

168. "Auden and MacNeice: Their Last Will and Testament" (1936), *Prose1*, 362 [also *Poems1*, 277]. See Chapter 1.

169. ALS from W. H. Auden to Christopher Isherwood, [July 1927], cited in Bucknell, introduction to *J*, xlix.

170. "As It Seemed to Us" (1964), *Prose5*, 151. Conor Leahy has discovered that Auden only applied for admission to read in Oxford's main academic library, the Bodleian, in mid-May 1927, toward the end of his second year at the university.

171. "We, knowing the family history" (1927), *Poems1*, 446.

172. "I chose this lean country" (1927), *Poems1*, 392–393; "On the frontier at dawn getting down" (1927), *Poems1*, 395.

173. "The Tower," Yeats, *Poems*, 198–200.

174. The friend was the poet Stephen Spender (1909–1995); see *WwW*, 58. Spender remembered Auden directing the remark at him, but here, as often, Auden was ciphering something very personal into an apparently objective statement. For more on Spender and Auden at Oxford, see Chapter 4.

4. THE ENGLISH KEYNOTE

Epigraph: Leed, *No Man's*, 107.

1. Frank Bradshaw-Isherwood's name was supposed to have been one of the roughly 55,000 inscribed on the arch by the time of this ceremony. In the event, the British authorities failed to include him at first. After protests from his widow, his name was placed on a list on one of the "addenda panels" in the upper galleries; see Parker, *Isherwood*, 270. Isherwood visited the gate and found his father's name on Armistice Day 1935.

2. "Menin Gate. War Memorial Unveiled," *Times*, 25 July 1927, p. 14. Sassoon in his poem "On Passing the New Menin Gate" calls the monument a "sepulchre of crime" that he hopes the dead will "Rise" to "deride" (*Poems*, 188).

3. Cited from the unsigned essay "Will Longstaff the artist" on the Australian War Memorial's website. Longstaff's painting is now usually known as *Menin Gate at Midnight* (1927). It is at the Australian War Memorial in Canberra.

4. "Leicester Galleries," *Times*, 6 March 1926, p. 12; "Art Exhibitions. William Blake," *Times*, 5 May 1927, p. 19.

5. "William Blake. A True Englishman. The New National Anthem," *Times*, 12 Aug. 1927, p. 11.

6. In 1932, Auden called himself a "Little Englander" in a letter to an acquaintance, Dorothy Elmhirst. See Chapter 6.

7. "William Blake. A True Englishman," p. 11.

8. Correlli Barnett, *The Collapse of British Power* (New York: William Morrow, 1972), 321.

9. Graves, *Good-Bye*, 263.

10. "Notes Regarding Details of Publication and Distribution," *The Enemy*, 2 (Sept. 1927), vii.

11. "Editorial Notes," *The Enemy*, 2 (Sept. 1927), xi–xxiii; emphasis in original. Lewis did not capitalize "french."

12. "Who stands, the crux left of the watershed" (1927), *Poems1*, 33–34. Critics identify this as Auden's first canonical poem. That is in part due to hints given by its author: somewhat portentously, Auden titled the poem "The Watershed" when he reprinted it in *The Collected Poetry of W. H. Auden* (New York: Random House, 1945). But Edward Mendelson points to a solid bedrock of bibliographical fact as the deeper reason for this understanding of the poem's significance: "His derivative early manners would persist in some of his poems for a few months more, but this was the moment when he found his own voice. In his first published volume, the 1930 *Poems*, he included two poems written before this moment, but he omitted them from the second edition published in 1933. From then on he never reprinted any poem he had written earlier than 'The Watershed'" (*EALA*, 40).

13. Freud, *Civilization and Its Discontents* (1930), *SE* 21:98.

14. Graves, *Unreason*, 2.

15. Katherine Bucknell, for instance, relates Auden's "failure to gain access to the natural world" in this poem to Auden's "early emotional experience" (introduction to *J*, xxvii).

16. On Cross Fell's summit is a cross-shaped stone shelter near an obelisk-like trig point that may be the "crux" Auden refers to in line 1 of the poem.

17. There are good discussions of the likely landscape of this poem by Edward Callan in his *Auden: A Carnival of Intellect* (New York: Oxford UP, 1983), 53 (it was Callan who first proposed Cross Fell as being the location of the poem), and more recently by Bucknell in *J*, 219n, and by Fuller in *Commentary*, 8–10. See also "A Visit to Alston Moor," *WHASN*, 2 (Sept. 1988), 1–2. On balance, the details seem to point to the poem being set on Cross Fell, Alston Moor. Cashwell (mentioned in the poem) is just over a mile away from Cross Fell. When Auden sent a draft of the poem to Isherwood, he called it "Rookhope," a place some twenty miles to the east of Cross Fell (see *J*, 219n).

18. See Chapter 2. In "Prologue at Sixty" (1967), Cross Fell is named as one of the places on Auden's "numinous map" of his "sacred" sites (*Poems2*, 628).

19. John Milton, *Paradise Lost* (1674), ed. David Scott Kastan (Indianapolis: Hackett, 2005) 12:369, p. 396 (from now on, cited as Milton, *PL*, with book and line numbers of the book followed by the page number in the edition).

20. *Ibid.*, 11:385–386, p. 361.

21. See *J*, 44–45, and Chapter 1.

22. See Chapter 2; and "A Literary Transference" (1939 or 1940?), *Prose2*, 46.

23. Howkins, "Discovery," 63.

24. I use the word "paragraph" instead of "stanza" to describe the poem's blocs of text because to call something a "stanza" implies that a poem is using relatively consistently sized, repeating units of a certain number of lines, organized around some obvious formal principle. That is not the case here.

25. "Nobody Comes," Hardy, *Works*, 3:55. Auden probably read the poem in what was then Hardy's latest collection, *Human Shows, Far Phantasies, Songs, and Trifles* (London: Macmillan, 1925).

26. Josef Breuer and Sigmund Freud, "The Psychotherapy of Hysteria," in *Studies on Hysteria* (1895), *SE*, 2:288, 291.

27. *Ibid.*, 2:293, 298–299; emphasis added.

28. "Analysis Terminable and Interminable" (1937), *SE*, 23:252; emphasis added.

29. Rivers, *Instinct*, 237; emphasis added.

30. *Ibid.*, 239.

31. Again, Eliotic language and thought survive Auden's abandonment of Eliotic surface style. "Comatose" evokes the simile of the evening sky "Like a patient etherised upon a table" in "The Love Song of J. Alfred Prufrock" (Eliot, *Poems*, 5). Fuller also notes language suggesting the presence of Eliot in the poem (*Commentary*, 10).

32. The "stimulation of the epicritic system is necessary to evoke the power of spacial discrimination." W. H. R. Rivers and Henry Head, "A Human Experiment in Nerve Division," *Brain*, 31 (Nov. 1908), 422.

33. Auden and Day Lewis wrote: "Emotion is no longer necessarily to be analysed by 'recollection in tranquillity' [an allusion to Wordsworth's preface to the 2nd ed. of *Lyrical Ballads*, where he writes that poetry "takes its origin from emotion recollected in tranquillity"]: it is to be prehended emotionally and intellectually at once," [Preface to *Oxford Poetry 1927*] (1927), *Prose1*, 4.

34. Graves, *Poetic Unreason*, 3.

35. John Denham, "Cooper's Hill," in *The Poetical Works of Sir John Denham*, ed. Theodore Howard Banks, 2nd ed. (1928; repr., Hamden: Archon, 1969), 77.

36. See Mendelson's account in *Poems1*, 547–548.

37. *J*, 187n, 229n.

38. For details see *ibid.*, 228n. Gabriel (Bill) Carritt (1908–1999) was one of four brothers who were the children of the communist activist Winifred Carritt (d. 1965) and E. F. Carritt (1876–1964), a moral and political philosopher who was a fellow of University College, Oxford. The Carritt brothers—Michael Carritt (1906–1990), Gabriel Carritt, Noel Carritt (1911–1992), and Anthony Carritt (1914–1937)—were known in Oxford as "The Golden Boys." See Deborah Baker, *The Last Englishmen: Love, War, and the End of Empire* (Minneapolis: Graywolf P, 2018), 52. Auden seems to have spent a considerable amount of time at their home on Boars Hill, just outside the city. Gabriel Carritt remained friendly with Auden well into the 1930s, and Auden wrote a number of poems in which he features, including: "Because sap

fell away" (1927; *Poems1*, 397–398); "Taller to-day, we remember similar evenings" (1928; *Poems1*, 49); "Between attention and attention" (1930; *Poems1*, 29), and perhaps "Nothing is asked of you, being beautiful" (1931; *Poems1*, 457). There is at least one other, so-far-unpublished poem, addressed to Carritt on the occasion of his birthday in May 1930: "Gabriel, fully occupied in either." The Carritt family makes an appearance in "Journal of an Airman" in *The Orators* (1930–1932), and Ode II in the same work is dedicated to Gabriel Carritt (*Poems1*, 87, 116). Gabriel's brother Anthony (of whom E. F. Carritt may not have been the biological father) was killed in the Spanish Civil War, and Noel Carritt was wounded in the same conflict. Michael Carritt, who is thought to have been a spy within the Indian Civil Service in the 1930s on behalf of the Communist Party of India, knew Auden at Oxford and later was in contact with John B. Auden in India.

39. Michael Spender (1906–1945) was a surveyor, explorer, and expert in the interpretation of aerial photography. He remained a figure at least peripherally present in Auden's life throughout the 1930s, eventually marrying the painter Nancy Sharp (1909–2001). Before she married Spender in 1943, Nancy Sharp was the wife of the painter William Coldstream (see Chapters 1 and 8) and the lover of the poet Louis MacNeice (1907–1963). Michael Spender, like Michael Carritt, was in touch with John B. Auden in India in the 1930s. Spender was killed as a result of an aircraft crash in Germany near the end of the Second World War.

40. "Suppose they met, the inevitable procedure" (1927), *Poems1*, 62. Auden explained the poem in an ALS to Isherwood of Sept. 1927, from which the quotations about "epic" here are taken. The letter is cited in *J*, 221n.

41. "The crowing of the cock" (1927), *Poems1*, 60–61.

42. "Because sap fell away" (1927), *Poems1*, 398–398.

43. "The colonel to be shot at dawn" (1927), *Poems1*, 787.

44. "The weeks of blizzard over" (1928), *Poems1*, 422. For the three names, see later in this chapter.

45. "Control of the Passes was, he saw, the key" (1928), *Poems1*, 36. Seamus Perry points out that Auden "allows just enough chiming to keep the possibility of rhyme barely present to our minds," and he links this formal feature to the vestigial possibility of connection between the poem's themes. See Perry, "W. H. Auden's 'The Secret Agent,'" *English Review*, 10.3 (Feb. 2000), 6.

46. Betjeman, "Oxford," *Tribute*, 44.

47. Wyndham Lewis, *Blasting and Bombardiering* (London: Eyre and Spottiswoode, 1937), 1. See also the Prologue.

48. "Soldier": "Will you turn a deaf ear" (1929), *Poems1*, 26; "bomb": "The spring unsettles sleeping partnerships" (1928), in *Paid on Both Sides* (1927–1929), *Poems1*, 13; "fighter": "Sometimes we read a sign" (before Sept. 1928), also in *Paid on Both Sides, Poems1*, 13.

49. "The houses rolled into the sun" (1927), *J*, 234.

50. "The weeks of blizzard over" (1928), *J*, 237.

51. See Bucknell's comments in *J*, 234n and 237n.

52. The poem is in *The Exeter Book* of Anglo-Saxon poetry; Auden's borrowing is pointed out by, among others, Fuller, *Commentary*, 15; and Bucknell in *J*, 239–240n.

53. Isherwood, *Lions*, 215; emphasis in original. See also Chapter 3.

54. "Suppose they met, the inevitable procedure" (1927), *Poems1*, 62. Letter to Isherwood cited in *J*, 221n.

55. The loans book for the English Faculty Library at Oxford records that Auden only joined the library on 20 Oct. 1927, at the start of his last year as an undergraduate. Thereafter, his borrowings between Oct. 1927 and June 1928 consisted exclusively of material from or about the medieval and Renaissance periods, including editions of poetry by Dunbar, Henryson, Malory, Skelton, Chaucer, the author of *Gawain and the Green Knight*, and Milton.

56. See the notes to "Nor was that final, for about that time" (1927), *J*, 224 [and *Poems1*, 396]; and "Control of the Passes was, he saw, the key (1928), *J*, 239 [and *Poems1*, 36].

57. Max Müller, *Lectures on the Science of Language* (1864), cited in Clare A. Simmons, "'Iron-Worded Proof': Victorian Identity and the Old English Language," *Studies in Medievalism*, 4 (1992), 208–209.

58. Thomas Carlyle, *History of Frederick II of Prussia called Frederick the Great* (1858–1865), cited in Paul Langford, *Englishness Identified: Manners and Character 1650–1850* (Oxford: Oxford UP, 2000), 20.

59. Ker added that this represented only one half of the Anglo-Saxon inheritance, the other being a literature "derived from Latin and turning into English the knowledge which was common to the whole of Europe." But his stress is on the fact that "the English in the beginning—Angles and Saxons—were heathen Germans who took part in the great movement called the Wandering of the Nations—who left their homes and emigrated to lands belonging to the Roman Empire and made slaves of the people they found there." Ker, *English Literature: Medieval* (London: Williams and Norgate, 1912), 21–22.

60. Stopford A. Brooke, *The History of Early English Literature: Being the History of English Poetry from Its Beginnings to the Accession of King Alfred* (New York: Macmillan, 1892), 5. "Widsith" is an Anglo-Saxon poem also known as "The Traveller's Song."

61. Ezra Pound, "Patria Mia," XI, *New Age*, 12.2 (14 Nov. 1912), 33.

62. J. R. R. Tolkien, "Philology: General Works," in F. S. Boas and C. H. Hereford, eds., *The Year's Work in English Studies*, vol. 5: *1924* (London: Oxford UP, 1926), 65; C. S. Lewis, "The Alliterative Metre" (1935), in *Rehabilitations and Other Essays* (London: Oxford UP, 1939), 119 (from now on, cited as Lewis, *Rehabilitations*).

63. See also Chapter 2.

64. J. R. R. Tolkien, letter to Christopher Tolkien, 6 May 1944, in *The Letters of J. R. R. Tolkien: A Selection*, ed. Humphrey Carpenter with the assistance

of Christopher Tolkien (London: George Allen and Unwin, 1981), 78. *The Silmarillion* (London: George Allen and Unwin, 1977) is a collection edited by Christopher Tolkien and Guy Gavriel Kay.

65. J. R. R. Tolkien, letter to L. W. Forster, 31 Dec. 1960, in *The Letters of J. R. R. Tolkien*, 303.

66. These lines are taken from the first, 1842 version of the translation and are cited in Andrew Wawn, *The Vikings and the Victorians: Inventing the Old North in Nineteenth-Century Britain* (Cambridge: Brewer, 2000), 187.

67. Chris Jones, *Strange Likeness: The Use of Old English in Twentieth-Century Poetry* (Oxford: Oxford UP, 2006), 49.

68. "The Alliterative Metre" (1935), Lewis, *Rehabilitations,* 127, 119, 128; emphasis in original. Shortly after finishing the alliterating *The Age of Anxiety* (1944–1947), Auden praised Lewis's essay and its explanation of alliterative meter in Ansen, *Table-Talk,* 61.

69. "Making, Knowing and Judging" (1956), *Prose4,* 484.

70. *A Certain World* (1968 [published 1970]), *Prose6,* 19.

71. Humphrey Carpenter, *The Inklings: C. S. Lewis, J. R. R. Tolkien, Charles Williams, and Their Friends* (London: George Allen and Unwin, 1978), 27. The Coal-biters study circle was a forerunner of the more celebrated Inklings group. The latter, more focused on original compositions, started meeting in Oxford in the 1930s, and Tolkien and Lewis would be members.

72. *Ibid. Kolbítar* can also be understood less idiomatically as "men who lounge so close to the fire in winter that they bite the coal." Educated at Emmanuel, Cambridge, R. M. Dawkins (1871–1955) was from 1920 a fellow of Exeter College, Oxford, and professor of Byzantine and Modern Greek. From 1916 to 1919, he had served as a naval intelligence officer in eastern Crete. Dawkins, who was unmarried, introduced Auden to the poetry of C. P. Cavafy, at that time a very coterie taste, in the late 1920s at Oxford. See [introduction to *The Complete Poems of Cavafy*] (1961), *Prose4,* 290. An expert on string figures, Dawkins also seems to have shown some examples to Auden. In "Auden and MacNeice: Their Last Will and Testament" (1936), Auden writes, "to Professor Dawkins who knows the Modern Greeks | I leave the string figure called the Fighting Lions" (*Prose1,* 370 [also *Poems1,* 285]; see also Mendelson's explanatory notes in *Prose1,* 795; and *Poems1,* 694). In "The month was April, the year" (1933), Auden imagines a ship that is an image of his psyche, and on it, "busy doing cat's cradles—[was] | The one they all called the Professor" (*Poems1,* 499). See Chapter 7. Fuller notes that Dawkins had published an article on string figures in *Annals of Archaeology and Anthropology* (1931): see *Commentary,* 184. J. N. Bryson (1896–1976), a lifelong bachelor and Oxford fixture, was a lecturer in English at Merton during this period.

73. Carpenter, *Auden,* 28.

74. Betjeman, "Oxford," *Tribute,* 44–45.

75. Bowra (1898–1971) had served in the Royal Field Artillery and fought on the Western Front from 1917 until the Armistice. See Chapter 3 for more about his destructive impact on Auden.

76. Fussell, *Abroad*, 4–5.

77. Tolkien, *Letters of J. R. R. Tolkien*, 55–56, cited in Garth, *Tolkien*, 42.

78. Graves, *Good-Bye*, 262; emphasis in original.

79. Two of the main studies of the war's impact on Tolkien's fiction are Hugh Brogan, "Tolkien's Great War," in Gillian Avery and Julia Briggs, eds., *Children and Their Books: A Celebration of the Work of Iona and Peter Opie* (Oxford: Clarendon P, 1989), 351–367; and Garth, *Tolkien*.

80. See Chapter 1.

81. "The Homecoming of Beorthnoth Beorhthelm's Son," in J. R. R. Tolkien, *Poems and Stories* (London: George Allen and Unwin, 1980), 88. Carl Phelpstead notes that Tolkien wrote the poem sometime before 1935. See Phelpstead, "Auden and the Inklings: An Alliterative Revival," *Journal of English and Germanic Philology*, 103.4 (Oct. 2004), 441. At the end of the poem, as the "cart" carrying the dead lord's body, as well as Tídwald and Torhthelm, "rumbles and bumps on," Tídwald complains about the roughness of the ride: "Hey! rattle and bump over rut and boulder! | The roads are rough and rest is short | for English men in Æthelred's day" (Tolkien, "Homecoming," 100). Tolkien intends the reader to pick up a reflection on the natural roughness and bumpiness of the "road" of alliterative English meter. W. S. Landor's eastern European prince uses a similar metaphor to differentiate between Ovid's Latin smoothness and his own Gothic ruggedness: "Thine resembled a car running smoothly over the frozen river; mine the same car jolting upon rough masses of ice." See Landor, "Ovid and a Prince of the Getæ" (1855), in *The Complete Works of Walter Savage Landor*, vol. 2, ed. T. Earle Welby (London: Chapman and Hall, 1927), 213.

82. "Futility" (1918), Owen, *Poems*, 135. (Auden began reading Wilfred Owen, sporadically at first, around 1926, and he used the line "Was it for this the clay grew tall?" from "Futility" as the epigraph for his autumn 1926 poem "Consequences." *J*, 162.) In another linkage between the war and Old English poetry, David Jones (1895–1974), describing life in the trenches, alludes to the "white-tailed eagle at the battle ebb," a sea eagle hovering over corpses at the close of *The Battle of Brunanburgh*, as well as the "speckled kite of Maldon." See Jones, *In Parenthesis: Seinnyessit e Gledyf ym Penn Mameu* (1937; London: Faber and Faber, 1963), 54. In 1930, C. S. Lewis too tried his hand at an alliterative poem when he wrote "The Nameless Isle," a 742-line narrative set on an enchanted island. See Phelpstead, "Auden and the Inklings," 439.

83. C. S. Lewis, "The Dethronement of Power," *Time and Tide*, 22 Oct. 1955; cited in Garth, *Tolkien*, 311.

84. C. S. Lewis to Dom Bede Griffiths, 8 May 1939, in Lewis, *Collected Letters*, vol. 2: *Books, Broadcasts and War 1931–1949*, ed. Walter Hooper (London: HarperCollins, 2004), 258.

85. C. S. Lewis, *Surprised by Joy: The Shape of My Early Life* (New York: Harcourt, Brace, Jovanovich, 1955), 96.

86. Nevill Coghill, "The Approach to English," in Jocelyn Gibb, ed., *Light on C. S. Lewis* (New York: Harcourt, Brace and World, 1965), 58. *Dauber* was a narrative poem about the sea published by Masefield in 1912. The first part of "A Happy New Year," which Auden wrote in early 1932, is in rhyme royal (*Poems1*, 137–144). See Chapter 6.

87. Clive Hamilton [C. S. Lewis], *Dymer* (New York: Dutton, 1926), 47, 82.

88. Jones, *Strange Likeness*, 34–35.

89. "The Planets," in "The Alliterative Metre" (1935), Lewis, *Rehabilitations*, 131.

90. Lines 1305–1306 of *Beowulf*: "Nor was that a good exchange, that they on both sides should pay with the lives of friends!" See Fuller, *Commentary*, 20.

91. *Paid on Both Sides* (1927–1929), *Poems1*, 7 (from now on, cited parenthetically in the text). The "charade" survives in two main states. Auden began writing the poems that coalesced into *Paid on Both Sides* in Dec. 1927, and by around July or early Aug. 1928 he had finished a version that he thought good enough for amateur performance. However, he did not complete what he thought of as the second, final version until Dec. 1928. He then made a few changes in April 1929. But because the basic scenario of the charade had been set by the late summer of 1928 and because Auden completed thirteen (i.e., over half) of the twenty-two separate lyrics in the final version of the charade before Oct. 1928, for the sake of a clear focus I discuss the entire work in this chapter. Throughout, though, my analysis refers to the completed version. See Mendelson's textual history of the charade in *Poems1*, 551–552.

92. Auden's full phrase is "A parable of English Middle Class (professional) family life 1907–1929." Cited by Mendelson in the introduction to *Poems1*, xiii.

93. "The Pity of It," in *Moments of Vision* (1917), Hardy, *Works*, 2:294. The title is taken from words spoken by Othello to Iago (Shakespeare, *Othello*, 4.1).

94. Cunningham, *British*, 16. After relative neglect in the immediate aftermath of the war (the first moderately comprehensive book written in English about the war poets, T. Sturge Moore's *Some Soldier Poets*, published in 1920, does not even mention Owen), by the second half of the 1920s Owen (1893–1918) was rising rapidly in stature among younger poets and readers such as Auden. Samuel Hynes wrote that: "The poets who had served as soldiers were heroes to those who came after, and Wilfred Owen in particular became a sort of martyred saint, whose words 'the poetry is in the pity' were repeated like a prayer or a line of scripture" (*Auden Gen*, 23). The quotation is from Owen's 1918 "Preface" (Owen, *Poems*, 192). When Auden met people, such as Sacheverell Sitwell in 1927 (see Chapter 3), who had met Owen, he must have felt that he had got tantalizingly close to encountering Owen's ghost. Owen was

closer to Sacheverell's brother, Osbert Sitwell, but in the summer of 1918 Owen became interested in Sacheverell Sitwell's poetry, and he and Sitwell did meet at least once during that year, introduced by Robbie Ross and Siegfried Sassoon. See Dominic Hibberd, *Wilfred Owen: A New Biography* (London: Weidenfeld and Nicolson, 2002), 315, 406n8; Sarah Bradford, *Sacheverell Sitwell: Splendours and Miseries* (London: Sinclair-Stevenson, 1993), 84.

95. See "Preface" (1918), Owen, *Poems,* 192.

96. Peter Firchow makes this point in *W. H. Auden: Contexts for Poetry* (Newark: U of Delaware P, 2002), 42.

97. Donald G. Scragg, "The Nature of Old English Verse," in Malcolm Godden and Michael Lapidge, eds., *The Cambridge Companion to Old English Literature* (Cambridge: Cambridge UP, 1991), 55.

98. Heaney is discussing the style of *Beowulf.* See Seamus Heaney, introduction to *Beowulf: A New Verse Translation* (New York: Farrar, Straus and Giroux, 2000), xxviii.

99. "The Alliterative Metre" (1935), Lewis, *Rehabilitations,* 121.

100. G. A. Auden, "Encephalitis Lethargica—Its Psychological Implications," *Journal of Mental Science,* 71 (Oct. 1925), 647.

101. "Films of the Week. 'North of the Rio Grande,'" *Times,* 16 July 1923, p. 14.

102. "Election Day in Chicago. Police versus 'Gangsters,'" *Times,* 10 April 1928, p. 9.

103. "Another Gangster Shot in New York. Silver Coffin to Be Used," *Times,* 4 July 1928, p. 15.

104. Cited in Marilyn Yaquinto, *Pump 'Em Full of Lead: A Look at Gangsters on Film* (New York: Twayne, 1998), 19.

105. "W.H.A. to E.M.A.–No. 1" (1936), in *Letters from Iceland, Prose1,* 265. A subliminal influence of the gangster genre on *Paid on Both Sides* may be one reason for the often-noted fact that some of the characters in this play, ostensibly set in the North Pennines, have American-sounding names, in particular the patriarch of the Shaws, "Red Shaw."

106. "The Gangster as Tragic Hero" (1948), in Robert Warshow, *The Immediate Experience: Movies, Comics, Theatre, and Other Aspects of Popular Culture* (1962; Garden City: Anchor, 1964), 87.

107. In *The Real War (1914–1918)* (London: Faber and Faber, 1930), the military historian B. H. Liddell Hart (who fought at the Somme) self-consciously turned away from "the trend of recent war literature," which focused on the individual soldier. Andrew Frayn discusses the war-books boom in his *Writing Disenchantment: British First World War Prose, 1914–30* (Manchester: Manchester UP, 2014), 201–239.

108. Radclyffe Hall, *The Well of Loneliness* (London: Jonathan Cape, 1928).

109. Wyndham Lewis, *The Childermass* (London: Chatto and Windus, 1928).

110. Similarly, H.D. drafted her roman à clef set during the First World War, *Bid Me to Live*, in 1927, though it was only published in 1960. Auden wrote about *In Parenthesis* in "'The Geste Says This and the Man Who Was on the Field . . .'" (1962), *Prose4*, 408–411, calling it "the finest long poem written in English in this century" (411).

111. David Stevenson, *Cataclysm: The First World War as Political Tragedy* (New York: Basic Books, 2004), 462.

112. Samuel Hynes, *A War Imagined: The First World War and English Culture* (London: Bodley Head, 1990), 282. See also *ibid.*, 382.

113. Cited in Modris Eksteins, "Memory and the Great War," in Hew Strachan, ed., *The Oxford Illustrated History of the First World War* (1998; Oxford: Oxford UP, 2000), 315.

114. Stevenson, *Cataclysm*, 470.

115. See John Onions, *English Fiction and Drama of the Great War: 1918–39* (Basingstoke: Macmillan, 1990), 50–51.

116. Thus, between 1928 and 1933 Faber and Gwyer, then from 1929 Faber and Faber, published at least nineteen books of various kinds (poetry, memoir, history, fiction, and so on) centrally concerned with the First World War.

117. Hansen, *Unknown*, 267.

118. Denis Winter, *Death's Men: Soldiers of the Great War* (London: Allen Lane, 1978), 252.

119. On the millions of soldiers of color in the opposing armies, see David Olusoga, *The World's War: Forgotten Soldiers of Empire* (London: Head of Zeus, 2015).

120. Leed, *No Man's*, 189.

121. *Ibid.*, 185; Bourke, *Dismembering*, 109.

122. Hynes, *War Imagined*, 465.

123. Fussell, *GW*, 326.

124. Eliot's letter of 6 Jan. 1930 to E. McKnight Kauffer is cited in Haffenden, *Heritage*, 77.

125. [Siegfried Sassoon], *Memoirs of an Infantry Officer* (London: Faber and Faber, 1930), 117.

126. See, for example, Fuller's remark: "The Nower-Shaw feud represents a psychic split in one individual" (*Commentary*, 27).

127. See *Poems1*, 14–18.

128. Noted in Fuller, *Commentary*, 19.

129. For examples of references to "the Mill" and "the Farm" in the Belgium war quagmire, see Edmund Blunden, *Undertones of War* (London: Cobden-Sanderson, 1928), 124, 228.

130. Fuller identifies the Rookhope Smelt Mill in *Commentary*, 21. When Nower says that "we must fight to the finish," he echoes Secretary of War Lloyd George's famous words at the end of Sept. 1916 when rumors of a peace settlement were circulating: "The fight must be to a finish—to a knock-out." See

"'Never Again!' Battle-Cry of the Allies. No Time for Peace Talk. Mr. Ll. George's Warning to Neutrals," *Times*, 29 Sept. 1916, p. 7.

131. See Fuller, *Commentary*, 27–29.

132. Rivers, *Conflict*, 5.

133. *Ibid.*, 22. In this book, Sassoon is given the pseudonym Patient B. In Sassoon's war trilogy, published between 1928 and 1936, Rivers is the only significant character whose name Sassoon does not change from his real one.

134. Rivers, *Conflict*, 31.

135. *Ibid.*, 26. Rivers's account of the dream and his entire commentary about it are *ibid.*, 22–32.

136. "Layard" is John Layard (1891–1974), an anthropologist, pupil of Rivers, disciple of the American psychologist and educator Homer Lane (1875–1925) and former patient of a number of distinguished psychiatrists. Auden would meet Layard and be impressed by him in Berlin in 1929. In 1938, Layard was the person who recorded Auden's 1927 Yugoslavia dream (see Chapter 3). For more on Layard, see Chapters 5 and 7, as well as Jeremy MacClancy, "Layard, John Willoughby (1891–1974)," *Oxford Dictionary of National Biography* online (Oxford: Oxford UP, 2004).

137. "1929 Journal" (1929), fo. [58], NYPL. See Trigant Burrow, *The Social Basis of Consciousness: A Study in Organic Psychology Based upon a Synthetic and Societal Concept of the Neuroses* (London: Kegan Paul, Trench, Trubner, 1927), xvii–xviii (from now on, cited as Burrow, *Social*). Trigant Burrow (1875–1950), who had been analyzed by Jung, was the president of the American Psychoanalytic Association before being expelled from the organization, after criticisms by Freud and others of Burrow's unorthodox ideas on group dynamics. For more about Burrow's impact on Auden's poetry, see Chapter 5.

138. The gap of twenty years is unclear in the actual text of the play (*Poems1*, 8) because, as Auden admitted to a friend, he forgot to include this in the stage directions. See Mendelson, *EALA*, 54.

139. R. J. E. Tiddy, *The Mummers' Play: With a Memoir*, ed. R. S. Thompson (Oxford: Clarendon P, 1923), 3; Auden's copy is now at Emory University. The book by Tiddy (1880–1916) was prepared for publication after the war by his friends.

140. Wawn, *Vikings and the Victorians*, 334.

141. G. Auden, "Difficult," 157.

142. Fuller, *Commentary*, 34.

143. G. A. Auden, "The Madness of Ajax, as Conceived by Sophocles, Clinically Considered," *Journal of Mental Science*, 72 (Oct. 1926), 503. The quotation is from Arnold's poem "To a Friend" (1848?); see *The Poems of Matthew Arnold*, ed. Kenneth Allott and Miriam Allott, 2nd ed. (London: Longman, 1979), 111. See also Chapter 7.

144. G. A. Auden, "Madness of Ajax," 512.

145. "I chose this lean country" (1927), *Poems1*, 392. See Chapter 3.

146. Cited in *J*, 212n. Margaret Gordon Geddes (1899–1976) was the daughter of an army officer and his wife stationed in India. She had four husbands (Donald Tucker, Douglas Marshall, John B. Auden, and Gordon McDonell). She eventually became a story editor for David O. Selznick in Hollywood in the postwar period. Some writers have suggested that she was influenced by the French psychologist and self-help guru Émile Coué (1857–1926); see Bucknell in *J*, 247n; and D-H, *Auden*, 70–74.

147. Day Lewis, *Buried*, 151–152.

148. ALS from W. H. Auden to John B. Auden, [late July 1927], present location unknown. Eventually she seems to have analyzed John Auden in Paris in around 1929–1930. "When they were back on the street, Margaret asked him if he was enjoying his analysis. 'Very much.' 'Wystan answered in just the same resentful manner,' she said, sounding pleased." Cited in Baker, *Last Englishmen*, 41. After her queer, tubercular husband Douglas Marshall died, Margaret Marshall followed John B. Auden to India, where they were very unhappily married from 1930 to 1933.

149. ALS from W. H. Auden to Christopher Isherwood, [late March 1928?], Huntington.

150. ALS from W. H. Auden to David Ayerst, [summer 1928?], NYPL. It is not certain that Auden spent these three weeks of analysis in the care of Marshall, but it seems likely that he did.

151. Carpenter, *Auden*, 80.

152. Mendelson explains the composition history in *Poems1*, 551–552.

153. Carpenter, *Auden*, 81.

154. The house, Tapscott, which Auden had visited during April 1927, is near the village of Woodgate in Somerset. The nearest substantial town is Wellington. McElwee's widowed mother lived there, her husband, John McElwee, a retired deputy surgeon-general in the Royal Navy, having died in 1916. See also Chapter 3.

155. ALS from W. H. Auden to Christopher Isherwood, [Aug. 1928], cited in *Poems1*, 552.

156. For more on the ending of the engagement, see Chapter 5.

157. "To throw away the key and walk away" (1928), *Poems1*, 403. The lyric was later absorbed into the longer version of *Paid on Both Sides* (1927–1929), *Poems1*, 18–19.

158. There is another poem, written very close in time to "To throw away the key and walk away," that begins: "The spring unsettles sleeping partnerships" (1928), *Poems1*, 13. It too uses Owenesque pararhyme. Owen, who was born just on the English side of the Welsh border but who had roots in Wales, uses the term "pararhyme" for the technique of *proest*. Both Auden poems can be dated to Aug. 1928, but manuscript notations by Auden indicate that "To throw away" was written in Belgium and "The spring unsettles" when he got back to his parents' home in Harborne, Birmingham, in the second half of the month. Both are in the longer version of *Paid on Both Sides* included in *Poems* (1930), but only

"To throw away" appears in *Poems* (1928). On the use of pararhymes, see Mendelson, *EALA*, 59. Auden had earlier deployed a few Owenesque pararhymes in "I chose this lean country" (*Poems1*, 391–393; see Chapter 3), but there the slenderness of the lines, which evokes Yeats's style, partially disguises the relationship to Owen. In "To throw away the key," the connection is less camouflaged.

159. Mendelson gives a full account of the making of the book in *Poems1*, 785–786. The most up-to-date published account of the book's distribution is also by Mendelson: "A Revised Census of Auden's *Poems* (1928)," *WHASN*, 26 (Dec. 2005), 14–19. He estimates that around thirty copies were produced. Conor Leahy has tracked the distribution of various inscribed copies of Auden's next book in "Some Copies of *Poems* (1930)," *WHASN*, 41 (Feb. 2023), 5–19.

160. "As It Seemed to Us" (1964), *Prose5*, 157; see as well "Letter to Lord Byron" (1936), *Poems1*, 256 [also *Prose1*, 333].

5. STRANGE MEETINGS

Epigraph: W. H. Auden to Margaret Church, 12 Nov. 1941, quoted in Margaret Church, "For This Is Orpheus: or, Rilke, Auden and Spender" (MA diss., Columbia U, 1942), iii.

1. "Strange Meeting" (1918), Owen, *Poems*, 125.
2. Leed, *No Man's*, 20.
3. "Strange Meeting" (1918), Owen, *Poems*, 125–126.
4. *Ibid.*, 125.
5. "Reconciliation," in Walt Whitman, *Poetry and Prose*, ed. Justin Kaplan (New York: Library of America, 1982), 453.
6. Owen, "Strange Meeting" (1918), *Poems*, 126.
7. *Ibid.*, 126; ellipses in the original. The poem was first printed in the Sitwells' *Wheels* anthology in 1919. Sassoon then placed it first in the edition of Owen's poetry he published in 1920. Critics debate if the poem is finished or exists as a draft. I treat it as a completed poem into which, at the end, a feeling of brokenness has been artfully built.
8. Contribution to "What France Means to You," *La France libre*, 8.44 (15 June 1944), 94; emphasis in original.
9. Valentine Cunningham was one of the first literary historians to insist on the importance of Germany to English-speaking artists in the interwar period. See Cunningham, *British*, 346–348. For more on British hostility to France in the 1920s, see Chapter 4.
10. "Are the English Europeans?: The Island and the Continent" (1962), *Prose4*, 431. See also "As It Seemed to Us" (1964), *Prose5*, 144–145; and "Letter to Lord Byron" (1936), *Prose1*, 330 [also *Poems1*, 253]. See Chapter 1.
11. Isherwood, *Lions*, 181.
12. See "Consequences" (1926), *Poems1*, 418–419; and section 2 of "The Megalopsych" (1926), *J*, 199, 204n.

13. The poems, both of which were integrated into the second version of *Paid on Both Sides* (1927–1929), are "To throw away the key and walk away" (*Poems1*, 18–19), written in Spa, and "The Spring unsettles sleeping partnerships" (*Poems1*, 13), written in Birmingham. See Chapter 4. Auden wrote another important poem in Owen's slant rhymes in Berlin in Nov. 1929: "Because I'm come it does not mean to hold" (*Poems1*, 15). Other poems using this Owenesque technique include "Since you are going to begin today" (*Poems1*, 27–28), also written in Nov. 1929.

14. Cited in T. G. Foote, "W. H. Auden—Interview IV" (1963), unpublished typescript.

15. "To throw away the key and walk away" (1928), *Poems1*, 18–19; "The Spring unsettles sleeping partnerships" (1928), *Poems1*, 13.

16. Rothehütte, in the province of Saxony in 1929, was at the time a tiny collection of houses and farms in the Harz Mountains, just southwest of Stadt Elbingerode and sitting at the foot of the Brocken, the highest peak in northern Germany.

17. "Berlin, as Viewed from the Landscape" (1932), in Ernst Bloch, *Literary Essays,* trans. Andrew Joron et al. (Stanford: Stanford UP, 1998), 361.

18. Sergiusz Michalski, *New Objectivity: Painting, Graphic Art and Photography in Weimar Germany 1919–1933,* trans. Michael Claridge (Cologne: Taschen, 1994), 23.

19. Wilhelm Stapel, "The Intellectual and His People" (1930), in Anton Kaes, Martin Jay, and Edward Dimendberg, eds., *The Weimar Republic Sourcebook* (Berkeley: U of California P, 1994), 423 (from now on, cited as *Weimar Sourcebook*).

20. Edited by Friedrich Radszuweit, it ran monthly from 1925 to 1932 and is said to have had a circulation of around 150,000. See Mel Gordon, *Voluptuous Panic: The Erotic World of Weimar Berlin* (Venice, CA: Feral House, 2000), 90–92 (from now on, cited as Gordon, *Voluptuous*).

21. The Weimar Republic, the first constitutional federal republic in Germany's history, lasted from 1918 to 1933.

22. Cicely Hamilton, "Sun Bathing," *Week-End Review,* 7.165 (6 May 1933), 524.

23. Sabine Rewald et al., *Glitter and Doom: German Portraits from the 1920s* (New York/New Haven: Metropolitan Museum of Art/Yale UP, 2006), 54 (from now on, cited as Rewald, *Glitter*).

24. Michalski, *New Objectivity,* 54.

25. Hans Sahl, cited in Ian Buruma, "Faces of the Weimar Republic," in Rewald, *Glitter,* 17.

26. Wolf Von Eckardt and Sander L. Gilman, *Bertolt Brecht's Berlin: A Scrapbook of the Twenties* (Garden City: Anchor/Doubleday, 1975), 52. For more on Toller, see Chapter 8.

27. Cited in Piers Brendon, *The Dark Valley: A Panorama of the 1930s* (London: Jonathan Cape, 2000), 27.

28. Alexandra Richie, *Faust's Metropolis: A History of Berlin* (London: HarperCollins, 1998), 321.

29. Cited in Sabine Rewald, "I Must Paint You!," in Rewald, *Glitter,* 8.

30. Joseph Roth, "Farewell to the Dead" (1925) and "The Unnamed Dead" (1923), in *What I Saw: Reports from Berlin 1920–1933,* trans. Michael Hofmann (New York: Norton, 2003), 199, 79.

31. "Our Italy" (1952), *Prose3,* 321.

32. Von Eckardt and Gilman, *Bertolt Brecht's Berlin,* 149.

33. The cartoon is reproduced in *Berlin in Lights: The Diaries of Count Harry Kessler, 1918–1937,* trans. and ed. Charles Kessler (1971; repr., New York: Grove P, 1999), 354.

34. Gordon, *Voluptuous,* 202.

35. TLS from W. H. Auden to Patience [Kennington] (1910–1963), [Dec. 1928?], BL. Kennington and McElwee married in Dec. 1930. Patience McElwee became a novelist and author of books for young adults.

36. Siegfried Kracauer, "Murder Trials and Society" (1931), in *Weimar Sourcebook,* 740–741.

37. George Grosz, *George Grosz: An Autobiography,* trans. Nora Hodges (New York: Macmillan, 1983), 129.

38. Cited in T. G. Foote, "Preliminary Interview with W. H. Auden" [25 Jan. 1963], unpublished typescript.

39. Ernst Bloch, "Nonsynchronism and the Obligation to Its Dialectics" (1932), trans. Mark Ritter, *New German Critique,* 11 (Spring 1977), 30, 26.

40. See Gordon, *Voluptuous,* 195.

41. *Ibid.,* 171.

42. Magnus Hirschfeld, *Sittengeschichte des Weltkrieges* (Moral history of the world wars) (1930), cited in Gordon, *Voluptuous,* 11.

43. Parker, *Isherwood,* 162.

44. TLS from W. H. Auden to Patience [Kennington], [Dec. 1928?], BL. Auden calls *Paid on Both Sides* "the play" in a letter of Aug. 1928 to Isherwood (cited in *Poems1,* 552).

45. "Can speak of trouble" (1928), in *Paid on Both Sides* (1927–1929), *Poems1,* 8.

46. Ian Buruma, "Faces of the Weimar Republic," in Rewald, *Glitter,* 19.

47. Chris Bryant, *The Glamour Boys: The Secret Story of the Rebels Who Fought for Britain to Defeat Hitler* (London: Bloomsbury, 2020), 51–52.

48. Artur Landsberger wrote in 1929: "uproars and cocaine are the sociological comforts of the metropolis." Landsberger, "The Berlin Underworld" (1929), in *Weimar Sourcebook,* 732. For the prosaic details of Berlin nightlife, and especially gay nightlife, see Curt Moreck, "Stammlokale des männlichen Eros," in *Führer durch das "lasterhafte" Berlin* (1931; Berlin: Nicolaische Verlagsbuchhandlung, 1996), 130–156.

49. Cited in Otto Friedrich, *Before the Deluge: A Portrait of Berlin in the 1920's* (New York: Harper and Row, 1972), 130.

50. Wyndham Lewis, *Hitler* (London: Chatto and Windus, 1931), 21 (from now on, cited as Lewis, *Hitler*).

51. Gordon, *Voluptuous,* 51.

52. *Weimar Sourcebook,* 718.

53. Gordon, *Voluptuous,* 27–28.

54. *Ibid.,* 93.

55. Barbara Ulrich, *Hot Girls of Weimar Berlin* (Venice, CA: Feral House, 2002), 73.

56. Rewald, *Glitter,* 228.

57. Gordon, *Voluptuous,* 99.

58. Hirschfeld (1868–1935) lived at the institute with his partner and the institute's chief archivist, Karl Giese (1898–1938), whom Hirschfeld had met after Giese attended one of Hirschfeld's lectures.

59. Gordon, *Voluptuous,* 153.

60. *Ibid.,* 164–169.

61. *Ibid.,* 165.

62. "1929 Journal" (1929), fo. [3], NYPL. This is a combination of journal and notebook that Auden started keeping in April 1929 in Berlin and continued to use sporadically after he returned to England in July 1929. Many of the entries are undated.

63. Rudy Koshar, "'What Ought to Be Seen': Tourists' Guidebooks and National Identities in Modern Germany and Europe," *Journal of Contemporary History,* 33.3 (July 1998), 337.

64. Eugen Szatmari, *Das Buch von Berlin* (Munich: R. Piper, 1927), vol. 1 of the "Was nicht im 'Baedeker' steht" series. Auden alludes to this series in the title of his poem "Not in Baedeker" (1949), *Poems2,* 372–373.

65. Moreck, *Führer durch das "lasterhafte" Berlin,* 130–156.

66. Klaus Mann, *The Pious Dance: The Adventure Story of a Young Man,* trans. Laurence Senelick (New York: PAJ, 1987), 11. The original is Klaus Mann, *Der fromme Tanz: Das Abenteuerbuch einer Jugend* (Hamburg: Gebrüder Enoch, 1925).

67. Mann, *Pious Dance,* 75.

68. John Henry Mackay, *The Hustler: The Story of a Nameless Love from Friedrich Street,* trans. Hubert Kennedy (Boston: Alyson, 1985), 189. The original is Sagitta (Mackay's pen name), *Der Puppenjunge: Die Geschichte einer namenlosen Liebe aus der Friedrichstraße* (Berlin: privately printed, 1926).

69. Mackay, *Hustler,* 23, 130, 87.

70. *Ibid.,* 256.

71. "1929 Journal" (1929), fo. [61], NYPL (see also *ibid.,* fo. [25], for notes about another visit to the "Adonis-Diele").

72. Jens Dobler, *Von anderen Ufern: Geschichte der Berliner Lesben und Schwulen in Kreuzberg und Friedrichshain* (Berlin: Bruno Gmünder, 2003), 160–161. In April 1929, Auden visited another bar on the same street at Skalitzerstraße 49. See "1929 Journal" (1929), fo. [41], NYPL.

73. Christopher Isherwood, *Christopher and His Kind* (New York: Farrar, Straus and Giroux, 1976), 29–30 (from now on, cited as Isherwood, *C&HK*).

74. ALS from W. H. Auden to Christopher Isherwood, [30 Jan. 1961?], Huntington.

75. TLS from W. H. Auden to Patience [Kennington], [Dec. 1928?], BL.

76. For more on Otto Küsel (1909–1984), see later in this chapter. The other (partial) exception to this statement is the man referred to here as "Gerhart Meyer"—Auden writes about him in the "1929 Journal," and he is mentioned, along with "Kurt Groote," in a poem (part of a sequence) beginning, "It was Easter as I walked in the public gardens" (1929), *Poems1*, 37; see later in this chapter. Groote (or Grote) is apparently the inspiration for the March 1929 poem beginning "Love by ambition" (see *Poems1*, 32–33, 562). Auden saw Gerhart Meyer again in Berlin in 1955 and was disappointed by the physical changes that time had wrought.

77. "1929 Journal" (1929), fo. [70], NYPL.

78. *Ibid.*, fo. [39].

79. Mendelson, *EALA*, 578. The list is tipped into a notebook in the NYPL.

80. "Because I'm come it does not mean to hold" (1928), in *Paid on Both Sides* (1927–1929), *Poems1*, 15.

81. In a letter of 26 Jan. 1963 to William Channing West, Auden commented: "I was present, it so happens, at the Première of Die Dreigroschenoper." Since the opening night had taken place at the end of Aug. 1928, before Auden arrived in the city, Auden must have meant that he saw a performance from the original production's run, which starred Harald Paulsen and Lotte Lenya (later a friend of Auden's). The letter is cited in West, "Concepts of Reality in the Poetic Drama of W. B. Yeats, W. H. Auden, and T. S. Eliot" (Ph.D. diss., Stanford U, 1964), 108n37.

82. Medley, *Drawn*, 89.

83. Cited in David Mellor, "London-Berlin-London: A Cultural History: The Reception and Influence of the New German Photography in Britain 1927–33," in David Mellor, ed., *Germany: The New Photography 1927–33* (London: Arts Council, 1978), 124.

84. Cf. Fredric Jameson, *Fables of Aggression: Wyndham Lewis, the Modernist as Fascist* (Berkeley: U of California P, 1979), 89.

85. David Stevenson, *Cataclysm: The First World War as Political Tragedy* (New York: Basic Books, 2004), 462.

86. Hugh David, *Stephen Spender: A Portrait with Background* (London: Heinemann, 1992), 17. Spender's mother, Violet Schuster (1877–1921), came from a family of Germans who had converted to Christianity and had long lived in London. Isherwood's most famous evocations of the city come in *Mr. Norris Changes Trains* (1935), *Goodbye to Berlin* (1939), and *CH&K* (1976); and Spender's come in *WwW* (1951) and, intermittently, in *The Temple* (composed in 1929 but only published, in altered form, in 1988).

87. The novelist and short story writer Edward Upward (1903–2009) (see also Chapters 5–7); the poet and society figure Brian Howard (1905–1958); the poet and editor John Lehmann (1907–1987).

88. Patrick Seale and Maureen McConville, *Philby: The Long Road to Moscow* (London: Hamish Hamilton, 1973), 34–35. Like John Cornford (1915–1936), another dominant figure in Cambridge communism, Haden Guest (1911–1938) was killed fighting in Spain.

89. Deborah Frizzell, *Humphrey Spender's Humanist Landscapes: Photodocuments, 1932–1942* (New Haven: Yale Center for British Art, 1997), 13. In the 1930s, Humphrey Spender (1910–2005) worked for *Harper's Bazaar* and the *Daily Mirror* (as "Lensman") besides joining the Mass Observation movement in the decade's second half.

90. Norman Page, *Auden and Isherwood: The Berlin Years* (New York: St. Martin's P, 1998), 12–13. For Howard, see Marie-Jaqueline Lancaster, ed., *Brian Howard: Portrait of a Failure* (London: Anthony Blond, 1968), 230, 239–240. Howard's mother was hoping that Prinzhorn would be able to change her son's sexual orientation.

91. Cited in Brendon, *Dark Valley,* 90.

92. Repr. in translation in *Weimar Sourcebook,* 409.

93. Lewis, *Hitler,* 3, 193. The word "german" is lowercased in the original.

94. John Layard, "Autobiography: History of a Failure" [1967], box 59, folder 6–7, fo. 236, San Diego (from now on, cited with folio number as Layard, "Autobiography" [1967], San Diego).

95. Layard, "Autobiography" [1967], fo. 169, San Diego.

96. Layard believed that Rivers was "crypto-homosexual" but highly repressed. In Layard's autobiography, he recounts the episode in which Rivers rejected him. See *ibid.,* fos. 104, 115–116. See also Chapters 3 and 4.

97. ALS from David Ayerst to John Layard, 19 Nov. 1928, San Diego; "Biography," in the online "Register of the John Willoughby Layard Papers, 1897–1974" at the library website of UC San Diego. Layard (1891–1974) arrived in Berlin from Vienna, where he had been in treatment with Wilhelm Stekel. Lt. Peter Layard (1896–1918), who served with the Suffolk Regiment, was killed at Gomiécourt in the Pas-de-Calais in the last months of the war.

98. Layard, "Autobiography" [1967], fo. 201, San Diego.

99. "1929 Journal" (1929), fo. [5], NYPL; "The Fronny" (1930), *Plays,* 478; see also Chapter 6.

100. See Chapters 2–4.

101. "1929 Journal" (1929), fo. [5], NYPL. Mendelson gives a summary of Homer Lane's fundamental ideas in *EALA,* 55–59. Lane (1875–1925) was involved through much of his career with helping juvenile delinquents in an institutional context (which perhaps sparked some of Auden's interest, given his own father's professional duties). But Lane also treated individual patients. In 1913, he took charge of the Little Commonwealth near Batcombe in Dorset, a libertarian community for young people who had run into trouble with the

law. In 1917, Lane was accused of sexual misconduct by two of the home's residents. The Little Commonwealth closed in 1918, and Lane was hounded out of England. He died in Paris in 1925, officially of typhus, though Layard believed of a "broken heart" ("Autobiography" [1967], fo. 210, San Diego).

102. "1929 Journal" (1929), fo. [5], NYPL.

103. See Chapter 3.

104. Layard, "Autobiography" [1967], fo. 205, San Diego.

105. TLS from W. H. Auden to Patience [Kennington], [Dec. 1928?], BL.

106. Spender, *WwW*, 133.

107. "I Like It Cold" (1947), *Prose2*, 334. It is likely that this in fact happened in the first week of 1929 rather than the week between Christmas 1928 and the New Year. See also his allusion to reading *War and Peace* during a "penniless Christmas in a foreign city" in "Making, Knowing and Judging" (1956), *Prose4*, 486. In the context of this "penniless Christmas" and the New Year, it is worth noting that Auden mentioned in a letter to William McElwee that he had dreamed on the night of 30–31 Dec. 1928 that McElwee was staying at Cley next the Sea, a tiny village close to Auden's old school at Gresham's (see TLS from W. H. Auden to William McElwee, 31 Dec. 1929, BL).

108. "Written Whilst Walking Down the Rhine" (1929), in Stephen Spender, *Twenty Poems* (Oxford: Basil Blackwell, 1930), 15, reprinted and retitled as "In 1929," in Spender, *New Collected Poems*, ed. Michael Brett (London: Faber and Faber, 2004), 10.

109. Isherwood, *C&HK*, 5.

110. "In the year of my youth when yoyos came in" (1932–1933), *Poems1*, 477. See Chapter 7.

111. Isherwood, *C&HK*, 4. Parker describes the rich symbolic connotations of the nickname Bubi—"baby," "boy," and "rogue"—in *Isherwood*, 169.

112. Richard Read, *Art and Its Discontents: The Early Life of Adrian Stokes* (University Park: Pennsylvania State UP, 2002), 15.

113. Layard, "Autobiography" [1967], fo. 202, San Diego.

114. TLS from W. H. Auden to to Patience [Kennington], [Dec. 1928?], BL.

115. "1929 Journal" (1929), fo. [51], NYPL.

116. Sorley's poem was written in the first month of the war, Aug. 1914, and after his death at Loos in Oct. 1915 was collected in his *Marlborough and Other Poems* (Cambridge: Cambridge UP, 1916).

117. *Paid on Both Sides* (1927–1929), *Poems1*, 24.

118. "Under boughs between our tentative endearments, how should we hear" (1929), *Poems1*, 51.

119. Parker, *Isherwood*, 169–170.

120. Isherwood, *C&HK*, 5.

121. "Before this loved one" (1929), *Poems1*, 41–42.

122. In *EALA,* 121, Mendelson notes Auden's comparable "technical bravura" with intricate vowel rhyme in "That night when joy began" (1931), *Poems1,* 212.

123. See Chapter 4.

124. "1929 Journal" (1929), fo, [58], NYPL.

125. "Before this loved one" (1929), *Poems1,* 41.

126. "1929 Journal" (1929), fo. [7], NYPL.

127. *Ibid.,* fos. [21, 85].

128. Isherwood, *Lions,* 189. Eventually, after Auden threw up in the hat at a cinema, it had to be burned.

129. ALS (on a TS of the poem made by Edouard Roditi) from W. H. Auden to Edouard Roditi, [Nov. 1931], Library Special Collections, Charles E. Young Research Library, University of California, Los Angeles (from now on, referred to as Los Angeles); cited in Mendelson, *EALA,* 71, and in Fuller, *Commentary,* 66.

130. William Empson, "A Note on Auden's 'Paid on Both Sides,'" *Experiment,* Spring 1931, repr. in Haffenden, *Heritage,* 80.

131. "May with its light behaving" (1934), *Poems1,* 201.

132. Sotheby and Co., *Catalogue of Nineteenth Century and Modern First Editions, Presentation Copies Autograph Letters and Literary Manuscripts,* 16–17 Dec. 1974, [lot 255], 36. The book was Wilfred Owen, *Poems* (London: Chatto and Windus, 1921); the location of this copy is unknown. The book that Auden gave himself was a second impression of Owen's *Poems* (1920), issued by the original publishers, with the inclusion of an additional poem, "The End." Day Lewis was teaching at Larchfield Academy in Helensburgh. Auden would take over the job there from his fellow poet in the spring of 1930 (see Chapter 6).

133. "Under boughs between our tentative endearments, how should we hear" (1929), *Poems1,* 51.

134. For "bad conscience," see Chapter 1; "1929 Journal" (1929), fo. [99], NYPL.

135. "1929 Journal" (1929), fo. [24], NYPL.

136. *Ibid.,* fo. [15].

137. *Ibid.,* fo. [36].

138. *Ibid.,* fo. [33].

139. *Ibid.,* fo. [21]. For the viewing of the newsreel, see *ibid.,* fo. [16].

140. Grosz, *Autobiography,* 153.

141. "1929 Journal" (1929), fo. [17], NYPL.

142. Layard, "Autobiography" [1967], fo. 206, San Diego. Auden's comments about the matter are cryptic, but they seem to suggest he may have expected or even encouraged Layard to seduce Meyer. See "1929 Journal" (1929), fo. [17], NYPL.

143. Layard, "Autobiography" [1967], fos. 208–210, San Diego; "1929 Journal" (1929), fo. [17], NYPL. Layard had come very close to killing himself

before. Episodes included one in Vanuatu (at that time known as the New Hebrides) during the First World War and one in 1923, in Herefordshire, when he had decided to end his life with a shotgun but failed to act on the impulse (Layard, "Autobiography" [1967], fo. 135, San Diego). Layard's friend Margaret Gardiner (1904–2005) suggested that his self-harming in 1929 was prompted by a fixation on a young Italian woman, Etta de Viti de Marco (1898–1962), who had been in Homer Lane's circle in France at the end of his life (*Scatter*, 135–141). But there is no mention of de Viti de Marco in Auden's or Layard's accounts of this 1929 episode in Berlin. Francis Turville-Petre (1901–1942) was a gifted and extremely dissolute archaeologist, who was in Berlin seeking treatment for syphilis at Hirschfeld's institute. Turville-Petre had already established his professional reputation with the discovery in a cave in Upper Galilee in 1926 of a skull fragment known as "Galilee Man," deriving from a member of an extinct species of human. Auden may have met him in Berlin in the queer circles in which they both traveled, or they may have been introduced by Turville-Petre's younger brother, Gabriel Turville-Petre (1908–1978), who was a year behind Auden at Christ Church and reading English. Having taken a Third, like Auden, Gabriel Turville-Petre went on to become a distinguished scholar of Icelandic and Old Norse literature. Francis Turville-Petre's Berlin nickname was "Der Franni," which Auden and Isherwood anglicized as "The Fronny," the name Auden used for the title of his lost play of 1930.

144. "1929 Journal" (1929), fo. [17], NYPL.

145. Auden's comment on "dead bodies" is recorded in an ALS from Maurice Feild to Humphrey Carpenter, 28 Jan. 1979, Columbia.

146. "1929 Journal" (1929), fos. [15–49], NYPL.

147. Isherwood, *C&HK*, 8.

148. "Upon this line between adventure" (1929), *Poems1*, 30–31; and "Sentries against inner and outer" (1929), *Poems1*, 35–36. In an "unwritten poem," composed in prose thirty years later, Auden remembers "coming unexpectedly upon a derelict iron foundry in the Harz Mountains." "Dichtung und Wahrheit" (1959), *Poems2*, 477.

149. D. H. Lawrence, "The Social Basis of Consciousness by Trigant Burrow" (1927), in *Introductions and Reviews*, ed. N. H. Reeve and John Worthen (Cambridge: Cambridge UP, 2005), 335; emphasis in original.

150. In the last will and testament of the Fronny (written between Sept. and Nov. 1930), the eponymous hero of Auden's play leaves one hundred pounds to "the Neukölner Otter | Taken last August at Rothehütte | Whose sensitive hands now work in prison" (*Plays*, 480). In 1940, the state transferred Küsel (1909–1984) to Auschwitz where he became a *Funktionshäftling*, a prisoner functionary (i.e., one whose role, with very limited room for discretion, usually involved supervising forced labor). He escaped, was recaptured and sent back to Auschwitz, held in solitary confinement, and then, near the end of the war, was sent to the Flossenbürg camp in Bavaria. Küsel was incarcerated there when, among many others, the theologian and anti-Nazi activist Diet-

rich Bonhoeffer (1906–1945) was hanged on the camp gallows in April 1945. In 1958, Auden wrote a poem dedicated to Bonhoeffer, "Friday's Child" (*Poems2*, 492–493). Somehow, Küsel survived the death marches, starvation, executions, and disease, and after the Second World War he testified at the Frankfurt Auschwitz trials in the 1960s. At this point, it emerged that he had used his position in Auschwitz to do what he could to alleviate the suffering of some of the weaker inmates. See also Mendelson, *EALA*, 45n. It is unclear whether, after the brief idyll they shared at Rothehütte in 1929, Auden ever heard anything about the remarkable later life-history of Küsel.

151. Isherwood, *C&HK*, 8–10. Parker gives a good account of the madcap episode in *Isherwood*, 152. Isherwood and Berthold Szczesny were, as Isherwood wrote, to meet again "many times, in many different places," including in Berlin in 1933 and in 1947 in Buenos Aires, where Szczesny had become the modestly wealthy part owner of a factory (*C&HK*, 10; see also Parker, *Isherwood*, 566). Ehrenburg's exhilarated phrase "in our time" would reappear a short while later in Auden's 1930 poem, beginning "Consider this and in our time" (*Poems1*, 52). See Chapter 6.

152. The four parts were all written in 1929 and can be found in *Poems1*, 36–37, 37–39, 39–40, 40 (from now, cited parenthetically in the main text). Originally, Auden wrote the parts as a series of verse letters to Isherwood (see *Poems1*, 565). The sequence originally had no overall title. Auden gave it the title "1929" in *The Collected Poetry of W. H. Auden* (New York: Random House, 1945); see *Poems1*, 565. Michael Kilby describes Auden's drafts in a notebook now in NYPL in "Some Thoughts on '1929'," *WHASN*, 15 (Nov. 1996), 10–15.

153. *Poems1*, 29, 42–43. The first poem was written in Dec. 1927 in Oxford and the second in April 1929 in Berlin.

154. "1929 Journal" (1929), fo. [51], NYPL.

155. Cited in Howard Griffin, *Conversations with Auden*, ed. Donald E. Allen (San Francisco: Grey Fox P, 1981), 92.

156. "1929 Journal" (1929), fos. [51, 53], NYPL.

157. Fuller identifies the seasonal structure in *Commentary*, 59. In the version of the poem printed in *Poems1*, the third part has only forty-one lines. However, the poem, as originally printed in *Poems* (1930), contained an extra two lines in part 3. Following "But taking the first steps falters is vexed," line 11 of part 3 (*Poems1*, 39), Auden's poem originally read "By opposite strivings for entropic peace, | Retreat to lost home or advance to new" (cited in *Poems1*, 565), before continuing as in the version printed in *Poems1*: "Happy only to find home . . ." (39). The two lines I quote here were dropped by Auden in *Poems* (1933), the second ed. of *Poems* (1930).

158. Burrow, *Social*, 114. Auden may have come to Burrow's work through D. H. Lawrence. One of Burrow's students, Max Rosenberg, had introduced Lawrence to Burrow's writing and ideas around 1919–1920. Mendelson and Fuller also comment on the relevance of Burrow's work to Auden's poem in, respectively, *EALA*, 74, and *Commentary*, 62. Fuller notes that "To ask the

hard question" (1930) (*Poems1*, 50–51) borrows too from *The Social Basis of Consciousness* (*Commentary*, 83). Importantly, this shows that Burrow's ideas lodged in Auden's mind for longer than just the period when he was at work on the 1929 sequence.

159. Yeats, *Poems*, 180. The poem was written soon after the Easter Uprising in 1916 but only collected in *Michael Robartes and the Dancer* (1921).

160. Auden used the word again in a poem he wrote around the time he finished his 1929 sequence. This is the poem beginning "Which of you waking early and watching daybreak," written in Oct. 1929, which contains the line: "And freedom from all anxiety about money" (*Poems1*, 58). Thus, although Auden never uses the word "anxiety" in a poem before 1929, he then chooses to deploy it three times in one year as he inaugurates his own poetic age of "anxiety."

161. This is part of a verse letter that Auden wrote to Isherwood in April 1929. It was originally intended as the dedication to the play that he was then beginning and was calling "The Reformatory." (Later, after Isherwood became a coauthor, it was retitled "The Enemies of a Bishop.") The manuscript of this verse dedication is now in the Huntington; the lines are cited in Mendelson, *EALA*, 76 (see also *ibid.*, 45n). Auden also mentions, as one "necessary condition of the season's setting forth," the "death by cancer of a once hated master" (*Poems1*, 37)—E. A. Robertson, his housemaster at Gresham's and the person in charge of the annual Shakespeare play there, who died in Devon early in 1929; see the Prologue and Chapter 1.

162. "1929 Journal" (1929), fo. [29], NYPL.

163. *Ibid.*, fo. [15].

164. *Ibid.*, fos. [2, 4, 6, 8].

165. Emphasis added; cited in Katherine C. Bucknell, "W. H. Auden: The Growth of a Poet's Mind (1922–1933)" (DPhil. diss., Columbia U, 1986), 196.

166. John 19:30.

167. "Coming out of me living is always thinking" (1929), *Poems1*, 37–38. On the night of 1 May 1929 there was a running battle between police and left-wing demonstrators in the Neukölln area of the city, not far from where Auden was living.

168. He spent the period from around 18 May to 20 July 1929 in Rothehütte before returning, with perhaps a short visit to Berlin, to his parents' home in Birmingham via Amsterdam and Stockport. Otto Küsel (see earlier in this chapter) seems to have joined Auden in Rothehütte in early June 1929.

169. There is a recollection here of Wordsworth's "parent hen amid her brood" from the crucial fifth book of the poem: *Prelude* (1805), 5:246, p. 164.

170. *The Waste Land* (1922), Eliot, *Poems*, 55.

171. "Preface to Anabasis" (1930), T. S. Eliot, *The Complete Prose of T. S. Eliot: The Critical Edition*, vol. 4: *English Lion, 1930–1933*, ed. Jason Harding and Ronald Schuchard (Baltimore: Johns Hopkins UP, 2015), 132 (from now on, cited as *Prose*, vol. 4). A little further into his preface, Eliot talks about *Anabasis* as characterized by its "its logic of imagery" (*ibid.*, 133).

172. Yeats, *Poems,* 187.

173. Cited in "Soviet Militarism. Stalin's Denunciation of the League," *Times,* 6 Dec. 1927, p. 15.

174. The "dangerous flood | Of history" comes from "August for the people and their favourite islands" (1935), *Poems1,* 216; see Chapter 8. See, for the other references, Jan Knopf, *Brecht-Handbuch: Theater; Eine Ästhetik der Widersprüche* (Stuttgart: J. B. Metzlersche, 1980), 367; and Michael J. Sidnell, *Dances of Death: The Group Theatre of London in the Thirties* (London: Faber and Faber, 1984), 321n40 (from now on, cited as Sidnell, *Dances*), which also notes Lawrence's novel *The Rainbow* (1915), where a great flood divides past organic life from present mechanized existence, and Shaw's play *Heartbreak House* (1919), with Captain Shotover standing in as a drunken Noah.

175. Auden also staged a version of *The Deluge* at the Downs School in March 1934; see Chapter 7. "To Those Born Later" ("An die Nachgeborenen": "Ihr, die auftauchen werdet aus der Flut | In den wir untergegangen sind"), in Bertolt Brecht, *Poems 1913–1956,* ed. John Willett and Ralph Manheim, rev. ed. (1976; London: Eyre Methuen, 1987), 319.

176. See Chapter 4.

177. *Prelude* (1805), 7:4–9, p. 226.

178. "1929 Journal" (1929), fos. [74, 101, 107], NYPL. This is a common idea in Auden. For instance, he also implausibly suggests: "The only way to prevent sex being a greater source of discomfort than it need be is to recognize it as an anomalous hanger-on in man's journey away from nature" (*ibid.,* fo. [74]). Mendelson explores two theories that he says were competing in Auden's mind at the time he wrote this sequence of poems. The first was an individualistic credo that the mind "must divorce itself from its origins in nature" while the "body could be left alone to indulge its simple habitual pleasures." The second theory—adopted after Auden returned to England, according to Mendelson—was that the mind "must choose its own dissolution into unconscious unity. . . . Consciousness must return to its source in nature." He argues that Auden had a metaphor for each of these theories: for the first, his metaphor was *weaning;* for the second, his metaphor was *drowning* (*EALA,* 69–70).

179. "1929 Journal" (1929), fo. [111], NYPL. See Chapter 3.

180. Burrow, *Social,* 131; noted by Fuller, *Commentary,* 62.

181. Burrow, *Social,* 30, 115.

182. *Ibid.,* 117.

183. *Ibid.,* 132.

184. *Ibid.,* 119–120; emphasis in original.

185. *Ibid.,* 130.

186. This phrase is entirely in italics in the original. In re-citing it briefly here, I have removed Burrow's italics in order to highlight my own emphasis of his words about the "fallacy of . . . *against*" (*ibid.,* 118).

187. *Ibid.,* 129.

188. *Ibid.,* 125.

189. *Ibid.*, 40; emphasis in original.

190. "1929 Journal" (1929), fo. [65], NYPL.

191. Burrow, *Social*, 40.

192. The last line of this section of the poem is recycled from "Punchard" (1925), *J*, 99. See Chapter 2.

193. "1929 Journal" (1929), fo. [28], NYPL. The quotation here is apparently not a citation from Freud but a summary of arguments Freud made in *Beyond the Pleasure Principle* (1920), such as: the goal of life "must be an *old* state of things, an initial state from which the living entity has at one time or other departed and to which it is striving to return" (*SE*, 18:38; emphasis in original). This seems to be the first time that Auden wrote down a note while reading Freud. See Chapter 1.

194. Burrow, *Social*, 118.

195. "1929 Journal" (1929), fo. [99], NYPL.

196. J. W. Dunne, *An Experiment with Time* (London: A. and C. Black, 1927). Dunne (1875–1949) published a second edition of his book in 1929, and it seems quite possible (since this poem is based closely on actual events) that this is the version of the book that Auden was reading in the train.

197. "Who stands, the crux left of the watershed" (1927), *Poems1*, 34; emphasis added.

198. The moment is very similar to the blackbird's "sudden scurry" breaking up a reverie in "I chose this lean country" (1927), *Poems1*, 391–393. See Chapter 3.

199. Burrow, *Social*, 38. The "frozen buzzard" had appeared earlier in "Frost" (1925–1926), *J*, 113 (see Chapter 2), and in "We saw in Spring" (1927–1928), *Poems1*, 389.

200. Burrow, *Social*, 12.

201. *Ibid.*, 132.

202. "Papa Was a Wise Old Sly-Boots" (1969) [review of J. R. Ackerley, *My Father and Myself*], *Prose6*, 361.

203. Burrow, *Social*, 131.

204. Lewis, *Hitler*, 106–107; emphasis in original.

6. THE ENGLISH CELL

Epigraph: Wyndham Lewis, *Men without Art* (1934), ed. Seamus Cooney (Santa Rosa, CA: Black Sparrow, 1987), 103.

1. [Foreword to *W. H. Auden: A Bibliography*] (1963), *Prose5*, 80. For more on the discussions about what Auden's first poem might have been, see Chapter 2. Another early instance of Auden's use of "tarn" comes in the Wordsworthian "'The Road's Your Place'" (1925), *J*, 95. Again, see Chapter 2. In considering this late recollection of a lost sonnet about Blea Tarn, it is relevant to note that Auden was once more turning toward Wordsworth as an in-

spiration at the end of his life. In the 1970s, he even told a friend that he was contemplating writing a long poem "along the lines of Wordsworth's *Prelude*" (see Emma Kann, "Recollections of Auden in Austria," *WHASN*, 10–11 (Sept. 1993), 12).

2. *The Excursion*, 5:9–11; see Wordsworth, *Poems*, vol. 2, p. 158.

3. The 1805 version of the poem was first published in 1926 in an edition by Ernest de Sélincourt (1870–1943). De Sélincourt was a professor of English and an administrator at the University of Birmingham, and it is very likely that he was acquainted there with Dr. and Mrs. Auden and perhaps also with their youngest son. From 1928 to 1933 he was also professor of poetry at Oxford, and, along with Tolkien and others, he was on the board of examiners that gave Auden a Third Class degree in 1928.

4. *Prelude* (1805), 5:389–422, pp. 172, 174. The boy of Winander episode is the only extract from *The Prelude* that Auden and John Garrett included in their anthology *The Poet's Tongue* (1935). See Chapter 3.

5. *Prelude* (1805), 5:459–481, p. 176.

6. "It is time for the destruction of error" (1929), *Poems1*, 40. See Chapter 5.

7. Some critics believe that the lines "Will you wheel death anywhere | In his invalid chair" in the poem beginning "Will you turn a deaf ear" (1930), *Poems1*, 25, refer to the dying Lt.-Col. Solomon (1886–1930). That poem was apparently written in Sept. 1929 before Auden started living with the Solomons, but in at least two copies of *Poems* (1930) Auden wrote in the margin next to "Will you turn a deaf ear" a reference to the Solomons' address as if he connected the poem with their household. After Eton and Balliol, Peter Solomon (1921–2005) worked as a codebreaker at Bletchley Park during the Second World War. In the postwar period, he became a barrister and then, in 1961, he was the founder and first general secretary of Amnesty International. Peter's mother Flora Solomon (1895–1984) ran the Blackamore Press, a small, private publishing house, for which Isherwood, through Auden's intercession, while knowing little French, translated Baudelaire's *Journaux intimes* in 1930. Auden found this tutoring job through John Layard's friend Margaret Gardiner (see Chapter 5, note 143), who was a friend of the London-based philanthropist, publisher, and translator Manya Harari (1905–1969), Flora Soloman's sister.

8. Reported in Carpenter, *Auden*, 392. The house, at Hinterholz 6 in the village of Kirchstetten, about twenty-three miles due west of Vienna, is the subject of Auden's poetic cycle "Thanksgiving for a Habitat" (1958–1964), *Poems2*, 505–531. For more on Auden's purchase of a home in Austria, see the Prologue.

9. His return to the United Kingdom was not once and for all. Auden went back to Berlin in the summer of 1930 and then again for a short visit at Christmas of the same year, and he visited again during the summer of 1931 and again at the Christmas–New Year period in 1932–1933. Between 1928 and 1933, Auden spent about twelve months in Germany at the end of the 1920s and the start of the 1930s, with roughly ten of those months being in 1928–1929.

10. "Sir, no man's enemy, forgiving all" (1929), *Poems1*, 53.

11. For the title "Petition," see *Poems1*, 574. In the sonnet beginning, "Thou art indeed just, Lord, if I contend" (1889), Hopkins has the lines "but, sir, so what I plead is just" and "I that spend, | Sir, life upon thy cause." See Hopkins, *The Poetical Works of Gerard Manley Hopkins*, ed. Norman H. MacKenzie (Oxford: Clarendon P, 1990), 201. In the poem beginning "As the magnum is smashed on the stern when the liner is loosed," the "Epithalamion" (written in the summer of 1930) for Auden's now largely lost play, "The Fronny," a deity addressed as the "Lord" is asked to "be present, sir" (*Plays*, 485).

12. George Herbert, "Prayer," in *The English Poems of George Herbert*, ed. Helen Wilcox (Cambridge: Cambridge UP, 2007), 178. Thanks are due to Armen Davoudian for helping me to see this.

13. Mendelson cites some of the deprecatory comments Auden made (an "old warhorse," "trash," and so on) in *Poems1*, 575. See also Auden's remarks on the poem in the foreword (1965) to his *Collected Shorter Poems: 1927-1957* (1966), *Poems2*, 735. There is a longer, thirty-five-line draft version of the poem in a notebook used by Auden in 1929-1930, now in NYPL.

14. "Which of you waking early and watching daybreak" (1929), *Poems1*, 57.

15. *Ibid.*

16. *The Rock* (1934), Eliot, *Poems*, 162.

17. Naomi Mitchison (1897-1999) was a prolific writer of science and historical fiction—including, in the latter genre, the classic *The Corn King and the Spring Queen* (London: Jonathan Cape, 1931)—as well as of autobiography. In 1929-1930 in London, Auden was tutoring her son Murdoch Mitchison (1922-2011), later a zoologist.

18. Alison Falby, "Heard, Henry Fitzgerald [Gerald] (1889-1971)," *Oxford Dictionary of National Biography* online (Oxford: Oxford UP, 2004).

19. Gardiner, *Scatter*, 143.

20. See Chapter 1.

21. ALS from W. H. Auden to John Layard, 26 Feb. 1930, San Diego.

22. "It was Easter as I walked in the public gardens" (1929), *Poems1*, 37. See Chapter 5.

23. "Consider this and in our time" (1929), *Poems1*, 52 (from now on, cited parenthetically in the text).

24. "It was Easter as I walked in the public gardens" (1929), *Poems1*, 37; H.D., "Oread," in *Collected Poems: 1912-1944*, ed. Louis L. Martz (New York: New Directions, 1983), 55; Ezra Pound, "In a Station of the Metro," in *Personae: The Shorter Poems of Ezra Pound*, ed. Lea Baechler and A. Walton Litz, rev. ed. (New York: New Directions, 1990), 111.

25. "The End of the Line" (1942), in Randall Jarrell, *Kipling, Auden & Co.: Essays and Reviews 1935-1964* (New York: Farrar, Straus and Giroux, 1980), 79-80.

26. Milton, *PL*, 1:8, p. 10. Fuller points out that the "Supreme Antagonist" recalls the "Adversary" of "Taller to-day, we remember similar evenings" (1928), *Poems1*, 49, and the "devourer" of "It time for the destruction of error" (1929), *Poems1*, 40: see Fuller, *Commentary*, 74–75.

27. "Get there if you can and see the land you once were proud to own" (1930), *Poems1*, 44–46 (from now on, cited parenthetically in the text). Mendelson establishes the dating of the poem in *Poems1*, 569–570.

28. The Tennyson poems are "Locksley Hall" (1835) and "Locksley Hall Sixty Years After" (1886). Auden refers to his own poem as "the Locksley Hall poem" in a version he sent to Isherwood (cited in *Poems1*, 570). The formal properties of Auden's poem are the most conspicuous borrowing it makes from Tennyson—there are no corollaries in Auden to the wandering inner monologues, life history, and love stories in Tennyson's poems. However, Tennyson does use the phrase "boon companion" in "Locksley Hall Sixty Years After," which Auden picks up in "Get there if you can" (*Poems1*, 45).

29. "It was Easter as I walked in the public gardens" (1929), *Poems1*, 36–37. See Chapter 5.

30. Auden often returned in his poetry to the experience of dropping a stone down a shaft or well; he had written about it as early as "The Old Leadmine" (1924), *J*, 29–30. See Chapter 2.

31. ALS from W. H. Auden to George Auden, [late Feb.–early March 1939], Department of Special Collections and Western Manuscripts, Bodleian Library, Oxford University (from now on, referred to as Bodleian); printed in Judith Priestman, "An Unpublished Letter by W. H. Auden," *Bodleian Library Record*, 15.4 (April 1996), 325–329; emphasis in original. See citations from the same letter in Chapter 6 and in the Epilogue.

32. Søren Kierkegaard, *The Diary of Søren Kierkegaard*, trans. Gerda M. Andersen, ed. Peter P. Rohde (New York: Philosophical Library, 1960), 106.

33. "The Fronny" (1930) is a play now mainly lost, with only a few fragments surviving. See the reconstruction in *Plays*, 466–487, together with Mendelson's comments (*Plays*, 464–466).

34. "The Fronny" (1930), *Plays*, 471.

35. "California" (1922), *J*, 3; emphasis added. See Chapter 2.

36. "It is time for the destruction of error" (1929), *Poems1*, 40; "Sir, no man's enemy, forgiving all" (1929), *Poems1*, 53; "Which of you waking early and watching daybreak" (1929), *Poems1*, 57–58; "Consider this and in our time" (1930), *Poems1*, 52–53.

37. Carpenter, *Auden*, 111. Auden had visited the school in Feb. 1929 when Day Lewis was teaching there (see Chapter 5).

38. "What siren zooming is sounding our coming" (1930), in *The Orators*, *Poems1*, 118–120 (from now on, cited parenthetically in the text).

39. Peter Stansky, *Edward Upward: Art and Life* (London: Enitharmon P, 2016), 110. Before their first meeting, Upward and Auden had known each

other by letter from 1926 when, probably at the instigation of Isherwood, Auden sent Upward some of his early poems. Isherwood introduced them in person in a Soho restaurant in London in 1927 (see Katherine Bucknell, introduction to *J*, lix). Over the coming decade or so, Upward and Auden remained in contact, though they were not close. Upward received copy 9 of Auden's *Poems* (1928), which is now in BL, and, when sending Upward a copy of *Poems* (1930) in Oct. 1930, Auden wrote in a note: "I shall never know how much in these poems is filched from you via Christopher" (cited in *Poems1*, 548). Auden was interested in Upward's growing attraction to communism; he wrote a comic light verse poem called "Comrade Upward" (1931), *Poems1*, 521–522. In 1932 Upward shared with him a private journal, which seems to have impressed Auden, describing his reflections on political commitment. (After a period in the early 1930s when Upward attended meetings and contributed informally, he joined the Communist Party in 1934, only leaving in 1948.) In "Auden and MacNeice: Their Last Will and Testament" (1936), Auden publicly made Upward and Isherwood his literary executors (*Poems1*, 274; this was not merely a lighthearted joke, the decision is confirmed in an ALS from Auden to Isherwood, written in Dec. 1936 [Huntington]). When Auden and Isherwood decided to remain in the United States during the Second World War, Upward wrote a furious letter to Isherwood attacking Isherwood's pacifism and Vedantic beliefs. (Extracts from the exchange of letters between Upward and Isherwood are given in Stansky, *Edward Upward*, 234–235.) Mendelson suggests that it was after reading Upward's letter to Isherwood that Auden angrily dropped the dedication of "What siren zooming is sounding our coming" in the version printed in *The Collected Poetry of W. H. Auden* (1945) (see *Poems1*, 604). For more on Upward, see Chapters 5–7, and Bucknell, "Edward Upward (1903–2009)," *WHASN*, 32 (July 2009), 5–14. Although Isherwood and Upward remained close until Isherwood's passing in 1986, Auden and Upward were apparently never in touch again after the war. However, Bucknell comments that Upward said after Auden's death that "Auden appeared in his dreams 'more often than anyone else alive or dead'" (cited in *ibid.*, 11).

40. Fuller, *Commentary*, 113; Mendelson, *EALA*, 94. Mendelson gives an account of the book's composition history in *Poems1*, 584–585.

41. "The Composer" (1938), *Poems1*, 339; see the Prologue.

42. ALS from W. H. Auden to Naomi Mitchison, [12 Aug. 1931], NYPL.

43. W. H. Auden to T. S. Eliot, 2 Dec. 1931, cited in *Poems1*, 585.

44. Tom Driberg, *Ruling Passions* (London: Jonathan Cape, 1977), 58. See Chapter 3.

45. [Untitled review], repr. in Haffenden, *Heritage*, 112, 115. Hayward (1905–1965) had been editor of the school magazine, *The Gresham*. He published (unsigned) one of Auden's very earliest poems, "A Moment," written around March 1922, saying, "it shows great promise" (see *Poems1*, 404, 791).

46. Mendelson, *EALA*, 103; in a letter on 16 Aug. 1932, Auden explained to the dancer Gertrude Prokosch Kurath ([1903–1992], sister of the writer Frederic Prokosch [1906–1989], whom Auden knew slightly; see Chapter 7) that "The genesis of the book was a paper written by an anthropological friend of mine about ritual epilepsy among the Trob[r]ian Islanders [Auden's mistake for Malakulans]" (cited in *Poems1*, 586; the letter is in the poetry collection at the State University of New York at Buffalo). The paper is John Layard, "Malekula: Flying Tricksters, Ghosts, Gods, and Epileptics," *Journal of the Royal Anthropological Institute of Great Britain and Ireland*, 60 (June–Dec. 1930), 501–524. For more on Rivers, see Chapters 2–5.

47. Rehearsals had started by mid-Jan. 1931, and the production took place at Helensburgh's Victoria Hall from 26 to 28 March. Besides Danny, Auden also played the bit parts of "Man with a Coat" and "The Censor." See Conor Leahy, "Auden and the Helensburgh Amateur Dramatic Society," *WHASN*, 41 (Feb. 2023), 32–33.

48. The last line is an echo of Wilfred Owen's phrase, used in letters to Sassoon and to his mother, "my nerves are in perfect order." Cited in Owen, *The Poems of Wilfred Owen*, ed. Edmund Blunden (London: Chatto and Windus, 1931), 36, 38. See also Chapter 7, note 170, and Fuller, *Commentary*, 113.

49. This is the title in *The Collected Poetry of W. H. Auden* (1945).

50. The poem cannot be set in Helensburgh at Larchfield Academy, since the school did not have a courtyard and the school, and the town, did not have any buildings with enough stories to justify the idea of a "Roof-line" or a courtyard "far down" (*Poems1*, 115).

51. The reference to Greek also sensitizes readers to the adaptations Auden is making of Pindar's odes in book 3 of *The Orators*, in this case to Isthmian 2.

52. "The Mop" was the mother of a colleague at Larchfield, Arnold Snodgrass (d. 1962). Snodgrass is the man drunkenly saluting the rising moon earlier in the poem (see *Poems1*, 601). The "white surgeon" (an odd locution) is a reference to the physician who performed an operation on Auden in March 1930: see earlier in this chapter. Mendelson provides further identifications in *Poems1*, 601.

53. Foreword (1965) to the third ed. of *The Orators* (1966), cited in *Poems1*, 590. In one of the earliest public references to Hopkins's sexuality, Auden noted the "homosexual feelings" in "The Bugler's First Communion." See [A review of *The Poetry of Gerard Manley Hopkins*, by Elsie Elizabeth Phare] (1934), *Prose1*, 68.

54. "A Commentary," Eliot, *Prose*, vol. 4, 254.

55. Cited in Robert Skidelsky, *Politicians and the Slump: The Labour Government of 1929–1931* (London: Macmillan, 1967), 281.

56. D. S. Mirsky, *The Intelligentsia of Great Britain*, trans. Alec Brown (London: Victor Gollancz, 1935), 40–41.

57. ALS from W. H. Auden to Christopher Isherwood, [9 Oct. 1931], Huntington; cited in Mendelson, *EALA*, 32. For more of importance on Auden's interest in "groups" in the early 1930s, see Mendelson, *EALA*, esp. 124–125, 135–136; and Bucknell's introduction to "Auden's 'Writing' Essay," *AS1*, esp. 18–20, 23–32. "Writing" (1932) itself is in *Prose1*, 12–24.

58. Gardiner, *Scatter*, 142.

59. The source for most of these notions is D. H. Lawrence's *Fantasia of the Unconscious* (London: Martin Secker, 1923).

60. A "stage in my conversion": W. H. Auden to Henry Bamford Parkes, 6 Dec. 1932, Special Collections, Colby College, Maine, cited in *Poems1*, 587; "a favourable exposition": W. H. Auden to Gertrude Prokosch Kurath, 16 Aug. [1932], poetry collection at the State University of New York at Buffalo, cited in *Poems1*, 586.

61. "Personal fascism": written around 1941 into a copy of *Poems* (1934), cited in *Poems1*, 587; "pseudonym": foreword (1965) to the third ed. of *The Orators* (1966), cited in *Poems1*, 590.

62. Naomi Mitchison, ed., *An Outline for Boys and Girls and Their Parents* (London: Victor Gollancz, 1932). On publication, the book was attacked for being antireligious, pro-Soviet, and too explicit about sexuality. It sold poorly.

63. "Writing," *Prose1*, 13, 18. See also "Oxford" (1937): "Knowledge is conceived in the hot womb of Violence" (*Poems1*, 325).

64. Mendelson, *EALA*, 32.

65. "The Symbolism of Poetry," in W. B. Yeats, *Essays and Introductions* (London: Macmillan, 1961), 157.

66. Spender, *WwW*, 145. Spender recalls Upward looking very "much like the emissary of a Cause" when they met in Berlin.

67. Stephen Spender to John Lehmann, 26 Aug. 1931, cited in John Sutherland, *Stephen Spender: The Authorized Biography* (London: Viking, 2004), 131.

68. Cited in *ibid*.

69. Eliot, "Commentary" (1931), *Prose*, vol. 4, 254.

70. Isherwood, *Lions*, 78–79.

71. Quoted by Spender in *WwW*, 69.

72. "Get there if you can and see the land you once were proud to own" (1930), *Poems1*, 45; Ode IV (1931), in *The Orators, Poems1*, 126.

73. W. H. Auden to Michael Roberts, 11 Dec. 1931, NYPL, cited in Mendelson in his introduction to *Prose1*, xvi.

74. Rhyme royal is a stanza form, made well-known at the end of the fourteenth century by Geoffrey Chaucer in his poem *Troilus and Criseyde*, consisting of seven lines of iambic pentameter, rhyming either *aba bb cc* or *abab bcc*, giving the form a repetitive, circling feeling. It was later used by some of Auden's favorite writers, including William Morris and Yeats.

75. Auden to Roberts, 11 Dec. 1931, NYPL, cited in Mendelson, introduction to *Prose1*, xvi.

76. "There on the golf course are the tiny red flags, | There's tea being laid on the vicarage lawn" (*Poems1*, 138); "players of Badminton" (*Poems1*, 146).

77. "A Happy New Year," part 1 (1932), *Poems1*, 140 (from now on, cited parenthetically in the text).

78. Bucknell analyzes Heard's influence in her introduction to "Auden's 'Writing' Essay," *AS1*, 24–32.

79. W. H. Auden to Christopher Isherwood, 12 Feb. 1932, cited by Mendelson in *Poems1*, 612.

80. Fuller, *Commentary*, 180.

81. Ramsay MacDonald (1866–1937), prime minister in 1924 and then again from 1929 to 1935 in the National Government; Stanley Baldwin (1867–1947), Conservative politician and prime minister from 1923 to 1924, 1924 to 1929, and 1935 to 1937, and Lord President of the Council in the National Government from 1931 to 1935; Viscount Snowden (1864–1937), Chancellor of the Exchequer in the National Government from 1931 to 1935; Winston Churchill (1874–1965), Chancellor of the Exchequer from 1924 to 1929; Oswald Mosley (1896–1980), Chancellor of the Duchy of Lancaster from 1929 to 1930, founder of the New Party in 1931 (dissolved into the British Union of Fascists in 1932); Viscount Rothermere (1868–1940), tabloid journalism pioneer as proprietor of Associated Newspapers; Lord Beaverbrook (1879–1964), proprietor of the *Daily Express.*

82. George Saintsbury, *A History of English Prosody from the Twelfth Century to the Present Day,* vol. 1: *From the Origins to Spenser,* 2nd ed. (1923; repr., New York: Russell and Russell, 1961), 150.

83. (George) Derek Wedgwood (1912–1992) is referred to as "Derek my chum" in the Envoi to Ode IV (1931) in *The Orators, Poems1,* 126. ("Derek" is also the name of one of the airman's doomed followers in book 2 of the same work: *ibid.,* 104–107.) Two other poems that seem to derive from Auden's affair with Wedgwood are "That night when joy began" (1931), *Poems1,* 212; and the poem that begins, "To lie flat on the back with the knees flexed" (1933?), *Poems1,* 206, but that derives from a longer, unpublished draft poem, "To lie this hour in any position" (*Poems1,* 462–463), that was written before Auden left Scotland in 1932. See also Chapter 7. Wedgwood served in the Merchant Navy during the Second World War; he married Barbara Sidebottom in Cheshire in Dec. 1941.

84. Gerald Heard, *The Ascent of Humanity: An Essay on the Evolution of Civilization from Group Consciousness through Individuality to Super-Consciousness* (London: Jonathan Cape, 1929), 14 (from now on, cited Heard, *Ascent*). For more on Burrow's work, see Chapter 5.

85. Heard, *Ascent,* 23.

86. Gerald Heard, *Social Substance of Religion: An Essay on the Evolution of Religion* (London: George Allen and Unwin, 1931), 12 (from now on, cited as Heard, *Social*).

87. Heard, *Social,* 212.

88. John Betjeman, "The Death of Modernism," *Architectural Review,* Dec. 1931, pp. 172–174.

89. Heard, *Ascent,* 62–63.

90. *Ibid.,* 63.

91. For Dr. Auden's position on these issues, see Chapter 3.

92. Graham Greene, "Three Poets," *Oxford Magazine,* 10 Nov. 1932, repr. in Haffenden, *Heritage,* 115.

93. Hugh Gordon Porteus, *Twentieth Century,* Feb. 1933, repr. in Haffenden, *Heritage,* 120.

94. "Writing" (1932), *Prose1,* 12–24; "Private Pleasure" (1932), *Prose1,* 25–27.

95. "Problems of Education" (1932), *Prose1,* 27–28.

96. For this important 1939 letter to Dr. Auden, see earlier in this chapter.

97. "A Happy New Year," part 2 (1932), *Poems1,* 144 (from now on, cited parenthetically in the text).

98. T. E. Lawrence (1888–1935), popularly known as Lawrence of Arabia, was an archaeologist, soldier, and writer; at the time the poem takes place, he was serving in the RAF; Sir Thomas Horder (1871–1955) was the main physician for King George V and Prime Minister Ramsay MacDonald; Norman Haire (1892–1952) was Britain's most prominent sexologist in the interwar years. Mendelson gives explanations of the boys' and master's names in *Poems1,* 609. An early version of some lines in part 2, including the names, was written around Dec. 1930 in the dedication of "The Fronny," a poem that begins, "Run Favel, Holland, sprightly Alexis." Auden had then thought about including that poem as the final ode in *The Orators* before deciding against it (see *Plays,* 466; *Poems1,* 609).

99. Fuller was able to identify some of the inhabitants of the houses in *Commentary,* 160.

100. Auden had used the five-line stanza, technically a cinquain, in May 1931 in the poem in *The Orators* beginning, "There are some birds in these valleys" (*Poems1,* 107–108). A much earlier use came in "The Dying House" (1925), *J,* 96–97. See Chapter 2. "Now from my window-sill I watch the night" marks his deepest engagement so far with this somewhat-unusual stanza form.

101. "Writing" (1932), *Prose1,* 19.

102. Heard, *Social,* 89. Cited in Katherine Bucknell, introduction to "Auden's 'Writing' Essay," *AS1,* 25.

103. Heard, *Social,* 91.

104. *Ibid.*

105. Peter M. Sacks, *The English Elegy: Studies in the Genre from Spenser to Yeats* (Baltimore: Johns Hopkins UP, 1985), 267–269.

106. "Frost at Midnight" (1798), in Samuel Taylor Coleridge, *Poetical Works: Poems,* vol. 1, part 1, ed. J. C. C. Mays (Princeton: Princeton UP, 2001), 453.

107. Gardiner's "Meditation on the Future of Northern Europe" (1928) is cited in Richard Griffiths's *Fellow Travellers of the Right: British Enthusiasts for*

Nazi Germany 1933-9 (London: Constable, 1980), 144. For Rolf Gardiner (1902-1971), see also Chapter 5.

108. Gardiner was often associated during the interwar period with far-right figures and organizations in Britain, and he demonstrated a degree of sympathy with the Nazi regime in Germany. He is a central figure in Patrick Wright's *The Village That Died for England: The Strange Story of Tyneham*, rev. ed. (London: Faber and Faber, 2002) (from now on, cited as Wright, *Village*). Gardiner's account of the conversation with Auden in Jan. 1932, recorded in his diary, is cited in David Bradshaw, "New Perspectives on Auden: Rolf Gardiner, Germany and *The Orators*," *WHASN*, 20 (June 2000), 23.

109. The letter is cited in Bradshaw, "New Perspectives on Auden," 27.

110. See also the Prologue. Fuller describes some of the sources for Auden's Lords of Limit, two monitory watchers over human activity (*Commentary*, 159-160).

111. "In Memory of Major Robert Gregory" (1918), Yeats, *Poems*, 134.

112. W. H. Auden to John B. Auden, 14 Jan. 1932, NYPL; cited in *Prose1*, 742.

113. Heard, *Ascent*, 213-214.

114. ALS from W. H. Auden to John Pudney, 28 July 1932, NYPL.

115. This is from a section of the essay called "Summary," which Auden drafted but then did not include in the final version: see *Prose1*, 746.

116. Heard, *Social*, 214.

117. In writing about the "field of five or six, the English cell" in a school setting and relating the number in the "field" to the poem's stanza size, Auden might have had in the back of his mind Wordsworth's 1802 poem about the sonnet's "scanty plot of ground" and the beneficial effects of boundedness. That poem begins: "Nuns fret not at their convent's narrow room; | And hermits are contented with their *cells*; | *And students with their pensive citadels*" (Wordsworth, *Poems*, 2:586; emphasis added).

118. "The chimneys are smoking, the crocus is out in the border" (1932), *Poems1*, 200. This is probably another poem prompted by Auden's affair in Helensburgh with Derek Wedgwood (see earlier in this chapter).

119. Fuller calls it "perhaps the most significant of the new kind of fully argued and rhetorical poem that [Auden] had been writing for about a year." In it, he identifies the influence of writers "unafraid of magnificence," including Paul Claudel (1868-1955), "the great master of psychic geography, invocations and sea-voyages" who gave "this crucial lift to Auden's choric manner in 1932" (*Commentary*, 145). The sea and sea voyages are key elements of Claudel's gigantic, virtually unperformable play *Le Soulier de satin* (1929). Conor Leahy has established that Auden owned a copy of the English translation of this play: *The Satin Slipper: or the Worst Is Not the Surest*, trans. John O'Connor [and Claudel] (London: Sheed and Ward, 1931). This book is now in the Cadbury Research Library at the University of Birmingham. Mendelson notes that Auden wrote "Claudel" next to the poem in Chester Kallman's copy

of his collection *On This Island,* published in the United States in 1937 (*Poems1,* 635).

120. "In the year of my youth when yoyos came in" (1932–1933), *Poems1,* 477.

121. "It is time for the destruction of error" (1929), *Poems1,* 40; "A Happy New Year" (1932), *Poems1,* 137, 144; and "The chimneys are smoking, the crocus is out in the border" (1932), *Poems1,* 200.

122. "Prologue" ["O love, the interest itself in thoughtless Heaven"] (1932), *Poems1,* 183 (from now on, cited parenthetically in the main text).

123. W. B. Yeats, *A Vision: The Revised 1937 Edition,* ed. Margaret Mills Harper and Catherine E. Paul (New York: Scribner, 2015), 19. Yeats's famous phrase originally appeared in a different form in *A Packet for Ezra Pound* (Dublin: Cuala P, 1929).

124. This is slightly over half of the poem, which has fifteen stanzas in all. Auden first titled the poem "Prologue" when it was printed in the *New Country* anthology in 1933. To start with, he seems to have intended it to be the prologue to a never-written play, then to an "epic" he was writing in 1932–1933, which begins: "In the year of my youth when yoyos came in" (*Poems1,* 466–495; see Chapter 7). In the end, the poem became the prologue to Auden's 1936 collection, *Look, Stranger!* Mendelson has explanatory comments in *Poems1,* 634.

125. "Writing" (1932), *Prose1,* 13.

126. See Fuller, *Commentary,* 146. Mendelson supplies the stanza containing the line that Auden dropped before the poem appeared in print (*Poems1,* 648).

127. "Song" (1926), *J,* 161.

128. Fuller, *Commentary,* 146.

129. Dennis Hardy, *Utopian England: Community Experiments 1900–1945* (London: Spon, 2000), 153, 156. Dorothy Elmhirst (1887–1968) and Leonard Elmhirst (1893–1974) had married in 1925.

130. See Michael Young, *The Elmhirsts of Dartington: The Creation of an Utopian Community* (London: Routledge and Kegan Paul, 1982), 206–207.

131. See Carpenter, *Auden,* 137; D-H, *Auden,* 130.

132. See Hardy, *Utopian England,* 150.

133. ALS from W. H. Auden to John B. Auden, 11 April 1932, NYPL.

134. See Naomi Mitchison, *You May Well Ask: A Memoir, 1920–1940* (London: Gollancz, 1979), 118.

135. Auden calls himself a "selfish pink old Liberal" in "Letter to Lord Byron" (1936), *Prose1,* 328 [also *Poems1,* 251]. In the 1930s, shirts could be important signifiers of political affiliation: for example, black shirts were associated with fascism, red with socialism or communism (see Chapter 7), green with the Social Credit movement, and brown with the paramilitary wing of the Nazi Party.

136. Fuller, *Commentary,* 223. Fuller's comment is based on private information.

137. ALS from W. H. Auden to Dorothy Elmhirst, 3 April 1932, Dartington. Auden lent Elmhirst what he said was his only copy of the play "The Fronny." He asked for it back in June 1932, after which no further trace of the full text is known (see *Plays,* 464).

138. J. H. Grainger, *Patriotisms: Britain 1900–1939* (London: Routledge and Kegan Paul, 1986), 152. See also Chapter 4.

139. ALS from W. H. Auden to John B. Auden, 11 April 1932, NYPL.

140. "A Commentary" (1931) in Eliot, *Prose,* vol. 4, 359.

141. "Writing" (1932), *Prose1,* 746.

142. The incident of Newton and the apple is a commonplace but was first related in William Stukeley, *Memoirs of Sir Isaac Newton's Life* (1752). Auden might be remembering the phrase "eternal tie" from Hardy's poem "In Death Divided" in *Satires of Circumstance* (1914), where a buried corpse regrets that it is not in a grave beside the corpse of the person (gender unspecified) with whom it was in love while both were alive: "The eternal tie which binds us twain in one | No eye will see" (Hardy, *Works,* 2:28).

143. See Chapter 1. In fact, Auden's mother's side of the family seems to have descended from Gaunt's brother Thomas of Woodstock.

144. Shakespeare, *Richard II,* 2.1.

145. Auden was taken with the word "mole" (a breakwater). A little earlier, in Jan. 1931, he had used the word in Ode I of *The Orators:* "The pair walking out on the mole, getting ready to quarrel" (*Poems1,* 115).

146. "Dante" (1929), Eliot, *Prose,* vol. 3, 723.

147. See Ansen, *Table-Talk,* 34; emphasis in original.

148. "Dante" (1929), Eliot, *Prose,* vol. 3, 709 (emphasis in original), 727.

149. *Ibid.,* 706. Stare is another name for starling.

150. *Ibid.,* 705; emphasis in original.

151. *Ibid.,* 704; emphasis in original.

152. *Ibid.,* 702.

153. "Swinburne as Poet" (1920), in Eliot, *Prose,* vol. 2, 184.

154. Anthony Collett, *The Changing Face of England* (1926; London: Jonathan Cape, 1932), 91 (from now on, cited as Collett, *Changing*). Collett (1877–1929) was a journalist (contributing frequently to the *Times*) and a specialist in natural history. He served with the Post Office Rifles in the war and was badly wounded at Vimy Ridge in 1917. His early death is usually attributed to the effect of his injuries in France. For more on Collett, see Chapters 6 and 7.

155. *Ibid.,* 91.

156. In judging the tone of the solution that involves a "surgeon's idea of pain," it is relevant to note that in the run-up to the Oct. 1931 general election, Ramsay MacDonald's "National" coalition had campaigned (successfully) for a "doctor's mandate" to cure the ills of the country.

157. Evidence that Auden was aware of the doctrines of the diffusionists as early as 1930 comes from the will of "the Fronny" in Auden's 1930 play of the same name. There, the central character, borrowing from Auden's life

history, announces: "Item, to the diffusionist John Layard | For having raised me from the dead | Nothing but love" (*Plays*, 478–479; see also Chapter 5). For a basic description of diffusionism (sometimes called "hyperdiffusionism") and its doctrines, see Henrika Kuklick, "Diffusionism," in Alan Barnard and Jonathan Spencer, eds., *Encyclopedia of Social and Cultural Anthropology* (London: Routledge, 1996), 160–162. Rivers and Layard were diffusionists of a kind, and Heard may have encouraged Auden's interest in diffusionism too: for example, in *The Ascent of Humanity* Heard mentions and cites prominent members of the school such as Rivers, Grafton Elliot Smith, and W. J. Perry. In Chester Kallman's copy of *On This Island* (1937), next to the phrase "And out of the Future" in "Prologue," Auden wrote and then crossed out "Perry," a reference to the diffusionist W. J. Perry (1887–1949), who believed that the use of megaliths for cultural purposes originated in Egypt (see *Poems1*, 635; and Fuller, *Commentary*, 148).

158. H. J. Massingham, *Fee, Fi, Fo, Fum: or, The Giants in England* (London: Kegan Paul, Trench, Trubner, 1926), 13. Massingham (1888–1952) published widely on "English" and rural topics in interwar culture and shared many interests with Auden's acquaintance Rolf Gardiner (see earlier in this chapter). He joined Gardiner's right-wing "Kinship in Husbandry" circle, dedicated to rural revival, in 1941.

159. The completely fabricated notion that Merlin was the builder of Stonehenge, using menhirs brought from Ireland, first arises in Geoffrey of Monmouth's twelfth-century *Historia regum Britanniae* (History of the kings of Britain).

160. Massingham, *Fee, Fi, Fo, Fum*, 36.

161. Collett, *Changing*, 29.

162. See Ad De Vries, *Dictionary of Symbols and Imagery* (Amsterdam: North-Holland, 1974), 419.

163. Massingham, *Fee, Fi, Fo, Fum*, 39.

164. The most important exception to the disciplinary obsolescence of diffusionism in anthropology today is Martin Bernal's *Black Athena,* the controversial and still influential multivolume study that posits Egyptian and Phoenician roots for the civilizations of ancient Greece: *Black Athena: The Afroasiatic Roots of Classical Civilization,* 3 vols. (New Brunswick: Rutgers UP, 1987–2006). The intellectual interests pursued by Bernal (1937–2013) were in part a family affair. Bernal, son of Auden and Layard's friend Margaret Gardiner and of the communist scientist J. D. Bernal (1901–1977), was a grandson of the influential Egyptologist Sir Alan Gardiner (1879–1963), Margaret and Rolf Gardiner's father. Alan Gardiner was an important reference point for diffusionist scholarship. In addition, Margaret Gardiner had been romantically involved with the diffusionist anthropologist Bernard Deacon (1903–1927), another student of Rivers, who conducted fieldwork on Malakula (now Vanuatu) in the 1920s, somewhat later than John Layard. Deacon died of blackwater fever on Malakula, but Gardiner seems to have befriended Layard

through family, including her brother Rolf, and mutual acquaintances in anthropological circles. She traveled to Berlin in 1929 to help Layard during the aftermath of his suicide attempt and met Auden there (see Chapter 5, note 143).

165. Pound, "Affirmations, Vorticism," *The New Age*, 16.11 (14 Jan. 1915), 277.

166. Eliot, "Dante" (1929), *Prose*, vol. 3, 704.

167. For the first version of the line, see *Poems1*, 635.

168. The first poem Auden wrote after leaving Helensburgh also begins with water imagery: "The sun shines down on the ships at sea" (1932), *Poems1*, 205. The emphasis is quickly abandoned, however, as the poem proceeds. An early version of this poem was titled "To a Young Man on His Twenty-First Birthday" when it was published in May 1933. A pair of lines near the end of the poem say: "In your house tonight you are flushed and gay; | Twenty-one years have passed away." Although it is tempting to link this poem to Auden's Helensburgh lover, Derek Wedgwood, the dates do not match up: Wedgwood was apparently twenty in July 1932, when Auden wrote the poem. After 1937, the poem was never reprinted.

7. THE FLOOD

Epigraph: C. F. G. Masterman, *The Condition of England* (London: Methuen, 1909), 208.

1. See Chapter 6. Mendelson gives details of Auden's varying thoughts about the title and the placing of the poem in *Poems1*, 634–635. The first mention of its role as a prologue to something else comes in an undated letter that must have been sent near to the time of the poem's composition in May 1932. Writing to Isherwood and including a copy of the poem for him to see, Auden said it was: "a prologue to a play I'm writing" (cited in *Poems1*, 634). Auden's 1936 collection was named *Look, Stranger!* by mistake in Britain, but he corrected this for the American edition in 1937 by using the title *On This Island*. For more on this episode, see the Epilogue.

2. "Prologue" ["O love, the interest itself in thoughtless Heaven"] (1932), *Poems1*, 184.

3. Shakespeare, *Henry V*, prologue.

4. Layard, "Autobiography" [1967], fo. 118, San Diego. Perhaps Lane had in mind the idea that a group of men, sequestered alone at sea for long periods, would turn to homosexual activity. This seems to be at the root of the commonplace connection of the British Navy with "rum, sodomy and the lash." But Auden's image of the ship driving through the sea at night conveys something more than that—a wild, sensuous, even erotic, feeling.

5. "Prologue" ["O love, the interest itself in thoughtless Heaven"] (1932), *Poems1*, 184.

6. "Enter with him . . ." (1931), *Poems1*, 135–136; see also *Poems1*, 610.

7. "This lunar beauty" (1930), *Poems1*, 41. Mendelson writes that Auden annotated this poem as having been inspired by the unidentified "JC"; see *Poems1*, 568.

8. "That night when joy began" (1931), *Poems1*, 212. "That night when joy began" is the earliest poem to be retained in Auden's 1936 collection.

9. "What's in your mind, my dove, my coney" (1930), *Poems1*, 35.

10. Auden marked "DW" next to a printing of "What's in your mind": see *Poems1*, 563. See also Chapter 6.

11. W. H. Auden to D. P. M. Mitchell, sent in 1958 and cited in *Poems1*, 645. Among the best examples of Auden writing lovers' initials (along with dates of composition) into his books are the copies of *Poems* (1934) and *On This Island* (1937) that he marked for Chester Kallman around 1939. See *Poems1*, 563, 634.

12. "A shilling life will give you all the facts" (1934), *Poems1*, 195–196.

13. "Before this loved one" (1929), *Poems1*, 41–42. See Chapter 5.

14. Ode V (1931), in *The Orators, Poems1*, 129.

15. "A Happy New Year," part 2 (1932), *Poems1*, 146.

16. ALS from W. H. Auden to John Pudney, 28 July 1932, NYPL. See Chapter 6.

17. "The chimneys are smoking, the crocus is out in the border" (1932), *Poems1*, 199.

18. "A Communist to Others" (1932), *Poems1*, 196, 645. *Poems1*, 196–198, prints the complete version of the 1936 state of the poem. The 1932–1933 state can be reconstructed in its essential form by dovetailing together the text at *Poems1*, 196–198, with the cuts and revisions detailed at *Poems1*, 646–647. Here, I cite from the 1932–1933 version.

19. "Flyting" was a ritualized exchange of extravagant insults between two speakers, conducted in verse. As a social practice, it died out in Scottish and Gaelic cultures in the Middle Ages, but the tradition continued in printed verse.

20. Symons (1912–1994) later became a crime writer and was the author of a notable book on the 1930s: *The Thirties: A Dream Revolved* (London: Cresset P, 1960). His comment here comes from "'A Communist to Others': A Symposium," *AS1*, 178 (the symposium as a whole is in *AS1*, 173–195).

21. See Mendelson's notes to "A Communist to Others" (1932), *Poems1*, 647.

22. W. H. Auden to Henry Bamford Parkes, 6 Dec. 1932, Special Collections, Colby College, Maine, cited in *Poems1*, 587. See also Chapter 6.

23. See Wiener, *English*, 50; Howkins, "Discovery," 62–64; Krishan Kumar, *The Making of English National Identity* (Cambridge: Cambridge UP, 2003), 209–210.

24. H. J. Massingham, *Cotswold Country: A Survey of Limestone England from the Dorset Coast to Lincolnshire* (London: Batsford, 1937), cited in David Matless, *Landscape and Englishness* (London: Reaktion, 1998), 131.

25. Auden speaks about his "country background" in T. G. Foote, "W. H. Auden—Interview III" (1963), unpublished typescript. See Chapter 1 for descriptions of the rural world he lived in for most of the year as a child.

26. Howkins, "Discovery," 64.

27. Wright, *Village*, xiv.

28. Karl Baedeker, *Great Britain: Handbook for Travellers*, 9th rev. ed. (Leipzig: Baedeker, 1937), 230.

29. David Garrett Izzo, interview with John Duguid (who was at the Downs from 1934 to 1937): "The Student and the Master: A Pupil Recollects W. H. Auden," in Garrett Izzo, ed., *W. H. Auden: A Legacy* (West Cornwall: Locust Hill P, 2002), 37.

30. Tolkien and his colleague at Leeds, E. V. Gordon, had produced an edition of the poem in 1925, the year when Auden arrived at Oxford: *Sir Gawain and the Green Knight*, ed. J. R. R. Tolkien and E. V. Gordon (Oxford: Clarendon P, 1925). When Tolkien was young, he, like Auden, had had a family home in Birmingham, once part of the kingdom of Mercia. He told Auden many years later, implying that he had some sort of race-memory of his ancestors' origins, "I am a West-midlander by blood (and took to early west-midland Middle English as a known tongue as soon as I set eyes on it)" (Tolkien to Auden, 7 June 1955, in *Letters of J. R. R. Tolkien*, ed. Humphrey Carpenter with the assistance of Christopher Tolkien (London: George Allen and Unwin, 1981), 213). Tolkien, again like Auden, had an "intense identification with areas that had cultivated alliterative poetry during the Middle Ages, especially Iceland and the English West Midlands," such as the terrain once known as Mercia (Carl Phelpstead, "Auden and the Inklings: An Alliterative Revival," *Journal of English and Germanic Philology*, 103.4 [Oct. 2004], 449–450). Auden's almost unique first name, Wystan, was derived from the Saxon origins of the parish church in Repton, Derbyshire, the town where his father, Dr. Auden, had been born and educated (and died). The church is dedicated to St. Wystan, a Mercian prince, grandson of King Wiglaf, murdered in 849 because of his opposition to his mother's remarriage.

31. William Langland, *Piers Plowman: A Parallel-Text Edition of the A, B, C and Z Versions*, vol. 1: *Text*, ed. A. V. C. Schmidt (London: Longman, 1995), 2 [B version].

32. Naomi Mitchison, "Young Auden," *Shenandoah*, 18.2 (Winter 1967), 13. See also Mitchison, *You May Well Ask: A Memoir 1920–1940* (London: Gollancz, 1979), 124: "I went over to see him at Colwall, and we walked over the Malvern Hills. He quoted line after line from *Piers Plowman* and these seemed to go completely into the rhythm of these English hills, the rise and fall."

33. "A Happy New Year," part 1 (1932), *Poems1*, 138; see Chapter 6. See Chapter 4 for details of Tolkien's and Lewis's theorizing about the Englishness of alliterative meters.

34. See "In the year of my youth when yoyos came in" (1932–1933), ed. Lucy S. McDiarmid, *Review of English Studies*, n.s., 29.115 (Aug. 1978), 271.

The book was Allen H. Bright, *New Light on "Piers Plowman"* (London: Oxford UP, 1928).

35. Cited in Glenn Watkins, *Proof through the Night: Music and the Great War* (Berkeley: U of California P, 2003), 442n43. See also a reference in 1926 to Elgar as "our national minstrel," cited in Jeremy Crump, "The Identity of English Music: The Reception of Elgar 1898-1935," in Robert Colls and Philip Dodd, eds., *Englishness: Politics and Culture 1880-1920* (Beckenham: Croom Helm, 1986), 176.

36. "A Happy New Year," part 1 (1932), *Poems1*, 137, 138.

37. Auden told his old schoolmate John Hayward on 28 July 1932: "I'm getting to work now on a narrative poem in alliterative verse. God knows how it will turn out" (cited in *Poems1*, 496). One of his first references to the poem as "my epic" comes in an ALS from Auden to Naomi Mitchison, 18 Oct. 1932, NYPL; another is in a letter, probably written in the same month, to Isherwood: "tinkering at my epic which should be good if it doesn't get too dull" (cited in *Poems1*, 496). Of the two cantos he wrote (the second only partially done), the first was completed by Dec. 1932. He seems to have given up the poem around April 1933. It was unusual for Auden to abandon a poem completely. Even though, in this case, he quarried the poem extensively for later work, there is something anomalous about his decision to stop working on it altogether.

38. "In the year of my youth" (1932-1933), *Poems1*, 466 (from now on, cited parenthetically in the text). Throughout, unless otherwise noted, I follow the poem's punctuation and wording in *Poems1*. Mendelson glosses: "The Reinmuth object is an asteroid (later named Apollo), discovered in 1932 and rumored to be approaching Earth. The rector of Stiffkey [Harold Davidson] had recently been removed from his post for immoral acts" (*Poems1*, 496-497). For Ramsay MacDonald, see Chapter 6, note 81.

39. For example, the Lords of Limit appear in part 2 of "A Happy New Year" (1932), *Poems1*, 145 (see Chapter 6). Their presence has also been detected in the "gaitered gamekeeper with dog and gun" in "Who will endure" (1930), *Poems1*, 49.

40. The origins of Titt and Tool, the Lords of Limit, are mysterious, but they derive at least in part from D. H. Lawrence's last book, *Apocalypse* (Florence: G. Orioli, 1931). The song was reused in Auden's play "The Chase" (1934) and also printed as a separate lyric titled "The Witnesses," *Poems1*, 149-152. John Fuller provides a useful list of other phrases and passages that Auden later quarried from "In the year of my youth" for use in his plays "The Chase" (1934) and *The Dog Beneath the Skin* (1935) and in the "Commentary" (1938) to "In Time of War," as well as various other poems. See Fuller, *Commentary*, 128-130.

41. See Lucy S. McDiarmid's introduction to her edition of "In the year of my youth when yoyos came in" (1932-1933), *Review of English Studies*, n.s., 29.115 (Aug. 1978), 268-281; Fuller, *Commentary*, 128-131; and Mendelson, *EALA*, 141-145.

42. In canto 1, Sampson gives Auden a long sketch of this scheme over dinner in a restaurant. His speech starts, "That wave which already was washing the heart" and ends, "From the North Sea to the Alps was only a manoeuvre" (*Poems1*, 470–471). The most public, polished version of this historical schema comes in a section of the "Commentary" (1938) that Auden composed to accompany the sonnet sequence "In Time of War," which he wrote for his and Isherwood's *Journey to a War* (1939). The passage begins there with "This is one sector and one movement of the general war" and it ends with "Might mumble of the summers measured once by him" (*Prose1*, 682–685 [also *Poems1*, 309–313]).

43. "Lay your sleeping head, my love" (1937), *Poems1*, 337.

44. German sailors scuttled most of their country's High Seas Fleet at Scapa Flow in the Orkneys on 21 June 1919.

45. Mendelson, *EALA*, 90.

46. "Consider this and in our time" (1929), *Poems1*, 52; "Get there if you can and see the land you once were proud to own" (1930), *Poems1*, 45.

47. "Journal of an Airman" (1931) in *The Orators*, *Poems1*, 102; emphasis added. This part of *The Orators* was written in Helensburgh where, at the turn of the previous century, the television's primary inventor, John Logie Baird (1888–1946), had grown up and attended Larchfield Academy, the school Auden was now teaching at.

48. In his reference here to the belongings of two dead soldiers, Auden, perhaps a little tastelessly, is playing off Alexander Pope's description in canto 1 of *The Rape of the Lock* (1712–1717) of the jumbled array of objects on Belinda's dressing table: "Puffs, Powders, Patches, Bibles, Billet-doux" (Pope, *"The Rape of the Lock" and Other Poems*, ed. Geoffrey Tillotson, 2nd ed. [London: Methuen, 1954], 155).

49. "Prologue" ["O love, the interest itself in thoughtless Heaven"] (1932), *Poems1*, 184.

50. "In the year of my youth" is part of the tacit beginning of Auden's praise of novels and novelists that takes a more overt form in the mid-1930s, as in these lines from "Letter to Lord Byron" (1936): "novel writing is | A higher art than poetry altogether | In my opinion, and success implies | Both finer character and faculties. . . . The average poet by comparison | Is unobservant, immature, and lazy" (*Prose1*, 181 [also *Poems1*, 231]). See also Chapter 8.

51. "O-h-v" stands for "overhead valves"; Claudel-Hobson carburetors were in widespread use in cars in Britain in the early twentieth century, but there is also probably a complicated joke—about mixing "gas" with air—going on here in the reference to the French poet and playwright Paul Claudel's windy poetry, which Auden was enthusiastic about at the time. Fuller explores Claudel's influence on "Prologue" in *Commentary*, 144–145. See also Chapter 6, note 119.

52. Alexander Pope, postscript to The Odyssey *of Homer: Books XII–XXIV*, ed. Maynard Mack (London: Methuen, 1967), 387; emphasis in original. Auden quoted this sentence in his essay "Pope" (1936), *Prose1*, 151.

53. In *Poems1*, 489, the reading of the second line here is, "Letting them slip and [illegible in the manuscript] naked." My version is based on an

examination of the hasty scrawl in the notebook Auden used from 1932 to 1934 (now in Swarthmore College Library Special Collections), containing the text of the poem.

54. "Words" (1956), *Poems2,* 460.

55. ALS from W. H. Auden to John B. Auden, 16 Sept. 1932, NYPL.

56. "Problems of Education" (1932), *Prose1,* 28. The review appeared in the 15 Oct. 1932 issue of the *New Statesman.*

57. "The sun shines down on the ships at sea" (1932), *Poems1,* 651.

58. ALS from W. H. Auden to John B. Auden, 16 Sept. 1932, NYPL.

59. Probably connected to Auden's affair with Derek Wedgwood (see Chapter 6 and earlier in this chapter), which seems to have lasted from the autumn of 1930 until the spring of 1932. Auden's love poems start to become more celebratory than mournful around the autumn of 1931, in such works as "For what as easy" (1931), *Poems1,* 135; and "That night when joy began" (1931), *Poems1,* 212.

60. ALS from W. H. Auden to John B. Auden, 16 Sept. 1932, NYPL.

61. "Problems of Education" (1932), *Prose1,* 28.

62. ALS from W. H. Auden to Rupert Doone, 19 Oct. 1932, NYPL. "C.P." is the Communist Party.

63. ALS from W. H. Auden to Henry Bamford Parkes, 6 Dec. 1932, Special Collections, Colby College, Maine.

64. ALS from W. H. Auden to John B. Auden, 16 Sept. 1932, NYPL.

65. Cited in Carpenter, *Auden,* 142.

66. Cited in *ibid.,* 144.

67. E. J. Brown, *The First Five: The Story of a School* (Colwall: n.p., 1987), is a brief history of the school (from now on, cited as Brown, *First Five*). See also Gurney Thomas, "Recollections of Auden at the Downs School," *WHASN,* 3 (April 1989), 1-2. At various points between 1933 and 1937 Auden wrote three poems ("Lament," "Epilogue," and "Johnny") and a two-part travelogue ("In Search of Dracula") that were first published in the school magazine, *The Badger.* They are available, along with detailed annotatory arcana about characters at the Downs School during the time when Auden was there, in Katherine Bucknell and Nicholas Jenkins, eds., *W. H. Auden: "The Language of Learning and the Language of Love": Uncollected Writings, New Interpretations,* Auden Studies, vol. 2 (Oxford: Clarendon P, 1994), 18-31, 34-40 (from now on, cited as *AS2*).

68. Carpenter, *Auden,* 142. Geoffrey Hoyland (1889-1965); he had married Dorothea Cadbury (1892-1971) in 1919 and since 1920 had owned the Downs School (presumably purchased with what was originally Cadbury money). Dorothea was one of the daughters of the Birmingham chocolate tycoon George Cadbury (1839-1922) and his wife, the philanthropist and activist Elizabeth Cadbury (1858-1951). Curiously, a "little world" (Auden's phrase) was also a small world—Dorothea Hoyland's father, George Cadbury, a pacifist, was an old enemy of Dr. Auden: Cadbury, chair of the Birmingham

Education Committee, had tried unsuccessfully to remove from Auden's father the right of return to his municipal post when Dr. Auden enlisted during the First World War. See Richard R. Trail, "George Augustus Auden," in *Munk's Roll*, vol. 5: *1926–1965* (London: Royal College of Physicians, 1968), 16. Dorothea Cadbury served as a nurse in the war; her husband, Geoffrey, already a master at the Downs, was a conscientious objector.

69. See Brown, *First Five*, 52–53.

70. Parker, *Old Lie*, 269. The first phrase is often given as "Pax melior quam iustissimum bellum" (Peace is better than the most just of wars); the Horace phrase is from *Odes*, 3.2. See also Chapter 1.

71. Carpenter, *Auden*, 142.

72. Forge's remark comes in an interview with Cathy Courtney, available as a recording for the National Life Stories Collection posted at the British Library's "Sounds" webpage. (Edward) Maurice Feild (1905–1988) taught at the Downs from 1928 until 1954, when he left to join the Slade School of Art in London. The Slade was directed at the time by William Coldstream, whom Feild had met through their mutual friendships with Auden in the 1930s. See Chapter 8. In 1930, Feild married Alex (Alexandra) Dunlop (1904–1995?); they had one son, John (b. 1934). In 1937, in the Feilds' house in Colwall, Coldstream painted a medium-sized portrait in oils of Auden. Feild too made a number of portraits of Auden, including at least one in oils from 1937. He also painted Michael Yates (see later in this chapter).

73. See Mendelson's note on the composition history of the poem in *Poems1*, 496.

74. Fry (1927–2016) made this comment in an interview with Cathy Courtney, available as a recording for the National Life Stories Collection posted at the British Library's "Sounds" webpage.

75. ALS from W. H. Auden to Arnold Snodgrass, 21 Feb. 1933, NYPL, cited in Carpenter, *Auden*, 155.

76. APCS from W. H. Auden to Geoffrey Grigson, ca. 22 March 1933, cited in *Poems1*, 496.

77. ALS from W. H. Auden to John B. Auden, 16 Sept. 1932, NYPL.

78. "Problems of Education" (1932), *Prose1*, 28.

79. "The month was April, the year" (1933), *Poems1*, 497–502 (from now on, cited parenthetically in the text). Auden writes in Ode I (1931) in *The Orators* that he saw in "a vision | Life pass as a gull" (*Poems1*, 114).

80. For more on Dawkins, see Chapter 4. Dawkins was an expert on string figures; Fuller notes that he had published an article on them in *Annals of Archaeology and Anthropology* (1931). See Fuller, *Commentary*, 184. In "Auden and MacNeice: Their Last Will and Testament" (1936), Auden writes: "to Professor Dawkins who knows the Modern Greeks | I leave the string figure called the Fighting Lions" (*Prose1*, 370 [also *Poems1*, 285]; see also Mendelson's explanatory notes in *Prose1*, 795; and *Poems1*, 694).

81. Quoted in Farnan, *Auden*, 32.

654 | NOTES TO PAGES 397-401

82. Auden's first sestina was the poem beginning, "We have brought you, they said, a map of the country" (1931), *Poems1*, 94–95, in "Journal of an Airman," from *The Orators*, written not long after Empson's book was published.

83. William Empson, *Seven Types of Ambiguity* (London: Chatto and Windus, 1930), 45, 48, 50.

84. "Hearing of harvests rotting in the valleys" (1933), *Poems1*, 189 (from now on, cited parenthetically in the text).

85. "This lunar beauty" (1930), *Poems1*, 41; "Under boughs between our tentative endearments how should we hear" (1929), *Poems1*, 51.

86. Fuller points out that in this poem, as the word "islands" cycles back into visibility in successive stanzas, it means many things: "places of mysterious origin . . . and of equally unknown destination" but "also places to wish to be rescued from." This is because, he judges, "they represent the dangers of solipsism or an impossible dream of escape from society": Fuller, *Commentary*, 156. My claim is that Auden also loved and valued islands as well as rejecting them.

87. Gerard Manley Hopkins, "The Wreck of the Deutschland" (1875–1876), in *The Poetical Works of Gerard Manley Hopkins*, ed. Norman H. MacKenzie (Oxford: Clarendon P, 1990), 121; emphasis added. Auden reviewed an academic book about Hopkins in the *Criterion* in 1934 (see also Chapter 6).

88. Dobrée (1891–1974), pronounced Dob-RAY, had begun adult life as a professional soldier and ended it a well-established scholar of eighteenth-century literature with a professorship at the University of Leeds. Pukka, learned, and worldly, married but queer, he was a friend of Eliot and Herbert Read as well as of Auden. For more details of Dobrée's career, esp. in the 1930s, see Jason Harding, The Criterion: *Cultural Politics and Periodical Networks in Inter-war Britain* (Oxford: Oxford UP, 2002), 127–142.

89. Bonamy Dobrée, "New Life in English Poetry," *Listener*, 9.231 (14 June 1933), 958. The national component to Auden's imagination was noticed by other writers in the 1930s too. For example, the Marxist American literary historian F. W. Dupee (1904–1979), an editor of *Partisan Review*, wrote in 1938 that the "economic crisis [of 1930–1931], coinciding with the long-standing crisis in English culture, called forth in the first instance, not a socialist but a nationalist reaction from the young poets; and Auden was intensely conscious of himself as the prophet of a resurgent Britain." See Dupee, "The English Literary Left," *Partisan Review*, 5.3 (Aug.–Sept. 1938), 13.

90. ALS from W. H. Auden to Stephen Spender, [late June–early July 1933?], NYPL; see "Eleven Letters from Auden to Stephen Spender," ed. Nicholas Jenkins, *AS1*, 61–63. In citing the text of this important letter, I have left the spelling and punctuation exactly as they are in the original. The review Auden mentions is C. H. Madge, "Poetry and Politics," *New Verse*, 3 (May 1933), 1–4. Madge (1912–1996) seemed to be taunting Spender in his review by alluding in mocking fashion to the personal mobility that Spender's

limited private income made possible. There may already have been bad blood between Spender and Madge, reflected in the review. And it continued. Spender married Inez Pearn (1913–1976) in 1936. In 1939, she and Madge left their spouses and became a couple, marrying in 1942. In Dobrée's review, he had called Spender, with hints at less-than-total enthusiasm, "the most evident singer of them all."

91. For obvious reasons, this phrase has been the subject of critical dispute. The doyen of Auden scholarship, Edward Mendelson, argues that in "1933 it was still possible to use this term without referring exclusively to Nazism" (*EALA*, 300). In contrast, Valentine Cunningham claims that by "National Socialism both Auden and Spender can only have meant Nazism" (*British*, 236). It is possible to find historical evidence to support either contention. Certainly, the term "National Socialism" did not come into being with Hitler. For example, there was a short-lived, right-wing French "Socialiste national" party at the very start of the twentieth century, decades before Hitler's rise to power in Germany. See Eugen Weber, *Action Française; Royalism and Reaction in Twentieth Century France* (Stanford: Stanford UP, 1962), 69, 128. But Auden's use of "tendency" and "dangers" in the letter to Spender suggests he is describing something regrettable and retrograde in himself. And that tends to fit better with the idea that he was referring to an English analogue for German National Socialism. The German Workers' Party (DAP) changed its name to the National Socialist German Workers' Party (NSDAP) around March 1920. In *Hitler* (1931), a polemic roughly contemporaneous with Auden's letter, Wyndham Lewis asserted on the first page of his book that the "so-called Nationalsocialism . . . is the creation of Adolf Hitler" (Lewis, *Hitler*, 3). One of Hitler's more recent biographers, Ian Kershaw, writes of the period between 1923 and 1929, "for opponents and supporters alike, National Socialism came in these years to mean exclusively 'the Hitler Movement'" (Kershaw, *Hitler: 1889–1936: Hubris* [London: Penguin, 1998], 26). In June 1933, when Auden wrote to Spender, "National Socialism" had not had an opportunity to demonstrate many of its "dangers" anywhere outside Germany, though, of course, Auden was familiar with German life at first hand and would have been well aware of Nazi ideology, methods, and intentions. As far as I have been able to find, neither Mussolini nor Franco ever uses the phrase (perhaps to distinguish their own creeds from Hitler's), so what else could Auden be referring to when he talks about a tendency on his part "to Nationalism Socialism, and its *dangers*" (emphasis added) but some imagined, more tolerant English variant of German National Socialism as the latter existed in 1933?

92. The "personal fascism" remark was written around 1941 into a copy of *Poems* (1934), cited in *Poems1*, 587. See Chapter 6.

93. Ian Kershaw, *The "Hitler Myth": Image and Reality in the Third Reich* (Oxford: Oxford UP, 1987), 22.

94. Mendelson, *EALA*, 300.

95. "To T. S. Eliot on His Sixtieth Birthday" (1948), *Poems2*, 388. Auden is quoting *Hamlet* 2.2: "Use every man after his desert, and who shall 'scape whipping?"

96. "A Happy New Year," part 2 (1932), *Poems1*, 146; "Prologue" ["O love, the interest itself in thoughtless Heaven"] (1932), *Poems1*, 183; ALS from W. H. Auden to John B. Auden, 16 Sept. 1932, NYPL.

97. Preface to *For Lancelot Andrewes: Essays on Style and Order* (1928), in Eliot, *Prose*, vol. 3, 513. See the Prologue, note 87, and Chapter 3, note 83.

98. Eliot, *Prose*, vol. 5, 20. In later years, when challenged, Eliot sometimes tried to rationalize or explain away these remarks, never successfully.

99. ALS from W. H. Auden to T. S. Eliot, 26 April 1934, Faber and Faber archive.

100. "Out on the lawn I lie in bed" (1933), *Poems1*, 184–186 (from now on, cited parenthetically in the text). In the last line, Auden is using a euphonious-sounding archaic genitive ("The tigress her swift motions" = "The tigress's swift motions"). In much the same way, a phrase in "Sir, no man's enemy" (1929) reads "will his negative inversion" instead of "will's negative inversion" (*Poems1*, 53). The lines about the "nervous nations" and the "tigress" derive from an earlier poem about love. In the "Epithalamion" (composed in the summer of 1930) for the play "The Fronny," Auden writes that "the life" (meaning, roughly, sexual reproduction and physical growth) "shall outlast the tiger his swift motions. | Its slowness time the heartbeat of nervous nations" (*Plays*, 486; see also Chapter 8, note 48).

101. Cited in Foote, "W. H. Auden—Interview III."

102. "Easily, my dear, you move, easily your head" (1934), *Poems1*, 206.

103. See Auden's [introduction to *The Protestant Mystics*] (1963), *Prose5*, 42–69; the section on the Vision of Agape is on pp. 57–59. Mendelson's extended account of this poem is in *EALA*, 151–166. As early as 1970, at a point when mention of Auden's private life was off limits, Fuller had drawn the connection between "Out on the lawn" and the *Protestant Mystics* essay in his *A Reader's Guide to W. H. Auden* (London: Thames and Hudson, 1970), 99–100. *The Protestant Mystics* was edited by the Catholic author Anne Fremantle (1909–2002), whom Auden had known since at least 1931.

104. Mendelson, *EALA*, 151; emphasis in original. The title of the poem has varied subtly. It was called "Summer Night" when first printed in the *Listener* in 1934. (Probably not coincidentally, this was the same periodical in which the Dobrée review, a year earlier, referred to Auden and poets associated with him as "communists with an intense love of England.") Then, after a decade in which it was reprinted without a title, Auden titled it "A Summer Night, 1933" in *The Collected Poetry of W. H. Auden* (1945). It became "A Summer Night" in *Collected Shorter Poems: 1930–1944* (1950), and subsequently stayed that way. The fact that Auden made these many small changes to the title indicates that he saw significance in the exact wording.

105. [Introduction to *The Protestant Mystics*] (1963), *Prose5*, 57. The three other teachers may have been Hilda Woodhams (the school's music teacher), Margaret Sant, and Ross Coates.

106. Heard, *Social*, 213–214.

107. On Heard's unease with his sexuality, see Peter Parker, *Ackerley: The Life of J. R. Ackerley* (New York: Farrar, Straus and Giroux, 1989), 111. On Heard's argument about hunger versus sexual need, see Heard, *Social*, esp. 31–32; 110–112. See also Bucknell's introduction to "Auden's 'Writing' Essay," *AS1*, 26.

108. [Introduction to *The Protestant Mystics*] (1963), *Prose5*, 58.

109. For "Paradise Row" and Auden's bed, see Brown, *First Five*, 43, 49. One pupil, John Bowes (see also Chapter 8, note 164), recalled Auden lying outside on a bed "strewn with blankets heaped one on top of the other (and the floor carpet on top of the lot)" in "Downs Days Remembered," *WHASN*, 13 (Oct. 1995), 20.

110. Wright, *Village*, 142.

111. As seen in Chapter 5, in 1929 Auden had described the atmosphere in Berlin with Isherwood and Berthold Szczesny as "sexy": see "1929 Journal" (1929), fo. [7], NYPL. The rareness of the word is striking. For example, I have not been able to find "sexy" in encyclopedic modernist classics of the everyday from this period, such as *Ulysses* (1922) or *Finnegans Wake* (1939). The American poet Genevieve Taggard (1894–1948) included the line "In the eyes of sexy women and of snakes" in "Two of a Kind: Marriage à la Mode," dated by her "Bennington, Vermont, 1933." See Taggard, *Collected Poems: 1918–1938* (New York: Harper and Brothers, 1938), 66. Taggard's poem was apparently not printed until after 1933, so Auden cannot have known about it when he was working on "Out on the lawn." It seems that, besides Auden's and Taggard's, no other English-language poem written before the Second World War includes the word "sexy."

112. "A Happy New Year," part 2 (1932), *Poems1*, 146.

113. Brown, *The First Five*, 23. There is no date given, and the photographer is uncredited. The opposite page (p. 22) shows a picture of the Downs' dining hall, where Auden sits among the pupils with an adult colleague or friend.

114. The full context of the line is this: Arnold attributes a special temperamental balance to the "mellow glory of the Attic stage": "be his || My special thanks, whose even-balanced soul, | From first youth tested up to extreme old age, | Business could not make dull, nor passion wild; || Who saw life steadily, and saw it whole." See "To a Friend" (1848), in *The Poems of Matthew Arnold*, ed. Kenneth Allott and Miriam Allott, 2nd ed. (London: Longman, 1979), 111. See also Chapter 4.

115. E. M. Forster, *Howards End* (1910), ed. Paul B. Armstrong (New York: Norton, 1998), 191.

116. Shakespeare, *The Tempest*, 3.2.

117. "Easily, my dear, you move, easily your head" (1934), *Poems1*, 206–208; ALS from W. H. Auden to Olive Mangeot, [early 1935?], private collection.

118. Among the many poems strongly associated with this love are: "The earth turns over, our side feels the cold" (Dec. 1933); "Easily, my dear, you move, easily your head" (Nov. 1934); "Dear, though the night is gone" (March 1936); "Fish in the unruffled lakes" (March 1936); and "Lay your sleeping head, my love" (Jan. 1937) (*Poems1*, 191–192, 206–208, 213, 212–213, 336–337); and, later, "First Things First" (1957); "Iceland Revisited" (1964); and "Since" (1965) (*Poems2*, 481–482, 536–538, 583–584). See also Mendelson, *EALA*, 197n.

119. "Epilogue" first appeared in *Day by Day* (1977), repr. in Robert Lowell, *Collected Poems,* ed. Frank Bidart and David Gewanter (New York: Farrar, Straus and Giroux, 2003), 838.

120. Never the most accurate of self-chroniclers, Auden at one point implied that his love for Yates had begun in 1932. It is more likely, however, that it began a year later. Michael Yates (1919–2001) was one of five brothers (including two sets of twins), born in Sale, a suburb of the northern city of Manchester. His father was a solicitor. He later described his family life as "claustrophobic" (Yates, "Iceland 1936," *Tribute,* 60). Yates was educated at the Downs School, where he met Auden, who taught him English, and Maurice Feild, who taught him art. In the autumn of 1933 he moved to Bryanston, then still a relatively small, new school, where he eventually became head boy before leaving in the summer of 1937. As a schoolboy, Yates was especially interested in painting; he later became a successful stage designer for television. There are reproductions of pictures of him by Maurice Feild in *The Art Room* (n.d.) at the Downs and a *Portrait of Michael Yates* (about 1932?) in *Painting the Visible World: Painters at the Euston Road School and at Camberwell School of Arts & Crafts 1930-1960* (London: Austin / Desmond Fine Art, 1989), 24, 3. (The identification of Yates in *The Art Room* is tentative.) One of these paintings may have been bought by Auden, who paid Feild for what seems to be a now-lost portrait of Yates. He stuffed some pound notes into the art master's pocket as he took the picture.

Auden went on holiday with Yates (and Peter Roger, one of Auden's more causal lovers; see later in this chapter) to central Europe in the summer of 1934, and then he spent a holiday with Yates and his family on the Isle of Man in Aug. 1935 (see Chapter 8). He traveled in Iceland with him, the poet Louis MacNeice, and a Bryanston school party in June–Sept. 1936. Yates features prominently in *Letters from Iceland* (1937), the travel book Auden and MacNeice wrote about the trip; there is a photograph of him there, taken by Frazer Hoyland, Geoffrey Hoyland's half brother, in *Prose1,* 348. Auden and Yates's affair appears to have ended around 1938, but Auden recommended Yates to the English scholar of drama Allardyce Nicoll (1894–1976), who at the time was head of the Yale Drama School. Auden saw Yates several times, both in New Haven and in New York, during 1939. (While Yates was at Yale, he introduced

Auden to his friend, the poet Owen Dodson [1914–1983], also a Yale student at the time.)

Yates served as a lieutenant in the Royal Marines during the Second World War and was captured in 1941 at Suda Bay on Crete. He spent the rest of the conflict in Oflag X-C in Lübeck and Oflag VII-B in Eichstätt, Bavaria, two German prisoner-of-war camps. In Oflag VII-B, he was heavily involved in stage designs and acting for productions, including *Hamlet* and *Macbeth*, put on by the prisoners. The Yates family paid an extremely high price during the war. Aside from Michael Yates's service and imprisonment, his twin brother, Flying Officer James Yates of the Royal Air Force Volunteer Reserve, was killed somewhere in the English Channel or in northern France while piloting a Spitfire on 8 April 1943. And one of his younger brothers, Lt. David Yates (1922–1944), a Royal Marine commando, was drowned coming ashore under heavy fire at Juno Beach on D-Day, while Anthony Yates (b. 1922) fought with the Lancashire Fusiliers in the Burma campaign. (Any service details for Yates's older brother, Peter Yates [1915–1973?], are unknown.)

In the postwar period, Michael Yates began the main phase of his professional career as a stage designer with the Carl Rosa Opera Company. He then worked for several television companies including the BBC, Rediffusion, and LWT, rising to be head of design at the latter. Michael Yates married Margaret (Marny) Wood (1919–2017) in 1955. In the postwar period, Yates kept quite closely in touch with Auden until Auden's death, and he and his wife visited Auden in his summer homes almost annually for many years— Auden's posthumous book *Thank You, Fog: Last Poems* (1974) is dedicated to Michael and Marny Yates (*Poems2*, 689). Michael Yates retired in 1979. A good account of his life and his career as a designer for television is Dennis Barker, "Obituary: Michael Yates: Designer Who Brought Style to Television Drama," *Guardian*, 18 Dec. 2001, p. 18. See also "Michael Yates," *Times*, 21 Jan. 2002, p. 18; and [Edward Mendelson], "Michael Yates," *WHASN*, 22 (Nov. 2001), 39.

Long referred to only in indirect, veiled terms by Auden scholars, Yates was first, probably inadvertently, outed as Auden's former lover in Thekla Clark's 1995 memoir of her friendship with Auden and Chester Kallman. See Clark, *Wystan and Chester: A Personal Memoir of W. H. Auden and Chester Kallman* (New York: Columbia UP, 1995), 129. Recently, writers have become more open on the matter in glosses and asides. For example, Peter Parker refers to Yates as Auden's "teenage lover" in *Isherwood*, 304, and Mendelson's notes in *Poems1* are straightforward. But the story itself has never been told. Yates wrote two short, unrevealing accounts of his friendship with Auden: "Wystan Auden 1907–1973," *Badger* (Downs School), 47 (Autumn 1974), 34; and "Iceland 1936," *Tribute*, 59–60. In his last years, he talked publicly, if still very briefly and circumspectly, about his relationship with Auden in the BBC television program "Tell Me the Truth about Love," first broadcast in March 2000.

121. ALS from W. H. Auden to Stephen Spender, [late June–early July 1933?], NYPL; see "Eleven Letters from Auden to Stephen Spender," ed. Nicholas Jenkins, *AS1*, 61–63.

122. "Here on the cropped grass of the narrow ridge I stand" (1933), *Poems1*, 202.

123. Isherwood, *C&HK*, 4. See Chapter 5.

124. In a late review of J. R. Ackerley's *My Father and Myself*, Auden comments that "all 'abnormal' sex-acts are rites of symbolic magic, and one can only properly understand the actual personal relation if one knows the symbolic role each expects the other to play" ("Papa Was a Wise Old Sly-Boots" [1969], *Prose6*, 363).

125. "Love had him fast, but though he fought for breath" (1933?), *Poems1*, 214.

126. Lincoln Kirstein, unpublished MS diary, Lincoln Kirstein Papers at the Jerome Robbins Dance Division of the New York Public Library for the Performing Arts. Thanks to Martin Duberman for alerting me to this reference.

127. "Easily, my dear, you move, easily your head" (1934), *Poems1*, 207–208.

128. Carpenter, *Auden*, 176. Peter Roger (1911–1976) spent most of his life working outdoors. He was perhaps similar in temperament to Auden's oldest brother, Bernard Auden (see Chapter 1). Roger was deaf in one ear, which seems to have affected deeply his interactions with others. In "Auden and MacNeice: Their Last Will and Testament" (1936), from *Letters from Iceland*, Auden bequeaths: "My Morris-Cowley to carry chickens in | To Peter Roger, with a very fine large goat" (*Prose1*, 371 [also *Poems1*, 285]). Peter Roger had a brother, David Roger (ca. 1923–1941), who was at the Downs School for at least part of the time when his (much older) brother was working as a gardener at the school and when Auden was a teacher there. During the Second World War, Peter Roger was employed as an agricultural laborer; David Roger was serving as a leading aircraftman in the RAF Volunteer Reserve when he was killed in/over Wales in Oct. 1941. After their affair at the Downs ended, perhaps around 1935, Auden and Peter Roger (like Auden and Yates) remained in touch. Auden saw Roger in England in 1948 and then again in 1951 on Ischia in the Bay of Naples. Some of this information was kindly provided to the Auden Estate by David Godby, Peter Roger's nephew, and by Andrew Biswell.

129. Andrew Forge interview with Cathy Courtney, available as a recording for the National Life Stories Collection posted at the British Library's "Sounds" webpage.

130. "Prologue at Sixty" (1967), *Poems2*, 629. Auden wrote up the trip in lightly comic style as "In Search of Dracula" (1934) for the Downs School magazine, *The Badger*, where it appeared in two installments in autumn 1934 and spring 1935 (see *Prose1*, 72–77).

131. "Easily, my dear, you move, easily your head" (1934), *Poems1*, 206.

132. The boy Auden spoke to was Humphrey Kay (1923–2009), later life a professor of hematology at the University of London, cited in Alisdaire Hickson, *The Poisoned Bowl: Sex, Repression and the Public School System* (London: Constable, 1995), 112. Auden taught at the Downs from around the start of Oct. 1932 until July 1935; he returned to fill in for an absent master from around May until late July 1937.

133. Katherine Bucknell, "Some Notes on a Meeting with Stephen Spender, 4 June 1992," *WHASN*, 13 (Oct. 1995), 11. This is probably the same pupil to whom Auden wrote with unfortunate results in 1934 after Jones (and Yates) had moved on to Bryanston. See Chapter 8.

134. One pupil at the Downs remembered Hoyland as "a very strong, firm man, an athlete." See David Garrett Izzo's interview with John Duguid (at the Downs from 1934 to 1937), "The Student and the Master: A Pupil Recollects W. H. Auden," in Garrett Izzo, ed., *W. H. Auden: A Legacy* (West Cornwall: Locust Hill P, 2002), 35. A good summary of Hoyland's religious and educational career is contained in Nigel Lemon, "'The Dust and Joy of Human Life': Geoffrey Hoyland and Congregationalism," *Journal of the United Reformed Church History Society*, 8.10 (May 2012), 610–623.

135. Reported in conversation by Andrew Forge (1923–2002) to Edward Mendelson, probably in the 1970s, and recorded by Mendelson in contemporaneous typed notes on the conversation. In an interview with Cathy Courtney (available in the National Life Stories Collection posted at the British Library's "Sounds" webpage), Forge commented that although Hoyland "was married and had a son, [he] was a suppressed homosexual who, as time went on, found it harder and harder to keep himself clearly defined." Forge said that pupils would relate to one another their experiences with Hoyland: "Later on, the whole thing fell apart in a great scandal, and he was declared to have had a nervous breakdown and retired." The artist Anthony Fry, also at the Downs in the 1930s, referred to Hoyland's propensities in another interview with Cathy Courtney, also available as a recording at the same National Life Stories Collection source. Was this normal behavior for a 1930s English headmaster? Forge's comment to Mendelson when he recalled the headmaster's actions was, "Very rum!" It would seem not. The Downs's governors did not approve. The son of another former pupil, who was at the Downs during Auden and Hoyland's time there, corroborated to me Forge's and Fry's comments about Hoyland. Hoyland's "problems," this source said, were the reason why "eventually, the governors persuaded him to retire." Brown writes that Hoyland ceded his position as headmaster in 1940 "on health grounds" (*The First Five*, 59). He was succeeded by his half brother, Frazer Hoyland (1908–1981), who held the position until 1952.

136. Bucknell, "Some Notes on a Meeting with Stephen Spender," 11.

137. Consult the Forge interview with Cathy Courtney, available as a recording for the National Life Stories Collection posted at the British Library's "Sounds" webpage.

138. John Catlin, *Family Quartet* (London: Hamish Hamilton, 1987), 135. If the recollection by Catlin (1927–1987) is accurate, this visit, otherwise unrecorded, probably took place in Oct. 1938.

139. Examples include "Lucky with day approaching, with leaning dawn" ("Doom is darker and deeper than any single dingle"; 1930); "Whose life is lucky in your eyes" ("Night covers up the rigid land"; 1936?); and "His lucky guesses were rewarded well" ("He watched the stars and noted birds in flight"; 1938), *Poems1*, 27, 209, 298.

140. The poem's idea of "luck" and its connection to love links it to another strongly associated with Yates, beginning "Easily, my dear, you move, easily your head" (1934). There, Auden insists that when the lovers are together: "*Lucky* to love the new pansy railway, | The sterile farms where his looks are fed, | And in the policed unlucky city | *Lucky* his bed" (*Poems1*, 207; emphasis added). The suggestive phrase "new pansy railway" alludes to a miniature railway with a 9½-inch track gauge constructed in the grounds of the Downs School.

141. *Leaves of Grass* (1855) in Walt Whitman, *Complete Poetry and Collected Prose,* ed. Justin Kaplan (New York: Library of America, 1982), 30–31. A kelson is a crucial structural member in a ship's hull, something like the backbone of the vessel, fitted directly above its keel.

142. Forster's novel was written and intensively revised on and off between 1913 and around 1960. It was eventually published in 1971.

143. Philip Gardner cites from Forster's correspondence about the book with Isherwood in April–July 1933 and with Spender in Aug. 1933. See Gardner's "Editor's Introduction" to E. M. Forster, *Maurice* (1971), ed. Philip Gardner (London: André Deutsch, 1999), xxxv–xxxviii. For more on Isherwood's reading of the novel, see Parker, *Isherwood,* 255. For more on Spender's, see John Sutherland, *Stephen Spender: The Authorized Biography* (London: Viking, 2004), 92. Spender had previously given Forster his own frank and at the time unpublishable *The Temple* (1929) to read.

144. Isherwood, *C&HK,* 126–127; Parker, *Isherwood,* 222.

145. Edward Upward and Isherwood had apparently discovered Forster's work, and in particular *Howards End,* in early 1926 (see Parker, *Isherwood,* 129–130). Auden too read *Howards End* in 1926: see *J,* 236n.

146. Forster, *Maurice,* 207. See also the Prologue.

147. Fuller notes the source in Smart: see his *Commentary,* 149.

148. "Writing" (1932), *Prose1,* 19.

149. See *Poems1,* 184.

150. David Trotter, *The Making of the Reader: Language and Subjectivity in Modern American, English, and Irish Poetry* (New York: St. Martin's P, 1984), 114–115. Cunningham, too, commenting on Henry Green, discusses the power of deictics, "extremely prevalent in other texts of this period, in Auden's and Dylan Thomas's poems just as much as in T. S. Eliot or D. H. Lawrence" (Cunningham, *British,* 10).

151. For Antonio, see Shakespeare, *The Tempest,* 2.1; and for Stephano and Trinculo, *ibid.,* 2.2.

152. "Sir, no man's enemy" (1929), *Poems1,* 53; see Chapter 6.

153. "Love had him fast, but though he fought for breath" (1933?), *Poems1,* 214.

154. ALS from W. H. Auden to Frederic Prokosch, [4 Jan. 1937], NYPL.

155. For comments on Sonnet 109 and on the phrase "my all," see Helen Vendler, *The Art of Shakespeare's Sonnets* (Cambridge, MA: Belknap P of Harvard UP, 1997), 464–465.

156. "The fruit in which your parents hid you, boy" (1933), *Poems1,* 159. Using Mendelson's textual notes in *Poems1,* 618, I cite the version published in 1933. Auden cannibalized the last lines here for use in his poem "Journey to Iceland" (1936), *Prose1,* 186 [also *Poems1,* 262]. Auden at first intended to collect this 1933 poem in 1936, but he dropped it from his book at the page-proof stage. For "Sir, no man's enemy," see Chapter 6.

157. Around 1935 this line was revised, perhaps judiciously, to "Turn not towards me lest I turn to you" (see *Poems1,* 619).

158. Mendelson describes the genesis of the sequence and lists its contents in *Poems1,* 619–620.

159. The two poems unpublished in any context in Auden's lifetime are "Dear to me now and longer than a summer" (1933?), *Poems1,* 506–507; and "One absence closes other lives to him" (1934), *Poems1,* 507–508.

160. "That night when joy began" (1931), *Poems1,* 212; and the poem which in the sequence begins "To lie flat on the back with the knees flexed" (1933?), *Poems1,* 206, but which derives from a longer, unpublished draft poem "To lie this hour in any position" (*Poems1,* 462–463) that was written before Auden left Helensburgh in 1932.

161. "Dear to me now and longer than a summer" (1933?), *Poems1,* 506. This never-published sonnet was the thirteenth poem in the sixteen-poem sequence he sent to Isherwood in 1934.

162. "Friend, of the civil space by human love" (1933), *Poems1,* 505–506; Mendelson, *EALA,* 223.

163. "Friend, of the civil space by human love" (1933), *Poems1,* 505.

164. "Here on the cropped grass of the narrow ridge I stand" (1933), *Poems1,* 201–205 (from now on, cited parenthetically in the text).

165. Forster, *Howards End,* 127.

166. Collett, *Changing,* 94. The Sugar Loaf is a hill in the Black Mountains, just northwest of Abergavenny in Wales. Collett seems also to be the source for Auden's remark later in the poem that "Here . . . looked north before the Cambrian alignment." Collett writes that the Malvern range "does not conform to the newer orientation of British hills from north-east to south-west, but stretches due north and south" (*ibid.,* 94).

167. Dominic Hibberd, *Owen the Poet* (London: Macmillan, 1986), 126. Hibberd notes that Owen owned a copy of *The Dynasts* (*ibid.,* 230).

168. "The Show," Owen, *Poems*, 132. Jon Stallworthy suggests that the imagery of Owen's airborne perspective is probably derived from chapter 1 of Henri Barbusse's *Le Feu* (*Under Fire*, 1916).

169. "Hearing of harvests rotting in the valleys" (1933), *Poems1*, 189–190.

170. Auden reuses a phrase, "nerves in order," from Owen's letters. Owen himself wrote it twice in a final sequence of searing letters from the front written during his last month. To his mother on 4 Oct. 1918, he wrote, "My nerves are in perfect order." To Sassoon on 10 Oct. 1918 he wrote, "I cannot say I suffered anything; having let my brain grow dull: That is to say my nerves are in perfect order." These letters are cited from Owen, *Selected Letters of Wilfred Owen,* ed. John Bell, 2nd ed. (Oxford: Oxford UP, 1998), 352 (see also Chapter 6, note 48). Auden owned Edmund Blunden's edition *The Poems of Wilfred Owen* (London: Chatto and Windus, 1931), in which extracts from Owen's letters are quoted.

171. The ending strongly recalls the ending of "I chose this lean country" (1927), where Auden's speaker, his "corpse | Already wept," nonetheless passes "Alive into the house" (*Poems1*, 393).

172. See M. J. Sidnell, "Auden and the Group Theatre," *Plays,* 503. In London in Feb. 1934, the Group Theatre had presented a version of *The Deluge* that Auden lightly adapted from an original source (*Plays,* 496); see Chapter 5. It is probable that Auden used the same version of the play for his production at the Downs.

173. See Mendelson, "Auden on the Air," *Prose1,* 727. For the "Do we read too much and think too little?" discussion, Auden was paired with Wing Commander E. G. Hilton, an RAF officer, test pilot, and frequent broadcaster. (Hilton was killed in 1937 when he and his copilot crashed their plane during an air race at Scarborough in front of a thousand people.)

174. A D'Yrsan (a French car with three wheels) is mentioned as being driven at Oxford by Auden in V. M. Allom, "W.H.A.: A Further Tribute" (1975), Columbia; see Chapter 2, note 159.

175. The letter is dated 9 Jan. 1935, and the text is available in John Haffenden's edition of the Eliot-Hale letters on the tseliot.com website (see Chapter 3, note 57). Frank Morley (1899–1980) was a Faber and Faber director and a friend of Eliot.

176. Mendelson's account of the evolution of *The Dog Beneath the Skin* is in *Plays,* 553–554.

177. *The Dog Beneath the Skin, or, Where Is Francis?* (1935), *Plays,* 191. Some elements of this chorus had been drafted as early as the summer of 1934 in "The Chase," a work that was the forerunner of *The Dog Beneath the Skin* (see *Plays,* 111). The lines about "the Dutch Sea so shallow" and "the deep water that divides us still from Norway," which were also drawn from Collett's *The Changing Face of England,* 9–10, were added in 1935, after Auden had flown to see Isherwood in Denmark. For Collett, see earlier in this chapter and also in Chapters 6 and 7.

178. "1929 Journal" (1929), fo. [99], NYPL. See Chapter 5.

179. Quoted in Carpenter, *Auden,* 176.

180. Austin Wright's account was created from a letter written to Maurice Feild in 1977, later revised in collaboration with Humphrey Carpenter and cited in Carpenter, *Auden,* 176.

181. ALS from W. H. Auden to James Yates, [May / June 1935], NYPL. Between 1926 and 1929, Mann (1905–1969) was married to the German actor Gustaf Gründgens (1899–1963). After her wedding to Auden in 1935, she and Auden saw each other occasionally (see Chapter 8), and they remained married until her death in 1969; in her will, she left him a small bequest.

182. "38 More Germans Lose Citizenship," *New York Times,* 12 June 1935, p. 9.

183. Gunna Wendt, *Erika und Therese: Erika Mann und Therese Giehse: Eine Liebe zwischen Kunst und Krieg* (Munich: Piper, 2018), 253–254. Sources in the literature on Erika Mann differ slightly on the dates of her denationalization and her journey to Britain. I have mainly relied here on the version offered in one of the more recent studies.

184. Alec Bangham (1921–2010) became a distinguished biophysicist who did important research on liposomes. Smoking was acceptable in the young in the 1930s: once teenagers started to earn money, which could easily begin by the age of fourteen, buying and consuming cigarettes was considered an initiation into adulthood: see Martin Pugh, *"We Danced All Night": A Social History of Britain Between the Wars* (London: Bodley Head, 2008), 221 (from now on, cited as Pugh, *Danced*).

185. Wendt, *Erika und Therese,* 256.

186. ALS to Spender, 28 June 1935, NYPL; see "Eleven Letters from Auden to Stephen Spender," ed. Nicholas Jenkins, *AS1,* 67. By "till the ceremony," Auden probably meant something like "until she arrived in Malvern a few days earlier to prepare for the marriage ceremony." Erika Mann arrived in the country on 12 June 1935, and she met Auden in Colwall a couple of days before the wedding. On 14 June 1935, she and Auden went on a visit to C. Day Lewis's home at Box Cottage in Cheltenham, Gloucestershire. They were married in Ledbury the next day. Katherine Bucknell has discovered that the wedding probably took place in the Ledbury Registry Office, which was then housed in the offices of a firm of solicitors, Orme Dykes, in Banks Crescent, Ledbury.

187. Thomas Mann, *Tagebücher 1935–1936,* ed. Peter De Mendelssohn (Frankfurt am Main: S. Fischer, 1978), 120.

8. IMAGES IN THE DARK

Epigraph: Friedrich Nietzsche, *The Gay Science: With a Prelude in Rhymes and an Appendix of Songs* (1887), 2nd ed., trans. Walter Kaufmann (New York: Vintage, 1974), 251; emphasis in original.

1. "In Search of Dracula" (1934), *Prose1*, 73; *The Dog Beneath the Skin* (1935), *Plays*, 191. *The Dance of Death* (see *Plays*, 81–107) was staged for Group Theatre subscribers in two "club" (i.e., private) performances in the spring of 1934. It became part of the Group Theatre's public season in the autumn of 1935.

2. "Phantasy and Reality in Poetry" (1971), *Prose6*, 710.

3. "Out on the lawn I lie in bed" (1933), *Poems1*, 185; see Chapter 7.

4. "August for the people and their favourite islands" (1935), *Poems1*, 214 (from now on, cited parenthetically in the text).

5. See Parker, *Isherwood*, 305–306, for details of the celebration.

6. Auden later used the name in his satirical ballad about a bank cashier who murders his wife. Before his marriage, the character, Victor, lives at the Peveril, a "respectable boarding-house" ("Victor" [1937], *Poems1*, 360).

7. See Chapter 7, note 120 for details about the lives of the Yates brothers.

8. *Poems1*, 36–40, 565; see Chapter 5, note 152.

9. W. H. Auden, *Look, Stranger!* (London: Faber and Faber, 1936), 63. Yates's copy is in a private collection. See also the Epilogue.

10. "A Happy New Year," part 2 (1932), *Poems1*, 146. See Chapter 6.

11. Auden had written a verse letter to Isherwood in April 1929 in which he called the novel the "most prodigious of the forms," following Henry James's claim in the preface to *The Ambassadors* (1903), included in James, *The Ambassadors*, vol. 1 (New York: Charles Scribner's Sons, 1909), xxiii, that the novel was "under the right persuasion, the most independent, most elastic, most prodigious of literary forms." But that comment never appeared in print in Auden's lifetime (it is cited in Mendelson, *EALA*, 45). Auden's public reverence for the novel is developed after 1935 in such poems as part 1 of "Letter to Lord Byron" (1936), *Prose1*, 181 [also in *Poems1*, 231] and "The Novelist" (1938), *Poems1*, 338. See also Chapter 7.

12. Parker, *Isherwood*, 132.

13. After Auden published an anthology of Tennyson's poetry in 1944, he wrote to Isherwood: "So glad you like the Tennyson; I think of it as very much *our* book, as every page is crammed with our private associations" (ALS from W. H. Auden to Christopher Isherwood, 18 Nov. [1944], Huntington; emphasis in original).

14. Isherwood describes the visit briefly in *C&HK*, 81–83; see also Parker, *Isherwood*, 222–223.

15. The reference to the "animal brother and his serious sister" is puzzling since Yates had four brothers and no sisters (see Chapter 7). Presumably, this is a reference to some fellow holiday makers.

16. Mendelson writes: "In a list of poems in Auden's 1936–1937 *Ascent of F6* notebook this may be the poem listed as 'The island'" (*Poems1*, 661).

17. "The earth turns over, our side feels the cold" (1933), *ibid.*, 191–192. Mendelson gives the place of composition as the Audens' home at Wesco and

dates the poem to Christmas Day, 1933 (*ibid.*, 641). The phrase "would-be lover" suggests that Auden's and Yates's sexual relationship had not yet started by Christmas 1933.

18. See Chapter 7.

19. "Yeats as an Example" (1948), *Prose2*, 388. For more on Auden and the Robert Gregory poem, which was collected in *The Wild Swans at Coole* (1919), see Chapter 6.

20. "In Memory of Major Robert Gregory" (1918), Yeats, *Poems*, 132–135.

21. [Introduction to *The Poet's Tongue*] (1935), *Prose1*, 108.

22. "Gentleman versus Player" (1933), *Prose1*, 33–34; emphasis in original. Auden seems to be citing from the one-volume abridgement (1931) of Churchill's six-volume *The World Crisis* (1923–1931), his "huge comic history of the war," as Auden put it.

23. "Preface" (1918), Owen, *Poems*, 192.

24. For discussion of the setting of part 2 of "A Happy New Year" (1932), see Chapter 6.

25. Freud, "Fetishism" (1927), *SE*, 21:156.

26. *Three Essays on the Theory of Sexuality* (1905), *SE*, 7:155.

27. *La Fugitive* (1923): "l'amour . . . est un exemple frappant du peu qu'est la réalité pour nous." See Proust, *The Captive; The Fugitive* (vol. 5 of *In Search of Lost Time*), trans. C. K. Scott Moncrieff, Terence Kilmartin, and D. J. Enright (New York: Modern Library, 2003), 647.

28. See "Hamlet and His Problems" (1919), in Eliot, *Prose*, vol. 2, 125; emphasis in original.

29. Speech of 6 Oct. 1939 in the Reichstag, in *Hitler: Speeches and Proclamations 1932–1945*, ed. Max Domarus, vol. 3: *The Years 1939 to 1940*, trans. Chris Wilcox (Würzburg: Domarus, et al., 1997), 1847–1848. In the German: "Es gibt heute keine Inseln mehr."

30. H. A. L. Fisher, preface to *A History of Europe*, vol. 1: *Ancient and Mediaeval* (London: Eyre and Spottiswoode, 1935), [vii].

31. Fuller, *Commentary*, 175.

32. "Epithalamion" (1939), *Poems1*, 381. Elisabeth Mann (1918–2002) married Giuseppe Antonio Borgese (1882–1952) in Princeton on 23 Nov. 1939 with Auden in attendance—he read out his poem to the couple at the wedding reception that day.

33. The "real meeting" is a phrase from "Before this loved one" (1929), *Poems1*, 42; see Chapter 5.

34. "Sounding Auden," in Seamus Heaney, *The Government of the Tongue: The 1986 T. S. Eliot Memorial Lectures and Other Critical Writings* (London: Faber and Faber, 1988), 116.

35. Auden's old Oxford acquaintances A. S. T. Fisher (see Chapter 3), Eric Bramall (1905–1958), and Wilfred Cowley (1904–1965) were on the teaching staff at Bryanston. At the beginning of April 1935, Auden appeared to

believe he had a job there for the coming year, but then a short while later, by his own account he wrote a letter to Michael Paget Jones, another old Downian now at Bryanston and probably one of the Downs headmaster Geoffrey Hoyland's schoolboy former lovers (see Chapter 7). Hoyland was due to visit Bryanston to preach in the chapel. The letter joked about Hoyland's visit. Auden told a poet acquaintance that his message to Paget Jones contained "an unfortunate exhortation to put an onion in the chalice. Boy showed letter in pride to prefect, prefect in shock to headmaster" (see Carpenter, *Auden,* 174–175). Bryanston's headmaster, Thorold Coade (1896–1963), apparently canceled Auden's employment, perhaps using the letter as a pretext but probably having heard other rumors as well. As almost always, Stephen Spender's apparently limitless capacity for gossip may have extended only so far. It seems possible that he himself later had some kind of fling with Paget Jones (b. ca. 1921), who, in *WwW,* Spender says, "stayed with me during one of the worst nights of the Blitz" (320). Spender's "To Poets and Airmen" (1941?), an elegiac poem dedicated to Paget Jones, seemingly after the latter's death, advises him suggestively to "Remember for a flash the wild good | Drunkenness where | You abandoned future care." The poem is collected in Spender, *Ruins and Visions* (1942), repr. in *New Collected Poems,* ed. Michael Brett (London: Faber and Faber, 2004), 164–165.

36. The whole story is related in Carpenter, *Auden,* 174–175; and D-H, *Auden,* 120–121. The BBC job is mentioned in a letter to Michael Roberts of 22 April 1935, cited in Carpenter, *Auden,* 175.

37. Auden came back to teach at the Downs for a single term in the early summer of 1937. Wright (1907–1987) went to Cambridge as an undergraduate, but he met Auden at a lunch party in Cecil Day Lewis's rooms in Wadham in 1927, the year that Auden and Day Lewis were the editors of *Oxford Poetry.* (Day Lewis and Wright had been at Sherborne together.) Wright, who was queer, may have seen Auden occasionally in social circles in the first half of the 1930s, allowing Auden a pretext to be in touch in 1935 asking for a job. As Wright explained it, a bit leadenly, Auden had written that "he would like to get some experience of documentary film making." See Wright, "Britten and Documentary," *Musical Times,* 104.1449 (Nov. 1963), 779; see also Carpenter, *Auden,* 177. For a brief official biography of Wright, see Nicholas Pronay, "Wright, Basil Charles (1907–1987)," *Oxford Dictionary of National Biography* online (Oxford: Oxford UP, 2004).

38. ALS from W. H. Auden to Arnold Snodgrass [July 1935], cited in Carpenter, *Auden,* 178. "Pro tem" is a contraction of the Latin phrase *pro tempore,* meaning "for the time being."

39. "Here on the cropped grass of the narrow ridge I stand" (1933), *Poems1,* 202; see also Chapter 7.

40. "Madrigal" (1935), *Plays,* 421. Auden gave the piece the title "Madrigal" when he briefly submitted it along with some other verse written for film to *New Writing* in Jan. 1936 (see *Plays,* 665). He also used this title when

he collected the poem in *Another Time* (1940). A lurcher is a crossbred dog, typically mixing a greyhound with a herding dog such as a terrier. They have long associations with hunting and poaching activities.

41. *Plays*, 508. Mendelson gives the story of the production and prints the surviving texts of songs and skits in *Plays*, 503–509. Andrew Forge comments that Auden had a "very deep, beautifully flexible voice which could move into the falsetto at a moment's notice." Forge attended the 1934 Revue and recalled Auden's performance of "Rhondda Moon" in his interview with Cathy Courtney, available as a recording for the National Life Stories Collection posted at the British Library's "Sounds" webpage. The Rhondda Valley was one of the most important coal-mining areas in South Wales, and as the industry declined in the early decades of the twentieth century, the social damage there was enormous. In 1932, unemployment for men in the area stood at around 62 percent. The Rhondda Valley, just across the Welsh border from Herefordshire, is only about fifty miles southwest of Colwall. During Auden's time at the Downs School, he was involved with fund-raisers for Rhondda citizens in Dec. 1932, Dec. 1933, and probably also in Dec. 1934 (with the Revue). Auden used another version of "Rhondda Moon" in his and Isherwood's play *The Dog Beneath the Skin* (1935); see *Plays*, 261–262. Auden also mentions the "wreck of Rhondda" in "New Year Letter" (1940), *Poems2*, 34.

42. Hannah Arendt, "Remembering Wystan H. Auden . . . ," *New Yorker*, 50.48 (20 Jan. 1975), 39. See the Prologue.

43. Auden is cited in Elizabeth Sussex, *The Rise and Fall of British Documentary: The Story of the Film Movement Founded by John Grierson* (Berkeley: U of California P, 1975), 65 (from now on, cited as Sussex, *Rise*), saying the "'Coal Face' poem was the first thing I did" for the Unit.

44. See Mendelson's note in *Plays*, 666.

45. "Madrigal" (1935), *Plays*, 421 [also *Poems1*, 367]. I am citing here from the first printed version of the poem, published in the program released for a showing of the film at the Film Society in London on 27 Oct. 1935 (not from the slightly different one used in Auden's *Another Time* [1940] and printed in *Poems1*). Auden's poem is aware of the fact that the working week for miners lasted for six days in the 1930s, with only Sundays off.

46. Shakespeare, *Othello*, 1.1.

47. Auden met Cunard (1896–1965) in Paris in mid-April 1937, and she published a limited edition of his poem "Spain" in early June of that year. At around this time, Auden wrote to thank her for the copies of the edition that she had sent to him and in the same letter—evidently Cunard had also given him a copy of the pamphlet—he commented: "I did enjoy Black Man White Ladyship so much." Partially quoted in *Auden Bibliography*, 29.

48. *Plays*, 421. Auden's directive, organizing mode with lovers in poems had first emerged in the context of a dramatic marriage ceremony. In the "Epithalamion" (1930) for "The Fronny," a speaker sententiously instructs the groom

and bride: "But approach now, Alan" and "Receive him, Iris, now; obey, sur-render, | Admit the new life from the strange outsider" (*Plays*, 486). For more on the "Epithalamion," see also Chapter 7, note 100.

49. "Here on the cropped grass of the narrow ridge I stand" (1933), *Poems1*, 202–203.

50. Stephen Spender was an avid photographer too, and Spender's brothers, Humphrey and Michael, were even more deeply involved with cameras. Humphrey (see Chapter 5), the youngest Spender brother, originally trained as an architect but soon became a professional photographer. In Berlin, he used a Leica, recommended to him by Michael, who had also been in Berlin, working for the Leitz Company, which made Leicas. Optics, maps, and cameras fascinated Michael Spender (see Chapter 4), who had known Auden at Gresham's. For a brief, entertaining overview of cinema fashions in the 1930s in Britain, see Alan Jenkins, *The Thirties* (London: William Heinemann, 1976), 46–59. For a more extended treatment, see Jeffrey Richards, *The Age of the Dream Palace: Cinema and Society in Britain, 1930–1939* (London: Routledge and Kegan Paul, 1984).

51. "1929 Journal" (1929), fo. [5], NYPL. See also Norman Page, *Auden and Isherwood: The Berlin Years* (New York: St. Martin's P, 1998), 146. Page's chapter on Weimar cinema, from which I glean occasional details in what follows, offers a good conspectus of the kinds of films that Auden, Isherwood, and the Spender brothers saw in Berlin in the late 1920s and early 1930s. See Page, *Auden and Isherwood*, 146–172.

52. "1929 Journal" (1929), fo. [16], NYPL.

53. See Peter F. Alexander, *William Plomer: A Biography* (Oxford: Oxford UP, 1989), 165, 186.

54. Isherwood, *Lions*, 85–86; Parker, *Isherwood*, 89, 227n4.

55. Parker, *Isherwood*, 78.

56. *Ibid.*, 89.

57. Isherwood, *C&HK*, 5. See also *ibid.*, 34, where he recounts his thrill at seeing the film star Conrad Veidt (1893–1943), most famous for his performance as Cesare the somnambulist in *Das Kabinett des Doktor Caligari* (*The Cabinet of Dr. Caligari*, 1920, dir. Robert Wiene), at a Christmas ball in Berlin in 1929. Isherwood had seen at least one of Veidt's "homosexual" films, either *Anders als die Anderen* (*Different from the Others*, 1919, dir. Richard Oswald) or the film's remake, *Gesetze der Liebe* (*Laws of Love*, 1927, dir. by Magnus Hirschfeld and Richard Oswald), at Hirschfeld's Institut für Sexualwissenschaft in Berlin (see Chapter 5). Auden and Isherwood were also enthusiastic about Veidt's performance in *Der Student von Prag* (*The Student from Prague*, 1926, dir. Henrik Galeen). Page points out that Auden and Isherwood saw the film together and that a specter in their play "The Enemies of a Bishop" (1929) is based on a figure in the film (*Auden and Isherwood*, 148–149; see also Mendelson, introduction to *Plays*, xviii). Auden mentions *Der Student von Prag* in "In Search of Dracula" (1934), *Prose1*, 75. For more on Isherwood and Szczesny, see Chapter 5.

58. See Parker, *Isherwood*, 216. As Parker notes, all three of these films were first released while Isherwood was in Berlin.

59. Isherwood, *C&HK*, 2; Isherwood, *Lions*, 299.

60. Stephen Spender, "The Express" (first printed in *Poems*, 1933), in *New Collected Poems*, ed. Michael Brett (London: Faber and Faber, 2004), 19. See David Mellor, *Germany: The New Photography 1927–33* (London: Arts Council, 1978), 116.

61. Paul Swann, *The British Documentary Film Movement 1926–1946* (Cambridge: Cambridge UP, 1989), 90; Rachel Low, *The History of the British Film 1929–1939: Documentary and Educational Films of the 1930s* (London: George Allen and Unwin, 1979), 79.

62. Cited in Sussex, *Rise*, 65.

63. Slater (1902–1956) may have been chosen for this job since he was reporting during 1935 on the state of the Welsh coal industry. He wrote a play about a miners' strike, *Stay Down Miner*, which opened at the Westminster Theatre in May 1936. Following their collaboration on *Coal Face*, Britten wrote a chorus for Slater's play's final scene. Later, Slater was the librettist for Britten's opera *Peter Grimes* (1945).

64. J. B. Priestley, *English Journey: Being a Rambling but Truthful Account of What One Man Saw and Heard and Felt and Thought during a Journey through England during the Autumn of the Year 1933* (London: William Heinemann / Victor Gollancz, 1934).

65. Ian Aitken, *Film and Reform: John Grierson and the Documentary Film Movement* (London: Routledge, 1990), 99.

66. W. H. Auden, "Memoir of Benjamin Britten," unpublished MS (probably written in the 1960s), private collection.

67. Cited in Sussex, *Rise*, 76.

68. See Humphrey Carpenter, *Benjamin Britten: A Biography* (London: Faber and Faber, 1992), 66–67.

69. Basil Wright, "Britten and Documentary," *Musical Times*, 104.1449 (Nov. 1963), 779.

70. "It was from Britten, too, that I first heard the name of Alban Berg. We went together to a memorial concert just after his death—I had a tummy upset and threw up in the street" (Auden, "Memoir of Benjamin Britten"). Berg had died in Vienna on 24 Dec. 1935.

71. The three film projects they worked on in 1935 were *Coal Face*, *Night Mail*, and "Negroes" (the latter was never released in the form they intended—see later in this chapter), while in 1936 they worked on *The Way to the Sea* (*Plays*, 421, 422–423, 424–428, 430–432). "Our Hunting Fathers" was premiered at the Norfolk and Norwich Triennial Musical Festival in Sept. 1936 ("The Creatures" is in *Poems1*, 324). Auden later wrote of Britten (1913–1976): "What immediately struck me as someone whose medium was language, about Britten the composer, was his extraordinary musical sensitivity in relation to the English language" ("Memoir of Benjamin Britten"). Auden's collaboration with Britten stretches

beyond the chronological boundary of this book, but some of the main projects they worked on together in the next few years are as follows: Britten wrote the music for Auden and Isherwood's *The Ascent of F6,* which opened in Feb. 1937, and for their *On the Frontier,* which opened in Nov. 1938 (the published version of the play was dedicated to him); Britten also wrote incidental music for Auden's radio broadcast "Hadrian's Wall," performed in Nov. 1937 (*Plays,* 441–455); starting in 1937 and lasting into 1940, Auden and Britten created words and music for cabaret songs mainly performed by the singer Hedli Anderson (Auden wrote many more texts than Britten eventually used; see *AS2,* 67–101, for some examples); Britten set another five, previously written Auden poems to music in the "On This Island" song cycle he composed between 1937 and 1938; he also took inspiration from (and probably some instruction from Auden about) Arthur Rimbaud's poetry—a selection of which he set to music in his "Les Illuminations" cycle in 1939. After both Auden and Britten found themselves in the United States at the start of the Second World War, they collaborated on an operetta, *Paul Bunyan* (1939–1941; *Libretti,* 3–46), and in 1940, Britten set a version of Auden's "Song for St. Cecilia's Day" (1940; *Poems2,* 256–258) as "Hymn to St. Cecilia." The main phase of this important artistic partnership ended in a massive, slow-burning row that began just before Britten returned to the United Kingdom in April 1942 while Auden remained in the United States. In the aftermath of that row, Britten was the friend whom over the course of his lifetime Auden most regretted losing.

72. Cited in Richard R. Trail, "George Augustus Auden," in *Munk's Roll,* vol. 5: *1926–1965* (London: Royal College of Physicians, 1968), 16.

73. Christopher Isherwood, *Goodbye to Berlin* (London: Hogarth P, 1939), 13; Mendelson, *EALA,* 578–579 and 579n.

74. Auden called the play a "Masque" in letters to friends: ALS from W. H. Auden to Nevill Coghill, 24 April 1933, NYPL, cited in Mendelson, *Plays,* xx, 534. For more on Medley and Doone, see Chapter 3, note 87.

75. For "The Summer holds: upon its glittering lake | Lie Europe and the islands," see *Plays,* 191; and see also Chapter 7.

76. [Review of R. L. Mégroz, *English Poetry for Children*], (1934), *Prose1,* 71. Yates was born on 20 July 1919; the review was sent to T. S. Eliot on 1 May 1934: see *Prose1,* 755. Auden may have associated painting with a lack of sophistication; Fuller cites an inscription (in French for unexplained reasons) that Auden made for Feild in one of his books while he was teaching at the Downs, describing painting as "cet art plus primitif, auquel le corps sain est plus éxcitant que les malaises de l'ésprit" (this primitive art for which a healthy body is more exciting than the diseases of the spirit) (see Fuller, *Commentary,* 253). For more on the Feilds and on Michael Yates, see Chapter 7.

77. Mendelson, *EALA,* 578–579 and 579n.

78. Bruce Laughton, *The Euston Road School: A Study in Objective Painting* (Aldershot: Scolar P, 1986), 28.

79. William Coldstream, "A Portrait," *Tribute,* 58.

80. For Michael Davidson, see Chapter 2. Probably wrongly, Bruce Laughton dates the meeting between Auden and Coldstream to early in 1926 in *Euston Road School*, 28. In his biography of Coldstream, Laughton suggests that the pair was taken by Davidson and Browne to see the film version of *White Cargo*. See Laughton, *William Coldstream* (New Haven: Yale UP, 2004), 7. This cannot be the case since the film based on Gordon's play was not released until 1929. Coldstream himself noted that it was the "play" *White Cargo* in conversation with Stephen Spender in 1975: see Spender, *Journals 1939-1983*, ed. John Goldsmith (London: Faber and Faber, 1985), 295.

81. Coldstream is cited in Spender, *Journals 1939-1983*, 295. I cannot trace this line in Auden's surviving work, but see "Motherhood" (1925-1926), *J*, 123.

82. For the prospectus, see *Plays*, 491-492; for the "Prologue" (1933), see *Plays*, 493-495.

83. Sidnell, *Dances*, 55, 271. Nonetheless, the link cannot have been that close in the early 1930s. When Coldstream was asked, in April 1934, just after he joined the GPO Film Unit, to find samples of poets' work in "free verse" for possible use in a film about the GPO Savings Bank, he apparently wrote to a close friend, Dr. John Rake, for advice about the job instead of applying at once to Auden. See Laughton, *Euston Road School*, 111.

84. In conversation with Mark Glazebrook, Coldstream, whose later recollections about events from the 1930s were often vague, remembered meeting Auden again around 1935 or early 1936. See Glazebrook, "Talking to Coldstream," *London Magazine*, n.s., 16.1 (April-May 1976), 92.

85. Jenny Pery, *The Affectionate Eye: The Life of Claude Rogers* (Bristol: Sansom, 1995), 35, 66. Claude Rogers (1907-1979) and Elsie Few (1909-1980) were married in 1937. Margerie Few (1914-2003) was Elsie's younger sister. Coldstream has a slightly different version of the story in Glazebrook, "Talking to Coldstream," 92. Coldstream or Alberto Cavalcanti (1897-1982), the Brazilian-born director who had joined Grierson's organization in 1934, having been alerted to Britten's name, contacted the musicologist Edward Clark about Britten's whereabouts.

86. Ross McKibbin, *Classes and Cultures: England 1918-1951* (Oxford: Clarendon P, 1998), 425.

87. "What I Look For" (1932), repr. in John Grierson, *Grierson on the Movies*, ed. Forsyth Hardy (London: Faber and Faber, 1981), 39.

88. Cited in Ian Aitken, *Film and Reform: John Grierson and the Documentary Film Movement* (London: Routledge, 1990), 60.

89. *Ibid.*, 174-175.

90. Montagu Slater, "The Purpose of a Left Review," *Left Review*, 1.9 (June 1935), 365; cited (incorrectly dated "May 1935") in Aitken, *Film and Reform*, 175.

91. Carl Jung, "New Paths in Psychology" (orig. "Neue Bahnen der Psychologie," 1912), in Jung, *Two Essays on Analytical Psychology*, 2nd ed., trans. Gerhard Adler and R. F. C. Hull (Princeton: Princeton UP, 1966), 246-247.

92. Cited in Carpenter, *Auden,* 178. He revised the verse in the autumn of that year. See Harry Watt's and Basil Wright's accounts of the revision process. Watt and Wright are cited in Sussex, *Rise,* 71–72. Watt (1906–1987) was a documentary and feature film director who began work at the GPO Film Unit in 1936 and would make several well-known propaganda documentaries, such as *London Can Take It!* (1940), during the Second World War.

93. Mendelson notes that "the actual direction was mostly by Watt" (*Plays,* 666). It has also been suggested that a famous sequence in *Night Mail,* the moment when the mailbag is grabbed from the speeding train by an assemblage of gantry, net, and hook, may have been influenced, or even shot, by Humphrey Jennings (1907–1950), the experimental filmmaker who was also working at the Unit at this time. There is a similar scene in Jennings's *Locomotives* (1934 or 1935). See Anthony W. Hodgkinson and Rodney E. Sheratsky, *Humphrey Jennings: More than a Maker of Films* (Hanover: UP of New England, 1982), 16. Hodgkinson and Sheratsky also suggest that the opening and closing images of pitheads used in *Coal Face* may have been shot by Jennings (*ibid.,* 14).

94. See David Mellor, *Germany: The New Photography 1927–33* (London: Arts Council, 1978), 116.

95. John Grierson, "First Principles of Documentary" (1932), in *Grierson on Documentary,* ed. Forsyth Hardy, rev. ed. (Berkeley: U of California P, 1966), 149.

96. Cited in Sussex, *Rise,* 70.

97. "Night Mail" (1935), *Plays,* 422 [also *Poems1,* 175]. I quote here from the version representing the earliest published text. From now on, all references are to *Plays* only and are cited parenthetically in the text.

98. Arthur Elton, "Realist Film To-Day," *Left Review,* 2.9 (June 1936), 430. Auden mentions Elton briefly in *Letters from Iceland* (1937), comparing him to a "fine bull" he saw there (*Prose1,* 280).

99. Ode IV (1931), in *The Orators, Poems1,* 125.

100. Harry Watt, cited in Sussex, *Rise,* 71.

101. ALS from W. H. Auden to Stephen Spender, [late June–early July 1933?], NYPL; printed in "Eleven Letters from Auden to Stephen Spender," ed. Nicholas Jenkins, *AS1,* 62. See Chapter 7.

102. TLS from W. H. Auden to unidentified correspondent, 8 Nov. 1937, Harry Ransom Humanities Research Center, University of Texas at Austin (from now on, referred to as Texas).

103. Caroline Elkins, *Legacy of Violence: A History of the British Empire* (New York: Knopf, 2022), 126; Pugh, *Danced,* 395, 398.

104. "Out on the lawn I lie in bed" (1933), *Poems1,* 185; emphasis added. See Chapter 7.

105. "Hongkong" (1938), in "London to Hongkong," Auden and Isherwood, *Journey to a War* (1939), *Prose1,* 498 [also *Poems1,* 295].

106. "Travel-Diary" (1938), in Auden and Isherwood, *Journey to a War* (1939), *Prose1*, 629. HMS *Birmingham* was a light cruiser attached to the Royal Navy's China Station.

107. Elkins, *Legacy of Violence*, 356. Elkins gives, as examples of such films, *Clive of India* (1935), dir. Richard Boleslawski, and *Rhodes of Africa* (1936), dir. Berthold Viertel. Viertel (1885–1953), who was an Austrian exile, had given Isherwood his first job in London screenwriting in 1933: an assignment to rework the script for *Little Friend,* which Viertel directed in 1934.

108. See Britten, *LFL,* 1:376, 380.

109. A later project, released under a different title and made by different filmmakers, used some of the music and language created by Britten and Auden in 1935, but neither was involved in this revived version of the film. Very little evidence survives of Britten and Auden's original ideas and plans. Mendelson describes what is known about "Negroes" in *Plays,* 669–670. In addition to *Coal Face, Night Mail,* and "Negroes," Auden also worked in 1935 on "Air Mail to Australia" (an unmade film), *Beside the Seaside* (1935), and *Calendar of the Year* (1937). He also may have been involved in 1935 in planning for a "documentary" (again unmade) "about English Middle Class family life"; see *Plays,* 672.

110. Laughton, *William Coldstream,* 34; Britten, *LFL,* 1:380n3. Coldstream remembered that Auden or Britten chose lines from William Blake's poem "The Little Black Boy" in *Songs of Innocence* (1789) for inclusion. The lines appear in "Negroes," *Plays,* 426 (from now on, cited parenthetically in the text).

111. See earlier in this chapter.

112. Most of these rivers in Africa are easily identifiable with the name forms that Auden uses. However, the "Nune" is the Nun in southern Nigeria; the "Komoe" is now usually spelled Komoé and is in Burkina Faso and the Ivory Coast; the "Ogowe" is now usually spelled Ogooué and is in the Republic of Congo and Gabon.

113. Elkins, *Legacy of Violence,* 292.

114. After work on the film had stopped, Auden adapted the chorus for use in his and Isherwood's play *The Ascent of F6* (1936–1937), *Plays,* 622, 643, 648, 652.

115. *Plays,* 672.

116. Thomas Mann, *Tagebücher: 1935–1936,* ed. Peter De Mendelssohn (Frankfurt am Main: S. Fischer, 1978), 197. Auden was with the Manns for the weekend of 12–13 Oct. and returned to England on 14 Oct. 1935.

117. Britten, *LFL,* 1:376. One of the scenes that in 1940 Auden imagines no one who has lived through the 1930s could rid themselves of is "stumbling through his outraged mind | The Abyssinian, blistered, blind" ("New Year Letter," *Poems2,* 15). "Blistered" and "blind" here refer to the Italians' use of poison gas on the Ethiopians.

118. Cited in Sussex, *Rise,* 71–72. Some of Auden's most memorable lines did not make it into the version of the poem used for the film. In particular,

"Uplands heaped like slaughtered horses" and "this country, whose scribbled coastline traps the wild Atlantic in a maze of stone, | And faces Norway with its doubled notches" are only known because of a typescript titled "3 Fragments for Films" which, as Mendelson notes (*Plays,* 667; *Poems1,* 629), Auden submitted in 1936 to *New Writing* and then withdrew (*Plays,* 667–668 [also *Poems1,* 630–631]).

119. "Out on the lawn I lie in bed" (1933), *Poems1,* 184.

120. Cited in Sussex, *Rise,* 71.

121. See Wright's own account of how Auden wrote to him asking for a job: "Auden wrote to me. . . . Grierson said, 'Don't be a fool. Fetch him'" (cited in *ibid.,* 65). See also Carpenter, *Auden,* 177–178.

122. Basil Wright (1907–1987) was wealthy enough to subsidize to the tune of £3,000 Grierson's *World Film News* periodical, which was launched in March 1936. See Kevin Ingram, *Rebel: The Short Life of Esmond Romilly* (London: Weidenfeld and Nicolson, 1985), 115n.

123. Carpenter, *Auden,* 184. See also *Plays,* 672.

124. William Coldstream, "A Portrait," *Tribute,* 58.

125. W. H. Auden, "Memoir of Benjamin Britten."

126. "Letter to William Coldstream, Esq." (1936), *Prose1,* 345 [also *Poems1,* 267]. Coldstream later told Spender that he and Auden had been "very irreverent about the pieties of Grierson and used to leave their office and go to the pub saying how much they hated the British worker" (Spender, *Journals 1939–1983,* 295).

127. See *Prose1,* 762. The leave turned out to be something more since Auden resigned in mid- to late March 1936 in a letter sent from Portugal, where he was working with Isherwood on what became *The Ascent of F6* (1936–1937). See ALS from W. H. Auden to William Coldstream, 25 March 1936, Tate Archive, London, in which he mentions: "I've just sent in my notice."

128. [Review of Paul Rotha, *Documentary Film*] (1936), *Prose1,* 129.

129. *Ibid.,* 130. Edward Mendelson notes that a strainingly lighthearted rebuttal of Auden's review appeared in the April 1936 issue of Grierson's magazine *World Film News.* According to the column printed there, "film assistant" Auden was attacking his documentary "masters" when he made his criticisms. It claimed that "documentary forces its serfs to live and learn with workmen under working conditions, few operators in other arts come as close." And it concluded that as "Auden's own apprenticeship matures he may feel less despondent" about documentary's future. See *Prose1,* 761. Mendelson suggests that Grierson, "the Chief" himself, was the author of the article. This seems likely, and if not Grierson, then Auden's erstwhile friend, and Griersonian right-hand man, Basil Wright, is another strong possibility. Wright's *Oxford Dictionary of National Biography* entry describes him as "one of the most devoted, unquestioning, and faithful members of the British documentary movement and a follower of its mercurial and magnetic leader, John Grierson." See Nicholas Pronay, "Wright, Basil Charles (1907–1987)," *Oxford Dictionary of National Biography* online (Oxford: Oxford UP, 2004).

130. For example, emphasizing the camera's capacity to register detail, Auden said in his lecture (which exists only in a report of the talk and not in a text prepared by Auden himself): "If a peasant is photographed at work in a meadow the scene is definite because it is localised naturally by the visual detail present in the shots" ("Poetry and Film" [1936], *Plays*, 511; *Prose1*, 712), while in his review he wrote that "On the screen you never see *a* man digging in *a* field, but always Mr Macgregor digging in a ten acre meadow" ([Review of Paul Rotha, *Documentary Film*] [1936], *Prose1*, 129–130; emphasis in original).

131. "Poetry and Film" (1936), *Plays*, 511; *Prose1*, 713.

132. "Poetry and Film" (1936), *Plays*, 511–512; *Prose1*, 713.

133. "August for the people and their favourite islands" (1935), *Poems1*, 216. Note the cunning internal rhymes in Auden's stanza about Isherwood: "nature *clear*," "*near*er insight," "expanding *fear*."

134. "Poetry and Film" (1936), *Plays*, 512; *Prose1*, 713–714.

135. "Look, stranger, at this island now" (1935), first published as "Seaside," *Listener*, 14.362 (18 Dec. 1935), 1110; see *Poems1*, 187–188 (from now on, cited parenthetically in the text).

136. See *Plays*, 670: *Beside the Seaside* (1935), dir. Marion Grierson. Marion Grierson (1907–1998) was John Grierson's youngest sister. Auden was "on loan" for this film, which was produced by the Strand Film Company on commission from the Travel and Industrial Association of Great Britain. A year or so later, in Dec. 1936, he and Britten worked briefly on another "sea project": "The Way to the Sea," dir. J. B. Holmes. See *Plays*, 671. J. B. Holmes (1901–1968) also directed a film about coal mining called "The Mine" (1936) for Gaumont-British Instructional.

137. ALS from W. H. Auden to Stephen Spender, [late June–early July 1933?], NYPL; see "Eleven Letters from Auden to Stephen Spender," ed. Nicholas Jenkins, *AS1*, 62. See Chapter 7.

138. Anderson, *Imagined*, 7. My reading of Auden's poem and of the relation that it sets up between strangers derives from Freud's analysis in *Group Psychology and the Analysis of the Ego* (1921; Freud, *SE*, 18:69–143) of the libidinous ties originally uniting the "primal horde" and now binding people together in modern institutions like the church, the army, and the nation.

139. "A Happy New Year," part 2 (1932), *Poems1*, 146; emphasis added.

140. ALS from Auden to Spender, [late June–early July 1933?], NYPL; see "Eleven Letters from Auden to Stephen Spender," ed. Nicholas Jenkins, *AS1*, 63.

141. Fuller, *Commentary*, 152.

142. The "pluck | . . . of the tide" is from Auden's favorite, Anthony Collett: "cliffs fall, capes push seaward, or drift at the tide's pluck" (Collett, *Changing*, 9). For more on Collett, see Chapters 6 and 7.

143. Erwin Panofsky, "Style and Medium in the Moving Pictures," *Transition*, 26 (1937), 125.

144. "Memorial for the City" (1949), *Poems2*, 367.

145. Tallents, *The Projection of England* (London: Faber and Faber, 1932), 11–12. Tallents (1884–1958) was secretary of the Empire Marketing Board between 1926 and 1933. He was the public relations officer at the GPO from 1933 to 1935 (and thus ultimately one of the GPO Film Unit's overseers) before leaving to become controller of public relations at the BBC in 1935. Richard Falcon wrote: "The 1930s saw the development of questions of national image in the cinema in Britain and the increase in importance of the recognition of the ambassadorial aspects of a national film culture." See Falcon, "Images of Germany and the Germans in British Film and Television Fictions: A Brief Chronological Overview," in Cedric Cullingford and Harald Husemann, eds., *Anglo-German Attitudes* (Aldershot: Avebury, 1995), 70.

146. "Notes," Part II, in *The Double Man* (1941), in *Poems2*, 75.

147. Cited in Steve Ellis, *The English Eliot: Design, Language and Landscape in* Four Quartets (London: Routledge, 1991), 81.

148. A similar strategy is played out in other early poems, such as "Who stands, the crux left of the watershed" (1927), *Poems1*, 33–34: "Go home, now, stranger . . . | Stranger, turn back again."

149. Most of the other poems in the book are untitled too. A few lyrics are labeled with the vague "Song," one is called "Casino" (*Poems1*, 211–212; see the Epilogue), and the first and last poems are given the generic titles of "Prologue" and "Epilogue" (*Poems1*, 183–184, 216–217).

150. "A Happy New Year," part 2 (1932), *Poems1*, 144.

151. These lines contain another example of Auden's strategy of fusing inner and outer worlds. The "channels" suggest primarily the tubes in the interior of the ear, but they also, particularly when juxtaposed with "the chalk cliff," hint at the crucial stretch of water, the English Channel, that makes Britain a (kind of) island.

152. See *Poems1*, 14–17 (Auden calls the character "Father Xmas").

153. Barbara Evans, "Calendar of the Year," on p. 37 of the booklet accompanying the two-disk DVD set *We Live in Two Worlds*, vol. 2 of the GPO Film Unit Collection (BFIVD759) (London: British Film Institute, 2009).

154. "The Creatures" (1936), *Poems1*, 324. Mendelson gives the story of Britten's song cycle and Auden's participation in the project, along with the texts used, in *Poems1*, 440–443.

155. The six poems are "Let the florid music praise" (Feb. 1936), *Poems1*, 187; "Dear, though the night is gone" (Feb. or March 1936?), *Poems1*, 213; "Night covers up the rigid land" (March 1936?), *Poems1*, 209; "Fish in the unruffled lakes" (March 1936?), *Poems1*, 212–213; "Underneath the abject willow" (March 1936?), *Poems1*, 209–210; "Stop all the clocks, cut off the telephone" (April 1936?), from *The Ascent of F6* (1936–1937), in *Plays*, 350 [see also *Poems1*, 366, for a revised version, titled "Funeral Blues," printed as a freestanding poem].

156. For more on the "up-to-date" mode in Auden's poems, see Chapter 7.

157. "Let the florid music praise" (1936), *Poems1*, 187.

158. "Dear, though the night is gone" (1936), *Poems1*, 213.

159. "Prologue" ["O love, the interest itself in thoughtless Heaven"] (1932), *Poems1*, 184.

160. "The earth turns over, our side feels the cold" (1933), *Poems1*, 191.

161. "Hearing of harvests rotting in the valleys" (1933), *Poems1*, 190; "A Happy New Year," part 2 (1932), *Poems1*, 146; "Just as his dream foretold, he met them all" (1934), *Poems1*, 194.

162. Cited in Mendelson, *EALA*, 282.

163. "Dear, though the night is gone" (1936), *Poems1*, 213. The poem was called "The Dream" when it was printed in the April–May 1936 number of *New Verse* (see *Poems1*, 660). Auden removed the title when he collected the poem. (The poem is on just one page in *Poems1*, so any further page references here are superfluous.)

164. TS, undated, NYPL. "M" is Michael Yates; "bowes" is John Bowes, a pupil of Auden's at the Downs School (see *Plays*, 545 and Chapter 7, note 109). Bowes wrote about Auden in "Downs Days Remembered," *WHASN*, 13 (Oct. 1995), 19: "Each member of the class was set the task of writing a poem and then reading it aloud. When my turn came, it met with total scorn and adolescent ribaldry. Wystan would have none of it. I was told to recite it again. He then made some comments and ended by saying, 'I liked that very much indeed and I shall include it in my next book.'" Auden used a quatrain by Bowes as the epigraph to his unpublished play "The Chase" (1934); see *Plays*, 108. Mendelson gives more details in *Plays*, 545. The dream typescript, although unsigned, is almost certainly by Auden himself, but it (as opposed to the dream itself) is undated. It is part of the cache of papers that formerly belonged to Auden's New York friend and for a while his secretary Howard Griffin (1915–1975). In transcribing the typescript here, I have (very slightly) cleaned up the punctuation and have not reproduced deletions and insertions, all of which seem to have been made by Auden when he misspelled something that he immediately went on to type out correctly. It seems likely that the typescript dates from the period when the dream occurred.

165. "Out on the lawn I lie in bed" (1933), *Poems1*, 185; see Chapter 7.

166. See Chapter 7.

167. "Night covers up the rigid land" (1936), *Poems1*, 209.

168. "Poetry and Film" (1936), *Plays*, 511–512; *Prose1*, 713.

169. "Fish in the unruffled lakes" (1936), *Poems1*, 212–213.

170. *Ibid.*, 213.

171. "Remembering W. H. Auden . . . ," *New Yorker*, 50.48 (20 Jan. 1975), 39. See the Prologue.

172. The notebook, mainly used between 1942 and 1944, is now in Special Collections at the State University of New York at Buffalo. The lists are on fo. 2; Katherine Bucknell describes the notebook thoroughly in her introduction to *J*, xxxxvii.

173. David Impey (1917–2007) read mechanical sciences at Downing, Cambridge, between 1936 and 1939; sometime in the first half of the 1940s he married, and after the war he became a businessman. I am grateful to John Impey, David Impey's son, for discussing his father with me with great sensitivity.

174. *Poems1*, 660. During his relationship with Yates, Auden had earlier been simultaneously involved with Peter Roger (see Chapter 7), and in the autumn of 1934 he had a quick affair with a schoolmaster friend, John Garrett (1902–1966), whom he may have met through Auden's old Oxford tutor Nevill Coghill. Auden and Garrett compiled an anthology of poetry for schools together in late 1934 and gave it the camp title of *The Poet's Tongue*. The introduction to the book, probably written mainly by Auden, is [Introduction to *The Poet's Tongue*] (1935), *Prose1*, 105–109; see also Chapter 7.

175. "Dear, though the night is gone" (1936), *Poems1*, 213.

176. Mendelson gives details of the textual history of *The Ascent of F6* (1936–1937) in *Plays*, 598–602.

177. W. B. Yeats to Rupert Doone, 13 and 18 April 1937, NYPL; cited in Carpenter, *Auden*, 216; and Sidnell, *Dances*, 198.

178. *The Ascent of F6* (1936–1937), *Plays*, 624–625.

179. Cited in T. G. Foote, "W. H. Auden—Interview II" (1963), unpublished typescript.

180. Grautoff (1917–1974) was a sixteen-year-old star of Weimar theater and film when she went into exile with Toller (1893–1939) in 1933.

181. "W. H. Auden sah jung und nett aus. Ein besonderes Gesicht, lächelnd-lachend": *Die Göttin und ihr Sozialist: Christiane Grautoffs Autobiographie—ihr Leben mit Ernest Toller; Mit Dokumenten zur Lebensgeschichte*, ed. Werner Fuld and Albert Ostermaier (Bonn: Weidle, 1996), 89.

182. Isherwood, *C&HK*, 240. Isherwood also wrote about Toller in "The Head of a Leader" (1953), collected in Isherwood, *Exhumations: Stories, Articles, Verses* (New York: Simon and Schuster, 1966), 125–132.

183. Mendelson: "Auden had collaborated with Toller in the 1930s, providing freely adapted versions of some of Toller's lyrics for use in the English translations of his plays *No More Peace!* (1937) and *Pastor Hall* (1939)": see *Poems1*, 776. Herbert Murrill (1909–1952), who had worked on the music for *The Dance of Death* and *The Dog Beneath the Skin*, provided the music for *No More Peace!*

184. See *Auden Bibliography*, 128. The monologue, called "The Demagogue," was a version of "The Dictator's Song" from the translation of *Nie wieder Friede!*

185. In Paris, the exiled novelist and journalist Joseph Roth (1894–1939), whom years of alcohol and anxiety had left "with hardly any teeth, a liver like a sponge and a face the colour of ashes," heard the news of Toller's suicide and collapsed, dying two days later. See Florian Illies, *Love in a Time of Hate: Art*

and Passion in the Shadow of War, 1929–39, trans. Simon Pare (London: Profile, 2023), 289.

    186. "In Memory of Ernst Toller" (1939), *Poems1,* 375.

EPILOGUE

Epigraph: William Blake, *Jerusalem: The Emanation of the Giant Albion* (1804–1820), ed. Morton D. Paley (Princeton: William Blake Trust / Princeton UP, 1991), 170.

    1. Isherwood, *C&HK,* 239. I have corrected Isherwood's capitalization. For Neddermeyer, see also the Prologue and Chapter 8.

    2. Yeats wrote the poem in 1927 and collected it in *The Winding Stair and Other Poems* (London: Macmillan, 1933). For an assertion that Auden connected Yates with Yeats's poetry, see Mendelson, *EALA,* 215n.

    3. "In Memory of Eva Gore-Booth and Con Markievicz," Yeats, *Poems,* 233. Eva and Con had died, but Yeats speaks of them in the present tense.

    4. These Sintra poems are "Underneath the abject willow" (1936), *Poems1,* 209–210; "Epilogue" (1936), *Poems1,* 216–217; "As it is, plenty" (1936), *Poems1,* 195; "Casino" (1936), *Poems1,* 211–212; and perhaps (but not likely) "Since the external disorder, and extravagant lies" (1936), *Poems1,* 179.

    5. Isherwood, *C&HK,* 239.

    6. "Casino" (1936), *Poems1,* 211–212 (from now on, cited parenthetically in the main text). The Estoril casino was reportedly later the inspiration for the first James Bond novel, *Casino Royale* (1953).

    7. Auden, "Journal August 193[9]," [entry for 30 Aug. 1939], BL.

    8. See Chapter 8.

    9. The long-lines-short-lines quatrain pattern in these poems makes them look a bit like what critics have identified as Auden's first attempts at writing syllabics in later poems such as "Where do They come from? Those whom we so much dread" (1939), *Poems1,* 340–341; and "In Memory of Sigmund Freud" (1939), *Poems1,* 378–380. In the Freud elegy, for example, the syllabic pattern is (mostly) 11-11-9-10. Faber published Marianne Moore's *Selected Poems* in 1935, and Auden seems to have begun reading her in that year. When he did, her work seemed to him "so strange" (ALS from W. H. Auden to Marianne Moore, 14 Nov. 1939, Philip H. and A. S. W. Rosenbach Foundation, Philadelphia; see also Mendelson, *EALA,* 415–416). It is possible that the poems Auden wrote in Sintra—"weakened," unassertive, meandering, slightly ragged—in some fashion reflect an early, very partial understanding of Moore's metrics But, although these Sintra poems look similar to Auden's 1939 syllabic poems, the lines have a highly variable number of syllables and a recurring number of stresses (or, in Auden's preferred term, "beats"). In the case of "Casino," the first two lines in the quatrain have five stresses, and the second two

lines have four. In the case of "Epilogue" (see later in this chapter), the quatrain's first two lines have five stresses, and the second two have (mostly) three. In other words, both pieces are essentially camouflaged accentual poems. But the lines' highly variable numbers of syllables mean there are no truly recurring patterns of stressed and unstressed syllables because the placing of stresses within the line varies dramatically. In this sense, these 1936 Sintra poems are best described as halfway to being written in syllabics, borrowing a "look" from an American female poet to help break Auden away from the patriarchal, stressed assertiveness of the later Yeats and the Elizabethan English poets who stand behind Yeats's late manner.

10. Isherwood, C&HK, 239.

11. ALS from W. H. Auden to George A. Auden, [late Feb.–early March 1939?], Bodleian. There is another citation from the same letter in Chapter 6.

12. "As it is, plenty" (1936), Poems1, 195.

13. Ibid.

14. Another example of Auden ironically portraying himself as a family man and a person in business would come in "A Household" (1948), Poems2, 380–381. Auden annotated "As it is, plenty" as being based on the Somerset Maugham story "His Excellency" from Maugham's Ashenden: Or the British Agent (London: William Heinemann, 1927). See Poems1, 644. Auden gave "As it is, plenty" the title "His Excellency" when he collected it in The Collected Poetry of W. H. Auden (1945). Fuller (Commentary, 162), one of the few to have written about the poem, points out that in the summer of 1936, during a trip that MacNeice, Yates, and Auden made to Iceland, Auden reported they read out Somerset Maugham stories to each other and "the best one was called His Excellency" ("Letter to William Coldstream, Esq." [1936], Prose1, 349 [also Poems1, 269]).

15. "As it is, plenty" (1936), Poems1, 195.

16. See Fuller, Commentary, 162.

17. "From scars where kestrels hover" (1929), Poems1, 47; "Before this loved one" (1929), Poems1, 41–42.

18. "Underneath the abject willow" (1936), Poems1, 209–210; "I chose this lean country" (1927), Poems1, 391–393; "Night covers up the rigid land" (1936), Poems1, 209. "Lacrimae Rerum" is printed with a translation by David Constantine in "The German Auden: Six Early Poems," AS1, 4–5. See Fuller, Commentary, 170, where he is thinking of poems such as "Song" ["The crocus stars the border"] (1926), J, 126.

19. The Ascent of F6 (1936–1937), Plays, 350.

20. Britten set the poem to music for the play, and after Auden rewrote the poem, Britten, probably in the summer of 1937, revised his setting to fit this new text. Titled "Funeral Blues," they envisaged it as a cabaret song to be performed by Hedli Anderson (1907–1990), a member of the Group Theatre company. Anderson recorded "Funeral Blues" in 1938 and included it in her cabaret performances, and Auden collected the freestanding version of the

poem in *Another Time* (1940). But the poem remained relatively obscure and was hardly discussed by critics until John Hannah (as Matthew) recited the poem over his lover's coffin in *Four Weddings and a Funeral* (1994), dir. Mike Newell. Prompted by Hannah's moving performance and by the success of the film, the extraordinary second life of this poem began, in part as a vehicle for mourning at the time of the Princess of Wales's funeral in 1997 and in part through the poem's very widespread grassroots adoption at contemporary funerals. That story lies outside the scope of this book. But it is important to register with respect the significance of Auden's poem for many people who are not habitual poetry readers but who have been reached and moved by Auden's words in the context of their own lives. Respect to Auden too, who was able to write words that moved these people.

21. "Funeral Blues" [1937 version], *Poems1*, 366 (from now on, cited parenthetically in the main text). Mendelson gives the poem's history in *Poems1*, 762–763.

22. "Out on the lawn I lie in bed" (1933), *Poems1*, 184–185.

23. "Sentries against inner and outer" (1929), *Poems1*, 35–36.

24. "Archaic Statue of Apollo" (1908), in Rainer Maria Rilke, *Ahead of All Parting: The Selected Poetry and Prose of Rainer Maria Rilke*, trans. Stephen Mitchell (New York: Modern Library, 1995), 67. In the German: "Du mußt dein Leben ändern."

25. Cited in *Poems1*, 632. Mendelson's account of the history of the book, including its title, can be supplemented with Nicholas Jenkins, "Vin Audenaire," *WHASN*, 25 (Jan. 2005), 18–23. The title of the play that Auden and Isherwood were writing in Portugal changed from *The Summit* to *The Ascent* to *The Ascent of F6* during their work together. By the time Auden left Sintra on 17 April 1936, they had settled on the latter, the title that the first edition of the play was published under in Sept. 1936. See *Plays*, 598. In Sintra, Auden and Isherwood also seem to have discussed a (moneymaking) plan to write a composition book for schools. It never came to anything.

26. Two exceptions to this rule are *The Collected Poetry of W. H. Auden* (1945) and *Collected Shorter Poems: 1930-1944* (1950) where, in a jarring and ultimately short-lived gesture, Auden organized the books by alphabetical order of the poems' first lines.

27. See Chapter 7.

28. "Prologue" ["O love, the interest itself in thoughtless heaven"] (1932), *Poems1*, 183; "Casino" (1936), *Poems1*, 211.

29. "Out on the lawn I lie in bed" (1933), *Poems1*, 184; "Casino" (1936), *Poems1*, 211; and "Epilogue" ["Certainly our city—with the byres of poverty down to"] (1936), *Poems1*, 217.

30. "Prologue" ["O love, the interest itself in thoughtless heaven"] (1932), *Poems1*, 184.

31. "Epilogue" ["Certainly our city—with the byres of poverty down to"] (1936), *Poems1*, 216-217 (from now on, referred to as "Epilogue" and cited

parenthetically in the text). Another example of Auden's poems in 1936 reaching back to an earlier stage in his career is that the lines here about the "sinister tall-hatted botanist" infecting the drinking water with the "plague" were drafted first for a never-published but intensively quarried poem written in Helensburgh in 1932 beginning, "To lie this hour in any position" (*Poems1*, 463). The poem here also borrows heavily from another poem that Auden drafted but never managed to get published: "Poem" ["'Sweet is it,' say the doomed, 'to be alive through wretched'"] (1934), *Poems1*, 162–165. Auden borrowed lines and images from this unwanted poem and inserted them in several other places in his work, including *The Ascent of F6* (1936–1937) and here (see *Poems1*, 621).

32. For Eliot's ideas about "The Hollow Men," see the Prologue.

33. Cited in *Poems1*, 663. Auden's remark about the borrowing from Hölderlin is inscribed in Kallman's copy of *On This Island*, now in Texas. (For Kallman, see also the Prologue and Chapter 6.) The first time that Auden mentions Hölderlin is in his account of the trip that he, Michael Yates, and Peter Roger made to the Carpathians in the summer of 1934 (see Chapter 7). On their way, they stopped at Schloß Eisenberg (Schloss Jezeří to Czech-speakers) in the Erzgebirge, in what is now the Czech Republic, to meet Prince Maximilian von Lobkowicz (1888–1967), a lawyer, diplomat, and enemy of the Nazis, and his British-born wife, Gillian Hope, Princess Lobkowicz (1890–1982). Auden wrote: "Talked about Hölderlin and the Prince gave a marvellous imitation of Hitler" ("In Search of Dracula" [1934], *Prose1*, 74). It does not sound as though in 1934 Auden had yet become very interested in the German poet.

34. Stephen Spender, "The Short Ones," *New Writing*, 1 (Spring 1936), 116. See Fuller, *Commentary*, 177.

35. Aside from the visit from Ernst Toller and Christiane Grautoff described in Chapter 8, Auden and Isherwood had, in the often-overlooked Neddermeyer, a native German speaker with them the whole time they were in Sintra.

36. Auden makes no attempt to use the meter of the asclepiadian line and the associated stanza form that Hölderlin himself deploys. (For the technically inclined, an asclepiadian line is an Aeolic line constructed of a glyconic extended by one or two choriambs.) Auden did make an attempt to write asclepiadians in a late poem, "In Due Season" (1968), *Poems2*, 609–610.

37. Auden explained his generation's interest in German culture in 1941: "In Spender's case, of course, it was strengthened by the fact that he was partly German himself. It so happened that he went to Bonn and met there Professor Curtius who had been responsible for introducing writers like Joyce and Proust to Germany, and now introduced Spender to Rilke and Holderlin." Letter from W. H. Auden to Margaret Church, 12 Nov. 1941, cited in Margaret Church, "For This Is Orpheus: or, Rilke, Auden and Spender" (MA diss., Columbia U, 1942), iii. Auden refers here to the months at the end of 1930 when

Spender studied in Bonn with the German philologist and literary historian (and gravely wounded war veteran) E. R. Curtius (1886–1956).

38. "Psychology and Criticism" (1936), *Prose1*, 130–133. The review was published in *New Verse* in April–May 1936.

39. ALS from W. H. Auden to Norman Holmes Pearson, [Feb.–May 1943?], Beinecke Rare Book and Manuscript Library, Yale University.

40. Louis MacNeice, "The Tower That Once" (1941), in *Selected Literary Criticism of Louis MacNeice,* ed. Alan Heuser (Oxford: Clarendon P, 1987), 122. Heuser points out that the "dictum" is taken (slightly misquoted) from Thomas Mann's essay "Goethe und Tolstoi" (1921, revised in 1924–1925). The later version was printed in translation in Mann's *Three Essays,* trans. H. T. Lowe-Porter (London: Martin Secker, 1932), 136, which Auden read. In "Goethe and Tolstoy," Mann declares that "our socialism, which has all too long allowed its spiritual life to languish in the shallows of a crude economic materialism, has no greater need than to find access to that loftier Germany which has always sought with its spirit the land of the Greeks . . . it will not truly rise to the height of its national task until—if I may be allowed the extravagance—Karl Marx has read Friedrich Hölderlin: a consummation which, by the way, seems in a fair way to be achieved." And in the "Culture and Socialism" essay from his *Past Masters,* also known to Auden, Mann wrote, "What would be needed . . . would be an alliance, a compact between the conservative culture-idea and revolutionary social thought: to put it pointedly, as I have elsewhere done once before, an understanding between Greece and Moscow. It would be well with Germany, I repeat, she would have found herself, as soon as Karl Marx shall have read Friedrich Hölderlin. Such a contact, moreover, is about to be established." Thomas Mann, *Past Masters and Other Papers,* trans. H. T. Lowe-Porter (London: Martin Secker, 1933), 214.

41. Christopher Isherwood, "German Literature in England," *New Republic,* 98.1270 (5 April 1939), 254.

42. "Prologue" ["O love, the interest itself in thoughtless Heaven"] (1932), *Poems1,* 183.

43. "A Happy New Year," part 2 (1932), *Poems1,* 146.

44. It shows how much Auden was preoccupied with the phrase about the "really better | World" that he also used it in a prose piece he probably wrote in Sintra, [Review of *Questions of Our Day,* by Havelock Ellis] (1936), *Prose1,* 134: "He is, in our time, one of the greatest of those—there are never, perhaps, very many, but always more than we think—who towards the really better world have turned their faces."

45. The original: "Absolute Abstraktion—Annihilation des Jetzigen—Apotheose der Zukunft, dieser eigentlichen bessern Welt, dies ist der Kern der Geheiße des Xstenthums" (Absolute abstraction—annihilation of the present—apotheosis of the future, of this really better world, this is the core of Christianity's behests). See Novalis, *Das Allgemeine Brouillon* [*The General Rough*

Draft] (1798–1799), in *Werke, Tagebücher und Briefe Friedrich von Harden-bergs*, vol. 2: *Das philosophisch-theoretische Werk*, ed. Hans-Joachim Mähl (Munich: C. Hanser Verlag, 1978), 711.

46. Thomas Mann, "Freud's Position in the History of Modern Thought," *Criterion*, 12.49 (July 1933), 549–570. In the same issue, Auden had two poems—"To ask the hard question is simple" (1930), *Poems1*, 50–51; and "Hearing of harvests rotting in the valleys" (1933), *Poems1*, 189–190—as well as a review of William Dunbar's poems, *Prose1*, 39–40. This Mann essay (which repeats some material in the "Culture and Socialism" essay cited earlier) was collected in his *Past Masters and Other Papers*, published in English by Secker in Oct. 1933. Auden mentions Mann in print for the first time in "The Group Movement and the Middle Classes," probably written late in 1933, *Prose1*, 51. Thereafter, Auden regularly cites from *Past Masters*, as I will do here.

47. Mann, *Past Masters* 178. Mann also cites the phrase again on p. 180 of the same collection.

48. See *J*, 223; and the Prologue. Fuller notes that Charles Miller, Auden's roommate when he lived in Michigan in the early 1940s, said that the phrase "Hermetically sealed" in Auden's 1929 poem "Will you turn a deaf ear" (*Poems1*, 26) was borrowed from Mann's *Der Zauberberg* (*The Magic Moun-tain*) (1924); see *Commentary*, 53. Fuller also suggests that Auden's line about "The bugger magician with his Polish lad" in Ode IV (1931) of *The Orators* (*Poems1*, 125) is a compound reference to Mann's long stories *Death in Venice* and *Mario and the Magician* (1929) (*Commentary*, 118).

49. "'Sweet is it,' say the doomed, 'to be alive though wretched'" (1934), *Poems1*, 163.

50. "Are the English Europeans?: The Island and the Continent" (1962), *Prose4*, 431. See the Prologue and Chapters 1, 3, and 5.

51. Ronald Hayman, *Thomas Mann: A Biography* (New York: Scribner, 1995), 422–424.

52. Donald Prater, *Thomas Mann: A Life* (Oxford: Oxford UP, 1995), 249.

53. Edouard Korrodi's article was "Deutsche Literatur im Emigranten-spiegel" (German literature as reflected by émigrés), *Die Neue Zürcher Zei-tung*, 26 Jan. 1936. Mann's reply, "Ein Brief von Thomas Mann" (A letter by Thomas Mann), appeared there on 3 Feb. 1936. Mann's open letter was quite widely disseminated both in the original and in translation, as, for example, in "Thomas Mann's View of Emigre Writers," *New York Times*, 8 March 1936, pp. 8, 20–21. For convenience, I cite from this American translation in my discussion here.

54. "Thomas Mann's View of Emigre Writers," 8.

55. *Ibid.*, 20.

56. *Ibid.*, 20–21.

57. Thomas Mann, *Tagebücher 1935–1936*, ed. Peter De Mendelssohn (Frankfurtam Main: S. Fischer, 1978), 250: "Ich habe nach 3 Jahren des Zögerns

mein Gewissen and meine feste Überzeugung sprechen lassen. Mein Wort wird nicht ohne Eindruck bleiben."

58. Donald Prater, *Thomas Mann: A Life* (Oxford: Oxford UP, 1995), 249. The German government announced on 3 Dec. 1936 that Mann and his wife, Katia Mann, along with their four youngest children (Golo, Monika, Elisabeth, and Michael), had forfeited their citizenships. Erika and Klaus, the two older children, had already been denationalized, as had Heinrich, Thomas's brother. (Eighty-seven other Germans were denationalized in Dec. 1936 at the same time as the Manns.) After the German government's announcement, Mann received so many telegrams, letters, and phone calls of congratulation that he was moved to comment, "It is almost as it was after the Nobel Prize" (cited in *ibid.*, 429). The Nazi decree, a result of "injuring the German reputation by a lack of loyalty to the German Reich and people," was widely reported abroad. See, for instance, "93 Germans Deprived of Nationality: Thomas Mann and His Family Penalized," *Times*, 4 Dec. 1936, p. 15. The Manns' home in Germany was confiscated in the following year.

59. "Nobel Prize and Expatriation," in Ernst Bloch, *Literary Essays*, trans. Andrew Joron et al. (Stanford: Stanford UP, 1998), 44.

60. *Ibid.*, 46.

61. "Journal August 193[9]," [entry for 30 Aug. 1939], BL.

62. "August for the people and their favourite islands" (1935), *Poems1*, 216.

63. "Journey to Iceland" (1936), *Prose1*, 186 [also *Poems1*, 262].

64. Auden picked up this list of healers' names in "Certainly our city" from the March 1934 poem in triplets, "'Sweet is it,' say the doomed, 'to be alive though wretched'" (*Poems1*, 162–165). Auden took the 1934 list and very carefully pruned it for his new poem, dropping not only Marx but also English-speaking figures such as the physicists J. J. Thompson and Ernest Rutherford.

65. Simpson is the subject of a good, brief life by Andy Croft, "Simpson, John Frederick Norman Hampson [known as John Hampson] (1901–1955)," *Oxford Dictionary of National Biography* online (Oxford: Oxford UP, 2004).

66. Erika Mann, *Briefe und Antworten*, vol. 1: *1922–1950*, ed. Anna Zanco Prestel (Munich: Edition Spangenberg, 1984), 92–94. The German original is "Mein Mann is ein Tyrann. . . . Er bestellt mich bald hier, bald dorthin. . . . Mein Mann ist ja äußerst eigensinnig und hartköpfig und es macht ihm große Freude, to introduce his wife,—Ehe ist Ehe, was kann man da machen, obwohl ich ja bekanntlich keine Kinder will. . . . Morgen muß ich wieder nach Birmingham (häßlichste Stadt!), meine Schwiegereltern erwarten mich" (My husband is a tyrant. . . . He orders me here, then there. . . . My husband is extremely stubborn and implacable and it gives him great pleasure to introduce his wife—marriage is marriage, what can you do about it, although as you know I do not want any children. . . . Tomorrow I have to go back to Birmingham (ugliest city!), my parents-in-law are expecting me).

67. Klaus Mann, *Tagebücher 1936 bis 1937,* ed. Joachim Heimannsberg, Peter Laemmle, and Wilfried F. Schoeller (Munich: Edition Spangenberg, 1990), 75.

68. Golo Mann to Humphrey Carpenter, 10 May 1979, cited in Carpenter, *Auden,* 296.

69. Details of the marriage and subsequent celebrations come primarily from a superb account by the novelist and critic Walter Allen (1911–1995), who attended the ceremony. His description is in Allen, *As I Walked Down New Grub Street: Memories of a Writing Life* (London: Heinemann, 1981), 55–58.

70. *Ibid.,* 57.

71. *Ibid.,* 58; P. N. Furbank, *E. M. Forster: A Life,* vol. 2 (London: Secker and Warburg, 1978), 213. Probably in July 1936, Auden completed "Alfred: A Cabaret Sketch" (*Plays,* 437–439) for Giehse (1898–1975)—Mendelson suggests it may have been a wedding present (*Plays,* 674). Giehse was to give the inaugural performance of the role of Mother Courage in the first production of Brecht's *Mutter Courage und ihre Kinder* (*Mother Courage and Her Children,* 1939), staged in Zurich in 1941. Simpson and Giehse apparently kept up with each other for a while (Giehse visited Simpson at his employers' house in 1939, for example), though they were not as close as Mann and Auden in the years after their marriage.

72. Allen, *As I Walked Down New Grub Street,* 58.

73. "Since the external disorder, and extravagant lies" (1936), *Poems1,* 179.

74. "Coming out of me living is always thinking" (1929), *Poems1,* 38; "August for the people and their favourite islands" (1935), *Poems1,* 216.

75. Yates's copy of *Look, Stranger!* (London: Faber and Faber, 1936) is in a private collection. See Friedrich Hölderlin, "Sokrates und Alcibiades," in *Selected Poems and Fragments,* trans. Michael Hamburger, ed. Jeremy Adler (London: Penguin, 1998), 19. Auden quotes the phrase about the wise bowing to the beautiful in "Letter to Lord Byron (1936), *Prose1,* 356 [also *Poems1,* 260], and the whole of Hölderlin's second stanza in a 1938 review of *A.E.H.,* a memoir by A. E. Housman's brother, Lawrence ("Jehovah Housman and Satan Housman," *Prose1,* 439), among other places.

76. Mendelson explains the book's production history in *Poems1,* 632–633; see also Nicholas Jenkins, "Vin Audenaire," *WHASN,* 25 (Jan. 2005), 18–23.

77. Cited in *Poems1,* 632. The sales manager at Faber in 1936 was W. J. Crawley (1886?–1965), who later became a director of the firm.

78. Cited in *Poems1,* 632–633. Eliot's suggestions were *Certainly Our City: Poems 1936, Some Possible Dream, Into the Undared Ocean,* or *Look! Stranger.*

79. "Look, stranger, at this island now" (1935), *Poems1,* 187.

80. "The Composer" (1938), *Poems1,* 339. See the Prologue.

81. For "indifferent redeemer," see "One absence closes other lives to him" (1934), *Poems1,* 508; for "National Socialism" and "national emblems," see ALS from W. H. Auden to Stephen Spender, [late June–early July 1933?], NYPL; "Eleven Letters from Auden to Stephen Spender," ed. Nicholas Jenkins, printed in

AS1, 62, and see Chapter 7; for "mouthpiece of an epoch," see ALS from W. H. Auden to George Auden, [Feb.–March 1939], Bodleian, and see Chapter 6.

82. R. W. Seton-Watson, *Britain in Europe, 1789-1914: A Survey of Foreign Policy* (Cambridge: Cambridge UP, 1937), 37.

83. Masefield is cited in Carpenter, *Auden,* 223; Muir refers to Auden as one of the "poets of genius" in "Sixteen Comments on Auden," *New Verse,* 26–27 (Nov. 1937), 23; Keynes's remark is reported by Woolf in *The Letters of Virginia Woolf,* vol. 6: *Leave the Letters till We're Dead,* ed. Nigel Nicolson and Joanne Trautmann (London: Hogarth P, 1980), 197. The following year, 1938, Cyril Connolly too referred to Auden as a "poet of genius," in *Enemies of Promise* (1938; Boston: Little, Brown, 1939), 173.

84. Wyndham Lewis, *Blasting and Bombardiering* (London: Eyre and Spottiswoode, 1937), 4–5.

85. "A Commentary" (1937), Eliot, *Prose,* vol. 5, 563.

86. John Masefield, *The Old Front Line: or, The Beginning of the Battle of the Somme* (London: William Heinemann, 1917), 11. Masefield's "paths to glory" is a slight misquotation of Thomas Gray's "paths of glory" in "Elegy Written in a Country Churchyard" (1750): "The paths of glory lead but to the grave."

87. *News Chronicle,* early ed., 24 Nov. 1937, p. 1. After Masefield (1878–1967) died, civil servants advising the prime minister, Harold Wilson, considered Auden for the now-vacant role of Poet Laureate, a crown appointment. The idea was rejected on the grounds that Auden could no longer write with national representativeness because he had renounced his British citizenship.

88. "Remarks," *New Verse,* 28 (Jan. 1938), 14. It was never exhibited. It is possible that the *objet* was made by the poet David Gascoyne (1916–2001). Gascoyne recorded in his journal entry for 8 April 1937 hearing a rumor that Auden had been awarded the King's Gold Medal: "I can't believe this," he wrote with shock, also noting that he was told that "when [Auden] heard the news he waved his arms in the air with pleasure." See Gascoyne, *Collected Journals 1936–42* (London: Skoob, 1991), 75. Gascoyne contributed three prose poems (later retitled "Three Verbal Objects") to *Surrealist Objects and Poems* (1937), the catalogue for the exhibition of the same name that opened at the London Gallery in Nov. 1937. However, Gascoyne's involvement is uncertain: the pig's trotter was a favorite Dalí motif, and other surrealists in their art made use of, or reference to, dead animals.

89. Shakespeare, *The Tempest,* 2.2.

90. The next Christmas that Auden spent in the country was in 1972, and that was to be his last Christmas of all—he died in Sept. 1973.

91. Medley, "Gresham's School, Holt," *Tribute,* 41. See also the Prologue.

92. *The Tempest,* epilogue.

93. "August for the people and their favourite islands" (1935), *Poems1,* 216.

94. "To The Memory of My Beloved, the Author Mr William Shakespeare: And What He Hath Left Us" (1623), in Ben Jonson, *The Complete Poems,* ed. George Parfitt (New Haven: Yale UP, 1982), 265.

EXPLANATION OF AUDEN'S TEXTS AND EDITIONS

    1. See *Poems2,* 731–736, 751–752.

    2. *Ibid.,* 734.

    3. Edward Mendelson, "Editor's Preface," in W. H. Auden, *Collected Poems,* ed. Edward Mendelson, 3rd ed. (New York: Modern Library, 2007), xxi.

    4. For Auden's comment (in a letter written in Nov. 1963), see *Poems1,* 575.

    5. *Poems1,* 413. "Portrait" had appeared in the Oxford student magazine *Cherwell* in May 1926. L. A. G. Strong (1896–1958), who was a friend of W. B. Yeats and who happened to be teaching at a school in Oxford at the time, edited the anthology that "Portrait" appeared in; the book was published in New York by Dodd and Mead.

    6. "Night Mail" (1935–1936), *Plays,* 423 [also *Poems1,* 176].

    7. Mendelson, preface to *Poems1* [vii].

CREDITS AND PERMISSIONS

Every effort has been made to identify copyright holders and obtain their permission for the use of copyrighted material. Notification of any additions or corrections that should be incorporated in future reprints or editions of this book would be greatly appreciated.

IMAGE CREDITS

Fig. 1   Photographer: Harry Hodges Tansley; image now in the care of Gresham's School Archives and used by courtesy of Gresham's School, Holt.

Fig. 2   Smith Archive / Alamy Stock Photo.

Fig. 3   Private collection, © Estate of Stanley Spencer. All rights reserved. 2023 / Bridgeman Images.

Fig. 4   © Estate of John Bicknell Auden, National Portrait Gallery, London.

Fig. 5   W. H. Auden, Correspondence with Anne Bristow, Frederick R. Koch Collection, Beinecke Rare Book and Manuscript Library, Yale University.

Fig. 6   Reproduced from Humphrey Carpenter, *W. H. Auden: A Biography* (Boston: Houghton Mifflin, 1981), fig. 10 in photo insert after p. 176.

Fig. 7   Box 91, CI 3109, Christopher Isherwood Papers, Huntington Library, San Marino, California.

Fig. 8   © National Portrait Gallery, London.

Fig. 9   *Calendar of the Year,* General Post Office / Empire Marketing Board Film Unit, 1937.

Fig. 10   Box 91, CI 3109, Christopher Isherwood Papers, Huntington Library, San Marino, California.

QUOTED MATERIAL

Quotations from W. H. Auden's unpublished manuscripts, typescripts, and letters are printed with the permission of the Estate of W. H. Auden.

The quotation from an unpublished journal by Lincoln Kirstein is printed with the permission of the New York Public Library (Astor, Lenox and Tilden Foundations).

Quotations from emails by John Lanchester are printed with permission.

Quotations from John Layard's unpublished manuscripts and typescripts are printed with the permission of the Estate of John Layard.

The quotation from an unpublished journal by Selden Rodman is printed with the permission of Carole Rodman.

Quotations from an unpublished letter by Oliver Sacks are printed with the permission of the Oliver Sacks Foundation.

ACKNOWLEDGMENTS

Years went by as I researched and wrote this book. In that time, so many people helped me with it. *The Island* took not so much a village as a small town. It has only been completed because of the sustained kindness, understanding, and selfless efforts of a large number of friends, strangers, colleagues, and family members. No words of mine can properly express the scale of my indebtedness. But what follows is my effort to recognize at least some of those who brought the book into the light.

Among the people whose friendship, conversations, and examples have sustained me are Timothy Garton Ash, Eavan Boland, Katherine Bucknell, Miranda Carter, Terry Castle, Dan Chiasson, Jed Esty, Shangyang Fang, James Fenton, Mark Ford, Prue Fuller, Jonathan Galassi, Louise Glück, Jorie Graham, John Haffenden, Saskia Hamilton, Langdon Hammer, Seamus Heaney, Richard Davenport-Hines, Christopher Hitchens, Richie Hofmann, Alan Hollinghurst, Mick Imlah, Laleh Khadivi, John Lanchester, Edna Longley, J. D. McClatchy, Paul Muldoon, Bernard O'Donoghue, Heather O'Donoghue, Peter Parker, Jahan Ramazani, Peter Sacks, Hannah Sullivan, Noah Warren, and Clair Wills. Comments and insights that these friends kindly gave me, often just in passing, have lodged in my mind and guided me, in a few cases through decades. It is painful to acknowledge that some of these memorable spirits are no longer here. Including their names, alongside those of the living, is more important to me than ever.

I owe a special debt to Cheryl Gore-Felton for what and how much she knows. And, while I was writing in Mariposa, my friends Don Florence and Henry Warden brightened the already sunny days with their optimistic outlooks and their generosity.

At Stanford, Vaughn Rasberry, Blakey Vermeule, and Alex Woloch made substantial contributions through their patient, constructive, far-seeing engagement, as did Adam Johnson, Elizabeth Tallent, and many other friends in Stanford's Creative Writing Program, who welcomed me during the years I spent with them. I have been blessed to work with a group of outstanding readers and writers while they were pursuing graduate studies at the university: I think especially of Lorenzo Bartolucci, Armen Davoudian, Harris Feinsod, Jesse Nathan, and Claire Seiler. I am grateful to each of them for their company and their informed intelligence. Lorenzo and Armen read the entire manuscript and offered acute suggestions that raised the level of the book. Warm appreciation is also owed to my research assistants of long ago, Eve Hill-Agnus, Renée Allyson Fox, Joey McGarvey, and Nhu-Y Phan.

I gratefully acknowledge that work on *The Island* was supported by fellowships from the Commonwealth Fund, the American Council of Learned Societies, and the Stanford Humanities Center.

While I was shaping this book, I had the good fortune to work with Bill Swainson. Bill's expertise and pragmatism made a great impression on me; his help was a crucial factor in my turning a corner with the project. I also had a number of knowledgeable correspondents who were generous with their responses to my questions: John Impey, Conor Leahy, Seamus Perry, Oliver Sacks, Alan Wakefield of the Imperial War Museums, Heiko Weissbach of the Forschungsstätte für Frühromantik and the Novalis-Museum at Schloss Oberwiederstedt, and Jonathan Wood. *The Island* drew as well on the skills and knowledge of many great librarians and archivists. Among them, I must single out Tim Noakes and Ben Albritton of Stanford Libraries, along with Mary Munill and Hilary Thorsen of Stanford's Interlibrary Borrowing service; Heather Smedburg and Jennifer Donovan of UC San Diego Library's Special Collections and Archives; and Carolyn Vega of the Henry W. and Albert A. Berg Collection at the New York Public Library. Invaluable help came also from Joan Arthur of the English Faculty, Oxford University; Emma Marsh and Anna Petre of the Oxford University Archives; Laura Sweetenham of Bryanston School; and Clare White of St. Anne's College, Oxford.

Kate Edgar of the Oliver Sacks Foundation, Izzy Farmer of Gresham's School, Baron Layard of Highgate, and Carole Rodman have all been gracious in helping me understand things better and in agreeing to the use of copyrighted materials.

That this book has appeared is to a great extent due to my agent, Melanie Jackson, and her coagent, Peter Straus. Disregarding all practical considerations, and even common sense, Melanie has had faith in me, encouraged me, fought for me, and figured things out (while finding time to laugh with me, as well). I think about her wonderful support, week after week, month after month—my deepest respect and gratitude to her and to Peter.

At Harvard University Press, I got an advanced education in little more than a year. With acute literary sensitivity, Emily Silk, this book's remarkable editor, worked with finesse, commitment, and energy through many drafts, even as she was also blazing a trail for *The Island* across the terrain where a long, sketchily formatted Word file turns into a beautiful printed object. She has made my writing here better in fundamental ways. In that endeavor, alongside Emily, I also had the good luck to work with a circle of special colleagues who tactfully, patiently kept this author moving forward and not backward: Jillian Quigley; Stephanie Vyce; Annamarie McMahon Why, who designed the book's jacket; Lisa Roberts, who designed its interior; the production editors, Julia Kirby at Harvard and John Donohue at Westchester Publishing Services; the copyeditor, Andrew Katz; and the indexer, Enid Zafran. I would also like to thank George Andreou and Sharmila Sen for their wisdom and intelligence in guiding the enormously complex undertaking that is Harvard University Press and thus making the publication of books like this one possible. I have been equally lucky at Faber and Faber, where gratitude is especially due to Paul Keegan, who accepted this book for publication, and to Matthew Hollis, Lavinia Greenlaw, Jane Feaver, and Lavinia Singer.

The poet and Auden scholar John Fuller was the person who introduced me to Auden's work and fired my interest. John gave me so much more than this, but he gave me this, too. In addition, like a hand coming down out of the sky, his *Commentary* on Auden's poetry has saved me at more moments of critical despair than I care to own up to.

There is a group of treasured, steadfast friends and extraordinary, passionate authors who over the years have shaped my imagination, taught me that thinking and feeling are not separable, and given me the best personal models I could ever have of what it means to be committed to writing, art, and scholarship. They are Lincoln Kirstein, Alexander Nemerov, and Helen Vendler.

One other person belongs in that group. Every reader of Auden, every writer on Auden, is in Edward Mendelson's debt. His knowledge of Auden's work and life is unrivaled. (Auden told a friend that Professor Mendelson knew more about Auden than Auden did. And I believe that thought has to be true.) His many remarkable editions of Auden's writing, and his own profoundly intelligent and cogent expositions of the meaning of Auden's poetry, have forever widened understanding of this great artist's achievements. Over decades now, Edward Mendelson has been unstintingly generous to me in sharing what he knows, never more so than when he disagreed with what I was saying or writing—as, for example, he sometimes disagreed with things that I was writing in this book. He held nothing back: he read my sentences intensively, giving me his frank opinions, his expert advice, the benefits of his vast learning, and his acute insights. My admiration is unqualified, while my thanks are inadequate.

At the sharp end of most authors' acknowledgments come family members, and this is the case here. I got so much from my father, Richard Jenkins, and my mother, Mary Jenkins. My sister, Kate Brazil, and my brother, Tom Jenkins, have shared everything vital with me. My beloved wife, Siri Huntoon, and our sons, Hugo Jenkins and Owen Jenkins, inspire me with their lives and comfort me with their love. Besides contributing far more to this book than I ought ever to have asked for, they have shown me what "the really better world" is, and they have brought me to it.

Finally, I write out the names of the two people, contemporaries of Auden, to whom *The Island* is dedicated. They are my grandmothers. Thinking of them reminds me of how much that is good and important about people does not routinely get written down in books. That recognition fills me with a sharp sense of regret and a desire to create an exception now.

Enid Browne (1902–1955) I never met. After a long, painful illness, her life ended before mine began. Her absence haunted me as a child, and I believe that it made me a person determined to try and recover something of the past. She lived and died in modest circumstances. But, missing her without knowing her, I was not willing to see the record of her time here fall into oblivion. One of my lasting ambitions has been to see at least the bare minimums of her precious existence—her name and her birth and death dates—memorialized in a book issued by a great publisher.

Joy Holmes (1907–1977) was born in the same year as Auden. She matriculated at Oxford as a "home-student" while Auden was an undergraduate at Christ Church. He got a Third and made himself into a truly great poet. After the deaths of her parents, she had to cut short her studies to return home and care for her younger siblings. Joy Holmes read poetry to me when I was a child. These sessions are among my most intense experiences of warmth and togetherness; they were the moments when a feeling for the magical power of words started to grow inside me. Now, when I silently read a poem, even one she could never have known, I feel that I can hear her voice.

Without these two people, this book would never have been started, let alone finished. In a real sense, it is theirs as well as mine. I am happy and grateful that their names are the first and last substantive entries in *The Island*. My love to you, Enid Browne and Joy Holmes.

INDEX TO AUDEN'S TITLES AND FIRST LINES

Note: Page numbers in *italics* indicate figures. When a poem by Auden had no title during the period covered in this book, the poem's first line is used here. Media and genres other than poetry are noted. Twelve major poems and sequences (preceded here by *) are analyzed in the General Index.

GENERAL INDEX

Note: Page numbers in *italics* indicate figures. All of Auden's works referred to in *The Island* are listed in the separate Index to Auden's Titles and First Lines. Where needed, media and genres other than poetry are noted. The General Index includes subject analysis for selected major poems and sequences by Auden.

abandonment felt by Auden while father in WWI, 15–16, 71–74, 77–78, 96, 117, 133, 139, 188, 249, 517, 597n198
Abercrombie, Patrick, 561n95
Ackerley, J. R.: *My Father and Myself* (autobiography), 660n124
Action Française, 165, 603–604n80
Adorno, Theodor, 6, 8
Aeneas, 597n207
Aeschylus, 555n21
Aitken, Ian, 466
Albert I (Belgian king), 197
Aldington, Richard: *Death of a Hero* (fiction), 233
alienation / aloneness / isolation: in Auden's "A Happy New Year," 341–342; in Auden's "Casino," 507; in Auden's "Friendship," 13, 34; in Auden's "I chose this lean country," 187–188; in Auden's "Letter to Lord Byron," 15–16; Auden's longing for connection, 399, 509, 531; in Auden's "The Megalopsych," 168; in Auden's "Out on the lawn I lie in bed," 422–423; in Auden's "Prologue," 365; in Auden's "Who stands, the crux left of the watershed," 202, 205–207, 209; English desire for, 533; isolation assuaged by receiving a letter, 470, 471; isolation of islands, 398; loneliness as poetic theme, 31; loneliness of Auden's later years, 31
Allen, Walter, 527, 529, 688n69
alliteration, 217, 219, 221, 223, 227, 272, 381, 384, 388–389, 487, 615n68, 650n37; alliterative tradition of Old and Middle English, 379, 649n30, 649n33
Allom, V. M., 595n159, 606n110
aloneness. *See* alienation / aloneness / isolation
ammonites in Auden's "Prologue," 366, 368–371

Anderson, Benedict, 482; *Imagined Communities,* 23, 569n54
Anderson, Hedli, 672n71, 682n20
Anglo-Catholicism, 27, 43, 44, 46–47, 48, 166, 393, 436, 567n25, 567–568n38
Anglocentrism. *See* Englishness; nationalism and national belonging; pastoral Englishness
Anglo-German Naval Agreement (1935), 440
Anglo-Saxon poetry, 216–224, 508, 517, 614n59
animals in Auden's poetry: in "Casino," 506, 507; cattle in "'Lead's the Best,'" 158; in "The Creatures," 490–491; farm dogs in "Frost," 141–142; in "Fish in the unruffled lakes," 498–499; frogs in "It was Easter as I walked in the public gardens," 284, 285, 289; hare in "Who stands, the crux left of the watershed," 206–207, 211–212; small animals in early works, 105–106, 115, 116, 158; squirrels in "The Dying House," 125–126. *See also* birds
anthologies, Auden's poems included in, 541. *See also titles of specific anthologies*
antimetropolitanism, 346–347, 351, 359–360, 401
antimodernism, 11, 206, 221
antisemitism, 46, 252, 404, 447, 521, 601n57
antiwar sentiment, 231–232, 652n68
anxiety and fear as motifs: anxiety as personal issue for Auden, 129–130; Auden's anxieties about academic work at Oxford, 176, 194; Auden's Bowra nightmare (1927), 177, 189–193, 212; in Auden's "California," 101; Auden's early forebodings of catastrophe, 145–146, 175; Auden's early years beset by microaggressions related to his sexuality, 111; Auden's first use of word "anxiety," 285, 632n160; in Auden's "Frost," 143; in Auden's "I chose this lean country," 170;

anxiety and fear as motifs (*continued*)
in Auden's "It was Easter as I walked in
the public gardens," 284, 285, 632n160; in
Auden's "Out on the lawn I lie in bed," 408;
Auden's panic about delivering inaugural
lecture at Oxford (1956), 609n158; in
Auden's "Which of you waking early and
watching daybreak," 632n160; "nerves in
order," 433, 639n48, 664n170; war-related
anxiety, 112
Appletreewick (Yorkshire): first surviving
northern poem set by Auden in, 130; travel
(1927) with Day Lewis, 168–170; visit
(1923) to Medley's family, 130, 168
Aquinas, Thomas. *See* Thomas Aquinas
Arendt, Hannah, 5, 16, 252, 298, 454, 499
Aristophanes: *The Frogs* (drama), 555n21
Aristotle, 179
Arnold, Matthew, 204; "Dover Beach," 204;
"A Summer Night," 413; "To a Friend,"
243, 413, 620n143, 657n114
Arts and Crafts movement, 50, 255, 568n42
asphyxiation in George Auden's "An Unusual
Form of Suicide" and in Auden's "On the
frontier at dawn getting down," 182–183,
186–189, 608n138
assonance, 325, 370, 487
Auden, Bernard (brother), 16, 42, 54, 68, *71*,
341, 566n19, 570n61, 573n100, 660n128
Auden, Constance (mother): arguing with
husband over his affair, xi, 15, 70, 78; ashes
of, scattered in Threlkeld churchyard,
595n157; in Auden's Bowra nightmare
(1927), 190, 192–193, 207; Auden's fondness for, 176; in Auden's maritime dream
(1933), 395–396; Auden's sexuality as
concern for, 256; born at Salthouse,
Norfolk (1869), 80; calligraphy and
embroidery, love of, 50, 462; crucifixes
and, 79, 568–569n48; death (1941), 72;
death of her father, 73; dominant figure
in marriage with George Auden, 184;
dressing up in drag for masquerade, 54;
family heritage, 361, 600–601n41, 645n143;
as Francophile, 47, 587n21; German
musical influences and, 19; influence on
Auden's identity, 11, 55; leaving Solihull
house during WWI, 59; Erika Mann,
Auden's wife, meeting, 527, 687n26;
marriage to George Auden (1899), 42;
miscarriage prior to Auden's birth, 41;
musical interests shared with her children,
19, 45, 55, 67, 462, 558n56, 572n82; nostalgic

for holistic past, 49; oratorio written by
Auden for ("For the Time Being"), 45; in
patriarchal society, 48; poetic nature of, 47;
religious nature of, 43, 46–48, 190; temperament of, 47, 190, 396; turbulent relationship with Auden, 158–159, 181, 190;
Wesco family home associated with, 299
Auden, Geoffrey (cousin), 68, 576n147
Auden, George (father): affair with Ann
Haverson, xi, 15, 70, 72, 78, 184, 577n157;
ambition for son to be "mouthpiece of an
epoch," 322, 345, 533; ancestry of, 595n160,
649n30; ancient grave inscriptions recorded
at Gallipoli by, 57, 115; archaeological
and mythological interests of, 49, 51, 131,
569n56; Auden connecting to Hardy and
Edward Thomas, 119–120; in Auden's Berlin
dream (1929), 282; in Auden's maritime
dream (1933), 396; Auden's references to,
directly and indirectly in his poetry, 163,
243, 591n102; Auden's reverence for, 176;
Auden's sexuality as concern for, 256; as
Birmingham's first school medical officer,
41, 44, 50–51, 181, 569nn59–60; George
Cadbury as enemy of, 652–653n68; on
child development and illnesses, 40, 72, 179,
180–181; compared to Bowra in Yugoslavia
nightmare (1927), 192; death (1957),
577n163; death of his father, 73; "Dionysiac"
potential of illness, interest in, 578n165;
dressing up in drag for masquerade, 54, 316;
early medical practice of, 41, 51, 566n10;
encephalitis lethargica, contracting, xi,
72, 578n165; eugenics as interest of, 52,
571n68; extrascientific interests of, 51;
geological interests of, 78; German connections for Auden through, 249, 517;
Heard holding views in opposition to,
344; honorary degree from University of
Birmingham, 180; influence on Auden's
identity, 11, 15–16, 52, 102–103, 517; *Lancet*
obituary (1957) for, 51; on maladjusted
children in wake of WWI, 68, 179; Erika
Mann, Auden's wife, meeting, 527, 687n26;
marriage to Constance Bicknell (1899), 42;
medical interest in feeble-mindedness and
antisocial habits, 51–52, 178–179, 180,
570n61; medical writing by, 72; name
"George" used for murdered father in *Paid
on Both Sides*, 237–238; Norse cultures and
literature as obsession of, 49, 131, 158, 217,
219, 600n41; Pennines walking tour with
Auden and son John (1922), xii, 131, 586n7;

sources for, 14–18, 39, 332, 373, 492–493, 516, 639n46; stanza of five lines in, 123–124, 345–346, 642n100; subsequent revisions of published works, 539–540; syllabics in later poems, 681n9; texts and editions, explanation of, 539–543; "three" (divisions and patterns) as significant to structure of, 100, 283, 284, 318, 325, 354, 366, 423, 442, 483, 493, 498; T-shaped stanza form, 325; "up-to-date" poems, 384, 398; verbal patterns, 272; visual images in compared to film images, 480–481; as voice of Englishness, 11, 21–22; vulnerability in, 98, 102, 122, 145, 175, 195; working-class voices in, 149, 151; WWI as presence in, 14–18, 44, 58, 65, 73, 91, 96, 112–113, 116–117, 126, 132, 136, 155, 157–158, 196, 212, 213, 296–297, 326, 383, 447, 520. *See also* influences on Auden; word choices in Auden's poetry; *specific motifs*; *Index to Auden's Titles and First Lines*
Auden, William (great-great-great-grandfather), 595n160
"August for the people and their favourite islands," xv, 440–452; Auden comparing film medium to word imagery in poetry, 480–481; Auden praising Isherwood's austere art as novelist, 442, 446–447, 481, 602n65, 666n11; Auden's description of Isherwood's physical appearance (with fetishistic mention of "adult pen"), 442, 444, 448–449, 530; Auden's doubts about character of poets in, 442; Auden's verse epistle for Isherwood's thirty-first birthday, 441, 471; Auden writing from Isle of Man holiday with Yates family, 441–444; called "occasional" work, 445; compared to "A Happy New Year," part 2, 447; dangerous flood looming, 445, 448, 503, 633n174; dictated by Auden to Yates, 441–442; fetishism and, 449; final stanza's structure of contracted sentences, 524; forebodings and dangers lurking in, 447–450; Forster, Spender, and Klaus Mann at Isherwood's birthday party, 441; historical events as triggers for writing poetry, 445, 448, 451; impossibility of shutting out history, 447–450; "The Island" as early title for, 444, 666n16; on Isle of Wight visit by Isherwood and Auden (1926), 442–443; Lane's teachings transmitted through Layard to Auden and Isherwood, 443; nature of Auden's relationship with

Yates after his Downs School departure, 444–445; outcast status of homosexuals and, 444–445, 450; Owen's influence in, 447; as poem dividing early Auden from Auden of the later 1930s, 451–452; on Rügen island visit of Auden to Isherwood (1931), 443; significance of islands in Auden's imagination evident in, 444; spying fantasy of Auden and Isherwood, 443; three-part structure of, 442; "To a Writer on His Birthday" as first title for, 441; Yeats's influence in, 445–446, 447
Austria: Auden's death in Vienna (1973), 31, 559n59; Auden's home in Kirchstetten, 312, 559n59, 635n8; Auden's travel with McElwee to (1926–1927), 164; Kitzbühel, travel to, xii, 19, 164, 184, 559n59; Salzburg Festival trip, with father (1925), xii, 19, 184, 249, 282, 517, 594n138
Ayerst, David, 150, 156, 194, 265, 598n16

Bach, J. S., 19, 45, 115
Bacon, Francis, 264
Baedeker guides: to Berlin, 258, 625n64; to Great Britain, 378
Bagnall-Oakeley, Richard, 584n250, 586–587n15
Baldwin, Stanley, 157, 341, 641n81
Bangham, Alec, *437*, 438, 665n184
Barbusse, Henri: *Le Feu* (fiction), 136, 664n168
Barker, Pat: *Regeneration* (fiction), 589n60
Barnett, Correlli, 199
baroque, 529
Barrie, J. M.: *A Kiss for Cinderella* (drama), 328, 639n47
Batsford (publisher): "English Life" series, 30
Battle of Maldon (Old English poem), 216, 221
Battle of Scimitar Hill (1915), 56–57, 222
Battle of the Somme (1916), 96, 218, 235, 535
The Battle of the Somme (film), 136
BBC: Auden's broadcasts of his poetry, 440; Auden's first broadcast (1934), xv, 434, 664n173
Beaverbrook, Lord, 341, 641n81
Beer Hall Putsch (1923), 252
Belgium: Auden's travel to Spa (1928), 244; Menin Gate Memorial to the Missing (1927), 197, 610n1; theater of destruction in WWI, 69, 110, 112, 128; trench warfare in, 136
belonging and conforming, 155. *See also* nationalism and national belonging
Benjamin, Walter, 16

Eliot, T. S. (*continued*)
Auden as influence on, 315, 403; Auden's
first meeting with (1927), xii, 212, 605n87;
Auden's first submission of poetry collection to (1927), xii, 167, 212, 605n87;
Auden shocked by views of, 404; on
Auden's *Paid on Both Sides*, 235; Auden's
possible allusion to ("Thomas Prologizes"), 601n54; as Auden's publisher, xii,
25, 144, 212, 327, 530; austerity associated
with, 162, 602n65; British citizenship of,
27, 166, 604n81; celluloid ear as gift to
Auden (1935), 434; classical and Romance
influences on literary culture of, 220–221;
cosmopolitanism of, 163, 165; face powder
and obscuring himself, 602nn61–62;
as father figure for Auden, 193; on
Georgian ethos, 106; Georgianism of title
"Little Gidding," 107; on Georgian poets,
107; gossip about, 161, 602n63; as influence on Auden, 144–145, 159–165, 170,
175, 188, 205–206, 235, 289–290, 365,
612n31; on insularity as new paradigm
("enforced insularity") and rejection of
international modernism, 23, 27, 107,
144, 165–167; as "invisible poet," 602n61;
literary history's construction of, 161,
601–602n57; on "logic of the imagination,"
290, 632n171; London as home of, 41; on
modernism and its 1926 demise, xii, 25,
26–27, 145; objective correlative concept of,
449; Orwell's *Down and Out in Paris and
London* rejected by (1932), 263; pastiches
of, by Auden, 165; on poet as chemist,
162–163; political and social views of, 107,
161, 165–167, 402, 403, 601n57; secretiveness of, 161, 167, 602nn61–62; sexuality
of, 161, 601–602nn57–59; title suggestions
for Auden's *Look, Stranger!*, 530–531,
688n78; on visions and dreams, 370
Eliot, T. S., works by: *After Strange Gods: A
Primer of Modern Heresy* (prose), 403–404;
Anabase by St. John Perse (trans.), 604n82;
"Ariel" poems, 167, 212; *Ash-Wednesday*,
604n85; "Ben Jonson" (prose), 162, 602n65;
Clark lectures, 166; *The Criterion* ("Commentaries" and editorship [prose]), 26, 82,
160, 163, 166, 172, 175, 235, 238, 327, 331,
337–338, 359, 519, 534, 654n86; "Dante"
(prose), 362–363, 370; *Ezra Pound: His
Metric and His Poetry* (prose), 602n65;
For Lancelot Andrewes (prose), 166; *Four
Quartets*, 107; "The Hollow Men," 26, 166,
516; "Journey of the Magi," 27, 166–167,
212, 604n82; "Last Words" (prose), 26,
27, 166–167; "Little Gidding" (in *Four
Quartets*), 107; "The Love Song of J. Alfred
Prufrock," 612n31; "Marina," 167; "The
Metaphysical Poets" (prose), 159; *Murder
in the Cathedral* (drama), 434; *Poems:
1909–1925*, 25–26, 516; "Reflections on
Contemporary Poetry" (prose), 106, 107;
The Rock (pageant), 315; *The Sacred Wood*
(prose), 162; Sweeney poems, 160–161;
"Tradition and the Individual Talent"
(prose), 162. See also *The Waste Land*
Elkins, Caroline, 675n107
Elmhirst, Dorothy, 356–359, 368
Elmhirst, Leonard, 356–357
Elton, Arthur, 468
Empson, William, 275; *Seven Types of
Ambiguity*, 397
energy: of Auden's 1927–1930 poems, 167;
Auden's description of writing verse and,
423; of Auden's "I chose this lean country,"
170–171, 173; of Auden's "Out on the lawn
I lie in bed," 409; of Auden's poem for
Night Mail (film), 468; Auden's "Prologue"
losing momentum before regathering, 366;
of Auden's "Who stands, the crux left of
the watershed," 201, 204; spark in Auden's
"The Creatures," 491
England: of 1920s and 1930s in Auden's writing,
9, 22–23; 1926 as critical year for literary
culture in, 24–28; as Albion of Blake's
imagination, 198, 505; Auden returning
from Sintra to (1936), xvi, 526; Auden
returning to rural England in "Who stands,
the crux left of the watershed," 200,
206–207; Auden's aspiration to redeem, 127,
323–324, 330–331, 334, 355, 364–367, 376,
430–433, 492, 532–533; Auden seeing
cultural crisis in "Here on the cropped
grass of the narrow ridge I stand," 432–433;
in Auden's "I chose this lean country,"
168–175; Auden's instinct to depart, 502,
507, 537; Auden's last Christmas in (1937),
until 1972, xvi, 536, 689n90; in Auden's
"Prologue" vs. "Epilogue," 514–515; choice
of, Auden making, 168–175, 282–283, 340;
cultural trend toward introspection and
apoliticism, 517; film-going by Auden and
friends in, 459; Germany and German
literature of importance to Auden's generation in, 517–518, 684n37; "Heritage Britain"
iconography, 30; Labour government

Helensburgh, Scotland. *See* Larchfield Academy
Hemingway, Ernest: *A Farewell to Arms,* 233
Henning, Magnus, 526
Henry VIII (Shakespeare), 199
Herbert, George, 313; "Prayer," 314
Hesse (Germany), 288
heterosexuality: Auden seeking to develop
    "heterosexual traits," 244; Auden's engage-
    ment to Sheilah Richardson, 245, 298;
    heterosexual love and marriage in *Coal
    Face,* 457; heterosexual marriage, Auden's
    fears of, 298, 303; marriage with Erika
    Mann, xv, *437,* 438, 451–452, 457, 517,
    665n181, 665n186; sex with Petzold, 19–20
Heuser, Alan, 685n40
Hirschfeld, Magnus, 254, 257–258, 625n58,
    630n143, 670n57
history: historical events as triggers for
    Auden's poetry, 9, 360–361, 433, 445, 451,
    555n26; impossibility of shutting out,
    447–450; indirect presence of war-related
    events, 17; water connected to, 290;
    WWII's forebodings and, 276, 450. *See
    also* First World War
Hitchcock, Alfred, 264
Hitler, Adolf, 8, 17, 252, 264, 331, 401, 439,
    503, 527, 655n91; "no more islands," 450,
    667n29. *See also* Nazism
Hodge (archetypal English peasant), 154,
    599n23
Hodgkinson, Anthony W., 674n93
Hölderlin, Friedrich, 516–518, 522, 684n33,
    684n37; "Die Kürze" (translated by
    Spender), 516, 518; "Sokrates und
    Alcibiades," 530
Hölderlin stanza, 516, 522, 684n36
Holland, Auden and Isherwood in (1929), 280
Holmes, J. B., 677n136
Holst, Gustav, 46
Holywell Press, Oxford, 246
Homer: Auden's use of Homeric epithets, 367,
    373, 494, 497; Bowra's study of, 609n159;
    Odyssey, 142, 367, 373, 387, 597n207
Home Rule for Ireland, 53–54
homosexuality. *See* queerness
Hopkins, Gerard Manley: Auden on, 639n53;
    Auden's review of book on, 654n86; as
    influence on Auden, 168, 313, 331, 353, 396
Hopkins, Gerard Manley, works by: "The
    Bugler's First Communion," 639n53; "Thou
    art indeed just, Lord, if I contend," 636n11;
    "To what serves mortal beauty," 331; "The
    Wreck of the Deutschland," 396, 399

Horace, 394, 653n70
Horder, Thomas, 345, 642n98
Housman, A. E., 104, 510
Howard, Brian, 263, 264, 627n87, 627n90
Howkins, Alun, 204, 589n54
Howson, G. W. S., 4–5, 81, 83–85, 554n13
Hoyland, Dorothea, 393–394, *415,*
    652n68
Hoyland Geoffrey, 393–394, *415,* 436,
    661n134, 668n35; in and out of the closet,
    419, 661n135
Hughes, Ted, 58, 96, 110, 140; "The Dream
    Time," 58; "For the Duration," 110;
    "National Ghost" (prose), 96, 140
Hughes, William, 58, 96, 218
human evolution as theme, 292–293, 295,
    633n178
Huxley, Julian, 100, 111, 587n19
Hyndman, Tony, 500–501
Hynes, Samuel, 14–15, 108, 232, 617n94

Icarus, 30
Iceland travel (with MacNeice and Yates,
    1936), xvi, 7, 531, 658n120, 682n14. See
    also *Letters from Iceland*
"I chose this lean country," xii, 168–175,
    664n171; alienation / aloneness / isolation
    in, 187–188; anxiety in, 170; birds in, 170,
    172, 174–175, 194, 634n198; death as motif
    in, 170, 173, 175; dream in, 170, 174–175,
    606n108; eclipse of sun in, 169; Eliot's
    modernism and, 145, 170, 175; enjambed
    trimeters used in, 172; Graves's influence
    on, 171–173, 175; half rhymes used in,
    622n158; Isherwood mentioned in, 174,
    244; Margaret (psychoanalyst Margaret
    Marshall) mentioned in, 174, 244; mascu-
    linity in, 173; remote landscapes repre-
    senting nation as synecdoche, 171–172,
    200; return to northern rural world in,
    169; silence and passivity in, 174–175;
    "Underneath the abject willow" borrowing
    from, 510; written in Appletreewick
    (1927), 168; WWI suffusing, 172–173;
    Yeats's influence on, 172–173, 175
identity: Auden becoming "English poet,"
    312, 404; Auden's father absence, effect on
    Auden, 73–74, 77–78, 139, 188, 517,
    597n198; father's role in forming, 11,
    15–16, 52, 102–103; as theme in Auden's
    early writing, 33, 283–284, 305, 532. *See
    also* nationalism and national belonging;
    outcast as motif

poet must be clinically minded, 162; Auden's description of physical appearance of (with fetishistic mention of "adult pen"), 442, 444, 448–449, 530; on Auden's early poetry, 109–110; Auden's first commercially published book of poems (1930) dedicated to, 529; on Auden's forebodings of catastrophe, 146; Auden sharing appreciation of Tennyson with, 666n13; in Auden's "I chose this lean country," 174; in Auden's list of "great emotional milestones" (1947), 463; in Auden's *The Orators*, 330; Auden's poem for Isherwood's thirty-first birthday ("August for the people and their favourite islands"), 440–452, 480–481; on Auden's secretiveness about queerness, 16; Auden's submission of sequence of sixteen love poems to (1934), xv, 414–417, 428–429, 433, 445, 662n140; in Berlin (1928–1929), xiii, 258–261, 263, 270, 320; Bubi (Szczesny) relationship with, 270–273, 416, 459, 631n151; camera-like art of, 480–481; China travel with Auden, 420; continuous travel from 1936 on, 503; "Cosy Corner" as favorite bar of, 259, 260; in Denmark, Auden's visit to (1935), 434; on Eliotic poetry by Auden, 163–164; on English fascination with Germany after WWI, 20, 518; father (Frank Bradshaw-Isherwood) killed in WWI, 68, 111, 158, 197, 610n1; as filmgoer, 458, 459; Forster and, 422, 441, 662n143, 662n145; on General Strike, 156–157; homosexual romanticism of, 338; introducing Auden to Upward, 638n39; Isle of Wight trip with Auden (1926), 442–443; London as home of, 41; Mann family and, 435–436; on meeting disabled veteran, 110; on Moxon (character in Mortmere fantasy), 557n45; Nagasaki travel with Auden (1938), 17; Neddermeyer and, 500–501, 505; possible photo from Auden's "Dracula trip" and, 418; reconnecting with Auden (1925), 157, 600n39; repressed shame of missing WWI, 157–158; at Repton, 81; in Rothehütte with Auden and Küsel (1929), 279; at Rügen island, Auden visit to (1931), 443, 666n14; at St. Edmund's with Auden, 59, 75, 78, 579n178; in sexual relationship with Auden, 162, 442, 602n64; in Sintra, collaborating with Auden on *The Ascent of F6*, xv, 501–502, 505, 508; symbolic reconciliation of making love to German boys and, 268;

Toller and, 502–503, 680n182; in United States during WWII, 638n39; Upward attacking as pacifist, 638n39; Veidt and, 670n57; Viertel and, 675n107; writings about life in Berlin, 626n86; on WWI in minds of young writers of mid-1920s, 155
Isherwood, Christopher, works by: *The Ascent of F6* (drama, with Auden), xv, 500–504, 505, 507, 511–512, 526, 672n71, 675n114, 676n127, 682n20, 683n25; Baudelaire's *Journaux intimes* (trans.), 635n7; *Christopher and His Kind* (autobiography), 559n60, 626n86; *The Dog Beneath the Skin* (drama, with Auden), xv, 431, 435, 463, 650n40, 664n177; *Down There on a Visit* (fiction), 630n143; "The Enemies of a Bishop" (drama [originally "The Reformatory"], with Auden), 632n161, 670n57; "Gems of Belgian Architecture" (fiction), 65; *Goodbye to Berlin* (fiction), 463, 559n60, 626n86; "The Head of a Leader" (prose), 680n182; *Journey to a War* (travel book, with Auden), 472, 651n42; *Lions and Shadows* (autobiography), 67, 78, 136, 155, 157, 162, 228, 459, 557n45, 559n60, 602n64; "Lions and Shadows" (unpublished early novel), 157; *Mr. Norris Changes Trains* (fiction), 626n86
Ishmael (biblical), 127
the island: Auden's feelings toward, 398, 444, 471–472, 481–482, 654n86; Eliot using motif of, 107, 166, 604n85; England as "fortress" and "our little reef," 355, 362, 403, 518; forebodings of coming war from continent (1939), 450; Gresham's School functioning as, 3; national imaginary of, 12, 28–29, 531–532; Shakespeare's *Richard II* and "this sceptered isle" monologue, evoked by Auden, 361–362; Soviet spies' use of code name "The Island" for Britain, 29, 561n93; as symbol for English identity in interwar period, 28, 35. *See also* insularity
Isle of Man holiday, with Yates and his family (1935), xv, 441–442, 443–444, 450, 503, 658n120
Isle of Wight: Auden family holiday in (1917), 67, 130, 576n138; Isherwood and Auden visit (1926), 442–443
isolation. *See* alienation / aloneness / isolation
Italian invasion of Abyssinia (1935–1936), 447, 476–477, 675n117

significant friend to Auden, 317; suicide attempts or ideations, xiii, 277–278, 286, 629–630n143, 647n164

lead, meanings of, 135

lead mining, 70, 75, 78, 99, 130–135, 138, 151–152, 154, 165, 200, 237. *See also* miners and mining

Leahy, Conor, 598n4, 610n170, 622n159, 643n119

Leavis, F. R., 30

Leed, Eric J., 13–14, 28, 110, 135, 196, 247, 596n177

Léger, Fernand, 596n175

Legg, Stuart, 470

Lehmann, John, 263, 519, 627n87

Lewis, C. S.: in counter-Bowra group of dons, 221; deprecating his war experience despite lingering memories, 222–223; in *Kolbítar* (Icelandic for "the Coal-biters") circle, 219–221, 615n71; Old English scholarship at Oxford and, 217–223, 379; at Oxford as don, 111; on Sheldonian Theatre concert on day after raucous Armistice Day celebrations (1922), 600n36; WWI experiences of, 218, 222–223

Lewis, C. S., works by: "The Alliterative Metre" (prose), 227, 379, 615n68; *Dymer* (published under pseud. Clive Hamilton), 223; "The Nameless Mile," 616n81; review of Tolkien's *The Lord of the Rings,* 222

Lewis, Wyndham: among favorite authors of Auden, 14; anti-French sentiments of, 199–200, 264–265; on Berlin's immorality, 256; calling Auden a national institution, 534; on cultural shift in England to abrasive and combative mode, 215; "Men of 1914" phrase of, 25, 560n77; on modernism, 24–25; on national solidarity, 304–305; Porteus and, 344; on radical movement of youth, 20–21, 337; on WWI's impact in British life, 14

Lewis, Wyndham, works by: *Blasting and Bombardiering* (autobiography), 14, 25, 560n77; *The Childermass* (fiction), 232; *The Enemy* (periodical), 20–21, 199–200; *Hitler* (prose), 264–265, 655n91; *Men without Art* (prose), 309

Liddell Hart, B. H., 618n107

"life goes on" poems, 185

Light, Alison, 25

light as motif, 385–386. *See also* sun and sunlight as motifs

The Listener: Auden's "Out on the lawn I lie in bed" published in (1934), 413, 656n104;

Auden's review of Rotha's *Documentary Film* (1936), 479–480, 676n128; on *Poems* (1930), 399–400

literary modernism. *See* modernism

Little Caesar (film), 230

Little England and Little Englanders, 28, 198–199, 358–359

Llewellyn Smith, Harold, 603n75

Lloyd George, David, 619n130

Lobkowicz, Maximilian and Gillian von, 684n33

Lodge, Oliver, 113

London: Auden living in and working as private tutor (1929), xiii, 41, 282, 298, 311, 636n17; Auden living with Coldstreams in (1936), xv, 478–479, 492, 498; Auden living with Wright in (1935), xv, 478; "horrible London," Auden's dislike of, 41, 311–312, 478

Longford, Lord. *See* Pakenham, Thomas

Longley, Edna, 606n102

Longstaff, Will, 197, 233, 246; *Immortal Shrine (Eternal Silence)* (painting), 197; *Menin Gate at Midnight* (painting), 197, 610n3

"Look, stranger, at this island now," xv, 481–488; anonymity of speaker vs. impersonality of modernism, 486; Auden as the poem's "director," 484; authoritativeness of speaker in, 485–486; connections to cinematic projection of national brand in, 485; filmmaking origins and camera-aesthetic of, 482, 484–485; hints of diaspora in, 488; insularity in, 486–487; internal complexity of, 487; "Madrigal" compared to, 484; nationalism and national belonging in, 481, 483, 486; "Seaside" as original title, 481; seeing as motif in, 484–485; "small field" in, 483, 484, 486; stillness in, 487; stranger in, xv, 481–488, 490, 492, 677n138; sunlight and, 481; three-part structure of, 483; as waking dream, 488, 492; written for film, 481–482

Loraine, Percy, 264

Lords of Limit (mythological figures), 22, 348, 352, 382, 482, 643n110, 650nn39–40

love: Auden's "Before this loved one" and, 270–277; Auden's "The chimneys are smoking, the crocus is out in the border" and, 375; Auden's "Dear, though the night is gone" and, 497; Auden's early cynicism toward, 374–375; Auden's "A Happy New Year," part 2 and, 374–375; Auden's list of "great emotional milestones" (1947), 463, 499; Auden's "Out on the lawn I lie in bed"

Schuyler, James: "Wystan Auden," 8
Schwarz, Bill, 25
Schwarzschild, Leopold, 520–521
Scottish Psalter, parody of, 335
Scrutiny articles by Auden, 344
The Seafarer (Old English poem), 216, 217
"Seaside," 481–482. *See also* "Look, stranger, at this island now"
Second Battle of Ypres (1915), 197
Second Boer War (1899–1902), 60, 358
Second World War (WWII): Auden poetry generated from, 276; considered as standard historical reference point for Auden, 17; in Europe, 8; violence in Weimar Germany in period leading to, 34, 251, 252, 254, 277, 282, 288, 294; Yates as prisoner of war during, 441, 659n120
Sedbergh School (West Riding), 212–213, 331
seeing. *See* sight
senses, poetry invoking, 171, 210, 385–386, 487
sequence poem in four parts (1929), xiii, 280–304; "It was Easter as I walked in the public gardens" (part 1), 282–288, 289, 302, 317, 318, 321, 603n78, 608n138, 626n76, 631n153, 637n26; "Coming out of me living is always thinking" (part 2), 283, 288–289, 292–298, 301, 529, 631n153; "Order to stewards and the study of time" (part 3), 283, 290, 298–301, 631n157; "It is time for the destruction of error" (part 4), 283, 290, 301–304, 310, 324, 354, 355
—Auden's self-critique in part 3, 299–300; George Auden's top hat box in Berlin dream, 282; autobiographical details in, 283; Berlin dream of new model of poem, 281–282; birds in, 290, 296, 300–301; Burrow's influence on, 284–285, 293–298, 302; man like chicken in part 1, 286, 290; city setting of parts 1 and 4, 283; creativity linked to water in, 291–292; crucifixion references in part 1, 287; death and rebirth in, 282–283, 286–287, 298, 301–302; doom and despair in, 283, 299, 301–302; drowning as motif, 290, 303–305; ducks in part 2, 288, 290, 292–293, 295; Dunne and, 299–301; echoes of "Who stands, the crux left of the watershed" in, 299; Eliot's *The Waste Land* and, 289–290; first and last parts displaying correspondences and symmetries, 283; first poetic use of word "anxiety" in part 1, 285, 632n160; first two parts written in Germany, 281; foreboding at end of part 1, 288; formal structure of

parts, 283; "fresh hand" in part 1, 284, 286, 288, 303, 321; frogs in part 1, 284, 285, 289; happiness in part 2, 297; heterosexual marriage, Auden's fears of, 298, 303; human evolution as theme, 292–293, 295, 633n178; last two parts written in England, 281, 298; Layard in part 1, 286–288; "logic of the imagination" and, 290; "lolling bridegroom" of final line of part 4, 303; love's failure to offer security in, 300, 302; May Day riots (Berlin) and, 282, 288, 294; meditative walk as poetic motif, 284–285; Meyer in part 1, 286–288; "1929" as title later given to, 631n152; as occasional poems, 445; originally intended as cycle of verse letters to Isherwood, 441, 631n152; Owen's "Strange Meeting" and, 298, 304; as pivotal poem in *Poems* (1930), 280; pronoun "I" used in all four parts, 281, 283, 284; pun on "analysis" in part 1, 287; rain as motif, 284, 288–290, 303; revolutionary flood or tide (flood of history) in, 291–292; rural setting of parts 2 and 3, 283, 295; sadness of part 4's ending, 303–304; seasonal organization, 283; simile of colonial expatriate returning home, 297; stillness as symptom of Freudian death wish in, 297; train travel in part 3, 298; transition between German parts and English parts, 298; as valediction to easy reconciliation with Germany, 281, 296–297, 304; Wall Street Crash and part 4, 282, 301; water imagery in, 288–293, 303; "weeping man" in part 1, 283, 284, 286–288; "Who stands, the crux left of the watershed" compared to part 3, 299; WWI presence in, 296–297; Yeats's influence on, 283
Seton-Watson, R. W., 533
sexual encounters (Auden's): affairs with young men in 1930s, 11; Auden's list of "great emotional milestones" (1947), 463; in Berlin with German boys, 260–261, 451, 459; with Betjeman while at Oxford, 600n33; with Crossman while at Oxford, 598n16; with his brother John, 131; with Isherwood, 162, 442, 602n64; with Küsel in Berlin, 278–279; with Layard in Berlin, 266, 268–269, 277–278; Layard's perception of Auden's sexual masochism, 268–269; with Meyer in Berlin, 277–278, 281; with Pieps in Berlin, 260, 273; with prostitute while attending Gresham's, 82; purported celibacy of Auden, 163, 176;

Yeats, W. B. (William Butler): on Auden and
Isherwood's *The Ascent of F6* (drama),
501–502; compared to Auden, 172–173,
175, 285, 336, 347; compared to Graves,
173; to hold "in a single thought reality
and justice," 355; home at Thoor Ballylee
in County Galway ("Norman tower"), 172,
446; as influence on Auden, 172–173, 175,
184, 188, 195, 290, 445–446, 447, 622n158,
682n9; on memories of early life, 39;
modernism and, 144–145; occasional
works transformed into serious reflective
poems by, 445; Owen and, 447; rhyme
royal, 640n74; subsequent revisions of
published works by, 539; walking poems,
285
Yeats, W. B., works by: "Among School
Children," 31; "Easter, 1916," 285,
632n159; "In Memory of Eva Gore-Booth
and Con Markievicz," 505, 507, 517,
681n2; "In Memory of Major Robert
Gregory," 347, 348, 445–446; "Meditations

in Time of Civil War," 606n102; "Nineteen
Hundred and Nineteen," 173, 606n102;
The Player Queen (drama), 291; "The
Second Coming," 290; "The Symbolism of
Poetry" (prose), 336; *The Tower,* 606n102;
"The Tower," 172–173, 184, 187, 195, 347,
606n99, 606n102; *The Winding Stair,* 505,
681n2
Yorke, Henry ("Henry Green"), 156
Yorkshire, 70, 77, 580n186; Auden family in
York, 41. *See also* Appletreewick
Yugoslavia: Auden's Bowra nightmare in
(1927), 177, 189–193, 207, 212; Auden's
travel with father to (1927), xii, 176–177,
180, 184, 188–189; Auden's unhappiness
throughout time in, 177, 193–194; Auden
wishing "I was dead" in Yugoslavia, 188;
poems Auden wrote at time of travel in,
608n152

Zola, Émile: *Germinal* (fiction), 136
Zörgiebel, Karl, 294